presented at times more like a novel or a documentary . . . There is in fact, something for everyone here and with no less than sixty well-paced chapters, the book can either be taken on in a giddy steeplechase, or dipped into again and again. Either way, it will not disappoint.'

Iain Gale, *Scotsman*

# IN THESE TIMES

*Living in Britain Through*
*Napoleon's Wars*

1793–1815

JENNY UGLOW

ff

FABER & FABER

For Hermione and John

First published in 2014
by Faber & Faber Limited
Bloomsbury House
74–77 Great Russell Street
London WC1B 3DA
This paperback edition first published in 2015

Typeset by Faber & Faber Limited
Printed and bound by CPI Group (UK) Ltd, Croydon, CR0 4YY

A CIP record for this book
is available from the British Library

ISBN 978-0-571-26953-2

FSC
www.fsc.org
MIX
Paper from
responsible sources
FSC® C101712

2 4 6 8 10 9 7 5 3

# CONTENTS

Map xi

1. Who tells the news?  1

I : STIRRING, 1789–1792

2. Down with Tom Paine!  13

II : ARMING, 1793–1796

3. The universal pant for glory  27
4. Flanders and Toulon  39
5. Scarlet, shoes and guns  46
6. British tars  56
7. Trials and tribulations  67
8. Warp and weft  78
9. Money, city and country  88
10. 'Are we forgotten?'  101
11. High life  109
12. Four farmers  120
13. Portsmouth deliveries  130
14. Bread  139
15. East and west  151

# CONTENTS

III : WATCHING, 1797–1801

16. Invasions, spies and poets  163
17. Mutinies and militia  172
18. Cash in hand  182
19. At sea and on land  191
20. The powerhouse  200
21. 'Check proud invasion's boast'  210
22. Ireland  224
23. The Nile and beyond  233
24: 'The distressedness of the times'  243
25. God on our side  254
26. 'Good men should now close ranks'  268
27. Denmark, Egypt, Boulogne – peace  276


IV : PAUSING, 1801–1803

28. France  289
29. New voices  297
30. 'Always capable of doing mischief'  309
31. Albion  318


V : SAILING, 1803–1808

32. Into war again  335
33. 'Fine strapping fellows'  346
34. Press gangs and fencibles  355
35. Panic and propaganda  365
36. 'Every farthing I can get'  378
37. The business of defence  384
38. Trafalgar  395
39. All the talents  407
40. Private lives  420
41. Abolition and after  430
42. Danes and Turks  438

CONTENTS

43. Orders in council  444
44. Land  455


VI : FIGHTING, 1809–1815

45. 'Caesar is everywhere'  469
46. Scandals, Flanders and fevers  481
47. Going to the show  490
48. Burdett and press freedom  499
49. 'Brookes's and Buonaparte', Cintra and Troy  505
50. Storms of trade  513
51. The coming of the sheep  524
52. Sieges and prisoners  535
53. Luddites and protests  545
54. Prince, Perceval, Portland  554
55. Three fronts  566
56. Sailors  575
57. Swagger and civilisation  582
58. 'We are to have our rejoicings'  595


VII : ENDINGS, 1815 and beyond

59. To Waterloo and St Helena  615
60. Afterwards  624


Principal events of the wars  643
Acknowledgements  653
Sources and abbreviations  655
Select Bibliography  657
Notes  665
List of illustrations  709
Index  713

Principal places for
*In These Times*

# 1. WHO TELLS THE NEWS?

The cathedral city of Canterbury had a barracks on the downs nearby until it closed, when the Argyll and Sutherland Highlanders left, in March 2013. In the last fifty years soldiers have gone from here to the Falklands, the Gulf War, Iraq and Afghanistan. This is my home town and I have seen feelings veer over time from antipathy – squaddies barred from pubs – to respect and sympathy – 'help for heroes' – and back to suspicion again. 'One does wonder, though, *why* they joined the army in the first place?' asked a woman, looking sideways at me on the bus. Not so different then, from the way people spoke about Wellington's 'scum of the earth', the heroes of the Peninsular War. The first barracks here were built for them in Military Road by a young speculator of dubious reputation. He made a fortune.

In the twenty-two years from 1793 to 1815, with a brief gap in 1802–3, the French Revolutionary Wars and the Napoleonic Wars touched people in every part of Britain. Boys who were babies when the wars began fought in the Peninsula and at Waterloo. Because of the way recruiting and balloting were organised, every village, every 'hundred', had to list its men, and men from one in five families were directly involved, in the army and navy, the militia and volunteers. As the years passed, so the bullish, flamboyant figure of Napoleon came to dominate so strongly that the whole conflict was given his name and Boney became the bogeyman of children's nightmares.

The period has been labelled in different ways – the Romantic Era, the Age of Wonder, the Age of Scandal, the Age of Cant – yet behind all those lay a country at war. And as I thought about the men who marched away I began to wonder, how did the wars affect the lives of people in Britain, not those who fought, but those at home looking on, waiting, working, watching?

This book is an attempt to pursue that question by following a few people and families. It is a cavalcade with a host of actors – a crowd biography, if such a thing is possible. It moves from fields and farms to dockyards and foundries, theatres and fairs, drawing rooms and clubs. It follows the back and forth of war and domestic politics, seeing how news reached the people, how fear bred suspicion and propaganda fuelled patriotism, how victories were celebrated and the dead were mourned, how some became rich and others starved. The big names are here – Pitt, Fox, Nelson, Wellington, Wilberforce and others – but history is not a matter of individual lives, however power-ful or heroic. It is multi-layered, with many facets. At some times in this story conflict at home seems more pressing than battles abroad, with the state silencing free speech, spies sending reports, the militia firing on crowds. In Ireland that conflict was deadly. For some people the reports and rumours of victories and defeats and the accounts of Napoleon's lightning marches were like a huge running serial that they could not get enough of. For others they were a muddle of con-fused events in places with difficult foreign names, humming in the background, slipping off the side of the page. The wars were like per-manent bad weather, so all-surrounding that people stopped referring to them and merely said 'in these dismal times', 'in such troubling and dangerous times' or simply 'in these times'. They affected everyone, sometimes directly, and sometimes almost without their knowing it, and in the process the underlying structures of British society ground against each other and slowly shifted, like the invisible movement of tectonic plates.

To sketch the bigger picture, the telling swerves from general to particular, from the state of the wool trade or the action of a military campaign to a man tilling a field, a woman sitting on the stairs. And although the wars and the political disputes are areas of collective action – regiments and crews, parties, crowds and mobs – the detail of those lives also suggests how separate our lives are, even when we call ourselves a 'nation'. What has a widow tramping to see a wounded son to do with a countess gambling in St James's? How does a south Wales ironworker connect with a country banker, or an elderly clergyman in his study? What 'world' do they share?

The war rumbles beneath the late poems of Burns, and colours the work of Scott, Wordsworth, Coleridge and Lamb, Clare, Byron and Shelley; it affects Maria Edgeworth and Jane Austen; it prompts moral outpourings from Hannah More and angry articles from Cobbett and Leigh Hunt; it inspires paintings by de Loutherbourg and Turner. The prints of Gillray, Rowlandson, the Cruikshanks and fellow satirists are a version of the history in themselves, biased and brilliant. These names have endured. But men and women of all classes wrote letters, diaries and memoirs. And many thousands, from women applying for parish relief to relatives looking for places for war orphans, left no record but signed their name only with a cross, on documents still in the archives. Among the crowds, here are some of the voices in this book:

The Heber family of Shropshire and London, clergymen and
     bibliophiles
William Harness, soldier, and his wife Bessy
James Oakes, prosperous citizen of Bury St Edmunds
The Gurney family, Norwich bankers with many children and
     cousins
Samuel and Hannah Greg, of Quarry Bank Mill in Lancashire
The Hoare family, private bankers in Fleet Street
The Galton family, gunsmiths of Birmingham
William Rowbottom, Oldham weaver
Boys: Samuel Bamford from Manchester, William Lovett from
     Penzance, Thomas Cooper from Gainsborough, future
     Chartist writers and leaders

John Marshall, linen-mill owner from Leeds

Aristocrats: Amabel Hume-Campbell, Countess de Grey, and
her friend Agneta Yorke; Lady Jerningham and her daughter
Charlotte; Sarah Spencer, later Lady Lyttelton

Betsey Fremantle and her sister Eugenia Wynne

Mary Hardy, from a Norfolk brewing family

Farmers: James Badenach of Aberdeen, Randall Burroughes
from Suffolk, William Barnard of Essex

Robert Pilkington of the arms depot at Weedon Bec,
Northamptonshire

Sailors: Jane Austen's sailor brothers Francis and Charles;
Lieutenant Thomas Gill; the Scottish seamen, John Nicol and
Robert Hay

William Salmon, a young merchant mariner from the Bristol
Channel

Thomas Perronet Thompson from Hull, soldier, briefly Governor
of Sierra Leone

The Hutchinson family, farmers from County Durham, and their
cousins the Monkhouses from Cumberland

The Longsdon family, farmers and textile merchants from
Derbyshire

James Weatherley, factory boy in Manchester

The Chambers brothers, William and Robert, growing up in
Peebles and Edinburgh

\*

What did newspaper readers in a provincial town know, or think, about
their country at the start of the 1790s? They were told, repeatedly,
that Britain was a great power despite losing the American colonies
only a decade or so before. The humiliation made the older generation nervous of war, yet the American conflict was also an arena where
soldiers and sailors, contractors and arms-makers proved themselves
and learned lessons. Since then, horizons had widened and trade had
grown: travel books offered graphic accounts of distant countries and

wild tracts still to be explored. People read of wars in India, trading posts in the East Indies, sugar and slavery in the Caribbean, rivers in Africa and new convict settlements in Australia. They began talking of 'empire'. And at home, they had become surprisingly fond of their king, George III, celebrating his recovery from a bout of madness in 1788 with tears and relief, and disapproving, by contrast, of the Prince of Wales and his extravagant ways.

When war came, the London and provincial papers carried full reports of debates and immensely detailed – if late and often inaccurate – accounts of military and naval actions, copied from despatches in the official *Gazette*. Although papers carried a heavy tax and were expensive, news spread fast. Men and women interested in politics and the progress of the war devoured papers, pamphlets, and monthly and quarterly journals, discussing them in the book clubs that met in many towns, collecting eclectic libraries of history and travel, romances and philosophy, sermons and verse. These were social as much as literary gatherings: the Birmingham Book Club, which had been going since the mid-1770s, had a group portrait painted in 1792, showing a convivial bunch of radical tradesmen with clay pipes and tankards on the table, and not a book to be seen.[1] In all clubs, members argued over their purchases, especially political works. In Jane Austen's *Northanger Abbey*, written in the late 1790s, General Tilney, a keen book club member, despatches the young women to bed, explaining, 'I have many pamphlets to finish before I close my eyes, and perhaps may be poring over the affairs of the nation for hours after you are asleep.'[2]

The news was part of daily life for many middle-class families. Mary Russell Mitford was five when the war broke out. Despite her family's financial problems as her father gambled his way through her mother's fortune, they could always afford their paper. As a toddler Mitford was perched on the breakfast table 'to read some Foxite newspaper, "Courier" or "Morning Chronicle", the Whiggish oracles of the day'. As a reward her mother would read the ballad of the Children in the Wood, 'and I looked for my favourite ballad after every performance, just as the piping bullfinch that hung in the window looked for his lump of sugar after going through "God save the King". The two cases were exactly parallel.'3 The leisured classes who could not afford a daily paper took one weekly, or relied on the *Evening Mail*, which arrived every Monday, Wednesday and Friday. Friends and relatives commented on war news in the press as something shared. During the Revolutionary Wars, from 1793 to 1802, the Revd Reginald Heber exchanged letters almost every week with his sister Elizabeth in London. Elizabeth and her sister Anne sent groceries like Bohea tea, nutmeg or pyramid sugar to the Shropshire family, and looked after their sons when they went to school in the south. Their affectionate letters were often sprinkled with the phrase 'You will have seen in the papers', usually accompanied by expressions of horror at French excesses or the riotous populace at home.

Less well-off families sometimes shared subscriptions. William Chambers's father, an avid reader of the twice-weekly *Edinburgh Star*, could not afford to subscribe: 'All he could do was to be a member of a club to take in the paper, which was handed about to one after the other, each member being allowed to have it in turn for a certain number of hours.'4 Men also read the news in subscription reading rooms, coffee houses and taverns, which took a wide range of papers. Visiting Glasgow in 1802, Dorothy Wordsworth found 'the largest coffee room I ever saw', in the piazza of the Exchange. 'Perhaps there might be thirty gentlemen sitting on the circular bench of the window, each reading a newspaper,' she wrote in her journal, looking like 'men seen at the extremity of the opera-house, diminished into puppets.'5 The linen-mill owner John Marshall also admired the room, brilliantly lit with candles, and rarely with fewer than a hundred people in it. 'There are 1100 Subscribers to the Coffee Room at 28/- a year,' he noted carefully. 'They take London & Edinburgh papers & journals, country papers & 9 copies of the Sun, Star & Courier & all the monthly publications.'6 Although this was exceptional, most manufacturing towns and ports, even small ones, had reading rooms, sometimes with one room for British and one for foreign papers. At Teignmouth, the public library took the London papers, including the Hunts' weekly *Examiner*. In London, papers were hired out by the hour then sent to the provinces, an annoyance to the government, since vendors sent them back as 'unsold', dodging the tax.

The progress of the war and the battles of politics were played out, too, in songs and ballads, plays and processions. Queues formed round print-shop windows to see the latest satires, and pedlars carried broadsheets with crude woodcuts of ships and guns and John Bull in his many guises.

J. Elwood, a print shop window, 1790

Workers read the papers aloud in taverns, so that even the illiterate could follow the news.[7] When Alexander Aikin visited the great copper mine in Parys, Anglesey, on a mild summer Sunday in 1797, he saw 'a circle of men gathered around a point of rock on which was seated the orator of the party reading a newspaper aloud and commenting upon it'.[8] But still, local and personal concerns came first: weather and wages, bread and board, children and love affairs. The sailor John Nicol found this when he borrowed the papers from the owner of a quarry where he was hiding from the press gang.

[ 7 ]

'The other workmen assembled in my cottage on the evenings I got them and I read them aloud,' he remembered. 'Then we would discuss the important parts together. When they spoke of heavy taxes I talked of China. When they complained of hard times I told them of West Indian slaves – but neither could make any impression on the other.'[9]

As the men (and some women) marched and sailed off to war, letters from soldiers and sailors were longed-for events. 'I could almost have jumped out of the window to snatch the letters from him,' wrote Sarah Spencer, waiting in the bow window in the sunshine for the messenger who collected their letters from the post, and might bring one from her midshipman brother.[10] As letters circulated, family and friends often found their accounts at odds with the official despatches. From Flanders in 1794, Major William Harness wrote home to his wife, complaining about the inaccuracies of the press and the lack of trust in the army:

I can easily suppose that this event will give place to infinitely less probable reports in the English Papers; for we have seen that credulous Country put in alarm from accounts that deserve as little attention, by the flaming Editor of a Newspaper, whose ignorance of the geography of the Country, of position, and dispositions, can only be equalled by his absolute blindness of the force, even of ourselves. My Bessy will never let her judgement be drawn away by these hired pervertors of Truth.[11]

This tirade was prompted by Bessy telling him that she had been reading the *Courier*. 'That iniquitous paper', he raged. 'What a diabolic Trade do these despicable wretches rest their subsistence upon!' 'All read of war,' Coleridge wrote in 'Fears in Solitude', 'The best amusement for our morning meal!'

Alternately trusting and distrusting the papers, people made their own records. In letters, diaries and memoirs they tried to make sense of the times, as well as recording their daily lives. William Rowbottom, a hand-loom weaver, living in Burnley Lane near Oldham, was approaching forty at the start of the war. Almost every day he wrote in his vellum-bound notebooks, in sloping copperplate. He rarely wrote of himself, his brothers and sisters, his wife Anne – or Nanny – and their six children.[12] Instead he recorded local events, as a conscious historical exercise. He loved statistics – the number of households, the records of births, marriages and deaths. He listed prices – meal, flour, pease, malt, treacle, butter, bacon, soap, salt and candles – and marked their rise and fall. His politics are clear: on 26 December 1797, he wrote, 'Died the great patriot who put a stop to general Warrants, John Wilkes Esquire FRS'; on 14 July 1800, 'Died Crispin Clegg, tailor of Royton, a person formerly attached to the Cause of Freedom.' He used the word 'patriot' in its old sense of one speaking for the country against a cabal of ministerial and court interests, the way the Tory Samuel Johnson had used it, in 'Patriotism is the last refuge of a scoundrel.' In his account people march past, ballad-singers, grocers, blacksmiths and innkeepers; they die from old age, consumption and fever; they kill themselves for love or for the shame of bankruptcy; a mother, holding her baby in her arms, leans too close to the spindle on her spinning wheel. These daily losses seem more terrible than the impersonal lists of numbers lost at sea or in battle. But behind everything rolls 'this disasterous war'.

At the other end of the social scale, diarists, letter-writers and memoirists among the aristocracy and gentry also recorded events. Betsey and Eugenia Wynne, for example, began writing their diaries in exercise books on the same day, when they were eleven and nine, and Betsey kept hers up, with one pause, until she died in her eightieth year. The Wynnes lived abroad after Betsey's high-living father met financial trouble in the mid-1780s, but in 1796, alarmed by the progress of the French army, they left Florence and sailed from Livorno on the *Inconstant*. In Naples a few months later, Betsey married the frigate's captain, Thomas Fremantle, their wedding organised by Emma, Lady Hamilton. Sailing with the fleet after the attack on Tenerife in which Nelson lost his arm, the nineteen-year-old Betsey nursed both her badly wounded husband and his commander: as

Thomas reminded her years later, remembering Nelson, 'the first note he ever wrote with his left hand was to you.'[13] So Betsey's diaries move from sea battles and crowded ports to London parties and politics, the love-lives of her sisters, Eugenia, Harriet and Justinia, and the years of bringing up her nine children, waiting for letters from Thomas, her '*caro sposo*', to 'my dearest Tussy', as he called her, when he sailed off to war again.

Some of Betsey's elite set were wild and improvident, some were pious, some brilliant, some boring, some wealthy, some drowning in debt. But they all wrote constantly. They wrote in the morning and the afternoon and in the early hours, in studies and boudoirs, clubs and their country houses. They wrote at home and on the road – many coaches had fitted writing desks. They sent notes across town and wax-sealed letters to the country; they wrote to children at school, to friends they had seen an hour ago, and to their soldier and sailor sons and husbands. Opening the thin, closely written sheets, men on campaigns read accounts of balls and outings, pets and horses, the hay crop and the filling of the beer casks, like news from another world.

# I : STIRRING

## 1789–1792

... shaken the forests of France, sick the kings of the nations,
And the bottoms of the world were open'd, and the graves of
    archangels unseal'd:
The enormous dead lift up their pale fires and look over the
    rocky cliffs.

WILLIAM BLAKE, *The French Revolution*, 1791

## 2. DOWN WITH TOM PAINE!

On Boxing Day, 26 December 1790, the Revd Reginald Heber, in his rectory at Malpas in Cheshire, settled down to write to his sister Elizabeth. Living comfortably off inherited estates in Yorkshire and Shropshire, Heber disapproved profoundly of the liberal ideas of nonconformist leaders like Richard Price and Joseph Priestley. 'I have sent for Mr Burke's book on the French Revolution which everybody reads,' he told his sister, 'and I hear everybody but your Prices and Priestleys and rank Republicans and King-Killers approves.'[1] When it arrived, he read it with 'uncommon pleasure and admiration'.

The book was *Reflections on the Revolution in France*, a passionate polemic greeted with such enthusiasm that it shot through eleven editions within a year. Most people in Britain had welcomed the fall of the Bastille in 1789, seeing it as a symbol of the overthrow of absolutism, edging their traditional enemy nearer to British constitutional rule. The Whig leader Charles James Fox rejoiced: 'How much the greatest Event it is that ever happened in the World! & how much the best!'[2] The national and provincial papers were approving, some warmly so. Joseph Gale's *Sheffield Register* hailed 'twenty-six millions of our fellow creatures bursting their chains and throwing off, almost in an instant, the degrading yoke of slavery', adding that other governments must take note.[3] William Pitt, who had led the British government since he became First Lord of the Treasury in 1783, at the age of twenty-four, was determined, however, not to take serious note, being more concerned with his mission to solve the huge national debt lingering after the American war. He felt sympathy for the French government, he told the House of Commons, but 'the present convulsions . . . must, sooner or later, terminate in general harmony and regular order.' They might even make France a better neighbour. With 'freedom resulting from good order and good government', he declared breezily, 'France would stand forward as one of the most brilliant Powers in Europe; she would enjoy just that kind of liberty which I venerate.'[4]

Within a year doubts set in. How would the members like it, Burke asked the House of Commons in a speech on army estimates in February 1790, 'to have their mansions pulled down and pillaged, their persons abused, insulted, and destroyed; their title deeds brought out and burned before their faces, and themselves driven to seek refuge in every nation throughout Europe'.[5] And all this for no other reason than that they were born gentlemen, and men of property? In November, in his *Reflections*, Burke argued that if the French aristocracy were wiped out, the balance of the constitution would vanish, allowing an unprincipled democracy to emerge: this would lead to licence, then to the rise of demagogues and a new despotism.[6] Worse, the revolutionary spirit was infectious: it could spread across the Channel if not checked. Since Burke had supported the American Revolution, his old allies in the Commons were startled and derisory, and pamphlets and books poured from the press to show his errors. Mary Wollstonecraft wrote *A Vindication of the Rights of Men* at such red-hot speed that it appeared only a fortnight after Burke's tract. In it she attacked his version of the Revolution as the work of a heated imagination, coloured by wild metaphors, and argued that rights should be conferred because they were just, rather than traditional; the social contract must be based on sympathy and reason rather than custom.

A pamphlet war followed, and in March 1791, Thomas Paine published the first part of the *Rights of Man*. In Paine's analysis, the lauded virtue of hereditary monarchy was a fable, a legend woven by those who clung to power. Countering Burke's belief that the nobility

were the 'natural' leaders, he argued that each nation, each generation, should have the right to choose its own form of government:
the deposition of Louis XVI was therefore justified. Part Two of the
*Rights of Man*, published the following February, used the example of
America to argue for a republic approved by the people. When the
book's price was reduced to sixpence so that working men could buy
it, the government panicked. Paine fled to France and was convicted
of seditious libel in his absence. But nothing could stop the spread of
his ideas, anathema to the Revd Heber and his family.

Eighteen years later, in Coleridge's journal *The Friend*, Wordsworth
looked back on the Revolution, 'As it appeared to enthusiasts at its
commencement', in a passage that he included later in his autobiographical *The Prelude*:

> Bliss was it in that dawn to be alive,
> But to be young was very heaven!, oh! times,
> In which the meagre stale forbidding ways
> Of custom, law, and statute, took at once
> The attraction of a country in Romance!
> When Reason seem'd the most to assert her rights.

'To be young' was the key: to feel that doors were opening, dreams of
freedom could be realised, the yoke of habit thrown off, the encrusted
laws of state overturned. The whole world could be changed.

The French Revolution, with its promise of a new political order,
fitted the exuberant mood when 'Reason' was unveiling different patterns in the universe itself and in the solid-seeming material world.
People thrilled to the finding of a new planet, Uranus, discovered
by William and Caroline Herschel in 1781. Amateur astronomers
looked through their telescopes at a night sky ever expanding, while
botanists peered through microscopes at the tiniest operations of
seeds and tissue. People watched balloon flights soar into the sky,
and experimented with electricity and new-found gases. All these
gave dizzying perspectives. But even this intellectual excitement now

began to seem dangerous. Burke implicitly linked science and the Revolution as potentially explosive. 'When I see the spirit of liberty in action, I see a strong principle at work; and this, for a while, is all I can possibly know of it,' he wrote. 'The wild gas, the fixed air is plainly broke loose: but we ought to suspend our judgments until the first effervescence is a little subsided, till the liquor is cleared, and until we see something deeper than the agitation of the troubled and frothy surface.'[7]

Alarm increased as events raced on in France. In late June 1791, Louis XVI and Marie Antoinette fled from Paris, aiming to take refuge in Austria, where Marie Antoinette's brother, Leopold II, was emperor, and mount a counter-revolution. They were recognised and arrested in the small town of Varennes, and brought back to Paris under guard. Their flight changed everything, hardening opinion against the king, who had not only rejected the Revolution but was, it seemed, planning to join the enemies of France. At the end of September, the French National Assembly was dissolved, and a Legislative Assembly established. As the British loyalists heard of the doings of the French sans-culottes, their fear of the mob grew. Disquieted by talk of 'frenzy', 'madness' and 'agitation', they turned nervously to assurances of order, a strong government, and trust in a strict overruling Providence. Repression, not revolution, was in the air.

As well as arguing about the Revolution's political rights and wrongs, people feared that it might draw Britain into war. In mid-February 1792, calming this apprehension, Pitt stifled appeals to increase military funding: instead he cut the budget of both army and navy. He also repealed a tranche of taxes, increasingly hopeful that the national debt was gradually being repaid. The present prosperity might not last, he told the Commons, 'but unquestionably there never was a time in the history of this country, when, from the situation of Europe, we might more reasonably expect fifteen years of peace, than we may at the present moment'.[8]

A month after this blithe speech, Leopold II of Austria formed an alliance with the King of Prussia against France, inviting the other European powers to join them. Approached by both sides, Pitt declined to intervene. If he had, would that have saved Louis, branded as a traitor for colluding with his country's enemies? On 20 April 1792, the Assembly in Paris declared war on Austria. Immediately, Austria and Prussia, soon joined by Russia, took to the battlefield. (Despite their vows to avenge the Bourbons, critics saw this move as prompted more by a desire to expand their own territories while France, they thought, was weak.) In July a Prussian army crossed the French border, led by the Duke of Brunswick, who issued a manifesto promising to restore the king and condemn all rebels to death. More violence towards the royal family would, Brunswick said, provoke an 'ever memorable vengeance by delivering over the city of Paris to military execution and complete destruction'.[9] This merely roused the revolutionaries to fresh fervour; if there was no chance even of a modified monarchy, they had nothing to lose. They must win the war.

In Britain, there were already societies formed to debate political reform, like the gentlemanly Society for Constitutional Information, founded by Major John Cartwright in 1780. Now others sprang up, like the London Corresponding Society, started by the Scottish shoe-maker Thomas Hardy in January 1792, and the Society of Friends of the People, organised by the playwright and politician Richard Brinsley Sheridan, with Charles Grey, Lord John Russell and opposition Whigs. All these wrote to support the French. In London and the provinces, clubs abandoned the old reformist language, with its appeal to Saxon liberties, Magna Carta and the Commonwealth, in favour of the rhetoric of French egalitarianism and Paine's *Rights of Man*. Opposing them, government spokesmen propounded a new 'patriotism', supporting Church and King.

By now Pitt had dropped his insouciant unconcern, disquieted by events abroad and the reform clubs at home. In May a Royal Proclamation banned 'tumultuous meetings and seditious writings'. 'You see there is a proclamation issued, not before it was wanted,' Elizabeth

Heber wrote to her clergyman brother; 'God preserve us from the wicked devices of republicans and dissenters of all denominations.'[10] The *Sun* and the *True Briton*, founded with ministerial help, stirred up fears, and the placeman John Reeves formed the Association for Preserving Liberty and Property against Republicans and Levellers, which spawned two thousand branches. In Bath, hundreds signed a typical 'loyal declaration':

That the wild doctrine of equality newly propagated is unknown to the English Constitution, is incompatible with Civil Society, and only held forth as a Delusion to mislead the lower ranks of the people, to poison the minds of his Majesty's subjects, to subvert all distinctions, to destroy subordination between Man and Man, and to substitute Anarchy in the place of our mild and happy Government.[11]

In Manchester, Samuel Bamford's father, a Wesleyan and a reformer, read Paine's *Rights of Man* and *Age of Reason*. Inspired, he formed a group with his brother and friends – an apothecary, two weavers and a shoemaker – who 'met at each other's houses, to read such of the current publications as their small means allowed them to obtain, and to converse on the affairs of the nation, and other political subjects'. They were quickly labelled 'Painites' and 'Jacobins' (after the revolutionary French Société des Amis de la Constitution, known as the Club des Jacobins from the Dominican convent where they met, in the Rue St Jacques). The five-year-old Bamford, sitting on the doorstep and watching the decorated carts pass by in the processions during the annual Wakes Week holiday, noticed a figure teetering on the back of the last cart. The crowd threw stones at it, shouting:

'Tum Pain a Jacobin' – 'Tum Pain a thief' – 'Deawn wi o' th' Jacobins' – 'Deaawn wi'th Painites' – whilst others with guns and pistols kept discharging them at the figure . . . Poor Paine was thus shot in effigy on Saturday, repaired, re-embellished and again set upright on Sunday; and murdered out-and-out on Monday – being again riddled with shot, and finally burned. I, of course, became a friend of Thomas Paine's.[12]

The previous year had already seen Church and King riots in Birmingham, when the dissenting leader Joseph Priestley's house and laboratory were burned. Now more loyalist riots flared. The poet William Cowper, although he had laid aside his early sympathy for the revolutionaries, was one of those who feared the government's encouragement of such demonstrations. The wisest thing, he mused, in a letter to Lady Hesketh, 'is to let those crackers sleep if they are disposed to do so. Fired as they may be today on the right side, you cannot be sure that they will not prove equally combustible on the wrong tomorrow.'[13]

Every month the press reported new French excesses and carried reports of crowds jeering and spitting as aristocrats were wheeled to the guillotine, whose blade had sliced down for the first time that spring. British sympathisers in Paris began to grow wary. The aspiring surgeon Astley Cooper, who had gone there in June with his new wife Anne to study under leading French surgeons, and had listened avidly to the debates of the National Assembly, was in the streets on 10 August when a crowd stormed the Tuileries and slaughtered the Swiss guard. Next day, in blistering heat, he and Anne wove through the crowds watching Louis XVI and Marie Antoinette taken to prison. In the Tuileries courtyard they found mutilated bodies piled high: another English visitor described the many beautiful ladies, 'walking arm in arm with their male friends . . . contemplating the mangled naked and stiff carcasses'.[14] Soon the Coopers and many others left Paris. A month later, fearing that imprisoned men would rise up in support of the foreign armies, National Guardsmen and others launched a wave of prison massacres. On 20 September, a formidably armed French force led by General Charles-François Dumouriez met Brunswick and his Prussians at Valmy near Reims and forced them into retreat. Next day, France was proclaimed a republic.

In November the French defeated the Austrians again at the battle of Jemappes, and soon afterwards the National Convention issued the 'Decree of Fraternity and Assistance to all People', promising fraternal help to all those who wanted to regain their 'liberty'. The exhilarated republican armies swept on: in the north they took Brussels, and in the east they took Savoy. At the start of December the Convention put Louis XVI on trial.

Some British citizens stayed on in France. Mary Wollstonecraft, who wrote her *Vindication of the Rights of Woman* in response to French debates about women's education and role, reached Paris that December. Sheltered by being registered as the wife of the American Gilbert Imlay, she lingered in France until 1795. But most British visitors turned hastily towards the Channel. Wordsworth had been in France since November 1791, joining other young enthusiasts like James Watt junior and Tom Wedgwood, and feeling inspired by the revolutionary fervour of Helen Maria Williams. He also fell in love with Annette Vallon in Orléans. He waited in Paris until Annette sent him news of the birth of their daughter Caroline, then he returned to England, pleading lack of money. His sadness would last for years. When he wrote the first drafts of *The Prelude* he remembered how in Paris that year, he had seen 'the Revolutionary Power'

> Toss like a ship at anchor, rocked by storms . . .
> I stared and listened with a stranger's ears,
> To Hawkers and Haranguers, Hubbub wild!
> And hissing Factionists, with ardent eyes,
> In knots, or pairs, or single . . .

It seemed that the inspiring energy of 1789 was metamorphosing into darker passions and factions. But still, sympathetic British delegations took addresses to the Convention celebrating French victories. The Society for Constitutional Information offered more than words, donating a thousand pairs of shoes for the 'soldiers of Liberty', saying that they intended to send a thousand pairs each week for the next six weeks.[15] Whether or not those shoes ever reached the French armies, they caused horror in Westminster. And while the young clown Joe Grimaldi entertained the crowds at Sadler's Wells in pantomimes like *The Sans Culottes and the Grand Culottes*, around the country the streets were increasingly tense. 'December 7', wrote William Rowbottom, 'the people of Great Britain much divided and great commotions and strife concerning Paines' "Rights of Man"'. In the following week, in a three-day riot in Manchester, the Church and King mob attacked Unitarian chapels, besieged reformers' houses and trashed the offices of the radical *Manchester Herald*. At the same time, a rumour reached the Home Office that French Jacobins, disguised as priests and even as waiters, were plotting with British radicals to storm the Tower and the Bank of England.[16] The government called for the Tower to be strengthened and brought troops into the capital. In parliament Fox and Sheridan dismissed this as a hoax, a shadow terror created by Pitt to frighten people into attacking dissenters and republicans. Measures were passed to increase the army and navy, stop grain exports to France, and vote through an emergency Aliens Bill to remove 'undesireable' foreigners.

During a discussion of this Bill in late December, in a gesture that soon became famous, Burke flung down a dagger on to the floor of the House of Commons, describing it as the pattern for three thousand knives ordered by Jacobins among the Birmingham metalworkers, 'a sample of the fruits to be obtained by an alliance with France'. Picking up the blade and holding it high, he stormed: 'It is my object to keep the French infection from this country, their principles from our minds and their daggers from our hearts . . . When they smile, I see blood trickling down their faces; I see their insidious purposes; I see that the object of all their cajoling is – blood!'[17]

While the Alien Office set about keeping the 'French infection' out, French émigrés poured across the Channel. The royalist refugees were often surrounded by a romantic aura, like the Marquise de Beaule, who dressed as a sailor on a fishing boat and smuggled her maid across in a trunk, or the twenty-one-year-old, pregnant Comtesse de Noailles, who hid in a coil of rope, dressed as a boy. When she reached Brighton her old friend Maria Fitzherbert whisked her off to watch a cricket match with the Prince of Wales.[18] But the refugees were also marked by tragedy. Jane Austen's cousin, Eliza, who had married

James Gillray, *The dagger scene, or Plot discover'd*. Burke flings the dagger,
Fox and Sheridan recoil and Pitt's hair stands on end.

Jean-François Capot de Feuillide, a captain in Marie Antoinette's
dragoons, had been in London with her small son Hastings at the
storming of the Bastille. While she stayed in England, her husband
returned to France, anxious that his land might be confiscated. He
was guillotined in March 1794.

Fanny Burney, staying with her sister at Mickleham in Surrey,
described the take-over of nearby houses like Juniper Hall, which was
occupied by aristocrats, most of them reformers who had initially welcomed the Revolution. Among them was the Comte d'Arblay, whom
Fanny would marry in 1793, despite her father's disapproval. 'As my
Partner is a *French man*,' she admitted to a friend:

I conclude the wonder raised by the connection may spread beyond my
own private circle: but no wonder upon Earth can ever arrive near my own
in having found such a Character from that Nation. – This is a prejudice

certainly impertinent & very John Bullish, & very arrogant; but I only share it with all my Country men, & therefore – must needs forgive both them & myself![19]

Soon they had a son, Alex, and moved to a small cottage in the country. Not far away, the Abbey School at Reading, run by M. Saint-Quentin and his English wife – where Jane and Cassandra Austen had gone in the 1780s and where Mary Martha Butt, later the prolific author Mrs Sherwood, was now a pupil – was rapidly becoming a small French colony. Mrs Sherwood remembered how when one girl, without thinking, struck up the revolutionary song '*Ça ira!*', 'It will be fine', on the piano, the Marquise St Julien 'flew out of the house and into the street, wringing her aged hands and crying aloud like one deranged'.[20] Not surprisingly, since one version ran,

> *Ah, ça ira, ça ira, ça ira*
> *Les aristocrats à la lanterne.*

James Aitken, *Hell Broke Loose, or, The Murder of Louis*, 1793. As the guillotine descends, flying devils sing '*Ça ira*'

There was some confusion with regard to 'aliens'. Émigrés found work in every corner of the country (Humphry Davy was taught French in Penzance by a refugee from the Vendée, and John Keats by the Abbé Beliard at Enfield), but *The Times* suggested that French servants should be dismissed and French milliners sent home. The fear of espionage grew, particularly around the naval dockyards. The Revd Heber's cousin Mary received a letter from her friend Mrs Drake, lately staying on the coast. 'The number of French people at Southampton and Portsmouth was scarcely credible, they came in such shoals,' she wrote.

But they were never admitted, either Man or Woman, into the *Dock-yard*, and there was a double guard ordered to mount *there* on acct. of the french, and I think it was very proper for it was not possible to be sure that they were all Emigrants and persecuted people, as Spyes and ill-designing people very probably might come over in such a multitude.[21]

The new Alien Office, set up allegedly to hunt these foreign spies, was, however, soon spying on supposed rebels at home.[22] There were arguments in the press, rows in assemblies and meetings, and much table-thumping in taverns and radical clubs. When William Rowbottom began his new diary for 1793, he noted:

This year comenced with very temperate wheather for the Season, but peoples minds far from temperate for a kind of frenzey as burst out amongst the people of this land under the cover of loyalty and shielded by the cryes of Church and King . . . The effigy of Tom was burnt &c in most of the towns and villages in England. In Oldham on New Year's Day his effigie was with the greatest solemnety brought out of the dungeon and placed in a cart and from thence – atended by a Band of Music playing 'God Save the King' besides sixty two musketiers – was taken to the gallows erected over a large Bonfire in the street where he was for some time hung by the neck and then let down to the fire and then consumed to ashes.[23]

The tensions between loyalists and reformers, in parliament and the wider nation, became an escalating fight that framed many people's experience. The polarisation that marked British attitudes throughout the war years was laid down before the conflict even began.

# II : ARMING

## 1793–1796

Who will not sing, GOD SAVE THE KING,
Shall hang as high's the steeple;
But while we sing, GOD SAVE THE KING,
We'll ne'er forget THE PEOPLE!

ROBERT BURNS, 1795

# 3. THE UNIVERSAL PANT FOR GLORY

In the *Gentleman's Magazine* in the spring of 1793 the poet Anna Seward, an earlier supporter of the Revolution, lamented events in Paris. 'O, that the French had possessed the wisdom of knowing Where To Stop,' she cried.[1] It seemed, as the French hurtled on, that the British would inevitably be drawn into war. Pitt and his cousin William Grenville, the Foreign Secretary, had tried to stave off the conflict, negotiating hard to get the French to guarantee that they would not invade Holland. In Britain the conservative gentry and magistrates and the loyalist associations were all for war, while reformers and radicals, industrialists and merchants were generally against. While *The Times* trumpeted the need to fight to preserve the 'British Constitution', the opposition *Morning Chronicle* warned of sliding into a war fought on principle, when there was no threat to national security but great danger to trade and prosperity.

At the start of the new year rain and hail lashed the south, but in early February the weather cleared: snowdrops were flowering and the first thrushes began to appear in the gardens. In the streets, meanwhile, men were selling penny broadsides, handbills and pamphlets describing Louis XVI's death on 21 January. Prints showed a kingly martyr bidding farewell to his sobbing family, and depicted his gory end. The rulers of Europe saw his execution as a threat to every crowned head, especially as the Convention had announced that all conquered territories would be declared republics. In Britain people poured their outrage into letters and diaries. 'Janry 26, Saturday' wrote Parson James Woodforde:

The King of France Louis 16. inhumanly & unjustly beheaded on Monday last by his cruel, blood-thirsty Subjects – Dreadful times I am afraid are approaching to all Europe – France the foundation of all of it – The poor King of France bore his horrid fate with manly fortitude & resignation – Pray God he may be eternally happy in thy heavenly Kingdom. And have mercy upon his Queen.[2]

Crowds wore mourning, or black crêpe bands, and Church and King mobs were out in force. To conservatives like the Revd Heber the execution of a king was the ultimate horror: 'surely this heinous crime will draw down the Vengeance of Heaven on this devoted Race of barbarians.'[3] He rejoiced that effigies of Tom Paine were 'shot through and through and then burnt', and that his own children were joining in: 'Tiddy, Tom and Missy amused themselves yesterday in dressing up two figures to represent Tom Paine and Demourrier which they carried about stuck upon their hunting poles all day long, and in the evening suspended them from the balustrade at the top of the stairs, where they are still hanging.'[4]

In late January the National Convention rejected Grenville's peace proposals, and when the news of Louis's execution reached London, Pitt expelled the French ambassador. On 1 February the Convention declared war on Great Britain and the Republic of the United Netherlands.

On 12 February the House of Commons was packed: the Militia Bill was read for a second time, the business of Canal Bills was dealt with and the Accounts of the Commissioners of the National Debt. Pitt then rose to his feet to acknowledge that 'War has been declared on us':

The event is no longer in our option, for War has not only been declared, it is at our very door, War that aims at the total ruin of the freedom and independence of Great Britain . . . It now remains to be seen whether, under Providence, the efforts of a free, brave, loyal and happy people, aided by their allies, will not be successful in checking the progress of a system, the principles of which, if not opposed, threaten the most fatal consequences to the tranquillity of this country, the security of its allies, the good order of every European government and the happiness of the whole human race.[5]

As the MPs stepped out into a rain-drenched night, Britain was at war.

In the past century Britain had often fought France: in the War of the Spanish Succession from 1702 to 1713, the wars of Jenkins's Ear and the Austrian Succession from 1739 to 1748, the Seven Years War from 1756 to 1763 and the American War of Independence, from 1775 to 1783. Yet in some ways this was a completely new enemy, its armies not the hired troops of an absolute monarch but the people of a revolutionary nation. It was easy to underestimate the passion, and fear, that drove these soldiers on. In early 1793, when the French had reached Brussels and opened the river Scheldt to trade through Antwerp, in competition with Amsterdam, Pitt and his ministers were less concerned with countering the republican menace than with practical imperatives. The urgent need, they agreed, was to stop the French marching into the Netherlands, threatening North Sea trade and the Dutch-held Cape of Good Hope, a vital calling-point on the British run to India.

Pitt gave Grenville the task of welding together an alliance with Austria, Russia and Prussia, and making separate agreements with Spain and Portugal, Sardinia and an array of Italian and German states. At thirty-three, Pitt already had nearly ten years' experience in government, but none in handling a nation at war. He was, however, good at managing money – and he needed to be, since the costs, even of a short war, would be high. But if they could raise funds to pay for the army and navy and provide subsidies for foreign allies, he and his cabinet were convinced the 'First Coalition' must prevail. France looked weak and in disarray, while Austria and Prussia were well armed. The war, Pitt declared, should not last very long.

\*

The news spread quickly. On 15 February 1793, three days after Pitt made his speech in the Commons, James Badenach, farming near Stonehaven south of Aberdeen, was writing his diary, describing the morning snow and the long day's work, ploughing to sow barley and oats, planting horse chestnut and ash trees along the bank, and draining the bog for a new plantation. He recorded the prices of the day, corn and fodder, hay and oats, 'all kinds of manufacture very brisk & high & Servants Extravagant. The French War may Alter Them. Early spring flowers rather backward – No Crocus or Snowdrops yet.'[6] War meant a tightening of belts, a threat to trade, a humbling of servants.

The first thing that confirmed the changes to come was the beat of the recruiting drum, sounding in town squares, on village greens, at country fairs and city markets, as it had in wartime for a hundred years and more. Like travelling players, announcing their arrival with a drum, the regiments sent out a small band – a captain, a sergeant and a corporal, with their drummer and two private soldiers. When they planted their flag, the drummer took up his batons, and as the crowd gathered the captain leapt on to a bench, a chair or a cart and cajoled them into enlisting, offering a bounty and the prospect of booty ahead.

'We had to strut about in our best coats,' remembered Thomas Jackson of the Coldstream Guards, 'and swaggering, sword in hand, drumming our way through the masses, commingled with gazing clodpoles, gingerbread mechanics, and thimble-rig sharpers.'[7] When William Harness, a regular soldier, was recruiting in Sheffield, he set off with three or four other officers, as he told his wife Bessy:

Then follows a Cart with a Barrel of ale with fidlers and a Man with a Surloin of Roast Beef upon a pitch fork, then my Colours of yellow silk with a blue shield with a reath of oak leaves and trophies, and in Silver letters on one side 'Capt. Harness's Rangers', on the other 'Capt. Harness's Saucy Sheffielders'.[8]

The sergeant, corps, drums and fifes followed. 'You can conceive the stir in a prosperous place like this all this noise must make. I am become very popular.'

Harness was one of many officers recruiting their own companies. He had been in the army for thirteen years, saving money to marry his 'adored Bessy', Elizabeth Biggs, in 1791. During her long wait Bessy took up botany, tried to run a book club in her home town of Aylesbury, and loyally made him shirts. Once married, they settled on his half-pay in Dronfield, near Chesterfield in Derbyshire, in a cottage with a garden and orchard, and when the war started they had a two-year-old, Charles, and a baby, Jane. In 1793, William raised enough men to form a company in the new 80th Regiment of Foot.

William and Elizabeth Harness

The cajoling and bribing and bullying were needed, since army life offered few solid benefits. Army service was unlimited – once in, you were there for life. That life might be short, since disease as well as battle cut men down, and it was certainly brutal, with harsh punishments for petty misdemeanours. The very poor, or the desperate, were the first to be tempted. Magistrates sent many others as an alternative to gaol. The French army used conscription, calling on every class, as Wellington would later say, notoriously, 'but our friends . . . are the very scum of the earth':

People talk of their enlisting from their fine military feeling – all stuff – no such thing. Some of our men enlist from having got bastard children – some for minor offences – many more for drink; but you can hardly conceive such a set brought together, and it really is wonderful that we should have made them the fine fellows they are.[9]

Regardless of the hard life, the idea of fighting with a regiment had a certain dashing attraction. Many memoir-writers testified how the moment they joined up changed their lives for ever. One recruit, Thomas Jackson, wrote, 'I now saw myself a new figure – my head being trimmed to order, and crimped with hot irons; my blood red coat, white small-belows, with black leggings; belted and armed; and with a long leather cue, or tail, fashioned to my pole. A strange metamorphosis, thought I to myself, since the day before.'[10]

Countless boys and young men enlisted to get away from drudgery. In Norfolk, James Woodforde's servant was one of those who felt the tug of glory:

May 10, Tuesday . . . On going to bed to Night, our Boy Tim Tooley who was supposed to have been gone to bed was not to be found – All his Cloaths gone also. It is thought he is gone to Norwich to enlist himself, as his Head has long run on a Soldiers Life – His being at Norwich last Saturday & then offered ten Guineas if he would go for a Soldier, determined him.

May 16, Monday . . . My late servant, Tim Tooley, called on us this morning, He came from Norwich with a Cockade in his Hat, and says he has entered himself in the thirty third Regiment of Foot – Poor Fellow, he appeared happy & looked well – I paid him what Wages were due to him and half a Crown extraordinary – in all – 17:6.[11]

Debt-ridden students also fled to the army, including Samuel Taylor Coleridge, who signed up secretly as a private in the 15th Light Dragoons in a moment of guilt-ridden frenzy, as 'Silas Tomkyn Comberbache'. He couldn't ride well, had rusty equipment, found himself nursing a man with smallpox and after three months of misery was extricated by his brothers, discharged as 'insane'.

The promise of pay in hard times was the principal draw, and the offer of a bounty of several guineas on joining. But the bounty often vanished immediately in buying uniform or paying debts. Even with a meagre increase in 1792, army pay was less than a quarter of what a man might earn as a hand-loom weaver, or a tenth of that brought home by a skilled worker after a week in the dockyards. Desperate for troops, the army stepped up recruiting and employed 'crimps', civilians who kidnapped men, forced them to sign up and held them in 'crimp houses' until they were marched off to a regiment. In September 1794, Londoners rioted and tore down the crimp houses; a year later, in a new round of protests, crowds pelted 10 Downing Street with brickbats.[12]

The man responsible for building up the army was Pitt's close friend and drinking companion Henry Dundas, the bluff, fifty-one-year-old Scottish lawyer and politician who had been Home Secretary since 1791 and would be officially appointed as Secretary for War in 1794. In finding men, Dundas had little difficulty with officers, since the army was a chosen career for younger sons of the aristocracy and gentry. But since army commissions were bought, not won by merit or seniority – a cause of much later controversy – this did not necessarily mean the officers had any experience. By 1793, for example, Arthur Wellesley, later Lord Wellington, had stacked up commissions in five regiments without seeing a stroke of action, spending his time drinking, gambling and piling up debts.[13] Aged twenty-four when war was declared, he obtained yet another commission, becoming a major in the 33rd Foot.

The officer class was thus a mix of veterans and entirely untried men. As for the ranks, after the American war the army had been cut to a minimum. In 1793 there were fewer than forty-five thousand men in the cavalry, foot guards and line infantry, and two thirds of these were already serving overseas, chiefly in India or Canada.[14] In the past, when the British fought on the Continent, they had used German mercenaries and now they followed this tradition by hiring twenty thousand troops from Hanover and Hesse. But Dundas also needed to raise new British regiments, no easy task. He turned first to his powerful connections in Scotland. Despite the high cost, Highland magnates were keen to raise regiments, both to gain access to power in London, and to widen their influence through granting and selling commissions to the gentry: in the first two years, the Earl of Breadalbane, the Duke of Gordon, the Countess of Sutherland, Sir James Grant and the Chief of the Mackenzies raised several battalions.[15] In comparison to the size of the population, more soldiers and far more officers would come from Scotland than from any other part of the British Isles. Ireland too provided many early recruits, and Scots and Irish soldiers amounted to half the British army in 1794.

Men were leaving fields and factories, farms and homes, to join the army. And they were also leaving to join the militia, the first line of home defence, organised by the Lords Lieutenant of the counties. A month before war was declared, William Rowbottom noted that 'owing to the expectancy of an approaching war the lots for this part of the Lancashire Militia were this day drawn at Rochdale'. In late January the pace quickened for both army and militia:

Middleton, January 23rd, this day the New Militiamen for Manchester and Middleton Divisions were sworn in at the Bull's Head Inn here, and owing to the probabilety of a war substitutes were hired from 5 guineas and a half to 10 guineas.

Manchester, January 26th, the Recruiting buisness goes on with the greatest alacrity, in this place there being no fewer than 54 recruteing parties of different Regiments.

Manchester, February 10th, it is as true as it is extrordinary that upwards of 1200 yong men enlisted in the different coars here in the course of the last 7 days as apeared in Harrops & Wheelans Manchester papers.[16]

The militia was an old institution, dating, it was said, back to the time of Alfred. Since the Civil Wars the British people had been wary of a large standing army under the control of a king, and the county militia was partly designed to balance this centralised force as well as being a professional reserve. The regiments were raised by ballot from men aged between eighteen and forty-five, and the numbers in each county had been set by the Militia Act of 1757. This now posed a problem since industrial towns were growing fast: the percentage of men taken by ballot in Dorset, say, was one in seven, while in Lancashire it was one in forty-five.[17]

A militiaman was bound to serve for five years. There were exemptions for peers, university dons, clergymen and dissenting ministers, apprentices and clerks, men who had children, even men who were too short (under five feet four), while men could buy themselves out with a £10 fine, or provide a substitute, offering a bounty. But from the start, the militia, like the army, drew unemployed men and those seeking excitement: 'Oldham, March 8th,' wrote Rowbottom. 'Such is the rapid decrease of fustian weaving and the universal pant for glory that Thomas Dobson, James Cheltham and James Wolstoncroft of Northmoor entered into the Derbyshire Militia this day.'[18] When the recruiting officer came back in June so many men flocked to him 'that his order was soon stacked and it is supposed he might have had hundreds more, had he wanted them'.

In the county towns, magistrates worked at all hours, swearing in militiamen and arranging for transport and lodgings. Local inns were commandeered as billets, much to the innkeepers' annoyance, as they had to throw out their normal guests, and the bills were paid late, and rarely in full. Backed by the townspeople they begged for proper barracks to be built, and soon an official barrackmaster general took on this massive task. Barracks, the government reasoned, would make it easier to move militia regiments to police disturbances in areas remote from their own homes, where they were less involved. Radicals like John Thelwall understandably saw this as an 'alarming attempt to separate the soldiery from that mass of fellow citizens of whom they are a part; to whom they are allied; and whom it is their duty to protect in the full enjoyment of their liberty and happiness, and not to be made the instruments of their oppression and ruin'.[19]

At the start of the war there were only seventeen permanent infantry barracks: within twelve years there would be 168, for 133,000 men.[20] But the regiments still descended on small towns. From Newport in the Isle of Wight, the Revd John Gill, with his daughters Sophia and Charlotte, tracked his son Jack's progress around Britain with the Shropshire Militia. They worried about him, as the Revd Gill admitted in November 1794: 'I dare say, my dear Jack, you are by this time weary of Camp and long to get into good and comfortable Winter quarters . . . But we must submit our wishes to the Will of those in power: this you know I always do, as a lover of my Country and my King.'[21] Soldiers and militia filled the towns, drinking and brawling and devouring provisions. Ratepayers complained bitterly, since the daily allowance for the wives and children of militiamen – paid at one day's labour at the local level – came out of the poor rates.[22] In April 1794 the Oldham overseer paid the allowance to 'upwards of seventy wives whose husbands are at this time soldiers'.

Alarmed by the prospect of invasion, within three weeks of war being declared, local gentry in the coastal counties began organising volunteer patrols and sending peremptory requests to the War Office for 'Arms and Accoutrements for their use during the continuance of hostility'.[23] The idea of arming the people made many commentators nervous: Pitt himself called it a dangerous experiment. But then came a startling move in France, the first real sign that a whole nation could go to war, rather than professional soldiers fighting on the country's behalf. In August 1793 the National Convention announced a *levée en masse*. Just as the Revolution had given rights to the people, so the people, the Convention decreed, had an obligation to defend the state. All able-bodied men should be available to fight: unmarried men between eighteen and twenty-five were called up immediately, making up an army of almost eight hundred thousand men, trained within a year. Beyond that, everyone was expected to serve in some way:

The young men shall fight; the married men shall forge arms and transport provisions; the women shall make tents and clothes and shall serve in the hospitals; the children shall turn old linen into lint; the old men shall betake themselves to the public squares in order to arouse the courage of the warriors and preach hatred of kings and the unity of the Republic.[24]

This was a jolt to the British way of thinking, prompting the government to consider how best to use their own people. Conscription was ruled out as too divisive, and recruitment, militia ballots and volunteering were stepped up.[25] In March 1794, they sent out a call, through the Lords Lieutenant of the counties, to 'Gentlemen of Weight or Property' to form infantry and yeomanry troops to defend their local areas.[26]

At this stage volunteering was a game for the elite. Wealthy merchants, manufacturers and professionals as well as peers and gentry began to raise troops. Here too, the Scots were among the first. In Glasgow, citizens raised a staggering £13,938 14s 6d for the volunteer fund. Charlie Walker, owner of a famous shop at the Gallowgate Bridge, formed the Glasgow Grocers Corps, nicknamed the Sugaraloes; Samuel Hunter, editor of the *Glasgow Herald*, founded the kilted Highland Regiment; Mr Geddes, who owned the Verriville glass works and pottery, had a corps called the Anderston Sweeps. During their three weeks' drill 'the musical bands in the evenings discoursed music in front of the residences of their colonels, which drew around them large crowds of citizens'.[27] Here, and south of the border, colonels took immense pleasure in designing uniforms, with trimmed waistcoats and slim breeches, close-fitting jackets, and helmets with cockades and badges. One side effect was the new craze for boots, hitherto farmer's footwear, worn by gentlemen only for hunting, now adopted even by Beau Brummell and the Prince Regent.[28]

There was something intoxicating about such display, and women too longed to be involved. A correspondent from Edinburgh wrote an open letter to 'Mr Urban' of the *Gentleman's Magazine*, insisting, with tongue in cheek, that 'Softness, delicacy, benevolence, piety, and, I may add, timidity (the guardian of virtue), are the natural characteristicks of women'. He damned the fashion for masculine dress, exclaiming that in Scotland, and sometimes even in England,

I have often seen them with short petticoats, short coats with epaulets, a Highland bonnet and feathers, and even with a sword by their side . . . But even this infringement, indecent and disgusting as it unquestionably is, is not quite as bad as that of learning them military exercise. Yes, Mr Urban, it is a fact that, in this town, since the corps of volunteers were embodied . . . the military fever has so far seized on several young and beautiful females as to make them submit to be drilled and exercised (privately of course) by a common serjeant.[29]

Could anything be more indelicate 'than for ladies with their petti-coats kilted, to submit to be taught the movements of a soldier by a Highland man without breeches'? They must leave military duties and the defence of our national dignity 'to their fathers, their bro-thers, and their countrymen'.

Dashing as they looked in their tight coats and shiny boots, the volunteers were, however, hardly reassuring as a military force. Many signed up without realising how strenuous the duties were, forget-ting their age, corpulence and frailty: one Scottish cavalry volunteer resigned, as he was, he said, 'so severely hurt in my private parts by the sudden halting'.[30]

## 4. FLANDERS AND TOULON

When the French Armée du Nord, led by General Dumouriez, marched from Antwerp to invade Holland, William V of Orange begged Britain for help. Less than a month after war was declared, on 25 February 1793, four battalions of the Guards, set sail to Flanders to aid the Austrians. Their commander, on the king's insistence, was his second son, the twenty-nine-year-old Frederick, Duke of York. The order came so suddenly that officers out recruiting in the country only just reached London in time, as one recorded in lively doggerel for the *Annual Register*, describing his rush into the London coach from Devon halfway through supper, his pulling soldiers from the alehouses, and the dash down to Greenwich:

> Our march interrupted by whiskeys and gigs,
> Mad drivers, mad oxen, and obstinate pigs,
> Men boxing, dogs barking and women in tears,
> Harsh concert that threaten'd the drums of our ears.
> Midst a bustle, dear Richard, beyond all compare,
> At length we arriv'd at the Hospital-square.[1]

Although the head of the column arrived in good order, many of the men behind them, plied with drinks from well-wishers, had to be scooped up and stacked in carts. Still, it was a day of pageantry and patronage. Crowds gathered early in the dark, windy morning to wait for the dignitaries to roll up in their carriages. Queen Charlotte and all six of her fair-haired daughters, aged from nine to twenty-six, came bowling down the London road in two large coaches, alighting beaming and smiling under their feathered Gainsborough hats. They were followed by their uncle, George III's brother, the Duke of Gloucester, and his family, and by their brother Prince William, Duke of Clarence, in a spanking coach and six. William – the Whiggish sailor prince, who had served in the American war and in the West Indies – was not given a ship in this conflict. He was in disgrace, both for falling downstairs drunk and, more seriously, for roundly opposing the war in the House of Lords. Much of the whispering in the crowd concerned his liaison with the actress Dorothy Jordan, rather than his naval service. (Two years before the *Morning Post* had reported, 'Her terms are a £1200 a year annuity, an equipage, and her children by all parties provided for.'[2])

Finally, at eleven, flanked by the Prince Regent and the Duke of York, the king rode in to the strains of the national anthem – as the officer poet put it,

> Our sov'reign, God bless him! Belov'd and rever'd,
> Benignantly smiling, amongst us appear'd.

He waved his cocked hat as each regiment marched past and then, while the royals took a late breakfast, the troops piled into boats and uniformed Greenwich pensioners rowed them out to the transports moored in the river. The last boatload left at three o'clock, the king waved his hat, the queen and princesses waved their handkerchiefs, and the coaches swept them back to London.

A haze of glamour surrounded the men who marched away that summer. Watching the regiments in their camps people felt that they too were taking part. In August, at a camp near Brighton, the troops staged a dramatic mock invasion. It was, wrote the *Morning Chronicle*, impossible to describe the effect:

the sublime appearance of those military talents displayed by the different commanders; the different positions taken by the troops; the rapid movements of the cavalry, now in lines, crowning the brows of the hills; now in columns, descending in fast gallop down the steeps, or along the sides of these beautiful swells of ground; the firing of cannon and musquetry, and the immense crowds of spectators, were wonderfully pleasing; and displayed as gay and festive a sight, as can possibly be imagined.[3]

The quality drove down from London in their carriages and the gentry from their estates. The spectators ranged from clergy and lawyers to traders selling food and quack medicines. Brighton camp retained its allure throughout the years of war, as Jane Austen noted in *Pride and Prejudice*, conjuring up for Lydia Bennett 'every possibility of earthly happiness'. In streets thronged with officers:

She saw herself the object of attention to tens and scores of them at present unknown. She saw all the glories of the camp – its tents stretched forth in beauteous uniformity of lines, crowded with the young and gay, and dazzling with scarlet; and to complete the view, she saw herself seated beneath a tent, tenderly flirting with at least six officers at once.

The fictional Lydia had many real-life counterparts, in all classes. In Lancashire, Rowbottom wrote wryly, 'As proof of the influence which the Military have over the fair sex a young woman possessed with less vertue than beauty, decamped from the Cotton Tree Old- ham with one of the train of Artilery, but by the timely influence of her friends, this afair was quashed in its infancy.' As with Lydia, these friends made sure the affair was squared: next day the couple 'were privatly married at Stockport'.[4]

The Duke's continental foray was successful at first. The Austrian armies, under the Prince of Coburg, defeated the French twice, winning back much of the Austrian Netherlands. They they drove south, besieging the border fortresses of Valenciennes, Condé and Mainz. Reading the news while he sat in Cheshire suffering from rheumatism in his shoulder, Reginald Heber told his sister that he

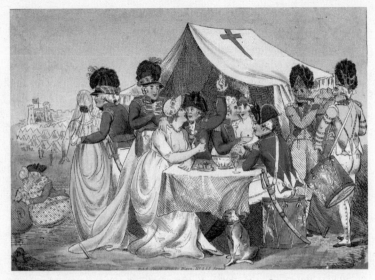

Anon., *The Wags of Windsor, or Love in a Camp*

hoped 'that a Warm Bath and Pump will drive it as successfully and speedily as the Austrians have driven the French Scoundrells out of Brabant'.[5] The whole Heber family were watching events keenly. Ten-year-old Thomas wrote solemnly to his brother Richard, then a student at Oxford, 'Papa and Mama say you are an Idle Gentleman Commoner not to answere their Letter – I think the Loyal people in Oxford must be glad that Dumourier has withdrawn himself from Williamstadt. We rejoice at it very much.'[6] Meanwhile Richard wrote to his aunt Elizabeth, his 'dearest Pop', to whom he was devoted, confessing that he saw events in France as a 'dreadful catastrophe . . . devastation is all that can be expected for months to come. Sorry am I that we have been compelled to take an active part in the war against these wretches – however it is to be trusted, that such confrontation will speedily affect some reinstatement of something like order & tranquillity.'[7]

Everyone hoped for a speedy end. Soon they learnt that the Duke of York was pushing the French back in the Pas de Calais, and in late May, that he had taken command of the siege of Valenciennes, vital for its position on the Scheldt, flowing north to Antwerp. In London, Ann Michelson, a middle-aged woman who enjoyed sending social and political news to her friends and relatives in the country, reported that she had just seen Lady Dalrymple, 'who may this moment be a widow; with tears and trembling she read me part of a letter she received last Saturday from her husband.'[8] She need not have worried: Dalrymple, commanding a battalion of grenadiers, emerged safe, and was made a major-general. Wives and families everywhere circulated letters that described each stage of the conflict as it happened. Among the Guards in that first campaign was William Knollys, eighth Earl of Banbury, who wrote more than a hundred long letters to his mother, his pen dashing quickly over the hardships of army life, poor food, sleeping on hard ground, cold nights walking about to keep warm. There was plenty of entertainment in the towns they passed through, he told her, dances and plays and even pretty nuns. But as his mother and sisters read his letters they could also pick out threads that would be woven into soldiers' accounts all through the war: a distrust of the press, who seemed set on undermining their achievement; a frequent sense of total confusion; and an awareness of the threat to local people. From a camp near Valenciennes, 'having been in a Continual bustle, owing to the awkwardness of our Situation & the turbulence of the times of this Country', Knollys wrote:

When our business is over no one can possibly tell, for our orders are given one Hour, we march the next, & even our Field Officers are ignorant . . . the villages through which we march are plundered, fine Edifices destroyed, so that we sleep in Stables, Churches & whatever we can find – I am sorry to tell, that the Combined Armies distinguish neither Friends or Enemies in their Progress, and Devastation marks our Advance, in deed it is almost impossible to avoid it, for when our soldiers starve & literally we have no Provisions provided, it is impossible to stop them from taking what they can.[9]

That summer, the troops sweated in another heatwave, reaching ninety degrees. In Paris in June, a coup put Maximilien Robespierre and the Jacobins in power, sealing the fate of Marie Antoinette and many others. So when British troops finally stormed the ramparts of Valenciennes on 28 July there were loud celebrations. At Astley's Amphitheatre in London, Philip Astley, an old soldier who had tried to volunteer at the start of this war at the age of fifty-one, staged a bold re-enactment of the siege, including the firing of a cannon that had been captured there.[10]

In August the Duke of York's forces headed towards Dunkirk. The signs were good and French morale was low: General Dumouriez had defected to the Austrians, while other generals who failed had been summarily recalled – some to the guillotine. But this month the news of the French *levée en masse* brought the prospect of thousands of fresh volunteers, while the Flanders campaign was undermined by Dundas recalling troops to redeploy to the West Indies or the Mediterranean and by York's conflicts with his allies. As the French troops pressed forward again it seemed that the British might be cut off and surrounded. In early September the London papers revealed that York had been slowly withdrawing from Dunkirk under cover of darkness, abandoning guns and stores. After dining with the duke in Belgium, Sylvester Douglas, later Lord Glenbervie, wrote in his diary that he had talked 'with considerable earnestness' about his complaints against the ministers and especially the Duke of Richmond, head of the Ordnance, 'in the affair of Dunkirk. His heavy artillery which had been promised did not arrive until three weeks after the time.'[11] When it did come, it was worse than useless. But why, critics asked, was no naval squadron there to support him?

In the south of France too, British hopes rose – and then fell. The Jacobin coup had prompted counter-revolutionary uprisings in the Vendée, Lyons, Marseilles and Toulon. In August the sixty-year-old Lord Hood, a veteran of the Seven Years War and the American war and now admiral of the Mediterranean Fleet, responded to a request from the Toulon rebels and took the port with a combined force of British, Spanish and French émigré soldiers. This dazzling move promised to destroy France's naval strength in the Mediterranean and give Britain a southern French base. But in September, the same month as York's retreat from Dunkirk, the revolutionary army laid siege to Toulon. After three months the French troops drove out the British garrison, their artillery commanded by an unknown officer, twenty-four-year-old Napoleon Bonaparte.

As the soldiers ran to the ships, with women and children screaming and scrambling on to the boats, Captain Sir Sidney Smith tried to burn the Arsenal and scuttle the French fleet. In the process he blew up two British gunboats. 'Having now set fire to everything within our reach, exhausted our combustible preparations, and our strength, to such a degree that the men absolutely dropped on the oars, we directed our course to join the fleet,' Smith explained to his admiral.[12] It was not a glorious moment.

# 5. SCARLET, SHOES AND GUNS

When the war began, government stocks dipped, losing a fifth of their value. There were many bankruptcies – 'Have you heard of the terrible Crash among the Bankers at Chester and Liverpool?' asked the Revd Heber; '. . . everybody is sorry for the Chester Bankers who it is said are taken in for at least sixty thousand pounds, between Caldwell of Liverpool & Forbes, a Banker in London who it is said decamp'd for France the Land of Rascals with seven hundred thousand Pounds', intending to buy church lands.[1] 'In Wheelers *Manchester Chronicle* of August 31st,' noted William Rowbottom, 'it apeared that since January last owing to these dismal times no less than 873 Commisions of Bankrupsey had been issued out.'[2] Many merchants and manufacturers were anxious about the intricate lines of credit that supported their trades, but others rubbed their hands – while large-scale building works like the crescents of Bath ground to a halt, builders, for example, looked forward to big contracts for barracks, fortifications, arsenals and wharves.

A horde of army contractors leapt into action. Soho Square in London, built in the late seventeenth century, was home to politicians and colonels and clergy, congregating in London during the parliamentary session. Slowly the merchants moved in, like young John Trotter. He had been an army contractor during the American war, and when it ended he pointed out that it was ridiculous to sell off military stores and then buy them again more expensively at the first hint of alarm. Instead he offered to store them himself. This was agreed, and in 1785, aged twenty-eight, he set up his business at number 5 Soho Square. With the new war, Trotter acted fast, moving into number 7 Soho Square and using numbers 4, 5 and 6 to build a warehouse. Soon he was channelling all the stores the government might demand: tents and camp kettles by the hundred, knapsacks and canteens by the thousand. Within five years he was doing so well that he bought Dyrham Park in South Mimms in Hertfordshire, the estate of Admiral Keppel's son William – house, park, home farm and land.[3] Other army agents, keen for a slice of the action, soon shouldered into the square: John Crawford, John Dickson, Benjamin Andrews and the Duberley brothers, 'Contractors to the Armies'.[4]

There were grand tailors too in Soho Square, taking in orders for the regulars, the militia and the flashily dressed volunteers. In October 1798 James Duberley, Trotter's neighbour, handed one militia colonel a bill for £1369 9s 4d, for clothing supplied over the past year.[5] Behind the tailors came the wool and cloth merchants, supplying 'scarlet' for officers, 'red' for the ordinary soldiers and militiamen and superfine broadcloth for the yeomanry volunteers, the cream of the local gentry. (A crisis came when the vital cochineal from Mexico for the red dye, imported through Spain, was cut off by the war.) The London tailors sometimes hired out the work to a mass of poorly paid workers: Messrs Silver & Co. used women and children in the city and the counties around to make the favourite 'frilled or full-fronted linen shirt'.[6] But on the whole the masters employed journeymen tailors, who were paid by the day or for piece-work, and who clung to their rights, being divided between 'flints' who worked by day, and 'dungs' who worked by night, usually for lower wages. They formed one of the strongest of the journeymen's unions, operating from 'houses of call', informal labour exchanges in pubs in the City and the West End where they waited until a job came their way. In these days of high demand, they did not have to wait long, and their wages of around a pound a week increased yearly until 1813, almost the end of the war.

They were doing so well that colonels who wanted resident tailors to accompany their regiment or militia corps found it hard to persuade them to leave London for country wages.

Like the tailors, shoemakers were never short of work. Many were independent: a man might work in his shop, measuring feet and cutting out the leather – a skilled job – while the stitching was done by his wife and children at home. But now that each soldier was, in theory at least, supplied with two pairs of shoes plus spare soles and heels, there was a sudden demand for thousands of pairs and shoemakers began to work on a new method, using standard sizes. The demand put pressure on prices and upset the market. The navy supplier Mr Murray complained in 1793 that prices had risen fast, not just from the increase in the cost of leather, 'but from the very uncommon demand for the last 5 or 6 months having rendered that Article not only dear but very scarce'. Matters were made worse, he said, by 'a demand for upward of 30 thousand pairs of shoes for the said Militia, which are at this time manufacturing in different parts of the country, but has taken from us many useful journeymen and has occasioned an increase in wages'.[7] A great distribution of orders followed, with London contractors providing cut uppers and sole leathers, then sending them out to the shoemaking districts of Northamptonshire and Staffordshire to be stitched, packed in baskets and carted back to London.

Every battalion in the army, every ship in the navy, also needed arms and ammunition, maps and charts. A list of stores and equipment supplied to each ship ran from 'iron ordnance with carriages' though axle trees, trucks, ladles and sponges, heads and rammers, spikes, round shot and grapeshot with boxes to hold them, down to 'hand grenadoes', powder measures, muskets and bayonets, pistols, cartridges, flints and oil.[8] The body responsible for supplying all these was the Ordnance Board, a medieval institution that still had its headquarters in the Tower of London, with additional offices in Palace Yard, Westminster. Since its chief officer, the Master General, was usually a statesman or soldier and was often away, the practical work was done by members of the

Board – the Lieutenant General, Surveyor General, Clerk of the Ordnance and Clerk of Deliveries – and their staff. One of their respon-
sibilities was the production of maps, often surveys of ports and other
militarily strategic spots, and in 1793, the pioneering 'Trigonometrical
Survey' team began working on maps of the southern counties, as part
of the 'Ordnance Survey' put in place two years before.[9]

The Board had its own industrial plants, like the gunpowder mills
at Waltham Abbey and Faversham, but its oldest and most famous site
was the 'Warren' at Woolwich Arsenal, the base for the Royal Military
Academy and for the Royal Regiment of Artillery, the Gunners. After
Ordnance reforms in the 1780s, the whole stock was now regularly
tested and weak guns condemned. New gun locks, brought in in 1793
– a decade before the French used them – allowed naval gunners to
sight more accurately, looking down the barrel and allowing for the
pitch and roll of sea. Woolwich took pride in its great foundry, built in
the American War for casting brass guns.[10] The casting was dramatic
and dangerous, with glowing metal pouring into moulds stacked in
earth in the great pit, and the boring of the cannon was absolutely up
to date, with a new, horizontal boring machine.

Cannon manufacture in the Royal Brass Foundry, Woolwich

The Ordnance had yards at all the ports, and the Arsenal was regarded as one of the wonders of the day. One visitor in 1798 described it as 'the *Palladium* of our Empire, where one wonder succeeds another so rapidly that the mind of a visitor is kept in a continual gaze of admiration'.[11] The Royal Artillery made their tests of new cannon as spectacular as possible, staging dramatic displays before huge crowds on Woolwich Common and the marshes, firing off different types of guns, rockets and smoke bombs at flags, mock fortresses and specially built earth banks, with the shots roaring like thunder and sparks and flames shooting high into the London sky.[12]

In 1793, however, the Board faced a problem: they needed over two thousand extra cannon quickly, and around the same number as replacements each year. From the start, they relied on private contractors. Orders for cannon and for the shorter, lighter carronades went out to big gunfounders like Walker & Co. of Rotherham, who rushed into work, laying down the cannon moulds in pits by their furnaces, pouring in the molten iron, cooling, fettling and cleaning the great guns, sending them down by boat to be tested. The cannon balls were also made here in circular moulds, finished by hand, with men chipping away at the heavy metal spheres to make them perfectly round so they would fly as straight as a gunner could aim.

Musket-making surged too. Along the lanes and alleys and over the roofs of Birmingham in the winter of 1792–3 the frost glittered, hard as steel. Yet within the open workshop doors men sweated in their shirts, sleeves rolled up, necks open, making handguns and muskets. The town hummed with the tapping of chisels, the ringing of hammers on anvils, the stamping of dies and punches, the shaving of steel. The ledgers in the gunsmiths' offices bulged with slips of paper, orders ready for clerks to write up. Birmingham workshops had produced swords and weapons since Cromwell's Commonwealth and gunmakers now clustered in the streets and lanes around St Mary's Church. Here the back gardens of elegant Georgian houses became a maze of workshops, places for skilled men to hire a room, or make do with a few feet of bench space. The hub was Steelhouse Lane, where John Kettle ran two cementation furnaces, converting iron into steel by heating it with carbon packed into airtight chests. Further down the lane, the Galtons' family firm was turning out hundreds of guns a week.[13] Samuel Galton senior, once a draper's apprentice in Bristol, had begun by making gun barrels and locks in the 1750s in the company run by his father-in-law, James Farmer, and had then bought up warehouses and workshops in neighbouring streets. His profits rose steadily, from government contracts during the American wars and from selling guns to the Africa traders, who often exchanged them for slaves.

At the start of the wars the Ordnance bought ten thousand muskets from Liège as well as placing orders with the Birmingham makers, the Galtons, Grices, Ketlands and Whatelys. Both sets of makers found it hard to keep up with demand. The brusque Duke of Richmond complained in frustration to Dundas that 'all our Workmen have failed us in respect to the time they agreed to send in supplies'. As for Liège, the people there were 'very dilatory', could not work to a pattern, 'and although the bore is the same, scarce any two of the musquets are similar'.[14] Although there were talented British designers, like the gunsmith Henry Nock, it would take too long to introduce new, experimental models.[15] Gunmakers were asked to send in anything they could make and they flooded the Tower with cheap guns of all shapes and sizes. As they had often done in the past, the government turned to the East India Company, which had supplies for its own private army and now agreed to transfer its current stock of arms and empty its warehouses. (It helped that Henry Dundas was also president of the India Board of Control, the government's official liaison with the Company.) So great was the urgency that one Indiaman in full sail down the Channel was diverted into Portsmouth and five thousand stands of arms were requisitioned. In Birmingham the gunsmiths' district rattled with business, making muskets, carbines and pistols, and sending gun barrels and locks to London to be 'set up' at the Tower.[16] The Galtons, in particular, worked on larger and larger orders, including an unusual request for 5,100 'French pattern' muskets at the high price of twenty-five shillings each.

For eighty years the gunmakers had a regular system of filling orders for the Ordnance. The Ordnance officials signed contracts for different components, supplying patterns and negotiating separately with individual manufacturers – barrelmakers and lockmakers, the furniture makers who made the brasswork, and the 'small-work men' who supplied pins, screws and triggers. When the finished parts were delivered to the Tower, they were sent out to 'rough stockers and set-ters up' who put the weapons together, sometimes including the bay-onet. But depending on demand, Birmingham firms like the Galtons sometimes assembled the muskets themselves. The only problem was that the government was slow to pay, and some makers still preferred to deal with the East India Company, the Hudson's Bay Company or the Royal Africa Company, who were not so strict on quality and came up with the cash more quickly. The big contractors negotiated with the small masters, who in turn negotiated with the artisans: bills and credit slips surged across the town and the outlying districts.[17] There were no guilds here to dominate the industry and specialised workshops took on different parts of the process. At the barrel rolling mill, men shaped the finished steel plates round a cylindrical mandrel, welded them along their length to make the barrel and then smoothed and planed the rough barrels, inside and out. At another workshop, using water power or a hand-turned crank, they bored the barrels, finishing them to a precise internal gauge. Larger gunmakers like the Galtons had their own boring mills, but sent the barrels out to be ground to a smooth finish at a grinding mill.[18]

Different workers made the gun locks, shaping and fitting more than a dozen parts, while other workshops made the wooden stocks, the best for the army, from German or Italian walnut, the rest from beech, for the cheaper guns of the African trade. Behind every trade lay the tool-makers and their tools, even special cutters for making bullet moulds. There was a poetry to the making, a host of names: 'stock-makers, barrel welders, borers, grinders, filers, and breechers; rib makers, breech forgers and stampers; lock forgers, machiners and filers; furniture forgers, casters, and filers; rod forgers, grinders, polishers, and finishers; bayonet forgers, socket and ring stampers, grinders, polishers, machiners, hardeners, and filers; band forgers, stampers, machiners, filers, and pin makers; sight stampers, machiners, jointers, and filers; trigger boxes and oddwork makers'.[19] Then came the 'setters up', the jiggers – who tested the fit of lock to stock – and the stockers, percussioners and screwers, smoothers, polishers and engravers. Everywhere small boys ran between the workshops and warehouses carrying the parts ready for the next stage. Finally the three parts – lock, stock and barrel – were assembled and sent to the Ordnance, and from there, often haphazardly, to the regiments that needed them.

After four years of war the Ordnance adopted the East India Company's standard firearm, the India Pattern Musket or a version of the standard military weapon affectionately known as 'Brown Bess'. This was a smooth-bore musket, a muzzle-loading flintlock, fired by sparks from striking steel into a small pan holding gunpowder on the side, the flash leaping through a touch-hole into the barrel.[20] It was slender and 'elegant' – strange term for a weapon of death – with a thirty-nine-inch barrel and a range of eighty to a hundred yards. When fitted with bayonets, these muskets were between five and six feet long, often taller than the soldiers who carried them. On the battlefield the infantrymen fired in mass volleys then charged with their bayonets, using the gun like a pike. The Brown Bess, while effective, was not technically advanced, but it was still demanding to make, since it required the correct stiffness of spring and delicate setting of the flint, and the Board cajoled the Birmingham makers to turn over to this pattern by giving them a higher payment for longer credit.

When the Galton company took this on, the man in charge was Samuel Galton junior – Samuel John to his family. Now in his forties, he had joined the company at seventeen and when he was twenty-one, in 1775, his father had put £10,000 into his business account and made him manager of the Steelhouse Lane firm. A year later he was a partner and by the 1780s he had quadrupled his investment. He and his wife Lucy, from a Scottish branch of the Barclay family, had five sons and three daughters and a house full of noise, music and books. Lucy was clever and humorous, knowledgeable about plants, birds and insects, a reader of Homer, Dante and Milton. Samuel was bulky and serious, with a piercing glance from beneath heavy brows. His daughter Mary Anne remembered how 'he was usually occupied for a few hours every day at his house of business in Birmingham; but from about one o'clock, when he usually returned, he was chiefly engaged at home in intellectual pursuits; and of these he had an endless variety'.[21] A former student at the dissenting Warrington Academy, he was a great supporter of Joseph Priestley, a friend of Matthew Boulton and James Watt, and a member of the Lunar Society, writing on optics, colour, canals and birds, and building up a fine library and collection of scientific instruments. As his wealth grew he moved his family to a mansion at Great Barr, just outside Birmingham: they spent their summers here and the winters in town.

Like all who supplied the army, Galton was raking in money. His profits grew year by year, and the £10,000 he had, when his partnership began, rose to £139,000 by 1799, a fortune made from war. But his gun-making put him in a difficult position. He and Lucy both belonged to old Quaker families, related by marriage to the Darbys, Gurneys, Lloyds and other powerful clans. And the Quakers were pacifists. At the Yearly Meeting in 1790 the Birmingham Meeting had issued a firm statement:

If any be concerned in fabricating, or selling Instruments of War, let them be treated with in love; and if by this unreclaimed, let them be further dealt with as those we cannot own. And we intreat that when warlike preparations are making, Friends be watchful lest any be drawn into loans, arming, or letting out their Ships, or Vessels, or otherwise promoting the destruction of the human Species.[22]

Galton's attitude caused tension, and he felt the strain. To Mary Anne, his character, 'earnest and impetuous, was not one of repose, and the various elements of which it was composed issued in conflict rather than rest'.[23] In 1795, accused of 'fabricating, and selling Instruments of War', he and his father were formally investigated by the Meeting and threatened with 'disownment'. A visit to examine them was arranged, headed by men they had known for years: Sampson Lloyd, merchant and banker, Joseph Gibbins, a metal merchant, and the jeweller James Baker. Furious, Galton answered forcefully, pointing out that the family had made guns for seventy years, without any rebuke, and arguing that making arms did not necessarily imply an approval of war: indeed guns were vital for defence and for keeping the peace. He would give no pledge about abandoning the business, but would, he said, 'reserve to myself, a perfect Independence on that head'.[24] On 10 August 1796, Galton was disowned by the Society of Friends, the formal body of the Quaker movement. Although his father now retired, Galton defiantly continued his trade. But he still wore his broad Quaker hat, and he and Lucy went to Meeting, as they had always done, to the end of their lives.

# 6. BRITISH TARS

After the setbacks of the failed siege of Dunkirk and the loss of Toulon, Pitt was determined to take a closer interest in the detail of campaigns. Wilberforce remembered him haring back and forth to Downing Street, and finding him in Westminster, 'a great map spread out before him'.[1] But if the Prime Minister was troubled about the army, there was no doubt, in the press and in the minds of the people, that the strength of Britain would lie, as it always had, in its navy.

Sailors were often viewed with suspicion, as if they carried a threat of danger, but the 'honest tar' – so named from his canvas jacket coated with tar to make it waterproof, the old tarpaulin – was already a symbol of defiance. When the fleets were in port the towns were thronged with sailors, officers in uniforms with cocked hats and hardened seamen with their rolling walk, flaunting oiled pigtails, short jackets and white trousers, embroidered down the seams with ribbons. Just as the military camps enthralled people, so did displays of naval power. In June 1793, Parson Woodforde took his niece Nancy to the Panorama in the Leicester Fields, 'a fine deception in painting of the British & Russian Fleets at Spithead . . . It was well worth seeing indeed, only one Shilling apiece – I pd.– 0.3.0. We stayed about an Hour there – Company continually going to see it.'[2]

Although there was some tension between the Admiralty, who

controlled naval manning, appointments and strategy, and the Navy Board, who built and kept up the ships, the navy was in fighting trim, at least with regard to warships. After the end of the American war in 1783, Pitt's government had granted money for shipbuilding and launched new ships regularly. Then, at the end of the decade, during a dispute with Spain in 1789 over rights of navigation in the Pacific, a Spanish warship had anchored in Nootka Sound, a favoured base for whalers on Vancouver Island. Impounding British ships, arresting sailors and pulling down the British flag, the Spaniards claimed their country's right to the whole of America's west coast up to Alaska, which would be left to the Russians. Alarmed, the Admiralty speeded up the repair and arming of the fleet. The Spanish crisis was eventually resolved by negotiations but since then the navy had taken priority in government spending. At Portsmouth an impressive system of dry docks was built, where ships could be repaired and have their copper sheathing renewed, using an entirely new type of hard-rolled alloy bolt. This was developed by the industrialist Thomas Williams, owner of copper mines in Anglesey, factories in Birmingham and smelting works in Lancashire, who maintained his monopoly of coppering ferociously, making himself a millionaire.[3] And while the naval dockyards repaired the ships, a host of private yards took over their building and visitors crowded to see new warships on the stocks.

Yet the Admiralty itself was far from efficient. The second Earl of Chatham, Pitt's elder brother, who had been First Lord of the Admiralty for the past fifteen years, was notoriously lazy, a late riser who missed so many Admiralty Board meetings because of 'ministerial concerns' that he became known as 'the late Lord Chatham'. When Pitt tactfully removed him in December 1794, hundreds of Admiralty letters were allegedly found unopened in his home.[4] He was replaced by Lord Spencer, a Whig of the old school. Methodical and efficient, Spencer set about tidying up the chaos – encouraging promotion by merit and pushing through the appointment of talented officers. He appointed Jervis to lead the Mediterranean Fleet and Duncan to the North Sea and recognised Nelson's talent at an early stage. To a certain extent the navy regulated itself: promotion could not be bought, as in the army, but was acquired through 'interest' or won by glory. In these early years of the war popular captains could still take their crews from ship to ship like feudal lords and corruption was not only endemic but viewed as essential: if a captain had the money to bribe a dockyard superintendent to give him the supplies he needed, so much the better.

For the families of naval officers, war brought anxiety but also hope of advancement and riches. When the sailors were away, often on long missions of months and years, their letters home were treasured and passed round, the replies carefully numbered so that those who received them could see if the sequence was broken, a packet lost at sea, abandoned in a wreck, burnt in a battle. Francis and Charles Austen, born in 1774 and 1779, the youngest of Jane Austen's six brothers, both went into the navy. From the Royal Naval Academy at Portsmouth, Francis joined the frigate *Perseverance* in 1789 and then Admiral Cornwallis's flagship the *Crown*, sailing in the Indian Ocean and becoming a lieutenant just before his nineteenth birthday. Following him, Charles became a midshipman in 1794 under Captain Thomas Williams, who was married to an Austen cousin, and joined in the capture of a French frigate, the *Tribune*, a first taste of glory.

Francis was authoritarian, precise, and a devout evangelical; Charles was easy-going, loved by his men. But both their careers showed the importance of influential allies such as Thomas Williams, and Admirals Bertie and Gambier, connections through their brother James's marriage. Like many concerned parents, the Revd Austen pressured the Admiralty contacts who might help his sons. In 1798 Jane wrote excitedly to Cassandra, with a delight she later gave to Fanny Price in *Mansfield Park* when Henry Crawford intervenes with his admiral uncle to win promotion for Fanny's brother William. Telling Cassandra that Admiral Gambier was optimistic about Francis being made commander, Jane ended, 'There! – I may now finish my letter, & go & hang myself, for I am sure I can neither write nor do anything which will not appear insipid to you after this – *Now* I really think he will soon be made . . .'[5] A few days later she reported Frank's appointment to the *Petrel* sloop at Gibraltar. 'This letter is to be dedicated entirely to Good News,' she said. And as soon as she had 'cried a little for Joy', Cassandra must also take in Charles's move to a frigate he had longed for, and her father's offer to cover her current expenses: 'If you don't buy a muslin Gown on the strength of this Money, and Frank's promotion, I shall never forgive You.'[6]

While officers clawed their way up, the Admiralty was desperate to boost the number of crews, relying more and more on the Impress Service, the press gang. To 'impress' – to stamp or seal – meant to register a recruit, and the press gang was an old institution, recently reorganised, with over sixty rendezvous stations in the ports and in industrial towns inland.[7] In addition, captains could press men from ships captured at sea. Technically the officers on land were only allowed to impress watermen and seamen, but they could also take 'volunteers', enabling magistrates and constables to hand over troublesome drunks and minor felons. Above all the gangs wanted trained seamen. Immediately they met resistance, particularly in the merchant ports of the north-east, like North Shields and Whitby. Two weeks after war was declared, sailors and ships' carpenters wielding axes and tools and women hurling stones saw off the Tyneside gang with a traditional humiliation of their jackets turned inside out. 'On Tuesday last', the *Newcastle Courant* reported, 'the sailors of this port dismissed the press-gang from North Shields, with the highest marks of contempt; – with their jackets reversed. They were conducted by a numerous mob to Chirton-Bar, and who, on parting, gave them three cheers, but vowing that, should they ever attempt to enter Shields, they should be torn limb from limb.'[8]

Whitby, with its river and harbour sheltering under the old abbey, had 250 boats, some sailing to the Mediterranean or America and others whaling in the Greenland seas: four thousand men from the town had served in the American wars, and the townsfolk were determined that this would not happen again. As soon as the warrant officer, Captain Shortland, set up his rendezvous, a crowd of a thousand men and women attacked it, broke down the doors and ran the gang out of town.[9] Men and women played an equal part. Two ringleaders, Hannah Hobson and William Atkinson, were tried at York assizes in March under the riot act: Hobson was transported and Atkinson hanged.

Experienced sailors lived in fear of the gangs. John Nicol, a Scottish sailor, now nearly forty, had served in the navy during the American war, then worked on a whaler off Greenland, on a merchantman in the West Indies and on the *Lady Juliana*, transporting female convicts to Australia. On the way he fell in love with a convict, Sarah Whitlam, who bore him a son but disappeared in Sydney Cove and was never seen again. Much of his life was spent hunting for her. In 1794 when his ship reached Gravesend and 'a man of war's boat came on board to press any Englishman there might be', Nicol and a friend hid among smothering bags of cotton, while their captain swore that all his hands were Portuguese. Borrowing a cocked hat from a customs officer, Nicol slipped off board, wary of informers among the watermen who rowed him and the waiters who served him. In the end he changed his mind, and a landlord informed on him with his own connivance, as a way of getting him to sea again to search for Sarah. The landlord 'got the six guineas allowed the bringer, which he returned to me. He was from Inverness, as honest a man as ever lived.' This was the start of years of naval voyaging, to the Cape of Good Hope, then to Java and China, and back to Norway and the North Sea.

Sometimes, through an odd stroke of luck, the gang was the door to an officer's career. In late 1794 the Revd John Gill was worried about his second son, Tom, a merchant seaman who had been on a trading voyage to Nevis and Martinique, had nearly died of fever, lost his money gambling, and was now a prisoner of the French in Guadeloupe. From there Tom was handed over to an American captain and got a passage home, surviving a shipwreck off the north Welsh coast and walking to London, straight into the arms of the gang. As he stepped on to London Bridge, he wrote, 'I was collared by two stout men, who soon gave me to understand they were part of a press gang purposely stationed there to catch such stray birds as poor me. Resistance was quite vain, for there were a dozen of them round me in a moment.'[10] By chance, the captain who questioned him knew his home in the Isle of Wight, and since they had naval friends in common, put him down as able seaman but told him to consider himself a midshipman, a junior officer. Joining the fleet at the Nore, the anchorage off Sheerness where the Medway meets the Thames estuary, Tom sailed on into the war.

In its drive to strengthen the navy, the Admiralty also turned to the government's great ally, the East India Company, which had its own 'Marine', a fleet of armed ships a hundred strong, that worked alongside the navy in Indian waters. These armed Indiamen with their well-trained crews could easily be converted into ships of the line. The Company also raised three thousand sailors and offered transport ships for troops and supplies, while its shipbuilding programme provided many trained shipwrights. In return the government protected the Company's interests, hardly a worry for parliament, as between sixty and a hundred MPs were substantial owners of India stock, including an increasing number of Company directors and nabobs enriched by their stay in India. This protection annoyed the cotton manufacturers, who lobbied hard to end the Company's monopoly. Samuel Greg of Quarry Bank Mill wrote angrily to his friend William Rathbone in Liverpool, noting that Dundas was stressing the Company's ability to carry goods more cheaply than independent traders, but hoping that the whole business would be discussed openly, and 'the Interests of the Body of the Kingdome weigh'd against that of a few Rapacious & Corrupt Individuals, for I cannot consider the Company in any other light'.[11]

All the merchants trading overseas now needed protection from the navy, and in its desire to build strong links, the City bestowed honorary freedoms, gold boxes and swords on successful captains. In 1794 the Lord Mayor of London and the corporations of other trading and industrial towns also opened subscriptions for extra bounties for volunteers: £5 for an able seaman, £2 10s for an ordinary seaman, and £1 10s for a landsman, who had never gone to sea before. But the captains' dreams of riches went further than City rewards. The granting of prize money for captured ships and cargoes, laid down in the Cruizer and Convoy Act of 1708, offered a dream of fortune that could be shared – to a degree – by the lower deck as well as the officers. Captured ships were valued at special prize courts, then merchantmen and their cargoes were sold at auctions and warships bought by the Admiralty: an enemy merchantman was worth about £2500 in prize money, and a privateer, often a pirate ship, around £1250. The proceeds were divided by eighths, according to formal rules: the captain got a quarter, lieutenants and captains of marines shared one eighth, warrant officers like the boatswain and gunner and master's mates another, and junior officers and midshipmen another. The rest of the crew took equal shares in a quarter. Above this, however, if the captured ship was sighted while a squadron sailed in formation, the final eighth went to the admiral or commander as his 'flag-eighth'– a rule that led to many frigate captains lurking independently where they thought the treasure ships might run, well away from their squadrons, so that they could claim this for themselves.

Prize courts were slow, disputes could last for years and lawyers' expenses bit into the promised gold. But sometimes dreams of wealth came true. When the *San Iago*, a Spanish galleon sailing under French colours, was captured in 1793, carrying specie worth a million pounds, the Commander in Chief, Lord Hood, scooped a royal £50,000, while £30,000 went to each of the four captains in his squadron, lesser amounts to officers and much smaller sums to the crews. In April the following year Captain Edward Pellew, sailing off Guernsey in the *Arethusa*, took two French frigates in a blaze of gunfire. Pellew's commander, Sir John Borlase Warren, received the largest slice of prize money but the rest, shared among all five frigates of the Western Squadron, prompted some legendary celebrations. In Plymouth five 'Harrythusers' hired a coach, packed it with women, a fiddler and organ grinder, and a good supply of grog, and careered round the town for days until the money ran out.[12]

George Cruikshank, *Sailors on a Cruise*: the crew of the Arethusa spend their prize money in style

\*

In the late autumn of 1793 Lord Howe brought the Channel Fleet into port for Christmas, avoiding the winter storms. The fleet did not set sail again until next May, when it set out to escort a merchant convoy heading for the East Indies, a billowing cloud of canvas. Off the Lizard, Howe sent some of his ships with the Indiamen, then led the rest in search of the French Atlantic Fleet, rumoured to be protecting a convoy bringing American corn to Brest.

As fast-sailing sloops dashed back to the Channel, different reports came through. On 10 June the *Gazette* announced that Howe had met the French, and next day the London papers explained that he had sighted them on 28 May, four hundred miles west of the Isle of Ushant at the tip of Brittany, but had lost them again in two days of thick fog. Finally, on the morning of 1 June, battle was engaged. Seven French ships were captured and one sunk, her crew rescued by the boats from the British ship *Alfred*. Howe had defied the conventional pattern of combat where the ships sailed in parallel lines, raking each other with their broadsides. Instead, manoeuvring to get favourable winds, the 'weather-gage', he told his captains to turn, swoop down and engage their immediate opposites, then sail through the French line and cut off their escape – a tactic Nelson later borrowed. Not all the captains understood or followed these orders, and the convoy itself escaped, carrying the precious grain to a starving France, but in the ragged chaos the victory was undoubtedly Howe's.

As news spread slowly across the country, householders and inn-keepers lit candles and lamps in all the windows. When the fleet returned to Spithead George III and Charlotte, and three princesses, visited Howe's flagship. But tourists like the London fencing master Henry Angelo, who visited the ravaged, dismasted prizes in Ports-mouth found disturbing scenes:

When we went below deck, the scene was truly frightful; on each side were hammocks on the floor, with numbers of dying and wounded . . . At this moment I fancy I see their pale faces and black beards. Here great havoc must have been made, as the shot appeared, from the grooves on the deck, like that of a ploughshare on the earth, to have raked through the cabin, from stern to stem. Our curiosity did not last long; the smell, with the sight of the dying, and the groans of the wounded, soon put an end to our naval visit.[13]

Two days later, with his friend the artist Thomas Rowlandson, Angelo watched wounded prisoners being loaded into carts, groaning as the jolting 'made their wounds appalling'. Many were boys, some not more than twelve, and several had lost both legs. In the evening they went to Forton prison, where Angelo found the misery too much to bear but Rowlandson lingered, drawing a French prisoner's wretched death, 'a ghastly figure, sitting up in bed, a priest holding a crucifix before him'.

Sailors' accounts gave a grim view of what a naval battle meant: the gun teams sweating below in choking smoke; the flash and recoil of cannon and carronades, firing like thunder. On deck, masts and spars cracking and falling, with ripped sails and tangled rigging; shots crashing through the timbers sending huge jagged splinters that pierced flesh like spears; shouted commands, yells, shrieks of the wounded; the smell of gunpowder, blood and burning.

Such scenes were not mentioned in the celebrations, which set a pattern for the rest of the war. The Bury St Edmunds merchant James Oakes, after soberly recording the death of a local man, George Heigham, on the *Royal George*, noted on 18 June:

*This evening very unexpectedly* the town was illuminated on acct of the Victory gaind over the French Fleet the 1st June never havg had any Rejoycing in the Town on the Acct. It was pretty general considering the short Notice. – Ringing of Bells – firing of Guns &ca. All was not over before 2 O'Clock in the Morning.[14]

Although critics in London clubs held that 'Black Dick' Howe had left the officers who had disagreed with his orders off the honours list, showing a woeful disregard for custom, the battle was immediately called 'the Glorious First of June'. Seizing the moment, Drury Lane mounted Sheridan's sensational *The Glorious First of June*, with the stage turned into a sea. 'Nothing can surpass the enchantment of this exhibition', wrote one critic:

The vessels are large, perfect models of the ships they represent, and made with such minute beauty as to be worthy of a place in the most curious collection. All the manoeuvres of the day are executed with nautical skill, – the lines are formed; they bear down on each other; the firing is well managed, and kept up warmly, for some time on both sides.[15]

The performance ended with fireworks proclaiming 'RULE BRITANNIA', with showers of fire streaming from each letter. The play itself, though, had some surprising twists, since it showed the sailor hero William deserting to help the Russetts, the family of his dead shipmate Henry. The tangled plot involves a rackrent landlord and an unscrupulous lawyer, but at the end all is resolved and William goes back to sea, his desertion justified. In one swoop Sheridan blended naval brotherhood with the landsman's fears of poverty, persuading his audience that if rights were respected, justice might indeed prevail.

The 'Jolly Jack Tar', manly, yet tender in his sympathy and capacity for sacrifice, became a central figure in wartime theatre, much appreciated by the sailors themselves. A relaxation of the Licensing Act in 1788 had led to a burst of provincial theatre building and Plymouth, for example, had two theatres, one in town for the gentry, the other near the docks for the navy.[16] The sailors treated the playhouses like ships, with gallery aloft and pit below. They found work helping to hoist scenery, being men who 'knew the ropes', and stories abounded of them taking plays literally, shouting support and jumping on stage. The nautical song, like Charles Dibdin's 'The Heart of a Tar', became a part of every evening's entertainment:[17]

> Your lords, with such fine baby faces,
> That strut in a garter and star,
> Have they, under their tambour and laces,
> The kind honest heart of a tar?

In the later stages of the wars, Robert and William Chambers, at school at Peebles, had a teacher who often came to school extremely drunk. 'When elevated to a certain pitch, he sung a good song about Nelson and his brave British tars; and this in itself, in the heat of the French war, extenuated many shortcomings.'[18]

# 7. TRIALS AND TRIBULATIONS

In 1794 Robert Burns, hailed as Scotland's national bard and feted in Edinburgh and in London, was a nervous man. Two years earlier, before Britain entered the war, radicals had planted liberty trees on market crosses around Scotland to celebrate French victories, and on the king's birthday riots had broken out in Edinburgh. The protestors burned effigies of the Lord Advocate, Robert Dundas, nephew and son-in-law of Henry Dundas, an attack on both the Scottish Whig dynasty and the Westminster government.

Burns knew many reformers and progressive thinkers. His doctor and friend William Maxwell was one of the founders of the London Corresponding Society; he corresponded with Mary Wollstonecraft, with the Liverpool reformer William Roscoe and with members of the United Irishmen, and he sent poems, anonymously, to the opposition *Morning Star*. But Burns was now in his early thirties, a married man with children, trying to hold on to his post as an excise officer. He knew that hints of Jacobinism could cost him his job. When accusations of radicalism were laid against him in January 1793 he had written to his superior, Robert Graham of Fintry, defending himself against the charges as 'brought by Malice and Misrepresentation'.[1] He had never asked for '*Ça ira*' in the playhouse, he said, although people around him were clamouring for it, 'nor ever opened my lips to hiss, or huzza, that, or any other political tune whatever'. He had, he admitted, been 'an enthusiastic votary' of the French Revolution but his feelings had changed when France attacked Holland. 'As to REFORM PRINCIPLES', he wrote, with some ambiguity, 'I look upon the British Constitution, as settled at the Revolution, to be the most glorious Constitution on earth, or that perhaps the wit of man can frame.' The problem was that Britain had deviated from those principles, and 'an alarming System of Corruption has pervaded the connection between the Executive Power and the House of Commons'. He got off with a reprimand, but in private he held to his views. A month after these protestations of loyalty, and a week after Britain and France went to war, he sent his friend Alexander Cunningham a 'political catechism', including 'Politics is a science wherewith, by means of nefarious cunning, & hypocritical pretence, we govern civil Polities for the emolument of ourselves & our adherents.'[2]

Burns was wise to be wary. In Edinburgh the previous November, when Scottish radical groups had tried to hold a 'British Convention' – a term uncomfortably echoing the French – magistrates arrested the leaders, including the Unitarian minister Thomas Fyshe Palmer of Dundee, William Skirving of Edinburgh and the lawyer Thomas Muir from Glasgow, and charged them with sedition. On bail, Muir visited France and Ireland, where he met the leaders of the United Irishmen. In February 1793 he was declared a fugitive from justice and the following August he was captured landing in the far west of Dumfries and Galloway. Burns was at work in Dumfries as Muir was brought through on his way to Edinburgh. At his trial, Muir conducted his own defence before Scotland's 'hanging judge', Robert McQueen, Lord Braxfield, whom the Scottish lawyer Henry Cockburn described as 'a little, dark creature, dressed in black, with silk stockings and white metal buttons, something like one's idea of a puny Frenchman, a most impudent and provoking body'.[3]

Braxfield would have hated to be thought a Frenchman. In his summing up, he told the jury that the question was to decide the prisoner's guilt: 'Now, before this can be answered, two things must be attended that require no proof: First, that the British constitution is the best that EVER was since the creation of the world, and it is not possible to make it better.'[4]

Muir was sentenced to fourteen years' transportation in Botany Bay. (He escaped in 1796 and fled to France, appealing to the French to liberate Scotland.) His colleagues in the Convention were also transported, Palmer for seven years and Skirving and two delegates from the London Corresponding Society for fourteen. Braxfield's judgement was crucial in tilting future charges from 'sedition' to the more serious charge of treason.[5] A year later, when Joseph Gerrald, another British Convention member, claimed that the rights he argued for echoed the teaching of Christ, Braxfield nodded to the jury and said in broad Scots, 'Muckle he made o' that; he was hanget.'[6]

In June 1793, the cobbled streets of Dumfries saw 'patriotic' riots and on the king's birthday the people of nearby Ruthwell burned Tom Paine in effigy. But on 30 August, the day set for Muir's trial, Burns wrote to his friend George Thomson saying that he had been musing on the tradition that the old tune 'Hey tuttie taitie' was Robert Bruce's march, played at the battle of Bannockburn in 1314, when his small force routed the English. This thought, Burns wrote, 'warmed me to a pitch of enthusiasm on the theme of liberty and independence'. When 'Scots wha hae', entitled 'Bruce's Address at Bannockburn', was published in the *Morning Chronicle* the following May it was clear to many that it was about the present struggles as well as those of Scotland's past:

> By Oppression's woes & pains!
> By your Sons in servile chains!
> We will drain our dearest veins,
> But they *shall* be free!
>
> Let the proud Usurpers low!
> Tyrants fall in every foe!
> LIBERTY's in every blow
> Let us DO – or DIE!!!

So may God ever defend the cause of TRUTH and Liberty, as he did that day! – Amen![7]

Edinburgh's old town baffled strangers like the actor Charles Dibdin, climbing 'in winding directions from among that throng of streets, where loaves, stockings, pitchers, hats, cabbages and numbers of other incongruous particulars were painted against the houses to denote the occupations of their inhabitants, who live up stairs into one street, and down stairs into another, burrowing like so many rabbits in a warren'.[8] But the crowded town also held bookstalls, learned societies and students. The classical New Town, designed forty years before, now extended as far as Charlotte Square, from where, remembered Henry Cockburn, you could look across a grassy field down to the Water of Leith and listen to the call of the corncrakes.

Walter Scott, whose father was a good friend of Lord Braxfield, was an advocate here. Scott was thirty in June 1794 and he was quick to join the forces of order when riots began in Edinburgh on the king's birthday, as they had the year before. Four days later, he wrote to his aunt Christian Rutherford, telling her that if they met he could describe:

*how* near a Thousand gentlemen (myself among the number) offered their services to the Magistrates to act as *Constables* for the preservation of the peace . . . *how* they were furnishd with pretty painted brown *battons* – *how* they were assembled in the Aisle of the New Church and treated with Claret and sweetmeats – how Sir John Whiteford was chaced by the Mob, and how Tom, Sandy Wood, and I rescued him . . .'[9]

Later that year, a cache of arms, supposedly collected by a former government spy, Robert Watt, was discovered in Edinburgh, appearing to prove contacts with Ireland and suggesting a foiled uprising. Scott went to the trials of Watt and his accomplice Downie, 'which', he said 'displayd to the public the most atrocious & deliberate plan of villany which has occurrd perhaps in the annals of G. Britain'.[10] Grabbing his seat early, he sat in court from seven o'clock until two the next morning, providing himself with 'some cold meat & a Bottle of Wine'. In November he witnessed Watt's hanging, watching as his head was cut off as a traitor and shown to the crowd. He was rather disappointed that Downie was not hanged too.

Although the trial of Watt and Downie was used to bolster government arguments about conspiracies, the fate of Muir and his colleagues roused widespread protests about Pitt's repression of radical opinion. The Foxite Whigs held that the French Republic had been driven into war by Europe's absolutist rulers. Pitt's government, they declared, were now using the war to bolster the power of the Crown and their own aristocratic clique, reducing the influence of the Commons and suppressing free speech. Outside parliament, dissenters and manufacturers such as the Rathbones and Roscoes of Liverpool formed the 'Friends of Peace', convinced that the government's war policies were a threat to civil liberty, imposing hardship on the poor and middling classes.

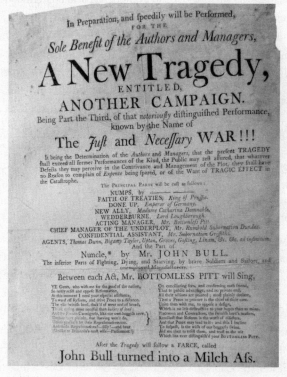

Mock advertisement for 'A New Tragedy', Manchester 1794

For the past two years men had been prosecuted for speaking out. John Frost, a lawyer and a member of the London Constitutional Society, who had dared to say in a coffee house that all men should be on the same footing and there should be 'no kings in this country', was put in the pillory and sent to Newgate for six months. A Baptist minister in Plymouth, William Winterbotham, was sentenced to four years for saying that the Revolution had opened people's eyes, and that if George III did not observe the laws, he had no more right to the throne than the Stuarts.[11] But juries did not always comply with the government's wishes. In February 1794 Daniel Isaac Eaton was prosecuted for publishing a speech by John Thelwall in his journal *Politics for the People*, calling for universal suffrage and an end to the war. The speech included a story about a cockerel, King Chaunticlere, beheaded for despotism: 'A haughty sanguinary tyrant, nursed in blood and slaughter from his infancy, fond of foreign wars and domestic rebellions, into which he would sometimes drive his subjects, by his oppressive obstinacy, in hopes that he might increase his power and glory by their suppression.'[12] Eaton, who had already been prosecuted unsuccessfully for selling Paine's works, was acquitted amid much laughter when his defence lawyer suggested that it was the Attorney General who was guilty of seditious libel, since it was he, not Thelwall, who was implying that 'Chaunticlere' must be George III.

Two months later, the manufacturer Thomas Walker and nine other Manchester reformers, charged with conspiring to overthrow the king, constitution and government, were all acquitted and the informant was convicted of perjury.[13] But in Oldham on Easter Monday, when the bachelors and married men played football (the married men won), a group calling for reform still had to fight off 'a merciless mob' attacking them as Jacobins.[14]

Though shaken by the Scottish trials, opponents of the war were determined to fight on. In April, while Walker's trial was going on in Manchester, the London Corresponding Society called a huge general meeting at Chalk Farm: 'the crowds that Packed there were inconceivable and beyond all my ideas,' reported one spy.[15] They planned, they said, to call their own 'General Convention of the People'. After other spies reported secret drilling and caches of arms, the government suspended habeas corpus and on 12 May constables arrested Thomas Hardy, Secretary of the London Corresponding Society, and other activists, including Thelwall, Thomas Holcroft and the veteran reformer John Horne Tooke. When Wordsworth told his friend William Mathews that he disapproved of 'monarchical and aristocratical governments, however modified', his brother Richard advised him, 'I hope you will be cautious in writing or expressing your political opinions. By the suspension of the Habeas Corpus Acts the Ministers have great powers.'[16] They did: after more arrests many radicals fled the country or went into hiding.

Two weeks after Hardy and the others were imprisoned in the Tower, the news arrived of the Glorious First of June. During the celebrations, a loyalist mob hurled stones and bricks at Hardy's home, and his wife, six months pregnant, was badly bruised as she fled: on 27 August she died in childbirth and her baby was stillborn. Hardy lost his livelihood, and his family.

So far no charges had been made. Finally, on 2 October, thirteen of the men arrested were indicted, not for sedition, but for high treason, which carried the barbaric punishment of hanging, drawing and quartering. In late October the *Morning Chronicle* carried an anonymous article arguing that the prosecution was shaky: the Treason Act specified rebellion and regicide, and made no mention of campaigning for reform or criticism of government. All Britons had a right to free speech. The author of the article was William Godwin. In 1793, in his *Enquiry Concerning Political Justice*, trying to stay above the rows around the *Rights of Man*, Godwin made the point that if people could be educated to use their reason fully and freely, exercising their private judgement in public life and debate, they could, eventually, hope to eradicate bad leadership: government, he argued, was formed on opinion.[17] Now, when Daniel Eaton published Godwin's argument about the Treason Act as a pamphlet, it influenced public opinion and anticipated to some degree the sharper legal arguments of the defence lawyer, Thomas Erskine.[18]

When the trials began at the Old Bailey in November, angry crowds gathered to support the defendants. From their office in Fleet Street, near Hardy's shop, the clerks at Hoare's bank watched as John Scott – the Attorney General, afterwards Lord Eldon – was mobbed on the corner of Chancery Lane. 'The mob', Eldon wrote, 'kept thickening around me, till I came to Fleet Street, one of the worst parts of London that I had to pass through':

and the cries began to be rather threatening. 'Down with him!' 'Now is the time, lads,' – 'Do for him!' – and various others, horrible enough. So I stood up, and spoke as loud as I could – 'You may do for me, if you like, but, remember, there will be another Attorney-General before eight o'clock to-morrow morning, and the King will not allow the trials to be stopped.' Upon this one man shouted out, 'Say you so? you are right to tell us. Let's give him three cheers, lads!' And they actually cheered me, and I got safe to my own door.[19]

Despite the government's attempt to pack the juries, in their separate trials the first three defendants – Hardy, Tooke and Thelwall – were quickly acquitted. After Hardy left court, the crowd unhooked the horses from his carriage and pulled it down the Strand to Westminster and Pall Mall. An embarrassed Pitt was called as a defence witness at Tooke's trial and asked to confirm that in 1782, before he came to power, he himself had called for parliamentary reform at large public meetings – one of the charges against Tooke.[20]

The year before, Thelwall had thrilled an audience of doctors at the Physical Society at Guy's Hospital with an ambitious lecture, not about the war, but about new vitalist, materialist theories concerning the physiological basis of life.[21] This was alarmingly atheistic to many, but several doctors who heard him, including Astley Cooper and Peter Holland, were among the cheering crowds outside court after the acquittals; their teacher at St Thomas's, Henry Cline, was a character witness for Thelwall and a close friend of Tooke. Yet the trials had an impact, and both young doctors had to suppress their views to keep their jobs. Thelwall himself continued to write, but left the Corresponding Society and masked his political speeches as lectures on classics. Tooke dropped his demand for universal suffrage, but remained a mentor to radical politicians of the years to come. Godwin, worried that his picture of unjust institutions in his novel, *Things as They Are: or, The Adventures of Caleb Williams*, published this year, might bring a charge of seditious libel, dampened his tone. Many of the popular debating societies closed down.[22]

The doctor, inventor and poet Erasmus Darwin, whose own lines welcoming the French Revolution had been reprinted in Eaton's *Politics for the People*, felt the climate to be cold. Lamenting his friend Josiah Wedgwood's death in early 1795, he joked that the world was only meant for the devil,

who seems daily to gain ground upon *the other gentleman*, by the assistance of Mr Pitt and our gracious – I dare not mention his name for fear that high treason may be in the sound; and I have a profess'd spy shoulders us on the right, and another on the opposite side of the street, both attorneys! And I hear every name supposed to think different from the minister is put in alphabetical order in Mr Reeve's doomsday book, and that if the French should land these recorded gentlemen are all to be imprison'd to prevent them from committing crimes of a deeper dye.[23]

America was the only place of safety, he thought, and what did a man past fifty want anyway? 'Potatoes and milk – nothing else. These may be had in America, untax'd by Kings and Priests.'

No more was heard of the planned 'Convention of the People', and radical opposition was largely suffocated. Newspapers like the *Sheffield Iris, Chester Chronicle, Morning Post* and *Newcastle Chronicle* dropped support of revolutionary aims and suppressed their criticism of the war. The nation must resist 'even that heavenly boon, *Liberty*,' declared the *Newcastle Chronicle*, 'if it be attempted to be crammed down our throats by *foreign bayonets*.'[24] But the fight still went on, and in defiance of this silencing satirical handbills still appeared on walls and in taverns attacking the subsidies to the allies and 'Mr Bottomless Pitt'.

*

Many radicals, like Burns, held on to their beliefs in private while being careful in public. Aged only thirty-six, Burns was often ill and was anxious about getting a pension to help his children if he died: it was important to look loyally 'patriotic'. He turned up, with many of his close friends, as well as Alexander Findlatter, his superior in the Excise, to the crowded meeting in the courthouse on 31 January 1795, chaired by the deputy lieutenant of the county, to discuss the formation of the Royal Dumfries Volunteers. There was no pay, and yet the minute book specified an elaborate uniform:

a blue coat half lapelled with red cape and cuffs, and gilt buttons with the letters R.D.V. engraved on them; a plain white Cassimere vest, with small gilt buttons; white trousers made of Russia tweeling, tied at the ankle; white stockings; a black velvet stock; hair to be worn short, or turned up behind; a round hat turned up on the left side with a gilt button, a cockade, and a black feather; their shoes to be tied with black ribbon . . .[25]

Volunteering could be expensive, but it offered a release from the militia ballot and it showed your loyalty. Burns swore the oath of allegiance and joined the regular drills. A month later, the *Dumfries Weekly Journal* carried his poem, beginning:

> Does haughty Gaul invasion threat?
> Then let the loons beware, Sir,
> There's WOODEN WALLS upon our seas,
> And VOLUNTEERS on shore, Sir.

But the ending of this poem, 'We'll ne'er forget the People', made the message less straightforward. And although this song was published as 'The Dumfries Volunteers' under Burns's name in the *Edinburgh Courant* on 4 May, at the same time a rather different poem appeared anonymously in the *Glasgow Magazine*, a vernacular rendering of liberty, fraternity and equality:

> A Prince can mak a belted knight
> A marquis, duke, an' a' that;
> But an honest man's abon his might,

Gude faith, he maunna fa' that!
For a' that, an a' that,
Their dignities an' a' that;
The pith o' sense, and pride o' worth,
Are higher rank than a' that.[26]

The following spring, despite bathing in the famed salt water of Ruthwell spring, among the reedy marshes fringing the Solway, Burns was mortally ill. On 1 June 1796 he wrote to Maria Riddell, with whom he had a long, up and down, flirtatious relationship, telling her that he was racked by rheumatism:

Would you have me in such circumstances copy you out a love-song? No! if I must write, let it be Sedition, or Blasphemy, or something else that begins with a B, so that I may grin with the grin of iniquity, & rejoice with the rejoicing of an apostate Angel.

– All good to me is lost:
– Evil, be thou my good![27]

He had never paid for his volunteer's uniform, and when the tailor David Williamson, seeing his customer was dying, presented his bill, Burns flew into a rage, humiliated by having to beg the sum from friends. Towards the end, according to his editor and biographer, the poet Allan Cunningham, he pleaded with a fellow volunteer, 'John, don't let the aukward squad fire over me?'[28] But they did. On Monday 25 July 1796, soldiers in uniform lined the streets to St Michael's Church: the volunteers, the Cinque Port Cavalry and the Angusshire Fencibles. The cavalry band played Handel's Dead March, the volunteers, with black armbands, were the pall bearers, and the fencibles fired three volleys over his coffin in the open grave.

# 8. WARP AND WEFT

Cotton, calico, wool, worsted, silk and linen. The textile industries spread like a net from north to south, from the bleaching fields of Glasgow to the hills of the West Country, with spinners, weavers and finishers, bleachers and dyers, merchants and masters. Loss of men and new excise and customs duties hit all Britain's industries during the war but textiles were in the headlines most often, beset by problems of disrupted trade and by disputes between masters and workers over customary rights and the onward drive of the machines.

The father of William and Robert Chambers, who came from a line of Glasgow woollen clothiers, had moved fifty miles south-east to Peebles by the Tweed and set up a business in cotton, with as many as a hundred looms working for him, selling his cloth to Glasgow merchants. Robert's earliest memories were of their small house, with its ground floor full of looms and its attic full of yarn, and of watching the swing of the weavers' treadles and listening to their gossip and songs. Other weavers worked in their own homes. Peebles was then a single street of thatched cottages, a place where porridge cooled on the window sills, the smell of peat smoke filled the air and the click of the shuttle was heard everywhere. In the evenings 'the gray old men came out in their Kilmarnock night-caps, and talked of Bonaparte, on the stone steps beside their doors'.[1]

By now the Scottish cotton industry was losing out to Lancashire, where the damp climate was ideal for spinning the brittle yarn. To add strength to the cotton, weavers added 'fustian', wool or linen yarn, to make the warp. In Oldham in mid-1793, the weaver William Rowbottom fumed: 'The relentless cruelty exersised by the Fustian Masters upon the poor wevers is such that it is unexampled in the annals of cruelty tyaraney & oppresion for it is nearly an imposability for weavers to earn the common necesaries of life so that a great deal of familys are in the most wretched and pitiable situation.'[2] At the end of the year he was no more optimistic. 'December 31st, the year concludes with a cold boistress day and the callamitys and miseryes of the poor too heavey to bear, and when it will mend human wisdom cannot tell.'[3] Then trade revived again. 'It is with heartfelt pleasure', reported Rowbottom in August 1794, 'that we hear callicoes nan-keens roe moll napkins and all sort of light goods are at this time rapidly rising, their wages likewise. Hats are increasing prodigiously, but poor strong Fustian remains in its former misserable sittuation.'[4] For a short time the upward trend continued, but by the following January prices for piece-work had dropped again. This roller coaster swooped on throughout the war.

The Oldham weavers relied on Manchester, 'the heart of this vast system, the circulating branches of which spread all around it', as the dissenting scholar John Aiken described it in 1795.[5] Travellers arriving from the south, through the rich countryside of Cheshire, were often appalled by the town's noise and the narrow crowded streets: a 'great *Hot-Hell*' in the words of the visitor John Byng.[6] But the wealth was also creating a new town, with an infirmary in Piccadilly, a theatre, a concert room and assembly rooms as well as the renowned Literary and Philosophical Society, the 'Lit & Phil'. Manchester merchants imported raw cotton from the West Indies and the American colonies through Liverpool, and sent it out to be spun into yarn. Then they gave the yarn to weavers, paying them piece rates, and exporting the woven cloth to Europe, Russia and America as well as selling it in the home market. In 1794, ten-year-old John Fielden and his three brothers were working for ten hours a day in a small family business run by his Quaker father Joshua: once a week father and sons took their woven cloth the twenty miles to Manchester. A little later, Samuel Bamford and his brother, aged eight and ten, also trekked back and forth to Manchester from their uncle's house a few miles away in Middleton. Outside schooltime, Bamford helped his aunt spin while his elder brother helped his uncle at the loom: as he grew older Bamford walked into Manchester himself to hand over the heavy wallets of finished work and receive fresh yarn.

For some domestic workers, however, life was changing. As the Wigan magistrate John Singleton noted, the war meant that more women were now involved. 'Altho' numbers of our people are gone for soldiers and sailors there is still an increase in Looms for if a man enlists, his Wife turns Weaver (for here the women are weavers as well as the men) and instructs her children in the art of weaving.'[7] Year after year, Rowbottom noted the predominance of women. At the Rushbearing in 1795, 'a finer day never came from heaven', and on the Monday of the festival the fine weather, with 'the sky serene and clear not a cloud to be seen', brought out 'an uncommon deal of people in genaral, two nymphs to one swain the war having drained the towns of men, so that but one recruiting party apeard wich was the Windsor Forristers Horsemen drest in green.'[8]

Home weaving would continue well into the next century but spinning, women's traditional province, had already become increasingly mechanised. The latest developments, like Crompton's Spinning Mule, whose enormous hand-turned wheel worked the spindles back and forth across the machine carriage, producing strong, fine thread, required greater power and the frames were too big for a cottage. To use them, innovators built mills in the valleys where the fast streams could turn waterwheels. The next great leap was steam – over fifteen years before, Matthew Boulton had written to James Watt: 'as the people in London, Birmingham and Manchester are Steam Mill mad, therefore let us be wise, and take the advantage.'[9] Now factory after factory was putting in engines.

The divisions were never clear. Linen, wool and cotton mills clustered beside each other. Farming and industry mingled: weavers kept cows and ran smallholdings, farmers built fulling mills. In Little Longstone in Derbyshire, a hamlet of grey limestone cottages on an old packhorse route three miles from Bakewell, the Longsdon family had farmed for many generations, winning rights to graze their sheep on Longsdon Moor when they swapped some land with Bess of Hardwick in the seventeenth century.[10] It was a prosperous area, with local lead mining and shoemaking as well as farming. James Longsdon sold wool to Yorkshire clothiers, but over the past twenty years he had also moved into the cotton trade, going into partnership with the neighbouring Morewood family, distributing cotton yarn to local weavers, collecting the finished fustians and checks and taking them to sell in Manchester thirty-five miles away.[11] In the mid-1780s, he invested his new bride's dowry in a carding mill, a warehouse, a bleaching croft and workers' cottages. Although the partnership with the Morewoods ended, the families remained friends. The Morewoods set up a merchant house in London, and sent their sons as agents to Russia and America, while Longsdon farmed, ran the cotton spinning with his manager Ralph Finch, and opened his own Manchester warehouse. In the early 1790s, he had three small sons, James, John and William, and to him their future was clear: farm, mill and trade.[12]

During the war years, as thousands of acres of common land were enclosed on the sides of the Lancashire and Yorkshire valleys, speculators and manufacturers rushed to buy plots. The new mill owners were not all men: at Keighley, in the Aire valley in Yorkshire, the entrepreneurs of the 1790s included Rachel Leech, who set up a mill on her brother's land, Ann Illingworth, who built a mill for her son, and Betty Hudson, whose son-in-law managed her mill at Dam Side, 'for the rage was so great to embark in the business of cotton spinning', wrote one Victorian local historian, 'that not only the leading gentlemen and land owners of the neighbourhood, but ladies also embarked in the enterprise, doubtless being lured by the prospect of acquiring wealth'.[13] Textile manufacture doubled and redoubled, then doubled again.

The masters who had invested in large mills now had to work out how to manage hard times. Robert Peel, the son of a Blackburn calico printer, a shrewd businessman, passionate about mechanical devices, had been in charge of the company since his mid-twenties, starting new calico-printing works at Bury and Burnley, adding bleaching works, and then sending cotton out to hand-loom weavers from Lancashire to Paisley. In 1790, aged forty, he had put in steam power and bought an estate of four thousand acres near Tamworth in Staffordshire, where he built a large integrated factory for both spinning and weaving. In the same year he was elected MP for Tamworth: his son, also Robert, would later become Prime Minister.

Peel employed over seven thousand people and his profits were running at £70,000 a year. He was already a giant of industry, and newcomers like the Irish Samuel Greg, who built his mill at Quarry Bank in the 1780s, watched his progress closely. In contrast to the Anglican Peel, Greg came from a dissenting, Unitarian background: his father, Thomas, had helped to make Belfast a major port, and his uncles, the Hyde brothers, were key figures in the linen industry in both Northern Ireland and Lancashire. At the age of eight Sam was sent to live with the Hydes in Manchester, and when they died he inherited their fortune and their valuable web of connections and credit. These connections were boosted when he married Hannah Lightbody, daughter of a Unitarian cotton merchant in Liverpool, whose sisters also married into the cotton aristocracy.[14] Greg was a radical, one of the thirteen Manchester Lit & Phil members interrogated in the purges of 1794. In person he was informal and down to earth, very different from the iron-firm, loyalist Peel. But at the start of the war both men found business growing, with less continental competition and more exports to America.

Over the next few years they ran their factories with military discipline, using cheap pauper labour. Local children like James Weatherley found work as scavengers, keeping the machinery clean from the 'dirt and flyings' that clogged them. Small, nimble-fingered children could run under the heavy machines. 'We have to do it while the Machines are working,' wrote Weatherley:

which is often very dangerous if you are not very sharp and wide awake you would be caught by the straps Drums shafts Pulleys rollers or Cog wheels which may make you minus a limb or two or perhaps your Life I knew several that were killed in the Factorys and some badly hurt by loseing an arm and scores that have lost more or less of their fingers I have had many a rap and squeeze but never lost a limb.[15]

He kept this up for two years and more, working alongside parish apprentices sent north from the Foundling Hospital and London workhouses, listening to their dialect, 'a kind of low London Slang such as I have heard used by the cab and watermen in London'. They were poor, miserable-looking, pale-faced creatures, he thought, their plight 'as bad or worse than American Slavery'.

George Walker, factory children in Yorkshire

Peel employed parish apprentices and so did Greg. His water-powered Quarry Bank Mill in the sandstone gorge at Styal had no large local workforce to call on, so he built houses and brought labour in. His Apprentice House was well run but the hours were long and accidents frequent. One boy, Thomas Priestley, looked after two machines each spinning fifty threads, guiding the threads, twisting them when they snapped, and learning to oil the machine.

Our working hours were from 6 am in summer and winter until 7 in the evening. There was no night workers. We had only ten minutes allowed for our breakfasts, which were always brought up to the mill for us – two days in the week we had an hour allowed us for dinner, while the machines were oiled . . . and other days we were allowed half an hour for dinner, when the boys worked overtime they were paid 1d an hour . . . During the time working, and there was a great deal of cotton in the machine, one of the wheels caught my finger and tore it off, it was the forefinger of my left hand. I was attended by the surgeon of the factory Mr Holland and in about 6 weeks I recovered.[16]

Quarry Bank, which had its schools and doctor (Elizabeth Gaskell's uncle, and Astley Cooper's old friend, Peter Holland), was better than many other places. When the Birmingham Poor Law Guardians visited their parish apprentices at Peel's factories in 1796, they found long hours, misery and homesickness, brutality, poor clothing and food: noticing that the children had no shoes or stockings, they were told that 'if they gave them shoes they would run away'.[17] Six years later Peel promoted the Health and Morals of Apprentices Act 1802, the first factory legislation in England, making him a hero to later factory reformers. This was philanthropic but also shrewd, since if profit was the bottom line then care of workers was as crucial as tending machines. The debate then turned to 'free labour', the children sent to the mills, not by the parish but by their parents. What right did the state have to interfere with their choice? The argument raged for years, to the furious disbelief of commentators like Coleridge:

But *free* Labour! – in what sense, not utterly sophistical, can the labour of children, extorted from the wants of their parents, 'their poverty but not their will consenting', be called *free*? . . . If the labour were indeed free, the contract would approach, on the one side, too near to suicide, on the other to manslaughter.[18]

Across the Pennines, the Yorkshire worsted and wool industries had far overtaken those of the traditional wool counties of the West Country and East Anglia. Each district had its specialism. The villages around Huddersfield wove broad and narrow cloth and fancy woollens with names like beaverettes, honleys and kerseymeres; weavers further north produced plainer, undyed white cloth; in the Wharfe and Aire valleys they wove mixed cloth; in the high moors around Halifax they made lightweight worsted, 'shalloons, calimancoes, camblets and tammies'.[19] Worsted yarn was made of long fibres, easier to spin on the frame, so power machines like those in the cotton industry could be used earlier and mill owners built large factories. Woollen fibres were shorter, finer and silkier, and had to be strengthened by scribbling and carding before they could be drawn out and spun into yarn. The final dressing – raising and shearing the cloth – was done by skilled croppers and dressers in Halifax, Wakefield and Leeds. All these towns had cloth halls, but Leeds was the chief centre, where the merchants bought the cloth from country weavers before finishing it in their own premises. Sales took place twice a week in the White Cloth Halls, and in the arcaded market for mixed or coloured cloth (dyed in the wool before weaving). The 'irregulars', clothiers who had served no formal apprenticeship, set up stalls on the ground floor of the new Music Hall in Albion Street, quickly called 'Tom Paine's Hall'. Upstairs was a gallery, lecture room and concert hall for 850 people, with huge chandeliers.

The merchants who patronised the concerts lived far from this noisy district. Several had moved into Park Square and South Parade, new houses with libraries and butlers' rooms, coach houses and stables. But since 1791, at Bean Ing, just west of the square, thirty-year-old Benjamin Gott had been building the largest factory in the industry, and its smoke floated straight into the elegant parlours (including those of his own house, in Park Lane, where he lived with his wife Elizabeth, 'a woman of infinite charm'.)[20] Gott was an engineer's son who had worked his apprenticeship with a leading merchant firm, Wormald and Fountaine, becoming a junior partner in 1785. Within three years the two elderly partners died, leaving Benjamin as senior partner before he was thirty. In his new factory, his revolutionary scheme, copying the Lancashire cotton mills, was to bring all the processes under the same roof: spinning, weaving and finishing. In 1793 he installed a forty-horsepower coal-fired steam engine, the first in a Yorkshire mill, built locally in agreement with Boulton and Watt. Within five years he had a workforce of eighteen hundred and, struggling to fill all his orders, he leased the water-powered Armley Mills, a mile along the Leeds Canal. At the same time he worked on as a merchant, and in 1799 he became Mayor of Leeds.

When small local clothiers saw Gott's Bean Ing mill, they took fright, thinking that other wealthy Leeds merchants would try to take over their business. They need not have worried. Most merchants, sons of dynasties who had intermarried and formed partnerships over the years, were too aware of their status to dirty their hands with engines and looms. Instead they put their money into consols and bonds and lived off their investments, particularly canal shares whose dividends could run into thousands. With the proceeds they bought estates, calling in John Nash to improve their houses and Humphry Repton to design their gardens.

If Gott, a good Tory, emulated Robert Peel, Yorkshire also had its parallel to Samuel Greg in John Marshall, a linen-mill owner with strong Unitarian connections. Marshall was thirty-eight in 1793. The son of a Leeds draper, he had joined with two partners and used his own capital and loans from fellow Unitarians, family and friends, to start spinning flax. First he snapped up a licence on newly patented machines from Darlington, experimenting with modifications and noting every step in his 'Experiment' books. After a young engineer, Matthew Murray, helped him to improve these, he took out a patent, sold the drapery business and moved to a large four-storey mill at

Water Lane, across the river Aire, where labour was plentiful, coal cheap and canal links good.

Jack Marshall talked to everyone and made notes on everything, from alkalis, bleaching, bobbins and crank steam engines to pulleys, tumbling-shafts, waterwheels, windows and wood. He jotted down the names of expert 'mechanicks' – spindle makers, steelworkers, boilermakers, millwrights and fitters – from all over Lancashire and Yorkshire. But the war posed a threat:

The sudden shock that was given to mercantile credit brought us to a stand . . . We had a large stock of flax, the payments for which were becoming due, our book accounts were of small amount, and in the entire stagnation of trade which ensued, we could neither sell our goods nor obtain payments. Our Bankers called on us to reduce our account which we were unable to do and equally so to provide cash for the workmen.[21]

At first his spirits sank, particularly at the thought of the loss to his mother, 'who had entrusted me with her all'. But Marshall was canny about figures and people. The 'losses' allowed him to buy out his first partners and to join up with the Benyon brothers, wool merchants from Shrewsbury, to build even larger mills. In June 1794, he ordered a twenty-eight-horsepower engine from Boulton and Watt. By the end of the year, twelve hundred spindles were spinning in his Leeds mills.[22]

As these powerful men forged ahead, skilled workers began to watch them, anxious for their livelihood. Already, in 1792 angry workers had destroyed all the power looms and spinning mules in the Grimshaw brothers' mill in Manchester and burnt it to the ground. As mechanisation drove on, so more riots and protests would follow.

# 9. MONEY, CITY AND COUNTRY

Among bankers across the country, the war caused a near panic. In March 1793, there was a run on local banks and by mid-April over a hundred country banks had failed. It was impossible to get cash or credit, so vital to eighteenth-century trade, as one contemporary noted:

many whom the assistance of even a moderate sum of money would have enabled to surmount their difficulties, could not obtain any accommodation; for, in the general distress and dismay, everybody looked on their neighbour with caution, if not with suspicion. It was impossible to raise any money upon the security of machinery or shares in canals, for the value of such property seemed to be annihilated in the gloomy apprehensions of the sinking state of the economy.[1]

In London a meeting of eleven City financiers, chaired by the Lord Mayor, Sir James Sanderson, recommended the issue of Exchequer Bills to allay anxiety about cash. Advised by John Julius Angerstein of Lloyds, Pitt agreed to ease the credit panic by circulating more bills and allowing the Bank of England to issue notes for £5, rather than the minimum £10.

In Hoare's bank at 37 Fleet Street, almost opposite the entrance to Fetter Lane, the partners decided on a strategy. From now on, they would tell their aristocratic customers that they could lend nothing without solid collateral and promise of early repayment, and they would be stricter on overdrafts and repayments of loans. Letters went out with hinted reminders of old debts or outright refusals of new loans, always couched in the politest of terms. On 7 June 1793, having honoured the Earl of Thanet's draft for £12,000, they wrote tactfully, 'We wish you in every respect to consult your own Convenience as to the time of replacing the Money overdrawn on your Account.'² On 18 June, an apologetic letter was sent to Oliver Farr, agent for Lord Rivers: 'we are extremely concerned that it will not be in our Power to advance the sum Lord Rivers requires.' The partners had, they said, been 'refusing all applications whatsoever', would have been happy to accommodate him '& only lament that the present situation of Public Affairs renders it necessary for us to decline lending any Money at this present Juncture'. To Lord Rivers himself, they explained that 'the very great distress occasioned by recent failures & the consequent stagnation of Money have obliged us for some Months past, to decline advancing all sums of Money whatever'. They then begged for the indulgence received from 'all our other Friends'.

And so it went on, with more requests for indulgence, more and more laments about 'the peculiar Situation of the times'.³ The following year, when Sir John Hussey Delaval wanted a loan of £10,000 the senior partner Henry Hoare would not countenance it unless Sir John paid off three bonds on which he already owed interest. In the Memorandum Book he wrote briskly, 'If he gets the £10,000 he pays them off. Didn't get it.'⁴ The tactics proved surprisingly successful, and Hoare's gained customers rather than lost them.

They had been in Fleet Street since Richard Hoare moved from Cheapside in 1690. Their old banking house was marked by the sign of the Golden Bottle over the door, a gilt case rumoured, quite untruthfully, to contain the leather bottle that Richard had carried when he first came to London with half a crown in his pocket, as if he were Dick Whittington – in fact he was the son of a Smithfield horse dealer, born and bred in the city. The current head was forty-three-year-old Henry 'Harry' Hoare, known as 'Henry Hoare of Mitcham' from his Adam-style house Mitcham Grove, across the river on the Surrey side, with parkland, hothouses and dairy, 'good hunting at a small distance, good shooting and fishing'.[5] The junior partners were his cousins, the brothers Hugh, Charles and Henry Merrick Hoare, jointly known as 'the Adelphi'. They were aged thirty-one, twenty-six and twenty-three respectively, although their sober letters never sound so young.[6] Their half-brother, Sir Richard Colt Hoare, had inherited the Wiltshire mansion of Stourhead from their grandfather, 'Henry the Magnificent'. He had left on a long Grand Tour after his wife died six years ago, returning as a passionate antiquarian, devoted to his library, local history and his ravishing estate.

Hoare's Bank in Fleet Street, with the golden bottle fixed to the pediment over the door

From their front windows, the Hoare partners gazed down on a noisy street where different worlds collided. Lawyers hurried in and out of their chambers in the Temple, stretching down to the river; customers strolled into the booksellers or stared at print-shop windows; messengers ran to the *Morning Advertiser*, or the publishing house started by John Murray in the 1760s and inherited this year by his son, John Murray II. Just up Chancery Lane was Nando's coffee house, and nearby was Mrs Salmon's Waxworks, where the new proprietors – keeping the Salmon name – displayed wax kings and queens and the splendours of a Turkish seraglio. Further along, on the northern side of Fleet Street, was the shop of Thomas Hardy, bootmaker, secretary to the London Corresponding Society. Next door to Hoare's was the Mitre, where Johnson and Boswell had met, now Macklin's Poets' Gallery, where the print seller Thomas Macklin showed paintings commissioned to illustrate famous English poems, published monthly as engravings. It was an expensive venture and Macklin was hit badly by the war, which stopped the sale of his prints across the Channel.

Several private banks were dotted down Fleet Street and the Strand to Charing Cross, a busy corridor between the City and Westminster and the West End, all dealing with wealthy landed customers in need of mortgages and loans, or, if they were flush, a safe home for their deposits. Some borrowed to cover their gaming debts and high spending; others to improve their estates or arrange marriage settlements. Each bank had its distinctive clientele: Praed & Co. in Fleet Street had the West Country and Cornish business; Drummond's catered for army agents, Gosling's and Child's for East India Company tycoons; Coutts' dealt with the aristocracy and never with industry; Wright's in Covent Garden looked after the Catholic gentry and Herries Bank in St James's Street, further west, issued cheques for smart travellers setting out on the Grand Tour.[7]

The rule at Hoare's was that one partner was in attendance at all times. They took turns, living in the rooms above the bank for several weeks or months at a time. Harry, small, slight and suffering from bouts of rheumatic fever – but able to hang on to power until he died at the age of seventy-eight – was rarely there, but messengers dashed down to Mitcham, and he oversaw every major transaction. Within the bank, around ten clerks did the day-to-day work. Some lived in, and these were much sought-after posts, held on to with pride: the senior clerk, John Noble, worked here for fifty-two years between 1758 and 1810. A cook and two servants looked after them and laundry maids and other helpers came in daily. The regime for the Hoares' 'Gentlemen of the Shop' was strict: there must be at least one clerk in the bank all the time, even on Sundays and Christmas Day 'which is in every respect to be considered a Sunday'. They had to attend, properly dressed, from nine o'clock, and after the bank closed at five they must stay on until the balance was right. They must not pay drafts on the accounts of gentlemen whose credit was not good, and if they did so 'to excess' they would personally have to make good the deficiencies. Every day at least one clerk went up to the City, going round the brokers.

Their salaries rose early in the war from £80 to £100 for juniors, and from £140 to £160 for seniors, and then stayed at those rates for sixty years. There were perks, like free board and lodging and a Christmas Fund, and extra pay came from a fund based on commissions from the buying and selling of stocks. This was not to be sneezed at as the Brokerage Fund averaged over £3000 between 1799 and 1809, with half going to the two senior clerks and the rest divided among the others. But there was no pension, as John Willoughby had realised in 1788 when he began to set aside 2½d out of every shilling for his old age, gradually increasing this to 6½d. He kept records of all his expenditure and income – fruit and coal, candles and fish and salt and pepper – and, after thirty years, he wrote in his neat notebook, 'Independent and left off saving'.[8]

The heart of City dealing was still the Royal Exchange, between Threadneedle Street and Cornhill, where merchants and brokers met in the wide colonnades and courtyard to deal in commodities and foreign bills. Opposite was the Bank of England, whose workmen were building a new Stock Office, designed by the Bank's architect John Soane. On the eastern side was the Stock Exchange, still a relatively small affair on the corner of Threadneedle Street and Sweetings Alley. All around, in streets and alleys, were the halls of the City companies. And in Leadenhall Street was India House, bursting with business, soon to be expanded and rebuilt. It was here that Charles Lamb worked every day for thirty-three years from 1792. Often profoundly depressed by the monotony, Lamb did his best to play the part he later described with dry affection as 'the Good Clerk', clean and neat, up early so that he can be first at his desk, with his quill behind his ear: 'His whole deportment is staid, modest and civil. His motto is "Regularity".'[9]

The City was home to merchants, banks and brokers. Francis Baring, son of an Exeter wool merchant, had run his business in Queen Street, Cheapside, for forty years, acting as agent in overseas trade from Britain and Europe to the West Indies and North America. When the French invaded Holland and Dutch capital flooded into London, Hope & Co., Baring's great ally in Amsterdam, moved to the City and the links were cemented when Baring's daughter Dorothy married Pierre César Labouchère, one of Hope's leading traders. By now Baring was effectively a merchant banker – though the term was not used until later – carrying accounts for merchants, financing foreign business, placing shipping insurance at Lloyd's and acting as a British base for foreign companies. Baring's also accepted drafts drawn to finance transactions, the start of the 'acceptance business', involving bullion, bills of exchange and foreign currencies.

More traditional banks, accepting deposits and operating their own credit systems, often acted as go-betweens, arranging for country banks in richer rural areas to discount the bills of British industrialists, buying them at a lower face value and receiving interest until the payment date. The City banks, in turn, dealt with the brokers, who bought and sold stock for clients, and with the jobbers who dealt on their own account. Dealing was noisy and wild. In the Tuesday and Friday markets for foreign drafts and payments, brokers scurried round the Exchange, fixing different rates for bills from Amsterdam and Hamburg, Portugal, Spain and Italy, Dublin and the West Indies, and dealing in government stock and bills from the Exchequer, the Navy and Victualling Offices and the Boards of

Ordnance and Transport. The supreme specialists were bill brokers like the Dutch-born Benjamin and Abraham Goldsmid in Capel Court, and their elder brother Asher, a partner in the bullion brokers Mocatta and Goldsmid. They kept a fast sailing boat at Harwich so that they could carry express messages and receive rapid intelligence from their continental agents, and their high reputation abroad made them the government's chief liaison with the City. Yet like all the Jewish dealers they battled against anti-Semitism, in the sneers of their fellow brokers, in political speeches, in articles, poems and satirical prints.

Britain was richer than France and better organised financially, largely because parliament could monitor the accounts of the Treasury Commissioners and could challenge waste and ask questions, giving taxpayers confidence. Yet the nation was still deep in debt. After the American war the national debt had risen to £243 million – ten times the government's annual income – and had stayed at that level until 1793. (Theories vary, but to calculate today's equivalent for the 1793 sum the Bank of England reckons that one should multiply by 123, amounting to nearly £30 billion.) The interest charges alone reached £8 million (£984 million today). To deal with this Pitt had introduced his much-mocked 'sinking fund', setting aside £1 million to invest each year, trusting that it would grow to pay off the debt. But while the ploy looked promising in peacetime, war was now making the debt soar.[10]

To find money for the army, navy, armaments and home defence, and for subsidies to foreign allies, particularly Prussia and Austria, Pitt increased taxes and raised loans, largely through consols, 'consolidated annuities', paying 3 per cent to investors.[11] His needs were huge, and he had to float loans of up to £20 million per year. For these immense sums he turned to the merchant bankers and brokers. The first to take on large-scale war loans was the Scottish banker Walter Boyd, who had previously run a bank in Brussels, working with the Austrian administration in the Netherlands, and had then opened another bank in Paris. A month after war was declared, he started a London company with Paul Benfield, a wealthy Indian nabob of extremely doubtful reputation, now living in ostentatious style in Grosvenor Square. In May 1794 Boyd contracted for a £3 million loan to Austria, for the war in the Netherlands. After difficult negotiations, he offered to raise an £18 million loan for the British government in a consortium with Goldsmid's and two other banks, if they would guarantee a separate loan of £6 million to Austria. Pitt accepted the offer, in a deal that *The Times* called 'the greatest money negotiation that ever took place in this or in any country at one time'.[12] The arrangements for payment to Austria were the stuff of story. As well as sheaves of bills, millions were sent abroad in silver dollars, Louis d'or and foreign bullion. Since French privateers roamed the Channel, the shimmering coins were packed into barrels and sent on navy frigates to Hamburg, then carried in disguised, armed barges and wagons to Vienna.

In November the following year, Boyd and Benfield won a further contract for another £18 million loan, with government safeguards against loss and with no competition allowed from the other loan houses. Just down the road, Harry Hoare was suspicious, and also wary of being diminished in the face of so many millions, as the partners recorded in their memorandum book: 'Dec 10th Messrs Goldsmid called to offer a Share of the Loan amounting to £60,000 in their List upon our signing the usual Engagement to make the Payments. It was judged improper by HH to put down the Name of Messrs H in a Brokers List for so small a sum.'[13] But in the end they accepted, 'provided our Name did not appear in it': instead it appeared under the name of their broking clerk, John Morgan. The whole affair smacked of underhand dealing. Just before Boyd put this stock on the market in December 1795, Pitt announced a message from the king, concerning rumours of peace: the stock's value almost doubled. 'The annual subsistence of a hundred and fifty thousand inhabitants of Great Britain', thundered the *Morning Post*, 'has been at one blow, given by Mr Pitt to gorge the voracious maw of a gang of

Loan Contractors.'[14] Fox damned the transaction as 'disgraceful' and Pitt was forced to agree to a parliamentary inquiry.

The following year, when Boyd, Benfield & Co. won yet another loan, for which over fifteen City banks had offered but received no answer, there was more outcry. As the *Morning Chronicle* put it, 'to talk of competition is ridiculous. There is but one booth in the fair.'[15] Writing to Drummond's after a meeting to discuss this, William Hoare said that his father Harry was 'happy to find that the general opinion of the parties present there yesterday, upon the application of Messrs Boyd B. & Co, perfectly concurs with his own ideas; he is indeed decidedly averse to having any concerns in a loan where there is no competition.'[16] Soon the major private banks would have nothing to do with Boyd.

Boyd's dealings were stratospheric, but all industrialists, landowners and traders relied on credit and loans. Outside London a spreading hinterland of country banking had developed as wealthy merchants, goldsmiths, attorneys and others began making loans, taking money on deposit and exchanging bills. The number of country banks multiplied: in 1784 there were 119 banks outside London, by 1797 this had grown to 230, and in the boom and bust of the next decade they would reach 470 by 1804 and 800 in 1809.

Among them were the Quaker banks, such as Lloyd's in Birmingham, Backhouse's in Darlington and Gurney's in Norwich, all with links to the City bank of Barclay, Tritton & Co., who paid their notes, accepted drafts, bought stock and undertook other transactions on their behalf.[17] The Gurney bank, established in the 1770s, was the pre-eminent bank in East Anglia, holding the accounts of yarn dealers and brewers, shipping agents and farmers, town corporations and local politicians. Founded in 1770, it was run officially by Bartlett Gurney, but most of the work was done by his cousins John and Joseph, whose elder brother, Richard, also had shares. Politically, the family were Foxite Whigs, liberal reformers, but the three brothers were very different characters: Richard was virtually a country squire, Joseph was a strict Quaker, keeping a stern diary of self-examination, and John was far more easy-going. When John's wife died in 1792, he had entrusted his eleven children to his oldest daughter, seventeen-year-old Kitty, unconcerned that they wore bright clothes, were rude to neighbours or joined hands across the road to hold up the Norwich coach. While the boys went away to school the girls studied at home at Earlham Hall, reading Rousseau, Voltaire and Paine, and sketching with the Norwich artist John Crome. Clever and forceful, they drank in the radical ideas of the Norwich Unitarian James Alderson and his daughter Amelia, who was a friend of Thomas Holcroft, John Horne Tooke and the Godwin circle, and would marry the painter John Opie in 1798. The Gurneys were well-known figures, not least because of their support for reform. But their political opinions made no difference to their careful, clever banking.

One of the Gurneys' regular East Anglian clients was James Oakes of Bury St Edmunds. Oakes was fifty-one when war broke out, plump and prosperous, a member of the corporation, a trustee of the town's charities and a long-serving Justice of the Peace. His father had moved south from Manchester and he still had relations

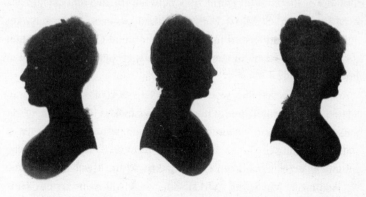

Silhouettes of the Gurney sisters, Hannah, Elizabeth and Richenda

in the Lancashire cotton trade, while two of his sisters were married to Liverpool merchants. But his mother came from an old Bury family of substantial clothiers, and he served his apprenticeship with his uncle, Orbell Ray, who left him the business. He and his wife Elizabeth brought up their four surviving children – Maria, Orbell, James and Charlotte, now in their twenties – in a large brick house in Guildhall Street. The family lived in one wing, and the other was the 'banking office', with a room above to entertain customers on market days, and wool warehouses and sorting rooms behind. Both sons were married, and while James became a clergyman nearby, Orbell joined the business.

Bury was an old abbey town, the seat of the county assizes and quarter sessions, typical of many provincial towns, where merchants and professional men met in corporation business, debating societies, book clubs and Masonic meetings, and their families mingled at concerts and card parties, assemblies, race meetings and fairs. About eight thousand people lived here, busy with yarn-making, brewing and malting, and in the countryside around lay the estates of powerful families, the Fitzroys, Dukes of Grafton, and the Herveys of Ickworth, Earls of Bristol. On Sundays the townsfolk strolled in their finest down the avenue of lime trees between the two parish churches of St James and St Mary. They liked their closeness to Newmarket and the races, and looked forward to the annual October fair, when leading citizens gave dinners and the Norwich players performed at the theatre.

In 1793 however, they were worried. The yarn makers had miscalculated: seeing war coming, they had overstocked. Now their warehouses were full and customers short. 'Wednesday Janry 16', wrote Oakes: 'Meeting of the Yarn Makers: a *Considerable* Reduction in the Spinning Wages agreed on. I dind at Mrs Mills. Met Coll Bunbury, Mr Adamson, Mr Smith, Mr Hockley, staid till near 10 O'Clock. Marching Orders for the Militia came down.'[18] A week later, with heavy underlining, he recorded the execution of Louis XVI. Then, on 1 February, 'At home alone. War declared by France against England.'

Soon Oakes and fellow merchants met to talk over 'the propriety of petitioning his Majesty not to prosecute the war being so particularly injurious to the Manufact. & trading Interests of the Kingdom'.[19]

Oakes's own small yarn-combing factory, Ray, Oakes & Co., was in St Andrew's Street behind his house, where he built cottages for workers and bought the Green Dragon pub as a kind of social club.[20] Nearby was a meadow where horses grazed and hay was cut. He was an old-fashioned paternalistic employer, strict but kindly, and was alarmed that he might have to turn off hands. In June 1793 he lamented, 'I never met with a more depressed Markett, never sold one Bundle of Yarn notwithstanding every possible Endevor. This is the 4th Month of attending at Norwich without being able to make any Sales.' Business slowly picked up, but he was already looking elsewhere – to banking – to make his family secure.

One of his many roles was political agent for Lord Euston, the Duke of Grafton, and through his patronage Oakes had been appointed receiver general of the land tax for West Suffolk: 'Took in 119 Parishes, abt £8,800,' he wrote cheerfully in October 1794. 'We finishd before 8 O'Clock & agreed to a farthing.'[21] He paid in the tax money through Gurney's in Norwich and their linked bank, Barclay, Tritton in London.[22] In the year before the war, Oakes's balance with the Gurneys had risen to £30,000. Holding the tax payments until they were paid into the Exchequer, as all receivers did, gave him thousands to invest – enough capital to start a bank himself. The Bury New Bank opened on Michaelmas Day 1794, the first and busiest day of Bury Fair. Squashed down the side of his diary page, nearly lost in the margin, was a brief entry, surrounded by stars: 'Open'd my bank.'[23] His son Orbell joined him and the Gurneys sent their chief clerk to help them set up proper bookkeeping. Two years later he would finish with the yarn trade altogether.

Banking was a pleasure to such a man of method, who kept his stock books and letter books, estate books and journey books in perfect order. His diaries were part of this ordering of life. But he also enjoyed the bustle of wartime, dining on turtle with the West Kent

Militia and going to the subscription ball. 'A most brilliant Appearance,' he wrote cheerfully, 'abt 90 Ladys & Gentlemen, 26 couple of dancers. We got home abt 3 O'Clock.'[24] He noted all the parades of the militia and volunteers and the plays they sponsored at the theatre, like George Colman the Younger's comedy *The Battle of Hexham* and the farce *Sprigs of Laurel*, for which 'The House completely filld & many disappointed of Place.'[25] And the soldiers also brought romance. Oakes's daughter Maria met her husband, William Gould, a clergyman's son, when the North Gloucestershire Militia were stationed here. Gould became an officer in the marines, and they lived on his half-pay until Oakes bought him a half share in a Yarmouth brewery, and later found him a safe job as barrackmaster at Yarmouth. The old working of interest and influence and the new effects of war – shaky markets and a town full of soldiers –made an impact not only on the town, but on family life.

There were moments of sadness, like the death of Oakes's first grandchild, Maria's baby son, Edward, in 1795 at the age of eight months, and of joy, like the birth of James's son in 1796. 'Dinner at my Son's being the Christening of his little Boy,' Oakes wrote. 'We all get to Dinner, 14 set down to table . . . Most of us staid till near one O'Clock in the morning.'[26] War or not, his family – and his bank – came first. But from periphery to centre, from the family firms of Oakes and Gurney to the grand private banks like Hoare's and the City brokers, all the money men were linked in a fragile interlocking system of credit. It was like an immense house of cards. And no one knew if the war would give it a push, and all would fall.

## 10. 'ARE WE FORGOTTEN?'

In late spring 1794, Henry Dundas ordered Francis Rawdon Hastings, Lord Moira, to head an expedition to defend Ostend, to prevent any possible threat of invasion. In Southampton, Moira's quartermaster William Napier was busy organising men and supplies, and his cramped quarters, shared with his wife Sarah and his daughter by his first marriage, were overrun with people. It was a novel mix of classes and types, as Sarah described:

Various and constant are the occupations of Major Napier, and constant and unremitting is his attention. Ceremony don't belong to his character and poverty makes us confine ourselves to cheap lodging with three small bedrooms and one parlour, into which are introduced 20, 30 or more people of various denominations from 8 in the morning till 11 at night . . . All march in at all hours on business. To this must be added 'les dames de la ville', now and then wives of officers, officers themselves sometimes on duty, sometimes as visitors, half a dozen very young men, who, belonging to the departments, call in and run in and out like children for a hat or a paper forgot.[1]

Amid this chaos Sarah herself organised and paid the recruiting officers, proud of every man they signed up.

Seven thousand troops hung around in Cowes until they finally sailed in June to join the Duke of York's forces. Other regiments were even slower to leave, including William Harness's 80th Foot, and the 54th Foot, whose new lieutenant-colonel, the eighteen-year-old Sir

Edward Paget, confessed to Harness that he was 'young at the business' and would welcome any hints. Harness's regiment were waiting in Guernsey, the officers billeted in the castle, whiling away the time going to balls and drinking cheap but excellent claret. From the moment they arrived, Harness was desperate for news from home. He had been two days on the island, he wrote, 'but I have not had the happiness to receive one word from my beloved Wife! My Bessy's own faithful heart will disclose to her the anxiety of mine.' He missed her, but 'in absenting myself from you Bess, I have the grateful consolation that I am improving the situation of our dear Children – oh my dearest wife that it were possible to have you with me without exposing you to sufferings even beyond those of separation.'[2] The men felt strangely cut off, with little public news – the sound of firing at sea suggested a battle between two frigates, but no one would tell them what it was. Begging Bessy to write, Harness told her that the best way to get a letter to him was via the smugglers, whose rapid postal service was an open secret: 'Major C. has given me the following address which greatly expedites the arrival of all English communication. "Capt. Harness 80th Regt. Guernsey to the care of Mr Tozer Brixham Devon". Let me hear often from you.'[3]

The regiments stayed in the Channel Islands for months while the allied armies drove the French back. But then came a French counter-offensive. In May and June 1794 the French pushed north again, overcoming the allies at the battles of Tourcoing near Lille and Fleurus in Flanders. (This was the first battle in which a gas-filled aerial reconnaissance balloon was used, prompting Napoleon to set up a Corps d'Aerostation and ballooning school.) After these defeats the Prussians headed back towards the east and the Austrians too began a strategic retreat. The Duke of York and his Hanoverian and British troops were forced to fall back, mounting a doomed attempt to defend Antwerp, leaving Moira's reinforcements as a garrison in Ostend. In Paris in late July, the coup of 9 Thermidor saw the end of Robespierre's power, tersely noticed by *The Times*: 'Robespierre has at length terminated his career at that *guillotine*, so often crimsoned with the blood of the innocent; and if we are to judge of the present and future by the past, the villains who succeed him in power, will most probably, in a short time, follow his example.'[4] It was the close of the most violent phase of the Revolution, but under the new leaders of the National Convention, the French armies marched on.

During the summer, Moira's troops rejoined the Duke of York on the Scheldt, but every month complaints about the slow progress became louder. Finally the regiments that had lingered in their barracks crossed to Flanders. They included the 33rd Foot, with the young Arthur Wellesley among the officers, and the 80th, with William Harness, now promoted to major. At home, following William's instructions, Bessy had been having coats made for Charles and Jane. They were 'of blue cloth or casimere with red collar and cuffs', with regimental buttons to match their father's, she told William, teasing him about keeping up appearances when visiting her brother-in-law: 'Our sweet Children, they must go with me. I cannot leave either behind, but the misfortune of it is that I cannot do without Mary, for the appearance of a *Major's Lady* and two Children without a Servant would be shocking.'[5]

In September 1794, the 80th landed at Flushing to join the troops protecting Antwerp and the Scheldt. Like many soldiers Harness often wrote in reassuringly conventional language: 'A Campagne in this delightful Country for an officer of my Rank furnishes much instruction, much to amuse the mind in its progress.' But the letters, like a journal, also allowed him to think over what he saw. In early October he reported that they were stationed in Bommel on the south bank of the Waal, and about to cross the river: 'We have the Meuse at present between the Enemy and us. The night before last they took possession of Fort St Andre, a small Island between that of Bommel and Bois-le-Duc. Our post is not considered as tenable, and it is supposed the Island, which is of great importance, will be given up.'[6]

Conditions were already grim. 'We continue dreadfully sickly having four hundred unfit for duty, including two hundred left in the General Hospital at Dort. Those Dye daily – it is a melancholy thing.' The colonel of each regiment was responsible for clothing, and many had scrimped on the sums given them so that they could make a profit for themselves. Some privates marched without coats, in linen shirts, supplemented with flannel waistcoats given by their officers. Often they had no decent shoes. Across Britain, groups of well-off women provided warm clothing, organised collections and arranged depots. Only a rush of donations saved more soldiers from dying of cold.[7] Writing from Cheshire, the Revd Heber reported:

There was an Assembly at Chester on Friday for the purpose of raising a Sum for the purchase of flannel Shirts and Welch Stocking for our brave soldiers in Flanders, the Collection amounted to 170 Guineas. And a Benefit Play for the same Laudable purpose in which Mrs Siddons acted, produced seventy pounds more. These Collections have been very generous all over the Kingdom.[8]

The well-heeled British public, glowing with patriotic virtue, dipped into their pockets – as they would continue to do for the next twenty years.

In December Pitt recalled the Duke of York to London, tactfully confirming him as Commander in Chief but replacing him in the field with General Harcourt. But in Flanders the British still retreated fast. From Nijmegen, where they left behind much of their heavy artillery, and then from Arnhem, the tone of Harness's letters grew darker, describing plunder, robbery and assaults: 'A Lady running from her house, which had just been struck by a shell, had her Ear-ring pulled from her Ear by one of our Villains . . . The excesses of our Army are truly horrible.'[9] For a while, under constant bombardment, the British paused on the bank of the river Waal, so swollen with autumn rains that it was impossible for the French to cross. 'I am glad you have a map,' William told Bessy, helping her to place the Hanoverian and British posts.[10] But as temperatures dropped below zero, the rivers froze and the French cavalry and artillery drove forward in a surprise attack over the ice. The British were overwhelmed.

In December 1794 Moira returned to London, intensely frustrated at the suffering of his troops. By the end of the year all hopes of a short war were fading. The French had taken Belgium and pushed the Austrians back across the Rhine. In Italy they had cleared a path for invasion. In the Pyrenees they had driven off Spanish attacks. In the Netherlands, the frost was so intense that in January 1795 the French Hussars charged across the ice and captured the ice-bound Dutch fleet off the island of Texel at the mouth of the Zuider Zee. The Republic of the United Netherlands, which had been a British ally at the start of the war, accepted defeat and surrendered. On 18 January, the Dutch royal family fled, landing in fishing boats at Harwich and Yarmouth. Next day Holland was renamed the Batavian Republic, a client state of France: the Dutch too were now the enemy.

Only the navy could see this as a potential good, offering the chance of prize money for Dutch vessels snapped up in the Channel or rich merchant vessels taken in the East Indies. To most people it was a disaster. 'The French have taken all Holland,' lamented James Woodforde in his parsonage. 'Dread & terrible times appear to be near at hand – Pray God! deliver us and send us an happy Peace.'[11] Here too it was freezing. 'The ice in the Pond in the Yard which is broke every Morning for the Horses, froze two Inches in thickness last Night, when broke this morning.' In the worst winter for a hundred years, most of the British regiments moved slowly east, but the 80th were sent north to Friesland, finding no shelter, marching by night, sleeping with weapons at the ready, while exhausted soldiers froze to death. 'The miseries of the sick are too painful to write,' wrote William Harness. 'Seven were found dead in one Waggon . . . I am, my Bessy, little more than a Spectator of the wretchedness which surrounds me.'[12] It was hard for people at home to take all this in. When she heard in late January that this letter had arrived, Bessy's Aunt Croke merely wrote with exclamations of delight that William was still alive, and of disgust at the perfidy of the French and the detestable Dutch. Then without pausing she ran straight on to answer Bessy's questions about London dress: 'The hair is worn quite the same; the bonnets are very small and velvet most fashionable. I don't think full muslin sleeves are now worn, but will enquire. Your sattin gown will only want a very short waist, plaited very far back; three broad tucks in it are enough, – but more than four *must not be.*'[13]

Muslin sleeves were a world away from Friesland. Shivering, hoping for news of transports to take the soldiers home, Harness became emotional: 'I regret the endearing actions of our Charles! His present age is what calls out the fondness of a father. Our Daughter is unknown to me. I have an acquaintance to make with my own children.'[14] This letter was not sent until mid-February, when the regiment crossed the border into Hanover. The rest of the British regiments were also slowly arriving. In April 1795, the troops straggled into Bremen, and were at last shipped home. The campaign had cost the lives of twenty thousand men. No expeditionary force would touch continental soil for the next four years.

The seasoned fifty-year-old brigade commander Ralph Abercromby, who had led the long withdrawal, was knighted and hailed as 'Britain's greatest general'. But this was a bitter glory, won in defeat. Early in the campaign Abercromby had already written to the Duke of York saying that he felt 'a spirit was abroad which would certainly spread'. Indeed, he thought, it would be wise to withdraw from the war, adding that the old monarchies were worn out, 'and a new order of things was approaching, which would be felt throughout Europe'.[15]

Across Britain, the families and neighbours of the soldiers who had signed up so keenly were beginning to face the reality of war. Among his notes on the accidents of Oldham life and the sedition trials and riots, William Rowbottom had begun to list the dead, all familiar local boys and men. In May 1795, as the last survivors arrived back from Germany, news came of the death off Yarmouth, so nearly home, of James Needham, a grenadier in the 57th Regiment: 'He formerly resided in Maggot Lane, enlisted in January 1794. Was in Flanders in that ever-memorable Campaign. That year he had the misfortune to have his leg broke in the retreat of the combined Army and lying a long time without assistance was frostbit and was never well after. His age, 28 years.'[16]

Mourning their dead, the regiments returned. William Harness was back in Derbyshire for a few short weeks from May to July, from the hawthorn to the roses, playing with his children, fretting about their accents and their table manners and worrying that his wife was too lax: 'I almost doubt whether that affectionate Duty to a mother which is lost at five years old is ever really recovered.'[17] But his leave was brief. In June French émigré troops and three British regiments landed at Quiberon in Brittany to support the *chouans* (their name taken from a Breton screech-owl) who were fighting alongside the Vendée rebels. In July Harness joined the 80th, due to reinforce this campaign. But while they waited at Plymouth, held up by contrary winds, news came that the Quiberon troops had already been driven back to the sea. As people scrambled to get on to the British transports and gunboats, six thousand men, women and children were captured; and although they were promised that they would be treated as prisoners of war, General Hoche's troops shot over 750 royalist rebels, on orders from Paris. When Pitt declared defensively in the Commons that no English blood had been shed, Sheridan retorted, 'That is true but English honour has been shed from every pore.'[18]

Attempting to salvage something from the disaster, Harness's regiment and six others finally sailed in late summer, taking with them the Comte d'Artois, 'Monsieur', the younger brother of Louis XVI and prospective Charles X of France, who planned to join the rebels. Awaiting orders, the troops were left for months on the windy Île d'Yeu, twenty miles off the Vendée coast, their provisions exhausted, their spirits low. Why had no ships come from England, William asked Bessy, waiting for a packet to bring mail and for transports to bring supplies, 'Are we forgotten?'[19] In late December, having done nothing, the British soldiers were finally shipped home and soon the Breton uprising collapsed. This hopeless expedition has been described as 'the most disgraceful, in point of negligence and recklessness, that was ever thrust by a British Minister upon a British General': 'to consign three thousand infantry and two thousand cavalry, without any reserves of food or forage, in the month of September to a barren rock in the Atlantic, where there was no safe landing-place and consequently no assured communication with the outer world – this was something more than a blunder! It was a crime . . .'[20]

The year seemed full of British humiliations and French triumphs. Towns across Britain sent petitions deploring the war's cost in lives and money, and begging that the government would seek peace, which would unite the people more effectively than the introduction of 'new and oppressive Laws'.[21] In February 1795 Tuscany had come to an agreement with France, in April Prussia signed a treaty accepting occupation of the left bank of the Rhine, and in northern Spain French armies marched through Catalonia. When Spain too signed a treaty in July, this released French troops for more campaigns in Italy. In October, the British doubters who saw the European allies as fighting only for their own gains felt vindicated when Russia, Prussia and Austria finally suppressed a desperate Polish uprising and carved up Poland between them. The Polish state ceased to exist. 'It is with regret, we again allude to the Partition of Poland', sighed the *Times* leader on Christmas Eve, 'which reflects so much disgrace on the Empress of Russia and King of Prussia':

We have a private letter from Warsaw, which draws a very affecting picture of the unhappy state of mind of the unfortunate Stanislaus, when he was forced to sign the act, by which he abdicated his sovereignty. The Letter runs thus: – 'The King was in the utmost despair; tore his hair, and at first absolutely refused to sign . . . he said that his fate was even more wretched than that of Louis XVI.'[22]

Such articles placed the European sovereigns on a level with the king-killing republicans. Watching the troops limp home from Flanders and the Île d'Yeu, and dreading the coming winter and the food shortages that it might bring, people across Britain found it hard to rejoice.

# 11. HIGH LIFE

Amabel Hume-Campbell came from a stalwart Whig family. She was the daughter of Philip Yorke, second Earl of Hardwicke (whose brother Charles was made Lord Chancellor just before his death in 1770). Prodigiously clever, frustrated that she could not enter politics herself, Amabel wrote two studies of the French Revolution, and of French ambitions, in 1792 and 1796.[1] As she went through life she garnered a bevy of titles, her husband's and her own – Baroness Lucas, Lady Polwarth, Countess de Grey – but she always felt stoutly a Yorke. Her husband Lord Polwarth died when he was thirty, and by now, in her mid-forties, she had been almost fifteen years a widow, sturdily independent and a diligent letter-writer, as her scholarly, bluestocking mother Jemima had been. From her Putney villa and from the family home at Wrest Park that she would inherit in 1797, she wrote tartly to her sister Mary Jemima and her friend and aunt by marriage Agneta Yorke on social life, the war and Westminster politics.

Between groans about her housekeeper, outbreaks of flu, local feuds and the romances and scandals of their circle, Amabel often passed on royal gossip. The great topic of April 1795, pushing the war out of the headlines while the exhausted Flanders troops were trailing home, was the marriage of the Prince of Wales. His debts were gigantic – around £630,000, enough to fund an army – and parliament was reluctant to help, having shelled out vast sums to him over the past few years. When George III agreed that the debts would be paid and his allowance raised as soon as he married, the prince looked for a bride. The choice was Caroline, daughter of the Duke of Brunswick, and the omens were not good from the start. When she arrived in England, Caroline was met at Greenwich by Frances Villiers, Lady Jersey, a clever, malicious and widely feared woman, who was currently the prince's leading mistress. Then, when the prince first saw Caroline, he turned to his aide, allegedly over-powered by the way she smelled, saying, 'Harris, I am not well. Pray get me a glass of brandy.'

Describing their ill-starred wedding, another aristocratic letter-writer, Lady Maria Stuart, told her friend Charlotte Bedingfield that she and Lady Ailesbury had set out in a sedan chair to St James's around seven in the evening, trotting up 'between two hedges of per-sons who did nothing but stare at us and make remarks'. The drawing room was impossibly crushed:

Lady Ailesbury and I stood from the time we arrived till eleven without being able to obtain even a place to lean against. At last Lady A. got a seat and I a door place, just then they said the Royal Processions were coming in, from which we all ran to the middle of the room, and formed two lines between which there was not space enough for the Princesses to pass without great inconvenience in their hoops.[2]

There they stayed for an hour, while the prince and Caroline signed the register. The prince, she heard, was 'serious more than can be told', and one of the equerries told her that he had been so agitated during the ceremony that they expected him to burst into tears. When the royal family finally emerged,

they spoke to nobody as they passed by us, except the K. and Q. to a few old men. The Prince looked like Death and full of confusion, as if he wished to hide himself from the looks of the whole world. I think he is much to be pitied. The bride, on the contrary, appeared in the highest spirits, when she passed by us first, smiling and nodding to every one.

On the wedding night the prince fell into the bedroom fireplace drunk. According to his own account, in the days that followed, they had sex three times and that was that: Princess Charlotte was born nine months later. A year later he told Lord Malmesbury that he was sure he was not Caroline's first lover, and she showed 'such marks of filth both in the fore and *hind* part of her . . . that she turned my stomach and from that moment I made a vow *never to touch her again*.'[3]

Outside the court circles, Elizabeth Heber's servants had rushed to see the princess showing herself at the windows of St James's Palace, and thought her 'Beautifull . . . very lively and pleasing in her manner & she is allow'd in General to be a pretty little woman – may she long continue pleasing in the Eyes of her Lords & Master.'[4] That was a vain hope. Gossip leaked into the papers, and into Isaac Cruikshank's print *Oh! Che boccone!* ('Oh, what a mouthful!'), showing the shivering prince bracing himself with a bottle of Spanish fly.[5] Soon the understandably petulant Caroline won her own reputation for sexual voracity and a royal drama of one-upmanship began. A year after the wedding, Charlotte Bedingfield's mother, Lady Jerningham, told her the current state of affairs: 'The Reconciliation of the Princess remains suspended, it is a dreadful Scandal, and would be very much to be wish'd that it was over.'[6] George III became increasingly impatient with his son, and when Princess Charlotte was born in January 1796, he told the doctor, Mr Lockman, or so Ann Michelson reported to her friend Kitty Senhouse, 'he liked its being a granddaughter and he hoped there would be three girls first . . . it did not appear to me there was much more rejoicing at this birth, than if the Royal Cat had kittened.'[7]

The gossip was significant since the titled world was split between those who followed the king and those who belonged to the prince's raffish set. The former went to sober royal breakfasts and levees, lining up against the walls as George III and Queen Charlotte walked up and down to greet them. The latter flocked to Carlton House or to Brighton, where the prince was filling his new pavilion with sumptuous oriental designs, mirrors, lacquer-works and silks. But both sets were obsessed with land and money and title. Their close circles were enlivened by new blood when estates and titles passed to different branches, or when Scottish and Anglo-Irish grandees chose English wives, and as peers married women with far-flung estates their growing landholdings became so scattered that they never even visited some of them.

The land brought in vast wealth but it also swallowed cash in mortgages and improvements, which meant that it was vital to keep on good terms with your bankers. Coutts, bankers to George III, had hard times dealing with the debts of the Prince of Wales and the Duke of Cumberland but, like the other private banks, they clung on to their grand clients. The personal touch of the Hoare partners was particularly valued. On 16 March 1796, their memorandum book noted, the Duchess of Somerset came in and 'wished to speak to a confidential Person'. She owed ten thousand pounds and 'wished to borrow 7,000 of it on a transfer of Mortgage; or a Bond of Mr Grahams'. As it happened, only a year before they had bought exactly that amount for her Grace in Navy Bills and stock, and when Harry Hoare explained that these could be assigned as collateral, 'she was highly pleased'.[8] And so, no doubt, were they.

The family of the diplomat and lawyer David Murray, second Lord Mansfield, had held an account here for two generations. After he died in September 1796, his executors sat in the bank parlour, going over deeds, and after 'a good fire, chocolate and sandwiches, parted in excellent humour'.[9] Three months earlier, when the partners had been asked to buy £20,000 of Navy Bills for Mansfield, they had worried that he was already overdrawn and the sale of his current government stock would not clear the debt.[10] But now all was sunshine: his heir used his inheritance to build a Gothic palace at Scone, and agreed to sell another estate to pay off a huge loan from Hoare's of nearly £40,000. When he asked for another loan, 'Nearly fifty years attachment to the House', they wrote, 'claimed an immediate acquiescence.'

The great wealth of these men and women, who casually quoted sums that were almost incredible in comparison to the wages of artisans and tradesmen, still swayed British politics. Many MPs now had financial, industrial or trading connections but Westminster was still extraordinarily close-knit – one in four MPs was married to the daughter of another member, while many others were the sons or relations of peers, or had married into the peerage. The atmosphere was hectic, especially as parliament's workload grew in the war, with long debates, all-night sittings and a mass of committees. Lordly ministers in the Treasury, Foreign Office or War Office complained that they could hardly find time to breathe. And both Commons and Lords became increasingly enmeshed with the armed forces: many MPs were in the forces and at least half served as volunteers or militia officers. Outside Britain too, well-born youths, who knew little except Eton, hunting and balls, sped off to lucrative posts in colonies and captured islands.

Everyone hung on the news of battles and casualties and promotions, handing round the journal-like letters from soldiers and naval officers, although sometimes the gaps between these could be worryingly long. 'I am very much afraid you will have been under some anxiety,' Captain Thomas Fremantle wrote to his wife Betsey, 'as the last letters that went from us were entrusted to a Captain Petell who was taken by a French privateer and all the letters thrown overboard.'[11] Promotion in both the army and navy was intimately connected with patronage and thus with domestic politics; you could rise if your patron's party was in power, and stagnate when they were not. The four Fremantle brothers were opposition Whigs, largely reliant on the influence of William Grenville's brother, the Marquess of Buckingham – 'poor old Bucky', as Fremantle called him – and luckily Betsey, with her French mother and Catholic upbringing, became a pet of the Catholic Lady Buckingham. When Grenville's star rose, the Fremantles flourished and when it was in decline, they languished. The oldest brother, John, was a colonel in the Coldstream Guards until his death in 1805; William became influential in the Exchequer and the Commons; Stephen was a lieutenant-colonel and an Irish MP – he died in 1794, but his son John later joined the army and was Wellington's aide-de-camp at Waterloo. Thomas himself would end as a Knight of the Bath and commander in chief in the Mediterranean.

The life of the 'quality' was still an alternation of town and country, sprinkled with trips to newly fashionable seaside towns like Brighton and Weymouth, and to the spas. Bath was now slightly démodé compared to smaller spas like Tunbridge Wells or Cheltenham, but it was still a mecca. 'No place in England, in a full season, affords so brilliant a circle of polite company as Bath,' wrote Christopher Anstey in *The New Bath Guide, or, Useful Pocket Companion*:

The young, the old, the grave, the gay, the infirm, and the healthy, all resort to this place of amusement. Ceremony beyond the essential rules of politeness is totally exploded; every one mixes in the Rooms upon an equality . . . In the morning the rendezvous is at the Pump-Room; – from that time 'till noon is spent in walking on the Parades, or in the different quarters of the town, visiting the shops, etc; – thence to the Pump-Room again, and after a fresh strole, to dinner; and from dinner to the Theatre (which is celebrated for an excellent company of comedians) or the Rooms, where dancing, or the card-table, concludes the evening.[12]

Anstey's 'equality' was more wished for than real. Bath was ruled by snobbery, as Jane Austen showed comically in *Northanger Abbey*, which she began in 1798, and seriously in *Persuasion*, where Anne Elliot's old schoolfriend Mrs Smith lives in dark, noisy rooms in the lower, poorer part of the town. The toffs ignored impoverished ladies like Mrs Smith and gazed over the heads of Bath's shopkeepers, staymakers and servants, being far more interested in themselves. Eagerly devoured gossip flowed through scandal sheets like *The Town and Country Magazine* and *Bon Ton Magazine: or, Microcosm of Fashion and Folly*.

On their favourite country estates, they held gatherings for their tenants and parties for their friends, employed painters and engravers to commemorate their houses, and collected 'Picturesque views'. Joseph Turner (J. M. W., as he would soon style himself), who made his name at the Royal Academy in 1795 with watercolours based on tours of the West Country and Wales, soon had patrons among collectors like Sir Richard Colt Hoare of Stourhead. In the autumn and winter many families returned to London for the parliamentary session and the Season, which lasted while the royal family were in Town, from October or November until late spring. Three to four thousand aristocratic and gentry families mingled with mercantile and City circles in the booming, boisterous capital. Aristocrats and MPs moved into the new Portman, Grosvenor and Bedford estates (95 per cent of the Lords and 90 per cent of the Commons had houses in these estates in the 1790s).[13] Further south, older mansions ran along Piccadilly and south into St James's Square, and nearby, overlooking the park, was Carlton House, grandly refurbished by the Prince of Wales.

St James's Street was home to the great clubs: White's, the most exclusive, Boodle's for the country squires and shooting, and Brooks's, the most political: Fox and his allies had moved here in protest when Pitt was elected to White's ten years before the war. Club rivalries were played out in James Gillray's *Promised Horrors of the French Invasion*, where French troops thunder down St James's Street with the palace on fire behind them; dukes and ministers are hurled from the balcony of White's; a gleeful opposition sets up a guillotine outside Brooks's, and Fox belabours a naked Pitt, tied to a stake bearing a cap of liberty.[14] It was a very public world, used to seeing itself in the prints, and fond of buying them. Gillray's protector and landlady Mrs Humphrey moved from New Bond Street to set up opposite Brooks's in 1797, and other print sellers and publishers were all around: Samuel Fore's in Piccadilly, Ackermann's in the Strand and William Holland, the sole radical spirit, in Oxford Street. Nearby were the booksellers: Nicol's in Pall Mall, and Stockdale, Hatchard's (for the Tories) and Debrett (for the Whigs) in Piccadilly. The streets of St James's had every shop a man could desire, hatters and wine merchants, confectioners, cane and whip sellers, saddlers, wig-makers, cutlers and gunmakers.

Rakes young and old also joined private clubs and riotously informal

Gillray, *Promised Horrors of the French Revolution*, 1796

drinking societies. A few had their hair cut short, in the revolutionary style, but they still enjoyed the coarse eighteenth-century jokes of bums and farts and tits, the erotic prints found in backstreet shops, and the taverns, brothels and bagnios of Covent Garden and beyond. In the tense wartime atmosphere, they drank and gambled and duelled and showed off to an unprecedented degree. Members of the Four-in-Hand club, imitating their coachmen and parading in their livery, drove open carriages at top speed from Hyde Park to Slough, drinking at every inn. One or two notorious men, like the Prince of Wales's friend Lord Barrymore, and Pitt's cousin Lord Camelford, who had settled in London after a disastrous and violent naval career, still upheld the brawling libertine ways of the mid-century but few were so extreme. They preferred more formalised aggression, dropping into the boxing saloon in 13 Bond Street run by John 'Gentleman' Jackson, Champion of England after beating Daniel Mendoza in April 1795. Lord Byron later pasted his fire screen with prints of great fighters on one side and actors on the other. Jackson shared the rooms on alternate days with Henry Angelo the fencing master, whose father had taught George III and the Duke of York, had briefly been master of ceremonies at the Pantheon and also ran a school teaching etiquette, riding, fencing and dancing to 'young men of fashion'.[15] Angelo knew everyone, from Charles James Fox to Byron, his pupil from the age of twelve. In later life, when he retired after an injury fencing with the actor Edmund Kean, he poured his memories into a haphazard ragbag of anecdotes.

Polite families disapproved of the hell-raisers and raised their eyebrows at the over-refined dandies, dressed according to the rules of Beau Brummell's establishment in Mayfair's Chesterfield Street. And although both dandies and rakes sneered at soldiers as uncouth, returning soldiers could cut a figure too. William Knollys, who came back from Flanders before the terrible retreat, was worn out by the parties. 'It seems the Sun Burnt Soldier is in great Request,' he joked, abashed – or so he said – by smart women making passes at him and 'quite tired of this dissipated coffee-house way'.[16]

The women, meanwhile, paid calls, dropped into Wedgwood's new showroom, opened in 1796 in St James's Square, shopped in Bond Street, went to their dressmakers, had their portraits painted, drank tea, and danced at Almack's in King Street, with its formidable grand 'patronesses' and prohibition of any talk of politics or the war. The younger women now looked startlingly different from their mothers' generation. New fashions were regularly illustrated in the ravishing pages of Heideloff's *Gallery of Fashion*. Gone were the petticoats and corsets and hoops: in came the high-waisted, loose-flowing dresses, often revealing the breasts, which were lightly covered with necker-chiefs or shawls. Satirical prints showed nipples galore, blaming the new styles squarely on France. The prints also liked to compare high-born women to the other women their husbands and sons might know in Covent Garden and St Giles. And it was true that gambling, for one thing, was as intense among the high-born women as the low. But many aristocratic women were sober and worthy: they plunged into charitable work, went to literary salons, wrote novels and poems and political or educational pamphlets. Some simply languished,

Evening dresses in Heideloff's *Gallery of Fashion*, 1794

complaining of being simultaneously rushed off their feet and bored to death. And they wrote letters.

Lady Frances Jerningham, leaving her Norfolk estates for London in the Season, wrote almost daily to her daughter Charlotte, newly married to Sir Richard Bedingfield, from a local Catholic family: in the early days of the Revolution, Lady Jerningham gave a home to an exiled group of Blue Nuns from Paris. Her own position was freighted with Stuart and Catholic loyalties: her mother was the great-granddaughter of Barbara Villiers and Charles II, while her father's family, the Dillons, had been Jacobite exiles in France. They had become a powerful family there, and had formed an Irish regiment for the French crown. This was disbanded in 1791, and its last colonel, Frances's younger brother, Arthur Dillon, was guillotined three years later. Her brother Henry and nephew Edward both formed regiments of émigré and foreign soldiers to fight for the British, while her niece

Lucy, Marquise de la Tour du Pin – who was devoted to Frances – fled to America, then back to France and finally to England with her family.[17] Frances Jerningham had been educated in France herself, but she loved her Norfolk home, Cossey Hall, four miles outside Norwich, and was devoted to her warm-hearted husband, who took a great interest in his estate and wrote a paper on mangel-wurzels.[18] And in London, she was utterly at home in the British Hanoverian court. Writing to her daughter she mingled family affairs with gossip of routs, intrigues and fashions – in her case, a middle-aged compromise between old-fashioned hoops and new classical styles:

On Wednesday I had my third Rout: 96 visitants, and to entertain them, the two Damianis, Miss Wynne who has a very fine voice and sings in the best style, and Miss le Tourneur on the Harp. It all went off very well . . . On Thursday we went to the Drawing Room at three o'clock, and remained standing till six, in the most violent Crowd I ever yet saw: the three Rooms filled with hoops, and swords, and each step thro the Crowd bringing danger of suffocation. My dress is not at all dismal and very fashionable; the petticoat is white Crape, and a drapery up and down, one of white satin, the other of drab Crape like the Gown, and tassels of large white Beads, but not looking so close and heavy as my drawing. What hangs down is Like a Bell of Beads . . .[19]

If trimmings and trains were as gripping as battles and thrones, passions also ran high with regard to the war. Almost every family had someone close to them in the army or navy. This was, in a very personal sense, 'their war', since their property and status were so threatened by the French example. In 1795 a flurry of memoirs appeared – Louvet's *Narrative of the Dangers*, Madame Roland's *An Appeal to Impartial Posterity* and a new volume of *Letters from France* by Helen Maria Williams, who had been imprisoned at Paris for six weeks in 1794 with her mother and sister. All these books amplified newspaper reports of the humiliation of the aristocracy.[20] During this conflict Britain's elite would grow in power, but the Revolution had unnerved them and they clung now, more steadfastly than ever, to their titles, their rights of property and their whole way of life.

# 12. FOUR FARMERS

In the first week of January 1796, in Suffolk, Randall Burroughes sold most of his bullocks. A few of them were home-bred but mostly Scots and Irish stock bought at September fairs and fattened on East Anglian grass and turnips. Some went to market, some to a Norwich butcher, and the rest were put out to eat turnip tops and make muck for the farm. Next he slaughtered his bacon hogs, one of which weighed '18st 7lb. It was fed on grey peas split by a machine and to every bushel was mixed one of barley meal.'[1] In the same week he brought the sheep that had exhausted the meadow grass into the home farm yard. His men were out checking field drains, hedging, carting and ploughing fields now bare of turnips or reduced to stubble. There was work indoors – a new staircase in the dairy and granary – and in the garden: 'finished removing the filbert rows cut down to the new cucumber ground'.

While labourers left to join the army and militia, farmers carried on with their seasonal work, totting up the prices, trying to make a living. Burroughes, now in his mid-thirties, was doing well. He had two large farms, one bought after his father's death and the other acquired in 1792 when he married Anne Denton of Burfield Hall: three years later he and Anne moved into Burfield, building a townhouse for her widowed mother in Wymondham, or 'Windham' as he pronounced and usually spelled it. They had four children in the 1790s. While he concentrated on his two farms, he also rented out extra land to tenants.[2]

Like many farmers keen on 'improvement', Burroughes kept a journal. It was baldly factual and any sentiment was reserved for his horses, so vital for ploughing and harrowing, rolling and carting:

Horses: Poor old Carter was so ill as to require to be knock'd on the head. He had been an excellent horse sent to me at Browick, an old coach horse, being worn out many years ago but the excellence of his spirits kept in exertion to their utmost the powers of his body to the last hour & without any stimulus from the carters whip. His age approaching thirty. *Quiescet in pace.*

Every week was full, not of war news, but of daily tasks, costs and prices, rain and drought. In February his men were threshing the barley in the barn, ploughing fields for oats and laying muck, while his tenant George Bernard worked out deals for the sale of horses and bullocks with a dealer and a butcher: 'They continued together from 11 o'clock morning 'till near six in the evening, drank three bottles of port wine & two of ale but could not agree upon terms.' In spring the barley was sown and the cattle were turned out to the meadows. In July and August, when Napoleon was rampaging through Italy and making a treaty with Spain, they were cutting and stacking the hay, delayed by sudden storms of rain. Here and on farms across the country, the mowers were out at dawn, bringing their own rakes and scythes, working slowly across the fields, stopping for an hour or two at noon. Behind them came women and boys who strewed the hay to dry and raked it into rows in the afternoon, then gathered it into haycocks. Next day the mowing, spreading and raking resumed, with the haycocks turned and shaken. Flies swarmed, and the horses stood in the shade, ready to carry the haycocks away to be made into stacks, thatched to keep off the rain. Burroughes's mowers were paid one shilling and sixpence per day '& 3 pints of beer'.

He won a reputation for being tough, sacking men if he thought they cheated him, but also fair, putting up wages when the work was harder or longer than expected. His farm servants, hired by the year, stayed with him for many years, either living in the farmhouse or in a tied cottage. He repaid their loyalty by keeping them on in old age: one of his 1798 harvesters was 'E. Plunket an old man to be paid at the *quantum meruit*', as much as he merits. Plunket also earned money threshing, ploughing, weeding, harrowing and gardening. A year later, his usefulness fading, he was noted as 'an old workman continued out of charity'.[3]

But if Burroughes respected the independence of the old labourers, giving them work rather than alms, in these hard times he began paying his ditchers and drainers, cowmen and threshers, by the day or on piece rates. He listed their tasks and noted their surnames – Elmers, Barnes, Reeve, Tayler, Plunket, Bunn, Lanham, Tite, Hudson – but they rarely stride into the foreground of his diary. They were always there at harvesting time, when a team of men and women worked together, cutting, binding, gathering, raking and stooking, with scythe, sickle and hook, expected 'to begin soon after five o'clock in the morning & not to leave off 'till seven at night'. There was beer every day and a feast at the end, and on feast days and holidays they had time off and went out with their 'purse clubs' or friendly societies. In mid-September, when the harvest was done, the barley all in, the clover cut and raked and the turnips hoed, 'they had their frolic':

I gave them £2 2s 0d in money & half a leg of beef weighing about 2 stones. All the helpers partook thereof. At home also the maids who had performed the additional labour with great willingness and diligence had a little reward. Mrs Moy was allow'd to invite some of her acquaintances and Andrew Turners family. I gave them 3 bottles of ale 3 of porter 2 of white wine one of rum for punch and they separated after a cold supper about ten o'clock.[4]

The year wore on, the farming round unaffected, or so it seemed, by the war. But it was, in fact, having a profound effect. Burroughes was turning over more land to barley and oats and especially wheat, capitalising on the high price in the market, sending most of his 'combs' – four-bushel loads – to the local mill to be ground into flour and meal, and some to grain dealers in the town.

The drive for improvement in which Burroughes took part was

encouraged by the Board of Agriculture, established at the start of the war in 1793 with a galaxy of lords on its committee. Its brief was to enquire about land ownership, the state of the soil, crops and machinery and the advantages gained from enclosures. The Board was the brainchild of the ferociously hard-working Sir John Sinclair, who acted as its unpaid president, while the good-humoured, energetic Arthur Young was its secretary. Young had been farming since the late 1760s, and became known for his volumes of *Tours* in the different regions of England, and later of Ireland, which included his accounts of progressive farmers and landlords. In 1784 he had founded the journal *Annals of Agriculture*, and although its circulation was only in the hundreds, its ideas spread widely. Long tours in France had, however, transformed him from a liberal into an anxious conservative, determined to protect British agriculture. To get a comprehensive picture, at the Board he commissioned a series of county reports, or *General Views*, writing several himself. Sinclair was even more impassioned. He owned large estates in Caithness and in the 1790s he compiled his detailed *Statistical Account of Scotland*, a compendium of information on geography, economy and society and history that would eventually grow to twenty-one volumes.

Putting the new theories and practices into effect, while keeping the old paternalist ways, could be a difficult balancing act. But the Board would have approved of Randall Burroughes, who was keen on draining his meadows and grubbing out hedges to make larger fields, and noting the density of seed used in each. He took to heart the recommendations of Arthur Young and of works like *The Complete Farmer: or, a General Dictionary of Husbandry*, now in its fourth edition. But he went his own way when he felt that the advice did not suit his soil, breaking the recommended pattern of four-year rotation – wheat followed by turnips, turnips by barley, barley by clover and grasses – by following wheat with peas, or even, against all accepted custom, sowing one money-making grain crop after another. And he was dubious about the newly popular breeds of sheep such as the Southdowns, recommended by Young and bred since 1793 by the great local 'improver'

Thomas Coke of Holkham, whose famous sheep-shearings attracted gentleman farmers from across the country. But Southdowns were hard to procure pure, thought Burroughes, and 'A gentleman declared to me he heard Mr Coke say he could keep 3000 South Down sheep upon the same ground which afforded feed for no more than 1500 Norfolk Sheep. Querey.'

Burroughes counted his profits, and bought more land and farms. In ten years' time he would have over a thousand acres. He was also a Justice of the Peace and served at one stage as Deputy Lieutenant of Suffolk. When he died in 1817, his memorial in Wymondham Abbey would record him as kind, generous and sincere, 'in the discharge of his public duties intelligent and firm at the same time mild and lenient'.[5]

Further east, just inland from the north Norfolk coast, William and Mary Hardy were running their farm and brewery. William had been an excise officer in West Yorkshire before he was transferred to King's Lynn and married Mary, from a long-established local family, the Ravens. In a manner typical of the upwardly mobile 'middling classes', set on advancing fortune and status, they then rented a farm and William managed a small maltings near Norwich, building a wherry to take his malt to Great Yarmouth, from where it could be carried to London. In 1781 he bought a brewery and fifty acres at Letheringsett, moving here with Mary, their two sons, Raven and William, and their daughter, Mary Anne. Soon he added a corn mill, causing noisy disputes with the local miller, and now he was looking keenly at men who were bringing in steam power. Raven, an attorney's clerk, died in 1787, aged twenty, but their second son, William, became their head brewer at seventeen. In his mid-twenties and full of youthful energy, he increased the range of brews, sought buyers as far as Lancashire and Tyneside, and installed great casks in a new vat house. At its opening, his mother noted proudly, 'Wm invited a Party of 20 Gentlemen & Ladies to tea in the New Mash Vat' (a customary celebration for new vats, although the guests would have needed ladders to climb in and out).[6]

Mary Hardy had been keeping her diary for the past twenty years. Like Randall Burroughes, she recorded the drifting snows, foggy mornings and sudden droughts, the gales driving wrecked ships on shore and blowing down the chimney stacks, as well as the haymaking and harvest frolics. She noted accidents (many) on the roads, murders and cricket matches and domestic happenings like the buying of a looking-glass or the monthly washing day. The Hardys were stout Foxite Whigs and kept a sharp eye on the papers. William even suggested that Mary should use her diary to note national as well as local and personal events, and at the opening of parliament in January 1794, when the King's Speech was followed by a quick amendment calling for the end of the war, he copied in the account from the London papers, listing the names of the '62 Vertuous Members who voted in the great contest for PEACE against 297'.[7] A month later, Mary herself carefully copied a list of Pitt's proposed taxes on bricks, slate, glass, British spirits and imported rum and brandy, all important for farmers and brewers.[8] Her account of daily life was scattered with notes of disasters in Flanders and repression at home:

*May 23, Friday.* A cold Showry day. Mr Hardy & Wm. at home all day. The Girls walked up to Holt afternoon, drank tea at Mr Jennis's. From the News Papers, the British Troops Defeated with great loss in France. Many people taken up in England for Sedition & Treason, the Habeas Corpus Act Suspended.

*May 24, Saturday.* A cold day . . . Mr Smith of Blakeney was killd going from Market Morn 2, fell from his horse in a little run of Water in the lane going from Holt to Cley.

*May 25, Sunday.* A cold day. All went to our Church fornoon, Mr Burrell preachd. Robt. Traven came to dinner, went hom after tea, Mrs Forster came an hour in the eveng. The British Troops & Allies defeated in Flanders yesterday & this day se'nnight.[9]

For all the Hardys' approval of Foxite demands for peace, in June 1795 they snapped up the contract to supply beer to a new camp on the coast. This caused much excitement:

*June 8, Monday.* Wm and M.A. rid up to Holt foornoon to see a Rejement of Artillary come into town which are to be encamped at Weyborn near the Sea . . .

*June 9, Tues.* A very close foggy day. Mr. Hardy & I walked up to Holt foornoon to se another Regiment of Artillerry expected at Holt. They did not come . . .

*June 10, Wed.* Mr Hardy I & M.A. rid up to Holt in Chaise to see the Rejiment of Artillary come in, we came home to dinner.[10]

Next day they followed the regiment from Holt to the coast, and continued to visit the camp once it was set up, joining the crowds to see parades and field days. The Hardys were doing well, and their household and labourers at the Christmas and Whitsun feasts numbered fifty to sixty people. In 1797 they took time off to make trips to the sea, and to watch the famous cricket match between 'Norfolk and All England' in July. That September, Hardy senior turned most of the business over to William, keeping the house and an annuity. When William took over, the Letheringsett brewery was producing 2,100 barrels of strong beer each year, for over forty public houses, including twenty-five tied houses, bound to take beer only from them.[11] And although they continued to farm, buying more and more acres, it was the brewery that made the family rich – William junior eventually bought Letheringsett Hall nearby, and become, like Randall Burroughes, a prosperous local citizen.

Farmers everywhere hoped to profit from the war. At Whiteriggs near Stonehaven, just south of Aberdeen, James Badenach was making money by selling hay to the dragoons stationed down the coast at Montrose, sending all he could spare, loading his carts and borrowing wagons from his neighbours. Like the East Anglian farmers, Badenach had his sheep and cattle, his turnips and clover. Being so far north, he cut his hay a little later in July, swearing at the six-monthly hiring fair that took away his workers. He was also a naturalist, noting the first toad of the year, the coming of swallows and swifts. He kept

an immaculate weather diary, his neat writing recording the fog drifting in from the North Sea, the 'hurricanes' and sudden snow in May
that blasted early potatoes, the longed-for mild spells and autumn
rains, and the winter storms, like the '*FURIOUS* Gale of Snow & drift
which Stopped all work without doors & also prevented watering the
Young Cattle'.[12]

Badenach was a member of the Edinburgh Philosophical Society,
and, like Burroughes, a determinedly progressive farmer. In the late
eighteenth century, improvement became an obsession in Scotland,
whose experts were determined to move the country from peasant,
subsistence farming to a 'scientific agriculture', geared to the markets.
Over the past fifty years, the agriculture of the Lowlands had already
changed. In the 1780s, when Andrew Wight toured Scotland for the
Commissioners of the Annexed Estates, the lands taken from Jacobite
landlords after the '45 rebellion, he was impressed by the landlords
who were using new methods of rotation, drainage, enclosure and
manuring with lime and dung. 'While the bulk of our farmers are
creeping in the beaten path of miserable husbandry, without knowing better,' he wrote, 'or even wishing to know better, several men of
genius, shaking off the fetters of custom, have traced out new paths
for themselves, and have been successful, even beyond expectation.'[13]

One of the commissioners, Henry Home, Lord Kames, had advo-
cated all the new methods in *The Gentleman Farmer, Being an attempt to
improve agriculture, by subjecting it to the test of rational principles*. The word
was spread by the *Transactions* of the Highland and Agricultural
Society and reinforced by the twenty volumes of Sinclair's *Statistical
Account*. 'There is no country in Europe', wrote the Ayrshire soldier,
MP and landowner Colonel Fullarton, 'where men, possessing property in land, have so generally applied their skill and capital, to the
encouragement of husbandry and the introduction of new modes of
cultivation.'[14] At the same time ironworks and cotton mills were being
built in the Lowlands, and new coal mines opened. With coal at hand,
people were less reliant on peat for fuel, and many bogs and moors
were drained, dug up, and planted with crops and trees.

The traditional small tenancies and communal grazing had all but disappeared in the hills of the Lothians and the uplands of Dumfries and Galloway and the Borders, whose cattle filled the markets of northern England. Here and on the grain-growing, pastoral east coast there were now large and medium-sized farms, with a clear hierarchy of landlord, tenant farmers and wage labourers. The life of the old 'ferm touns', the villages that had been the centre of life and work for small tenants and cottars, vanished as the big farmers swallowed their land for cattle and cereals.[15] Around Aberdeen, where Badenach farmed, landlords created systems of crofts and smallholdings as some form of compensation, so that families could stay on and take seasonal work. All these changes happened gradually, with little resistance apart from occasional outbreaks of sabotage, theft and arson. It would be different when 'improvement' stretched north into the Highlands.

Meanwhile, in his valley on the eastern edge of the Peak District, James Longsdon farmed land handed down through generations. As his cotton-spinning business grew he bought and rented more land, building up to 450 acres. He still sold wool to the Yorkshire mill own-ers, including Benjamin Gott, but he saw more profit in cattle, buy-ing bullocks and heifers from the fairs at Tideswell and Ashbourne, Bakewell and Chesterfield, fattening them over the summer and sell-ing them for slaughter in the autumn. Local landowners like Sir Joseph Banks, as well as the Board of Agriculture, encouraged Derbyshire farmers to develop good drainage systems and make watering places for cattle on the moors, to avoid poisoning from the lead mines.[16]

By 1799, Longsdon's three sons were all at the Revd Ashridge's school at Chesterfield, not far away – James was thirteen, John eleven and William nine. As the eldest, James would inherit the farm and he already had his own stock, according to custom. While their mother Elizabeth worried about the boys' clothes and whether they had enough to eat and told them news of their cousins, their father had more serious things to say. He was 'glad to hear you are all good boys and mind your Books and Mr Ashridges instructions':

I have to inform James that I have sold his Heifer with two others. She was valued at £12, less than I expected, but the extreme wetness of summer has been greatly against fattening Cattle, especially the younger sort. Now we have, thank God, fine weather and the latter part of my Cattle are likely to turn out better than I some time since expected.[17]

Had Mr Ashridge threshed his wheat? If so, he must be pleased, now corn was so dear. 'You must look about if you cannot find out a nice Barren Cow or two for the next Season, or a pair or two of good Bullocks that have had some Turnips.'

James would grow up with a stream of such letters. With Elizabeth's plum puddings and clean shirts, and messages of love from their sisters, came his father's stories of journeys in search of good stock at fair prices. At one point he sent his cowman Joseph Higginbotham to Lancashire and over the estuary sands to Ulverston, to meet a Quaker, Joseph Salthouse, whom he heard had 'just purchased a Lot of fresh Cows'. Joseph came back with '11 cows 7 Heifers & 4 Oxen':

They are nice Cattle which Joseph has brought, particularly some of the Cows and the 4 bullocks, & I like them, but they are dear . . . Now I have told you what I have bought I will tell you what I have sold. Goddard came on Thursday & I sold him the 4 Bullocks under Geo Shaw's care and the little Heifer bought of your Uncle. 3 bullocks were reckoned £24 but the little one bought going to Bakewell Fair not so much . . . If you consider what I valued them at on 1 January you will easily perceive the Turnips have paid well this year.[18]

Farming was a passion, but in wartime it was also an endless calculation, of weather and markets, crops and stock and sales.

# 13. PORTSMOUTH DELIVERIES

In the terrible winter of 1794–5, gales lashed the southern coasts. The ships anchored off Portsmouth, tossing and rolling even in the calm waters of the Solent, were waiting for supplies of fresh beef. But they faced a problem. The agent victualler in the naval yard had stopped all deliveries by the yard's hoys, the large barges used for freight, and instead each ship had to send its own boats ashore to the quay by the slaughterhouse. There was fierce competition, since each boat was loaded in order of arrival and now boats were being sent off at four in the morning to get a good place in the queue. Once there, the sailors waited in the cold for three hours or more, stamping their feet to keep warm, since the clerk who issued supplies did not begin work until seven-thirty. If the wind was in the wrong direction, the swell was such that boats had to move round the Point to a more sheltered landing, leaving the sailors to heave the beef over their shoulders, carry it through narrow gates, often blocked by others going in and out with their loads, and then stagger with it down across the beach.

Sometimes fifty or sixty boats jostled and crashed in the harbour, with nine sailors to each, reaching for their oars, tumbling from their seats. Crowds gathered to see, and officers complained that it was impossible to stop onlookers persuading crews to desert or plying them with drink. There was, complained Vice-Admiral Graves of Spithead, 'a struggle and contention not easily described'.[1] Sweating after loading the beef, the men rowed out through the wind, suddenly chilled to the bone. In rough seas, their overladen boats could easily capsize.

The local agent scribbled his comments on the back of the admiral's letter, perhaps as notes so that the Victualling Board could respond. They had used larger hoys to take the beef out in the past, he noted, but in windy weather some had been stoved in and beef lost overboard. And if the tides were wrong, the meat had to wait overnight on the hoys and could go off in hot weather. Taking it back and salting it rarely cured it, and the victualling department got the blame. Then came the management concerns: the hoys could only be used for meat, they were expensive to rent, and the three clerks who had to see them loaded overnight could do no work in the day. In other words, sending out hoys was a waste of time and money when the sailors could get the stuff themselves. As a small sop to the outraged captains, a vague note was added about rebuilding the landing stage and putting in more cranes.

A long line of people trailed back from the ships to the pastures where the cattle had once grazed: the sailors, the Portsmouth clerks, the slaughterhouse men, the agents who bought the meat, the farmers who fattened the cattle and the drovers who brought them down from their distant northern rearing grounds.

Although the British fleet had other anchorages – off the Downs near Deal, at Plymouth and Yarmouth, in the Medway off Sheerness – many sailors and landsmen saw Portsmouth as the navy's real home. William Cobbett vividly remembered his youthful sight of the sea and 'the grand Fleet . . . riding at anchor at Spithead':

From the top of Portsdown, I, for the first time, beheld the sea; and no sooner did I behold it than I wished to be a sailor. I could never account for this sudden impulse; nor can I now; almost all English boys feel the same inclination: it would seem, that, like young ducks, instinct leads them to rush on the bosom of the water.[2]

Captains made rich by prize money built new houses around this viewpoint on Portsdown Hill, their windows gazing out over the fleet. Within the ramparts, where townsfolk took their Sunday walks, the narrow lanes of the old town ran off the High Street, with the Platform at its seaward end, where people gathered to watch the boats pass. Stunned by the crowds of sailors, shopkeepers and dockyard workers, innkeepers and prostitutes, William Wilberforce, passing through in late June 1794, found it a 'shocking scene', where 'wickedness and blaspheming abound'.[3]

Portsmouth was also the headquarters for one of three marine divisions. These were the sea-going infantry, looked down on by sailors as ignorant landlubbers who would believe anything, hence 'Tell it to the marines'. On board they provided covering fire in action, guarded the powder and the guns, patrolled the wardroom and turned out with their bayonets at floggings. On land, they policed the streets and guarded the docks. About a third of the port's entire population worked in the dockyard. There was great demand for labour, especially when the fleet was laid up for repairs in the winter months. While a farm worker a few miles inland was earning a shilling a week, the shipwrights' wages were six shillings and sixpence: two months out of three they worked double tides, for double wages, and could earn an extra two shillings and sixpence a week as night watchmen. As Frederick Eden commented when he surveyed the poor of the country in the late 1790s, 'Watermen, at present, have constant employment; but in peace this class of men is almost starving. Tailors, shoemakers, and other tradesmen, more particularly publicans, are in full business: in short, war is a harvest for Portsmouth; and peace, which is so ardently wished for in most parts of England, is dreaded here.'[4] Yet these good wages were hardly enough. Take one example, said Eden, totting up the sums as he wrote: they had questioned a dockyard worker, aged thirty-five, with a wife and children aged eleven, seven and three: her earnings were no more than fifteen shillings, and while his, with double tides and extra jobs, could reach £36, after subtracting expenses for rent and food you were left with 'Surplus of earnings, £8 8s.':

The man could give no account of his other expenses, but says they do not exceed his earnings. The sum however of 8 guineas seems very inadequate to provide five persons with the other necessary articles of food they must want, fuel, cloathing &c. No milk is used in this family. They generally breakfast on tea, and sometimes on bread and cheese. A joint of meat is provided once a week; but bread, with a little cheese, constitutes the principal part of their diet.

In 1796 several hundred dockyard workers formed a co-operative to overcome the monopoly of millers and bakers supplying bread and ship's 'bisket', building their own mill and bakehouse. Their union was so successful that other yards followed and within five years a single combination spread across the royal dockyards at Deptford, Woolwich, Chatham, Portsmouth and Plymouth.[5]

The Victualling Board with its seven commissioners was one of four Boards run by the Admiralty.[6] The oldest and most senior was the Navy Board, where Samuel Pepys had laboured nearly 150 years before, but the Victualling Board, like the Sick and Hurt Board and the Transport Board, was old enough, having been established at the end of the seventeenth century. In 1794 its brief was extended to cater for the army overseas, as well as the navy. The chairman was responsible for cash and the other commissioners supervised stores, brewhouse, cutting house, bakehouse, cooperage and transport. In the years of the war, the numbers of officers and clerks in the Board's London office in Somerset House swelled from sixty-five to 105, with clerks scurrying though the corridors, poring over maps, settling orders and accounts – often years overdue – breaking their quills in writing minutes, and shepherding contractors and agents into the cramped lobby, where they waited to be seen.

Like the Ordnance, the Board worked through contractors who could buy in large quantities from local suppliers or even from abroad. Through these contractors the victualling yards in the main ports bought in cereals, wheat, oatmeal, pease and flour, fresh and salted beef and pork, cheese, oil and butter (much of this bought cheaply in

Ireland), beer, malt and vinegar. Wine, raisins and brandy came from southern Europe; rum, molasses and sugar from the West Indies; rice from India and beyond. All these were, in theory, allocated according to rule. The Navy Board decided on the number of men needed for each ship, ranging from over eight hundred for the largest warship, and five or six hundred for a seventy-four-gun ship of the line, down to thirty for a gunboat. And although ships rarely sailed with their full complement of men, the size of the fleet grew year by year.[7] The Admiralty set a monthly budget per man and allocated rations according to a strict plan: a pound of bread (the hard bread known as 'bisket') and a gallon of beer every day, four pounds of beef, two pounds of pork and two pints of pease each week, plus three pints of oatmeal, six ounces of butter and twelve ounces of cheese, with occasional substitutes, like wine or spirits instead of beer, or chickpeas and lentils replacing the dried peas.

The Victualling Board's yard at Deptford sent out supplies to around half of the fleet – the ships based at Deptford, Woolwich, Chatham and at stations abroad – while Portsmouth and Plymouth looked after another third, and smaller ports like Dover or Yarmouth, or the rare victualling ports abroad, such as Gibraltar, supplied the remainder. Deptford was huge. The brewhouse was one of the first to use a steam engine, and the twelve ovens, with their twelve teams of bakers, turned out bisket by the ton. In the cooperage, carpenters and coopers made thousands of casks to hold everything from salt beef to butter.

From 1797, each warship was supposed to carry twenty oxen, housed in impromptu stalls between the guns on the main deck, but this hardly touched the need for salted meat. To meet the demands of the army and navy, each year the number of beasts sold at Smithfield market increased. The cattle made their slow journey down from Scotland, Wales and the north-western counties, crowding the autumn roads, plodding steadily on, to be fattened before market on the turnips of Norfolk and Suffolk. John Clare remembered the Scottish drovers, a breath of mountain liberty with their blue caps and scarlet tassels, coming down the Great North Road past Helpston, and shepherds staring as they passed:

> To witness men so oddly clad
> In petticoats of banded plaid.[8]

Pigs too were driven in, from the fields around London, where around forty thousand a year were reared and fattened on waste from the city's breweries.

The vast slaughterhouse at Deptford could hold 260 beasts at a time, while 650 hogs swung from the hooks in the hanging house. In the yard, where the cutting house operated only during the cool autumn and winter months, they were dressed, salted and packed, and the marrow bones and shins of the oxen were given to the Sick and Hurt Board to make 'portable soup', a strong tablet of jellied, dried stock.[9] There were many specialist tasks and names: randers cut the carcasses into strips, messers cut the strips into regular 'mess' pieces of two, four or eight pounds, and salters packed it into casks, using rock salt from Cheshire, shipped down from Liverpool. Here too the war brought work spreading far beyond the yards – for workers in the salt mines, for men in the timber yards supplying wood and staves for barrels, for the small merchant convoys and the dock workers on the city quays.

The bakehouse too became increasingly specialised, so that tasks followed each other, like a modern production line. A few years after it was built, a visitor watched them producing the tons of ship's bisket. One man worked the flour-and-water dough in a huge machine, then a second sliced the dough with a large knife for the five bakers:

the first, or the moulder, forms the biscuit two at a time, the second, or marker, stamps and throws them to the splitter, who separates the two pieces and puts them under the hand of the chucker, the man who supplies the oven, whose work of throwing the bread on the peel must be so exact that he cannot look off for a moment; the fifth, or the depositor, receives the biscuits on the peel and arranges them in the oven.[10]

The aim was to put seventy biscuits a minute in the oven, and this was done 'with the regularity of a clock, the clacking of the peel operating like the motion of a pendulum'.

Occasionally the Board bought directly from producers: distillers sold their vinegar, millers built mills near the ports, local bakers provided sacks of bisket. In Kent, the market gardener William Patton supplied vegetables to Chatham, John Rigden brewed and delivered beer to ships in Faversham Creek and Whitstable Bay, while the farmer John Hughes sent fresh beef to the Whitstable vessels.[11] Usually, however, everything worked through middlemen, contractors and agents. The big contractors were often London businessmen, who employed subcontractors who knew about local farmers and sources of supply. The firm that provided the beef for the sailors staggering down to the landing stage at Portsmouth in 1795 was run by Peter and William Mellish, wholesale butchers from Smithfield. Their father had supplied the navy in the American war, building up close contacts with Deptford.[12] Living in their large brick house by the riverside, among a warren of narrow lanes with names like 'Labour-in-vain-street', the Mellish brothers became leading figures in the Butchers' Company, and they had their own ships tied up at Shadwell Dock, acquiring several vessels as securities for debts.[13] On the Isle of Dogs, where they fattened their cattle, they built wharves and shops and even a pub, the King's Arms.[14]

A whole network of contractors grew up. Many, like the Mellishes, had begun during the American war, including the London merchant Charles Flower, later Lord Mayor, Jordaine and Shaw, who supplied butter and cheese and salt meat from Ireland, and the Dunkins and the Knights, corn factors of Borough.[15] Everything was put out to tender and competition was tough, but the merchants were at least confident of being paid, if very slowly. They formed partnerships to spread the risk, assigning contracts and sharing ships, working with elaborate systems of credit at home and abroad, across Europe and the Baltic, down to the Mediterranean and over the Atlantic. There were plenty of openings for corruption, small backhanders and petty embezzlement, with goods winding across country through odd, informal channels. The Revd James Woodforde, a man who loved his food, was more than happy to receive 'a fine large Somersett Cheese', a present from his nephew, who had got it from a relation of his wife, 'by name – James Jules, a great Dealer in Cheese and employed for Government in that way – and is getting a good fortune by it.'[16] The cheese was even stamped with the king's arms.

In the winter of 1794–5, when the sailors were fighting for their beef in Portsmouth, the bad weather also caused trouble at Great Yarmouth. Once the Netherlands were under French control, the Admiralty decided to use the port, a fishing town with an extra trade in exporting wheat and flour, as the base for its blockade of the Dutch fleet, to stop it sailing south to join the French at Brest. But the shallow waters meant that larger vessels had to anchor offshore, and supply boats faced the dangers of strong tides and sandbanks, and swamping in northerly gales as they set out from the quays to reach the ships.[17] In these difficult conditions it could take five weeks to provision the

William Daniell, Yarmouth from Gorlstone, looking towards the exposed anchorage of the Yarmouth Roads

whole fleet. There was no depot or proper victualling yard here, and the Board's supervisors were easily dominated by contractors with good knowledge of local sources. The leading local man was Samuel Paget, only twenty in 1794, who supplied beer, bread, bisket and vegetables and arranged their carriage out to the Roads. Paget had been a teenage clerk to an earlier agent before winning the contract himself, borrowing from local merchants and traders, taking over the warehouses and hiring heavy square-sailed keels to carry flour and bisket down the river Yare from the mills at Norwich.

One of the greatest problems was supplying the thousands of tons of fresh water that the warships needed. In some places this was solved by bold engineering projects, encouraged by Samuel Bentham, inspector general of naval works, including a reservoir at Plymouth dockyard and a huge well at Portsmouth, pumping fresh water from a depth of 274 feet. But ships at the Nore, or off the Downs in the Channel, relied on water-ships moored in the Thames estuary, filled by smaller transport ships bringing water from the river's upper reaches, beyond the tidal limit. In Yarmouth, where Sam Paget won the water contract, there was always a shortage of barrels, and in high winds the water-carrying ketches would tumble against the ships' hulls, causing much damage. It was hard to keep the hungry, thirsty navy happy. One Yarmouth boat was sunk in a squall when she had unloaded her water and was suddenly lightened, and a month later a violent gale drove sixteen supply boats ashore, swamping and ruining their cargoes. That day even Sam Paget – a 'rather small, active handsome man', as his son remembered him, 'a good cricketer, a good speaker, gentle, calm, busy all day', found it hard to keep his composure.[18]

## 14. BREAD

In 1795, as the allied campaigns in Europe crumbled, what good news there was came from far away: the British seized Ceylon and took Cape Town from the Dutch. These distant events seemed irrelevant to the poor of Britain. The harvest had been ruined by a summer drought, making the ground hard and dusty and almost slippery to walk on. The wheat ripened early but was thin and hard to thresh. The New Year began with a frost so severe that Parson Woodforde found the milk pans in his dairy at Weston Longville, a few miles from Norwich, a solid mass of ice, and the chill 'froze apples within doors, tho' covered with a thick carpet. The cold today the severest I have ever felt.'[1] On it went, and at the end of February the black frost was still there. Woodforde, who had been suffering from gout, his agony comforted by red wine and water with nutmeg and sugar, fully intended to go to church, he confessed, 'but the Weather still continuing so severe, and much Snow on the Ground, I thought too dangerous for me to venture to go into a damp Church and Walking upon Snow, having not left off my flannel lined second Gouty Shoes, therefore sent word to my Parishioners, that there would be no Service'.

The harsh winter that was freezing the retreating troops in Flanders brought great snowfalls interspersed with floods, making it impossible for winter wheat to flourish and threatening the harvest to come. In late January 1795, Randall Burroughes, farming his three hundred acres and noting the fierce frost and snow and the rapid thaws that made his meadows like a little sea, heard that a band of labourers had turned up at his brother James's estate demanding that local land-owners 'should raise the price of labour in the winter half year to 1s 6d per day & in the summer to 2s', threatening violence if they were refused.[2] Fearing trouble, Randall rode over, to find that James had already called the neighbouring squires and farmers to a meeting, and had asked for help from the militia from Norwich 'if necessary'. When about two hundred farmers turned up, the labourers backed down, and 'there was no appearance of any tumultuous assembling of the people, so that all the threatening vanished into ayr'.

But the trouble was not quite over. In late February, the poor of a nearby village turned on the directors of the local workhouse and Randall could see that distress was growing. In early March, he wrote:

Upon Thursday night was a great fall of snow which the frost detained. Upon Saturday night another fall of snow. Weather all the time very cold. For the fortnight past I have ordered that milk be reserved for labourers on account of the high price of provisions so that about a pint of it with oatmeal boiled therein to the amount of about two pints is added.[3]

Milk and oatmeal were not enough, so cheese was added too, 'and a great relief it seems to be.'

In the West Country the demands from the port and dockyards at Plymouth, the fleet in Torbay and the convoys to Flanders and the West Indies had sucked in all available stocks and pushed up prices. In April, Mr Elford, a country gentleman, wrote to the Duke of Portland pointing out how badly the area was affected by the fleet at Plymouth:

from which market and that of the Dock Twenty-five thousand inhabitants more than usual were fed for several months: a number nearly equal to all the stationary inhabitants of both those places. During their continuance here, after the vicinity had been much drained of oxen, sheep, corn and potatoes, supplies were drawn from the several counties of Somerset, Dorset, Gloucester and Worcester.[4]

Watching the local corn sold to agents, leaving none for the people, the tinners of Cornwall and the weavers of Devon took to the streets and lanes. The first move made by angry people, here and elsewhere, was to keep the price of food in the markets down to pre-war levels and to persuade – or force – the farmers, millers and market traders to accept this. There were furious gatherings in Truro, Penzance and Plymouth: magistrates called in militia from other counties and rioters in Truro were dispersed by a bayonet charge. Some gentry and mine owners bought grain for their own workers, but gangs of miners still set upon grain dealers. Near Chudleigh in Devon, labourers wearing skirts to look like housewives marched through villages crying, 'We cannot starve,' and wrecked a mill that supplied the fleet. The ringleader, a blacksmith, Thomas Campion, was tried at the August assizes and hanged at the same mill 'with great ceremony'.[5]

Not every protest was a riot nor every crowd a mob, but there were rumblings of trouble from Northumberland to Land's End. The butchers were targeted too. In Bury St Edmunds, people began seizing meat from the butchers' stalls, wrote James Oakes, '& Obliging them to sell off at their prices. Some Meat was taken away without anything being paid for it – much Confusion ensued.' The justices swore in about forty extra constables, who read out a proclamation demanding good order in the market place. Later, however:

At 7 in the Eveng the Gentn Farmers &ca to the Number of 150 or 200 mounted their horses & rode thro many Streets in the Town till full 8 O'Clock. Many Stones at length being thrown & Mr Smith wounded by one we quitted our horses & returned to the Guild Hall. The Major of the West Kent came & informed the Alderman & Justices that his Magazine where all his Powder & Ball were lodged were threatened to be taken possession of & as he apprehend'd Danger should mount a Pickett Guard of 50 men.[6]

At ten o'clock the Riot Act was read, and the people went home.

Here and elsewhere, the militia were brought in to keep the peace, but in many places they joined the crowds, in part to protest about their own meagre rations. In April 1795 four hundred men of the Oxfordshire Militia trashed the town of Newhaven for two days, drinking as they went, seizing and selling meat and attacking farms and mills. Thirteen of these men were court-martialled. A further ten thousand men from the regiments and militia stationed nearby were marched to watch the punishment. Three were flogged, with a terrible three hundred lashes each, while two more, judged to be the leaders, knelt on their coffins and were shot by ten of their comrades.[7] Henry Austen, the Oxfordshire's regimental paymaster, who had been away at the time of the riot, was among the witnesses. Fearing mutiny, Pitt moved fast to increase army rations. But this did not help the general shortages.

Better-off citizens set up subscriptions and local papers listed alternatives to wheaten bread – brown bread, rye bread, potato flour. As prices rose, wages fell or remained stagnant. When the radical MP Samuel Whitbread introduced a bill proposing a minimum wage, Pitt countered with his own ideas for reforming the Poor Law and pushed other counties to adopt a measure being introduced in several places – notably in May in Speenhamland in Berkshire. By the Speenhamland scheme, as it became known, designated 'paupers' received poor relief fixed in relation to the price of bread. Since the cost of this fell on ratepayers, they turned to other methods of dealing with the poor and particularly to workhouses, paid for by parish funds rather than poor rates. All over the country workhouses were built: 'We all walkd up to see the House of Industry,' wrote Mary Hardy in north Norfolk, and later, 'drank tea at the New Workhouse'.[8] The Houses of Industry were designed to take all ages, but were filled largely by children, prompting the creation of Schools of Industry: soon there would be around twenty-one thousand children in such schools.[9]

Samuel Bamford's parents were in charge of the workhouse in Manchester, an echoing building with separate sleeping rooms for men and women, girls and boys, a lying-in room, and a huge basement with a weaving shop, a lunatic ward, a lock-up, 'a wash-house, a dead-house, a pin manufactory and a shoemaker's shop'.[10] Epidemics tore through the crowded dormitories where the sick lay shivering beneath thin blankets. In 1795 Bamford's sister, brother and mother and uncle all died of smallpox and he himself was dangerously ill. When Sir Frederick Eden visited here, he wrote, 'a malignant fever now rages with great violence in the house, and renders it unsafe to enter it'.[11] It was the crisis of 1794–5 that prompted Eden to write his pioneering survey, *The State of the Poor*. Making his own enquiries, sending out questionnaires to clergymen and employing an investigator to travel round England, Eden collected details of the work, wages, diet and dress of paupers and labourers in all parts of the country. Since he worked in insurance he was interested in Friendly Societies and was robustly critical of current laws and regulations, and of the vermin-infested workhouses and Schools of Industry whose children and paupers were hired out to manufacturers at starvation rates.

The Revd John Stonard, tutor to Pitt's nephews, the Stanhope boys, was an arch conservative, yet even he could see how grim the situation was. 'I see a good deal of the poor,' he wrote to Richard Heber, eldest son of the Revd Reginald Heber, 'and I know they can hardly live. It is with them a life of starving to death':

Much as I hate all popular tumult and piously as I deprecate all popular government, I should not wonder and I declare I could hardly blame the lower class of people if they were to make, which God forbid, some desperate and dreadful effort to better their condition. It is not the romantic and absurd notion of French liberty that will entice them to such an attempt; the desire of life and the hard struggle which men make to pursue it, it is this alone will impel them to rise against their Governors.[12]

By midsummer prices of wheat and flour were so high that bakers stopped working and bread ran out in Birmingham, Newcastle, Hull and Sheffield. People attacked granaries and set up barricades to stop grain moving from rural areas to the cities and ports, and gangs of women, some linking arms, others throwing stones and shouting, stopped wagons leaving the market towns. In Oxford crowds tried to stop the corn going by canal to Birmingham; in Bath and Tewkesbury they held up the flour barges; in Yorkshire they almost closed the rivers Aire and Calder.[13]

There were rumours of farmers stockpiling grain and tales of smuggled exports, particularly when supplies were sent to sustain rebel forces in Brittany as part of the war effort. As riots grew more threatening over the summer of 1795, the responses became more drastic. In Sheffield in June, troops fired on a crowd, killing two and wounding many more; in Manchester in July the cavalry dispersed crowds for three days running, slashing with their swords; in Rochdale in August, the infantry killed two old men. In Sheffield, a handbill issued a call to arms:

Treason, Treason, Treason. The People's humbugged. A Plot is discovered, Pitt and the Committee for Bread are combined together to starve the Poor into the Army and starve your Widows and Orphans . . . And may every wearer of a Bayonet be struck with heaven's loudest thunder that refuses to help you . . . Sharpen your Weapons and spare not.[14]

Then, suddenly, prices fell. 'Joy appears in every countenance on the rapid fall of Meal and Flour,' wrote Rowbottom. For six weeks the weather was fine, and the harvest was safely gathered in. Insects buzzed, fish glittered in the brooks, birds sang so sweetly 'they would have convinced the most rigid atheist of the Blessings of the Almighty God', Rowbottom thought. But he was a realist: 'it should not be forgot,' he added, 'that fleas were very numerous and very much anoyed poor people in bed i'th night.'[15]

It was a brief lull. As the shortages started again, the government abandoned *laissez-faire* principles and intervened. This gave at least one dealer the chance to make a fortune. Like the butcher William Mellish, the grain trader Claude Scott made a mint out of the war through opportunistic dealing and knowledge of the markets. Gossip had it that Scott had started out as a boy by offering to do the books for old Ben Kenton, who kept the Magpie inn at Whitechapel.[16] He came to know the London docks and the traders and became a corn factor in Southwark, often supplying the Privy Council with information about the movements of grain.[17] By now he was a wealthy merchant-importer, controlling about a quarter of the trade in the

London wheat market of Mark Lane, which was run by a close-knit band of fewer than twenty men, who dealt chiefly with the flow of grain from Kent and East Anglia.

At the start of the war Scott bought up stocks of grain from abroad. He knew, as he told the Board of Trade, that the American harvest had been poor, that Canadian grain had gone to Spain and Portugal, and that while the Baltic crop was good, exports from those countries were banned and it would be tricky to get licences from their governments. In December 1794 he had written to the Treasury noting that while corn was 'scarce and dear' at home, he thought he could get large supplies abroad.[18] They asked him to import as much as possible, in the utmost secrecy. Slowly he built up his stocks, pressing the Foreign Office to negotiate Prussian export licences and leaving the Board of Trade to fix Canadian deals while he scoured the Baltic.[19] Progress was painfully slow. By June and July 1795 he still feared he would never be able to bring in enough. When the cargoes arrived he released the wheat carefully and slowly on the London market, trying to keep the price steady. To begin with the sale was limited to the capital – millers drove in from sixty miles away – and then grain was sent out to the provinces, in response to desperate requests. Over the following winter the import strategy seemed to work, although many grain merchants resented the government intervening in their trade. In January 1796 Scott also bought fifty thousand quarters (a quarter being eight bushels, a measure of volume, not weight) of Polish wheat to supply a new West Indies expedition. From March onwards, when he began selling in bulk, prices were gradually driven down, and many farmers who had been holding back stocks finally released them. Soon there was a different kind of crisis, as the big corn factors and merchants in the ports were unable to shift the imported wheat.

Scott made vast profits. In these two years alone, he was paid the extraordinary sum of £1,250,000 as advances, which he invested in East India stock. He made even more from fees when he was given the post of government agent, disposing of goods seized on neutral ships. He and his son Samuel (who married an heiress) signed the 'loyal London merchants' declaration' and subscribed £50,000 to the City's loyalty loan. Soon Scott bought an estate near Bromley and five years later both he and Samuel became MPs, in safe seats under the patronage of a Wiltshire landowner.

British radicals linked bread shortages to the war and to corruption and cabals among the leisured rich. After the acquittals at the treason trials, membership of the reformist London Corresponding Society briefly revived, and the society held large open-air meetings on St George's Fields, Southwark, in June 1795. That autumn, on 26 October, John Thelwall and others addressed great crowds in the fields around Copenhagen House, an Islington pub, and sent a 'remonstrance' to the king. 'The shopkeeper, the mechanic, and the poor ploughman, all suffer together,' Thelwall proclaimed.[20] To remove the corruption that was destroying them, 'we ought all to unite heart and hand together'. The crowd roared approval before dispersing into the city streets, some walking back past Bedlam and Moorfields, and on past the Swan and Hoop inn and livery stables, where three days later, on a night of full moon, John Keats was born.

Thelwall addresses the crowd in Gillray's *Copenhagen House*

At the end of that week, James Woodforde and his niece Nancy were among the many who went to St James's Park to see the king drive to the House of Lords in his state coach 'with eight Cream-Coloured Horses in red Morrocco-leather Harness'. The park, noticed Woodforde, 'was uncommonly crouded', and he was sorry to say,

that his Majesty was very grossly insulted by some of the Mob, and had a very narrow escape of being killed going to the House, a Ball passing thro' the Windows as he went thro' old Palace-Yard, supposed to be discharged from an air Gun, but very fortunately did not strike the King or Lords – On his return from the House to James's Palace, he was very much hissed & hooted at, and on his going from St. James's to the Queens Palace in his private Coach he had another very lucky Escape, as the Mob surrounded his Coach and one of them was going to open the Door but the Horse Guards coming up very providentially at the Time, prevented any further danger.[21]

The king was using a private carriage because the state coach had been abandoned and vandalised in Pall Mall: a royal groom lay crushed beneath its wheels. By the time it was returned to the mews every window was broken and pieces of glass were being sold as souvenirs in the streets.[22] The crowd grew so thick that Woodforde and Nancy found it hard to escape from the park, squeezing through a narrow passage into Pall Mall and then crossing over 'under the Heads of Horses that were in the Coaches which stood quite close one to another all up the Strand', before collapsing into their inn: 'Dreadful Work was expected to be done to night.'

Although there were shouts of 'No Pitt, No War, Bread, Bread!', the window of the royal coach was probably broken by a pebble, rather than a bullet. But in Woodforde's view and that of conservatives up and down the country, the crowd were all 'the most violent & lowest Democrats'. The hunt was out to find the alleged culprits and loyalist papers like the *True Briton* howled for legislation to suppress public meetings. On 6 November, the government introduced the Treasonable Practices Bill and the Seditious Meetings Bill. When Thelwall came back to address another rally at Copenhagen House a few days later he spoke at one of the last public meetings for several years.[23]

Despite furious opposition from Sheridan and Fox, and widespread petitioning and submission of addresses from protestors – which suggested that a broad swathe of people thought Pitt was overstepping the mark – the two 'Gagging Acts' were passed six days later. Under the Treasonable Practices Act (never used, the existing legislation being quite flexible enough) it became a treasonable offence to incite hatred of the king, or even to imagine his death, in speech or on paper. Other clauses specified that anyone bringing the king, government or constitution into contempt faced seven years' transportation. The wording was so vague that this 'contempt' for government could be applied even to an objection to a local turnpike, let alone opposition to the war. Meanwhile, the Seditious Meetings Act, closing down lecture halls and restricting unlicensed meetings to fifty people, clamped down on lectures, silencing intellectual argument as well as stopping public gatherings.[24]

Fox and leading Whig supporters stayed away from parliament in protest. If complaint was silenced, Fox warned, the only alternative for protestors would be violence. Petitioners bombarded parliament protesting against the attack on liberties. The war, declared the London Corresponding Society, was being waged solely 'for the manifest purpose of destroying the Liberties of France, and insulting those of the British'.[25] Even normally cautious people felt that the repression was going too far. In Bury St Edmunds, James Oakes made an entry in his diary, starred for importance: 'Signd a Petition to the House of Commons against the Bill pendg in parliament to prevent Seditious Meeting & the better preservg his Majesty's Person against the Attack of ill desposd people. *Signd principally by the Dissenting Party.*'[26]

That autumn the young poet Robert Southey whisked Coleridge down to Bristol, where he met Wordsworth and began to consider becoming a Unitarian minister. His friends decided that the best place for him to start was Bath, but before he even began, Coleridge startled his 'large and enlightened audience' by refusing to wear a preacher's black gown, climbing into the pulpit in bright blue coat and white waistcoat.[27] Taking the text 'When they shall be hungry they shall fret themselves, and curse their king and their God and look upward' (Isaiah 8:21), he then delivered an impassioned lecture on the Corn Laws. Pleased with himself, Coleridge announced that he would not mind giving a second sermon that afternoon, on the hair-powder tax, another measure to restrict the use of flour. But by then, having had enough of politics, the congregation had shrunk to seventeen, and the Bristol bookseller Joseph Cottle buried his head in his hands as the citizens of Bath flung back the doors of their pews and left. Yet this apparently frivolous issue – people who chose to pay the guinea tax were called 'guinea-pigs' – did raise questions about luxury, taste and taxes. The tax speeded up the abandonment of wigs, which had already begun as men adopted short 'French' haircuts, a style linked to the reformist views of Fox and leading Whigs like John Russell, Duke of Bedford. *The Times* joked that a club had been formed 'called the Crop Club, every member of which is obliged to have his head cropped . . . the new crop is called the Bedford Level.'[28] Verses, pamphlets and cartoons imagined penurious barbers forced into the army. 'What a change!' wrote one critic. 'To behold a troop of feminine frisseurs converted into a company of valiant guards – their songs transformed into muskets and their powder bags into cartridge boxes!'[29]

More seriously, in December the gentlefolk of Bury St Edmunds held a meeting, poorly attended, noted James Oakes ruefully, to decide how to regulate their own intake of wheat. This did not necessarily mean restraint. In line with Pitt's suggestion that people should eat meat to save bread, the following spring Parson Woodforde and cronies enjoyed a dinner given by Squire Mellish, of salmon with shrimp sauce, mutton, tongue, breast of veal and 'the best part of a Rump of Beef', followed by spring chickens, sweetbreads, jellies, 'Maccaroni – frill'd Oysters', '2 small crabs' and a dish of eggs. 'N.B. No kind of Pastry,' noted Woodforde, 'no Wheat Flour made use of . . . and even the melted Butter thickened with Wheat-Meal – and the Bread all brown Wheat-Meal with one part in four of Barley Flour.'[30]

The poor, however, did not even have brown wheatmeal. Near

Aberdeen, James Badenach noted that there was no oatmeal either. 'The Price of Grain Precarious at Present,' he noted, 'Meal scarce & scarcely to be got & threatened Mobbings &c.'[31] A county meeting was held, but by March 1796 the meeting's agenda had shifted from shortages to roads. In June Badenach wrote in excitement, 'Rode Some Miles on the New formed TURNPIKE road benorth Stonehaven which will be pleasant Instead of the Dreary present One.' Beyond the turnpikes the rutted roads were full of people on the move, many thrown out of parishes because they could prove no right to their poor relief. Beggars turned up at the doors of country vicars like Wood-forde, who had his own reasons for disapproval: 'To one John Turner an old decayed Fisherman with a petition, gave 0:1:0 – He was the Man that brought me once some very indifferent Spratts.'[32]

William Henry Pyne, a group on the road

Vagrants haunted the lanes and woods. They wrote no letters or diaries, and their only records are parish books and assize court transcripts. They appear, though, in Wordsworth's poems and in Southey's 'English Eclogues' and 'Botany Bay Eclogues', showing the poor sinking into crime and despair. They are there in William Pyne's drawings of rural life and in George Morland's paintings. After winning fame with sentimental scenes, in the 1790s Morland shunned polite society, drank and was always in debt and often joined the gypsies, poachers and army deserters on the tramp. In his paintings they huddle beneath trees or by an alehouse door, the women wearing the red cloaks given them by the Poor Law officer, clutching babies, fearful of the men who loom over them, resting, just for a while, in their travels on the road.[33]

# 15. EAST AND WEST

In Westminster new alliances had formed. In June 1794 the Whig grandee the Duke of Portland had left Fox's party, becoming Pitt's Home Secretary, and taking most of his followers with him, including Burke: this was a fundamental split in the Whigs, a disaster for Fox and a triumph for Pitt, who now had a huge majority. In the general election in the early summer of 1796, only sixty-six seats were contested, although the Foxite Whigs still campaigned for peace and removal of the repressive legislation. In Norwich, Richard Gurney's son Hudson, who had just come of age, stood as proxy for his father's rich cousin Bartlett (both men had left the Quakers and could stand for public office). 'All my aspiring was to be the author of one good poem,' Hudson said, and, 'should luck favour, London and Parliament'.[1] The war had brought hard times to Norwich weavers and they were ready to support him against the ministerial candidate, William Windham. Hudson's young cousins, the many children of John Gurney of Earlham, were in a whirlwind of excitement, rushing to the market place to find a window to watch from. 'This morning I thought of nothing but the election; I was so interested in it,' wrote eleven-year-old Louisa. 'Norwich was in the greatest bustle. We had blue cockades and I bawled out of the window at a fine rate – "Gurney for ever!" Hudson was tossed in the chair. He looked most handsome. I never saw him so handsome or so well.' In the evening, they heard that Windham had won. 'I cannot say what I felt, I was so vexed. Eliza and I cried. I hated all the aristocrats; I felt it right to hate them. I was fit to kill them.'[2]

Louisa was swift to apply political to personal. A few weeks afterwards, angry that her sister Richenda was treated differently just because she was two years older, she scrawled, 'there is nothing on earth I detest so much as this. I think children ought to be treated according to their merit, not their age. I love democracy, whenever and in whatever form it appears.'

Pitt's aristocratic cabinet, free from any whiff of democracy, was juggling two main war policies. The initial plan had been for a double onslaught: the army would support the troops of Austria and Prussia on the Continent, while the Royal Navy would strike at the French fleet and carry marines to seize the rich French sugar islands of the West Indies. This broader attack, thought Pitt, would at once blight the French economy and compensate, at least in part, for Britain's loss of the American colonies. But he dithered, unsure whether to back the continental war, defeating the French by force of arms, or to try and weaken French power by taking their colonies, blockading their ports and driving them into negotiations. Unable to plump for a single aim he tried, unhappily, for both. In the colonial war, after the precarious victories in Ceylon and South Africa, more troops had sailed out, east to India, south to the Cape, west to the Caribbean. All these brought casualties: in March 1795 a letter from Plymouth arrived in Oldham, telling of the deaths of the tailor James Cowper and shoemaker Matthew Barnes, in the 91st Regiment, which had sailed to the Cape of Good Hope. Next day another letter announced the death in the West Indies of the wheelwright Thomas Butterworth, in the 13th Regiment.[3] As the months went on many more such letters arrived. Across Britain the post was both longed for and dreaded.

So far there was no official arrangement to inform relatives of a soldier's death, or to let him send home his pay. It was not until 1797 that the Duke of York ordered commanding officers to report the names of the dead to the War Office, and not until 1809 that family members could petition for a dead man's effects. But a sailor could send half his money home each month, usually to his wife or mother, and in 1796 the navy set up the Allotment Office to record the details of all the seamen who were allotting wages to their families: the commanding officer had to help each man fill out the forms in triplicate, giving his name, that of the recipient and their address, and the number of children, specifying the number of boys.[4] One copy went to the Navy Office, one to the official who would distribute the money, and the third to the woman herself. Every month she would turn up to receive the money from the designated tax collector, bringing the form and a pass signed by the minister or churchwarden to prove her identity. The amounts were small but vital, £5 or £6 each month. If the man was killed or died, she came back to the same official to receive a lump sum, including back pay, and any uncollected prize money – sometimes as much as £150, enough to change a life.

Newspapers gradually brought home the global nature of this war. British ships sailed in every sea, from the Arctic to the South Pacific – in fighting squadrons, as escorts for convoys or convict ships, on solitary prize-hunting cruises, and on missions to remote islands in coral seas where the navy hoped to find a base. As they sailed, they gathered information about the war, about trade, about different cultures, and also about the natural world, bringing back specimens of fish, birds and mammals. Some naval men made the charting of distant seas and coasts their special mission. Matthew Flinders, son of a surgeon from Boston in Lincolnshire, had joined the navy shortly before the war. He had been on the *Bellerophon* at the crisis of Nootka Sound in 1789 and he had fought against the French on the Glorious First of June. All this time his father kept a detailed diary of family life: the birth of his daughters, the weather, the children's schooling, Christmas celebrations, as well as the expense of fitting Matthew out for sea and the receipt of his letters from Tenerife or the Cape of Good Hope. Then came a significant entry, a visit from Matthew before he sailed for the 'New Settlement of New Holland', later 'Australia'.[5] After the Glorious First in 1794, Flinders had moved with the *Bellerophon*'s lieutenant, promoted to captain, to the *Reliance*, which was now due to carry the new governor, John Hunter, to New South Wales. For the next five years he used all his spare time to explore and survey the nearby coasts with the ship's surgeon, George Bass, finally proving the existence of the strait between the mainland and Van Diemen's land – Tasmania – which Flinders suggested should be named 'Bass Strait'.

While Flinders surveyed, ships were carrying soldiers to different quarters of the globe. In April 1796 William Harness set off again, packing his bags two weeks before the birth of his third child, Jemima. He had spent three months at home after his fruitless time on the Île d'Yeu, and now his regiment was sailing south to the Cape. Bessy Harness got out her maps again, to follow her husband's letters about the wild interior of South Africa, mountains 'on whose summits rest Clouds that the eye cannot pierce', rich crops of grain springing out of sand and ostrich eggs of excellent flavour.[6] From the Cape the regiment went to Ceylon, and the Derbyshire circle passed round a new set of letters, about pots baked in the sun, plantains, shaddocks and cocoa nuts, turtles and pearl fisheries and palanquins. Sometimes a parcel arrived with presents, a shawl for Aunt Croke, shells for the children, muslin for Bessy, bead necklaces for the girls. The pain of separation was intense. Harness wanted to know every detail of their lives, and needed to be reassured that they loved him and missed him, while Bessy wrote that his son Charles said: 'tell Papa to come home; tell him there is peace and I am sure he will *begin to come home tomorrow*.' He could hardly remember his father's face, 'but I very well remember watching him down the lane when he went away'.[7]

Soldiers away for years followed their children through letters like these. Like countless other wives Bessy Harness recorded each step and William responded: he was pleased that at four Charles was learning to read, and wondered if he might be able to write him a note when he was five. And was Jane now also beginning her letters? When Charles was six and put into long trousers, Bessy sent a full account to Trincomalee:

I first intended he should wear a Green Jacket with nankeen Trousers like his Cousins; but Boy's dresses are made so short waisted that they will not look well. So since the hot weather began he has worn all Nankeen and his green Cloth is put by for the Winter, and he is the prettiest made gentlemanly young fellow you ever saw. His Clothes were beautifully made by a Man at Chesterfield.[8]

Charles's hair would not curl, but that did not matter 'for Gentleman's Children are generally cropt'. Soon he went to school, learning grammar and geography, searching – like his mother – for places on the map, and reading Mrs Trimmer's *History of England* with Aunt Croke.

In time Charles received his own letters, directed to 'my very dear Boy' and sent from addresses like the 'Palace of Bangalore'. Harness sent his son exotic stories of the east: of long marches in the heat, of children and elephants:

They are very good natured animals and, as you have been told, very sagacious. My keeper used to set down his child who was about three years old between the Elephant's forelegs, and trunk, and put him in his charge. The child would try to get away but the Elephant would, after he had got a few yards, put his trunk round him and place him again in his seat. He was an Elephant nurse.[9]

In her diary, Bessy made notes on the progress of Charles and Jane and two-year-old Jemima: smallpox inoculations and first shoes, early efforts at sewing. She kept a note of William's letters, often received many months after they were written, and of her letters to him. While he wrote of elephants, dust and sun, she told him of household events: the 'Great Wash' five times a year, the brewing of ale, tea with neighbours, visits from friends, rubbers of whist, rabbit for dinner, walks in muddy lanes. Neatly, she entered her accounts: a halfpenny to the beggar, a shilling for the poor children's school, sums for straw bonnets.

Although the British government was always concerned with affairs in India, its main goal at this point was to seize the French islands in the West Indies. Some of those captured in the first year of the war – Martinique, Guadeloupe and St Lucia – were soon lost, and the campaign in Santo Domingo was faltering. In November 1795 Ralph Abercromby, hailed for his leadership in Flanders, had been given command of a new expedition to the Caribbean. It began with disaster. A huge flotilla of 236 warships, transports and store ships, their holds heavy with bricks for barracks in Santo Domingo, sailed from a calm Spithead straight into ferocious Channel gales: several ships foundered and hundreds of lives were lost. A further attempt also met violent storms and after seven weeks at sea the tattered remnants of the fleet returned to different British ports. Writing to her friend Kitty Senhouse in Cumberland in January 1796, Ann Michelson began by asking about the Cumbrian weather, saying how she had read of the storms and tempests and high tides in the north. 'The newspapers are full of melancholy events,' she went on. 'Where the devastation of the West Indies expedition will end no one can say; as out of two hundred and twenty sail, only as yet fifty are accounted for.'[10] Admiral Christian had brought forty disabled ships into Portsmouth, crammed with sick soldiers, and the Duke of York had gone down to see them disembark, moving other troops on, 'that the poor wretches may be directly put into quarters'.

Seventy-eight ships straggled as far as Barbados, and once Abercromby's campaigns began, his gains were impressive. In April 1796 he retook St Lucia – restoring slavery, which the French governor had abolished the year before – and leaving Colonel John Moore in charge. Next he captured the Dutch colonies of Demerara and Essequibo, ensuring good sea-island cotton from Guyana for British mills.[11] In St Vincent, he put down a revolt led by the French radical Victor Hugues, in the aftermath of which five thousand black Caribs were deported to an island off Honduras. From October 1796 the British were fighting the Spanish as well as the French and the rebels. This was bad news for the government, but good news for the navy, who saw Spanish treasure ships, merchant vessels and privateers as rich prey. Abercromby then headed to Trinidad, with a fleet of eighteen warships, and in February 1797 the Spanish governor surrendered. Another target was Santo Domingo, largely controlled by Toussaint L'Ouverture, who had led the great slave revolt five years before.

Santo Domingo eluded Abercromby, who fell ill after a failed attack on Puerto Rico and resigned his command. He was a complicated character, a liberal who had refused to serve in the American war, sympathising with the colonists' grievances and sure that the war was provoked by the king and his incompetent ministers, and had welcomed the French Revolution and supported mediation until war was finally declared. With regard to slavery, his sympathies were with the abolitionists, but as an officer he set these aside. Above all he was concerned for his own men, as he had been in Flanders. With the wet season came thunder and lightning, 'distressful visitings of thick clouds of musquitoes', bringing the terrible 'yellow jack', a malaria-like fever affecting the liver and kidneys and inducing jaundice, weakness, black vomit, hallucinations, coma and death.[12] Army doctors followed the Dutch in treating it with emetics, opium and quinine, and Abercromby set up sanatoria, modified the uniforms and stopped drills under the pitiless sun, but he could do little to help: men died in their hundreds from fevers and constant ulcers. By now the government had already sent thirty-five thousand soldiers to the Caribbean and within five years the number would rise to eighty-nine thousand. At least half – up to forty-five thousand men – died in the islands, most from 'that ardent, and merciless destroyer, the yellow fever'.

As men sailed and marched abroad, sea battles and campaigns in Europe brought hundreds of prisoners of war to Britain: French, Dutch, Spanish and West Indian. For the first year of the war the Admiralty's Sick and Hurt Board had taken responsibility for prisoners, then the Transport Board took over, placing local agents in charge of each prison and parole depot. The French prisoners were usually exchanged within a year or two, although while they were here there were constant arguments with the French agent in London about paying for their keep – technically the money for prisoners of war was sent by their home government. There was also a rigid division between officers and men. The officers were given a passport to a particular parole depot, an alphabetical net flung over the south and west of England, from Alresford, Ashburton and Ashford to Peterborough and Tavistock. Local magistrates arranged for them to be billeted in houses or inns, and they gave their *parole* – their word of honour – not to escape, to obey an evening curfew and to walk no more than a mile from the town. Townsfolk put up milestones to mark the limit, like the stretch of road near Derby still known as Frenchman's Mile, or picked out special features like the tree at Whitchurch, which became known as the Honour Oak.[13]

By contrast, the unlucky rank and file were crammed into prison hulks at Portsmouth, Plymouth or in the Medway. The hulks had been used as convict ships for a decade, ever since American independence had stopped transportation to the Atlantic colonies. Most were dismasted men-of-war, designed to hold four hundred men but now often packed with eight hundred or even twelve hundred, with beams set up to sling rows of hammocks on every deck. The prisoners were guarded by marines, and sometimes by fellow inmates. The windows were unglazed, but the air was stifling, even in winter, and many suffered chest complaints and epidemics of smallpox, measles, dysentery and typhus. Local people sailed out to watch the prisoners exercise on the upper deck, which they called, ironically, *le parc*, or came on board to see them. They were curiosities, like lions in the Tower or madmen in Bedlam. Women visitors, the prisoners noted, were particularly callous in their remarks.

There were also land prisons, usually near the ports: Forton in Gosport, Portchester Castle near Portsmouth, Mill Prison at Plymouth. The Transport Board, overwhelmed, soon realised that more were needed and in December 1796 planned a new prison at Norman Cross in Huntingdonshire, seventy-odd miles from London up the Great North Road. It was built quickly of wood, leaving newspaper readers open-mouthed at the speed. London men made the framework and carriers took it to Norman Cross, where five hundred

Pyne's watercolour of prison hulks

carpenters and labourers worked seven days a week to assemble the walls and huts. From spring 1797 prisoners landed at Yarmouth or Lynn came here by water and road, while others tramped slowly from the south coast, lodging each night in barns and warehouses. Local papers reported bands of three hundred and six hundred marching through the towns, stared at by crowds as they passed.[14]

On the hulks and in the prisons, men taught each other languages, reading and writing (many prisoners who arrived illiterate could read and write when they left), and made gloves, hats and sweets to sell, and marquetry and straw-work boxes, toys and trinkets. Above all they worked in bone, cleaning the tons of beef and mutton bones that piled up outside the prison kitchen, and carving ships, fully rigged and decorated in minute detail, houses complete with furniture, dolls and mechanical toys, and developing a profitable line in obscene carvings. Betsey Fremantle, visiting Portchester Castle with her husband soon after her arrival in England in 1797, noted in her diary that the three thousand French prisoners there were 'very industrious and make all kinds of little works. We bought a Guillotine neatly done in bone.'[15]

The models were wonderful and the French craftsmen entertaining. But the most eye-catching figures were the black prisoners. It was proving difficult to house the captured French soldiers in the Caribbean, many of whom were freed slaves, described briskly in official papers as 'troublesome brigands and Negros taken in arms'.[16] Abercromby sent back four thousand prisoners in 1796 and when they arrived at Portchester, the governor, Sir William Pitt, decided, with evident distaste, not to allow their officers parole. 'The Blacks, who were called the officers', he explained, were 'violent in their behaviour and savage in their disposition, and doubtless many of them had been placed in that situation from having been conspicuously eminent in acts of rebellion and barbarity.'[17] It would be wrong to let them roam the countryside, especially in places where paroled French officers spread 'principles subversive to the Government'.

The misery of the West Indians alarmed observers. They were constantly attacked and robbed by European prisoners, 'considering themselves as a superior race of beings to the unfortunate blacks'.[18] They suffered from the English climate, with catarrh, pneumonia, dysentery, and the mortality rate was high. In the icy winters, wrote Commissioner Otway of Portchester, their state was 'truly melancholy'. Many were crippled by frostbite, with 'the loss of toes, fingers etc . . . many others I apprehend will meet a similar fate if detained in this country, as it is absolutely impossible to guard people of that description from the effects of a climate so very different from their own.'[19] To keep them warmer, some were moved from the stone cells into the crowded prison ships. Others, however, met a stranger fate: in April 1796, two West Indians in Mill Prison, Plymouth, were released to serve with the North Devon Militia.

# III : WATCHING

## 1797–1801

Thro' wood and dale the sacred river ran,
Then reach'd the caverns measureless to man,
And sank in tumult to a lifeless ocean;
And 'mid this tumult Kubla heard from far
Ancestral voices prophesying war!
    The shadow of the dome of pleasure
    Floated midway on the waves;
    Where was heard the mingled measure
    From the fountain and the caves.
It was a miracle of rare device,
A sunny pleasure-dome with caves of ice!
             COLERIDGE, 'Kubla Khan', 1797

# 16. INVASIONS, SPIES AND POETS

By the end of 1796 almost everyone longed for the war to end. The cost in lives and money had been great, and the gains seemed small. Napoleon and his Armée d'Italie were driving the Austrians out of Lombardy. After the battle of Lodi in May, British spirits had fallen, imagining that Italy, too, would now be blocked to trade. In Manchester Hannah Greg, writing to William Rathbone, noted, 'This town has been much agitated by the bad news from Italy. I think in matters of business the People here have not such good nerves as you Liverpool Merchants. However I believe the alarm here has pretty solid foundation.'[1] In August Spain signed the Treaty of Ildefonso with France, and in October declared war on Britain, forcing British fleets from the Mediterranean. In early December news arrived that the Anglophile Catherine the Great of Russia had died, causing more alarm, since her heir, Tsar Paul II, was known to favour France. Hearing of Catherine's death, Pitt wrote to Dundas, 'I am afraid much good is not to be expected from the new Emperor. It is difficult to say whether one ought to regret most that she had not died sooner or lived longer.'[2]

Fears of invasion grew. 'Serious apprehensions are entertained by many in high rank of the French invading England some time this Autumn,' Woodforde wrote in September. 'Preparations are making.'[3] In November, when Pitt mentioned the possibility of invasion openly in the Commons, he noted, 'As Mr Pitt is prime Minister, it is much credited throughout the whole Country, and creates a general alarm.' In London smart crowds rushed to see Macready in *Hamlet*, or took boxes at the Opera. There were dramas and delights, like the plans for the marriage of the Princess Royal, now nearly twenty-nine, to the stout, solid Duke of Wurtemberg. But as winter approached the British public were weary and worried. Pitt had tried in vain to negotiate with Paris the previous year and in September, in defiance of sceptics in the cabinet and the belligerence of George III, he sent James Harris, Lord Malmesbury, back to Paris to try again. For two months Malmesbury hovered there, discussing terms with the Directory. By November he was impatient, noting the new political figures waiting in the wings, including the young general Napoleon, 'a clever, desperate Jacobin terrorist'.[4] Then, on 19 December, Malmesbury was told he must leave.

Unknown to Malmesbury, four days before, General Lazare Hoche – infamous in Britain for the slaughter of prisoners at Quiberon – had sailed from Brest with seventeen ships of the line and twenty-six transports, carrying fifteen thousand seasoned troops. The British papers soon carried reports from Dutch sources that the fleet had sailed. Their destination, however, was still unsure.

Hoche was in fact heading for Ireland, believing an insurrection was at hand as the long-standing tensions in the country made it ripe for trouble. The bulk of the population were Catholic farmers and peasants, with small groups of Presbyterians among the linen workers of Ulster and the lawyers and merchants of Dublin and Belfast. But Catholics of all classes were held back by old penal laws preventing them from holding office or even buying land. It was the long-term English settlers, the heirs of the 'Ascendancy' who had lived in Ireland since the settlements of the Tudors and of Cromwell, who ran the country and dominated the recently established Dublin parliament.

In 1791, the charismatic Dublin lawyer Wolfe Tone had put forward a cogent argument for an independent united Ireland, reforming the Irish parliament and removing legal disabilities from Catholics. Tone and fellow thinkers then founded the United Irishmen, a group of secular, egalitarian, constitutional reformers inspired by Tom Paine and the example of France. The society, said one of the founders, William Drennan, should unite people 'in one grand pursuit, alike interesting to all, by which mental prejudice may be worn off, a humane and philosophic spirit may be cherished in the heart as well as the head, in practice as well as theory'.[5]

None of Westminster's measures could satisfy all sides. In 1793 Pitt and the leader of the Dublin parliament, Henry Grattan, managed to push through a Catholic Relief Act, granting a vote to all Catholics with a forty-shilling freehold. Protestants were enraged, and became more so in January 1795 when the new Lord Lieutenant, William Fitzwilliam, who passionately believed that Ireland's problems could only be solved if Catholics had equal rights, set in motion a plan for full emancipation. Rapidly stopped by Pitt, Fitzwilliam resigned and his replacement, Lord Camden, aided by his young stepson, the Irish MP Robert Stewart, Viscount Castlereagh, quickly moved to appease angry Protestants. With this apparent encouragement they took up arms, forming the Orange Order and causing thousands of Catholics to flee Armagh. In response a new, vehemently nationalist organisation, the Defenders, began stockpiling arms and building up links with the United Irishmen.

Respectable businessmen by day became United Irish conspirators by night; spies were everywhere, orchestrated from London; servants and labourers broke into houses at night to steal arms. The army and militia roamed the countryside, billeted on a resentful people; the government banned 'seditious' meetings and partially suspended habeas corpus. Richard Lovell Edgeworth was living with his large family in Edgeworthstown in County Longford, busily working on designs for a new telegraph system. In 1796 he became an Irish MP and set about campaigning for better education and an end to the magistrates' bias against Catholics. As he told his old friend Erasmus Darwin, 'The lowest order of the people has been long oppressed, and horrid calamities may ensue.'[6]

Links were now being forged with France. Wolfe Tone, who had emigrated to America in 1795 after a crackdown on the United Irishmen, had been in Paris since the spring. In the summer Arthur O'Connor, one of the leaders of the United Irishmen, and the idealistic young Lord Edward Fitzgerald, son of the Duke of Leinster and a former member of the Irish parliament, negotiated with the French Directory from Hamburg.[7] Their joint approaches convinced the French that an Irish uprising was imminent and an invasion feasible.

The French plan was apparently to launch a three-pronged invasion, the main thrust through Ireland, with diversionary landings in the south-west and the north-east of England. But things soon went awry. Hoche intended to land his men in Bantry Bay, but his fleet, with Wolfe Tone on board, was scattered by ferocious gales. When he reached Bantry Bay he had already lost eight ships and on Christmas Day 1796 a new gale forced them out to sea. By the time they reached Brest, a dozen French ships had foundered and thousands of soldiers and sailors had drowned.

Had Hoche managed to land he would have found little organised resistance. Hearing of the fleet's approach, army regiments and militia rushed down from the north, primed with whiskey as they staggered through the blizzards. Castlereagh, in his role as Lieutenant-Colonel of the Londonderry Militia, was appalled at the lack of intelligence and organisation. There were only eighteen hundred troops in the south, stationed in Bandon, twenty miles from Bantry, useless, he thought, 'to oppose any attempt of the enemy to take Cork by *coup de main*'.[8] In Dublin Castle his wife Emily and Lady Camden were busy stitching flannel jackets for the frozen men, but on 29 December he could write with huge relief to Emily, 'I am just arrived to find the wind has saved us the trouble of driving away the French: there is not a ship left in Bantry Bay. God preserve you. I am happy to give ease to your mind.' The French catastrophe brought jubilation on the British mainland: at the end of the month a one-act musical, *Bantry Bay; or, The Loyal Peasants*, was playing in Covent Garden, to the great entertainment of the crowds – and the royal family, who saw it on 20 February.[9]

The weather also halted the second French plan, an attack on New-castle across the North Sea. But in late February 1797 the third prong of this trident, designed to spear the West Country and take Bristol, was finally launched. Rebuffed from the Somerset coast by fierce tides and treacherous waters, the French landed instead on the Pembroke-shire coast near Fishguard. This was not, however, a conventional force. Their commander was the Irish-American Colonel William Tate, an enemy of Britain ever since his family had been murdered by pro-British native Americans during the War of Independence. Seek-ing revenge, Tate was now leading a small *légion noire*, almost wholly made up of convicts.

William Daniell, 'The Approach to Fishguard'

As they sailed into the Irish Sea a retired sailor, Thomas Wil-liams, spotted four warships off St David's Head, recognising them as French even though they flew the British flag. Within minutes the alarm was raised. Local people rushed to tell the militia captains and John Campbell, Lord Cawdor, Governor of Milford Haven, quickly gathered five hundred members of the militia and trundled three old cannons to the coast, while volunteers poured into Fishguard armed with rakes, old muskets, pikes and spades. The French were already disorganised. As soon as their troops reached shore many of the unwilling convict recruits immediately deserted and set out to loot nearby farms. One local heroine, Jemima Nicholas – *Jemima vawr*, or Jemima the Great, 'a tall, stout, masculine female, who worked as a shoemaker and cobbler' – took her pitchfork and captured twelve terrified men, marching them to captivity in Fishguard Church, and thereby winning a government pension of £50 a year.[10] When French officers turned up at the inn where Cawdor had his headquarters, hoping to negotiate, Cawdor, a good card player, declared that with his 'superior force' he would accept only an unconditional surrender. If no such surrender was made the next day on Goodwick Sands, he would attack.

In the pale morning light his rough troops waited on the sands with almost the entire population of Fishguard on the cliffs behind, including many women, wrapped in red flannel cloaks against the wind. Mary and John Mathias, writing to their sister in Swansea about the 'great Confusion' around their home, told her that there were 'near four hundard women in red falnes [flannels] and Squier Gambel went to ask them were they to fight and they said they were and when they com near the french put down their arms . . . they thought the women to Be a Rigment of Soldiers.'[11] By two o'clock, disconcerted by the militia and the apparent redcoats on the cliff, Tate had surrendered, and by four, having piled their arms on the beach, the French prisoners were marched away. According to Cawdor, as he drove his French prisoners back through Wales, 'the women were more clamorous than the men, making signs to cut their throats, and desiring I would not take the trouble of carrying them further'.[12] Not all the women were so hostile: two young Welsh girls working in the Golden Tower Prison near Pembroke, where four hundred captives were sent, fell in love and brought in tools to help their lovers dig a tunnel. Thirty men escaped, taking the girls with them, boarded Cawdor's sloop and sailed to France, capturing a coaster in mid-voyage and abandoning Cawdor's yacht to drift on to the Pembrokeshire rocks. When they reached St Malo, the girls married their French soldiers. In 1802, during the Peace of Amiens one couple came back and opened a pub, only to hurry back to France when war resumed.

The Fishguard invasion had its comic side, and it was probably intended less as a serious assault than as a harassing tactic, to drive the British to the negotiating table, but it proved that the French could indeed invade. People now looked at every merchant ship with suspicion and were ready to find spies everywhere. In August Dr Daniel Lysons of Bath, repeating tales his cook had heard from a servant at Alfoxden in the Quantocks, wrote to the Home Office about the dubious doings of 'an emigrant family' there. A government agent, James Walsh, was sent down to investigate, deciding that their friendship with John Thelwall, who was there that summer, made it almost certain that the Alfoxden group – William and Dorothy Wordsworth and Coleridge – were disaffected radicals spying for France. They went for walks at night and kept looking out to sea; they asked if the river was navigable (Coleridge was planning a poem titled 'The Brook'). In Coleridge's colourful account Walsh heard them discussing Spinoza: 'At first he fancied, that we were aware of our danger; for he often heard me talk of one *Spy Nozy*, which he was inclined to interpret of himself, and of a remarkable feature belonging to him.'[13] After this fuss, the Wordsworths were told that their lease would not be renewed in July the next year. A few years later, when Wordsworth looked back to this period in *The Prelude*, he compared Pitt's repression and spies to the open terror of Robespierre in Paris.[14] 'Our Shepherds', he wrote angrily, 'Thirsted to make the guardian Crook of Law/A tool of Murder':

> Giants in their impiety alone,
> But in their weapons and their warfare base
> As vermin working out of reach, they leagued
> Their strength perfidiously to undermine
> Justice, and make an end of Liberty.

It was a time of intense emotion. Dorothy's friend Mary Hutchinson came to stay for several weeks, escaping the family farm in County Durham where she had nursed her sister Margaret in the last stages of consumption. Charles Lamb visited in July, heartbroken after the tragedy of the previous year when Mary Lamb, 'my poor dear dearest sister', had stabbed her mother in a fit of madness: she would be in his care from now on. Coleridge, despondent about the cool reception of his *Poems on Various Subjects*, was increasingly unhappy with his wife Sara Fricker, Southey's sister-in-law, and now had a son, Hartley, and a baby, Berkeley, to support. In the autumn he and Wordsworth worked intensely on their poems, but Coleridge was still seeking a way to make a living, and in January 1798 he applied for a post as Unitarian minister at Shrewsbury. William Hazlitt, aged eighteen, heard him preach a sermon there 'on the spirit of the world and the spirit of Christianity'. It was a deliberate assault on militarism delivered to a congregation of landowners, most of whom were now keenly raising volunteers. 'Coleridge rose and gave out his text "And he went up into the mountain to pray, HIMSELF, ALONE",' remembered Hazlitt,

and when he came to the two last words which he pronounced loud, deep, and distinct, it seemed to me who was then young, as if the sounds had echoed from the bottom of the human heart, and as if that prayer might have floated in solemn silence through the universe . . . The sermon was upon peace and war; upon church and state – not their alliance, but their separation.[15]

Freed from the ministry by an annuity offered by the young Josiah and Tom Wedgwood, heirs to the pottery wealth, Coleridge came south again.

A new plan was for Coleridge, Wordsworth and Dorothy to spend two years in Germany. In the spring and early summer of 1798 Wordsworth and Coleridge worked on their poems, reading them to Hazlitt when he came to visit. These embodied a different kind of radicalism, in the use of ballads and the 'language of common men', where liberty lay not in political movements but in the inner workings of the poet's mind, and in humanity's relation to nature. At the end of June, Wordsworth and Dorothy walked to the Wye valley and then to Bristol. As they stepped onwards, Wordsworth was composing a poem as he walked, added at the last moment to the collection. When *Lyrical Ballads* was published, Coleridge and the Wordsworths were in Germany. Their early excitement at the Revolution had vanished. But 'Lines Composed a Few Miles above Tintern Abbey', looking back to Wordsworth's first visit to the Wye, suggested that if the spontaneous excitement of youth had passed, maturity could bring deeper reflection and release from 'the weary weight/Of all this unintelligible world':

> . . . a sense sublime
> Of something far more deeply interfused,
> Whose dwelling is the light of setting suns,
> And the round ocean, and the living air,
> And the blue sky, and in the mind of man,
> A motion and a spirit, that impels
> All thinking things, all objects of all thought,
> And rolls through all things.

# 17. MUTINIES AND MILITIA

By March 1797, when the country was shuddering at the Fishguard landing, Pitt's promised short conflict had stretched to four years. George III was inundated with petitions urging him to dismiss the ministers who were waging this 'long, disastrous, unjust and unnecessary war'.[1] Reports in the papers were a jumble of good and bad. 'Victorys obtained last month', began Rowbottom, listing those of both sides in his diary on 22 March:

February 14th Admiral Sir John Jervis with 15 sail of the line defeated the Spanish fleet of 27 sail of the line. On the 18th Admiral Harvey and Sir Ralph Abercromby captured the island of Trinadad – took one 74-gun ship and the enemy burnt an 84 and two 74-gun ships to prevent them falling into the hands of the English and victoryous General Bonapart at the head of the invincible Republicans totally defeated the Austrian Army and captured the impregnable City of Mantua.[2]

This new name – Bonaparte, or Buonaparte, keeping the Italian spelling – was scattered through the press. For the past year *The Times* had published translations of his bulletins, commenting on their arrogance and damning the excitement of alleged sympathisers. 'The insolence which prevails in General Buonaparte's Proclamation to his army, is equalled only by the exaggerated enthusiasm with which some of our Jacobin prints celebrate the exploits of that young warrior,' stormed one leader.[3]

With the Italian conquests came a hoard of art treasures, and in early March 1797, Napoleon's letter announcing that he was sending ten standards taken from the papal armies to Paris suggested to many that the dashing general was also a consummate thief. Technically, as he made clear, his looting was legalised by the appointment of commissioners and scholars sent to collect confiscated works. 'The Commission of Learned Men', he announced, 'has made a good harvest at Ravenna, Rimini, Pecaro and Cona, Loretto and Perugia; the produce will be immediately expedited to Paris. With this, joined to all that shall be sent to you from Rome, we shall have all that is beautiful in Italy, with the exception of a few pieces of art at Turin and Naples.'[4]

But while the young warrior and his invincible republicans were charging through Italy, collecting sculptures and paintings as they went, the British public could still take comfort in the thought that they had the best of the French at sea. Admiral Jervis's victory at the battle of St Vincent on 14 February was held up as an example of British pluck and daring matching Howe's 'Glorious First', and it also gave the country a new hero. Jervis had intercepted Spanish ships off Cape St Vincent, the south-western tip of Portugal, driven off course as they were sailing to join the French at Brest. As the British ships sailed through the Spanish line, raking each vessel with broadsides, the young Commodore Horatio Nelson hooked his ship *Captain* on to the Spanish *San Nicolas*, boarded it and used it as a bridge to leap across to a second ship, the massive *San Josef*.

Tom Gill from the Isle of Wight, who was there on the *Colossus* under Captain George Murray, wrote home excitedly, but when the Revd Gill and his daughters read his account, it seemed far more confusing than the papers suggested. Even in later recollections, Tom remembered more chaos than heroism. First, after a signals error, they were rammed by another British ship, the *Culloden*, and although the ship's carpenters patched the hole rapidly, the damage 'interrupted the working of four of the guns, and this, unluckily, was the side we were forced to present to the enemy soon after'. In the actual engagement, after they beat to quarters and stood by their guns, they waited in silence as the great ships came together, not firing until they were almost alongside, but by that time their fore-topgallant yard was shot away, the main mast and bowsprit damaged, the rigging cut to pieces and the sails ragged with holes. The sailors on board had little sense of the general battle: 'to describe it is impossible. An individual may know tolerably well what is going on in his ship, but no more.'[5]

The country preferred to hear of Nelson's bravado and Jervis's skill, rather than of confusion and blood. When James Oakes heard of the victory on 4 March, in the middle of a stormy time at his bank in Bury St Edmunds, he found it worthy of much underlining and many stars. 'At this Critical Juncture,' he wrote, it was 'perhaps the most providential & happiest Event that could have happened to this Kingdom & considering the wonderful superiority of Numbers & weight of metal one of the most glorious victories ever obtaind.'[6] Oakes and men like him thoroughly approved when Jervis was made Earl St Vincent and Nelson was knighted. The supreme showman, Nelson requested the Order of the Bath rather than a barony because he wished to display its fine red ribbon. The Spanish fleet never recovered.

The navy was the pride of the nation, but it was facing unsuspected trouble. To solve the shortage of men in the army and navy, an order the previous spring had decreed that no merchant ships should recruit crews, and then three Quota Acts were passed, decreeing that the counties in England and Wales should raise nearly ten thousand men. The seaports were to find another twenty thousand and the Scottish counties and towns a final eighteen hundred.[7] The number actually raised fell far short of what was hoped and later more Quota Acts were passed, demanding another six thousand men from coastal counties for the navy and roughly the same amount from the rest of the country for the army.

The basic sailor's wages had not been raised for 140 years. This concerned naval officers, especially when their own pay was increased but the men's remained the same. Injured sailors received pitiful compensation and long-serving seamen were still waiting for prize money promised, sometimes as long ago as the American war. Yet they saw prize money pouring into the pockets of admirals and Navy Board officials: Lord Arden, Registrar of the High Court of Admiralty, made £19,000 in 1797 from his percentage of the prizes that came before his court.[8] The radical-leaning frigate captain Thomas Cochrane reckoned that Arden's sinecure equalled the pensions paid to compensate for the loss of '1022 Captains' Arms; or . . . 488 pair of Lieutenants' legs'.[9] The sailors were angry, too, at conditions of service, especially the harsh floggings. Lieutenant Francis Austen noted without comment in his log for December 1795 in the *Glory*, 'Punished P.C. Smith forty-nine lashes for theft', and the following month, 'punished sixteen seamen with one dozen lashes each for neglect of duty in being off the deck in their watch'.[10]

Since the Admiralty paid little attention to their petitions, early in 1797 the sailors of the Channel Fleet appealed directly to their former commander, the popular Lord Howe, now nursing his gouty foot in Bath. Howe quietly sent these appeals on to the Admiralty, whose response in April was to ask Admiral Hood, Viscount Bridport, to order the Channel Fleet at Spithead to sail at once to prevent trouble in the port. To Hood's astonishment on 15 April the sailors refused, giving a defiant three cheers. They would sail if the French did, they said, but otherwise not until the Admiralty met their demands. Supported by many officers, these demands were entirely reasonable: higher wages, a greater share in prize money, the end of pursers' embezzlement of supply budgets, a better medical service, full wages for wounded men, guaranteed shore leave – and indemnity for their leaders. In the need to get the fleet to sail, the Admiralty accepted their requests and George III agreed to pardon the mutineers. But poor communication and a delay before the wages were actually paid led the men to believe that the agreement was being ignored. This prompted a second Spithead mutiny on 7 May, when the fleet again refused to sail. After heated discussions, Admiral Colpoys, on the *London*, ordered his marines to fire on the mutineers and several were killed. In retaliation, the seamen captured Colpoys and his officers, but spared their lives and put them ashore before taking over the fleet.

The mutiny spread to other ports, from Yarmouth in the east to Plymouth in the west. The stars that covered James Oakes's diary were dark ones. 'Very bad news by the Post from the Fleets at Plymouth & Portsmouth. A renew'd Mutiny among the Sailors & some Lives lost between the Officers & Sailors . . . we have our Apprehension that from this Mutiny of the sailors may be dated the Commencement of a Revolution in this Kingdom.'[11] His daughter Maria's husband, William Gould, prepared to set off for Portsmouth with his militia regiment. Only the arrival at Spithead of the persuasive Lord Howe, a master of tact and the only man they would trust, who was rowed from ship to ship explaining that the pay was indeed on its way, restored some peace. The crisis ended with declarations of mutual regret, lavish shipboard feasts for Howe and the delegates, and rousing renditions of 'Rule Britannia' from all the ships. On 17 May the Channel Fleet put to sea.

The offer accepted at Spithead was also made to the fleet at the Nore. But the Nore was a clearing house for new recruits and its ships were full of landsmen brought in under the Quota Acts, many of them opposed to the government and skilled in arguing their case. Led by Richard Parker, self-styled 'President of the Delegates of the Fleet', the Nore mutineers made more wide-ranging demands, in appeals salted with democratic rhetoric. They did not wish, they said, 'to be treated like the dregs of London streets, nor the Footballs, Shuttlecocks and Merry Andrews of a set of Tyrants who claim from us their Honours, Titles and Fortunes'.[12] What they wanted was simply their 'Liberty, their invaluable Priviledge . . . the Pride and Boast of Brittains – the Natural Rights of all'. Many people reading the reports in the papers thought the sailors' spokesmen sounded like 'Jacobins', and blamed the Irishmen who had been arrested in repressive sweeps of radicals and sent by magistrates to join the fleet. The Irish were not, in fact, the leaders of the mutinies, but around fifteen thousand

Defenders and United Irishmen were indeed sent to the navy between 1793 and 1796 – more than enough to alarm the loyalists.[13]

Soon other crews joined the Nore mutineers. On May Day in the Yarmouth Roads, where the Dutch fleet was provisioning, the crew of the *Venerable* climbed into the rigging and shouted three cheers as a signal for revolt. Admiral Duncan, employing both ferocity and tact, managed to calm his own mutinous crew on the *Venerable*, and a week later he also subdued that of the *Adamant*, marching aboard, grabbing a sailor and dangling him over the side, shouting, 'My lads – look at this fellow – he who dares to deprive me of command of the fleet!'[14] But several Yarmouth ships still sailed to the Nore. To keep up the blockade on the Dutch navy, Duncan set off in the *Venerable* with only the fifty-gun *Adamant* and the frigate *Circe* to back him. On the blockade he managed to trick the Dutch into believing the whole squadron was there by disguising his vessels to look like different ships each day, and sending signals to non-existent ships over the horizon. When the three ships came back, the Yarmouth merchants, organised as usual by Samuel Paget, took up a collection of £54 to reward their loyalty, which was spent on porter and vegetables for the crews.[15]

Meanwhile at the Nore the authorities cut off supplies. In return the seamen blockaded the Thames, seizing food and water from passing merchant ships. Troops were put on standby, the army at Tilbury exchanged fire with the fleet and on 6 June the mutineers were declared rebels, although offers of pardon were made to those who surrendered, apart from the leaders. Pitt introduced two emergency bills against encouraging sedition in the forces and communicating with the mutineers. Slowly, ship by ship, the Nore men gave in, and the mutinies were over by the end of the month. Some of their leaders escaped – perhaps to France – but others were court-martialled and twenty-nine were executed, including Richard Parker, the 'President of the Fleet', who was hanged from the yardarm of the *Sandwich*, watched by his wife Ann from a small boat nearby. Afterwards she took his coffin secretly to the Hoop and Horseshoe tavern on Little Tower Hill, where scores of people came to see his body. Fearing riots, the magistrates ordered that he be buried in the vault of St Mary Matfelon in Whitechapel: a hero to some, a villain to others.

In the subsequent inquiry by the London magistrates Aaron Graham and David Williams, the police opened sailors' letters to hunt for Jacobin involvement, but found that only one loving family had wished the sailors success. Instead Graham and Williams read warnings from a host of disapproving relatives and friends who stressed the danger from France, the great traditions of the navy, the glorious British Constitution and the need for sacrifice. One or two even hoped that the ringleaders would be executed. Graham and Williams were both convinced that although educated 'quota men', new to the service and therefore doubly sensitive to the injustices they found, might have led the mutineers, the uprisings were simply a demand for their rights, with no tinge of rebellion against the state or disapproval of the war.

On shore the disputes continued. In Portsmouth during the mutiny soldiers were wary of the theatre, packed with militant sailors. Gradually they braved the danger, with groups of officers going together, in uniform. One night a large band of Irish soldiers were in the gallery with 'many disorderly sailors' and their 'dissolute female companions'. James McGrigor, then a young army surgeon with the Irish 88th Regiment of Foot, and later Wellington's surgeon general, described the scene:

We called for 'God Save the King'. This was the commencement of a trial between the parties; the sailors and several of the inhabitants resisting the loyal song being sung. However, we carried it, and the soldiers turned out the malcontents. After this, the song was sung, I believe, half a dozen times in the course of the evening, every individual standing up and joining in the chorus.[16]

Yet if the soldiers won, the sailors had many sympathisers. Their views echoed through the street ballads in ports like Newcastle and Liverpool. The *Morning Post* and the *Courier* both published 'Mutiny at Portsmouth', by the 'Widow of a seaman', celebrating it as an expression of true British liberty:

The Genius of Britain went hovering round,
For she fear'd that Fair Freedom was fled,
But she found, to her joy, that she was not quite gone,
But remain'd with the Fleet at Spithead.[17]

In May, a handbill was posted in barracks across the country, urging soldiers to act for themselves, as the sailors had done, and attacking the ministry and parliament. If they were genuine 'fathers of the nation',

Would they mock us with a pretended addition to our pay, and then lock us up in barracks, to cheat us and keep us in ignorance? Would they not rather considering the price of everything wanting for our families at least double our pay?

Why is every regiment harassed with long marches, from one end of the country to the other, but to keep them strangers to the people and each other?

Are we so well cloathed as soldiers used to be? Ask the old pensioners at Chelsea College, whether horse or foot? Ask them too, if it was usual when there were fewer regiments, for colonels to make a profit out of soldiers cloathes? Don't colonels now draw half their income from what we ought to have, but of which we are robbed?[18]

Although the army and police hunted for the men who had pasted the handbills and offered a reward for information on the writer, they had no success. But they were swift to increase army pay.

The army did not mutiny, nor did the militia, but the government was taken aback at the resentment towards balloting for the militia. People tolerated regular recruitment and men actively enjoyed being volunteers. But the militia ballot seemed unfair, a random yet legal stealing of men, almost on a par with the press gang.

There was a baffling number of new Acts, and in July 1797, just after the naval mutinies were over, Scottish artisans, traders and labourers were outraged by a new Militia Act for Scotland, calling for a ballot of six thousand men, who would be conscripted for five years and fined if they failed to show up. Men resented the arbitrary break in their working lives and distrusted the Westminster government, fearing (rightly) that the militia would be used against dissidents. They were suspicious, too, despite promises to the contrary, that they would be sent overseas or drafted into the regular army. Riots against the Act spread northwards from the Borders. Crowds threatened officials, broke ballot boxes and tore up the parish Attestation Registers that listed every able-bodied man aged between nineteen and twenty-three, with notes on their appearance – tall or short, fair or freckled, ruddy or pale.[19] The poor schoolmasters who had to make up these lists were heckled and assaulted. In some cases villagers seized the register of baptisms and tore out leaves so that no one could use them to show their liability to serve.

The situation was made worse by the fact that the militia were the very force that had to hold back these protesting crowds. They included the Cinque Port Dragoons, one of several militia regiments stationed around Edinburgh, commanded by a future Prime Minister, the twenty-seven-year-old Robert Banks-Jenkinson, who had become Lord Hawkesbury the year before, when his father was made the first Earl of Liverpool. Originally the Dragoons were a regiment of fencibles – local troops raised to defend their nearby coastline – but for a year now they had been in Scotland, far from home, free from any real military discipline, nervous among hostile people.

On 29 August John Adams was walking towards the small mining town of Tranent, a few miles east of Edinburgh. He was on his way to collect some medicine for his wife, ill after the birth of their daughter, and was carrying two shillings in his pocket. The previous day local people, including the potters of nearby Prestonpans, had drawn up a proclamation calling for the repeal of the Militia Act, concluding: 'Although we may be overpowered in effecting the said resolution, and dragged from our parents, friends and employment, to be made soldiers of, you can infer from this what trust can be reposed in us if ever we are called upon to disperse our fellow-countrymen, or to oppose a foreign foe.'[20] That evening, the schoolmaster who had drawn up the lists fled to take shelter with the minister, while a crowd ransacked his house, taking away the papers and telling his wife they would tear him apart if they found him. They then handed their proclamation to the commander of the recruitment squad, Major Wight, whose job was to draw the ballot. Hearing of the disturbance the Lord Lieutenant called out the Cinque Ports Dragoons and later the Pembrokeshire Militia, stationed at Musselburgh. Crowds of women met the troops, hurling stones and crying 'that they should have their brains knock'd out'. When they smiled another woman cried, 'Ay, you may laugh now, but it will be otherwise with you by and by!'

Wight and his team went on with the ballot, parish by parish. The cobbled streets were now full of men and women armed with sticks, stones and broken bottles. Tough colliers and salters confronted the troops, led by a young woman called Jackie Crookston, who carried the town drum, shouting, 'Nae Militia!' After trying to read the Riot Act, the frustrated Major Wight called out, 'Why don't you fire!'[21] The dragoons reached for their weapons, shooting several protestors, including Jackie. Then the cavalry, 'armed with pistols, carabines and swords', rode across the fields, firing and slashing at people unconnected with the riot. Twenty men, women and children were wounded and twelve were killed, including a nineteen-year-old girl, trapped in a lane, two woodmen, a carpenter, an eleven-year-old boy, out for a walk, and John Adams, on his way to buy the medicine.[22]

The militia were exonerated by the authorities, and a long letter from the magistrates to the Lord Lieutenant was printed in the weekly *Anti-Jacobin*, telling their side of the story and praising 'the temperate, firm, and spirited conduct of the Officers employed on this occasion. We have no hesitation in declaring, that to their exertions we owe the preservation of our lives, and that by their means only, we were enabled to discharge the duty prescribed to us by the Act of Parliament.'[23]

With mutinies and anti-militia riots it began to seem as if another war was being waged, not on the Continent or at sea, but at home.

# 18. CASH IN HAND

Even before the mutinies, the threat of invasion sparked by the Pembrokeshire landings made thousands panic. As soon as the news of the landing reached London, *The Times* reported, Pitt summoned Grenville and Dundas and called an emergency meeting with directors of the Bank of England.[1] As frightened people demanded their money from the country banks, those banks in turn asked for gold from the Bank.[2] The public were exhorted not to worry. An announcement on 20 February 1797 entitled 'The Bank', in the *Oracle and Public Advertiser*, spoke in forthright tones. This might seem like a crisis, it said. 'But as the resources of this country are immense, A FIRM RELIANCE ON GOVERNMENT in the day of danger, and an energetic support of PUBLIC CREDIT, will discomfit the enemy.'[3] But when the Bank's reserves dropped in a fortnight from £16 million to a low of £1.2 million, it was forced to suspend cash payments. 'Feb 28 Tues.,' Mary Hardy, on the Norfolk coast, jotted neatly in her diary between records of cavalry parades and the ploughing of newly enclosed heathland: 'The Bank of England and all the Banks in City and Country stopt payment today.'[4]

The Bank immediately restricted the issue of gold to £50,000, to be shared out among bankers as the Court of Directors decided. In London, rumours spread that Hoare's had been given a large supply, and Richard Stone of the 'Grasshopper' – later Martin's Bank – wrote as 'an old friend' begging for a loan as the Grasshopper was running low. Politely Harry Hoare refused. 'Your Letter gives me real concern and the more so as I fear it is not in my Power to extricate you from the difficulty under which you labour. Demand is now so great from all quarters that it is impossible to calculate what Inventions People will have recourse to for producing small Sums.'[5] Hoare's too had had a run of demands for gold and had not expected the stoppage, he said, and when they had asked, that very day, if the Bank of England was authorised 'to assist Bankers with a Sum sufficient to pay the necessary Transactions, they answered certainly not, nor did they know when, if ever, they should be permitted to issue it as heretofore'. One partner was away but they would talk tomorrow. In the meantime, could Stone tell them the lowest sum that might help him?

At this point, on the Saturday after the stoppage, Pitt held an unprecedented cabinet meeting, with the Bank directors in attendance, and the king agreed to a Privy Council meeting on Sunday. An Order in Council then allowed the Bank to issue notes without the need, or promise, to back them up with gold: the Bank, and the country banks, could issue notes of under £5, and the first £1 and £2 notes began to appear. It was hard for people to see these new notes as 'real' money – five years later a hatter's wife in Oldham used three £1 notes to kindle the fire, 'fortunately for the Bank of England', wrote Rowbottom drily. Hoare's also worried about having to deal in these new, cheap-looking small denominations. In exasperation, one partner noted, 'Something decisive should be adopted respecting the receiving & paying Bank Notes of £1 & £2 how far it is practicable to be particular in the Entries of them: the Bank having begun to reissue all their bank Notes promiscuously & many dirty ones which it is impossible to offer to Ladies particularly.'[6] As well as the issue of small notes, the Bank's large holdings of over a million silver Spanish dollars were counterstamped and issued as five-shilling pieces, or as near as possible, but these proved horribly easy to forge and were recalled in late September.[7]

*

Gillray, *Bank-notes, paper-Money, – French Alarmists*, 1 March 1797. Pitt the bank clerk waves a parcel of notes towards a loyal John Bull, while Fox, backed by Sheridan, shouts: 'Dont take his damn'd Paper, John! insist upon having Gold, to make your Peace with the French, when they come'

If private London banks reeled under the shock, the country banks suffered even more. On the day of the stoppage all the Norwich bankers including the Gurneys suspended business, and the Bury St Edmunds banks followed. 'A general meeting of the Inhabitants was call'd by the Alderman,' wrote James Oakes, '& many attended with the principal Merchants, Farmers & Others & an Agreement was signd by upwards of 100 to support the Credit of said Banks & Town by receiving their Cash notes as usual.'[8] This seemed to work well, but the bankers paid only in Bank of England notes, and not in cash 'as not a Guinea could be procurd from Town'. A week later, Orbell Oakes went to London to collect some of the new small bank notes from Barclay, Tritton & Co., and if possible some cash and overstamped Spanish dollars. Market day passed without many problems, but when Orbell returned without any notes Oakes feared his bank might collapse. It was saved by a generous loan of notes from a Newmarket bank, and after this Oakes began to think about issuing his own paper notes, for as little as £1, fifteen shillings and even one shilling.

He was right to be concerned. In the following week two Bury banks failed, including the respected firm of Spink and Carss: 'The Consternation & Confusion occasioned in the Town by this event passes Description,' Oakes noted. Savings were lost and business threatened, and he listed the names of people in the town who, it was feared, 'cannot keep their Heads above water'. He knew it was a matter of trust, of public confidence. He felt sure he could ride it out, as indeed he did, and in fact he profited from the scare, enjoying a monopoly of banking in the town for the next four years.

Not far away Parson Woodforde also noted the impact, writing on 16 March,

There being little or no Cash stirring and the Country Bank Notes being refused to be taken, create great Uneasiness in almost all People – fearful what Consequences may follow – Excise Officers refuse taking Country Notes for the payment of the several Duties – Many do not know what to do on the present Occasion having but very little Cash by them.[9]

On the other hand, this disaster almost paled in comparison to his alarm at his niece Nancy's 'feverish complaint' a fortnight later. The doctor, Woodforde wrote, 'strongly recommends Port Wine and to drink rather More than less . . . She has not drank less than a Pint for many Days.'

Gentry ladies might fortify themselves with port but the national cupboard was almost bare. The opposition jumped on the restriction of gold as an example of the government's ruthless exploitation of the Bank of England; in parliament Sheridan called the Bank 'an elderly lady in the city, of great credit and long standing, who had lately made a *faux pas* which was not altogether inexcusable. She had unfortunately fallen into bad company, and contracted too great an intimacy and connection at the St James's end of the town.'[10] In late May, Gillray, who had already had a crack at this subject, with Pitt thrusting bank notes on John Bull, took Sheridan's image and gave the Bank its lasting nickname in *Political Ravishment, or the Old Lady of Threadneedle Street in Danger!*, showing Pitt wooing the Old Lady when he really wants her gold. The joke ran on: seven years later a chatty column in *The Times*, full of theatre news, French horrors and bad puns reported, 'The musical amateurs are in great distress, on account of Mrs. Billington's cold, and consequent hoarseness. That Lady does not intend keeping her *notes* any longer out of *circulation* than is absolutely necessary. She will be very ready to exchange them for *cash* as speedily as possible.'[11]

As it happened, the freedom from the gold standard was crucial in allowing the government to pay its bills during the war, giving bankers enough flexibility to keep the credit wheel turning. Five years later, in his *Enquiry into the Nature and Effects of the Paper Credit of Great Britain*, the banker Henry Thornton showed that the increase in paper money was not the sole cause of current economic troubles; on the contrary, it had fostered the circulation of credit and proved that the Bank of England could intervene in times of instability and could regulate the country banks. Yet it was still widely believed that the new notes caused rapid inflation, and the gold standard was eventually restored in 1821.

In the spring of 1797, after the Fishguard landing, the mutinies and the bank crisis, Pitt decided to make new peace overtures in conjunction with Austria. But almost as soon as he sent George Hammond from the Foreign Office to Vienna in April, news arrived of the total defeat of the Austrians in Italy a few weeks before. By now Napoleon had marched across their border and when Hammond reached Vienna at the end of April, he found that the Austrians had already signed a peace treaty.

In June Pitt tried again, despite keen arguments with bellicose senior Whigs like Portland and William Windham. The patient Lord Malmesbury, who had tried so hard to negotiate in Paris the year before, was sent off to Lille in July, briefed to accept peace on almost any terms. But after two months of talks, the coup of 4 September ('18 Fructidor' in the revolutionary calendar) ousted the moderates in the Directory.

The new administration had far less desire for peace, and set impossible terms that involved Britain giving back all her conquests. By the end of the month Malmesbury was back in London. To appease the peace lobby the government made sure that the press carried every detail and date of his long discussions. After exchanging thirty-eight separate papers over many weeks, the *St James's Gazette* reported, the French negotiators, under new masters, declared that their hands were tied 'by the most positive orders of the Directory': 'I then, says Lord M., saw no advantage to be derived from prolonging a conversation which, after the positive declaration they had made, could lead to nothing: I therefore ended the conference by declaring my resolution to begin my journey at a very early hour the next morning . . .'[12]

At Hoare's Bank the letters refusing loans and requesting payments became more urgent, referring not to 'these peculiar' but to 'such dangerous and alarming' times. They had problems in their own house. At the end of 1797 they called an emergency family meeting of all the partners, when it was unanimously agreed 'that a Speculative Transaction in the Funds has taken place between Mr Morgan our Clerk & Mr Morris Stockbroker, on which there was a considerable Loss. It was resolved, that the above transaction was highly improper on the part of Messrs Hoare's clerk.'[13] John Morgan, whose name they had used on their huge investment in Walter Boyd's loan not long ago, was sacked, and Harry Hoare was deputed to explain the situation to him and to everyone in the bank. Unnerved by the thought of low reserves, Harry then decided to set up a 'sinking fund', as Pitt had done for the nation. A partners' meeting resolved to take £500 out of the profits each year, 'to be invested in Security for the Purpose of raising a fund towards the reimbursement of sums overdrawn in their book, & in case of surplus towards the rebuilding of the Premises at Fleet Street'.[14] In seven years, with clever investment, this rose to £9370 11s.

Dangerous times or not, there was no doubt that the Hoares were doing well. This year Harry's son, the evangelical-minded William, joined the partnership, and two of the younger partners, Hugh and

Charles, were looking for estates outside London to rival Harry's at Mitcham. In 1797 Hugh and his wife Maria moved from Barn Elms, where he and his brothers had grown up, to Wavendon House in Buckinghamshire, while Charles, concerned for his delicate wife, Fanny, bought the Luscombe estate in south Devon. A few years later Hester Piozzi's daughter Sophia Thrale, who married the third Hoare brother, Henry Merrick, explained to Gabriel Piozzi that she was going down to see Charles, 'who has a beautiful Seat near Dawlish, and a very amiable wife whose delicate Health does not allow her ever to quit the pure Air of that delightful Coast'.[15] Nash designed a pseudo-Gothic castle for them and Repton planned their gardens. When Charles was there, a special postboy ran back and forth to Dawlish to collect the early morning mail from the London bank.

The bank crisis and invasion alarms gave people yet more cause to blame the war for their hardships. At Whiteriggs in Scotland the farmer James Badenach was sure that the market in March 1797, with low sales of hay, grain and 'Fatt Bestials', was slack because thoughts of 'an Imaginary deficiency of Money, and of French Invasion of this Country absorbs & Employs the Whole thoughts of the Idle & Speculative defenders of the Realm'.[16] As the markets stayed flat he became more and more convinced: 'No demand however for Hay, or for any farm produce whatever & the prices constantly falling – Pork hath fallen nearly One Half & it is owing to Many Imaginary Conjectures about Political Matters, not properly understood, & deranged Mercantile Speculations of kinds.'

Suspicion of speculators was matched by anger against contractors who seemed to be profiting from the war, and against the expense of subsidies to allies. In August, William Rowbottom neatly copied out the information from the *Manchester Gazette*. 'The National Debt of Great Britain is £409,665,570, yearly intrest . . . £16,272,597. Expence of the war for last year . . . £62,357,312.'[17] The government too were worried. Pitt's critics persuaded him to appoint a Finance Committee, like the one that had checked overspending during the

American war, and over the years the new committee's reports showed vast sums seeping out because of fraud, lack of competitive tendering, a mass of sinecures and fees and an ancient, unchecked accounting system hopelessly in arrears.

The needs of Britain's allies also pressed on the government, and some of Pitt's dealings in the City were proving alarmingly shaky. In 1797 Walter Boyd was still the leading loan contractor and the banker to the Austrian government but he constantly over-reached himself. Too greedy for profit, he was damaged by the failure of a bank in Hamburg and of Charles Herries's bank in London, which crashed owing him £188,000.[18] Believing in the rumours of peace during Malmesbury's negotiations, he hung on to his own stock rather than selling it, and found himself unable to pay a promised advance on a large Austrian loan. Pitt and Dundas helped him out by taking money from the Navy Fund, giving it to Boyd interest-free and allowing him to 'loan' it back – at interest – to the government. As his problems grew he was left out of the next London loan syndicate, and his company was dissolved. Within two years Boyd would be bankrupt.

As well as raising loans through men like Boyd, Pitt brought in new 'assessed taxes' on virtually everything he could: on servants, gamekeepers, hats, ribbons and gloves, horses and carriages, shooting licences and cards, spirits and sporting dogs, newspapers and letter franks, wills and wig powder. Loyal citizens were horrified to find they were taxed on almost everything they owned, used, ate, drank, rode or read. The better-off squared their shoulders. Elizabeth Heber told her brother Reginald, who looked after her money:

I must trouble you again to assist with another hundred to enable me *to pay the assessed Taxes* otherwise I shall be Obligd to sell out of the Funds to great disadvantage . . . these are hard times for us all but we must be content to lessen our Property in Order to preserve the remainder for the French – Subscriptions for the defence of the country are going on with great Spirit in the Capital and distant countys which many convince the enemy we have still both resources & inclination to resist them should they dare to invade Old England.[19]

At the end of the year, after furious debates in parliament, Pitt trebled these taxes, rousing cries that although the rich seemed the target, the poor would suffer; servants and grooms and carriage makers would lose their jobs and farmers would go bankrupt. Appeals poured into the private banks: Lord Willoughby asked Hoare's for £700 or £1000 to pay his assessed taxes; William Ward asked for £100 to pay his land tax.[20] Even the moderately well-off were scrimping and saving. On 3 December 1797, a raw, cold and windy day, with a sharp frost, Parson Woodforde once again took stock after his good roast veal dinner:

The present times seem to prognosticate e'er long very alarming circumstances – No appearance of Peace, but on the contrary the French reject every Proposition to it and so inveterate are they against our Government, that they are determined to make a descent on England & the Taxes therefore on the above account are talked of being raised trebly to what they were last Year.[21]

The French descent on England was on everyone's mind.

# 19. AT SEA AND ON LAND

In the autumn of 1797, amid the financial gloom and the failure of the peace talks, the navy was again in the news. Once the mutinies were over, Admiral Duncan's fleet resumed its blockade of Texel, but the September high tides brought gales that sprang the yards and masts and created leaks that no pump could control. Almost all the ships limped home for repairs and provisions. Duncan's *Venerable* anchored in Yarmouth Roads in the early evening of 3 October. Within hours a supply boat was alongside with water and candles. Next day came the vegetables, the casks of beef, pork, molasses, flour, raisins, pease, oatmeal, cheese, butter, wine and brandy, everything to provision the fleet for another four months – the only thing lacking was beer.[1] The weather was calm, with just enough wind to fill the sails of the ketches as they ploughed back and forth.

While Duncan's fleet was provisioning the Dutch slipped out, carrying fifteen thousand troops, bound, it was said, for Scotland or Ireland. As soon as they were spotted, the newly supplied fleet set sail from Yarmouth, their decks cleared for action. On 11 October they crushed the Dutch in a swift sea battle near the village of Camperdown (Camperduin) off the north coast of Holland. In a chaotic struggle in shallow waters, with shots piercing the rigging and sails on fire, the British captured eleven Dutch ships and lost none. Duncan sailed back through gales so fierce that two of the ships he had taken were wrecked. This victory, celebrated across the country with extravagant illuminations, brought considerable rewards. A subscription for the Lloyd's fund raised £52,000 for the men involved, and even the critical *Morning Chronicle* declared: 'However much we may deplore the calamity, or condemn the impolicy of the war itself, it is with pride and pleasure that we witness the exploits of our defenders on our natural element, and that we see our Country saved against the incapacity of Government by the courage of our Tars.'[2]

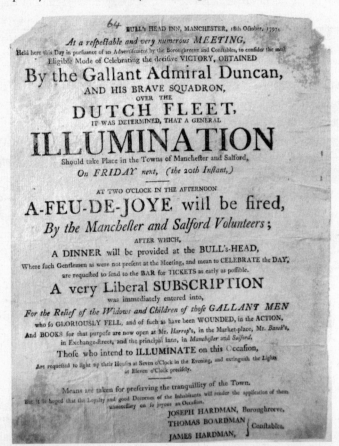

An advertisement for Manchester celebrations of Camperdown, 18 October 1795, a week after the battle

The following July, when Duncan returned to Yarmouth to resume command of the North Sea Fleet, the farmer Randall Burroughes was there – as one of his public tasks, he would soon join the Great Yarmouth Pier and Haven Commission. He had been at Lowestoft with his brother James's family and his usually stolid account of hoeing and harvesting gave way to excitement as he described the fencibles practising their gunnery:

On Wednesday I saw the Lea Fencibles excercis'd at the great Guns by Capt Killock in the morning. Went on board the contest gun boat Lieutenant Short, with 20 cannonades, 18 pounders & 28 pounders. Two guns were fired while our party was on board & I saw the ball soon after it had left the gun & ultimately fall into the sea. Our party Mrs Negus, my bro & sister, Henry & Mary their children, Mrs Short & son, & Matthew & Robert, two men servts. While at Yarmouth on Tuesday Adml. Duncan came there & was received with bells ringing & flags flying.[3]

As Burroughes said, the admiral was welcomed with the firing of guns, the ringing of bells and the hoisting of colours on the ships at the quay and on steeples and private houses: 'on his alighting from his carriage,' the *Norfolk News* reported, 'each person present testified their loyalty by repeated huzzas.'[4]

To the sailors there was, however, another hero. Sam Paget's organisation and speed before the battle – a whole fleet provisioned in five days – had astonished the sailors who remembered that the same work had taken five weeks the year before. At a later dinner to celebrate the anniversary of Camperdown, the townsfolk toasted Duncan's health. But the admiral, so Paget's son James was told, 'pointed to my father and said "That's the man that won the battle".'[5]

The war affected trades small and large, not only in ports around the coast, but in the villages and towns inland. In the countryside, labourers and tenant farmers padded out their income by working as weavers, shoemakers, lacemakers, linen bleachers. Robert Hay, living on a farm in Dunbartonshire, was only three when the war began, one of a family that eventually grew to include eleven children. His father John, hot-tempered but determined, brought in extra money as a weaver, and when the farm's lease was up in 1793 he went to work as a 'boiler' at his brother's small bleaching works in Renfrewshire. The family income included his wages of nine shillings a week, plus three shillings earned by the oldest daughter embroidering muslin at home, and one shilling and sixpence by her sister 'at darning with her uncle'.[6] Husband, wife and nine children had to get by on thirteen shillings and sixpence. Hay's mother kept the money in a drawer, running accounts with local grocers from one pay day to the next. Later, after a row with his brother, John Hay took up weaving in Paisley, the girls worked in a bleachfield and the eldest son as a farm labourer, while Robert and the younger children went to a cotton factory, beginning as scavengers then progressing to the loom. But Robert had been, very briefly, to school. He could read, escaping into books, falling in love with *Robinson Crusoe*, and three years later he would run away to sea.

More women and children were working as the war took men from country trades, as tanners and lime burners, brickmakers, basket weavers and wheelwrights. And the conflict also hit rural towns and villages in unexpected ways. Camperdown brought many prisoners, and a depressed agricultural town could find its fortunes transformed if it became a parole depot, housing foreign officers who paid for lodgings and food. On the other hand, a village that depended on crafts might find its livelihood threatened by skilled prisoners. Lacemaking was one of these crafts, especially thread lace, made with silk or linen thread, using bobbins attached to straw-stuffed pillows. This was a staple of country incomes around Honiton in Devon and in the East Midlands, Bedfordshire and Buckinghamshire. Village boys and girls went to lace schools at five and by eleven or twelve they could make enough to live on. This lacemaking, already threatened by knitting frames, now faced unexpected competition from the cheap prison labour.

The same went for straw hat makers and straw-plaiters. When trade with Italy stopped after Napoleon's conquests in 1796, Pitt slapped a heavy tax on imported straw, so that the making of 'Italian' hats with local straw became a lucrative cottage industry. This was especially so in the Midlands around Luton, close to the great prison of Norman Cross. Thousands of local people were employed in plaiting and bonnet making, mostly women and children, who went to 'plaiting school' from the age of three. In rooms packed with fifty or sixty children, icy in winter and stifling in summer, eight-year-olds could earn nine pence a week – of which two or three pence went in school 'fees'. Older girls, aged about thirteen, made a good three shillings – the same as Robert Hay's sister with her embroidery – a vital addition to a family's income. Some local grandees, like the Spencers at Althorp, patronised the craft as a charitable way of creating an income for the poor. At seventeen, Sarah Spencer wrote chattily to her grandmother that the girls of the village of Brington 'are going on so well – oh, so nicely! – with the straw work':

Do you know, that all the girls between eight and fourteen work at the straw work, and they begin at their cottage doors at five in the morning; some of them make two score a week; and there is a straw school, and everything delightful. My aunt and I are joint directors, and Mr Wolfe the agent, and a man at Dunstable the buyer . . .[7]

But the prisoners at Norman Cross soon began plaiting straw, undercutting the local workers, causing much misery. Everything was not quite delightful.

The lace and the 'scores' of coiled plait, twenty yards long, were sold to dealers who travelled the country and ran stalls at the markets. The markets were meeting grounds as well as places of business. For the shoemakers and plaiters, glove makers and wood turners, the year still kept its round of festivals. James Oakes in Bury and William Rowbottom in Oldham never failed to mention the fair. John Clare, remembering his childhood, wrote that 'the year was crowned with holidays'.[8] At Christmas children ran to the woods for ivy branches and the morris dancers performed plays. In spring came Valentine's Day, Shrove Tuesday and then April Fool's Day, tricking people into errands like fetching pigeon's milk. On St Mark's Eve, 24 April, girls baked a 'dumb' cake, ate it in silence at midnight and walked backwards to bed, to see 'the likeness of their sweethearts hurrying after them'.[9] May Day had races and dances round the maypole, and in Clare's village the first cow into the pasture wore a garland on its head, the last a thorn on its tail, and the garland was given at the end of the day to the Queen of the May. Then came the summer feasts for haymaking and the sheep shearing, and in the north the rushbearings, where clean rushes were carried to the church on flower-decked wagons to be strewn over the earth floors. Even in hard times, autumn fairs and harvest home had stalls of toys, sugar plums, lollipops and gingerbread – and then the year ran round to Christmas again.

There were fairs everywhere, from south to north: from Canterbury, where booths were stacked against the cathedral walls, and swing-boats, merry-go-rounds and 'shouting, kissing and screaming' crowds packed the Close, to Brough in Westmorland with its piper and fiddler, and the village of Pitlessie in Fife, the childhood home of David Wilkie, who painted the recruiting band among the fairgoers.[10] One of the greatest fairs, the largest in Europe in earlier days, was held on Stourbridge Common near Cambridge for a fortnight each September. Dairymen and women travelled here from Leicestershire and Derbyshire, Cheshire and Gloucestershire, bringing their cheeses. There were saddlers and harness makers, cloth traders from Yorkshire and the West Country, earthenware and china sellers from the Potteries, silk mercers and linen drapers, and booths of toys and musical instruments. A Limehouse grocer sold high-quality tea, soap, sugar and candles. He also sold pickles, and his pretty daughter was known as 'Miss Gherkin', or 'Little Pickle', until she grew more bosomy and graduated to 'Miss Mango'. The Norwich theatre company performed and there was 'the usual mixture of dwarfs and giants, conjurors and learned pigs'.[11]

For the traders who came to the fairs, and for manufacturers and farmers, communications were vital. The post roads span out from London like the lines of a spider's web to meet the country roads, and along the major routes the Penny Post made three deliveries a day, using fast coaches to carry their mail pouches, with an armed guard to protect against highwaymen. At sea, chartered mail packets sailed from Harwich to Germany and the north, and from Falmouth to Spain, Portugal and Gibraltar. The overseas mail continued, even during the war. And while orders and bills went by post and packet, the daily run of goods was carried across country on packhorses, wagons, canal barges, and small coasters travelling from port to port. A host of people made their living as carriers. Wagoners and bargees, their numbers depleted by the recruiting officers, the militia and the press gang, could now charge high for their labour.

The bargees who carried goods and coal on the canals were especially important. Built by gangs of itinerant navvies, the canals had snaked further and further across the land over the past thirty years: the Mersey–Trent canal had opened in the 1770s, with a connecting canal to the river Severn, and when the Severn–Thames canal opened in 1789, this meant rapid transport from north to south as well as east to west. A new burst of 'canal-mania' followed, in which the engineer was king. Since 1793 Thomas Telford had been working on the Ellesmere canal, joining the rivers of the Mersey, Dee and Severn, with its extraordinary cast-iron aqueduct over the Dee at Pontcysyllte. At the same time, John Rennie was engaged on the Kennet and Avon canal, with its bridges, aqueducts and seventy-eight locks, and on the beautiful stone aqueduct over the Lune, with its solid piers and graceful balustrades, on the Rochdale and Lancaster canals. The navvies had also been working since the war began on the Grand Junction Canal, linking the Midlands to the capital. The cost of carrying goods by water was a tenth, or even less, than that of using wagons and horses. Whole families lived on the barges, carrying cheese from Cheshire, iron from Shropshire, wood and wool, coal and cabbages, and now crates of arms and munitions.

Another floating community was that of the coastal trade. Every harbour had a fleet taking produce to other ports, down the west coast from Glasgow to Whitehaven, Liverpool and Bristol and across to Dublin, along the south coast to London, up the east coast to the Tyne, to Leith on the Firth of Forth and north to Aberdeen and Cromarty. Small towns like Bideford and Barnstaple in Devon, where the tidal Torridge and Taw flow together over the bar, had wharves and quays and boatbuilders, with ships bringing coal, pottery, herrings, malt, timber and hides and taking out timber, bark and ballast of estuary gravel. The streets were busy with chandlers' shops, and local boys went to sea young, learning bookkeeping, navigation and shipbuilding in a commercial school before serving apprenticeships on board. William Salmon, who was born in Bideford in 1780 and christened in Northam Church on the hill looking out over the sea, was now in his mid-teens. He had been an apprentice here since the war began and would progress slowly from trainee midshipman to master's mate and master, looking after the handling of the ship, navigating, and overseeing stores and ballast, water and sails and ropes.[12] At each small port he learned how its traders negotiated for cargoes, as well as the oddities of its tides and currents.

Warren Jane, across the Bristol Channel in Chepstow, where William Salmon would later work, mixed shipowning with several linked ventures. He had quays and warehouses and two pubs, the Mermaid and the Sailors tavern, and was also an apothecary, co-owner of a paper mill and a trader in timber and bark, wool and leather. Like his father before him, Jane was a trustee of the local almshouse and patron of charities, a dignified figure, living in a brand-new townhouse, built in 1796 opposite the castle. Brigs, hoys and sloops from Chepstow sailed over to Devon and west to Swansea (or 'Swanzey' as the Barnstaple port log book spelled it). But if the coasters sailed round Land's End they were at the mercy of the French privateers, swift luggers loaded with canvas, who lurked as near as two miles off the Devon and Cornwall coasts. Jane lost one ship to the French and another, trading further afield to the Baltic, to the Danes.

The profitable coastal trade thus carried its own wartime risks. Fast French privateers also haunted the North Sea coast between Hull and London, pouncing on so many vessels carrying farm produce that the

Cheesemongers' Company lobbied for warships to protect them.[13] For merchant seamen lost in these encounters or drowned in wrecks, there was little compensation. One Chepstow widow, Mary Farish, wrote miserably to the marine charity at Trinity House that 'as my family is large and most of them still very young I find it is with great difficulty I support them and myself comfortably and the allowance from Trinity house though small will be of material consequence'.[14] The rejoicing in Bideford and Chepstow at a victory like Camperdown was muted by the thought that with so many ships now in for repair, so many sailors dead and injured, and the press gangs hunting for good crewmen, their safety would be precarious again.

# 20. THE POWERHOUSE

Philip de Loutherbourg's sensational painting *The Battle of Camperdown* showed huge ships shattered and dismasted and others reeling and tilting, their sails aflame, against a sky black with smoke. But four years later he painted an equally dramatic scene with as much power as any battle. This was *Coalbrookdale by Night*, its glaring furnaces like a volcano showering the Shropshire countryside with sparks.

Since the 1750s ironworks had spread like streams of lava, fanning out from the Darby family's works on the Severn at Coalbrookdale and the Wilkinsons' blast furnaces close by at Broseley and at Bersham near Wrexham. These were run by the beetle-browed John 'Iron-Mad' Wilkinson, a temperamental giant now in his late sixties, who had long ago created new machines perfect for boring cannon and steam-engine cylinders. By 1796 his ironworks were producing an eighth of Britain's cast iron. As skilled workers moved across Britain to new foundries, a network of interlocking dynasties formed, with frequent marriages between leading families. Ironmasters copied each other. In Scotland the Carron company near Falkirk was the biggest provider of cannon, followed by the Walker brothers of Rotherham, who also specialised in steel made by Benjamin Huntsman's new crucible process. In Birmingham, the steam-engine entrepreneurs Matthew Boulton and James Watt, who had previously worked with John Wilkinson, opened their own Soho foundry with a flamboyant party in January 1796.[1]

A generation or so ago the Midlands ironworkers had seen the potential of south Wales, where mineral leases and coal were cheap. John Guest and his partners went from Broseley to Dowlais near Merthyr Tydfil, high up the Taff valley, 'bounded on either side by considerable heights, on the slopes of which the coal and iron seams stretch, more or less thick, from the foot to the top and up to the surface'.[2] The chalk, clay and sandstone they also needed for smelting were less than a mile away. Soon another Broseley man, Anthony Bacon, took over nearby at Cyfarthfa, bringing in Francis Homfray and his sons, Thomas, Jeremiah and Samuel, who went on to build their own works across the river at Penydarren. And when Anthony Bacon died, and the business was held in trust for his small son, Anthony Bacon junior, Cyfarthfa was taken over by Richard Crawshay, Bacon's London agent for ordnance contracts, another driving spirit.

Crawshay's life was like a chapbook romance: he ran away from Yorkshire after a quarrel with his father, apprenticed himself to a London iron merchant, married his master's daughter and won his starting capital in the lottery. At Cyfarthfa, he was one of the first to use Henry Cort's new puddling process, which involved stirring molten iron in a reverbatory furnace to make malleable bar iron. Each stage in the refining process produced iron of a different quality. Iron straight from the blast furnaces, 'pig iron', full of carbon and dross, was brittle and had to be heated until liquid and poured into a mould to make a firmer 'cast iron'. In the past this had then been worked into 'wrought iron' in charcoal-fuelled finery forges, or rolled into more solid bar iron, a slow and expensive business. Nearly 90 per cent of demand was for bar iron, and the puddling process allowed British foundries to make this consistently and cheaply, freeing them from reliance on Russian and Swedish iron. Even better, Cort's furnaces could burn coke. This had been used in blast furnaces for some time, but for refining the ironworkers had needed charcoal, and as supplies of British timber shrank, so costs rose. Cort had finally broken this barrier, as Wilkinson's workmen at Bersham crowed in their song:

That the wood of old England would fail did appear,
And tough iron was scarce because charcoal was dear.
By puddling and stamping he prevented that evil,
So the Swedes and the Russians may go to the devil.[3]

Crawshay was ahead of the game, making a private deal with Cort in 1788. Six years later, when young Anthony Bacon came of age, he bought him out, promising a royalty, which would lead to later rows. With supreme confidence, he had laid out £50,000 on new plant at Cyfarthfa and with two blast furnaces, eight puddling furnaces, three melting refineries, three balling furnaces and a rolling mill he was in a perfect position to supply wartime needs. He could also use the new canal that ran from Merthyr Tydfil to Cardiff and would eventually reach the sea. Each horse-drawn barge, guided by a man and a boy, could carry twenty-four tons of iron, the same amount that had previously taken twelve wagons, forty-eight horses, twelve men and twelve boys.[4] Since Crawshay was also the chief canal shareholder he raked in huge annual dividends, another source of his fortune. 'Moloch the Iron King', or 'The Tyrant', locals called him. When Turner came here in 1798, making atmospheric oil sketches for Anthony Bacon junior, showing waterwheels splashing and the great tilt hammer poised above glowing iron, Cyfarthfa was the largest ironworks in the country, perhaps in Europe.[5] South Wales looked set to be, as Gilbert Gilpin, the head clerk at Wilkinson's Bersham works, wrote excitedly, 'the Siberia of this kingdom', Siberia being not a bleak place of exile but the heart of Eurasian iron production.[6]

By the late 1790s Merthyr Tydfil had grown from a village to a town with a population of eight thousand, with rows of cottages, huts and sheds under its perpetual clouds of smoke, underlit with flame, making the night sky red. Visitors, seeing the streams of molten metal on the ground and the red-hot bars of iron like fiery serpents on the rollers, found it hard not to think of volcanoes, or classical infernos, or the biblical hell. Visiting Blaenavon ironworks near Abergavenny, Richard Colt Hoare felt that they offered a new, busily inhabited version of the picturesque and sublime, 'a perfect contrast to the deserted castles and solitary abbies we have lately been visiting'.[7] He was struck by the irregular, massive forms of the buildings and 'the noise of the forges, the fire and thick volumes of smoke occasionally bursting from the furnaces, the numerous mules, asses and horses employed in carrying the lime, coal etc., the many cottages and habitations all around'.

'Blaenavon Ironworks', Richard Colt Hoare's drawing of 1801

The use of steam engines to power furnaces, forges and rolling mills speeded up production so much that the coalfields could hardly keep up with the demand.[8] The cost of iron fell to almost half the price of Swedish iron and Britain began to export on a serious scale. After an initial dip the war had brought nothing but good for the ironmasters. Orders rolled in from the Ordnance Office for cannon and carronades, gun carriages and shot, steel swords and bayonets. The demand for precision in arms-making also forced improvements in the foundries, adding up to a transformation of the craft. The pressure of war brought innovations, like the boring of the cannon using a steam engine to act directly on a crank fixed in the centre of a shaft, with up to eleven horizontal borers working at the same time. 'Where sometimes orders of five thousand tons and more must be completed in a short time,' explained its inventor, 'it was necessary to bore and turn several at once.'[9] Other cannon-foundry devices included a portable machine that allowed a workman to drill precise touch-holes in two or three minutes, and a special truck to move small cannon about the foundry.

The war also made ironmasters think hard about their markets. Even when French conquests and British blockades closed official export routes, the iron and steel makers hunted for ways round restrictions. But as iron exports had always been low, the loss of their small continental trade was amply compensated for by their dominance at home, with less foreign competition. Lost exports were far outweighed by munitions orders and the soaring home trade, with iron needed for everything from girders and guns to stoves and saucepans. Some of the new civilian uses changed working patterns, and dazzled the imagination. Iron railroads for horse-drawn wagons, first made at Coalbrookdale in the 1760s, were now found in all the coal mines. In 1797 John Wilkinson launched a cast-iron barge on the Severn, amazing the watching crowds who were convinced it would sink, and in 1803 William Symington would build a pioneering steamship on the Clyde. Ornamental cast iron was appearing in buildings, beginning with John Bage's design for an interior iron frame for the linen mill that John Marshall and the Benyon brothers built in Shrewsbury in 1796. In the same year, following the example of Coalbrookdale's Iron Bridge across the Severn, bridge builders heaved up cast-iron girders from Rotherham to support the great bridge at Wearmouth, promoted by the Durham MP Rowland Burdon. The Wearmouth bridge was the largest single span in the world, and much of its design had been developed by Tom Paine, before politics swept him away.

Iron was everywhere, in small things as well as large. An advertisement for Seaton ironworks in the *Carlisle Journal* in 1802 declared that 'large assortments of the following articles are always kept upon hand, or manufactured upon the shortest notice':

machinery used in the various manufactures of woolen, cotton, flax and tow and also for steam engines; boiler's and bleacher's pans and curbs; brewer's mash vats and tuns; Bazellia stoves for halls, 'compting houses etc.; screw pins (malleable or cast iron) cut out of the solid, with brass or iron boxes suitable for paper mills, shipwrights, tobacconists, etc.; Register, Pantheon, Forest, Bath and Laundry stoves, neatly fitted; gin sheaves, wagon wheels, and rails, plates for collieries; every other article in the cast iron trade . . .[10]

The iron used for guns also made ploughshares, and lawn rollers. Early one June morning in 1794 James Woodforde sent his man Ben to Norwich to fetch his 'new Garden Roller of Cast-Iron'. Ben came back with mackerel for dinner, and the roller. 'It is a very clever Roller', Woodforde wrote happily, 'and is called the ballance Roller, as the handle never goes to the Ground – It is certainly very expensive but certainly also very handy – The Roller amounts in the whole to £4:0:0.'[11]

The iron magnates had interests in other metals, especially copper. Wilkinson held shares in Thomas Williams's vast Anglesey copper mines and smelting works, and both he and Matthew Boulton were partners in the Cornish Metal Company, which Williams also owned. Cushioned against the impact of war, indeed profiting from it, they were taken aback in 1796 when Pitt proposed a tax on coal at the pit head, plus an excise duty on pig iron of twenty shillings per ton. As they often did when threatened, rivals and competitors banded together, appointing a deputation to the ministry, including John Wilkinson, Richard Crawshay and William Gibbons, a Bristol merchant. Under their pressure Pitt not only dropped the excise but put up the customs duty, thus giving more protection against imports.

The ironmasters were often ruthless men, known for their tempers and long-held grudges (iron-willed, in fact). After John Wilkinson's younger brother William came back from France, where he had set up the smelting works at Le Creusot, the brothers quarrelled for years, with lawyers' fees swallowing up their profits. In south Wales,

Samuel Homfray was accused of seducing Richard Crawshay's eldest daughter, while Crawshay himself came near to blows with neighbouring ironmasters, and even with his own son William. After one visit Gilbert Gilpin told William Wilkinson, with some glee, that father and son would not sit in the same room: 'the young one however kept possession of the parlour, & the old gent took possession of the counting house & the business they were about was transacted by letters sent from the old Crawshay in the counting house to the young one in the parlour & vice versa.'[12]

Yet these prickly individuals also worked together to fix prices and control markets: 'They are in law one day & in a coach together the next,' wrote Gilpin of Jeremiah Homfray and Richard Crawshay. Their workers were tough too, brawny and strong, working twelve-hour shifts but earning good wages. Their employers protected them against press gangs and in the dark winters of the food shortages they subscribed generously to the relief of the poor. There were no bread riots here.

An exception to the rush of wartime profiteering was the oldest and most famous concern, Coalbrookdale. This was still the revered heart of the industry, and the juxtaposition of its wooded valley, winding walks, Doric rotunda and elegant iron bridge, with its demonic forges made people talk of heaven and hell combined. But the war placed Coalbrookdale in difficulties, due to the Quaker principles of its owners, the Darbys and the Reynoldses. Amid the uproar of the burning ironworks, their lives of tough commercial sense were tempered by calm meditation and determined philanthropy. Coalbrookdale was thus a curious place, a powerhouse of invention and of spiritual illumination, as well as of furnaces, iron and steel.

It was here that Betsey Gurney came to stay in 1798 and found the steely core to her own life. Betsey was the nervous, quiet, odd one of the wild Gurney sisters. She was thirteen when her mother died, stunned by grief, growing into a solemn, stern girl who filled her younger sisters with awe. One evening at Coalbrookdale she heard the elderly Deborah Darby speak, it seemed, directly to her. That evening, as she wrote in her journal, 'without looking at others I felt myself under the shadow of the wing of God':

D.D. then spoke – I only fear she says too much of what I am to be – a light to the blind, speech to the dumb and feet to the lame. Can it be? After the meeting my heart felt really light and as I walked home by starlight I looked through nature to nature's God . . . I know now what the mountain is I have to climb. I am to be a Quaker.[13]

A strange place, this fiery landscape, to see nature's God. But with some struggles, Betsey became a Plain Quaker. After she married Joseph Fry in 1801, she began preaching, working in London's 'Irish quarter'. Towards the end of the war, when her ten children were older, Elizabeth Fry began her famous work in prisons.

Richard Reynolds's son William, who took over the works in 1794, was an inspirational Quaker of a quite different sort. Like Samuel Galton he was disowned by the Society of Friends, not for war profiteering but for marrying his first cousin Hannah (although to the end of his life he wore his Quaker broad-brimmed hat).[14] During the war he stuck to the Quaker policy of not producing weapons of any kind, and while this affected his profits it gave him a kind of freedom, a time to experiment and invent, and to help other inventors around him. Reynolds was an intellectual, with broad scientific interests. He had his own laboratory, obtained a patent for making manganese steel (anticipating a much later development), surveyed the Shropshire canal and prompted the making of towpaths along the Severn. A 1790s scrapbook shows his fascination with engines, bridges and viaducts, including his work with Thomas Telford on cast-iron troughs for canal aqueducts. At the east end of the Ironbridge gorge he made a port, where in 1795 John Rose set up his Coalport porcelain factory. He encouraged James Sadler – more famous as a pioneering balloonist – to develop new rotative engines that might be applied to 'rowing boats with circular oars'.[15] Later Sadler worked for the Naval Board, setting up the first steam engine in Portsmouth dockyard.

Reynolds also encouraged the flamboyant Cornish engineer

Richard Trevithick, who came here in 1796 and in 1802, testing his high-pressure engines with Reynolds's iron boilers, and hoping to build a full-size locomotive. As for his high-pressure engine, Trevithick told his fellow Cornishman Davies Giddy:

The engineers abt this place all said that it was impossible for such a small Cylinder to lift water to the top of the pumps, and degraded the principals, tho at the same time they spoke highly in favour of the simple and well contrived engine. They say it is a supernatureal engine for it will work without either fire or water, and swear that all engineers hitherto are the biggest fools in creation.

All the local men came round. 'If I had 50 engines I cud sell them in a Day at any price I wod ask for them,' he crowed, 'for they are so highly plesd with it that no other engine will pass with them.'[16]

The energy of the iron furnaces and the inventiveness of industrialists like Reynolds drew the curious, the admiring, and the spies. Around Swansea alone, wrote the Swedish metallurgist Eric Svedenstierna, checking out the ground for his iron-making countrymen, there was 'such a profusion of copper works, coalmines, steam engines, ponds, canals, aqueducts and railways, that the traveller, on arrival, becomes quite undecided as to where he should first direct his attention'.[17] He went on to visit furnaces in Shropshire, the north-east and Scotland, and as he toured he made notes on other industries: on coal mines and canals, on Boulton's Soho factory and Keir's chemical works near Birmingham, on Sheffield cutlery makers and Newcastle mines, on Tyneside vitriol works, white-lead factories and Losh's pioneering alkali works, on Scottish distilleries, glasshouses, limekilns, soap factories and the paper mills.

Everywhere, from Cornwall to Inverness, industrial sites were springing out of fields and valleys and moors. Dorothy Wordsworth, heading north into Scotland with Wordsworth and Coleridge in 1803, passed thatched cottages with heather-covered hills behind. It was a mining village, built by the Duke of Queensberry, but beyond it loomed a building of grey stone, 'a kind of enchanter's castle':

When we drew nearer we saw, coming out of the side of the building, a large machine or lever, its appearance like a great forge-hammer, as we supposed for raising water out of the mines. It heaved forward once in half a minute with a slow motion, and seemed to rest to take breath at the bottom, its motion being accompanied with a sound between a groan and a 'jike'.[18]

It seemed, said her brother, to be like a creature 'making the first step from brute matter into life and purpose, showing its progress by great power . . . and Coleridge observed that it was like a giant with one idea'. Britain was full of such giants, lumbering into life, single-mindedly thumping away. But the supreme emblem of industrial strength remained the iron foundry, the birthplace of cannon, where molten metal, white-hot from the furnace, defied the darkness around.

# 21: 'CHECK PROUD INVASION'S BOAST'

The cannons from the foundries were needed. Despite the boost given by Camperdown, there were murmurings of disquiet in the press and in the cabinet. On 18 October 1797, the Austrians had signed the Treaty of Campo Formio with Napoleon Bonaparte, acting on his own, without instructions from Paris. The treaty, confirming proposals made earlier in the year, was a triumph for France: Austria ceded the Austrian Netherlands, its Italian territories, stretching from the Alps, around the east of Tuscany and south to the Papal States, and the region around Genoa, as well as clusters of islands including Corfu. As a sweetener Austria gained Venice (although not the Veneto), Istria and Dalmatia.

A confident Napoleon returned to Paris. On 27 October, now aged twenty-eight, he was given command of the Armée d'Angleterre, and rode to take up his position on the Channel coast. In London Pitt was weary and frustrated: he had blinding headaches and painful stomach cramps; his insomnia grew worse, he drank more and slept later, and lost his grasp of minutiae. Those in the know were so disturbed that they muttered about replacing him as Prime Minister with the Earl of Moira.[1] Foreign negotiations were left largely to William Grenville and his undersecretary, Pitt's protégé, the ambitious twenty-six-year-old George Canning. Cabinet meetings were tense, with Grenville as Foreign Secretary constantly at odds with Dundas as Secretary of War. Dundas, exhausted, begged to step down but Pitt would not let him go.

Sensing public disillusionment, the government mounted a double campaign, to trounce the opposition and renew horror at the French regime on one hand, and to raise morale and support for the war on the other. In the former cause, the first issue of the *Anti-Jacobin, or Weekly Examiner* appeared on 20 November 1797, dedicated to fighting Jacobinism in every form, whether it 'openly threatens the subversion of States, or gradually saps the foundations of domestic happiness', and to upholding the virtues of the 'just and necessary' war.[2] Many knew that Canning was the brain behind the paper and its successor, the monthly *Anti-Jacobin Review*. Illustrated by Gillray's cartoons satirising the Foxite Whigs and the whole range of 'Jacobin' culture, preachers and poetry, the *Anti-Jacobin* reached sales of 2,500 copies, and Canning's stinging parodies helped to drive Wordsworth and Coleridge and other intellectuals gradually away from radical politics. Women writers were pilloried too, including Mary Wollstone-craft, who had died in childbirth only two months before, and Mary Hays, who had stressed women's intellectual powers and desires in the *Monthly Magazine* and in her novel, *Memoirs of Emma Courtney*. In 1798, when Godwin's memoir of his wife Mary Wollstonecraft revealed her affairs, illegitimate daughter and suicide attempts, middle England was aghast. All such women, pronounced the Revd Richard Polwhele in the *Anti-Jacobin*, were unnatural rebels, 'Unsex'd Females', prone to 'Gallic freaks or Gallic faith':

> Survey with me, what ne'er our fathers saw,
> A female band despising NATURE's law,
> As 'proud defiance' flashes from their arms,
> And vengeance smothers all their softer charms.
> I shudder at the new unpictur'd scene,
> Where unsex'd woman vaunts the imperious mien.[3]

There were few outspoken women in the rest of the war years.

The sophisticated *Anti-Jacobin* was aimed at the London elite and at parliamentary circles, while the wider public were assailed by cheap tracts and loyalist broadsides and the radical presses were shut down. And while Canning and his crew went on the attack, Grenville hoped to boost the government by celebrating its naval victories. On 19 December 1797, the City of London organised a grand public tribute to the Glorious First of June, Cape St Vincent and Camperdown. Up to two hundred thousand people watched the sailors march to St Paul's with their flags and battle trophies. But on the way Pitt was heckled and jeered: he came home with a cavalry escort. The *Morning Post* called the spectacle 'a Frenchified farce', and in Oldham, summarising local papers, William Rowbottom copied out a squib, clearly by a seaman, posted opposite the Bank of England beneath a figure of Britannia:

> A vessel quite crazy and almost a wreck
> At her helm is a pilot unskild on the deck
> Without chart or compass who ne'er heaves the lead
> Who steers by his stars or false lights in his head
> The storm too increasing mids sholes and mids shelves
> Half the crew in dispair making rafts for themselves
> Provisions all out, the last water cask staved
> By a miracle only that ship can be saved.[4]

Despite its shock value, the *Anti-Jacobin* failed to persuade people that the real threat was at home, and the grand spectacle hardly cheered them that they were defeating the enemy abroad. The British public had followed Napoleon's progress through Italy with amazement and awe. Who was this young Corsican general who swept all before him? What were they dealing with?

There were still some passionate British Jacobins to whom Napoleon was the fiery leader the French needed. In late January 1798, the 'Secret Committee of England' reportedly wrote to the French Directory, 'We now only await with impatience to see the Hero of Italy and the brave veterans of the great nation. Myriads will hail their arrival with shouts of joy; they will soon finish the glorious campaign.'[5] But there were arguments even among republicans. Some saw Napoleon as the saviour of republican principles; others felt that the spirit of the Revolution had been lost, drowned by a desire for conquest. After French forces marched into Switzerland in early March, and the Directory abolished the cantons and proclaimed the Helvetic Republic, Coleridge wrote of his sense of betrayal in 'The Recantation: An Ode'. This was published in the *Morning Post* in April, and later retitled, more neutrally, as 'France, an Ode':

> Forgive me, Freedom! O forgive these dreams!
> I hear thy voice, I hear thy loud lament,
> From bleak Helvetia's icy caverns sent –
> I hear thy groans upon her blood-stain'd streams!
> Heroes, that for your peaceful country perish'd,
> And ye, that fleeing spot the mountain snows
> With bleeding wounds; forgive me, that I cherish'd
> One thought, that ever bless'd your cruel foes!

From the start of the year the people were bombarded with talk of Napoleon's invasion plans. He had constructed great rafts, it was said, a thousand feet long and able to carry sixty thousand cavalry, infantry and artillery, powered by windmills, with five hundred cannon on board – rumours spread to hearten the French public more than quell the British. More realistic reports filtered in that flat-bottomed boats were being built at Ostend, Dunkirk, Rouen, Le Havre and Calais, and that small boats and trading vessels were being commandeered from all the fishing ports along the Channel and Atlantic coasts.

As part of the wave of propaganda, the Poet Laureate, Henry James Pye, added a new verse to the national anthem, roared out in assemblies and at parades:

> Thou who rul'st sea and land,
> Stretch forth thy guardian hand,
> Potent to save;
> Lead forth our Monarch's host,
> Check proud Invasion's boast,
> Crush'd on our warlike Coast,
> 'Whelmed by our wave.[6]

Theatre audiences, stout men at dinners and crowds on the streets sang this anthem, and hummed new patriotic songs to jaunty tunes. On 12 February, Covent Garden followed a performance of Susannah Centlivre's comedy *The Busy Body* and the ballet *Joan of Arc* with a pageant displaying noble moments in British history: 'ALFRED disguised in the Danish camp as a Harper, and discovering himself to his desponding Countrymen, RICHARD COEUR DE LION imprisoned in Germany & liberated by the Voluntary Contributions of his fair Countrywomen'. Next came King John and Magna Carta; Henry III and the 'effects of the French invasion'; the Black Prince at Poitiers and Henry V, with 'The Triumphs of Agincourt and his Marriage with Catherine'.[7] These reminders of English victory, unity and magnanimity, ending triumphantly in marriage, were clearly for women as well as men.

In March Gillray's comic-horror *Promised Horrors* had shown St James's Palace in flames: now, in his *Consequences of a Successful French Invasion* a whip-wielding master proclaimed 'Me teach de English republicans to work'. Then, in April, London newspapers reported that the French fleet was preparing to sail from Brest, and people walking on the beach at Eastbourne claimed to hear firing in the Channel. The print makers stepped up their efforts. Gillray and other caricaturists, like Robert Newton, James Sayers and Isaac Cruikshank, produced fantastical scenarios of patriots and traitors: John Bull toppling Frenchmen like ninepins, or Fox winching the invasion fleet ashore. Pamphlets warned that a peaceful rural life would disappear.[8] They spoke too of the demonic trickery of the French – when they landed, their soldiers would first appear disciplined to win people's confidence: 'Like spiders, they artfully weave a web round their victim, before they begin to prey upon it. But when their success is complete they then let loose their troops, with resistless fury, to commit the most horrible excesses, and to pillage, burn and desolate, without mercy, and without distinction.'[9] Above all – a horror 'that will make your blood freeze in your veins' – they would violate women with savage ferocity. 'Will you, my Countrymen, while you can draw a trigger, or

Gillray, *Consequences of a Successful French Invasion*, 1 March 1798. The regulations on the board decree that at five in the morning 'the Hogs & English Slaves are to be fed', at midnight they are to be suppered and locked up. The first offence of laziness brings five hundred lashes, the second the guillotine.

handle a pike, suffer your daughters, your sisters and your wives, to fall into the power of such monsters?' Spies were said to be creeping round London, testing the mood, to see if the people would rise to support Napoleon, 'the bringer of Liberty'.[10] In the handbills he was no champion of liberty but an upstart, a monster, a butcher, a demon and a fiend.

The government was now hunting for money to pay for anti-invasion defences as well as for the navy and the army. In the Commons, Henry Addington, at this point Speaker of the House, put forward a proposal from the City that instead of paying taxes people might be invited to make voluntary contributions to the war chest of the same amount, or higher. This was taken up, not as an alternative to taxation, but as an extra source of funds. On 9 February 1798 the high fliers of the City plunged through crowded streets to meet at the

Royal Exchange to support the call for a Lord Mayor's Fund. As it was a public meeting everyone wanted to prove their worth, and the gathering raised over £46,000. The king then gave £20,000, the queen and Duke of York £5000 and the five princesses promised £100 a year as long as the war should last. Addington, Pitt and Dundas gave £2000 each. Subscriptions poured in from counties, towns and villages, regiments, schools and ships, and local funds were opened to support volunteer corps or to provide for the families of the dead and wounded. James Oakes, who had been worn down by grief after the death of his daughter Charlotte from consumption, a loss made even sadder by the death of Orbell's nine-week-old son, pulled himself up and joined a subscription among the Corporation for the Voluntary Fund, 'to express their Loyalty for their King & Country, it being now in agitation thro'out the Kingdome'.[11]

Even with all this voluntary effort there was not enough money. In April 1798 Pitt brought in a new land tax, assessed in each parish and reported to the county commissioners. Meanwhile, Henry Dundas, still Secretary for War, retreated to his Wimbledon villa to work on 'Proposals for Rendering the People Instrumental in the General Defence' – he was even said to have hunted out the state papers on preparations for defence against the Spanish Armada.[12] Lords Lieutenant were already required to send in details of all men of military age but this time Dundas was aiming to mobilise the whole nation.[13] His model was taken from William Clavell, High Sheriff of Dorset, who had used the ancient common law right of a sheriff – believed to date back to Alfred the Great – to raise a *posse comitatus*, a 'civil power'. The previous year, Clavell had ordered his Justices of the Peace to make lists, with the help of local constables, of all men between fifteen and sixty able to bear arms, excepting only clergymen, Quakers and invalids. He set up an office at the King's Arms in Dorchester, collecting the returns and allocating men to regiments which would meet at the market cross of each town. He also counted livestock and carts and enrolled smiths, carpenters and wheelwrights, horsemen as messengers and guides, and boys as helpers.

Buckinghamshire and Northumberland had already seized on Clavell's idea, and Dundas now used it on a nationwide scale, asking all the Lords Lieutenant to provide lists of men and livestock, with columns for oxen, cows, cattle and colts, sheep, goats and pigs, as well as horses, wagons, carts and corn mills. Every parish must decide on a rendezvous to collect cattle and provide a route map to drive them along the lanes. People would be paid – a shilling for every empty cart, nine pence for every sack of flour, two pence for a sack of oats, a penny for every ton of hay. A list of millers and bakers was also needed, to set up field bakeries so that 'an army of 30,000 men may, without difficulty, be supplied with bread, in any situation, at four or five days notice'. Companies of pioneers would repair roads and bridges for the home army and destroy others to stop the enemy advancing: 'In that case, these pioneers should, if possible, come provided with tools, of the following description, viz. six pick-axes, six spades, six shovels, three bill-hooks, and four felling-axes, to every twenty-five men.' Every detail, Dundas hoped, was covered.

The resulting Defence of the Realm Act, passed on 5 April 1798, also required county and parish officials to ask every man between fifteen and sixty about his willingness to fight in an invasion, and if he would do so outside his own area. Constables and schoolmasters filled their notebooks, vicars and curates checked them and deputy lieutenants compiled county returns, parish by parish. In this vision of mass warfare, everything depended on local co-operation, controlled, as it had been for generations, less by the state than by the landed gentry.

Men were told that they would not be moved around, but would fight with their own families, friends and neighbours. Working men with families were reluctant to serve, while others gave political or practical objections. By far the greatest number willing to fight came from the towns and industrial areas: country men found it hard to envisage leaving the land, or wanted to wait until after the harvest. Some regions did not answer in full but others gave detailed lists, a map of British working life. The prosperous village of Tingewick, near Aylesbury in Buckinghamshire, listed fifteen farmers, beginning with Joshua Caporn, who owned eight horses, two wagons and three carts. After the farmers came tailors, a weaver, six shoemakers, two staymakers, an excise officer, a wheelwright and two higlers, small traders in poultry and game. More names included a family of watch-makers, innkeepers, carpenters, blacksmiths, gardeners, masons, the butcher and the miller, the breeches maker and the turnpike man, a dozen servants and over fifty labourers. There they were, named for the state, with occasional annotations: 'one eye lost', 'one arm lost', 'lame', 'deaf', 'disabled'.[14]

Beacons were built. Wooden towers for the shutter, or semaphore, telegraph (developed six years before by the inventor Claude Chappe, in France) sprang up along the east and south coasts, so that minis-ters in Whitehall could be in rapid communication with the Downs, Portsmouth and Plymouth. It was said that the telegraph men were now so quick that news of an enemy fleet could fly from Yarmouth to the Nore in five minutes, and from London to Portsmouth in fif-teen. Complementing these, the Admiralty put up wooden signalling stations along the coast, using flags to warn of enemy privateers and ships.

Dundas also wrote to clergymen, asking them to explain the plan to their congregations and calm their fears. On Sunday 29 April, Mary Hardy noted that the vicar, Mr Burrell, 'harangd the people on taken up arms in defence of the Country, an Invasion being apprehended from the French'. Ten days later a town meeting was held at the vicar's house 'to contrive for the safety of the Inhabitants in case of an Invation from the French, which is much expected'.[15] While Bur-rell was bracing his parishioners, Londoners anxiously read through the 'Hints to Assist in the General Defence of London': blockhouses would be built in each square, and barricades in each street, 'the cor-ner houses to be supplied with hand-grenades'. As soon as news of an invasion arrived, all boats were to be moored on the north bank of the Thames. No foreign servants would be allowed. 'No Dutch boats to be allowed to supply the country with fish, as they carry back much useful information.'[16]

In Nether Stowey, in late April, Coleridge wrote his poem 'Fears in Solitude', exploring the tension between withdrawal and involvement, acknowledging that a man who wished 'to preserve/His soul in calmness' was yet bound to think of his fellow men:

> O my God!
> It is indeed a melancholy thing,
> And weighs upon the heart, that he must think
> What uproar and what strife may now be stirring
> This way or that way o'er these silent hills –
> Invasion, and the thunder and the shout,
> And all the crash of onset; fear and rage,
> And undetermined conflict – even now,
> Ev'n now, perchance, and in his native Isle.

But in the same poem, full of longing for a safe and peaceful country, he still attacked the corruption of the state and the greed for news of war:

> We send our mandates for the certain death
> Of thousands and ten thousands! Boys and girls,
> And women that would groan to see a child
> Pull off an insect's leg, all read of war,
> The best amusement for our morning meal.

\*

The scares of the previous year had already overcome the government's wariness about volunteers. At last, in Edinburgh, Walter Scott had been able to put on a uniform. His elder brother, John, was in the regular army and his other brother, Tom, had become a volunteer in 1794, but so far Scott's lameness had debarred him. Yet it had no effect on his skill on horseback and in February 1797, the month of the Fishguard invasion, he had been one of the first to join the Royal Edinburgh Volunteer Light Dragoons. He became the troop's quartermaster, secretary and paymaster. It was a gentlemanly business. Writing to Captain Patrick Murray, Scott reported that so far they had eighty men, 'each mounted on horses worth from 30 to 60 guineas a piece, armed equipped &c at our own expence . . . We can perform most of the common manoeuvres at the hard trot & Gallop – *I* mean such of us as have drilled from the beginning, that is about a fortnight ago.'[17]

They had also, he said, raised a body of tradesmen, 'arm'd cloathed & paid by the government', and a third corps for Highlanders was filling fast: 'in case of an invasion one & all will be the word'. Scott's corps were drilled for two or three hours each day by the officers of the Cinque Port Cavalry – the same troop that had accompanied Burns to his grave two years before, and had crushed the protestors at Tranent. Yet Scott, so excited by riding to the country's defence, was curiously coy about his personal ties with France. This year, when he married Charlotte Charpentier, daughter of a royalist refugee, he invented English parents for her called 'Carpenter', perhaps to fend off the disapproval of his Presbyterian father. She was born in France, he admitted, but 'has the sentiments & manners of an Englishwoman and does not like to be thought otherwise – a very slight tinge in her pronunciation is all which marks the foreigner'.[18] It was a strange wartime evasion.

On 4 June 1798, the king's birthday, Scott was riding in St Andrew's Square in Edinburgh with the Highlanders in their black feather bonnets, and other volunteers. 'The crowd of spectators', declared the *Edinburgh Herald*, 'attracted by the novelty and interest of the scene, was great beyond example. The city was almost unpeopled. Every house and every hovel displayed the verdant badges of loyalty as the procession passed.'[19] The only spot on this martial glamour was that the soldiers' large cocked hats were constantly knocked off at the command to shoulder arms, but 'the general picking-up thereof only added to the hilarity of the spectators'. On the same day there were parades across Britain. In Bury St Edmunds, Oakes walked with the corporation and clergy to the Guildhall, where Lord Brome's cavalry and Lord Hervey's infantry were lined up outside the Angel Inn and 'the Day passed off very pleasantly in all Company many loyal

Toasts & constitutional Songs'.[20] In Hyde Park the king reviewed eight thousand troops, accompanied by the Prince of Wales and the Dukes of York, Kent, Cumberland and Gloucester.[21] The artillery fired a twenty-one-gun salute and the troops presented arms, with drums beating and music playing. This became an annual event. Even when the rain poured and wind blew the royal party left 'amidst the joyous shouts and affectionate greetings of the people, who assembled on the occasion to the amount of upwards of 100,000, including all the beauty and fashion of the metropolis'.[22]

In the four months after April 1798 the number of volunteers doubled, reaching 116,000 by July. For the first time they included many labourers and artisans: the volunteer army was no longer a plaything of the propertied and professional classes. In Shropshire, Thomas Telford wrote to the Earl of Powis offering to put together a 'Band of Artificers and Pioneers' from his workmen on the Ellesmere canal, mechanics who could build machines, roads and bridges.[23] The Midland manufacturers were keen supporters of the Birmingham Loyal Association, smartly turned out in blue and white, while Bath tradesmen were delighted when the newly formed volunteers chose 'a scarlet jacket with black collar and lappels, white waistcoat and blue pantaloons edged with red'.[24] It took only a fortnight for the Bath paper to carry advertisements from canny agents and shopkeepers offering to sell the volunteers any flintlocks, pistols and swords they required.

Almost every part of London had its own troop. Harry Hoare plunged into volunteering with zeal. 'I did not enjoy much of Mr Hoare's Company, so occupied was he in arming and excercising,' wrote Hannah More, who went down to Mitcham in May 1798 with Harry's son William and his wife Louisa, her neighbours in evangelical Clapham. He rose at four thirty every morning, she explained, then:

trots off to town to be ready to meet at six the Fleet Street Corps performing their evolutions in the area of Bridewell, the only place they can find sufficient space, then comes back for a late dinner and as soon as that is over he goes to his Committees, after which he has a sergeant to drill himself and his three sons on the lawn until it is dark.[25]

Next year Harry became a captain in the Loyal London Volunteers: four of his clerks were members and the bank gave them £3 to £4 for 'military expenses'.

The uniforms of the capital were marvellously illustrated in eighty-seven expensive plates in *The Loyal Volunteers of London* in 1798–9. Such outfits were infinitely desirable. Henry 'Orator' Hunt – later a famous radical but in his youth a zealous loyalist from a well-off Wiltshire family – told the story of Captain Astley and Lieutenant John Poore, who set off to London to find an army tailor. 'Having been very particular in getting the taylor, breeches-maker, boot and even spur-maker, to fit them to a T, on the Friday they both appeared, accoutered from head to toe, at Edmonds's Somerset coffee house in the Strand, and really cut no small "swell" as they marched up and down the coffee room.'[26] They showed off in their full kit in the front boxes at Drury Lane, with broadswords by their sides. Next day they left the coffee house, eager to begin the campaign without waiting for the French and swearing that instead they would capture two notorious highwaymen on Hounslow Heath. But when a lone highwayman appeared, they froze, unable to grasp their pistols, and meekly handed over their purses.

In the country, the volunteers often gave a good excuse for a party. Betsey Fremantle – exclaiming in passing about their anxiety for her husband's soldier brother Jack 'as the French have landed in Ireland!' – went from her Buckinghamshire home in Swanbourne to Great Brickwell village to see the yeomanry display:

It was a great disappointment to everybody that the day was showery as it would have been a most charming sight, but the rain prevented our seeing the yeomanry making the sword exercises etc. – We dined under tents and had a charming ball and most elegant suppers. – Nearly all the county was there. We danced till past four o'clock in the morning.[27]

Everywhere, the volunteers pulled the crowds. In London, Joseph Farington had tickets when the Duchess of York gave the St James's Corps their colours, and was delighted to see how many fashionable people were there: 'The Duke & Duchess of York came abt. 3 o'clock. The Duchess was dressed in the uniform of the Corps Scarlet & Blue.'[28] Farington was also at Lord's cricket ground the following year when the wife of the governor of the Bank of England presented the colours to volunteers from the Bank and Somerset House. The parade was followed by a banquet in the Bank's rotunda and dividend rooms, where directors and clerks, officers and men shared tables and proposed loyal toasts.

'Here we are in the full tide of war,' wrote the French émigré Mallet du Pan in the summer of 1798:

Crushed by taxation, and exposed to the fury of the most desperate of enemies, but nevertheless security, abundance and energy reign supreme, alike in cottage and palace . . . The spectacle presented by public opinion has far surpassed my expectation. The nation had not yet learnt to know its own strength or its resources. The Government has taught it the secret, and inspired it with an unbounded confidence almost amounting to presumption.[29]

This was ludicrously rosy, but the confidence was indeed there to some degree, and if the poor saw no 'abundance', some investors did surprisingly well out of the invasion scares. The alarms brought 3 per cent consols down to half their price. Seeing this, Thomas Thompson of Hull, who had risen from being a clerk in the Wilberforce mercantile firm to become a wealthy Baltic trader, decided that 'if the French landed it mattered not whether he met his fate as a rich man or a poor one' and invested heavily in the funds.[30] When the invasion threat vanished and the consols' price revived, he made a killing and bought a country house, which he adorned with suitably military battlements – neighbours called it Cottingham Castle.

## 22. IRELAND

Despite the failure of Hoche's expedition to Bantry Bay, the United Irishmen were determined to free their country from British rule and went on with plans for a rising, hoping for help from the French. Supporters across Ireland began forging pikes, stockpiling them in barns and caves. But at every turn they met setbacks. In February 1798 Margate customs men stopped an Irish group embarking for France. They included Arthur O'Connor, editor of the United Irishmen's paper, *The Press*, whose account of atrocities by British soldiers, 'Address to the Irish Nation', had been published in the *Morning Post* the month before, and Father James O'Coigley, who had rashly pocketed a letter from the 'Secret Committee of England' inviting Bonaparte to invade. They were tried in Maidstone in April, and the newspapers ran full accounts, headed 'Trials for High Treason'.[1] A roll call of opposition Whigs appeared as character witnesses for O'Connor, including Fox, Sheridan, Moira, the lawyer Thomas Erskine, the Earl of Suffolk and the Duke of Norfolk, as well as Grattan, until very recently the leader of the Irish parliament, and Lord John Russell and Samuel Whitbread. O'Connor and three others were acquitted, but O'Coigley was convicted of treason. He would hang at Maidstone in October.

Soon after the Margate arrests, spies brought information that led, on 12 March, to the seizure of sixteen of the United Irishmen's eighteen-strong committee. Martial law was declared in Ireland, unleashing another round of arrests and violence. Ralph Abercromby, who was sent over as commander after he returned from the West Indies, expressed horror at the British troops, calling them 'formidable to everybody but the enemy', and telling his father angrily that 'Every crime, every cruelty, that could be committed by Cossacks or Calmucks have been transacted here'.[2] In April, finding his efforts to control the soldiers constantly thwarted by the Irish authorities, Abercromby resigned. His place was taken by General Lake, whose troops swept through the countryside searching for arms, instituting mass arrests, burning down houses and beating supposed conspirators.

That spring around five hundred thousand United Irishmen were waiting, over half of them ready and armed: some had muskets but most had scythes, spades, pitchforks and home-made pikes. After the March arrests, the remaining leaders, including Edward Fitzgerald, who was hiding from the law in Dublin, decided to keep to the plan for the uprising, set for 23 May. But a Catholic informer revealed Fitzgerald's hiding place, and on 19 May, after a bloody skirmish, Fitzgerald was shot, captured and taken to the New Prison, Dublin. He died of fever from his wounds on 4 June, aged thirty-four, and was long revered as a martyr to the cause. Towards the end of the war, Byron, who was nine in 1798, wrote in his journal, 'If I had been a man, I would have made an English Lord Edward Fitzgerald.'[3]

Frustrated, the leaderless United Irishmen led their own rebellion, without waiting for French help. This began with the battle of Leinster on 23 May and continued for a month, with clashes and skirmishes and staggered encounters, like the battle of Oulart Hill, where the determined Father John Murphy, 'a worthy, simple, pious man', so his followers claimed, led a band of pikemen in an attack on Colonel Foote's infantry. There were some early successes but at the bloody battle of New Ross on 5 June three thousand men died, and more in the aftermath when the army torched casualty stations in the town.[4] The violence was viciously sectarian (though some rewritings of history have denied this). In one instance, it was said, between one hundred and two hundred Protestants were herded into a barn and shot or burned alive; in another the rebels piked to death ninety-seven loyalist prisoners on Wexford Bridge. Protestant Orangemen and embattled army garrisons were equally savage, setting fire to houses, hanging men and boys by the roadside, terrorising towns and villages. When rebels surrendered their pikes they met floggings and barbarous 'pitch-capping': shearing the hair of 'croppies', who wore their hair short in the French style, and forcing a paper cap of boiling pitch on to their heads. Violence was part of the landscape. On 31 May, Frances Beaufort married Richard Lovell Edgeworth in Dublin. She was his fourth wife, a year younger than his eldest daughter, Maria, and was bracing herself to look after his many children. Driving from their wedding back to Edgeworthstown, she saw something on the side of the road. ' "What is that?" "Look on the other side – don't look at it!" cried Mr Edgeworth; and when we passed he said it was a cart turned up, between the shafts of which a man was hung – murdered by the rebels.'[5]

Watching Lake's policy of unbridled aggression some soldiers doubted the wisdom of their orders. In early June the twenty-one-year-old John Henry Slessor, whose family were British merchants in Oporto, was taking part in the defence of Antrim with the Royal Irish Artillery, 'dispersing the unfortunate, deluded rebels in all direction, and taking no prisoners . . . This was my first trial, my debut, and I must say, that after the thirst of blood was over, cool reflection did not much reconcile to my feelings such a horrible carnage of our own countrymen, but it was self-defence.'[6] The soldiers fought on, firing the thatched houses around them: 'how far such measures are politic,' he wrote drily, 'Government ought best to know . . . We constantly inflict martial law on the country people, flogging and even hanging.'

On 21 June, after fierce artillery bombardment which left hundreds dead, British troops encircled and defeated the main rebel force at Vinegar Hill in County Wexford. The leaders, Bagenal Harvey and Father Murphy, were both captured and executed, and within the next few weeks the uprising was crushed. It was too disorganised, too scattered: the Ulster men were slow to help and so were the western counties. The rebels had waited in vain for French assistance, and when it did come it was too little and too late. On 23 August a small contingent of French grenadiers commanded by General Humbert landed at Killala in County Mayo in the far west, capturing Ballina, Foxford and Castlebar and marching east. On 8 September veteran British troops surrounded them and Humbert surrendered. The prisoners were marched to Dublin and were swiftly exchanged and repatriated.

*The Queen's Own Royal Dublin Militia going into action at the Battle of Vinegar Hill, Wexford,* 1798: a cleaned-up, pro-government view

For the people on the fringe of the troubles, it was a strange and frightening time. In September, when the French landed, the Edgeworth family heard of friends blown up in the explosion of an ammunition cart, and of a band of three hundred rebels approaching their house. They took refuge in Longford, 'crowded with the yeomanry of various corps, and with the inhabitants of the neighbourhood, who had flocked thither for their protection,' remembered Maria Edgeworth.[7] Although the rebels sacked many houses, they were held back at the Edgeworths' inn by a man who said the landlady had lent his distressed wife the rent for her flax ground the year before. Such small things mattered. After news of Lake's victory the Edgeworths returned home to find their doors torn off and windows broken, yet their library untouched. 'Everything was as we left it,' wrote Maria, '– a map that we had been consulting was still open on the library table, a pansy in a glass of water, which one of the children had been copying, was still on the chimney piece.'

Six weeks later British frigates attacked a fleet sailing from Brest with four thousand men, while it was fighting the storms off Lough Swilly in Donegal, its planned destination. The exiled Wolfe Tone was captured along with 2,500 soldiers, including Tone's troop of United Irishmen recruited in France. Tone, found guilty of treason, requested death by firing squad. When this was denied he cut his throat in prison rather than be publicly hanged like a felon.

The rebellion was over, but the landing at Killala had proved again that the French could land forces in Britain. On the mainland, fears of republican support for any invasion led to repeated demands in the press and parliament for more rounding up of dissidents. But although Pitt and his ministers feared a wider conspiracy, and habeas corpus was suspended again after the arrests of the United Irish leaders in March, there was no real threat. The old radicals and republicans had been largely silenced since the Gagging Acts of 1795, and only one or two dared to speak out, like the schoolmaster William Clegg, who bravely published his pamphlet *Freedom Defended, or the Practice of Despots Exposed* in 1798. 'Who or what this Mr Clegg may be', fumed the *British Critic*, 'we neither know nor trouble ourselves to enquire; but a more completely jacobinical work never issued from the impure dens of that faction.'[8]

Clegg was linked to the United Englishmen, supporters of the Irish movement who established cells in Manchester, Liverpool, Nottingham, London and elsewhere, while the United Scotsmen gathered in Edinburgh and Glasgow. Although William Cowdroy openly published the United Englishmen's constitution and aims in

ROYALTY. People laughed at Gillray's dissolute Prince of Wales,
thrifty George III and salad-eating Caroline, but his cruder print
of Louis XVI, crying for vengeance as his blood pours skyward,
roused new loyalty to the crown.

DIARISTS AND LETTER WRITERS. James Oakes, and his diary for
February 1798; Francis Austen; and Richard Heber.

Hannah and Samuel Greg; John and Jane Marshall

SOLDIERS, SAILORS AND PRISONERS. The smart images of the
Birmingham Loyal Association, and Rowlandson's *Private Drilling*,
both 1798, reflect the mix of pride and amusement
that the volunteers provoked.

Rowlandson's Yarmouth crowd welcome the fleet after the Battle of Camperdown. But victories brought prisoners, many held in hulks like these in Portsmouth harbour, painted by a French prisoner, Louis Garneray.

HIGH LIFE. Gillray's leering swells take over the pavement and force women with veils, turban and feathers into the road. Below, plates from Heideloff's *Gallery of Fashion* display the walking dresses and theatre-going finery of the mid-1790s.

Favourite diversions: a crowd at Christie's auction rooms,
and a session at Henry Angelo's fencing academy.

Two explosive images of power, naval and industrial:
Philip James de Loutherbourg's dramatic *The Battle of the Nile*, and his painting of
the furnaces of Madeley Wood in *Coalbrookdale by Night*.

the *Manchester Gazette*, their meetings and oaths were illegal and they disguised their clandestine drills as social events. One London spy reported that the United Englishmen and Sons of Liberty, who were drilling at night in the garden of the Seven Stars at Bethnal Green, had 'a rule to begin singing as soon as they had done business, that people might have less suspicion of them and might think it a club'.[9] In the north, the movement's links with Ireland were strong. Manchester members had welcomed visits from United Irish leaders and raised funds for O'Coigley to go to France. In turn, O'Coigley brought pamphlets advocating the assassination of 'the petty tyrants of Manchester . . . and the rest would fear as they did in Ireland.'[10] But the Manchester group were eventually betrayed by their secretary, Robert Gray, who became a spy for a local magistrate. Hannah Greg of Quarry Bank Mill – who felt passionately about the Irish cause – had quickly spotted him as 'The Informer', telling William Rathbone that his incitement and 'spiriting them up' was behind much of the local activity.[11]

In April 1798, leaders of the United Englishmen were arrested in Manchester and London, with members of the London Corresponding Society. That month Hannah Greg wrote fiercely to the Rathbones about false reports and government-induced panic:

Let Justice be done, and let me add, let *truth* be *told* whatever happen. I am quite disgusted and discouraged at the difficulty of knowing what is the truth of facts that are even passing almost under one's own eyes. I seldom venture to repeat serious reports at more than second hand at the farthest – but now I find that even too far & that little less is safe than the testimony of your own eyes – nor do I know that even they ought to be trusted in the first moments of fear acting upon prejudice.[12]

In her view the government had 'succeeded in (what I imagine their principal purpose) filling the publick mind with consternation & a belief that a wide conspiracy to assist the French actually exists in the Country'. Many previous critics of the government, she thought, were pleased at the arrests of these 'dangerous Conspirators' and were almost frightened into being 'good subjects'.

The Gregs of Lancashire had visited Ireland three years before to see Samuel's family, and Hannah, outraged by the misery of the poor, had no doubt who was to blame: 'Certain will be the day of retribution – the crimes of this country and the crimes of old France are crying out and will be visited . . . to be Irish has always been sufficient to make anything obnoxious to the English Government.'[13]

In Belfast Samuel Greg's sister Jane was an outspoken member of dissident women's societies, including the United Irishwomen, and a close friend of Lady Londonderry, the wife of the chief secretary in Belfast. The women used their connections to carry messages but the post was often opened and in May 1797 the Belfast postmaster had reported Jane's involvement. Although her father managed to protect her from arrest, she was whisked away to stay with Samuel and Hannah in Manchester. Hannah sent William Rathbone a pamphlet arguing for a united Ireland, *The Appeal of the People of Ulster to their Countrymen*. She was enraged by the anti-Catholic, anti-Jacobin and anti-Irish feeling in the town and also afraid for her own family. Her daughter Ellen remembered nervously expecting a knock on the door, 'For my father was the only Irish gentleman in the town, and his sister Jane had been obliged to leave Ireland, being a friend of Lady Londonderry, and her letters might bring suspicion upon him. Invasion too was feared, and my mother kept all ready for flight along with her children.'[14]

Many of the United Englishmen and their sympathisers arrested in April were held without trial in the new Coldbath Prison in Clerkenwell, the 'English Bastille', for the next three years. Among their supporters in parliament was the young MP Francis Burdett, who spoke out against the curtailing of freedom of speech and of the press, and against the pressure on the judiciary to follow the government line. In November, responding to the pleas of prisoners, he visited Coldbath Fields. Soon he found himself denied access to all London prisons and when he raised the matter in the Commons, his appeal for an inquiry came to nothing.

The following year, parliament passed a new Sedition Act, aimed at suppressing the United Englishmen and United Scotsmen, and placing even stricter controls on public lectures and on the press. People were still ready to believe rumours of insurrection, their heads filled with government propaganda. In Jane Austen's *Northanger Abbey*, written largely during 1798–9, Eleanor Tilney is aghast when Catherine Morland hints that 'something very shocking indeed' will happen in London, 'more horrible than anything we have met with yet'. Whereas Catherine is hoping for the publication of a thriller like *The Mysteries of Udolpho*, Eleanor leaps to the conclusion that the coming horror must be a 'dreadful riot'. 'My dear Eleanor,' her patronising brother teases her, 'the riot is only in your own brain.' Instead of thinking of the subscription library, 'as any rational creature would have done', Eleanor's mind had leapt to potential danger to their eldest brother:

she immediately pictured to herself a mob of three thousand men assembling in St George's Fields; the Bank attacked, the Tower threatened, the streets of London flowing with blood, a detachment of the 12th Light Dragoons (the hopes of the nation) called up from Northampton to quell the insurgents, and the gallant Captain Frederick Tilney, in the moment of charging at the head of his troop, knocked off his horse by a brickbat from an upper window.

After the Irish uprising such fears were common, and prejudice against the Irish grew more intense. In Lancashire, where many Irish immigrants worked, they were labelled as drunken, violent and lazy – the opposite of allegedly sober English workers. Although there was more integration than appeared, the Manchester ghettos grew quickly, like 'Irish Town' by the river Irk, with its run-down terraced cottages. One man told Hannah Greg that he knew the local people believed all the Irish were Jacobins; it was a good thing they all lived in one quarter, he thought, 'or else they would all be murdered'.[15] A fiercely Protestant Orange movement was started in the north-west, largely by volunteers and militia who had been sent over during the rebellion. This grew to seventy lodges, organised like the Masons, mounting public parades and enrolling magistrates, magnates and gentry.

*

In the Irish rebellion of 1798 about thirty thousand Irish men, women and children died and two thousand government troops. In June 1799, exactly a year after the uprising, Frances Edgeworth, whose wedding day had been marked by the sight of a corpse hanging from a cart, gave birth to her first baby. The Edgeworths were staying with the Beddoes family in Bristol, and Maria Edgeworth wrote to her Aunt Ruxton, 'Good news, my dearest aunt . . . At nine minutes before six this evening, to my great joy, my little sister Fanny came into this world . . .'[16] Maria, who had turned not a hair in the face of rebels and French invaders, then took the baby down the slippery, uncarpeted stairs to show to its father, as Frances remembered:

but when she had descended a few steps a panic seized her, and she was afraid to go either backwards or forwards. She sat down on the stairs, afraid she should drop the child, afraid that its head would come off, and afraid that her father would find her sitting here and laugh at her; till seeing the footman passing she called 'Samuel' in a terrified voice, and made him walk before her backwards down the stairs till she safely reached the sitting room.

## 23. THE NILE AND BEYOND

In the late spring of 1798, when fears of a coming Irish rebellion were beginning to match those of a French invasion, the Kent folk scouring the French coast through their telescopes noticed new activity, and saw wagons moving. The papers began to carry reports of troops gathering, not on the Channel coast but at Toulon in the south. Bonaparte, they learned, had dashed south. On 24 April *The Times* carried an article headed 'FRENCH EXPEDITION TO EGYPT': 'It seems that General Buonaparte is to be the hero who is intended by the Directory as the Conqueror of the East, whither it is now generally thought by the best informed persons that the French expedition to the South is directed, proceeding by the route of Egypt'.[1] The report quoted a long speech from one of the Deputies, waxing lyrical about a new colony in the country where Alexander had wished to place his seat of empire. But this, *The Times* noted, was not solely a military operation: 'There are 50 scientific men employed in this important expedition, among whom are 4 astronomers, 5 engineers, 3 naturalists, 3 mineralogists, 4 chemists, 1 geometrician, 1 botanist, 1 zoologist, 2 physicians and 3 surveyors. Their books and instruments have already been sent off from Paris.'

The expedition took the British government entirely by surprise, revealing the total failure of their elaborate intelligence network. It brought new anxieties, a suspicion that Napoleon was planning to take Egypt, then a province of the Ottoman empire under control of the Mameluke military caste, as a first step to India. A report from Talleyrand, who had been a minister for Louis XVI and was now Napoleon's Foreign Minister, confirmed this: 'Having occupied and fortified Egypt, we shall send a force of fifteen thousand men from Suez to India, to join the forces of Tipu-Sahib and drive away the English.'[2]

Pitt bowed to Austrian pressure and agreed to send a fleet to the Mediterranean, despite the risk of reducing naval protection against invasions in Ireland or across the Channel. On 19 May, the French fleet sailed from Toulon, carrying forty thousand men and a special observation corps with four balloons – and then it disappeared. For ten weeks the British fleet under Nelson, now a rear admiral, sailed up and down the Mediterranean and could find no trace of the French. The newspapers and monthly magazines found this 'remarkable', and their readers, like Hester Piozzi, echoed their words:

'tis nearly miraculous that 400 Sail should thus have *slipt unperceived* away from Admiral Nelson and his Fleet of *Observation*. The Bishop of St Asaph says that while We are gazing after them in the Levant – Tydings will arrive that they are on the Coast of Ireland – He may be right for ought I know, Things happen so very wide of all Expectation.[3]

The Levant was, however, the right guess. In June Napoleon's Armée d'Orient occupied Malta, and on 2 July they landed at Alexandria. Three weeks later they defeated the Mameluke forces at the battle of the Pyramids. Astonishing reports arrived that Napoleon had declared his conversion to Islam – in a misguided attempt to woo adherents he had apparently announced to Egypt that the French were Muslims, a claim that only added to his 'exotic' reputation.

But then came a reversal. On the evening of 1 August Nelson tracked the French fleet to Aboukir Bay, between Alexandria and the mouth of the Nile. The French believed they were only open to attack on the seaward side and that any battle would take place the next day. Confounding those expectations, Nelson attacked at once despite the gathering dusk. From the least expected direction, he sent one line of ships running between the French and the shore, firing as they passed, while the other line fired from the sea. The French centre blasted back, and the fighting was intense for three hours, until in the darkness Villeneuve's flagship *L'Orient* caught fire, exploding with a blinding flash and deafening roar. Although the French then tried to tack out of the bay, only two ships of the line and two frigates got away: Nelson's fleet destroyed the remaining eleven French warships and two frigates.

Among the British ships was the *Goliath*, picked out of the Cadiz blockade by Nelson for her fast sailing, and on board – as he had been at the battle of St Vincent – was the Scots sailor John Nicol. 'The sun was just setting as we went into the bay,' he remembered, 'and a red and fiery sun it was.'[4] Nicol was in the powder magazine with the gunner, stripped to the waist, firing broadsides. There were several women on board, who worked as hard as the men: some women were wounded and one died and was buried on a small island in the bay. Another, from Edinburgh, bore a son in the heat of the action.

The British public knew nothing of this. The *Leander*, carrying Nelson's first set of despatches to London, was captured by the French off Crete. For the next few weeks, reports reproduced from French papers described Napoleon heading to Cairo, unconcerned: no mention of a sea battle. It was not until 2 October that a second set of despatches arrived, and next day Nelson's own descriptions of the battle appeared in the *Gazette*. Writing personally to naval colleagues he praised his brave captains. He had been wounded in the head and carried off deck, but, he said, 'I had the happiness to command a band of brothers . . . Each knew his duty.'[5]

Gillray produced two prints, one showing Nelson scooping up a flotilla of tri-coloured crocodiles, Napoleon's newly chosen symbol, and the other the merciless *Destruction of the French Colossus*, where the giant form of France, decapitated and dripping blood, staggers back across the sea clutching a guillotine, with Louis XVI's head hanging from his neck. 'Shall the Works of a Wicked Nation remain?' demands

the caption, 'shall the Monuments of Oppression not be destroyed?
– shall the Lightning not blast the Image which the Destroyers have
set up against the God of Heaven, & against his Laws?'[6] By contrast,
Rowlandson's exuberant *Nelson Recreating with his Brave Tars after the Glorious Battle of the Nile* was a tribute more than a satire, showing the one-
armed, one-eyed hero lounging on deck, raising a glass to his cheering
men. The chorus beneath, with yet more 'huzzas', was an appeal to
the ladies:

> Put the Bumpers about & be gay
> To hear how our Doxies will smile
> Here's to Nelson for ever Huzza
> And King George on the Banks of the Nile.

The doxies did smile. The November *Lady's Magazine* carried a fron-
tispiece of Nelson's ships in battle, a feature on his life, extracts from
his despatches and an Ode from 'a Lady of Lynn', near his home at
Burnham Thorpe in Norfolk.

Rowlandson, *Nelson recreating with his Brave Tars after the Glorious Battle of the Nile*

There were the usual bell-ringings, bonfires, transparencies and illuminations and drunken parties. The twenty-year-old Humphry Davy,
travelling from Cornwall with his patron Davies Giddy to his new job
at the Pneumatic Institution in Bristol, reached Okehampton just after
the mail coach, decorated with laurel and streaming ribbons; from here
onwards he could hear cheering and at night all the villages they passed
glowed with candles.[7] In Suffolk, the Bury St Edmunds MPs donated
hogsheads of beer for the people to 'partake of the general Joy'.[8] In
London the battle prompted a new panorama at the *Naumachia*, a theatre in Fleet Street specially built to stage sea battles, while Thomas
Dibdin's *The Mouth of the Nile*, 'a new Serio-Comic Intermezzo of Pantomime, Song, Dance and Dialogue', drew crowds at Covent Garden.
Like his father Charles, Thomas Dibdin composed nautical songs, and
the Nile found a special place in his 'Dumplings for Bonaparte':

> They say that bold Nelson has stopt him awhile,
> And has dish'd his great fleet at the mouth of the Nile,
> *Huzza for brave Nelson, for brave Nelson Huzza, and –*
>
> Like them be steady and steady, boys, steady.
> On the first of August, let us never forget,
> 'Twas that proud day they engag'd at sunset,
> And of their supper Nelson gave them enough,
> But the dumpling from Norfolk they found rather tough,
> *Huzza for brave Nelson, for brave Nelson Huzza* etc.[9]

A day of General Thanksgiving was tabled for Thursday 29
November: prayers were read in church, ox roasts were held in the
towns. 'I gave my Servants this Evening after Supper some strong-
Beer and some Punch to drink Admiral Lord Nelson's Health on his
late grand Victory,' wrote Parson Woodforde in his flowing hand, having perhaps had some punch himself, 'and also all the other Officers
with him and all the brave Sailors with them, and also all those brave
Admirals, Officers and Sailors that have gained such great & noble
Victories of late over the French &c – &c.'[10]

Many families, however, mourned sailors and marines lost in the battle, and others worried about the wounded making their slow way home. Tom Gill's ship the *Colossus*, escorting eight ships from Lisbon, was wrecked in a gale off the Scilly Isles; the islanders, braving the surf in open boats, rescued all on board, 'the sick and wounded first, whereof many were from the battle of the Nile'.[11] But the government whipped up patriotic pride. The City of London, led by the Russian-born merchant, plantation owner and Lloyd's underwriter John Julius Angerstein, subscribed to generous rewards, and the East India Company gave Nelson a personal gift of £10,000. Smart Londoners dressed 'à la Nile', in Egyptian Mameluke cloaks. Even Jane Austen abandoned her white satin cap and borrowed a 'Mamalouc cap', modelled on Egyptian fez work, adorned with Nelson's emblem. It was 'all the fashion now', she explained, 'worn at the Opera, & by Lady Mildmays at Hackwood Balls'.[12] Britain became gripped by Nelson mania, celebrating him in statues, paintings, prints and songs, and copying his portrait on to tea-trays and jugs, earrings, brooches, fans, ribbons and shawls.

In 1799 Turner, determined to be elected to the Royal Academy, a hurdle he had so far failed to leap, chose the battle as the subject of one of his eleven paintings at the Summer Exhibition. His very title read like a blast to the critics: *The Battle of the Nile, at 10 o'clock when the L'Orient blew up, from the Station of the Gun Boats between the Battery and Castle of Aboukir*. Turner's painting (now lost) was not the only one. Four well-known marine artists tackled the battle, including the veteran Philip de Loutherbourg, who showed the *L'Orient* exploding like Vesuvius against a bloody sky, while sailors crammed into small boats rescued drowning comrades and carried the wounded ashore.

After the battle of the Nile, the Mediterranean was once more under British control, and Russia and Turkey were encouraged to enter the war against France. Britain rejoiced. The navy capitalised on this triumph, making sure to seal good relations with the people of the ports. The following autumn James Oakes and his Liverpool niece Susan were among the guests at a lavish dance on the *Ganges*, anchored in the Yarmouth Roads: boats ferried the gentry out, and they were piped aboard while the marines presented arms, every buckle and bayonet gleaming. Admiral George Tate, a commander in the navy of Catherine the Great and now Vice-Admiral of the Baltic Fleet, arrived, followed by the Bishop of Norwich and his wife. There was dancing under an awning on the quarterdeck, and tables laden with dishes and fruit, as well as claret, port, madeira and sherry. 'Dancing continued till 6 o'clock & the Company went off in Boats as they came, highly gratify[d] with their elegant Entertainment.'[13]

At the start of 1799, as the wind roared and snow drifted, holding up the mail coaches, William Rowbottom noted that recruiting was brisk again: 'through the Ministers determination on war'.[14] Deaths, disease and desertion had lost the army twenty thousand men, and now a new drive encouraged militiamen to join the regulars, with a guarantee that they would serve only in Europe, for five years or the duration of the war. In June over fifteen thousand seasoned men moved to the army and in October ten thousand more. Many had already served a long time, and were almost strangers to their homes. Jack Gill, whose brother Tom was sailing with Nelson's fleet, had not been back to the Isle of Wight for six years, and had not written for over a year. He did not want to know the reason for his silence, wrote his father, the Revd Gill, 'it is enough for me to feel neglect, and to experience the disagreeable perception, that you seem determined to drop all correspondence with me, and all regard for your sisters. It will however be out of your power to divest either them or myself of those natural affections.'[15] Jack wrote back, blaming post going astray, and his father mildly replied that it gave him 'much pleasure to hear that you are so well beloved in the regiment to which you have the honour to belong'. Now Jack was in Weymouth, within easy reach of home, and soon, to their great excitement, he did at last visit them 'after the very very long absence'.

The British fleet, however, did not come home. After the Nile the press reported Nelson's triumphant arrival at Naples, where he was met by an ecstatic royal family and stayed with the British ambassador, Sir William Hamilton, and his wife, Emma, thirty-three, voluptuous, famed for her picturesque poses and 'attitudes'. Only three days into his stay, Nelson wrote home to his wife, Fanny, that he hoped some day to introduce her to 'one of the very best women in this world'.[16] Eyebrows were raised, and over the next six months sceptics began to question Nelson's judgement. Lingering in Naples, he was instrumental, or so critics thought, in persuading King Ferdinand to confront the French. In November 1798 a Neapolitan army marched north and entered Rome, only to be driven back within weeks. As the French approached Naples, the royal family fled to Palermo in Sicily on Nelson's *Vanguard*, and in January 1799, local republicans seized the fortress and let the French in. Their short-lived republic was brutally suppressed five months later when the British fleet helped to return Ferdinand to power: five hundred republicans were imprisoned and ninety-nine executed, including the patriot Caracciolo, hung from the yardarm of the *Minerva*.

If Nelson's reputation was tarnished by events in Sicily, Napoleon's glitter was also looking scuffed. Deprived of support from the sea, he marched his army north from Egypt to Syria and Palestine, capturing Gaza and Jaffa. He was stopped in May 1799 when Turkish soldiers, helped by a British squadron under the maverick Sir Sidney Smith, trapped the French troops as they were besieging Acre, the old Crusader fortress on the coast.

Amid stories of atrocities – he was said to have massacred thousands of Turkish and Albanian prisoners in Jaffa and poisoned his own plague-stricken soldiers so they would not be a burden – Napoleon retreated to Cairo and slipped back to France. But his Egyptian venture sent ripples far beyond the Mediterranean. The previous year, the Secret Committee of the East India Company had informed its three presidencies in Bombay, Madras and Calcutta of Napoleon's intentions to use Egypt as a doorway to the east, saying that the Company was sending out four thousand trooops. Encouraged by Dundas, the new Governor General, Richard Wellesley (created Marquess Wellesley at the end of this year), was quick to turn his forces against Napoleon's potential ally, Tipu Sultan. Known as the 'Tiger of Mysore', Tipu followed his father in his fierce opposition to the East India Company, and his French-trained troops had already fought the Company's armies in bitter wars over the past two decades. As the Muslim ruler of a Hindu state, he was pilloried in the British press for his alleged cruelty to Christians. His new overtures to France (he sent an embassy to Paris and planted a liberty tree in his capital, Seringapatam) served as pretext for a fourth Mysore war, yet another attempt to crush him. In January 1799 the combined troops of the East India Company and the Nizam of Hyderabad marched with their camels and elephants across the border into Mysore. The Hyderabad army was led by Colonel Arthur Wellesley, the governor's younger brother, who campaigned in style, adding his own regiment, the 33rd, and bringing thirty servants and all his silver plate with him.

In May, after a long siege, they breached the walls of Seringapatam and Tipu Sultan was killed in the city's defence. His six pet tigers were shot and Arthur Wellesley, silver plate and all, moved into his palace. Swathes of territory were divided up between the East India Company and the Nizam of Hyderabad. Among the soldiers there was William Harness, temporarily Lieutenant-Colonel of the 74th Highland Regiment of Foot. 'The 74th has suffered in Officers', Harness told his wife:

But the prize articles and plunder is immense. Large Ingots of Gold have been sold by the Soldiers for ten Pagodas and very valuable Jewels for a Bottle of Brandy. In walking round the Fort my amazement is at every step heightened at the possibility of a Fortress of such strength, defended by half an Empire, falling before the courage and conduct of a handful of Determined Men. The carnage of a sacked capital can be imagined. Thousands threw themselves over the ramparts into the Cauvery. Its rapid stream is infected for miles . . . The money and Jewels that are now sealed by the Prize Agent exceeds a million Sterling.[17]

A hoard of Tipu's glorious possessions was brought to England, including a beautifully painted life-size wooden tiger mauling a European man, containing a mechanical pipe organ playing the tiger's growls and the victim's shrieks. At East India House, and eventually in the British Museum, the tiger attracted crowds, including John

Keats, who wrote of Tipu's 'Man-Tiger-Organ' in his last poem, 'The Jealousies'.[18]

Seringapatam spurred the usual extravaganza of prints and songs, and on 2 May 1800 William Godwin went with John Opie to see 'Porter's Seringapatam', a huge panorama at the Lyceum, painted by Robert Ker Porter, which caused a sensation in London.[19] But at the time of the siege itself, the theatrical hit was Sheridan's *Pizarro*, his adaptation of translations of Kotzebue's *Die Spanien in Peru*, starring John Philip Kemble, Sarah Siddons and Dorothy Jordan.[20] Audiences saw Sheridan's rendering of the Spanish conquest of Peru not as a parallel with British imperialism in India, or as a statement of support for the United Irishmen's fight to free their land, but as Britain threatened by French invaders. Kemble's speech as the Peruvian general Rolla roused audiences to a fever:

THEY by a frenzy driven, fight for power, for plunder and extended rule – WE, for our country, our altars and our homes. – THEY follow an Adventurer whom they fear – WE serve a Monarch whom we love – a God whom we adore.

. . . Be our plain answer this: The throne we honour is the PEOPLE'S CHOICE – the laws we reverence are our brave fathers' legacy – the faith we follow teaches us to live in bonds of charity with all mankind, and die with hope of bliss beyond the grave. Tell your invaders this, and tell them too, we seek no change; and least of all, such change as they would bring us.

The defence of people's rights and the anti-imperialist tone harked back to Sheridan's Foxite days but this was a thoroughly loyalist show: Wilberforce went to see it, his first visit to the theatre in twenty years, and so did Pitt and Nelson. On 5 June George III appeared in the royal box, enjoying, said *The Times*, 'the bursts of patriotic enthusiasm and exulting Loyalty' on his arrival, and being 'particularly gratified with the noble and animated address of Rolla to the Peruvians in support of their just rights as an independent and happy people, against the lawless encroachment and savage ambition of foreign invaders'.[21] The play was put on all over the country: in October James Oakes reported that it was the alderman's choice at the playhouse in Bury St Edmunds.

## 24. 'THE DISTRESSEDNESS OF THE TIMES'

In December 1798, as food shortages threatened again, householders were shocked to find that Pitt was planning an entirely new tax, not on land or assets, dogs or servants, but on income. Pitt's guess was that the total national income, from land rental, mines and canals and capital invested in trade, amounted to just over £100 million; his aim was to take a tenth. He proposed a general, though temporary, tax of 10 per cent – two shillings in the pound – on all annual incomes over £200. Those with incomes below £60 would be exempt and those earning between £60 and £200 would pay on a sliding scale, beginning at two pence in the pound. People would have to assess their own income, report it and swear that it was accurate. By Christmas Elizabeth Heber was worried. Responding to her brother Reginald's plea to send him books from Hatchard's, Elizabeth asked him again to 'send the Odd hundred remaining in the Bond . . . to enable me to answer *Mr Pitts demands the ensuing year*'.[1] She and her sister Anne resorted hopefully to the lottery. Their niece Mary later followed their example, asking Elizabeth to get her 'a Ticket in the Lottery for the Pigott Diamond & send it in the next letter. – Wish me good Luck & let this be a *great Secret* to all but Papa,' adding, as postscript, 'It is but 11,427 to one – & what is that if a Woman has Luck?'[2]

Although the bill met a barrage of opposition, it went through quickly in January 1799, swept along by the emergency. The tax was to be paid in six equal instalments from June. Income was declared under five headings: from land, from rents, from public securities and funds, from trade, professions, business and investments at home and overseas, and from employment. Many people found it hard to work out what their income actually was and puzzled over expenses. Some gave up and made completely false statements. Others asked their bank or local vicar to help them – 'Mr Burrell here in the Eveng to help Mr H & Wm. through the New Income Tax,' wrote Mary Hardy.[3] (Burrell's obituary noted that as a Commissioner for Taxes he had to 'digest the numerous and frequently contradictory Acts' and although a loyal government man, 'it was his practice always to stand between the tax-charger and the tax-payer' whenever he thought a demand was unfair.[4])

A tax on the income of the rich meant little to people whose children were hungry. On New Year's Day 1799 William Rowbottom noted, 'Roast Beef Pyes and Ale are not to be seen in the poor mans table on the contery it is graced with Misery and Want and a universal lowness of spirits and dejected countinance appear in every one.'[5] A few weeks later no one in his district could remember weaving being at such a low ebb, with wages falling and the cost of wheat and oats rising. It was a terrible time, with perpetual snow. When another fast day was announced, wrote Rowbottom, 'in consequence of the distressedness of the times the poor kept more fast days than the Rich although the Rich strickely adeered to His Majestys proclamation'.[6]

The freezing wind blew on through February and March and into April. 'Last night was one of the most terrifick nights ever remembered by the oldest person living,' said Rowbottom on 5 April, writing almost lyrically of gales and drifts and coaches stopped in their tracks. When the snow turned to rain, it froze within minutes on hedges and trees and roads. The cold was bitter everywhere: in Suffolk that month James Oakes wrote in red ink down the side of his diary, 'N.B. The Town has been remarkably distressd for Coals for 6 weeks or 2 months back; most of the Inhabitants oblig'd to burn nothing but wood &

Isaac Cruikshank's *A General Fast in consequence of the War!*, drawn in the
first hunger of 1794–5. The Archbishop of Canterbury guzzles, while
Spitalfield's weavers starve and poor clergy emigrate

Turf. This, added to the uncommonly cold Season, has made it most
distressing.'[7] In distant Germany, William and Dorothy Wordsworth
wintered out the coldest night of the century.

In the non-spring of 1799 the birds failed to sing. As late as mid-
May, snowdrifts lay on the fields. There was no hay for the horses,
livestock suffered and the price of meat rose. In the textile towns
of Lancashire, many small masters, unable to find credit, had been
laying off men and were facing bankruptcy, and the cotton weavers
began to form a solid organisation to petition for regulation of their
wages. In Yorkshire, the croppers protesting about the gig-mills that
let one unskilled man do the work of three experts set up a union, the
Institution, threatening to strike if the merchants took on a journey-
man who was not a member or had not served an apprenticeship.[8]
In response to the growing power of the unions, Pitt's government
passed the Combination Acts of 1799 and 1800, pulling together
a whole history of acts dealing with individual trades – one consequence being that workers across the country felt united for the first
time. The first Act decreed that anyone trying to strike or merely

meeting to discuss wages and conditions could be prosecuted. They would appear before a single magistrate – often an employer himself – and only one witness was needed. The second Act, responding to an outcry against the first, specified two magistrates instead of one, a mighty concession.

There were frosts in June and floods in July. In the Pennine valleys the waters rose so fast that loom-shops, houses, mills, weirs, dams, bridges, sheep and horses were all swept away. And the war knocked insistently on the door. In Oldham letters arrived 'from the East Indies giving an account of the death of John Needham and Benjamen Needham, Ammy Jones, William Butterworth and wife, all of the 12th Regement of Foot'.[9] All these men, and Butterworth's unnamed wife, had been on the long march across India to the siege of Seringapatam.

In September uncut hay rotted in the meadows and unripe wheat blackened. Storms and hail killed hens and geese and pigs. Workmen sold furniture and pawned clothes to feed their families. 'But even Fine Weather now will hardly repair the Harm that Bad Weather has done,' wrote Amabel Hume-Campbell:

I expect continually to hear of some Resolution for eating Brown Bread & leaving off Puddings Cakes & Pies, but to begin before others would be an affectation of singularity. I am surpriz'd there should have been less of those Self-Denials talked of than Four Years ago when the Harvest was not in fact so bad, but I take it the Rich do not care to begin Self-Denial when the Poor hardly thank them for it. At least I hear Sir Joseph Banks says he will eat Brown Bread when the Poor will consent to eat it.[10]

Pitt did indeed pass a Brown Bread Act, banning millers from selling anything except wholewheat flour. In Middleton, on the outskirts of Manchester, Samuel Bamford remembered: 'Our bread was generally made from barley, and tough, hard, dark-coloured stuff it was. Instead of wheaten flour, we had a kind of mixture which was nick-named "ran-dan" or "brown George", and sad rubbish George proved to be.'[11] The boys hid oatcakes made from adulterated meal 'as a delectable snack to be eaten at leisure'. But as Joseph Banks implied, the poor refused to eat brown bread. Brown George was so unpopular that the statute was repealed within two months.

James Oakes and his fellow justices and Poor Law Guardians in Bury St Edmunds ordered alternatives to bread for the 'out-poor', such as herrings, potatoes, rice and meal. Here, as in many towns, shopkeepers and small traders aggrieved at the rising poor rate urged the Guardians to 'Badge the poor' – under an old law of 1697 paupers could be made to wear a 'P' on their right shoulder. Oakes voted against this, noting that more and more people needed temporary help and it would be a very great hardship to badge them.[12] When Oakes's son Orbell was sworn in as alderman, he made a 'short but appropriate Speech on the present critical Times from the exorbitant Prices of every necessary of Life &c.', and then laid on a cold buffet for a hundred dignitaries – not for the poor – at the Angel Inn.[13] And on the great estates the Christmas largesse followed its old hierarchical pattern. Betsey Fremantle, staying at Stowe, recorded the private dinner on Lady Buckingham's birthday, 'and after we went to see the dance and supper that is given to all the neighbouring farmers – the Ladies danced with them till 10 o'clock.' Next day, 'Three hundred poor people dined here today on the remains of last night's supper.'[14]

The bad harvest and the impossibility of sowing winter wheat in the waterlogged ground made the new year look bleak. In his *Local Records* for 1800, John Sykes of Newcastle noted that in January the harvest was so backward that oats were still standing uncut across the southern parts of Northumberland:

In consequence of the failure of the above harvest, together with the effects of war, a great dearth prevailed, and wheat in Newcastle market was frequently sold at two guineas a boll, two Winchester bushels. A subscription was formed at Durham for assisting the poor of that city and its neighbourhood. The hall of St. Nicholas' workhouse was fitted up as a soup kitchen, and a great quantity of soup, &c., was distributed to the poor at a very moderate charge.[15]

A month later there was chaos in Sunderland market place when a dealer charged high prices for corn. People raked the gutter for dirt to pelt him with, and when he hid in the Fountain inn they hurled stones and brickbats through the windows and trundled his carts into the river. The Riot Act was read, the Justice of the Peace fled, and the militia were called out, loading their muskets.

The spring of 1800 looked promising, and the hay crop was good, the scent of the stacks drifting far over the fields. Yet the price of bread stayed high. By April, flour that had cost just over one shilling a peck at the start of the war was between four and five shillings. Labourers cut bacon, the cheapest meat, out of their diets. Nettles became popular, selling for twopence a pound, eaten with salt and pepper: 'Nettles, parliance, docks, green saus, water cresses &c are plucked up by the poor people as a substitute for potatoes,' wrote Rowbottom, 'and scores of poor wretches are wandering in a forlorn state eagerously picking up any sorts of vegetables which fall their way.'[16] Workers blamed bakers, bakers blamed millers, millers blamed dealers, middlemen and farmers, accusing them (often correctly) of making private deals or holding back stocks, banking on even higher prices. Some bakers certainly did well. J. M. W. Turner's uncle Jonathan went into business in Barnstaple this year, and twelve years later wrote boastfully to his brother that he now had a house worth £700, had bought a flour loft and had 'some money beside to carry on the trade so I leave you to judge whether I have done well or not and if I live and I be in business as long as you and brother Price I shall be cock of the walk'.[17]

The previous year, in Penrith, Joanna Hutchinson was writing to her cousin, eighteen-year-old John Monkhouse, apprentice to a London wine merchant. The nine Hutchinson children had been left orphans in 1785 and were largely brought up by their mother's sister Elizabeth Monkhouse in Penrith, where they became friendly with the young Wordsworths. In 1795 Joanna's elder brothers, Tom, John and George, in their early twenties, had taken over a family farm at Sockburn, in a great loop of the river Tees in County Durham: their sisters, Mary and Sara, looked after the house. The teenage Joanna

– 'Jobby' as her sisters called her – had stayed with her aunt, and now wrote about friends and romances, dances and hats. They were scrubbing and cleaning, she said, and worrying about money. Her brother John and friends Tanty Wilkinson and John Robinson were 'at present in the parlor, disputing upon Banking and Mr Robinson is as usual very *knowing*'.[18]

John Monkhouse, trying to settle in London, longed for such news. He thought of home often, he told his grandfather, even in 'the gayest City in Europe' and he did not see the food shortages when he imagined his family in the north: 'fancy you are smoking your pipe at the Barn Door Hannah spinning at the Window and the Bairns plucking Berries in the Garden.' He was living in Pudding Lane – 'what kind of pudding?' asked Joanna. His salary was low and he had to be thrifty as 'things are very high'. The washerwoman asked for two guineas – more than the rent of a cottage, 'but I would not comply with such an extravagant demand and chose rather to wash by the week which will cost about 6 guineas per year, a good Coat costs £3.3 and a pair breeches £1-5'. Though John was not one for religion, he liked his master, Mr Bush, and went with him every day to Rowland Hill Chapel in Blackfriars. Bush was a Methodist, a 'strong professor', and they had family prayers every night, 'but he is a bumbling hand at them', and he read grace 'before and after meat amidst the giggling of his Children who laugh at his pomposity'.[19] By September, John had tired of Bush: 'He knows nothing of gauging or of the strength or goodness of Liquors and all the Customhouse and Quay business he leaves to the management of people who know nought of it themselves.'[20] But John was forced to stay on, as 'places are so very hard to meet with unless Buonaparte gives those invincible allies of ours another good drubbing and forces them and Mr Pitt into a Peace then most likely the Trade will be brisk again. Every body here is anxious for Peace and many men who were strong Pittites heartily wish for the defeat of the Allies.'

When the new year came John moved to another firm, Lindley & Zimmerman, and took lodgings with a wig maker in Shoe Lane, off

Fleet Street. It was 'not a very genteel part of the Town', he admitted. A French teacher had the front room, which served as a sitting room for them both, and they moved the well-patched chairs when other French emigrants came round. Among them, he said, 'I speak nothing but French.'[21] But John also saw growing tension, even in the heart of the capital. 'The greatest distress prevails in London amongst the poor', he told Joanna, 'on account of the dearness of every kind of provision and were it not for the support of a few benevolent Institutes many families would actually starve for want.'

The troops and militia often sympathised, as they had in the shortages of five years before. In Devon the fencibles and volunteer yeomanry joined a Brixham crowd who went round local farms asking farmers to sell their grain more cheaply. When volunteers were asked to put down disturbances many refused and others did it with heavy hearts. Teesdale Cockerell, leader of the Pontefract Volunteers, described how he 'trembled at the Idea of Marching out against the Starved Poor, I really felt my self a Coward, & yet I knew it was a Duty I must display Energy in. I only was out twice & thank God the Appearance of the Corps threw a Panic upon the Poor Starved People.'[22] Walter Scott's cavalry troop were on duty in Portsburgh during the looting of a bread shop, and later he told his son-in-law John Lockhart, 'Truth to say it was a dreadful feeling to use violence against a people in real and absolute want of food.'[23]

People with secure incomes had now begun to feel the pinch: artisans, traders, small masters, schoolteachers and clerks, whose pride would never let them apply for poor relief. Rowbottom noted a spate of robberies. Fevers swept the workhouses and beggars filled the streets. Suicides rose.

19th April. Earley this morning John Lord of Uin Nook Northmoor cut his throat in a shocking manner and afterwards threw himself into a coalpit where he was found dead. It is supposed pressure of the times and he being at that time attacked with a fever that threw him into a state of frenzy.[24]

Ragged children picked potato peelings off the dunghills and beat off stray dogs competing for bones thrown out of kitchens.[25] In the view of Malthus, whose *Essay on the Principle of Population* had been published a couple of years earlier, there were too many of these children already – the problem of the rising population had to be faced. As William Blake wrote in *The Four Zoas*, this conviction made the authorities more determined to contain the growing 'mob', cloaking repression as charity:

> Compell the poor to live upon a Crust of Bread by soft mild arts
> Smile when they frown & when a man looks pale
> With labour & abstinence say he looks healthy & happy
> And when his children sicken let them die there are enough
> Born even too many & our Earth will be overrun.

As workers demanded the repeal of the Combination Acts, the government stance hardened and almost any meeting was seen as seditious. But in July 1800 the Revd Heber was less worried about radicals than speculators, telling his sister Elizabeth that after three weeks of fine weather in Shropshire they looked forward to a fine hay harvest. He felt that when there was 'so much Corn on Shipboard & in the Granaries it is shameful it should be withheld from the Market' and the price of bread kept so high. 'The cruel Speculators in this necessary Article of Man's Sustenance will, tis to be hoped, in the long run be disappointed in their Avaricious Views.'[26] In the autumn, although he still railed against 'Forestallers and Monopolizers of Every denomination', he had begun to worry that food shortages would fuel other political demands: 'That Peace and plenty may prevail at home, & that the pestilent movers of Sedition & Outrage may be disarm'd of every pretence for disturbing the tranquillity and violating the Laws of the Land, is a Prayer devoutly to be proferr'd to that Omnipotent Being who stilleth the raging of the Waves and the Madness of the People.'[27]

Hunger did indeed stir latent republican feeling, and posters and broadsheets once more looked to France as an example. In Somerset a local poet called on 'half starv'd Britons':

Then raise yr drooping spirits up
Nor starve by Pitt's decree
Fix up the sacred Guillotine
Proclaim – French liberty!²⁸

Trouble began in the north and spiralled down from Sheffield to Derby, across the Midlands from Leicester to Oxford and then into London. On 15 September, a crowd of two thousand gathered at the grain exchange in Mark Lane and when the militia dispersed them they roamed the streets, breaking bakers' windows and sacking merchants' houses. For three days the tumults continued. Claude Scott, who had done so well out of the hunger of 1795 and now controlled a quarter of London imports, threatened to stop dealing unless the authorities cracked down on the popular agitation against traders to lower their prices.²⁹ In parliament the Denbighshire MP Thomas Jones expressed the resentment of working people. 'Contractors and loan-mongers are the only persons who have not been impoverished by the war,' he declared: 'War is life to the contractor, and death to the landed man. War is life to the loan-jobber, and death to the peasant; life to the jobber, and death to the mechanic; life to the remitter, and death to the shopkeeper; life to the clothier and death to the labourer.'³⁰

Even conservative politicians, judges and clergymen accused 'engrossers and forestallers' of combining to keep prices high. Yet most middlemen were small traders rather than plutocratic villains. Young John Monkhouse was a useful London contact for his family, particularly his cousin John Hutchinson (Jack), a widower with two small girls. He was farming at Sockburn in County Durham but trying to become a dealer, cashing in during the shortages. In May 1799, he had told John Monkhouse:

I am going into the Butter Trade this summer & any of my Customers that you see you may tell them so – You may tell Mr Wilson that he need not be afraid of making money of his Hams – he may rest assured that in a little Time everything of Provisions will be extravagantly dear – The spring is so dreadfully backward there can be neither grass nor hay to feed with & all kinds of meat rise here every week. Bacon, I could sell any quantity if I had it

. . . Butter must be very scarce & I am determined to speculate in the Article as far as prudence & Cash will permit.[31]

The butter speculation was not a winner but the 'Bacon business' proved so successful that soon Jack asked John Monkhouse to help with 'sale of my pork'. But by December 1801, he was complaining that pigs were now scarce so farmers were keeping their prices up and shipping costs were high. 'Nick Nottle the great Bacon & Pork man at Penrith has failed,' he wrote, and now local banks were going under, '. . . & last week Mr Simpson & his Partner Taylorson of Stokesley were both arrested & sent to Prison'. The Simpson bank, opened only four years before, was soon declared bankrupt.[32] Not all middlemen made a fortune.

The pressure for peace grew. In Lancashire, defying the Gagging Acts, thousands flocked to great peace meetings.[33] Amid the hunger and anxiety, Thomas Spence published a pamphlet arguing that hereditary titles and private ownership of land should all be abolished. Describing an altercation with the Duke of Portland's forester, who stopped him collecting nuts in a wood near Hexham, he asked what had happened to the people's birthright. If the French invaders came, he asked, and 'jeeringly ask what I am fighting for? Must I tell them for my country? For my dear country in which I dare not pluck a nut? Would they not laugh at me?'[34] Rather than stand for that he would throw down his musket and say: 'let such as the Duke of Portland, who claim the country, fight for it, for I am a stranger and sojourner, and have neither part nor lot amongst them.' Arrested in late May 1801, Spence was found guilty of seditious libel, fined £20, imprisoned for a year and bound to find £500 for five years' good behaviour.

## 25. GOD ON OUR SIDE

In the hungry months, middle-class citizens everywhere handed out coals and doled out pea soup. In Bridgnorth, Shropshire, Mary Martha Butt – the future author Mrs Sherwood – and her sister 'went among the poor', as she put it, going to one house a day with enough bread, butter, tea and sugar for one meal, and sometimes with less practical, or palatable, items:

These articles we bought, with our own savings, at the shops as we passed along. Thus wore away the winter, and part of the spring, during which time I wrote two tracts, one entitled 'The Potatoes,' in which I well remember describing the day of judgment, invested with all its horrors. The motto of this story was 'this night thy soul shall be required of thee.' The other tract was called 'The Baker's Dream,' of which I forget the particulars.[1]

Mary Martha, a clergyman's daughter, was alert to the times. One of the surprises of this decade was the success of Hannah More's 'Cheap Repository tracts'.[2] The first had been published in March 1795 by the Bath printer Samuel Hazard, and the series had eventually swelled to 120 small books, sold for a penny or two, warning against drunkenness and idleness, gambling and lust, and recommending honesty and thrift. Above all they were designed to encourage the poor to accept their place and avoid the desire to rise above their station.

Hannah More was then in her early fifties. As a brilliant young woman she had made a name as a bluestocking and lively London playwright, but in later life became increasingly serious and set up Sunday schools and evening classes with her sisters near their home in the Mendips. Her views in her *Estimate of the Religion of the Fashionable World*, published in 1790, were close to those of her new evangelical friends, William Wilberforce, Zachary Macaulay and the bishop of London, Beilby Porteus. The idea for the tracts grew from her tale *Village Politics*, commissioned by Porteus, which lampooned Tom Paine's ideas in a fictional dialogue between a blacksmith and a mason. Writing to her old friend Elizabeth Montagu, More pointed out how eagerly village people waited for the hawkers and how avidly they read the chapbook tales of ghosts, highwaymen and heroes. More alarming still, they read the democratic urgings of Joseph Priestley and others, based, in her view, on the French *philosophes*. 'I begin to fear that *our* workmen and porters will become *philosophers* too,' she wrote, 'and that an endeavor to amend the morals and the principles of the poor is the most probable method to preserve us from the crimes and calamities of France.'[3] The potential appeal of atheism was almost worse. As she put it to Zachary Macaulay: 'Vulgar and indecent penny books were always common, but speculative infidelity, brought down to the pocket and capacities of the poor, forms a new era in our history. This requires strong counteraction.'[4] She would replace this French 'poison' with her own halfpenny papers.

To the astonishment of More and her backers, within three weeks three hundred thousand tracts were sold and within a year the number reached two million, an unheard-of figure. More wrote more than half of them herself, dishing out others to her sisters and friends, and explained their success as due to her subscribers: employers gave them to workers and servants; parish officials and visitors handed them out in hospitals, workhouses and prisons; clergymen thrust them on congregations; officers scattered them among the ranks. Her cleverest stroke was to persuade the pedlars and chapmen to take them, at first promising a commission and then paying them to hand the tracts out free. Although More's own series had ended in December 1797, the publishers issued seventy-three more over the next two years.

Religion was debated more fiercely in this decade than it had been for a generation. The fear of atheism felt by Hannah More was repeated constantly, given added impetus by Paine's *Age of Reason*, published in two parts in 1794 and 1795, a vigorous deistic – not atheistic – work. In his Preface Paine explained that he had been thinking of writing on religion for several years, and this would be his 'last offering' to the public. But it was important:

The circumstance that has now taken place in France of the total abolition of the whole national order of priesthood, and of everything appertaining to compulsive systems of religion, and compulsive articles of faith, has not only precipitated my intention, but rendered a work of this kind exceedingly necessary, lest in the general wreck of superstition, of false systems of government, and false theology, we lose sight of morality, of humanity, and of the theology that is true.[5]

His attack was not on faith, he said; 'I believe in one God, and no more; and I hope for happiness beyond this life.' He could not, however, accept unthinking belief in the truth of the Bible, and he went on to dissect the 'fables', absurdities, inconsistencies and 'downright lies' of Old Testament stories and New Testament miracles, urging the use of reason in place of belief in revelation.[6] This brought instant reactions both from churchmen and dissenters, including accusations that he was the tool of Satan. One horrified minister claimed Bibles had been burnt in Scottish manufacturing towns by readers of the *Age of Reason*.[7] And since Paine also attacked the close links – real and symbolic – between Church and King, to loyalists his book was an attack on the whole philosophy of subordination to the state, and was therefore seditious. At the same time his assault on the Bible alienated many supporters of rational dissent, disturbing their allegiance to ideas of reform and driving deist radicalism underground.[8]

The idea of revelation that Paine dismissed as nonsense was central to the current evangelical revival, which put a dramatic focus on inner conflict, on the work of the Devil, on redemption through faith – the leap from the darkness of the soul into a blessed light – and on the final judgement. It was profoundly emotional, full of hopes and terrors and a sense of being scrutinised by the all-seeing eye of God. At its heart was a conviction of original sin, with redemption made possible by the atonement of Christ on the cross. A human being, declared Wilberforce, is 'degraded in his nature and depraved in his faculties: indisposed to good, and disposed to evil; prone to vice – it is natural and easy to him; disinclined to virtue – it is difficult and laborious; he is tainted with sin, not slightly and superficially, but radically and to the very core.'[9] The central experience was conversion, a flooding of the soul with God's grace, a melting of the individual will.

Works and faith and constant self-examination must begin in the family, where husband and wife should bring up their children in the light of Christ (many of these children, like the historian Tom Macaulay, grew up to be markedly secular), and while the man, strong yet sensitive, went out into the world, the wife and mother must be a moral improver at home. Particular households showed the way like lighthouses, and the brightest of all was that of the banker Henry Thornton and his wife Marianne near Clapham Common, which became the centre of a community of friends, including William and Barbara Wilberforce, the barrister James Stephen, who married Wilberforce's widowed sister Sarah, and Zachary Macaulay and his wife, Hannah More's protégée Selina Hill. These powerful men, with connections to law, trade, banking and empire, joined forces with the clergyman Henry Venn and others to form a group that the witty commentator and cleric Sydney Smith sarcastically called 'the Clapham Sect' or 'Saints'. Their text, outside the Bible and their own sermons, was Cowper's *The Task* – a poem loved by Burns, Coleridge and Austen and many thousands of readers. The evangelical man would be the opposite of the city-dweller 'loose in morals, and in manners vain,/In conversation frivolous, in dress extreme'. Instead, wrote Cowper,

> I venerate the man whose heart is warm,
> Whose hands are pure, whose doctrine and whose life,
> Coincident, exhibit lucid proof
> That he is honest in the sacred cause.[10]

A conviction that the war was a judgement of God upon the sins of the nation boosted the movement from the start. As the Revd John Stonard wrote to Richard Heber:

I cannot regard the present scene or look forward to what is coming without the most awful feelings. I do on my conscience believe that the Divine Wrath is manifesting itself against the sinful nations of Europe. Whether the Vengeance of God, now that it is aimed against our transgressions will be appeased by anything short of our destruction as an Independent Nation, is among the secret things of Omniscience. But let us not run into the evils we may justly dread.[11]

In parliament the evangelicals had now become increasingly prominent. The charming, energetic and sociable Wilberforce, a close friend of Pitt, had been a Hull MP since he was twenty-one, and had experienced an evangelical conversion in 1785, writing in his diary, 'God almighty has set before me two great objects, the suppression of the Slave Trade and the Reformation of Manners.'[12] The title of his 1797 book made his stance clear: *A Practical View of the Prevailing Religious System of Professed Christians, in the Higher and Middle Classes of this Country, contrasted with Real Christianity*. Much of the *Practical View* proclaimed the corruption of the human spirit and the check that 'real' religion would place on worldly ambitions, the greed for 'magnificent houses, grand equipages, numerous retinues, splendid entertainments, high and fashionable connections'.[13] The French example was held up to horrify. What would happen if religion was discarded?

It is upon this very ground that the Infidels of a neighbouring country have lately made war against Christianity, with what effects the world has not now to learn. But suppose Religion were discarded, then Liberty remains to plague the world; a power which though when well employed, the dispenser of light and happiness, has often proved, and eminently in the instance of a neighbouring country, to be capable, when abused, of becoming infinitely mischievous.[14]

His final exhortation was to educate the young to avoid 'the present state of France; where, it is to be feared, a brood of moral vipers, as it were, is now hatching'.[15] (Serious as he was, Wilberforce could still be impulsive: in the month that *A Practical View* was published, he met Barbara Spooner in Bath, fell in love, proposed within a fortnight and married a month later: they moved into a new house built by Henry Thornton in the garden of his Clapham mansion. Six children were born there in the next ten years and Wilberforce loved and played with them all.)

Wilberforce built up a cohort of about forty members in the Commons, and evangelical influence was also strong in the army, navy and City. Its power showed in a rash of new societies, from the Church Missionary Society in 1799 and the Society for Promoting the Religious Instruction of Youth in 1800 to the nicely named Female Friendly Society for the Relief of Poor, Infirm, Aged Widows and Single Women of Good Character, Who Have Seen Better Days.[16] In 1802, Wilberforce would join the loyalist pamphleteer John Bowles in founding the Society for the Suppression of Vice, whose stated aim was the 'safeguarding of public morals'. But as critics noted, the society was happy to attack working-class gambling and drinking and clear away beggars and ballad singers, yet ducked immorality among the wealthy, whose patronage it sought. It was really, said Sydney Smith a few years later, a 'Society for suppressing the vices of persons whose income does not exceed £500 per annum'. Attacking immorality was one thing, but why deny the poor any pleasure? Why shouldn't they sing and dance, for example?

The trespass, however, which calls forth all the energies of a suppressor, is the sound of a fiddle. That the common people are really enjoying themselves, is now beyond all doubt: and away rush Secretary, President, and Committee, to clap the cotillon into the Compter, and to bring back the life of the poor to its regular standard of decorous gloom. The gambling houses of St. James's remain untouched. The peer ruins himself and his family with impunity;

while the Irish labourer is privately whipped for not making a better use of the excellent moral and religious education which he has received in the days of his youth![17]

Perhaps inspired by the new society, James Oakes, who liked a good drink, toured his town as alderman with the churchwarden and stopped at about twenty pubs, counting the drinkers 'all tippling during Divine Service'.[18]

In May 1799 a Commons debate confirmed the suspicion that if evangelicals were reformers, they were far from democrats. The topic was Lord Belgrave's Bill to stop the sale of newspapers on Sundays. Technically, by an odd conjunction of old laws, the only things that traders could sell were milk before nine o'clock and after four, and mackerel before or after divine service. Newspaper vendors must be arrested and gaoled, said Belgrave. 'It ought not to be forgotten', he went on, 'that we were the near neighbours of a nation, where irreligion had taken deep root, where the very name of a Sunday had been blotted out of the calendar; and that their practice, unless a legislative barrier were raised against it, would have an infectious tendency in this country.'[19] Defenders of press freedom spoke out. Surely reading the news was an innocent recreation? Many workers only had time to read papers on Sundays and a long gap between newspapers would make news stale. Might the noble Lord recollect, asked Sheridan, that people might think stale news as bad as stale mackerel? To which Wilberforce replied, sweeping aside such frivolity, that newspapers were not 'innocent recreation':

The people could only innocently recreate themselves by attending to their religious duties; and the due and regular observance of the worship of that day could alone mend their hearts, and fit them for that condition in which the reward of piety is everlasting happiness. If the publishing and selling of newspapers should be permitted, then might hundreds of other trades be carried on on the Lord's day.[20]

Well, said Sheridan, the greatest Sunday-breakers he could think of 'were His Majesty's Ministers, whose Sunday dinners so often forced the poor cook and hundreds more who assist on such occasions to set religion quite at naught'. This time the irreligious won, and on a third reading the Bill was rejected.

The resurgence of intense piety within the church and the dissenting sects was seen in the many new chapels, the spread of charities and an explosion of religious literature – over a hundred new religious journals between 1790 and 1820. It was not all harmonious. Evangelicals were often at odds with High Church Anglicans, although the Anglicans too pressed the poor to be resigned to their status, and had their own propagandists, like Sarah Trimmer (author of *Fabulous Histories, or The Story of the Robins*, promoting kindness to animals), who argued that admirers of the Revolution were conspiring against 'Christianity and all social order' and 'endeavouring to infect the minds of the rising generation, through the medium of *Books of Education* and *Children's Books*'.[21] But to many churchgoers, Anglicanism seemed complacent and flabby, and over the decade evangelicalism slowly won the contest, appealing to the lesser gentry and to merchants and manufacturers, not only because of its energy but because it gave them a status set by faith rather than lineage or wealth. The same applied to the rational, liberal Unitarians, whose congregations included leading manufacturers, merchants and professionals. Workers, on the other hand, flocked to the Baptists and Methodists, with their emphasis on personal piety and rejection of hierarchies, and their cottage and open field meetings and travelling preachers.

Many believers were happy to sample different sects, as long as they could hear a rousing sermon. Mary Hardy, from the Norfolk brewing family, stout and sensible and far from officiously pious, had begun going to Methodist services in the mid-1780s, giving up her fine clothes and flouncy hats for their simple plain dress. But she still went to the local church (though often disapproving of the vicar, the hospitable John Burrell, a firm Tory, keener on insect-collecting than sermons), and also trotted off to Baptist services and Quaker meetings, and to hear young evangelicals at Holt church. In the summer of

Mary Hardy in plain dress – but fine lace

1800, the Hardys and their daughter Mary Anne set out to London, where Mary's eye was firmly on church-going, of all varieties. The day after they arrived, the family had a triple dose: '*May 16 Fri*. Went to Shoreditch Church foornoon heard a missionary sermon. Mr. H. and M.A. went to the Jews' Synagogue. After tea we joined Mr Cook's and meeting.' Next day was Cripplegate Meeting, and then came Sunday:

*May 18 Sun*. A fine day. I went to a Chappel in Camomile Street Morng 7, heard A Sermon from Hebrews 11 Chaptr 25& 26 Verses. Mr Hardy, I, MA, Mr. Cook & Mr. Goggs went to Wesleys Chappel City Road, heard A Sermon there foornoon, went to Tooly St. Meeting with Mr. & Mrs. Cooke afternoon, heard Dr Reppon preach. Mr H. went with Mr Cook to a prayer meeting in the eveng. I & MA went to Bow Church, heard Mr Abdy preach.[22]

And so it went on, with sermons from every denomination, from the Baptist divine John Rippon to 'Mr Liberty, from Frome in Somerset' at Rowland Hill's famous chapel in Southwark, and the preachers in the great domed chapel in the former Pantheon, which had been taken over as a Methodist chapel by Selina, Countess of Huntington, and could hold up to 2,500 people. The text from Hebrews for the

sermon Mary heard in Camomile Street had admonished the congregation 'rather to suffer affliction with the people of God, than to enjoy
the pleasures of sin for a season', but she was not one for suffering.
She also went to the play and the pleasure gardens, to the exhibition
at Somerset House, to Fuseli's Milton Gallery in Pall Mall, and to
Barker's lavish panorama in Leicester Fields.[23]

Mary liked the leading role that women could play in the Wesleyan Methodists. A few years later in December 1808, three months
before she died, she would found a meeting house in her own village,
in the cottage of her washerwoman, Elizabeth Bullock. 'Mr King our
Traveling preacher came to dinner,' she noted on the day it opened.
'He preached from Acts 5 Chapt. 2 last Verse.'[24] That text was Peter's
address to the apostles at Pentecost, when 'suddenly there came a
sound from heaven as of a rushing mighty wind', and they spoke with
tongues of fire. The last verses run:

And all that believed were together, and had all things common; and sold
their possessions and goods, and parted them to all men, as every man had
need.

And they, continuing daily with one accord in the temple, and breaking
bread from house to house, did eat their meat with gladness and singleness
of heart, praising God, and having favour with all the people. And the Lord
added to the church daily such as should be saved.

The lure of a sharing community, however strict, could be very
strong. And although the numbers of nonconformists were still small
– by 1800 there were only around three hundred thousand in Britain's
ten million population – dissent formed the background of many future
reformers. The Chartist leader William Lovett remembered the long
Sundays in his Penzance childhood during the wars, when his otherwise
indulgent mother, 'belonging to the Methodist Connexion', enforced
strict attendance at chapel, with no books except Bible and Prayer Book,
and not even the relief of a walk. 'My poor mother', wrote Lovett,

thought that the great power that has formed the numerous gay sportive,
singing things of earth and air, must above all things be gratified with the

solemn faces, prim clothes, and half-sleepy demeanour of human beings; and that true religion consists in listening to the reiterated story of man's fall, of God's anger for his doing so, of man's sinful nature, of the redemption, and of other questionable matters, instead of the wonders and glories of the universe.[25]

Samuel Bamford's father, like Lovett's mother, had been 'a burning and a shining light' in the local Methodists and his aunt and uncle were great Methodist hymn singers and chapelgoers. As a boy Bamford longed to be converted, for the call to come. 'But there was no call for me,' he remembered wryly. What he really wanted, he realised later, was simply to get away from the hated bobbin wheel: 'I came to the conclusion that God never did nor ever would take the trouble to convince one of my condition, and that there was no religion in the world that could ever make a bobbin-winder content with his lot; – and so ended, at that time, my efforts for obtaining grace.'[26]

On two issues, dissenters, evangelicals and traditional Anglicans worked together: education and slavery. Thousands of children went to the Sunday schools set up in the 1780s by ecumenical committees, but over time the alliance had collapsed. In 1800 the Bishop of Rochester told his clergy regretfully that 'the Jacobins of this country' were, he was sorry to say, 'making a tool of Methodism': 'schools of atheism and disloyalty abound in this country; schools in the shape and disguise of Charity Schools and Sunday Schools, in which the minds of the children of the very lowest order are enlightened: that is to say taught to despise religion and the laws of all subordination.'[27]

Sometimes, to show their allegiance, the schools took to the streets, like the Anglican Sunday-school children who walked proudly in procession to Manchester's Collegiate Church on Whit Sunday. In Charlotte Brontë's *Shirley*, set in the later years of the war, Canon Helstone's school find their way blocked by 'the Dissenting and Methodist schools, the Baptists, Independents, and Wesleyans, joined in unholy alliance'. The dissenters sing lugubrious psalms but the Anglican children win with 'Rule Britannia': 'The enemy was sung and stormed down.'[28]

*The Cruel Treatment of the Slaves in the West Indies*, 1793

Setting aside their battles, enthusiastic Christians did, however, unite in the campaign to abolish the slave trade, which had grown in strength since the first committees were formed in the 1780s. Campaigning pamphlets and prints poured out. Before the war, in April 1792, after five hundred petitions were sent to parliament with seven hundred thousand signatures, Pitt himself had declared that he could think of no greater evil than 'the tearing of seventy or eighty thousand persons annually from their native land, by a combination of the most civilised nations, inhabiting the most enlightened quarter of the globe'.[29] There was no nation in Europe, he went on, 'that has, on the one hand, plunged so deeply into this guilt as Britain, or that is so likely, on the other, to be looked to as an example, if she should have the manliness to be the first in decidedly renouncing it'. Campaigners took heart, winning a Commons motion in favour of 'gradual' abolition. But Pitt's outrage was silently dropped when the war began.

The interests ranged against abolitionists were immense. Roughly one slaving ship a day left British ports, taking manufactured goods to Africa, carrying thousands of slaves from Africa across the Atlantic, crammed into their holds in intolerable conditions, and returning to Britain with tobacco and sugar. Many MPs and Lords had interests in the West Indies, and when pro-abolition papers like the *Leeds Intelligencer* and *Manchester Mercury* published harrowing evidence, a committee of the London Society of Planters and Merchants met in London to arrange a counter campaign.[30] Money from the West Indies was woven into British life, in banking and insurance, in the buying of country estates, in commerce and industry. The Galtons, for example, had long sold cheap guns to African traders to exchange for slaves. But how could this be, when prominent Quakers led the anti-slavery movement? This was one of the isues that had been raised when their fellow Quakers conducted the examination in 1796. Angrily, Samuel Galton answered that as far as his guns went, he could not be held responsible for their abuse: 'Is the Farmer who sows Barley, – the Brewer who makes it into Beverage, – the Merchant who imports Rum, or the Distiller who makes Spirits; – are *they* responsible for the *Intemperance*, the *Disease*, the *Vice*, and *Misery*, which may ensue from their Abuse?'[31] As for slavery, why should a gunmaker be held more responsible than those who traded in tobacco, rum, sugar, rice and cotton? But the argument continued, even in his own family. His daughter Mary Anne, who was eighteen at the time, was intensely religious, and abolition fired her whole being. At her grandfather's home at Dudson the campaigner Thomas Clarkson was a frequent visitor. 'In the evenings we often read pamphlets on the subject, or examined in detail the prints of slave ships and slave treatment,' she remembered, 'and both my cousins and I resolved to leave off sugar, as the only produce of slave labour within our province to discontinue.'[32]

Galton's anger that his trade was singled out for condemnation, when others were not, was beside the point, but it contained a sting. He had many friends and relations connected to the West India trades and their wealth appalled Mary Anne. The kindly, generous Liverpool merchants in particular, she wrote, lived in houses like palaces, with 'sumptuous drawing-rooms, rich with satin and silk'. At their parties, amid the brightly dressed, bejewelled women, she was stunned by the number of black servants:

almost all of whom had originally been slaves; this deeply moved my compassion, and when I saw the table laden with West India produce, in its various forms of fruit and sweetmeats, and saw the black servants looking on at the produce of a land, their native home, which they had left for us, and of which they might not partake, my heart often ached; and it is no wonder that my resolution was confirmed never to taste anything made with sugar, or to use other West Indian commodities.[33]

However much she was teased, she stuck fiercely to her protest. And her father stuck to his guns.

The tension in the Galton family was reflected in many others. Hannah Greg grew up among the Liverpool Unitarians, many of whom braved physical threats for standing out against the trade. Hannah herself wrote to William Rathbone: 'Surely in Ireland, in India and in Africa the English name must be for ever odious – expressive of Injustice, Arrogance and Cruelty.'[34] Yet while the men she admired, like William Rathbone, William Roscoe and the doctors James Currie and Thomas Percival, were abolitionists, her sister's husband was an African trader and her cousins, uncle and father sold cloth to the Africa merchants. Her husband, Samuel Greg, inherited a plantation in Dominica in 1796, leaving it to be run by local managers. After her marriage Hannah spoke out firmly on other issues, but on slavery she was silent.

She was not the only one. If Pitt had dropped the subject, so had the evangelical party in the Commons, pledged to support the ministry's effort in the war, particularly in the West Indies. Dissenting communities and Quaker groups kept up the fight, but as the century closed, many men in public life found it easier to focus on the wickedness of the poor, and the saving of one's soul, than to fight this particular godly fight.

## 26. 'GOOD MEN SHOULD NOW CLOSE RANKS'

War news filled the papers, as the conflict in Europe swung back and forth. In March 1799, at the battles of Ostrach and Stokach near the Black Forest, the Austrians defeated General Jourdan's Armée du Danube and drove the French back into Switzerland. Fitting this in with more pressing matters and dispensing with the difficult names, Mary Hardy wrote briskly, 'We all went to Mr. Z. Rouse's Sale. Bought a Large Dresser for £1-11-6, 2 blankets 7/- & Several other Articles to the amount of £6. Mrs Bartell dind here, Mrs Lebor & Miss Brathwait drank tea here. A Great Battle fought in Germany between the French & Austrians, the Austr. claimed the victory.'[1]

The British cabinet might have stood back from this land war if the passionate advocacy of Grenville as Foreign Secretary had not overridden Dundas's cautious warnings. Yet for once the news seemed positive. In Italy the Austrians slowly regained territory, with the help of the Russians under the powerful General Suvorov. The plan was that Austria would invade eastern France, Suvorov would defend Switzerland, and Britain would invade Holland. Attacked on all sides, France would falter. As part of the scheme, on 14 August Abercromby, who had been stationed in Scotland since his angry resignation in Ireland, sailed to Den Helder, opposite the island of Texel in north Holland, to join the Duke of York's forces and a section of the Russian army. The aim was to capture the Dutch fleet and promote an uprising under William, Prince of Orange.[2] All went well at first: the Dutch fleet surrendered, and the British took some territory inland. But help from Prussia and Sweden did not come and since the Dutch had flooded the surrounding polders there were no supplies. After weeks of hesitating, remembered in the nursery rhyme 'The Grand Old Duke of York', in mid-November the British troops left for home.

The outlook was bleak again. In the south, the Austrians were retreating and the Russian army was forced out of Switzerland in a terrible march over snowbound passes. And then all plans were shaken by events in France. Napoleon's return to Paris after the siege of Acre coincided with the *coup d'état* of 18 and 19 Brumaire, 9 and 10 November 1799, which swept away the Directory, replacing it with three consuls, Abbé Sieyès, Roger Ducos and Bonaparte himself, as First Consul.

W. Holland, *The Corsican Crocodile dissolving the Council of Frogs!!!*, November 1799. After Egypt Napoleon took the crocodile as a symbol: Holland shows him calling in his troops to throw out his opponents in the Council at St Cloud

Now Napoleon was no simple general, but head of the French government. In Britain he was an object of fascination and bafflement. Was he, as Pitt put it, 'the child and champion' of all Jacobin atrocities and horrors?[3] Or was he imposing order after revolutionary excesses? If so, why continue with the war? As to his religious views, was he a proponent of toleration or a restricter of religious rights? Was he a freethinker, an atheist or a Catholic? Was he a looter, a thief of culture, or a patron of the arts who was giving France, unlike Britain, a fine national collection?

His disillusioned radical supporters felt his elevation to power as a blow. In a leader, 'Advice to the Friends of Freedom', in the *Morning Post* in December Coleridge argued, 'Good men should now close ranks. Too much of extravagant hope, too much of rash intolerance, have disgraced all parties.'[4] Napoleon himself was merely 'a military despot, intoxicated with success'. Over the next few weeks, however, Coleridge mellowed: the coup might, he thought, be a shrewd temporary expedient, 'to exchange the forms of political freedom for the realities of civil security in order to make a real political freedom possible at some later period'.[5]

On Christmas Day 1799, emphasising his role as head of state, Napoleon wrote to George III and Emperor Francis II of Austria proposing peace in general terms, but Pitt's cabinet turned down his approaches, thinking France's position weak after the losses in the Middle East. On 3 February 1800, Charles James Fox came back to the Commons after a long absence, to attack this rejection. Bonaparte, he argued, was an extraordinary man, who had found France unsettled and taken control. He would not defend him, 'but how this House can be so violently indignant at the idea of military despotism is, I own, a little singular, when I see the composure with which they can observe it nearer home', especially in Ireland. As for atrocities, he feared, 'they do not belong exclusively to the French . . . Naples, for instance, has been, among others, what is called "delivered"; and yet, if I am rightly informed, it has been stained and polluted by murders so ferocious, and by cruelties of every kind so abhorrent, that the heart shudders at the recital.'[6]

*

As the new century opened, Britain was still very much at war. The only consolation for loyalists was the safety of George III, always held up as a contrast to the thrusting, ruthless Napoleon. Each outburst against the king, like the jeers and stone-throwing during the bread riots, only confirmed his popularity. A sudden attack on his life heightened this still more. On the evening of 15 May, while 'God Save the King' was being roared out at Drury Lane, an ex-soldier, James Hadfield, had drawn a pistol and fired at the royal box, before announcing, 'God bless your Royal Highness; I like you very well; you are a good fellow.' The shots missed by inches, and the king ordered the performance to continue. Elizabeth Heber expressed the dismay of all loyal, genteel families: 'You will have a full acct. in the papers of the two Shocking Attempts on the Life of our Sovereign, which wicked purpose God in his Mercy to this nation has defeated.'[7]

Hadfield was an old soldier who had been badly injured and taken prisoner at the battle of Tourcoing in 1794. When Sheridan, Drury Lane's owner and manager, interviewed him with the Prince of Wales and the Duke of York after the attack he appealed to the duke as his former commander in chief:

I know your Royal Highness – God bless you. You are a good fellow. I have served with your Highness, and (pointing to a deep cut over his eye, and another long scar on his cheek) said, I got these, and more than these, in fighting by your side. At Lincelles I was left three hours, among the dead, in a ditch, and was taken prisoner by the French. I had my arm broken by a shot, and eight sabre wounds in my head; but I recovered, and here I am.[8]

All the prints showed him as badly scarred and his barrister Thomas Erskine used his wounds to plead a defence of insanity at his trial for treason, thus avoiding the death penalty, and also making his actions seem less political, dispelling fears of a concerted plot. Hadfield would spend the rest of his life in Bedlam, apart from a brief and unsuccessful escape attempt, when he was picked up at Dover, en route for France.

*

If George III was unscathed, Napoleon seemed indestructible. In May, taken aback by an Austrian push towards Genoa, he left Paris and led his army in lightning forced marches through Switzerland to Milan, crossing the river Po and taking Pavia and Piacenza. At the battle of Marengo on 14 June he staved off an Austrian attack, with horrific casualties on both sides.

That summer, strengthened by their Italian conquests, the French proposed a naval truce. Pitt wavered. He was obviously ill, shaking so much that he could not hold a glass, but a naval truce was not an option: in this tense period, the navy were still the nation's heroes, celebrated in annual celebrations of the Glorious First, Camperdown and the Nile. Everyone was thrilled to see the ships and enjoy opportunities to go on board. On a trip to the West Country in 1800, the twenty-five-year-old Richard Heber stopped at Brixham to see the fleet in Torbay. The broad, sheltered bay, which had already become popular with the new fashion for seaside holidays, was a favourite anchorage for the Channel Fleet, with ships of the line and frigates moored offshore, sloops and cutters further in, and victualling boats and wherries darting back and forth to shore. Brixham was full of naval officers and their wives and sailors on shore leave for the day. Having friends in common, Heber was asked to dine with Admiral Jervis, now Lord St Vincent, on the *Ville de Paris*. The dinner was notable for the 'great variety of well-cooked dishes, and the best liquors from Cockagne cyder to Claret Frontignac', and when a storm broke, stopping him going ashore, he found himself slung up to the ceiling in a hammock:

Before mounting my pendant couch, however, I took advantage of the fineness of the night, to enjoy one of the most interesting walks I ever took on one of the proudest terraces that can be trode by an Englishman, the Quarter deck of a 110 gunship, commanded by Lord St Vincent, having in my view 26 line of battle ships.[9]

The sailors were welcoming to all, not just their admirals' guests. When Tom Gill joined Captain Tom Williams's crack frigate *Endymion* (in which Jane Austen's brother Charles was now a lieutenant), and they moored briefly at Cowes, he took his uncle and small cousins Rachel and Jane 'to see our frigate':

and every attention was shown them, and a dance got up for their amusement, and as our band was a very excellent one, music and good cheer was the order of the evening, and a most charming, delightful one it was. My dear little Cousin Jane was as playful as a fawn, and skipped about the ship, her hand in mine, inspecting every part of the deck, and never shall I forget the incessant questions she put to me.[10]

The *Endymion* was then heading for Lisbon, carrying 'two medical gentlemen going to Constantinople at the Sultan's request to vaccinate the Turks'. But soon Tom Gill moved with his captain to the *Vanguard*, and his voyages took him north. Trouble was brewing among the Baltic countries, aggrieved by the British stopping and searching their ships for supplies destined for French ports, and British sailors and marines would soon be drawn into action.

To those reading the *Annual Register* for 1800, it seemed a year of expensive dithering, with the British cabinet unable to make any definite moves. As the year turned, they saw no gains from the vast subsidies to their allies. The tsar had left the coalition in October, and in December Austria, defeated in a blinding snow storm at the battle of Hohenlinden near Munich, signed a treaty with France. And as well as concern over the war and the food shortages Pitt's government still had to confront Ireland's problems in the aftermath of the 1798 rebellion. The anxious, corpulent Viceroy, Lord Cornwallis, and his Chief Secretary, Castlereagh, were convinced that it was crucial to obtain religious and political rights for Catholics. Inevitably, in trying to appease Catholic anger, they made more enemies among the Protestants and the Anglo-Irish ascendancy. Both men saw union with Westminster, with equal representation for Protestants and Catholics in parliament, as the only solution to the sectarian tension, and Pitt too had long held this view, seeing union as the best way to prevent Ireland becoming a stepping stone for French invasions.

After the principle of union was agreed in the cabinet, Pitt and his team in Dublin worked tirelessly to persuade the Dublin parliament to vote itself out of existence, bribing, bullying and handing out peerages. Finally it did so. On 2 July in Westminster and 1 August in Dublin, twin Acts of Union were passed. These came into effect on 1 January 1801. A hundred Irish MPs were added to the House of Commons and four bishops and twenty-eight peers to the Lords. The Churches of England and Ireland were joined, there was a new flag for the 'United Kingdom', and a new royal seal and title for the king – although, to the dismay of devoted loyalists, this dropped the ancient claim to be King of France.

Now, Pitt hoped, he could move towards Catholic emancipation in Ireland. The idea was abominable to George III, and to some members of the cabinet: one of them, Pitt's Chancellor, Lord Loughborough, told the king of Pitt's plans. At a court levee on 28 January George III stormed at Dundas, declaring loudly that emancipation was 'Jacobinical', adding, 'I will tell you, that I shall look on every man as my personal Enemy, who proposes that Question to me.'[11] Pitt, who had so far always been able to persuade the king round to his views, was, perhaps, testing his power. But when he raised the subject, George replied that despite his 'cordial affection' for Pitt, he felt a sense of duty to the Coronation Oath as head of the Church of England, and this 'must therefore prevent me from discussing any proposition tending to destroy this groundwork of our happy Constitution, and much more so that now mentioned by Mr Pitt, which is no less than the complete overthrow of the whole fabric'.[12]

Faced with such determined royal opposition Pitt saw the end of his time in office coming. He had already groomed his old friend Henry Addington, the Speaker of the House of Commons, to be his successor. George III knew this, and knew too that Addington opposed Catholic emancipation. Early in February he asked him to form a ministry. The opposition *Morning Chronicle* crowed:

It appears that the reports by which the public have been agitated for some time were not without foundation. Mr Pitt's Administration, by which this country has been reduced from the proud station which it held at the commencement of his career, is dissolved; and a new cabinet is patched up from the fragments, of a kind the most extraordinary that it is possible to conceive.[13]

Weeks of uncertainty followed, during which the king suffered a short relapse into insanity and could appoint no new government, and Pitt seemed to be reconsidering his resignation. He was as forceful and eloquent in parliament as he had ever been, and the press and their readers were left unsure of what would happen. As *The Times* put it, 'The interests and passions of men, which too frequently bias or mislead their judgement, have doubtless alone given credit and currency to a variety of plans and pretended arrangements.'[14]

But on Saturday 14 March 1801 Pitt finally stepped down, after seventeen years as Prime Minister. All his close allies went with him, a tumble of familiar names: Grenville, Dundas, Windham, Spencer, Canning, Castlereagh and Cornwallis.

# 27. DENMARK, EGYPT, BOULOGNE – PEACE

Henry Addington, a doctor's son and a lawyer, looked an unpromising choice, too small, quiet and un-aristocratic to lead a country – cartoonists often drew him as a tiny man in clothes that were far too big for him. Aged forty-two, he was Pitt's exact contemporary and they had been friends since the age of seven; he was loyal, unassuming, devoted to his wife and their six children. He seemed pale in comparison to the emotional, driven Pitt, and it was generally thought that he would struggle in the Commons. As Canning quipped spitefully, 'Pitt is to Addington as London is to Paddington.'[1] Yet, hero-worshipped as he was, Pitt had not proved a great wartime leader. Britain had escaped invasion, but as Pitt himself was tugged in different ways by Dundas and Grenville, his government never formed a clear offensive policy. His lack of confidence showed in his constant, almost annual, attempts to make peace and in his repression of opposition at home. By contrast, Addington was efficient and moderate, and many MPs preferred his genial manner and plain speeches to Pitt's public eloquence and private dealings. On 25 March 1801, in his first speech as Prime Minister, Addington announced that he would try for peace. Knowing he could hardly raise funds for two more years of war, he made prompt approaches to Paris.

Addington could not, however, avoid conflict in the Baltic. This was triggered partly by the British searches of ships, but also by the capture of Malta the previous year, after which Tsar Paul, who was the 'Grand Master and Protector' of the Knights of St John, had been angered by British delays in restoring the exiled Knights. In mid-December 1800 the tsar persuaded Denmark, Norway, Prussia, Sweden and Russia to defy Britain's policy of stopping their shipping by forming a League of Armed Neutrality. This posed a danger to Britain's corn supplies from the Baltic as well as to much-needed timber and tar for the navy. Soon afterwards the tsar announced that he would seize all British property and ships in Russian harbours, and Prussian and Danish fleets launched a combined attack on Hanover to force the end of the British blockade. In retaliation, from January to March 1801 the British attacked Danish colonies in the Virgin Islands, while Admiral Sir Hyde Parker gathered a fleet at Great Yarmouth, hoping to break up the League before the Baltic ice thawed and the Russian ships could leave port.

In February Nelson joined Parker, and on 12 March the fleet set sail, only to hover outside Copenhagen during weeks of slow negotiations. 'I hate your pen and ink men,' Nelson raged to Emma Hamilton, 'a fleet of British ships are the best negotiators in Europe.'[2] On 2 April he finally won permission to attack, with Parker's division supporting him by threatening the forts further north.[3] The Danes had few warships ready to fight, but they sailed out and anchored, taking with them several old hulks, to form a long curving line of batteries across the harbour entrance. After more than three hours of fighting, facing heavy damage from the batteries and thinking that Nelson was trapped, Parker hoisted the signal 'Discontinue the Action'. This was the moment when Nelson, aboard his seventy-four-gun *Elephant*, allegedly turned to his flag captain, Thomas Foley, and exclaimed, 'You know Foley, I have lost an eye and have a right to be blind if I like, and damn me if I'll see that signal.'[4] His defiance was widely talked of in the fleet, adding to his legend.

No help came to the Danes from Sweden, whose ships were hampered by bad winds, or from Russia. As Danish resistance faltered,

Nelson sent in bomb vessels, despatching a note to Crown Prince Frederick threatening to set fire to all the captured ships and batteries. Knowing the death toll would be terrible, Frederick capitulated. In the battle the Danes lost nineteen ships and over a thousand men killed or wounded, the British around eight hundred. Bodies floated in the harbour among the burning debris, and the jetty by the customs house was covered with stretchers carrying horribly injured men, many of them lacking limbs. Bitterly, the Danes buried their dead in a mass grave at the naval cemetery.

Worried relatives in Britain longed for news: 'this delay is truly distressing as it keeps me in so much anxiety and suspense,' wrote Betsey Fremantle, whose husband Thomas was now commander of the seventy-four-gun *Ganges*. She waited with her children and sisters until, at last, on Thursday 16 April, a fortnight after the battle, the news came through:

Heard my sisters play on the pianoforte; they are both much improved. Tom and Emma are exceedingly riotous with their Aunts. This morning's post brought me the most delightful news from off Copenhagen, where the English have gained a complete victory. It seems to have been a most dreadful engagement on the 2nd inst., but thank God Fremantle is safe.[5]

On the same day, the well-informed Mrs Custance and her daughters came to visit James Woodforde in Norfolk, '& stayed upwards of an Hour' –

Brought us great News, that Lord Nelson had taken several Men of War from the Danes, had demolished Copenhagen, a great Part of it at least – The Danes defied him – They have of late behaved very shabby towards us – The Emperor of Russia also is said to be dead supposed to have been put to death – He had long behaved bad towards England – Dinner to day, Breast of Mutton rosted &c.[6]

The rumour from Russia was true, and official confirmation appeared in the papers on that morning. A few weeks before, on 24 March, Tsar Paul had been assassinated by members of his court. Before he died he was forced to abdicate in favour of his son, Alexander. Now the wheel of alliances turned again. The Anglophile Alexander made approaches to Britain and the League of Armed Neutrality collapsed.

The fleet stayed in Danish waters and Tom Gill sent long letters home by 'a brig homeward bound with despatches from Lord Nelson'.[7] The sailors were now tourists, sending descriptions of the scenery they could see on shore, the fertile countryside and the forts of Helsingborg and Cronenberg. These, the British papers said, posed a grave threat, but Gill assured his father, 'Our newspapers exaggerated as usual when they spoke of continued batteries,' as they had passed within point blank range of Helsingborg 'and were all at quarters ready to give our friends the Danes a second dose of British fire should they have dared to violate the armistice'. Beyond the castle all was calm. At Copenhagen itself, said Gill, 'Nelson has left several monuments of British resentment behind him, still visible in the wreck of the almost extinguished fleet.' Like most officers Gill felt he was fighting the foe of mankind, as he put it, and was deeply sentimental, sending emotional messages to his sisters Sophie and Catherine – 'tell them I lay my hand on my heart when I say as I do now, I feel myself their brother.'

On Sunday 3 May, Betsey Fremantle had more good tidings to write in her diary. 'Glorious news from Egypt in this day's paper. The French have sustained a compleat defeat. I wish all these victories may lead to Peace.'[8] At the start of the year, Sir Ralph Abercromby had been appointed as commander of the British troops in the Mediterranean, and after attempting an unsuccessful attack on Cadiz he was ordered first to Malta, then to Egypt, to flush out the French army that Napoleon had left there. After spending the first weeks of 1801 at Marmaris Bay, north of Rhodes, trying to cajole supplies from the Turks, making his Scottish and Irish recruits practise landing on the beachheads, and liaising with Admiral Keith to make sure that the navy and army could work together smoothly, Abercromby and his soldiers sailed south. The fleet of 175 ships included a few warships, forty troop ships and a host of transports, supplemented by boats gathered from the small ports of the Aegean and Adriatic – polacres, xebecs and feluccas.[9] They anchored two miles off Aboukir, and landed in a series of waves, with the soldiers packed so tightly into the boats that they could hardly move. It was a brilliantly daring operation, mounted in the face of French cannon and field guns. The sailor John Nicol, now serving in the *Ajax*, was in one of the flat-bottomed boats, each carrying a hundred soldiers, leaving the ships at midnight and rowing with muffled oars across sandy shallows, the water very still and all silent as death. The French were waiting, firing when they came within reach of grapeshot and sinking many boats. But the sailors rowed on and 'landed eight thousand men the first morning. We had good sport at landing the troops as the Frenchmen made a stout resistance. We brought the wounded men back to the ships.'[10]

On 21 March – while Nelson was at Copenhagen – British regiments drove the French back at Canope near Alexandria; in the eight years of fighting, this was the first real victory. But during the fighting Abercromby was struck down and his men carried him carefully aboard the *Foudroyant*, moored in the harbour. He had always been popular with his troops, and with the public, and the news of his death a week later inspired numerous paintings and prints.

Over the spring and summer English and Turkish troops took Cairo and besieged Alexandria. Among them were the troops of Edward Dillon's foreign regiment, formed in Italy in 1795, as well as soldiers from India, who landed on the Red Sea coast and marched across the desert. William Harness was there. 'We have seen few of the Army from England,' he wrote; 'they appear very dirty, starved and shabby, not having any wine or comforts, even cloaths, with them. They were surprized at our manner of living. We brought even Cooks for the Soldiers from India, and, much as we were put to it for carriage, took care to bring a few Dozens of madeira across the Desert.'[11] On 2 September, two days before Harness wrote his letter, General Menou had conceded defeat. Under the terms of that surrender, ten thousand French soldiers were repatriated in British ships but all the

French ships and cannon were handed over. The British also took away, despite Menou's defiance, the magnificent stack of Egyptian treasures collected by the French. These included the Rosetta Stone, discovered by a French soldier two years before, which was brought back to London and displayed in the British Museum in 1802. Harness also told his wife of the great efforts made to bring back the red granite obelisk of Cleopatra's Needle to present to George III — but this was a feat that would have to wait another seventy-five years.

To the people at home, the victories in Egypt meant more than a pile of treasures. For the first time, they saw how strong the Scottish regiments were: the 42nd, the Royal Highland Regiment (the Black Watch), the 79th, the Cameronians, and the 92nd, the Gordon Highlanders. A new mythmaking began, of the Highland soldier, kilt flying, leading the charge. The London Highland Society issued special medals, beginning with its medal for the Black Watch, decorated with a portrait of Abercromby. When a veteran returning from Egypt, wrote Sir John Sinclair, President of the Highland Society, was congratulated by a stranger on the achievement of his regiment: ' "How could it be otherwise", said he, "when our Officers told us, in Gaelic, to remember the Honour of our Country." '[12] The image of the dashing Highlander was so strong that the crowds who came to see the king and Prince Regent reviewing the Black Watch at Ashford, expecting striding giants, were taken aback to find small, wiry men in bonnets and kilts, sunburned and exhausted. But when the regiment marched back to Edinburgh, thousands poured out of the city to meet the Highlanders on the road and followed them, cheering, to the castle. Their glamour would grow as the wars went on.

There was, as always, a terrible cost. When the wounded men came home people were horrified at the sight of sick and maimed soldiers, many with badly infected wounds. During the wars, physicians often had to deal with new conditions, and when John Cunningham Saunders, one of Astley Cooper's students, opened his dispensary in Moorfields 'for the Relief of the Poor Afflicted with Diseases of the Eye and Ear' in 1805, he found that many of his patients were soldiers who had contracted trachoma during the campaign in Egypt.[13] But still, the Aboukir landing entered legend. Ten years later, six-year-old Thomas Cooper, a future Chartist leader, was living with his widowed mother in Gainsborough. She worked as a dyer, sweating over two large coppers in their downstairs room and making extra money by selling pasteboard workboxes from house to house. On her rounds she would leave Thomas with neighbours, including Thomas Chatterton, 'a pensioned soldier, who had lost his eyesight in Egypt'. As Cooper wrote years later:

Many fragments of the fairy, and witch, and ghost-stories, told by the beggars and wandering pedlars, remain in my memory; but I have a far more vivid recollection of the blind soldier's relations of the way in which he stepped out of the boat up to the waist in water, in the Bay of Aboukir, and how they charged the French with the bayonet, and under cover of the cannon from the ships drove the enemy back from the shore, and effected a triumphant landing.[14]

*

The British success in Egypt rattled the French, but in July 1801 there were rumours of new invasion plans, spread by Bonaparte to keep up the pressure. To reassure the public, Nelson was put in command of defences and naval action around the coast from Suffolk to Sussex. He was sure the enemy would aim at London and insisted that as soon as word came that they had sailed, all British boats of all sizes must gather in the Channel and Thames galleys and wherries must be ready to carry messages. 'If a breeze springs up our Ships are to deal *destruction*; no delicacy can be observed,' he wrote. 'Whatever plans may be adopted, the moment the Enemy touch our Coast, be it where it may, they are to be attacked by every man afloat and on shore; this must be perfectly understood. *Never fear the event.*'[15]

On 3 and 4 August Nelson went on the attack. With twenty-eight gunboats and five bomb boats he bombarded the French fleet at Boulogne harbour, a fruitless effort watched for hours, on a day of sparkling clarity, by crowds on the hills on both sides of the Channel. On the 15th he tried again, attempting to break into the anchorage at night. The French were well prepared, the British ships lost contact in the moonless dark and their sailors fell under a barrage of musket fire and grapeshot. Two days after the raid, *The Times* described Nelson visiting the wounded sailors in Deal, 'with that humanity which has characterised his naval career'. He shed tears at the funeral of two young midshipmen.[16] Among the casualties was his devoted aide, twenty-three-year-old Captain Edward Parker, who died, painfully, several weeks later. 'My heart is almost broke,' wrote Nelson.[17] He could not bear to see his body.

There were no more dashing raids. The uneasy mood continued until suddenly, on 2 October 1801, to widespread astonishment, a *Gazette Extraordinary* announced that preliminaries of peace had been signed the previous day. Throughout the summer the French envoy M. Otto, officially in London to arrange exchanges of prisoners, had been privately negotiating with Lord Hawkesbury, the new Foreign Secretary. Express posts careered out of London and the news reached the provinces only hours after it hit the London clubs. Lord Hervey, undersecretary to Hawkesbury, sent an express at midnight which reached James Oakes in Bury St Edmunds by ten in the morning. On business in Manchester, James Longsdon's partner at the cotton mill, Mr Finch, heard about the peace and rushed back to Derbyshire with the news. Longsdon wrote to his three sons at school:

I am thinking how rejoiced your young hearts would be at the sudden news of Peace. Treasure the Event in your memories. Some of the occurrences of the War have been so extraordinary that I think you will remember them when you are old for I hope there will be no similar scenes to contrast them with in your future days and that you will never more hear of Host's incamping against this happy Country, or see its Peace destroyed by civil War or the anarchy of foolish Republicanism.[18]

Finch had reported that in Manchester, 'every mind concerned in Trade is filled with bustle & speculation'. This was true of the City as well: the price of stocks soared even before the *Gazette* was published.

A week later news arrived that Bonaparte had ratified the preliminaries. 'General joy to the height of enthusiasm pervaded all over the country,' wrote William Rowbottom solemnly, 'where bells were ringing colours flying and cannons roaring and nothing but joy and happiness appeared in every countenance.'[19] The bonfire in Plymouth was so large that the flames could be seen for forty miles. The huge manufactory at Soho in Birmingham was lit by hundreds of coloured oil-lamps. Letters shimmered along the facade – 'PEACE – BY PERSEVERANCE, VALOUR, UNION AND MAGNANIMITY' – with side illuminations announcing 'Europe Reposes Free' and 'Commerce & the Arts Revive'.[20]

Illuminations at Boulton and Watt's Soho Manufactory

Over the next two months, cities and towns, villages and country mansions staged their own displays. In Derbyshire, Elizabeth Longsdon gave strict instructions to her oldest son James to bring his white waistcoat, white stockings and best pumps in his saddle bags when he came back from school for the local ball. In Cheshire the Heber family went to Sir Richard Hill's gala at Hawkstone, climbing up the hill amid the flashing of fire squibs and rockets.[21] In Suffolk the Oakes family watched the illuminations in the town and went to a celebratory dinner, 'a most handsome Cold Collation, wh. Hot Soups', followed by singing and a ball.[22] In the village of Letheringsett, the *Norfolk Chronicle* reported, the vicar, Mr Burrell, filled his twenty-four windows with lights 'representing 2 beautiful figures of Gallia and Britannia in the act of uniting hands under

the influence of Peace', while the Hardys' garden walk was decorated with a large transparency of 'War vanquished'. In the village
itself, the *Chronicle* continued, 'The Church, Workhouse & every Cottage was illuminated, a bonefire and Collours flying &c enlivened
the scene; the decorum and regularity of the Poor was worthy the
highest commendations, the Visitors from the neighbouring towns
as well as distant parts, were genteely treated & the day passed with
much pleasure.'[23] Mary Hardy, understandably tired, wrote less rap-
turously, '*Nov 24 Tues*. the Wind being reather high could not keep
many of the Lamps light. Several people dind here, the poor people
dind in Mr Burrell's little Barn.'[24] The wind whirled and the rain fell.

# IV : PAUSING

## 1801–1803

Is it a Reed that's shaken by the wind,
Or what is it that ye go forth to see?
Lords, Lawyers, Statesmen, Squires of low degree,
Men known, and men unknown, Sick, Lame, and Blind,
Post forward all, like Creatures of one kind,
With first-fruit offerings crowd to bend the knee
In France, before the new-born Majesty.
WILLIAM WORDSWORTH, 'Calais, August, 1802'

## 28. FRANCE

The terms of the Treaty of London, the basis of the Treaty of Amiens the following year, were set before the news of Abercromby's victory in Egypt arrived. To public dismay the French did astoundingly well. France was to withdraw from Naples and the Roman states, but would keep other gains such as Savoy, Nice and Piedmont, the territory west of the Rhine, and, most worryingly, Holland, which left Britain vulnerable to invasion. By contrast Britain handed over almost all that she had won, including the Cape of Good Hope, Egypt and Malta, which was returned to the Knights of St John. In the Caribbean, Britain kept Trinidad, but Tobago and Martinique went back to the French, and Curaçao and the Demerara and Berbice regions of Guyana to the Dutch. Pitt backed the terms, although many of his former cabinet, including Dundas and Grenville, were horrified.

So great was the desire for peace that as soon as the preliminaries were announced the British papers began presenting Napoleon not as a tyrant or bogeyman, which he had seemed only a year before, but as the restorer of harmony and order. Thomas Robinson, writing to his brother Henry Crabb Robinson, said the sudden shift in tone reminded him of 'the transformation in a pantomime, where a devil is suddenly converted into an angel'.[1] Now that he was supposedly not a direct threat, people declared themselves openly fascinated by the First Consul's daring marches and extraordinary victories, and by his swaggering, carefully cultivated image. There was a trade in facsimiles of his signature, in prints of his portrait and in busts – Byron had to protect his treasured bust of Napoleon against schoolfellows at Harrow when war broke out again.

Optimists expected the peace to last and happily anticipated lower taxes. Such hopes were dashed when Addington's first budget of 1802 put new taxes on malt, beer and other commodities to pay the interest on the growing national debt. 'I never should have been for the Peace', Amabel Hume-Campbell sighed to Agneta Yorke, 'if I had not thought the Spirit of the Nation Crush'd by the Weight of Taxes & I doubt it has recovered itself . . . I declare I hardly know any Lady but Yourself, who paying the Taxes out of her own Pocket, does not feel *that* Burden more than the Honor of the Nation.'[2] In April, nine months before he died, the Revd James Woodforde dutifully paid his income tax, hoping it would be repealed that month, 'it being universally disliked'.[3] And Addington did repeal the tax, saying that it should not rest on the shoulders of the public in peacetime, but should be reserved for more important occasions, which, he trusted, would not soon recur.[4]

'I recollect the Soldiers coming home,' wrote James Weatherley, who was eight at the time 'they said Peace was made and we should have Plenty of white Bread Cheap when it had been so very dear which made the People more Cheerful than usual.'[5] The regular army was virtually halved: at a wet Oldham fair, Rowbottom noted, 'their was one blesing observeable there was no recruiting Sergeant nor air renting Militaria Drum'.[6] But while many soldiers returned, others were sent to the West Indies, or to India, like William Harness's regiment, which went straight back from Egypt to fight in the Maratha wars. Across the country, the barracks emptied as militia regiments were sent home. Henry Austen resigned his commission in the Oxfordshires, married his cousin Eliza de Feuillide, whom he had loved for years, and became an army agent with another ex-officer. Soon they set up as bankers, making a clever start by handling the regiment's payroll.

Sailors went home too. The Admiralty cut the navy from 130,000 to seventy thousand men and took more than sixty ships out of commission. But men returning from regiments or ships often found it hard to find work. John Nicol, with pay in his pocket and prize money due, went home to Edinburgh, astonished at what he found after years away: 'I scarce knew a face in Edinburgh. It had doubled itself in my absence. I now wandered in elegant streets where I had left corn growing. Everything was new to me.'[7] He found it hard to settle, but then married a cousin and promised her never to go to sea again; they bought a house on Castle Hill and he took up his old trade as a cooper, making barrels for a soap factory in Queensferry.

In the lull, the new First Lord, Lord St Vincent – 'Old Jarvie', Admiral Jervis, who had terrorised his captains by constant bullying – set about pursuing abuses and corruption in the dockyards with equal fury. The accounts showed that officials had claimed for prices far higher than those paid, and this had eaten badly into the Navy Board's funds. Within a month or so of the peace preliminaries, there were lay-offs at the dockyards: three hundred shipwrights, five hundred labourers and 150 coopers and packers at Deptford, another three hundred or more men at Woolwich dockyard next to the arsenal. Those who lost their jobs were given a handout and promise of being first in line if more work came in. In the civilian shipyards, where these men were now eager to work, the shipbuilders promptly cut wages. There was trouble in the north and south, on the Tyne and the Thames.

Towns, villages and ports were full of returning troops, but also full of widows and of orphans. Slowly the state and charities began to see this. In 1798 Andrew Thompson started a small industrial school for sailors' children, the British National Endeavour, in Paddington Green, with Nelson as a patron and the City financiers Benjamin and Abraham Goldsmid. This was taken over by a committee led by the Dukes of Sussex and Cumberland and later moved to Greenwich as the Royal Naval Asylum. Then in 1801 the Duke of York founded the Royal Military Asylum for soldiers' children: at the height of the conflict this was home to a thousand boys and five hundred girls, all casualties of war.

*

The main joy, for many people, was that Europe was now open. The regular Dover–Calais mail packets began to sail almost at once. Coaches left from the City for Dover in the early hours, at half past four, and from Charing Cross every morning and evening. When they arrived in Calais English visitors were confronted by Gillray's satires mocking British ministers, pinned up in the passport office to provoke them.[8] As well as the packets, they crowded on to private yachts and fishing boats, then took the coach on the new road that Napoleon had built for his invasion – a mere two days' drive to Paris. To begin with, until the Peace of Amiens was formally signed in March 1802, travellers had to get a passport from the French representative, the overburdened M. Otto, and from the British Foreign Office; those coming the other way needed a visa from the British Ambassador in Paris. But red tape did not deter them. Even pedlars and vagrants set out for France.

Some of the most eager travellers to Paris were the old radicals and Foxite Whigs, among them the Duchess of Devonshire, the lawyer Thomas Erskine and Fox himself, who was Napoleon's guest at a grand dinner at the Tuileries. Merchants and manufacturers, looking forward to the reopening of European markets, also rushed to renew old contacts. Visitors to Paris in 1802 included eighty-one MPs, sixty-one peers and thirty-three peeresses, often with large families and phalanxes of servants. All the high-society crowd wanted to see the theatres and ballrooms, hotels and assemblies, daring fashions, cafes and *glaciers* and nightly fireworks. English nobles trooped along to parties given by Mme Recamier and asked General Menou, so recently defeated by Abercromby at Alexandria, to join them for dinner. Richard Heber, staying at the Hôtel de Paris, found the city with its tall houses and narrow streets not at all equal to London, but 'every spot one looks at acquires an interest, tho' often of a melancholy nature, from the late great events which have been passing in the Metropolis for the last ten years'.[9] The aristocracy had clung to their love of France throughout the war: they spoke French at parties, used French phrases in letters, bought French furniture and Sèvres porcelain, smuggled in French wines and brandy, adored the *haute cuisine* and served French dishes at their dinner parties. Now Paris fashions were available again, velvet hats and sable muffs, embroidered shawls and silk-lined cloaks. A shocked colonel reported that the French women's dresses were 'nothing more than Petticoats and Shoulder straps'.[10]

Artists, including Farington and Fuseli, Flaxman and Opie – bringing his wife Amelia – hurried over, eager to visit the Grande Galerie in the Louvre, packed with treasures from royal and noble collections in Italy and Austria: over the entry to the Louvre was the inscription *Les fruits de nos victoires*. William Hazlitt, twenty-four and determined to become a painter, was commissioned by his Liverpool patron, Mr Railton, to copy ten paintings for a fee of £105. He worked in the Louvre for three months, copying Titian, seeing Bonaparte in the distance, bumping into Fox. Thomas Girtin boarded the Dover packet in October 1801, leaving his eight-months-pregnant wife behind, and stayed for five months, drawing vivid scenes of Parisian views and life. He had hoped to exhibit his planned *Eidometropolis*, a huge panorama of London, but this had to wait for his return, when it opened at Wigley's Great Room in Spring Gardens in August 1802. By then Girtin was very ill. He died in November, aged just twenty-seven. Turner, his close friend, followed his coffin to the grave.

George Cruikshank's view of Napoleon's artistic ambitions

Turner himself had just come back from Europe. He had set off in July 1802, travelling with Newby Lowson, one of the Durham gentry introduced by his new patrons in the north. After landing at Calais in a gale – 'nearly swampt', wrote Turner in his notebook – they travelled in style, hiring a cabriolet and a Swiss servant in Paris and heading south to the Alps. En route Turner filled his sketchbooks with studies of the sublime: the Grand Chartreuse, Bonneville and Mont Blanc, the Reichenbach Falls, 'fragments and precipices very romantic, and strikingly grand . . . very fine thunderstorms among the mountains'.[11] Back in Paris Turner spent a fortnight sketching and making notes on Titian, Ruisdael and Poussin. With his fellow artists Fuseli, Flaxman and Farington he met Jacques-Louis David, who had just made a copy of his painting of Napoleon crossing the Alps, triumphant on his great white horse, to hang in the Invalides.

Even artistic encounters, however, carried risk. In September Benjamin West, President of the Royal Academy, brought *Death on the Pale Horse* to exhibit in the Salon, a work originally commissioned by George III but rejected as a 'Bedlamite scene'. Not only was he spotted talking to Napoleon, who admired the picture, but he also gave a breakfast for radicals, poets and artists, at which his guests included former American revolutionaries, English Jacobins and the United Irish leader Arthur O'Connor. Reports of West's doings caused uproar, the king was appalled, and he lost his stipend as royal history painter.

Engineers and scientists were also on the packet boats. James Watt came to inspect the Marly aqueduct and to bring home secrets of the French bleaching trade, and William Herschel came to be elected as an associate to the French Institute. Herschel's achievements were acclaimed across Europe and his much-admired reflecting telescopes in their mahogany cases were sold to German princes, to Napoleon's brother Lucien and to the Emperor of Austria. In 1806 the grandest of all, costing £3500, would be delivered to the royal observatory in Madrid.[12] Acknowledging his fame, Napoleon granted Herschel and his wife Mary an audience at Malmaison. It was a baking hot day and the First Consul was at his most ostentatiously informal, offering fruit ice creams and quizzing Herschel on astronomy, while flinging out opinions on the English, their inadequate police, terrible newspapers and excellent racehorses. In science, Herschel later told the poet Robert Campbell, 'he seemed to know little more than any well-educated gentleman, and on astronomy much less for instance than our own king'.[13]

Paris was full of celebrities. Richard Lovell Edgeworth and his daughter Maria were persuaded to come by Marc-Auguste Pictet, the Swiss translator of their *Practical Education*. Edgeworth and his wife Frances, with Maria and her sister Charlotte, travelled through Belgium and arrived at Paris in October 1802, where Maria found the sweep of recent, violent history marked in the very names of streets and squares. On the day they arrived, she wrote, they were in a magnificent hotel in the fine square,

formerly Place Louis Quinze, afterwards Place de la Revolution, and now Place de la Concorde. Here the guillotine was once at work night and day; and here died Louis Seize, and Marie Antoinette, and Madame Roland: opposite us is the Seine and *La Lanterne*. On one side of this square are the Champs Elysees.[14]

It was an eventful stay. They met industrialists and bankers, writers and scientists; Maria turned down a proposal of marriage; and her father, feeling very proud, became a member of the Societé pour l'Encouragement de l'Industrie Nationale.

Many émigrés went home, for good they hoped. Fanny Burney came with her husband, the Comte d'Arblay, who was trying to recoup his army pension and his property. When she eventually encountered Bonaparte, he was not what she expected – instead of looking like a bold commander or even the self-dramatising star who entertained Herschel, he seemed sombre. His pale face, she thought, was marked with 'Care, Thought, Melancholy, & Meditation'. He had the look of 'a profoundly studious & contemplative Man', wearing himself out with 'abstruse speculations, & theoretic plans, or, rather, visions, ingenious but not practicable . . . more the air of a Student than a Warrior'.[15]

William Wordsworth, too, was here on a personal mission. The poet and his sister Dorothy came to stay for a month in Calais to see his former lover Annette Vallon, whom he had left behind in 1792. He saw his daughter Caroline, now nine years old, and walked with her on Calais sands. This summer he was making plans to marry Mary Hutchinson, and wanted to reassure Annette that he would keep sending the small maintenance for Caroline. Looking across the Channel to the lights of Kent, he expressed his ambiguous response to the peace. In his poem 'Calais, August, 1802', he was aghast at the rush to see Napoleon, all those men and women 'of prostrate mind' drawn by the heady scent of power: 'Shame on you, feeble Heads, to slavery prone!'

But how much had these visitors really learned of France? The greatest sight was Bonaparte in his box at the Opéra, escorted by his guards, or at a parade on his white charger. As Maria Edgeworth wrote drily, they saw the review, and 'we *saw* a man on a white horse ride down the ranks; we *saw* that he was a little man with a pale face, who seemed very attentive to what he was about, and this was all we *saw* of Buonaparte.'[16]

# 29. NEW VOICES

The peace celebrations enraged William Cobbett. In October 1801 when the preliminaries were signed he refused to light candles, only to find a crowd attacking his house. 'The smashing of the glass, and the cracking of the woodwork of my house' were, he claimed, 'accompanied with shouts of "France for ever!" – "Huzza for BUONA-PARTE!" – "Huzza for the Republic!"' He was sure on one hand that the government had paid for the illuminations and on the other that nine out of ten people who put up transparencies were republicans, expressing allegiance to '*the cause of France!*'[1] His words were full of fear of the 'bad' mob, 'headstrong, noisy, growling, slothful, filthy in their carcasses, nasty and excessive in their diet and drink'.

Cobbett's was a relatively new voice, loud and strong, and it would boom on, changing from loyalist to radical, through the long war years and far beyond. In contrast to his inflammatory, hard-hitting prose, Cobbett looked deceptively bucolic, like an old-fashioned gentleman farmer, thought Hazlitt, 'easy of access, affable, clear-headed, simple and mild in his manner', with 'a good sensible face, rather full with little grey eyes, a hard square forehead, a ruddy complexion'.[2] Brought up on a farm near Farnham in Surrey, with nostalgic memories of his grandmother's cottage and his days in the fields, he had been a restless youth, trying to enrol as a sailor, then copying 'crabbed draughts' as a lawyer's clerk, and then joining the West

Norfolk 54th Foot. In the American war he served in Canada under Lord Edward Fitzgerald, later the martyr of the Irish rebellion, but while he respected Fitzgerald he clashed with other officers. Becoming a sergeant-major, he wrote, 'brought me in close contact at every hour with the whole of the epaulet gentry, whose profound and surprising ignorance I discovered in a twinkling'.[3] His attempts to bring a corrupt quartermaster and officers before a court martial brought trouble and he left for France with his wife Nancy in 1792, before going to America as a journalist for six years.

Cobbett made his name in the States as the anti-Jacobin 'Peter Porcupine', but when a libel case threatened in 1800 he brought Nancy and their two young children back to England. Soon after he arrived, Pitt gave him dinner and offered him the editorship of a pro-government paper. He refused, and launched his own, keeping his American title, *The Porcupine*, and supporting politicians like his friend William Windham, now Secretary for War in Addington's government, who argued for continuation of the war and suppression of radicals at home. After selling *The Porcupine*, which was absorbed into the propagandist *True Briton*, Cobbett started a weekly, the *Political Register*. Outwardly this looked independent; privately it was funded by Windham and his cronies.

The peace seemed the right time to start such a paper. In the provinces, newspaper editors revived former magazines, like the *General Magazine* of Perth, warmly received by one grateful reader, who felt 'there is no place where a literary journal is more wanted than in Perth. The bustle of business, and the jingling of tavern bells; political debates and the chit chat of the card table threaten totally to drown the voice of learning and the song of the Muses.'[4] At the end of the year this small paper produced a collection, *Miscellanea Perthensis*. Keeping well clear of politics, it included unpublished poems by Burns, and two by Wordsworth, as well as articles on the Mamelukes, the new classification of plants, imprisonment for debt, and the problems of Scottish agriculture.

If Perth could do this, Scotland's capital could do better. In October

1802 Archibald Constable, currently Scott's publisher, backed four members of the Edinburgh Speculative Society, the lawyer Francis Jeffrey, the economist Francis Horner, clergyman Sydney Smith and another lawyer, Henry Brougham, in founding the *Edinburgh Review; or Critical Journal*. All four were in their twenties and early thirties, 'excellent ages for such work', thought Henry Cockburn. The *Edinburgh* was highbrow, long and expensive at five shillings, but it made a splash from the start. It was full of lively polemic: Smith trashed Dr Parr's attack on Godwin, Jeffrey attacked the Lake Poets in a review of Southey's *Thalaba* as 'dissenters' to the rules of poetry, and Horner wrote a powerful article explaining Henry Thornton's ideas on paper money. It was also a truly professional journal, as Constable paid contributors ten guineas a sheet, double the current highest rate. 'Upon my word,' wrote Maria Edgeworth when her brother Henry joined the staff, 'it is a fine thing to be an Edinburgh Reviewer, £200 a year and ten guineas a sheet! Poor authors must hide their diminished heads. But it is always a better diversion to tear, than to be torn to pieces.'[5]

The *Edinburgh* quickly became the most influential political and literary quarterly in Britain, free of cant, slashing its chosen targets, campaigning for reform. Henry Cockburn remembered its effect as electric:

And instead of expiring, as many wished, in their first effort, the force of the shock was increased on each subsequent discharge . . . It was an entire and instant change of everything that the public had been accustomed to in that sort of composition. The old periodical opiates were extinguished at once. The learning of the new Journal, its talent, its spirit, its writing, its independence, were all new; and the surprise was increased by a work so full of public life springing up suddenly, in a remote part of the kingdom.[6]

It was particularly cheering, he felt, because so many thoughtful men were 'alarmed lest war and political confusion should restore a new course of dark ages'.

Another group also planned a new journal, very different in style. This year the Clapham evangelicals launched the *Christian*

*Observer*. Published by Hatchard's, it was firmly addressed to middle-class periodical readers – like those who might take the *Edinburgh* – rather than to the working people they had aimed to reach with the *Repository Tracts*. Its view of 'Public Affairs' contrasted the false view of 'liberty' propounded in the French Revolution, 'which no less restrains the licentiousness of the people than the despotism of an individual', to the 'true liberty' of the religious life.[7] In December 1802 a leading article begged readers to remember how lucky they were in the prosperity of their country and its spreading empire, yet how fragile this prosperity was. Napoleon's threat was small, the article declared, compared with that of evil at home, which could only be kept down by 'a religion out of which subordination, order, and morality, grow as from their natural root . . . then being strong in the favour of the Almighty, we shall be in little danger from our enemies'.[8]

The growling of Cobbett, the impassioned criticism of the *Edinburgh* and the admonitions of the *Christian Observer* rang through the war alongside the loyalist urgings of the *True Briton* and the acid satire of the monthly *Anti-Jacobin*. Leisured readers followed the daily and weekly papers for the news, crammed into columns of dense print alongside advertisements for houses, patent pills and auctions of pictures, and skimmed the monthly magazines and quarterly reviews for opinions and argument. Those with money joined subscription libraries and ordered books from their local shops, or had them sent from the big London booksellers, keeping up with new fiction, history, travel and natural philosophy, physics, chemistry and biology.

In the fields of chemistry and physics, the new voice was that of Humphry Davy, the impulsive young Cornishman, poet and scientist, whose experiments with laughing gas, or nitrous oxide, at Thomas Beddoes' Pneumatic Institution in Bristol had already caught public attention. In the *Anti-Jacobin* Canning's satire 'The Pneumatic Revellers' suggested that Beddoes and his friends spent their lives in intoxicated orgies under the illusion that nitrous oxide could enlighten the world: 'And they, every one, cried, 'twas a pleasure extatic;/To drink deeper draughts of the mighty pneumatic.'[9] But Davy shrugged off this label and moved to London, where in 1801 he was appointed Assistant Lecturer in Chemistry and Director of the Chemical Laboratory at the Royal Institution, founded two years before by Count Rumford.

The Royal Institution was the place to go, even more than the Royal Society: the ground floor had workshops for carpenters and tinsmiths and a kitchen for experiments with food for the poor, one of Rumford's passions. Above were reading rooms, with 'the best English and foreign journals for all the sciences, with the exception of theology and politics', and higher still was a lecture hall with seats for a thousand people.[10] Jumping on to the stage, Davy thrilled his audience, beginning with the gripping topic of 'Galvanism'. In January 1802, by now a professor, he caused a sensation with his introductory lecture to an unpromising-sounding course on 'Agricultural Chemistry', making lyrical claims for the scientific imagination and the dawn of new knowledge, which might even uncover the secret of life itself, enabling man 'to produce from combinations of dead matter effects which were formerly occasioned only by animal organs'.[11] The Institution's lectures sparked cartoons by Rowlandson (who made them seem sexy) and Gillray (who filled them with stinks), and the crush of carriages was so thick that in 1803 Albemarle Street was made London's first one-way street. Five years later the lectures were still a draw, although Davy's friend Southey noticed that 'part of the men were taking snuff to keep their eyes open, others more honestly asleep',

while the ladies were all on the watch, and some score of them had their tablets and pencils, busily noting down what they heard, as topics for the next conversation party. 'Oh', said J—— when he came out, in a tone which made it half groan, half interjection, 'the days of tapestry, hanging and worked chair bottoms, were better days than these! – I will go and buy for Harriet, the Whole Duty of Woman, containing the complete Art of Cookery'.[12]

Gillray, *Scientifick Researches! – New Discoveries in Pneumaticks! – or – an Experimental Lecture of the Powers of Air*, 23 May 1802. The lecturer is Thomas Young, Professor of Natural Philosophy, with Davy wielding the bellows

The secrets of physical life became a matter of intense debate. Following Davy's lectures on Galvanism, Galvani's nephew Giovanni Aldini, a professor of physics in Bologna, arrived in London, and a horrified audience at the Royal College of Physicians watched him apply electricity to the corpse of a hanged murderer, rushed from the gallows to the anatomy theatre. The muscles quivered, an eye opened. This was too much for the authorities, and the demonstrations were stopped, but they illustrated a concern with the body and its workings that was amplified by the horrors of war, as if sudden death on a massive scale brought a shared longing for resurrection of the lost. With the interest in the essence of bodily life came a fascination with the workings of the mind and the imagination. What did it mean to be human? How did the body relate to the mind? How could imagination and sympathy enable the self to relate to others? All these concerns ran through Coleridge's notebooks and through Hazlitt's first book, *An Essay on the Principles of Human Action*, published this year.

The peace was a time for looking outward too, for learning about the new inventions, steam locomotives, agriculture and medical advances, for a more intense appreciation of the natural world and a greater knowledge of distant regions of the globe. Lovers of country life read Gilbert White's *Natural History of Selborne* and Thomas Bewick's *Land Birds*, the first volume of his *History of British Birds*, decorated with its pungent vignettes of north country scenes. The second volume, on water birds, was impatiently awaited. Everyone, of all ages, in all places, read travel books. And as travellers, soldiers and sailors recorded their journeys, horizons widened. Matthew Flinders, whose *Observations on the Coasts of Van Diemen's Land . . . and New South Wales* of 1801 caught the attention of Joseph Banks and the Royal Society, soon set off again for Port Jackson and Botany Bay. This time he was sailing with the backing of the East India Company as captain of the *Investigator*, with his brother Samuel as lieutenant and a staff of a naturalist, an astronomer, a botanical artist and a gardener. Before he left he married Anne Chapelle, 'my Ann' – hoping to take her with him, but although he wrote home that 'Mrs F now begins to get the better of that qualmish sickness that the motion of a ship, even at anchor, usually excites', in the end the Admiralty did not let her go.[13] Flinders sailed on, naming the capes and creeks of the distant continent after his native Lincolnshire: in his notes he suggested the name 'Australia' but officialdom stuck to 'Terra Australis' for the next twenty years. Sailing back in 1803, Flinders called in at Mauritius and was arrested. Despite Banks's efforts to get support from the French National Institute, he was a prisoner there for seven years until the British took the island.

On their way across England, heading for the boat to the Continent in 1802, the Edgeworths stopped at Leicester. While they waited for dinner Richard Lovell Edgeworth – an ebullient and sometimes embarrassing parent – went to the circulating library. 'My father asked for "Belinda", "Bulls" &c.,' sighed Maria, 'found they were in good repute – "Castle Rackrent" in better – the others often borrowed, but "Castle Rackrent" often bought.'[14] Maria's parodic, multi-voiced *Essay on Irish Bulls* was a witty, experimental work about 'bulls' or blunders of speech, designed to make people think, in the aftermath of the rebellion and the Union, about nationality and gender and stereotypes. Her favourite critique of it came from 'a gentleman, much interested in improving the breed of Irish cattle', who sent for the book after seeing an advertisement 'and when he began to read the first page he threw it away in disgust: he had purchased it as Secretary to the Irish Agricultural Society.'[15] Maria Edgeworth remained popular in these increasingly evangelical times, despite her secular, liberal views. Her realistic Irish stories aimed to overturn prejudice. In 1800 her satirical *Castle Rackrent* exposed negligent Anglo-Irish landlords; the three-volume *Belinda*, published at the start of the peace, showed London high society and French refugees, with talk of slavery and Methodism and mercenary marriage. A subplot, the marriage of an African servant, Juba, to an English farm girl, would be firmly excised, with other questionable matter, when the novel was included in Mrs Barbauld's 'English Novelists' in 1810.

Reading, the great imaginative escape, was already coming under evangelical scrutiny. Reacting with alarm to 'the evils of classical literature', Mary Anne Galton had been horrified, when staying with the giddiest of her Gurney aunts, to find that the novels of Fielding and Smollett 'and various others of the same class, desecrated the library shelves'.[16] This was, perhaps, a covert attack on her own book-loving mother, Lucy, who read novels with delight all her life and happily sent volumes of travels and Mme de Genlis's stories to her son at school. True, Lucy Galton taught her children that the natural world was God's work, leaving her husband Samuel to explain the scientific laws. But her religious instruction was practical: give to the poor from sympathy, not for praise; make your prayers short as 'God will not hear you better, for using many words'; when the Bible says 'take no thought for the morrow it does not mean that you are not to provide dinner or clothes, rather don't look forward so much that you forget today'.[17] There was no reference to being 'saved', no admonition to feel humble.

Lucy Galton in her Quaker cap

Quaker though she was, Lucy Galton, like Maria Edgeworth, was a woman of the Enlightenment, of the eighteenth rather than nineteenth century. The Bible was not a book of lessons but of poetry, and it was the poetry she loved. In her sixties, horrified at hearing that an ill friend, Mr Courtenay, could not move from his room and was 'fixt, like an image, to one solitary chair', she took solace in the hope that 'his mind seeks other Worlds':

& is capable of flights, like the imagination of Milton. I hope he feels the force of Satan's observation in the inferno – I find it true –

> The mind is its own place, and in itself
> Can make a heaven of hell!

This is certainly true to a considerable extent; – the mind may train itself to take vast flights & leave the body behind – to create an Eden round it – or bring the gardens of Alcina.[18]

She could leap easily from a Miltonic Eden to the seductive garden of Renaissance romance. Had Courtenay read the Romance of Ariosto, she asked, or the new edition of the tragedies of Alfieri?

Poetry was a solace, and also a challenge. The old favourites were still widely read: 'reflect how we are Shut up here to read Thomson's Winter and Cowper's Task for four or five months,' lamented Hester Piozzi as winter closed in.[19] Burns's *Poems* and Robert Bloomfield's new *Farmer's Boy* sold ten, twenty times as many copies as the expanded edition of *Lyrical Ballads*, published under Wordsworth's name in 1801. That collection shocked critics, with its radical Preface declaring the intention 'to choose incidents and situations from common life, and to relate or describe them, throughout, as far as was possible in a selection of language really used by men'. The supposedly progressive Francis Jeffrey saw this as an outrage, since the 'language of the vulgar' must be entirely unsuited to poetry and to the expression of fine feeling: 'The love, or grief, or indignation of an enlightened and refined character is not only expressed in a different language but is in itself a different emotion from the love, or grief, or anger of a clown, a tradesman or a market wench.'[20]

Old voices, too, could still shock. The lionised poet of the 1790s, Erasmus Darwin, who had come to be regarded with suspicion as a republican and atheist, died in Derby this year. When his long poem *The Temple of Nature; or, The Origin of Society* was published posthumously in 1803, it summoned a great vista of change, from the birth of stars and the origin of consciousness to balloons, cotton mills and steam engines. Disconcertingly, it offered the first coherent British theory of evolution, describing life emerging from the oceans, crawling on to land, competing to thrive. The poem's view of a bloody evolutionary contest seemed particularly piquant in a time of shortages and battles: 'From Hunger's arm the shafts of Death are hurl'd', wrote Darwin, 'And one great Slaughter-house the warring world!' But Darwin was an eternal optimist. Sex, he believed, was the secret of progress: reproduction, the urge to life, would always conquer. All nature, he wrote hopefully, 'exists in a state of perpetual improvement'.

And now a new literary giant was emerging, one who looked back, not to patterns of natural development, but to the social and cultural heritage of a romanticised past. In February 1802 Walter Scott published the first two-volume edition of *Minstrelsy of the Scottish Border*. Since he had begun collecting poems and songs, ten years before, he had brought in collaborators who were not above 'improving' the texts they found, inventing verses, sharpening rhymes, smoothing rhythms. Manicured for a modern public, the ballads of the *Minstrelsy* sold out in six months. It was a perfect book for dashing volunteers, with its raids and battles and 'songs to savage virtue dear'.[21] The collection fitted too with the new admiration for the bravery of the Highland regiments, and with a slightly more refined taste for the feudal, now that the Gothic bestsellers of Ann Radcliffe and Matthew 'Monk' Lewis were beginning to feel a bit passé. The *Minstrelsy* was like an overture to the great body of Scott's work, profoundly conservative, looking to the Borders, and soon to the Highlands, as one historian has written, as places 'where antique values – feudal fealty rather than commercial contract, rude fierceness and unthinking courage rather than polite sensitivity, sacrifice rather than stratagem, straightforwardness rather than subtlety, and above all uncritical loyalty to one's leaders – had once resided before they had been destroyed by modern ideas of commerce and equality'.[22]

Middle- and upper-class families devoured the *Minstrelsy* and the *Lay of the Last Minstrel*, published three years later. Young Tom Macaulay could recite the whole *Lay* at the age of eight. But Scott's ballad tales also had something in common with the 'lowest' of popular literature, the pedlar's chapbooks that the evangelicals and Hannah More so disliked. Every child in artisan and labouring families knew these. As a boy, Thomas Cooper collected them from the 'number man', or travelling bookseller, the stories of Turpin and Nevison, the famous highwaymen, and 'Bamfylde Moore-Carew the King of the Gipsies' and especially 'the old ballad of Chevy Chase'. He repeated them when alone, he said, 'until they used to make me feel as warlike as did the sight of Matthew Goy when he rode into town with the news of a victory; or the array of the Gainsborough Loyal Volunteers when they marched through the town, on exercise-days, to the sound of the fife and drum'.[23] Samuel Bamford read the same books, gazing into the windows of Swindells the printer, and scraping together farthings to buy Histories of Jack the Giant Killer, St George and the Dragon, Tom Hickathrift, Jack and the Beanstalk, History of the Seven Champions, and the tale of Fair Rosamond'. His poetry, like Cooper's, included Robin Hood's songs and 'Chevy Chase'. John Clare too gained his early learning, he said, from the Psalms and the Book of Job, and the sixpenny romances, from 'Little Red Riding Hood', 'Jack and the Beanstalk', 'Zig-Zag' and 'Prince Cherry'. Like Bamford, he believed every page.

These boys, with little schooling, went on to read the varied canonical books of the day: Bunyan's *Pilgrim's Progress*, Defoe's *Robinson Crusoe*, Goldsmith's *The Vicar of Wakefield* and *History of England*, Smollett's *Peregrine Pickle*, Bloomfield's *Farmer's Boy* and Thomson's much-loved *The Seasons* (Clare walked to the nearest town to try and buy a copy of *The Seasons*, which he heard was on sale cheaply). William Chambers remembered how he and his friends 'were familiar with the comicalities of Gulliver, Don Quixote, and Peregrine Pickle; had dipped into the poetry of Goldsmith, and indulged our romantic tendencies in books of travel and adventure'.[24] And even the classical texts fitted their wartime world. In later life, stuck at a German spa, William Chambers had only one English book, Pope's translation of the *Iliad*, and could not help thinking, he said, 'that exactly fifty years had elapsed since I perused the copy from Elder's library, in a little room looking out upon the High Street of Peebles, where an English regiment was parading recruits raised for Wellington's Peninsular campaign'.

# 30. 'ALWAYS CAPABLE OF DOING MISCHIEF'

At the start of August 1802, Amabel Hume-Campbell's younger sister, Mary Robinson, Baroness Grantham, was writing to her son Tom, who had just left Cambridge and was taking advantage of the peace to travel in Austria and Switzerland. Mary had been widowed young and had brought her two boys up herself, and when Tom's letters came she made careful copies to pass round to family and friends. 'Indeed there is no expressing the entertainment they give me,' she said, 'nor how well they deserve the praises all those give them to whom I give extracts. Whether *scrawled* or not, I can make them out. We always feel interested (but especially with these two last from Switzerland) to have been on the very spots famous for the various actions of the late War.'[1]

Mary's chief excitements, however, were the preparations for Tom's coming of age and his engagement to Henrietta Cole, a perfect match, as her sister Amabel noted: 'she is easy, lively and good-humour'd, runs like a Lapwing and bounds like a Fawn'.[2] But as well as notes on wedding plans, Mary thought Tom would like some political news. She was a conservative Whig, a Pittite, of the kind slipping fast into being called 'Tory'. 'The General Elections have occupied the United Kingdom for some Weeks & are nearly over,' she told him. They had gone off quietly on the whole, with, 'as usual, scenes of uproar in some places, in a few with more evil intentions . . . such as Middlesex & Nottingham . . . several Democrates, such as Sir Francis Burdett have got in, who are always capable of doing mischief'.[3]

In the elections this summer, the first since the Union with Ireland, Opposition candidates found it difficult to make any headway. Thomas Fremantle stood unsuccessfully for Aylesbury, despite Betsey's efforts at entertaining agents and local bigwigs, hosting a breakfast for the freeholders and obeying her husband's instructions to avoid the Dillons and her 'Popery people'. The other candidates, she said, were 'spending a great deal of money in shameful Bribery, and Aylesbury is already a scene of confusion and riot'.[4] Addington gained a comfortable majority. But as Mary Robinson told Tom, the radicals triumphed in the hotly contested election of Francis Burdett in Middlesex. Burdett was a scintillating speaker, slim, handsome and charismatic, a fox-hunting squire, painted by Thomas Lawrence in romantic pose against an appropriately stormy sky. An admirer and follower of John Horne Tooke, he had become a popular hero after his championing of the Coldbath Fields prisoners in 1799, but he had also benefited personally from the old corrupt ways – his father-in-law, the banker Thomas Coutts, had bought him a parliamentary seat six years before for £4000, largely to save Burdett's marriage to his demanding daughter Sophia. (The Burdetts stayed together, had six children and moved into the Coutts family's grand Piccadilly mansion in 1802, although their marriage was fraught: all society knew of his affair with the radical hostess Jane Harley, Lady Oxford, who was also Byron's mentor and mistress.)

In Nottingham, which Mary Robinson also mentioned in connection with scenes of uproar, the framework knitters turned against their current MP, Daniel Coke, who had stopped supporting their opposition to the war. Instead they brought in their own candidate, the Unitarian Joseph Birch from Liverpool. When Birch won, the procession included a tricolour flag and other French symbols, including 'four and twenty Vestals (modern ones) cloathed in white and singing "Millions be free" and other revolutionary songs'.[5] The government pamphleteer John Bowles called it a 'Jacobin triumph'. Coke petitioned against the result, on the grounds that his supporters had been intimidated and the magistrates had failed to restrain the demonstrations, which had echoes of the French Revolution: his petition was upheld and he was re-elected, although the whole Nottingham corporation campaigned against him.

Unlike Nottingham's, most town corporations were stoutly Tory. They were pleased with the peace, ready to toast Napoleon as well as George III, Pitt and Addington. In September 1802, when James Oakes was elected alderman of Bury St Edmunds for the fourth time, his guests included the Marquess Cornwallis and the French agent M. Otto, as well as the local MPs, gentlemen, tradesmen and farmers:

The Honor of Monsieur Otto's Company was quite unexpected. Lord Hervey brot him down for the Day & only introducd him ½ hour before Dinner. It was particularly honourable for me to sit at the head of the Table between the two great Peace Plenipotentiaries & the Marquess & Mr Otto seemd to enjoy each others Company most exceedingly. Indeed it made the Day pass off wh uncommon Glee.

After Drinking the Royal Family, the first Consul was drank & met with unbounded Applause.[6]

Yet despite toasts to Napoleon, Tory citizens were still suspicious of 'Jacobin' disruption. This year Addington reinstated habeas corpus and released most of the imprisoned radicals, but many magistrates clung to the belief that the United Irishmen and their English supporters were plotting insurrection. In November 1802 spies named Colonel Edward Despard, one of the London Corresponding Society members freed from Coldbath Fields, as the leader of a plan to seize the Tower of London and Bank of England and to murder the king. The evidence was slight, but Despard was found guilty, despite an appeal from Nelson, with whom he had served in the West Indies during the American war. The jury recommended mercy, but the new Lord Chief Justice, Lord Ellenborough, damned Despard's 'atrocious, abominable and traitorous conspiracy' and sentenced him to be hanged, drawn and quartered, with six other defendants: two army privates, two carpenters, a shoemaker and a slater. Apart from the fifty-year-old Despard, all were young men with families. The barbaric punishment was commuted to hanging and in February 1803 around twenty thousand people turned up to see Despard swing on the gatehouse at Horsemonger Lane. The seven men were hanged together, and as each was cut down the executioner hacked off his head and showed it to the crowd, declaiming, 'This is the head of a traitor.'

Although this conspiracy was doubtful, there were certainly links between United Irishmen and British radicals and plans were indeed afoot for another Irish rising. In October 1802, a month before Despard's arrest, Robert Emmet, who had fled to France after the rebellion, returned to Dublin and began gathering weapons and explosives. His attempt to capture Dublin Castle in the following July was a fiasco. The weather was bad, the date was changed, most supporters went home and in the middle of the street fighting enthusiasts dragged the Lord Chief Justice of Ireland, Lord Kilwarden, and his great-nephew from their carriage and hacked them to death with pikes. Emmet, horrified by the violence, called the whole thing off and fled to the Wicklow hills. He was quickly hunted down and arrested, and at his trial for treason he vehemently repudiated any idea that he was linked to France. He would fight the French invader, he insisted, in a moving speech often quoted in later struggles for Ireland's independence: it was Ireland he cared about. 'Let no man write my epitaph,' he said, but 'let my character and my motives repose in obscurity and peace, till other times and other men can do them justice. *Then* shall my character be vindicated; *then* may my epitaph be written.'[7] As this was repeated, so the words acquired more emphasis: 'When my country takes its place among the nations of the earth, *then*, and *not till then*, let my epitaph be written. I have done.'[8]

Emmet was executed the following September, in Dublin's Thomas Street, the scene of the most intense fighting. After his trial Cobbett, once such a supporter of the government, rounded on Addington, claiming that Ireland was 'in a state of total neglect and abandonment', and publishing three letters under the name 'Juverna' (from the Irish judge Robert Johnson), blaming the Lord Lieutenant, Lord Hardwicke, for doing nothing despite prior warnings. The government and Hardwicke were enraged and Cobbett was charged with criminal libel. He was tried in front of Ellenborough, and it took the jury just ten minutes to find him guilty and fine him £500.[9]

In this troubled peace, the government was jittery, quick to crack down. At first there were no fears of general unrest. After a good harvest food prices dropped to their old customary levels, while trade revived in the textile towns of the north-west. In Manchester there was fierce competition for business. Samuel Bamford, working in the warehouse of a 'counterpane and bed-quilt manufacturer', watched the Scottish Grant Brothers across the road outrage neighbouring merchants by touting for customers, stopping traders in the street and asking them in to look over their 'stock of unequalled prints at the very lowest prices'.[10]

One of these Manchester merchants, buoyant at the thought of open markets in Europe again, was Nathan Mayer Rothschild. In 1799, aged twenty-two, Rothschild had arrived from Frankfurt, where he had been working as an agent with the family firm, getting commissions for British cotton masters in Brussels, Basle and Paris. 'I could speak nothing but German,' he told Sir Thomas Fowell Buxton years later. 'The nearer I got to England, the cheaper the goods were. As soon as I got to Manchester, I laid out all my money, things were so cheap, and I made a good profit.'[11] Using credit and capital from his father's firm he placed orders for cloth in Nottingham, Leeds and Glasgow, and also made good cash deals with local weavers. 'On Tuesdays and Thursdays', he wrote in December 1802,

the weavers who live in the country twenty miles round Manchester bring here their goods, some twenty or thirty pieces, others more, others less, which they sell to merchants here at two, three and six months' credit. But as there are generally some of them in want of money and willing to sacrifice some profit to procure it, a person who goes with ready money may sometimes buy 15 or 20 percent cheaper.[12]

Buying cheaply in bulk, he could undercut his competitors in any sales to the continent. His only worries were the constant haggling and long credit terms demanded by his customers: 'If I send off the goods it is two months before I can draw at 3 months date and then . . . I may be kept out of my money five or six months . . . it is very easy to get commissions but not quite so easy to get paid for them.'[13] Yet he did get paid, and this was the start of an extraordinary story, the rise of the Rothschild fortunes in England.

Lancashire was enjoying a new boom. In March 1802 Rowbottom exuberantly recorded the rise in piece-work rates: 'the country flourishes and all is joy and happiness.'[14] But in the west of England trade was not so good. As men returned from the war desperate for work, they were taken on cheaply, often to work the new machines. In protest, unemployed weavers and shearmen (skilled finishers like the Yorkshire croppers) attacked factories, set fire to clothiers' hayricks, cut down their trees and ambushed carts, hacking the finished cloth to pieces. In July 1802 one clothier, Thomas Tugwell, found a letter pushed under his workshop door:

Death or glory to you T.& M. Tugwell. We will burn you and your Horses we will Cut your heart out and Eat him, you ot to have your Dam heart cut out of your Body you will Go to Hell for Starveing the Poor thee Shot Shaw fly by night for some of you.[15]

Workers' leaders were arrested and large numbers of militia were drafted in, but the clothiers, seeing the mills burn, agreed to the shearmen's demands.

In Yorkshire Benjamin Gott took up the challenge. When news spread that he had taken on two new croppers above the age for apprenticeship, and was about to bring in gig-mills, his entire finishing department walked out, and once his fellow merchants supported him the strike hit the whole town. Determined to break it Gott tried to get croppers from the West Country, employing agents to scatter handbills:

WANTED IMMEDIATELY AT LEEDS, in Yorkshire. A NUMBER OF JOURNEY-MEN SHEARMEN, sober, steady, good workmen will meet with constant employment and good wages by applying to Messrs. Wormald, Gott & Wormald, and their manufactory NEAR LEEDS.

But no labour came. The Leeds men stayed out for four months, and cloth workers across the West Riding raised funds to keep them from starving. Left with piles of unfinished goods, Gott and the Leeds merchants caved in.

George Walker, 'Croppers'. The cropper's teasels, used to comb the wet cloth, are fixed to a wooden frame on the floor. He holds his shears in one hand and works a lever, a 'gig' on the upper edge, with the other

Now both sides turned to parliament. The West Country masters, frustrated by the workers' victories and their refusal to set aside the ancient apprenticeship rules and other old laws, petitioned for the laws' repeal. Supporting them, the Yorkshire merchants and manufacturers persuaded the Commons to bring in a Bill to suspend the most restrictive laws for a year. In response, angry cloth workers came to London. Yorkshire croppers dusted down their best clothes and took the cheapest coach or wagon down the Great North Road, while the domestic clothiers of Gloucestershire, Wiltshire and Somerset trooped in from the west. At the start of May 1803 they hovered around Westminster, waiting with their counsel to be summoned before a select committee of the House of Commons, set up to examine the Bill. Among them was Anne Edwards, a cloth drawer who repaired tears in finished cloth. Her independence rather startled the committee. 'Is your Husband here?' they asked. 'No, he has no Business here.'[16]

The cloth workers were grilled about every aspect of their lives, and, as the questions piled up, so their direction changed, concentrating less on wages and apprenticeships, and more on sabotage, trade associations and Benefit Clubs. 'Is there any secret article in the Wiltshire subscription?' 'No, there is not,' replied the weaver James Jones, it was for the sick and distressed: 'There was one of our Men who subscribed to the Expence, who had a very heavy Affliction on him, Rheumatism, that the Use of his Limbs was entirely taken away. The Man's Family were taken down in the Distemper, the Fever, and we gave him Two Guineas to support him.'[17] The committee pressed another weaver, Daniel Whitworth, about the strike at Gott's mill. Sensing danger, he trod with care: 'How often has Mr Gott's manufactory been destroyed since you knew Leeds?' – 'Never that I know of, except when it was set on Fire by Accident; it never has been offered to be destroyed or hurt the least in the World that I know of.'[18]

Such answers made little impact. Having gathered all the evidence into four hundred closely printed pages, the committee came down firmly on the side of the manufacturers. Their recommendations to suspend the laws outraged the cloth workers, but each year the laws were suspended again. Many workers felt that they were losing traditional rights and independence. They could see this even in the ideal 'factory colonies' being built by Robert Owen and Samuel Greg, with schools, chapels and shops, and rules governing all behaviour. As with Pitt's Health and Safety of Apprentices Bill, passed this year, such projects mixed philanthropy with commercial sense, as Owen later explained: 'From experience which cannot deceive me I venture to assure you your time and money so applied, if directed by a true knowledge of the subject, would return you not 5, 10 or 15% for your capital so expended but often 50 and in many cases 100%.'[19]

In Lancashire Samuel Greg, like Peel and Owen, kept pouring money into his factories, improving his waterwheels and spinning and weaving frames and regulating his workers' lives. Styal was a calm village, with no alehouses, no drunks and little trouble. But still, workers ran away: some went home to their families, a few became soldiers, others left because they could not bear it any more.

Hannah Greg had eight children before she was thirty-four but found time to run schools for the apprentices, following the precepts of Richard and Maria Edgeworth's secular *Practical Education*, recommending fresh air and play rather than rote learning. Her own children loved Quarry Bank, swimming in the cut and playing in the sandstone caves of the huge garden. In November 1801, at the start of the peace, eleven-year-old Bessy Greg described family days there:

Papa has given Thomas, Robert and me the upper cave and we have put up a ladder of ropes but mama says we must not get up it . . . Robert goes forward very fast in learning both to read and write . . . Sam has just become a scholar of Miss Bate . . . Hannah Mary is very cross for her teeth hurt her.[20]

Six years later, returning to Styal from Manchester, Bessy wrote in her diary, 'After tea we went to Quarry Bank, and the Children were very glad to see us. We went up to the Apprentice House; – all were very glad to see us.'[21] Neither she nor her mother were abashed by the gulf between their lives and the paupers'. This did not seem an injustice, of the kind that had made Hannah so angry in Ireland, or had roused her feelings about slavery – it was, instead, a natural division, like officers and privates, masters and men, the poor in their place, the rich in theirs. There seemed little reason why workers in this mill, or any others, should be willing to do mischief.

# 31. ALBION

The spring of 1802 was cold and wet, with frost and hail in May, but in midsummer the sun shone strong. In Grasmere Dorothy Wordsworth saw tumbling bullfinches among the blossom, the columbines and lilies and wild roses flowering, the scarlet beans 'up in crowds'.[1] In June she woke to find swallows nesting below her window – it was the time for summer tours. That August, while she and William were in Calais, others would come to the Lakes, seeking the romance of nature and the wild.

'London is become, especially of late, the trading metropolis of Europe, and indeed of the whole world,' declared Henry Thornton in 1802.[2] This was only one aspect of the city Charles Lamb loved. 'For my part,' he wrote, 'with reverence to our friends northward, I must confess I am not romance-bit about Nature.' Just as important to him was 'all the furniture of my world':

Streets, streets, streets, markets, theatres, churches, Covent Garden, Shops sparkling with pretty faces of industrious milliners, neat sempstresses, Ladies cheapening, Gentlemen behind counters lying, Authors in the street with spectacles . . . Lamps lit at night, Pastry cook & Silver smith shops, Beautiful Quakers of Pentonville, noise of coaches, drousy cry of mechanic watchmen at night, with Bucks reeling home drunk if you happen to wake at midnight, cries of fire and stop thief, Inns of court . . . old Book stalls, Jeremy Taylors, Burtons on melancholy, and Religio Medici's on every stall – These are thy

Pleasures O London with-the-many-sins – O City abounding in whores – for these may thy Keswick and her Giant Brood go hang.[3]

In this city with its very poor and its very rich and its unvarying seasonal round, Sarah Spencer, daughter of the Whig politician and book collector Earl Spencer, the First Lord of the Admiralty who had resigned with Pitt in 1801, would soon be presented at court. She was seventeen, and told her grandmother that she wore 'a white crape train and petticoat, with silver embroidery on the sleeves and round my waist, and on my head a very pretty bandeau of diamonds and five white feathers'. She went with her mother and her aunt Georgiana, Duchess of Devonshire, and remembered only the crush, all the girls assembled 'like a pack of cards, one leaning on the other, till we got near the Queen; then the crowd opened, the Queen put out her cheek and I kissed it, and then made a curtsey . . . But, as I said before, I really am not perfectly clear about it.'[4]

Sarah was one of a new generation of aristocratic women, all tireless letter-writers. She was shy, dominated by her tyrannical mother, as all the Spencer children were, and although she had no fear of balls and 'squeezes', as the packed parties were called, she longed to be out of town. Every summer over the next few years, the family set off on holiday, often to the sea. The royal family had made the seaside fashionable, George III with his family at Weymouth, and the Prince of Wales at Brighton. Five years hence, Sarah wrote that they might go to 'some sea place, perhaps not, and if we do I think Scarborough and Weymouth are hardly far apart enough to mention them as the extremities of our indecision. Every place on the British coast has an equal chance of our presence.'[5] The place she liked least was Brighton, 'a Londonish town full of fine folks, barouches, princes, theatres, and public lounging rooms'. The place she liked best was Ryde, on the Isle of Wight, with its view of the ships at anchor. Here they could wander past cottages and across the great field, which, she wrote one Sunday evening, 'was full of all the fashionable of Ryde, male and female, shewing off their best dresses, and enjoying the beauty of the evening, while two sets of boys, most of them in sailors dresses, were playing at cricket'.

At the seaside the Spencers and their circle nodded coolly at the rich tradesmen and provincial gentry. This summer the Galtons from Birmingham were also off to the sea. From Sidmouth Samuel Galton sent their servant Patty, Mrs Patterson, detailed instructions about putting their son Hubert on the Bath coach, making sure he had money and a notebook to write down expenses. In Bath Hubert must stay at the White Lion before getting the morning mail coach to Exeter where John the coachman would meet him. Travelling had rules, noted Galton, telling Hubert that he must take no wine or ale, 'only beer with half water', and must give the waiter sixpence and the Bath chambermaid a shilling.[6] It was a fussy, fatherly letter but Galton's anxiety was understandable. Looking back on his travels, William Rose Boughton of Shropshire wrote to his father, remembering

numerous journeys in stage coaches, in the course of which I travelled with a cargo of Mrs Mostyns Paraquites & Cacatoos (I do not know if I rightly spell the names of these horridly screeching Birds) and at another time with a Subject on the roof for the dissection Room at Oxford, besides having met with innumerable biped brutes and beasts.[7]

The Gurney families of Norwich also took off to the sea every summer, to their circle of houses near Cromer. And James Oakes and his wife took lodgings at Yarmouth for nearly a month in 1802 while their house in Bury was painted. They spent evenings with friends and went to the assembly and the theatre, but the main draw was the sea itself. Oakes drank the salt water and bathed in a seawater bath every other morning, 'wch promised to agree extremely well with me. Riding & walking 5 or 6 hours every day by the Sea-Side.'[8] Next year he went back, but dispensed with the seawater drink. Yet sadly, it was not Oakes who was ill but his wife, his 'dear Mrs O'. Soon after their return in 1803, after what sounds like a stroke, she died 'without a Groan or even a Sigh or the least Shew of pain'. She was sixty-four, and they had lived together 'with the truest Love & Affection' for thirty-eight years.

*

After Elizabeth's death Oakes took many more tours, leaving the bank in the charge of his son Orbell. He went not to the sea, but round the country, often for weeks at a time – to Liverpool and the Midlands, to Kent and Sussex and the Isle of Wight ('travelld 545 miles on horseback', he wrote proudly'[9]). Touring was the ultimate form of holiday for the middling orders, and as they travelled they liked to keep journals. They wanted to see two different kinds of things: picturesque scenery and heritage – meaning mountains and lakes, ruins, abbeys and country mansions – and the wonders of the modern, industrial, commercial world. Tourism was regarded as a form of personal education, but it was also a way of crystallising the sense of nationhood so needed in wartime, and a mode of spreading 'politeness'. Indeed travelling was a positive duty, or so the author William Mavor suggested in the introduction to his six-volume compendium of 'Tours' by various authors, *The British Tourists: or, Traveller's Pocket Companion, Through England, Wales, Scotland and Ireland*:

By the frequency of communication, an acquaintance with the practices of the most dexterous in business, with the modes of the most refined in manners, has been rapidly diffused over the great mass of people; and the various tribes and classes of men, who are subject to the same government, however remotely situated, are now either animated by example, or taught by contrast.[10]

James Oakes was, in many ways, a typical middle-class tourist, though he set out to improve himself rather than the people he met. He enjoyed country mansions, statues and paintings, gardens and hothouses and the 'enchanting and romantick' scenery of the Peak District, but he also liked the growing towns and ports, especially Liverpool, where his sisters lived, with its Custom House, its asylum for the blind, its Lyceum and Union Coffee House, 'most superb Rooms, also the Concert room, wch exceeds anything I ever saw'.[11]

When Eric Svedenstierna visited Liverpool on his tour in 1802–3, he too praised the fine buildings and country houses around, and the subscription library with its 'newspapers and journals in all languages'. The port, where huge quantities of cotton, coffee and sugar were unloaded, amazed him, but he was appalled by the continuing slave trade, despite the cosmetic 'improvements', the greater room and the presence of doctors aboard, which made conditions marginally better than on Dutch and French ships. Coleridge had felt the same thing two years before, writing to Tom Poole: 'The slave-merchants of Liverpool fly over the head of the slave-merchants of Bristol, as Vultures over carrion crows.'[12]

Travelling was a way of meeting new people, and in Liverpool Coleridge met the abolitionist William Roscoe, who was also a writer and lover of art. He had founded a Society for the Encouragement of the Arts twenty years before, organising the first public exhibitions outside London, and had published his well-received *Life of Lorenzo de' Medici* in 1796. Roscoe was 'natural, sweet, and cheerful', Coleridge told Poole, 'zealous in kindness, and a republican, with all the feelings of prudence and all the manners of good sense'. In this circle he also met William Rathbone, and James Currie, the campaigning physician to the Infirmary. Currie was a loyal Scot, and after Burns died in 1796 he had agreed to edit his chaotic papers: his four-volume edition of Burns's works, accompanied by a biography, appeared in 1800, appalling admirers with its revelations about Burns's drinking. In 1802, Richard Heber encountered exactly the same Liverpool circle. His father, the Revd Reginald Heber, told his sister Elizabeth that Richard had met 'poor Poet Burns Biographer, a Book which Richard brought with him from Town which is well written and has afforded us much entertainment'.[13]

The gentry travelled for pleasure, the merchants for business, the artists for inspiration. Even the militia, moving to their different barracks, sometimes seemed tourists in disguise, indulging in the same lust for striking landscapes and industrial wonders. In 1796, Jack Gill, serving with the Shropshire Militia, had marched from Edmonton to North Shields, writing from Matlock in Derbyshire on the way. 'It is quite plain that you have been a very great traveller', wrote his father the Revd Gill admiringly, and must have visited 'many beautifully romantic places':

You did not say whether you had a peep into the Devil's Arse! The wonders there I have much read of, and were I a young man, and journeying in that neighbourhood, I should be eager to see them. I have noted your track on the Map from your first commencing soldier to the place of your present station, and cannot but think with you that you have made a tolerably complete tour of England. As I find you are amongst the Collieries I shall expect to hear, together with other matters, of some subterraneous excursions which you and your Brother Officers may now make, in those dark and dreary regions.[14]

The Reverend had obviously been down mines himself and warned his son that if he did commit himself 'to the bucket' he might feel pleasure in the descent, but nothing compared to the wonderful sensation of coming up again.

Picturesque accounts of caves, mountains and ivy-covered ruins jostled in letters and diaries with scenes from the industrial present. Richard Heber's trip, for example, took him north from Liverpool to Scotland, where he called at New Lanark, to be guided round the cotton mills. The next stop was Paisley, to see 'a great many manufactures such a cotton-spinning, ribbon-weaving, Lawn-making, tanning etc.' The industrial gave way to the romantic as he sailed up Loch Lomond and drove to Oban before crossing to Mull and marching across the island on the 'rugged mountain sheep walk' that would be trodden by John Keats in the summer of 1818.[15] Then, almost as soon as he got back from Scotland, Richard headed to the other end of Britain, to Cornwall, where he went down a copper mine near Land's End, ladder after ladder into the depths, crawling along the adits, swallowing a glass of brandy and singing 'God Save the King' underground.

Such mines gave a new sense of the sublime. Richard Colt Hoare, visiting the spectacular Parys copper mine in Anglesey, whose great caverns were open to the air, found it almost impossible to describe 'the singularly romantic and picturesque scenes of this mountain'.[16] Colt Hoare, who left the banking to his cousins and brothers, had recently added two wings to his house at Stourhead, one to hold the collection of paintings brought back from abroad, and the other for his library, and was now planting broad-leaved trees and rhododendrons

John 'Warwick' Smith, *Junction of the Mona and Parys Mountain Copper Mines*, 1790

around his grandfather's lake and classical temples. A fan of the picturesque, he was also an antiquarian: every year he toured the British isles, sketching and making notes on its ancient monuments and ruins. This was a growing interest in Britain and during the war new antiquarian societies were founded in several provincial towns, their members contributing articles to *Archaeologica* and information for the new county histories, like Hutchinson's *History of Cumberland*, published in 1794. Colt Hoare's particular love was Wales, land of the bards and druids: he had a shooting lodge at Bala, and had provided the drawings engraved for William Coxe's *Historical Tour of Monmouthshire*, published in 1801. But he was equally fascinated by his own county of Wiltshire, undertaking the first excavations at Stonehenge and exploring its many barrows and ancient sites.[17]

Other tourists in 1802 thought the new much more interesting than the old. The Hardys left their Norfolk farm and brewery on a trip to Hull and York. While Mary walked on the Humber bank and heard every sermon in the chapels, her husband and son visited the breweries, comparing them to their own. Another business-holidaymaker was the linen tycoon Jack Marshall. His wife Jane Pollard, one of six daughters of a wool and flax merchant in Halifax, had been a close friend of Dorothy Wordsworth since childhood: Dorothy came to the Marshalls' wedding and the Marshalls went to the Lakes for their honeymoon. They stayed close, and Dorothy had written to Jane in excitement in the spring of 1800 when she and William were settling in to Dove Cottage in Grasmere, telling her of their boat on the lake, and the garden with its roses and honeysuckles and beans trained on threads up the wall. The Lake District became Jack's favourite place, and towards the end of the war he bought a house there, Hallsteads on the western bank of Ullswater. Here he bought land and raised sheep and was accepted in a way that, as a Unitarian and self-made man, he never could be in Leeds.

Most tourists to the Lakes stayed in comfortable hotels, rode over the passes on ponies, followed routes around the 'stations' designed for picturesque views, and glided on the lakes to hear cannon-fire echo off the crags. But, much as he admired the scenery, John Marshall's mind was always partly on his business. By 1800 Marshall's Leeds mills alone were making a hundred thousand bundles of yarn a year and he now had 150 looms there, weaving coarse cloth, hessian and canvas. On his Cumbrian trips he visited mills in Keswick and Ambleside, Wigton and Whitehaven and Egremont, looking for tips, new products and threats from competitors. 'The Cumberland checks', he wrote, 'are about half of them consumed in England, the other half exported to America & the West Indies & used in the Navy . . .'

Mrs Christie of Cockermouth bleaches her linen yarn by the chemical process at 5/- per Cumberland bundle equal to 3/- our 10 lbs. They make it a good colour but it turns to the yellow afterwards. They take a month to do it – they say they give it five weeks, & never lay it on the grass – They steep it in the liquor in tubs, abt. 1 cwt in each, & keep moving it about in the tub.[18]

When Marshall gazed at the scenery, he was also interested in how people made their living. His notes were a mix of the terse, the practical and the romantic, with plenty of the standard disappointments: 'To Ambleside – Saw the Waterfall – nothing without more water.'[19] He walked around Rydal Water and admired the reflections of Loughrigg; from Keswick he walked over Honister to Buttermere. At Coniston, he made notes on lead mines, and at Wasdale on the clergy: 'the parish priest has £20 a year, and at Wastdale Head there is another church, the parson of which has a salary of £25. They both live on their income without any other imployment, & are too idle to improve them by teaching a school, which is most wanted.' A life without work was inconceivable.

In 1802, going north to Dumfries, Glasgow and Paisley, his route overlapping with Richard Heber's, Marshall went to New Lanark, where his notebook was out in a flash, recording the size of buildings, number of apprentices and lists of rules. He observed dryly that 'Mr Owen, who now conducts the concern, has the management of the branch of the Bank of Scotland at Glasgow where he spends half his time'. He returned more than once, noting in 1807 that Owen now employed sixteen hundred people and was building many houses, but 'Mr Owen is said to be a very strict man & is not popular in the neighbourhood'.[20] Everywhere Marshall went, he picked up information.

Marshall and the Hardys had a definite purpose. But for most trippers, factories and mills were entertainment rather than business. Sophia Thrale's tour this year began with scenic Derbyshire and the 'gloomy horrors' of its caves, followed by modern Manchester with its cotton manufactures: 'very curious indeed & well worthy of observation – numbers of people employed and quantities of Children – all carried on by means of a Steam engine the mechanism of which we examined – the principal people earn from eighteen to twenty shillings per week – the noise unbearable & heat intense'.[21] With a secure income, Sophia could afford to be fascinated before she wafted away to more picturesque scenes, relieved to leave the calico-printing works, which 'pleased us extremely', but still 'the heat & stink dreadful'.

A few years later, on her way to see her sisters in Scotland, Betsey Fremantle drove through Nottingham, 'a frightful old Town, the streets narrower than any I ever saw, oppressive, smoaky, noisy, riotous from the number of people employed in the Manufactories, the inn detestable . . .'[22] But some people found the smoke and dirt an exotic change from their daily lives. One summer traveller in 1802 was fifteen-year-old Hannah Gurney, daughter of the serious Joseph Gurney of the Grove and cousin of the wilder Earlham tribe. She set out with her family to visit her mother's relations in the north-east and as she went, she dutifully wrote her diary. Hannah knew what she was supposed to see and feel excited by: scenery, ancient buildings, mills and mines. But she was also fascinated by every small, new detail of peacetime England. The first stop was Swaffham, where they had supper and were 'regaled not only with some very good chickens but with the singing of some gentlemen met to celebrate Lord Nelson's Victory at the Nile'.[23] Then came the fens with stiff boggy soil and ditches instead of fences, and then the Great North Road, where she sat on the coach box with her father, trundling through rich green countryside and watching the haymakers in the meadows. The trip took them north to cousins on the Tees, and a familiar Quaker community: they 'called on Bro. Richardson who is surrounded by a great many virgin daughters he went with us to see a manufactory of damask which is very simple, a boy standing on one side of the loom and pulling the threads that form the pattern.' At Brother Nevel's bleaching mill: 'We saw nothing particular in it except its making a disagreeable noise and smell we next went to his flower mill to be weighed & afterwards took a walk.'

This was interesting, but Hannah wanted the romantic and the picturesque too, and County Durham had satisfyingly dramatic places, like Hartlepool with its old forts and the caves of Crimdon beach, where the noise of the waves 'dashing into them like thunder produced a very grand effect'. The miller by the ferry let them change their wet stockings in his warehouse, something she never remembered doing before, she said, in the presence of sacks and ropes. She found romance on a hill gazing over Cleveland, with sea on one side and moors on the other, where the still air beneath the burning sun was suddenly disturbed by a whirlwind. She found it too in Tynemouth churchyard, where sailors were buried 'in order that their ghosts may enjoy the first sea breeze & the view of the ships' and where the castle's winding staircase made her shiver like Catherine Morland in *Northanger Abbey* (which Jane Austen was just about to send to the Bath publisher, where it would linger, unpublished, for ten years).

Tyneside was exciting in the modern mode. Around the coal mines, Hannah feared being scalded to death or mown down by engines, boilers and machines. While she was there, the discovery of coal in a deep seam at Percy Main caused wild rejoicings: 'almost before I was awake I heard a firing of guns as made me thoroughly glad there was a peace – it was rejoicing at the ropery for the little bit of coal that we saw yesterday.' The hunt for this seam had been hard and slow. The first shaft, sunk in 1796, was stopped by a vast quicksand, with water rushing in at a thousand gallons a minute. The water was dammed with a great cast-iron cylinder, or tub, and slowly the shaft reached the coal, 120 fathoms deep.[24] At the winning of Percy Main, Hannah Bates, one of the wagoners' wives, was queen of the day, sitting on a wagon of coal, with the pit-men walking in procession; dinner under a canopy was followed by dancing, where Mrs Bates was grabbed by a large man, black with coal, who gave her a 'most hearty kiss'. John Sykes's *Historical Register* also recorded the firing of guns, the band playing 'The Keel Row' as the coal was delivered to the boat, and the workmen's dinner of beef and plum pudding, strong beer and punch.[25]

Next day Hannah's eyes were open wide at celebrations of a different kind, as they watched a disbanded corps of volunteers present a silver cup to their colonel, grandly decked in his regimentals, '& deliver up those arms which have been so nobly used in defence of their king & constitution'. The chaplain made an incomprehensible speech, and the band played 'God Save the King, & then a huzza which was a very entertaining sight but we were forced to go away before it was quite finished because of dinner'. Like the much older Sophia Thrale, this fifteen-year-old had an entirely unselfconscious sense of superiority. On her industrial visits, she fraternised with the natives while airily floating above them. At the glasshouses of South

Shields she laughed at blowing a bottle after the pipe had 'been wetted by the coral lips of a man who chewed tobacco'; at a calico printer she and her sisters tried the work 'but as we did nothing but the same thing over and over again we grew terribly tired before one, when at last we were set at liberty'. Abandoning their repetitive task, they flew off to dinner again.

While Hannah explored the north-east, her Earlham cousins were over in the west, touring the Lakes and sketching waterfalls and mountains. But critics were beginning to disdain picturesque tourism, 'for which a new language has been formed', as Southey put it in the person of his Spanish visitor, 'and for which the English have discovered a new sense in themselves, which assuredly was not possessed by their fathers'.[26] Towards the end of the wars William Combe mocked it cruelly in *The Tour of Dr Syntax in Search of the Picturesque*, illustrated by Rowlandson's prints. 'I'm going further, on a scheme', the Doctor explains,

> Which you may think an idle dream;
> At the fam'd Lakes to take a look,
> And of my *Journey* make a *Book*.

Combe combined this hunt with the tourists' equally powerful love of the Gothic:

> A sad and ruined scene,
> Where owls and bats, and starlings dwell, –
> And where, alas! As people tell,
> At the dark hour when midnight reigns,
> Ghosts walk, all arm'd, and rattle chains . . .
> A castle, and a ruin too, –
> I'll hasten there and take a view.[27]

In these war years, however, the rapture over a misty past, ghosts and all, also reflected an unthinking, sentimental patriotism, a retreat into history that offered a validation of current national loyalty. For a people weary of war it was heartening to evoke an image of ancient 'Albion', a landscape of sacrifice, poetry and inalienable rights.

Rowlandson, *Dr Syntax Sketching the Lake*

Heading for poetry and grandeur, Sophia Thrale and her sister left the calico-printing works of Manchester and headed north to the Lakes. Sophia was determined to follow one of the recommended itineraries in Thomas West's 1789 *Guide to the Lakes*, arriving from the south across the treacherous tidal quicksands off Lancaster. She was rather irritated by the local reaction: 'The people of Lancaster endeavoured to impress us with some idea of danger in crossing these sands, but as we took the precaution of following the Mail which goes every Day, no degree of prejudice could possibly magnify it into a difficulty.'[28] Over they went, admiring, as West decreed, the view of mountains as they crossed, comforted by the presence of the modern mail coach yet thrilled by the thought of the danger from the shifting sands and flowing tide. Once across, they still followed West's route – Cartmel, Furness, Dalton, Coniston, Hawkshead, Bowness, the Langdales and Grasmere to Keswick. Here they stayed with friends at Crossthwaite vicarage, making trips to Borrowdale and sketching with Joseph Wilkinson, who would later illustrate Wordsworth's *Guide to the Lakes*. On 25 August 1802, a day of terrible Lakeland rain, a slightly stunned Sophia confided to her diary that 'There was Company to dinner, among them a Mr Cold-ridge who struck me as being remarkably clever, unfortunately a provincial dialect, but is a most brilliant converser and very entertaining'.

The brilliant Coleridge with his West Country burr was currently renting Greta Hall, five minutes up the road, with his wife Sara and their children. That summer Southey and Edith, Sara's sister, moved there too. For Coleridge, the Lakes were not a scene of romantic tourism. He was wretchedly unhappy, bothered by debts and his health was poor, solaced by more opium and the addictive Kendal Black drop, an opium painkiller which he mixed with a great deal of brandy. He was also increasingly estranged from his quick-tempered wife and obsessed with Sara Hutchinson, 'Asra', his muse. He had met her when the Wordsworths were staying with her family at Sockburn on their return from Germany: this year, in October 1802, Wordsworth would marry Sara's sister Mary, after his return from France.

The mountains were Coleridge's escape and inspiration. He had just made his foolhardy, exhilarating ascent of Scafell and his notebooks were full of images of water, wind and shifting light. At the end of September he wrote a study of the waterfalls for Sara Hutchinson, describing the falls of Lodore as a Miltonic epic: 'the Precipitation of the fallen Angels from Heaven, Flight & Confusion, & Distraction, but all harmonized into one majestic Thing by the genius of Milton, who describes it'.[29] By contrast, Buttermere's Halse Fall was the 'War-Song of a Scandinavian Bard'. What a sight it was, he wrote, 'to look down on such a Cataract! – the wheels, that circumvolve in it – the leaping up & plunging forward to that infinity of Pearls & Glass Bulbs – the continual *change* of the *Matter*, the perpetual *Sameness* of the *Form* – it is an awful Image & Shadow of God & the World.'

Up from London, Charles and Mary Lamb were also staying at Greta Hall in late August – were they at the dinner too? Back in Town, Lamb wrote, 'I shall remember your mountains to the last day I live. They haunt me perpetually,' and perhaps there really was, he thought, 'that which tourists call *romantic*'.[30] It did not take him long to realise that 'After all I could not *live* in Skiddaw: I could spend a year, two, three years among them, but I must have a prospect of seeing Fleet Street at the end of that time: or I should mope and pine away.'[31]

# V : SAILING

## 1803–1808

Fear not, my Peggy, stormy winds, nor fear th' exulting foe;
'Tis glory calls, my King commands, and Colin now must go:
He goes, but soon will come again, enrich'd with gold and
      fame;
Nay dry those tears, my bonny lass, to weep it were a shame.

*The crew's on board, the sails are spread, our conq'ring flag unfurl'd,*
*And England's Navy still shall be – the wonder of the world.*

Song, Anon., 'The Hull Packet', July 1800

## 32. INTO WAR AGAIN

The longed-for peace was fragile from the start. Napoleon demanded that the government should silence his British critics like Cobbett and take action against royalist émigré journalists. These included Jacques Regnier, who became editor of the *Courier de Londres* in 1802, and Jean-Gabriel Peltier, whose paper *L'Ambigu* attacked the First Consul in articles that seemed to call for his assassination. In France, and in all the countries under French domination, Napoleon, superb propagandist, had imposed an iron control of the press, issuing flamboyant bulletins of military success, banning mention of the Bourbons and toning down allied victories.[1] The British, by contrast, had no way of spreading information in mainland Europe except through these émigré papers, and even they were hard to distribute – smugglers dropped trunks full of newspapers on the French coast. Having tried in vain to bribe British editors, Napoleon demanded Peltier's expulsion. Addington insisted that this could not be done under British law (although the government expelled pro-French journalists under the Alien Act), and eventually Napoleon accepted that the most he could insist on was a criminal trial.

The widely reported Peltier case was taken as an example of Napoleon's continuing wish to dominate. It was hard to think his intentions were peaceable. As well as building up the French fleet and sending squadrons to patrol the eastern Mediterranean, his protectionist policies were closing ports in France, Belgium, Holland and Italy and blocking the trade that the peace was supposed to bring. He was also making his colonial aims clear, claiming part of south Australia as 'Terre Napoleon', and re-establishing slavery in the West Indies. He sent General Leclerc to subdue the rebels in Haiti, General Victor to the Mississippi and General Decaen to India, and negotiated a deal with Carlos IV of Spain to cede Louisiana to the French in return for lands in Italy for the Duke of Parma. Early in 1803 Francis Baring sent his son Alexander, who had worked in the States and was married to the daughter of Senator Bingham, the richest man in America, to arrange finance of $15 million for the sale of this vast tract of land to the American government – a deal that raised eyebrows in London.

Watching Napoleon's actions, a wary Addington refused to evacuate British troops from Malta and Egypt as the treaty had promised, and in this uncertainty, Pitt's followers called for his return. In May Richard Heber went to the 'numerous assembly at Merchant Taylor's Hall' to celebrate Pitt's birthday, and was, said his aunt, 'much pleased by the Songs which were well performed, particularly that written by Canning, The Pilot who weathered the Storm, which you will see in your paper'.[2] On 2 August 1802 Napoleon was made Consul for life, rather than for ten years. As autumn set in, there was a mood of growing anxiety, a sense that the country was drifting, entangled in industrial troubles and financial worries. In October, Wordsworth called on the spirit of England's great poet whose voice was 'like a star':

> Milton! thou should'st be living at this hour;
> England hath need of thee: she is a fen
> Of stagnant waters: altar, sword and pen,
> Fireside, the heroic wealth of hall and bower,
> Have forfeited their ancient English dower
> Of inward happiness. We are selfish men;
> Oh! raise us up, return to us again;
> And give us manners, virtue, freedom, power.

In the same month Coleridge wrote blistering articles in the *Morning Post* damning the 'dishonest' peace and wearily repeating his fear of Napoleon as a tyrant rather than deliverer of liberty to the French. It would be too much, he wrote, 'to anticipate any system favourable to national liberty from a young man who had formed his habits, feelings and political creed at the head of an army and amid the career of dazzling victories'.[3] Slowly, he moved towards a deep hatred of Napoleon as a man who had abused the trust of a country that had made him great.

The renewal of war began to seem unavoidable, and money was poured into raising more troops. Speaking in a debate on army estimates, Canning demanded support to confront the Bonaparte phenomenon, describing him almost with admiration. 'I cannot shut my eyes to the superiority of his talents, to the amazing ascendant of his genius,' he admitted. 'Tell me not of his measures and his policy. It is his genius, his character, that keeps the world in awe.'[4] He would certainly vote for the large military establishments proposed. 'But for the purpose of coping with Bonaparte, one great commanding spirit is worth them all.' Yet was there a politician left in Britain who had that 'great commanding spirit'?

Over the winter the tension increased. At Peltier's trial in February 1803, the prosecution, led by the Attorney General and the future Prime Minister Spencer Perceval, provoked a stirring speech from the defence counsel, Sir James Mackintosh, who presented the case as a tussle between Napoleon and 'the only free Press now remaining in Europe', a boast that must have provoked hollow laughter from the radical journalists in Newgate. The judge, Ellenborough again, was quite clear what the verdict should be. As Cobbett told Windham, 'Lord Ellenborough and the Attorney-General both told the Jury, that if they did not find him guilty, *we would have war with France*!!!'[5] Luckily for Peltier, war began anyway: his account of his trial became a bestseller and *L'Ambigu* was hired by the Foreign Office.[6]

On Thursday 10 March 1803, a fortnight after Peltier's trial began, James Oakes wrote a heavily starred and underlined entry in his diary.

Attended Guildhall. This morngs post brot us an acct. in the News Papers that a Message had been sent by his Majesty to both Houses of Parliament recommendg an immediate preparation for arming to keep pace with the French, there being at this time some very important matters in agitation. Stocks, on this acct., fell 8 or 10 Pct., Consols settled from 71 to 63 ½ & Omnium settled at 14 ½ from 31-2. A general Consternation prevaild.

In the same week Amabel Hume-Campbell was not surprised by Agneta Yorke's demand 'to hear some Politics', knowing she must be anxious 'after this Alarm of War which has burst like a Bomb amidst the Political World'. No one, it seemed, was certain what would happen, but one of Amabel's contacts at the Palace

believ'd the whole Bustle would end in a Vapour, & then a Story was told of a Report that a particular Explosion of Buonaparte's violent temper had lately happen'd. He had sent for Ld. Whitworth to an Audience & work'd himself up into a violent Passion against the English nation whom he call'd a Perfidious Nation, & said that if we did not give up Malta he had 400,000 Men ready to employ against us.

If true, she added, 'our present Bustle is intended to give him Flash for Flash, Dash for Dash'.[7]

It was widely known that Addington's long-suffering ambassador, Charles, Earl Whitworth, had been publicly abused by the Consul. Whitworth's despatch described a violent scene at the Tuileries, when Napoleon flew into a rage, which, as the *Annual Register* later reported, was 'terminated by the First Consul retiring to his apartments, repeating his last phrases, till he had shut himself in; leaving nearly two hundred spectators of this wanton display of arrogant impropriety, in amazement and consternation'.[8] Gillray cashed in quickly with *Maniac-Ravings – or – Little Boney in a Strong Fit*, showing a furious Napoleon overturning furniture, jumping up and down and spitting, 'Revenge! Revenge! Come Fire! Sword! Famine! Invasion! Invasion! Four Hundred & Eighty Thousand Frenchmen! British Slavery & everlasting Chains!'

Gillray, *Maniac-Ravings – or - Little Boney in a Strong Fit*, 24 May 1803

The calls for Pitt rose in volume and in April he came back to the Commons. His return horrified the followers of Fox, like the gossipy Thomas Creevey, MP for Thetford. 'This damned fellow Pitt has taken his seat and is here,' he wrote in May, 'and, what is worse, it is certain that he and his fellows are to support the war. They are to say the time for criticism is suspended; that the question is not now whether the Ministers have been too tardy or too rash, but the French are to be fought. Upon my soul! the prospect has turned me perfectly sick.'[9]

Whitworth was now told to deliver an ultimatum, demanding, among other things, French withdrawal from Holland and Switzerland, but on 10 May the British papers announced that he had been recalled. Eight days later (dressed in his uniform as Captain Commandant of the Woodley Cavalry Volunteers), Addington read a formal declaration of war in the House of Commons. Within the week, an ailing Pitt, yellow and thin, with a hollow cough, gave a damning denunciation of France and an electrifying call to arms. Sadly, there was no option, he said, between 'the blessings of peace and the dangers of war'. They must consider their lot as cast, by the decrees of Providence, and he trusted in the temper and courage of the nation, who must be prepared to meet war 'with that resignation and fortitude, and, at the same time, with that active zeal and exertion, which, in proportion to the magnitude of the crisis, might be expected from a brave and free people'.[10] It was a theme that he repeated emotionally in the debate on the Defence Bill in July: 'It is for our property, it is for our liberty, it is for our independence, nay, for our existence as a nation; it is for our character, it is for our very name as Englishmen, it is for everything dear and valuable to man on this side of the grave.'[11]

On 18 May, the day war was declared, the British navy captured two French frigates off southern Brittany and customs officials seized French ships in British ports: some sailors were taken prisoner, but no civilians. The move caught Napoleon unprepared and he was swift to retaliate. In Paris, British visitors began to pack their bags and find a post-chaise to Calais. Carriages were scarce, the roads were packed. Many, including the Edgeworths and Hudson Gurney, scraped out at the last minute, but for some it was already too late. In the early hours of 22 May, Napoleon issued an order that all English men still in France aged between eighteen and sixty were to be regarded as prisoners of war. In Calais, the cutter *Nancy* and the packet *Prince of Wales* were seized and their crews taken away.

In the end only a few hundred British subjects were caught in the haul, including tradesmen with stalls at an industrial exhibition in Paris. Women and girls were also detained: the pupils at a Rouen finishing school did not leave until July, finally brought home by a Prussian ketch. At first the situation for those detained did not seem too alarming. In October 1803, Hoare's received a letter from John Nicholls, an erratic Whig MP who had attacked Pitt for the 'heinous delinquency' of his quixotic war: he was now stuck in Toulouse, asking Hoare's to pay some rent he owed, and to give his son the certificates of American bank shares, and:

If the amount Mr W. Ladbroke has not paid on the £1000 which he retains on the most Frivolous Pretences have overdrawn you, I hope you will send me the Security you formerly sent on. Such Difficultys and Delays have occurr'd on my Requests to the French Government to be permitted to return to England that I have relinquished all thoughts for this winter.[12]

He hoped to come back in the spring, he said, but noted cheerfully that 'the Bordeaux Wine of this Year will be probably remarkably good: – as the Summer has been so hot', and virtually advised them to lay some down now. But by May next year, Nicholls was in the great fortress of Verdun, writing mournfully that he had sold his tree farm to Mr Ladbroke and now he needed money to pay bills of twelve thousand francs (a Hoare partner wrote neatly in the margin in red ink, '£489/16s'). In September he was still there, needing another six thousand francs:

The greater part of the English & the Detenus have within the last four days been removed from this place to Valenciennes. The Great Part in a State of Great Misery . . . I have obtained leave to go to Lyons, and I shall set out tomorrow. The expense of travelling there is not the only inconvenience – But it is a great Object to be out of a Depot.[13]

High-flown prisoners like Lord and Lady Boyle, sent initially to Verdun, won permission to live in Paris, where they greatly enjoyed the social life, while others patiently negotiated their release, like the Duke and Dowager Duchess of Newcastle who came home four years later. Distinguished visitors were released, including James Forbes, a Fellow of the Royal Society, helped by pleas from Sir Joseph Banks and Edward Jenner. Lord Elgin, returning from his spell as ambassador to Constantinople and stopping rashly at Orléans, was stuck in France until given parole in 1806, resisting Napoleon's cajoling suggestions that he could win his release by selling his antiquities to the Louvre.

Many British subjects, like Fanny Burney, staying with her husband M. d'Arblay, were detained for the next decade. As she wrote to her friend Fredy Lock, two weeks before war was declared, 'How to write

I know not – at a period so tremendous – nor yet how to be silent – My dearest, dearest Friends! if the War indeed prove inevitable, what a heart-breaking position is ours!'[14] Maria Edgeworth's brother Lovell was detained for the whole of the war, spending six years at Verdun. In 1809 a Mrs Coffy arrived at the door in Edgeworthstown, to say that she had seen him there, 'and that he was well, and fat, and a very merry gentleman'.[15] Theatrical visitors, too, were caught by the outbreak of war. Old Philip Astley senior had come to France to petition Napoleon – successfully – for £10,000 worth of property and years of back rent lost on his Parisian theatre. He was interned but sneaked out by pretending to be ill, obtaining permission to visit a spa, fleeing to the German border, hijacking a carriage and escaping from the coast of Schleswig-Holstein.[16] Astley was lucky: in the fortresses of Meaux, Melun, Nancy and Geneva British detainees whiled away the years, joined as time went on by other British civilians taken prisoner in Italy, or on captured merchant ships.

The mood at the start of the new war was very different from that of 1793. With Napoleon setting up camp again in Boulogne, pamphlets and articles did not talk about preserving Europe's monarchs against levelling sans-culottes, but about defending the country against a tyrant set on world empire, who would show no mercy to ordinary people. What did the opposition want? asked Southey: 'Their country asks the question. War? They have it; every man in the country says Amen, and they whose politics are most democratic say Amen most loudly and most sincerely.'[17] In April the army recruiting bands were drumming again in the countryside. Offering bounties of a meagre £7 12s 6d, they found it hard to get men, and the government turned to Scotland, as before, and to Ireland, where they took men primarily from Catholic areas as it was 'by no means desireable', wrote Lord Hardwicke, 'to bring away any of the Protestants of the North upon whom must be your great dependence, under God'.[18] In the later stages of the war Irish soldiers, dispersed among many regiments, made up about a third of the rank and file.

This time the army had a new element, the rifle brigades. These had been a long time coming: twenty years ago, in the American war, the British troops had been horrified and impressed by the way American woodsmen and hunters had picked off their officers and demoralised the troops. Unlike muskets, fired from chest level, with the men standing shoulder to shoulder and aiming great volleys in the hope that at least some shots would go home, rifles were sportsmen's guns, designed to fell moving prey. The spiralling inner grooves stopped the bullet from 'tumbling', and thus improved range and accuracy, while sights along the barrel could adjust long-range shots: the word 'aim' began to mean something. A single sniper or a group of skirmishers could spread out over the terrain, going ahead to target key officers. In 1798 the first British rifle battalion went into service in Ireland. Two years later Lieutenant-Colonel William Stewart and Colonel Coote Manningham began training a special rifle corps, and detachments of their marksmen joined Nelson at Copenhagen. In 1802 they were formally established as the 95th Regiment of Foot, with distinctive green uniforms – the Green Jackets. Now they marched to Canterbury to train.

Everywhere professional soldiers, on leave at half-pay during the peace, rejoined their regiments. At Shrovetide, the carnival time before Lent, a traditional time for weddings, Rowbottom noted a marked rise in marriages and in mill girls flaunting their finery: 'Ear rings are at this time a very prevailing passion and few of the fair sex are to be seen without their ears being ornamented with some body from the sluggish lead to the massy gold, scarsely any old granny or miss in her leading strings escape this fashion.'[19] Many wives and children went with the soldiers, unsure where they would be sent, in the British isles or abroad – to Italy or Egypt, the West Indies or India, Ireland or South Africa.

The previous year, Mary Martha Butt had published her second novel, *Susan Grey*, written for the girls in her Sunday-school class, in which a heroic orphaned girl resists the advances of a philandering soldier. It was a huge success, but despite its warnings, in June 1803 Mary Martha married her own soldier, her cousin Henry Sherwood, just back from the West Indies with his regiment, the 53rd. Their first year of marriage was one of wandering around barracks across England, from Ipswich to Sunderland, a place memorable for 'thick fogs, a stormy beach, stunted trees, and dull brick houses'. Eventually they were ordered south. Sailing down the east coast with her new baby daughter on a spruced-up collier, the *Charming Peggy*, horribly seasick amid the coal dust, Mary Martha found a saviour in Mrs Sergeant Strachan, a broad and clumsy woman of around thirty-five, with 'carroty' hair and freckles and 'the most decided and most fearful cast in one eye'. As to her dress, she wrote, 'I remember nothing but a cap with many bows, and an enormous pair of gilt drops which hung from her ears, but, such as she was, we should have been lost without her'. Mrs Strachan nursed Mary Martha and the baby and every woman there: she was married to her second husband, having buried her first in the West Indies, and 'she gave us a full and detailed account of six offers which she had had before her deceased husband had been laid in the ground'. It was a strange new life for a clergyman's daughter: 'When she brought me my tea the first morning, I thought it tasted very strangely, and I asked her what she had put into it. "Only a sup of brandy," she answered, "and it is what will do you more good than all the tea in the world without it."'[20]

This was a prelude to active service. In April 1804, Mary Martha learned that they were off to India, and decided it was safest to leave their baby behind:

'The last time I saw Mary', I find written in my journal, 'she was sitting on her nurse's lap. She was eleven months and eighteen days old. Oh, my baby! My little baby! She could then walk a few paces alone. She could call mamma, and tell me what the lambs said. Oh, this state of bereavement – this parting – this life in which we are dead to each other.'[21]

Each company could take out ten women, and Mary Martha, allowed to take a maid, chose Betty, their regimental servant's wife. Betty was sure of her passage, but when the women came to be mustered in the *Devonshire*, there was one too many:

lots were drawn on deck to determine which was to be sent home. I saw this process – I saw the agony of the poor woman that was to be carried back to shore. I saw her wring her hands, and heard her cries, and I saw her put in a boat and sent back to Portsmouth, and I felt, whatever my hardships might be, my trials were nothing compared to hers.

On the long four-month voyage round the Cape she was pregnant again. She would stay in India, following the regiment, for the next twelve years.

Other families, still at home, were waiting for news from the east. After the Egyptian campaign William Harness and his regiment had returned to India and had not returned during the peace. In September 1802 Harness, now forty-two, warned Bessy, 'You will expect to see me much changed; seven years will have wrought on a person that has always appeared advanced beyond my time of life. However I am not much more grey, and have not lost a tooth since I saw you. My Bessy will love her old husband.'[22] The following March the British troops began their long conflict against the Marathas, federated states whose soldiers had been drilled by French officers. Harness's brigade were in the front line when Arthur Wellesley, now a major-general, won the battle of Assaye, near Hyderabad, in late September 1803. In mid-December William wrote, 'The Marattas are rendered peaceful for a lengthy period and the British interests secured. It has detained me a year but it has given me some credit: it is the last I will pass from you.'[23] Although he assured his wife that he was only suffering a mild bout of fever, Harness was writing from hospital: he died on 2 January 1804. The news did not reach Derbyshire until May. Bessy Harness joined the ranks of war widows.

## 33. 'FINE STRAPPING FELLOWS'

As the soldiers set off, the militia were shaking out their uniforms and reporting to their bases. Thousands of men were swept up by a flurry of new Militia Acts and the prices offered to men who would agree to act as substitutes soared, reaching ten, fifteen, twenty-five and even forty-five guineas.[1] Then came a dramatic move, the Levy en Masse Act, passed in July 1803, which asked the Lords Lieutenant to submit lists of all men between seventeen and fifty-five, excluding Quakers, schoolteachers, clergy and invalids. These were to be divided into four groups, to be called up in order: unmarried men under thirty with no child under ten, single men between thirty and fifty, married men between seventeen and thirty with not more than two children under ten, and the rest. In the end, the national levy was never needed, but it made people nervous that men would be marched off, suddenly, without warning.

A month later came a different ballot, for an 'Army of Reserve' to comprise fifty thousand men in home-based battalions to back up fifty of the army's ninety-three regiments. Balloting for this was another huge task, impossible to get through in one day and made more difficult by the August harvest, when men left their parishes to help elsewhere. The desks of the Lords Lieutenant were drowned in papers; the overstretched magistrates, who had to enrol the men and oversee the payments to their families, were often hasty and careless;

the schoolmasters and clergy sent to count the people put it off as long as they could. By the end of the year, hopelessly short of their target, the government stopped recruiting for the Reserve.

In the textile towns of Lancashire, however, the recruiting bands for the army and militia were often seen as saviours. Their story was told in the ballad 'John o' Grinfilt', about a weaver who takes the bounty rather than let his family starve:

> So fare thee weel, Grinfilt, a soger aw'm made:
> Aw've getten new shoon, un' a rare nice cockade;
> Aw'll feight for Owd Englond os hard os aw con,
> Oather French, Dutch, or Spanish, to me it's o' one;
> Aw'll mak' em to stare, like a new started hare,
> Un aw'll tell 'em fro' Oldham aw coom.[2]

The John of Greenfield ballads became a staple of northern entertainment, adaptable to any situation.

Some groups tried to avoid recruitment. John Clare, noticing that gypsies often had a crooked finger, learned that their parents 'disabled the finger of every male child in wartime' to stop magistrates sending them to the army.[3] This was also a practice on the farms. Benjamin Harris helped his shepherd father in Dorset, and was learning to make shoes, so as to have another trade in bad times. One of the unlucky men drawn for the Army of Reserve, he was drafted into the 66th Regiment, leaving his elderly father 'without an assistant to collect his flocks, just as he was beginning more than ever to require one'.[4] His father tried in vain to buy him off or persuade the sergeant he would be no use – he too had broken his son's forefinger deliberately when he was a child. At his first posting in Winchester Harris was picked as one of the firing party of sixteen to execute an inveterate deserter. The execution, it was thought, 'would be a good hint to us young 'uns'. The shooting was done in the deepest silence, and Harris never forgot it, in all his years as a rifleman, serving in Ireland, in Denmark, the Peninsula and Flanders.

\*

Meanwhile the volunteer corps met again. As artisans and labourers volunteered, usually less from patriotism than to gain exemption from militia ballots, local corps changed from being largely middle-class to include a far wider range of men. In Manchester, James Weatherley remembered:

the Regiment my Father belonged to was called the fourth Class, or Old fogys on account of most of them being married men I recollect on the Parade days when they were turning out they would send out their wives to see if Mr so and so was ready as they could not for shame go to Parade singly but would wait until they could muster 7 or 8 to go together in the Group There would perhaps be one as fat as Falstaff and another as thin as the living Skeleton that was once exhibited in Manchester, one five feet five another six feet one bow legged and another inkneed.[5]

There were many jokes about Falstaff's band. But the towns were proud of their men. In Oldham, the Loyal Volunteers marching back from training in Preston were 'accompanied by a band of musick, bells ringing, and were welcomed to their homes amid universall acclamations of joy'.[6]

In the rush to volunteer 380,258 men were enrolled by mid-1804 – far outnumbering the army, navy and militia. The only disincentive came when the men had to swear a standard oath of loyalty: many refused, fearing the oath would make them 'real soldiers' and they might be sent away from their own districts. Some corps were huge and some tiny: the South Devon Volunteers had nearly 2,500 men, the Norfolk Mounted Rifles only twenty-four.[7] As Warden of the Cinque Ports, Pitt became a colonel, riding along the coast, drawing up plans for moving people and livestock and making notes on drilling. His niece Hester Stanhope, living with him at Walmer, told a friend, 'Mr Pitt absolutely goes through the fatigue of a *drill-sergeant*. It is parade after parade, at fifteen or twenty miles distant from each other.' It did the world for his health, she said, he was thin but strong and 'his spirits are excellent'.[8]

The troops were everywhere, in country, town and city. In Bury St Edmunds Orbell Oakes and Captain Benjafield raised two companies

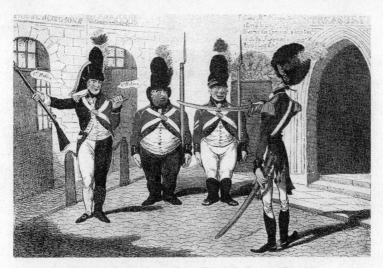

As Colonel of the Cinque Ports, Pitt drills Fox and Sheridan,
his former opponents, now volunteers

of a hundred men each: on 29 August James Oakes wrote, 'A meeting of the Deputy Lieuts to receive Lists from the Constable of the Army en Masse & to hear Appeals. I gave the Oath of Allegiance to my son's company of volunteers, nearly 100 of them in my yard.'[9] In Fleet Street Harry Hoare invested in expensive new 'drill Jackets and Pantaloons' for his men and hired a Sergeant-Major Jennings and Sergeant Birch to supervise drilling. He also laid out the considerable sum of £44 10s for twelve Brown Bess muskets – enough for all the clerks and two partners – from Henry Nock, the leading London gunsmith, whose shop was up the road in Ludgate Hill. (Nock ran a shooting ground in Blackfriars and a factory in Whitechapel, and supplied muskets to the king: when he died the following year, his son-in-law James Wilkinson took over, later turning to making swords, bayonets and razors – hence Wilkinson Sword.[10]) Hoare's muskets – still in their glass cases in the bank's lobby – were particularly fine, engraved with the bank's sign of a golden bottle and Nock's initials.

In Edinburgh, Walter Scott was drilling zealously. As Henry Cockburn saw it, this was neither a duty or a pastime, but an absolute passion, 'indulgence in which gratified his feudal taste for war, and his jovial sociableness. He drilled, and drank, and made songs, with a hearty conscientious earnestness which inspired or ashamed everybody.'[11] Scott's cavalry volunteers stuck a turnip on top of a staff to represent a Frenchman, and practised slashing at it with their sabres. Most were simply worried about falling off as they lunged, 'but Walter pricked forward gallantly, saying to himself, "Cut them down, the villains, cut them down" and made his blow, which from his lameness was often an awkward one, cordially muttering curses all the while at the detested enemy'. Other writers joined up, including men who had once spoken out against the war. Dorothy Wordsworth told her friend Catherine Clarkson that her brother William was going to Ambleside with 'the greatest part of the Men of Grasmere' to drill a couple of times a week.[12] It was a symbolic act, she noted, since if the French reached Grasmere the invasion would already have pretty much succeeded. A few miles away in Penrith, John Monkhouse told his brother that they had raised 'about a thousand, I daresay, to go under the general name of Inglewood Loyal Volunteers'.[13]

In his late teens Samuel Bamford found Middleton swarming with people, 'with fife and drum, and the constables parading for volunteers'. He put himself forward, got a shilling bounty, a billet and a black-and-red cockade. This horrified his Methodist – and perhaps pacifist – aunt, who said no one in the family had worn a cockade before, and Samuel was 'on the way to perdition'. It didn't matter, as the corps was never called on, even to parade.[14] There was a lot of flash and dash and wasted effort and local rivalry. In Manchester the Unitarian Joseph Hanson led Whig dissenters and radicals, while John Leigh Philips, from a powerful cotton merchant family, led the 'Church and King' Tories. When Hanson – who had formed his troop first – claimed his position as colonel commandant over all the local corps, Philips challenged him to a duel, and was only stopped at the last minute.[15]

Once again, manufacturers formed their own troops, like the Bury Volunteers, led by Sir Robert Peel and his partner William Yates. At

Belper Mills in Derbyshire Joseph Strutt's men wore feathered hats and scarlet coats with yellow facings, pleasingly cheap, Strutt found, 'as the materials were bought and the work done by local tailors, instead of through contractors'.[16] Local farmers contributed Strutt's wagons, which 'bore a number and the name of the corps on a tin plate, and had to be in attendance at every inspection', and were specially fitted with 'swinging seats attached to the side by leather straps'. This attention to detail was typical. As in 1798, volunteers were also recruited to drive livestock and supply food. In Bolton, the clerk John Holden noted in his diary how the constables went to every house:

To take down the names of every man that was able to bear arms, and in what Company he meant to serve in case of necessity of the French landing. Henry [of the] Union Building was to bake 100 in one day. Th. Mason in Bradshawgate was to bake 500 in one day and one night and to have four men to assist him.[17]

Brewers would be needed too, to supply horses, wagons and beer, and they also had their own volunteer troops. Elizabeth Heber reported that at Elliot's Stag Brewery next door to her in Pimlico, 'the dray men are drilled, morning and evening. They have strong beer given them when they have done their duty but the man who refuses to learn is turned away.' Mr Elliot had asked if her own two servants would join them, 'to which I can have no objection as it is now deemed necessary to oppose this daring invader by a Nation in Arms'.[18] At the same time, her nephew Richard had been asked to lead the Craven Corps at a family estate in Yorkshire. In August, before he went north, he was staying with Elizabeth and was, she told her brother, the Revd Reginald Heber in Shropshire, 'very diligently practising the Military Exercise Morning and Evening in our *little garden* under the direction of a drill Sergeant in the Guards – he does right to learn a soldiers duty tho I hope & trust he will never be calld into Action in the Field of Battle.'[19]

The tender correspondence between the now elderly Revd Heber and his sister was, however, drawing to an end. At the end of that month, as he explained, a fever had 'altogether made me as weak as Water and reduced me to the likeness of a Shadow that departeth'.[20] When he died in early 1804, Richard Heber, as the oldest son, inherited his Yorkshire and Shropshire estates. His younger brother, another Reginald, a Fellow of All Souls at the age of twenty-one, stayed in Hodnet in Shropshire, and led the local volunteers to the muster at Market Drayton. They got drunk, the weapons wouldn't fire, the town was 'a perfect brothel', and the drilling ended in a riot. Still, young Reginald reported to Richard:

I had forgot to tell you that on our march yesterday a very fine strapping fellow came running after us quite out of breath and in his shirt sleeves, and as soon as he could speak, prayed admission into the Company. He had heard the drum in the morning as he was riddling in a barn a little on the Hodnet side of Northwood and at once by a sudden start of patriotism, and without stopping to put on his clothes, followed us until he overtook us, which as we had near two miles start, did not occur till we were nearby Shrewsbury. So ardent and robust an adventurer was not of course refused.[21]

This ardent adventurer was called Ridgeway, aged about eighteen, and 'very respectable' once he put on his uniform.

Actors and musicians also turned soldier. The star of the panto-mimes and harlequinades, Jack Bologna, enlisted with the rifle corps raised by John Barber Beaumont, an insurance company director who was also an artist and a Royal Academician. Barber's corps spent Sundays fencing and shooting at targets at places like Montpelier Tea Gardens in Kennington, and won lofty patronage, becoming the Duke of Cumberland's Sharpshooters. Many went on to join the famous 95th Rifles.[22] But most actors were hardly fit for war. On exercises on the hills round Highgate and Hampstead, the 'now corpulent' singer Charles Incledon, 'round and green as a cabbage' in his rifleman's uniform, was so out of breath that he paid local urchins to carry his heavy gun and sword, while the grand romantic actor George Freder-ick Cooke, almost fifty and rarely sober, had to be pulled and pushed up every bank. Red-eyed, Cooke nearly shot a woman in a white apron, mistaking her for the target. Afterwards he felt not remorseful but pleased, having won a bet he made at the Cider Cellars at two o'clock that morning that he would still turn up to muster at Chalk Farm. One night, 'full of wine', he refused to go on stage despite a trail of pleading actors:

As they followed him about the stage beseeching him to dress for the character, his voice was heard in front, reviling them, in such terms as these, 'Out upon you, you vile mumming crew. Is this a time to practice your contemptible buffoonery? The enemy is at your gates – the citadel is in danger – I am studying the speech I shall address to the people of England for Dover Cliffs. Away with you – leave me to myself.'[23]

There was nothing to be done, except to say that Mr Cooke was 'taken suddenly ill', and put on another play instead.

The theatre itself profited from the new war. In 1803, in *Goody Two Shoes: or Harlequin Alabaster* at Sadler's Wells, Jack Bologna destroyed French balloons to stop an aerial invasion in a scene set at the North Foreland Lighthouse. Although Napoleon had actually dismantled his balloon corps in 1799, it remained part of the fantasy of his dominance of earth, sea and sky. The final scene, set in the Mall, saw a minuscule Napoleon taken prisoner. So 'Boneypart was pocketed'.[24] As Charles Dibdin wrote later, 'As far as my experience goes, theatres (in London at least) prosper most during War.'[25]

Around the same time, the Charterhouse organist and music professor James Stevens joined the St Sepulchre Volunteers, 'wishing to assist in the defence of my Country, now threated with invasion by *Buonaparte*'. He was hurt when a Charterhouse colleague laughed at his efforts to present arms and called out, 'Upon my word! Alexander the great!' Two months later he published a 'Loyal song, *He may come if he dare!*', originally composed for two of his girl music students, and the following week he played the organ for the swearing-in of the City of London Volunteers. Then it was his turn:

October the 28th. I marched with my Corps, the Middlesex St Sepulchre Volunteers, to Hyde Park. We all passed in review before his Majesty, and the Commander in Chief; after we had fired three vollies. The exertion of marching, and standing, such a long time, made me very ill, and gave me the Piles most terribly . . . I was so dreadfully tired with this violent exertion (as we were mustered at five o'clock in the morning) that I was obliged to go to Bed as soon as I had taken my dinner.[26]

This was the end of Stevens's volunteering. Getting a certificate of his 'incapacity to attend my military duty', he fled to Bath.

The Hyde Park parade of 1803, where Stevens suffered so badly, was the greatest of them all. George III reviewed twenty-seven thousand volunteers and a crowd of around half a million turned up to watch. Young Leigh Hunt was in the ranks of the St James's Volunteers, red-coated and smart for what *The Times* described as 'a glorious day for Old England'.[27] The fervour also spread to women, from housewives who sent petitions asking to be armed with pikes, to aristocrats like Lady Jerningham, who offered to raise six hundred women to drive cattle in Norfolk if the invasion came. More often, though, women offered domestic rather than martial help. In Manchester, James Wheeler noted, 'the witches of Lancashire . . . employed themselves in adding to the comforts and thereby to the efficiency of the soldiery'.[28] As well as sewing flannel clothing, 'the making of which was not entrusted to the hands of hirelings', they made and presented standards and cockades, and held parties for the soldiers, 'the hostess being ever foremost in dealing out good English cheer to the men, thus adding to the enthusiasm of the brave by the condescension of the fair'.

## 34. PRESS GANGS AND FENCIBLES

On the quays of Liverpool, a few days after war was declared, trade was lively. Watching with surprise, Eric Svedenstierna thought that the people had learned 'that if one must as a human being sigh over the misfortune of war, the business man can be very satisfied with the capital which the war brings'.[1] Ship owners had been busily equipping privateer vessels, and five were already rigged to go to sea. In the eight days after war was declared fifteen more were fitted out, and most returned quickly with fat French and Dutch prizes: 'also all the slave ships present, of 16 or 18 guns, were said to have made a cruise before their departure to Africa'.

More slowly, as the navy repaired and equipped its ships, the Admiralty sent out orders to commodores, captains and officers. Upheavals ensued for many families. Thomas Fremantle's *Ganges* was in dry dock at Portsmouth. In July Betsey packed their children into a coach and they all went down to join him there, travelling on roads so dusty in the baking heat that they were 'like deep sand the colour of brick dust'. The house her husband had taken was small, she wrote,

but tolerably clean and when we are settled we shall find it comfortable enough. We were not so on our arrival, the children being cross and tired, Nurse ill and obliged to go to bed where she was soon terrified at being attacked by a regiment of Bugs, and I could scarcely persuade her to lay down again. Fremantle has written for our Cook to come directly.[2]

Most officers itched to start on the chase for prizes, but some new recruits had more idealistic aims. Thomas Perronet Thompson, just down from Cambridge, the son of the Hull trader who had made a mint out of consols in the last invasion scare, joined the navy at the end of the peace with dreams of seeing the world 'as Captain Cook and Le Vaillant understood the term; the world of navigators, travellers and soldiers; the world where Bewick's Beasts ran loose, where strange countries were discovered and great battles fought'.[3] His Methodist mother, who wanted him to preach, and his father, who had planned a business career, were both appalled. In February 1803 he sailed on the *Isis* as a midshipman with Vice-Admiral Gambier to the Newfoundland station, revelling in bringing his first prize, a retaken West Indiaman, into St John's.

Young officers on the quarterdeck may have been keen, but it was harder to find crews to serve before the mast. Little had changed after the Nore and Spithead mutinies, and the flogging, poor pay, bad food and negligent care of the sick and wounded were still powerful deterrents. The government offered bounties and the great traders and insurers also chipped in. In July a group of merchants met in Lloyd's Coffee House and set up the Lloyd's Patriotic Fund for rewards for naval captures and gallantry, grants for the wounded and annuities for the families of the dead. Although Lloyd's subscribers were the main contributors, the Fund's prospectus sang of national co-operation, uniting all classes, 'the Mite of the Labourer combining with the munificent Donation of the Noble and Wealthy'. The aim, it said, was both to inspire sailors, soldiers 'and our Countrymen at Large', and to appall the enemy, who would see that the energy of Britain was '*irresistible, as its resources are incalculable*'.[4] This declaration, printed in *The Times* and issued as a broadsheet, became almost a national manifesto.[5]

To celebrate the fund, Charles Dibdin put on an entertainment, *Britons Strike Home*, in his little theatre on the Strand – with government backing and the loan of a complete military band. Adapting an old song set by Purcell, Dibdin praised the new Fund as a 'magnificent act' on the part of the Sons of Commerce:

Should Frenchmen e'er pollute Britannia's strand,
Or press with hostile hoof this sacred land;
The daring deed should every Briton arm,
To save his native land from dire alarm;
Her free born Sons should instant take the field,
The Altar and the Throne at once to shield.

*Britons, strike home! Avenge your Country's cause,*
*Protect your King, your Liberties, and Laws!*[6]

'Britons Strike Home' became the motto on the Lloyd's Fund seal. No one could ignore the vast mobilisation of the army, militia and volunteers, but the great hope, as always, lay with the navy. In August 1803 Sir Joseph Banks wrote to Nelson, then on the *Victory* off Toulon:

We are here Arming with a degree of Spirit & Enthusiasm as puts all chance of a successfull invasion out of the question. If some bounds are not set to the alacrity of all Ranks of People, we shall soon have as many millions of men in training here as Bonaparte has 100,000s of Troops. We are told also that the Emperor of Russia Grins Ghastly at the Corsican Tyrant. Thanks to your Lordship's exertions, and the animation of the People, we all now Sleep sound in our beds.[7]

Subscriptions were raised in every town, and the East India Company donated twenty armed ships to guard the Thames. Like the Company, Lloyd's, who dealt with insurance for shipping from across the world, had a close relationship with the Admiralty, advising on convoys, settling which ports they would sail from and when, and sharing intelligence gained from their foreign contacts. Some critics complained that the merchant shipping interest was affecting naval matters and consuming national wealth, a theme that roused Cobbett, for example, to an onslaught in the *Political Register* from July to December 1803. But the defence of merchant shipping was vital for trade. In Portsmouth merchant vessels now crowded the harbour, having run for port once war was declared. The engineer George Landmann watched as 'vast fleets of merchant ships' gathered, seeking the protection of convoys:

Thousands of sailors and passengers filled the streets, ships, and markets; the constant rattling of wheelbarrows full of luggage, the hallooing of porters accompanying them; the confusion created by the light carts passing to and from the landing place at the Point engaged in the carriage of live stock, butcher's meat, vegetables, groceries, liquors, crockery &c.; the crowds of officers of the navy and army about the doors and windows of the Crown and the Fountain inns . . .[8]

In Motley's Library there were queues for the Army and Navy lists and the Hampshire and London papers. Officers talked in doorways about the latest news, women hung on the arms of midshipmen, young ensigns showed off new uniforms, crews were rounded up from the taverns, and women gathered in cheery clusters to be rowed out to the ships.

Rowlandson, *Cattle not Insurable*

Yet the crews that gathered here were not enough. The press gangs hunted for still more men, looking particularly for sailors who had served before. Many had been dismissed in the peace and did not want to come back, and their wives, who had looked after families alone for years, often thrown on the parish, begged them to stay. In Edinburgh John Nicol's wife Margaret told him to hide, and 'was like a distracted woman and gave me no peace until I sold off my stock in trade and the greater part of my furniture and retired to the country'.[9] Not daring to sleep in his own house, Nicol went inland, working in the lime quarries and hiding from the gangs until the end of the war. At the other end of Britain, William Lovett's mother sold fish in Penzance market – his father, captain of a small trading vessel, had been drowned just before he was born. One of his earliest memories, apart from the illuminations for the Peace of Amiens, and the treat of eating raisins rescued from a wreck, was terror of the press gang. He remembered the cry that the gangers were coming, and the young men rushing out of town, and how, if the roads were blocked, you could see soldiers with drawn cutlasses, 'riding down the poor fishermen, often through fields of standing corn where they had sought to hide themselves'. One local heroine, a deaf girl called Honour Hitchens, saved her father from being dragged off by smacking the ganger across the face with a dogfish.[10]

Violence often followed the gangs. In early April, wrote *The Times*, Captain Wolfe, of the frigate *L'Aigle*, lying in Portland Roads, took a gang of sailors and marines ashore on Portland Bill and marched into the village:

They impressed Henry Wiggot and Richard Way, without any interruption whatever. The People of the Island took the alarm, and fled to the village of Eason, which is Situated about the centre of the island, where the people made a stand at the Pond. The gang came up, and the Captain took a man by the collar. The man pulled Back, on which the Captain fired his pistol; at which signal the Lieutenant of Marines ordered his men to fire, which being done, three men fell dead, being all shot through the head, viz. Richard Flann, aged 42, Alex. Andrews, 47 years, and William Lang, 26 years.[11]

Two of the dead were quarrymen and the third a blacksmith, shot at his smithy door. The gang killed two more people, including a young woman, Mary Way, shot in the back. They were said to be supported by the Mayor of Weymouth, provoking a lasting hatred of Weymouth people.

This was no isolated incident. In May, on the Thames, the Deptford gangs rounded up two hundred men, so many that those who could not be put aboard the holding ships had to be herded into the Tower. At Hungerford stairs coal-heavers pelted the gangs with lumps of coal and broken bottles. And so it went on, through the summer, autumn and winter. In November, when two Margate constables tried to stop the impressing of exempted men, the gang pressed the constables themselves and hauled them on board. In South Shields, a drunken lieutenant knocked the captain of a merchant ship on the head with his cutlass and dragged him to the rendezvous house. Anger spread at the humiliating treatment of the pressed men, locked in the holds until their ships sailed, crawling with lice, in air so foul that officers retched when they opened the hatches. Robert Hay, aged thirteen, leaving the mill in hope of a job in the merchant ships at Greenock, was grabbed and thrust into the hold of a guardship. Despite his father's pleas, there was no escape. Besides, said the captain, 'Your son, it is true, will not be of much use to us for some time, but if I can judge from the cut of his jib (eyeing me as he spoke, from head to foot) we have the makings of a smart fellow.'[12] Within a month, Hay was at sea, spewing with seasickness on a rain-washed deck.

The gangs met increasing resistance. Men were rescued from the tenders carrying them to the ships and mobs ran press-men out of town. The keelmen of the Tyne had been protected during the previous war, but now the protection was removed and the gangs, armed with short swords called hangers, seized shipwrights, tradesmen and gentry as well as seamen. The *Newcastle Advertiser* spoke out vehemently against these 'scandalous outrages' where men in useful trades were 'dragged like felons through the streets, beat and cut with hangers, and put on board a tender, merely because it pleased a set of ruffians called a Press Gang to do so'.[13] When the North Shields Regulating Officer impressed fifty Tyne men, their fellow keelmen went on strike, halting the coal trade, and their wives marched on the North Shields rendezvous house wielding pots and pans, broom handles and rolling pins. Finally the authorities negotiated a compromise, in which one in ten keelmen would enlist, with the coal owners and other keelmen raising a bounty for their families: in the end eighty men found as substitutes sailed down to the Nore.[14]

Ports like South Shields and Whitby became refuges where the gangs dared not tread: over a thousand sailors were said to be living in the North Yorkshire moors. At Whitby, in May 1803, townsfolk attacked the *Eagle* cutter which had come to impress men, killing two of the crew, and two months later a gang of women cursed and stoned the new regulating officer. A few months later, when the officer tried to press returning Greenland whalers, a great cry went up from the crowds on both sides of the river and the whaling boat's crew grabbed their harpoons, took to the boats and rescued their fellows, 'approved by loud huzzas from the shore'.[15]

It was not just working people who defied the gangs. In fishing towns and large ports, magistrates and leading citizens often joined in protecting their townspeople. Their motives were mixed: when the 'trowmen' of the river Severn left their barges to hide among the mine workers in the Forest of Dean, the Bristol merchants, who traded in goods sent down in those barges from the Midlands, found their trade so badly hampered that they sent angry pleas to the Admiralty. Bystanders could also be called in to help. When Mary Martha Sherwood was on her way from Newcastle to join her husband's regiment with other soldier's wives, lying seasick with her baby at the mouth of the Thames, she heard noise overhead, and a sailor rushed into her cabin and hid under the bed, concealed by the valance: 'I was made to understand immediately, by the captain's wife, that the poor fellow was hiding himself from a press gang, who were coming on board: and I was requested not to be offended.' The gang peered in, 'but seeing a lady lying upon the bed, though they looked keenly round, they did not enter. I lay quite still without speaking, and they walked out again, and made off, and we all gloried in having saved the poor fellow.'[16]

\*

One way of dodging the press, popular in the coastal towns, was to join the sea fencibles, the volunteer regiments formed to guard the shores. In Norfolk Mary Hardy noted that 'Rainham Rangers & Fakenham Volenters were sent to Yarmouth to Guard the Coast'.[17] The town had a parish meeting, as it had done only five years before, 'to consider the best plan to remove the Inhabitants to a place of safety in case of an Invasion on our Coast'. In Suffolk and on the south coast, there were constant false alarms. In August 1803 Betsey Fremantle at Portsmouth was astonished to see crowds on the beach, the yeomanry out, guns fired and signals flying. 'I was told it was supposed the French were effecting a landing as numbers of the flat bottom boats were seen making towards the shore.'[18] Next day she learned that it was only a fleet of coasters which had been becalmed behind the Isle of Wight. At Colchester later in the year, the poet and children's author Ann Taylor told her sister that when it was announced during a play that an enemy fleet was offshore, women fled shrieking from the packed theatre, and others rushed out of their houses 'screaming murder and in fact a scene of most alarming tumult and confusion . . . and I am afraid that in case of many more alarms or of actual invasion, the demand for salts vinegar, etc., etc., will be more than our perfumers will be able to supply.'[19]

For nine months, from July 1803 to April 1804, the Commander of the Southern District, General Sir David Dundas, set up his headquarters at Canterbury, convinced that the cathedral city and the port of Dover would be the key to a successful resistance. But the main defence was the Channel Fleet, now under Admiral William Cornwallis. Sometimes they cruised off Boulogne, and at other times they were moored in the Downs. But if the blockading squadrons formed the first line of resistance, they were supported on the coast itself by the fencibles, who were turning fishing vessels into small gunboats. These were the local heroes, celebrated in Wordsworth's sonnet of October 1803:

> Vanguard of Liberty, ye Men of Kent,
> Ye Children of a Soil that doth advance

Its haughty brow against the coast of France,
Now is the time to prove your hardiment!
To France be words of invitation sent!
They from their Fields can see the countenance
Of your fierce war, may ken the glittering lance,
And hear you shouting forth your brave intent.
Left single, in bold parley, Ye, of yore,
Did from the Norman win a gallant wreath;
Confirmed the charters that were yours before; –
No parleying now! In Britain is one breath;
We all are with you now from Shore to Shore: –
Ye men of Kent, 'tis Victory or Death!

Jane Austen's brother Francis was in command of the fencibles on the Kent coast from Deal to North Foreland, making detailed notes on defences and possible landing places, taking charge of a mere seventeen boats and 250 men. In his view, less rosy than Wordsworth's, the fencibles were almost useless: 'a non-descript half-sailor half-soldier as efficient as neither'.[20] The only consolation was that he met his first wife, Mary Gibson, in Ramsgate. They went on to have five daughters and six sons, three of whom joined the navy.

Francis Austen's gloom was shared by Vice-admiral Phillip, who toured the coast to check the fencibles and see how many might be moved into the navy. He found that when called upon, they often refused to muster, and although many were clearly navy material their fencible exemptions meant that none could be impressed – as far as he could see the 'pilots' of Hastings were actually organising cutters for smuggling. In Cornwall, around two thirds of the pilchard and mackerel fishermen were also sheltering from the navy in the fencibles, adding to their living by smuggling, hiding their boats in sheltered coves, and converting some into privateers with official letters of marque.[21] But the invasion threat was real to all the coastal men, and if a French army set sail they would man guns and launch boats without a word. Sir John Moore, reporting from Dungeness in one scare, reported that the fencibles were 'very cheerful – not at all dismayed at the prospect of meeting the French'.[22] The same went for the men in hiding from the gangs. John Nicol, safe in his Scottish quarry, begged the newspapers from the quarry owner and read them to other workmen, arguing about politics and triumphing at the news of victories. 'Every now and then I felt the greatest desire to hurra aloud,' he wrote, 'and many a hurra my heart gave that my mouth uttered not.'[23]

## 35. PANIC AND PROPAGANDA

The coast of Britain lacked real defences, as Napoleon well knew. A nation was very foolish, he announced, when it had no fortifications and no army, 'to lay itself open to seeing an army of ten thousand veteran troops land on its shores. This is the masterpiece of the flotilla. It costs a great deal of money, but it is necessary for us to be masters of the sea for six hours only, and England will have ceased to exist.'[1]

The British shivered at news of men and women trapped in Europe and at reports in the *St James's Chronicle* in July 1803 that toasts had been raised at a Calais dinner, 'To the barrack-master who shall issue the first billets at Dover' and 'To the first review of the French troops in St James's Park'.[2] Angry readers tossed their newspapers on the ground when they read that Bonaparte had ordered the Bayeux Tapestry to be brought from Caen and displayed in Paris as an example of a successful French invasion. Some householders in Kent, Sussex and East Anglia packed up their goods and headed inland, believing the warnings. 'People of the British Isles,' one broadsheet began: 'Let none affect to despise the idea that WE SHALL SHORTLY BE INVADED. Our Foe has pledged himself to it.' As they left, so the soldiers and militia marched in, housed in new barracks like the vast new buildings at Eastbourne and Pevensey, which could hold ten thousand men, or in camps with tents raised and flags flying. Soldiers packed the inns and men huddled in clifftop shelters ready to fire beacons to spread the alarm. Lady

Jerningham was spending the autumn in Norfolk at the family home at Cossey, an old rambling house with a great walled kitchen garden and deer park surrounded by woods of oak, beech and chestnut. It seemed so secure, but she exclaimed to her daughter Charlotte, 'Bonaparte's Invasion must, I am afraid, take Place, and what a Scene of Danger!'

I do not fear for my own personal Security, nor for Sir William's: but for the younger People who may find it necessary to defend themselves. I Cannot think of it without great terror. For quiet Housekeepers, the troop will (I Suppose) be under too good a Command for to have reason to fear private Riot, but what a State of Suspended Misery it would be. However I yet trust with a Confident Hope, that Providence will deliver us.[3]

Rumours spread like dust in the air. Napoleon was going to build a bridge from Calais, and his officers would hover above it in air balloons while the men tramped across; he was out there himself, disguised as a fisherman, spying on British ports; he was hiding in the mountains in Wales. Foreigners were suspect and so were lone travellers, especially if they carried sketching gear. Suspicion was levelled at unlikely groups, like the nuns from Marnhull in Dorset who were accused of harbouring one of Boney's brothers, sent to spy out British feelings, and of storing arms and ammunition. The local magistrate instituted a search of the convent, and the furious abbess announced with a nice irony that her nuns were even more surprised than they had been at the start of the last war, when their sister convent in France had received a similar visit, 'under the idea that Mr Pitt, the English Minister, was secreted there'.[4]

William Blake, who had moved to a cottage at Felpham in Sussex, was one victim of this new alarm. On 16 August 1803 he appeared before the Chichester justices accused of seditious language and assault on a soldier, John Scofield, whom he had thrown out of his garden. Scofield swore that Blake had said that 'The People of England were like a Parcel of Children, that they would play with themselves till they got scalded and burnt, that the French knew our Strength very well, and if Bonaparte should come he would be master of Europe in an Hour's time'.[5] Blake's wife Catherine ran out of the cottage, allegedly shouting that she would fight for Bonaparte as long as she could. Matters dragged on miserably until Blake was acquitted in January 1805. He saw the repression as mental as well as legal. 'Rouze up O Young Men of the new Age!' he called in the preface to his long prophetic book *Milton*, written between 1804 and 1810: 'Set your foreheads against the ignorant Hirelings! For we have Hirelings in the Camp, the Court, & the University: who would if they could, for ever depress Mental & prolong Corporeal War.'[6]

Ensconced in Boulogne, waiting to pounce, Napoleon reminded people of an oriental despot. Newspapers described his pavilion on the downs, erected in a day like a palace in story, with painted ceilings, long windows and wide views, and a telescope so strong that he could count the stones in Dover Castle. Around this were pavilions for staff officers and a city of huts on a grid of streets named after his battles, stretching over eight miles, with gardens and pyramids and arbours. With their own telescopes – if less powerful than his – sailors at sea could see batteries of guns and battalions of men. The contrast with George III, holidaying in a red-brick house in Weymouth, as he had done for several years, bathing in the sea and sailing on the royal yacht, was almost comical.

This time government propaganda was aimed less at the enemy within, the supposed republicans and Jacobins, than at the foe across the Channel. And even this enemy had changed: in the prints and broadsides the rabble of sans-culottes gave way to a single foe, Napoleon Bonaparte. To rouse confidence Gillray turned him from a threatening giant into a tiny, spluttering figure of fun: 'Little Boney'. But Boney was still a figure of terror. Sir Robert Wilson's *Narrative of the British Expedition to Egypt*, published in 1802, was a great source of such stories. True or not, they were useful in demonising Bonaparte's 'wanton inhumanity'.[7]

Pro-government publishers marshalled their forces on a greater scale than in the first invasion panic. Broadsides and ballads hammered home the consequences of invasion. The French armies, they said, would kill the men and rape the women: 'Every tar has his Sweetheart on shore and even she is held out to the Republican slaves as a lure to the venture.'[8] Over a hundred broadsides were published, cheaper than newspapers, easy to paste on to walls. Nearly all were produced and sold by a handful of London booksellers, many clustering in the same street, their names printed proudly in capitals at the foot of the page: 'JOHN STOCKDALE, 181 Piccadilly', 'JOHN HATCHARD, 190 Piccadilly', 'JOHN GINGER, 169 Piccadilly'. In the City 'JAMES ASPERNE, No. 32 Cornhill' called himself 'The Constitutional Bookseller' and published the *European Magazine*. Their common origins made the broadsheets feel like a synchronised government message, and many carried an appeal like that in Asperne's *Victorious Englishmen*: 'Noblemen, Magistrates, and Gentlemen, would do well by ordering a few Dozen of the above Tracts of their different Booksellers, and causing them to be stuck up in the respective Villages where they reside, that the Inhabitants may be convinced of the Cruelty of the CORSICAN USURPER.'[9] Other broadsheets were addressed to the clergy, suggesting they hand them out, scatter them in pews, pin them to the church door. They were collected into miscellanies, sold on market days, carried in pedlars' trays. Their contents ranged from sermons to songs, odes and comic dialogues between John Bull and Napoleon.

The poems and songs recalled British heroes – Richard the Lionheart, Henry V, Good Queen Bess and the Duke of Marlborough – and appealed to the spirit of Crécy, Agincourt and the Armada.[10] The theatres ran revivals of stalwarts like *Henry V*. Wordsworth followed this patriotic route in his 'Lines on the Expected invasion, 1803', looking back to the Civil Wars and summoning the heirs of both sides of that conflict to unite, those true to the royalist tradition of Falkland and Montrose and the republican followers of Pym and Milton:

> Come ye – whate'er your creed – O waken all
> Whate'er your temper, at your Country's call;
> Resolving (this a free-born Nation can)
> To have one Soul, and perish to a man,
> Or save this honoured Land from every Lord
> But British reason and the British sword.

Elizabeth and Napoleon: an appeal to the Armada spirit

Many broadsides were aimed at artisans and labourers, suggesting that they should set aside their grievances and accept that working for a British employer would be better than being a French-owned slave. New stories of atrocities were added to the crop from the last war, especially after the invasion of Hanover in May 1803, when the French were described as rounding up peasants, imposing huge fines and felling forests piecemeal. In Hanover, the pamphlets stressed, the people suffered whatever their class: Bonaparte did not, as Cobbett put it, observe 'the maxim of war to the palaces, peace to the cottages'.[11] Cobbett was the author of the official *Important Considerations for the People of this Kingdom*, which explained that the French had 'suspended their devastations' during the peace:

and now, like gaunt and hungry wolves, they are looking towards the rich pastures of Britain: already we hear their threatening howl; and if, like sheep, we stand bleating for mercy, neither our innocence not our timidity will save us from being torn to pieces and devoured. The robberies, the barbarities, the brutalities they have committed in other countries, though, at the thought of them, the heart sinks and the blood runs cold, will be mere trifles to what they will commit here, if we suffer them to triumph over us.[12]

Hannah More also produced suitable material, like 'The Plough-man's Ditty', answering that 'foolish question: What has the Poor to Lose?' Arms metaphorically akimbo, she offered a rose-tinted list of the things that would go: cottage, garden, orchard, regular wages – and gave a lurid list of what would come:

> I've a dear little wife
> Whom I love as my life;
> To lose her I should not much like, Sir;
> And 'twould make me run wild
> To see my sweet child
> With its head on the point of a pike, Sir.[13]

Her verses ended with the ploughman beating his ploughshare into sword or spear, determined to fight like a lion for Church, King, Law and Liberty and family, and 'rush on these desperate men, Sir'.

Several broadsides were addressed to women, urging them to cheer on their men. The author of *Old England to Her Daughters* – making a clear distinction between 'Ladies!', 'Women!' and 'Labouring Women!' – advised that ladies should not scream, faint or hamper their men by clinging to their arms; shopkeepers and housewives should be sober and strong, lock doors and keep servants in; working women could get in the harvest and care for the horses, and all women should, of course, sew, and nurse wounded soldiers.[14]

In the panic, middle-class evangelicals and nonconformists pondered tracts that deciphered the Scriptures to explain the course of politics and the war, while itinerant preachers harangued the poor. What was God's plan, these preachers asked, and was the war part of a grand Providential scheme? Some suggested that God was fostering the war to enable Britain to restore the Jews to Palestine, while others saw the British as now replacing the Jews as God's chosen people.[15] Some identified Napoleon with Antichrist, some with the creatures in Revelation who would punish the sinful world and crush the enemies of the Lord. But if this was a punishment, how then had Britain strayed? In Henry Andrews's solidly anti-Catholic astrological almanac *Vox Stellarum*, which sold a staggering 365,000 copies in 1802, the nation's many sins included 'Swearing and Lying, and Killing and Stealing, and Committing Adultery'. Yet Andrews went against the tide: in his view the worst sin by far was continuing to fight when the stars said no. The heavens demanded peace.

Unitarians and dissenting ministers placed more emphasis on public than personal sins: corruption, commerce, colonialism and the slave trade. But they still insisted that religion might save the nation. In his broadsheet *Advice Suggested by the State of the Times*, Wilberforce begged 'True Christians' to pray that God might avert Britain's ruin, and declared his 'true persuasion . . . that to the decline of Religion and morality our national difficulties must both directly and indirectly be chiefly ascribed'. His hope, he said, rested less on fleets and armies, or on 'the wisdom of her rulers, or the spirit of her people', than on 'the persuasion that she still contains many, who, in a degenerate age, love and obey the Gospel of Christ, on the humble trust that the intercession of these may still be prevalent, that for the sake of these, Heaven may still look upon us with an eye of favour'.[16] The Devon-born millenarian preacher Joanna Southcott, who had gathered thousands of fanatical followers, echoed this hope: 'if Bonaparte entered this nation, he should not conquer it; for the Lord would protect this nation from destruction, for the sake of Believers'.[17] Believing was more than a way to save the individual soul; it was a patriotic necessity, to save the nation.

There was fresh outrage in the British press in March 1804 when Napoleon sent soldiers across the border to kidnap the Bourbon Duc d'Enghien on neutral territory in Strasbourg, believing him, falsely, to be involved in a conspiracy. Even though the truth was soon clear, d'Enghien was summarily executed. In killing a Bourbon prince, Napoleon, who had once seemed the man to bring order after revolutionary outrages, was now a proven enemy of royal blood. All the crowns of Europe were at risk, including that of George III.

While all these alarms were sounded, some critics pointed out that there was a slight danger that the ferocious warnings might actually work the wrong way. In *John Bull and the Alarmist*, Gillray hinted that the massive broadside campaign might even be sponsored by the French – though in vain – to weaken British resolve. While Sheridan whispers that the 'Corsican Thief' is coming 'to Ravish your Wives & your Daughters', in the poem below, John Bull shouts, 'Let him come and be D—n'd! – what cares Johnny Bull!/With my Crabstick assured I will fracture his Scull!' The bills pasted on the wall behind sum up the warning propaganda: 'Live Free or Die Slaves', 'Consular Monster', 'Invasion of Great Britain Pillage Destruction Rapes Murder'. In his sonnet 'October, 1803' Wordsworth wrote:

> These times strike monied worldlings with dismay:
> Even rich men, brave by nature, taint the air
> With words of apprehension and despair.

Wordsworth took heart from his belief that thousands of working people – like Gillray's John Bull – were sure of an eventual victory. He was right, though, that 'apprehension and dismay' were as prevalent as the colourful volunteer parades.

Napoleon was quick to exploit this demoralisation. In January 1804 off Mauritius, a French squadron captured the East Indiaman *Admiral Applin*, sailing to Madras and carrying a hefty mailbag, including eighty letters. In retaliation for the publication of captured letters from their army in Egypt in 1799, the French government placed a carefully slanted selection in their newspaper the *Moniteur*, which was soon published in English in London, 'not without reluctance and regret'.[18] Written in the summer of the previous year, the mail ranged from a long letter from Grenville to Marquess Wellesley, detailing the low state of Britain and looking forward to seeing him next year 'supposing at that period you have still *a country to re-visit*!', to business letters from directors of the East India Company and personal letters

*John Bull and the Alarmist*, 1 September 1803: a defiant John Bull, with his pocket stuffed with volunteer lists, 'God Save the King' and 'Rule Britannia'

to families and friends. Most were full of laments about collapsing banks, rising prices, soaring taxes, scarcity of money, stagnant trade, the fall in price of Indian silk, anxiety about Ireland, fears for the rising national debt. 'You learn by the public prints the difficulties in which we are in,' wrote a Mrs Seton to her son: 'subscriptions are established for everything: all the articles of absolute necessity are at a higher price than ever. I fear the people, in their discontent, would join the French if they should endeavour to come; all the world has become military; great preparations for defence are made throughout all England. – The times are sad indeed.'

Several struck a note of impending crisis: 'When this reaches you,' one letter began, 'the grand blow will have struck! Two hundred thousand men upon the Calais coast wait only for orders from the conquering Bonaparte.' Miss M. Tomson added a note to her sister's letter to their brother in the 6th Regiment of Native Cavalry in India, saying how relieved she was that he was so far from the French, 'in the mean time, believe that I am well, though terribly frightened, I confess . . . all the world says I ought not to be alarmed, yet all the world agrees that certainly they will attempt an invasion, and will succeed: What a prospect!!!'

From Napoleon's point of view the most pleasing thing was the conviction in many letters that the invasion would definitely happen, any day. There was, however, a tone of stout resistance. 'When I have sold your goods, I will place them in the bank; for if that fails, every thing will fail,' wrote John Maid to a Mr Gordon:

but there is nothing to be feared. We have no dread of invasion, though we expect it every day. All the world is prepared for such an event, so that Bonaparte would have to kill at least a million of men before he could conquer England; and we have reason to hope, that so great a number of men would give him some difficulty, when, with arms in their hands, we should be determined to fight in defence of our lives.

John Nixon agreed. 'The fate of the invading army is, I believe, fixed,' he wrote, 'they will all be cut to pieces, or drowned, after one or two actions,' and so thought Mr Taylor, writing to a friend in the Calcutta Civil Service. Many lives would be sacrificed, he knew, 'but a Briton thinks nothing too dear for the defence of his liberty, especially when the aggressor is a devil in human form, whom I would kill whenever I could'.

For a year the people waited. The volunteers drilled, and people made plans. Not everyone dashed inland. In September 1803 the Gurney family had no intention of rushing home from Cromer. The weather was still fine and Richenda told Betsy, now married to Joe Fry and living in London, that she must imagine them before breakfast, with troutbeck bonnets and coloured gowns, 'running in all directions on the sands, jetty &c.'[19] In the morning they paid visits, read and wrote, went down to the sea to bathe, and then went for a ride or a walk. They ate in the kitchen, and spent the evening in music or games. But two months later, the sisters and their maids, Molly and Ellen, were beginning to worry. Their father John was off to Lynn and then to Liverpool. 'I think we shall be in a very unprotected state if the French should land whilst my father is away, without a single man or even boy to take care of us,' Priscilla wrote. They had a family conference, and made plans, if somewhat selectively:

It is, however, now finally decided that as soon as ever we hear the news of their arrival we six sisters, Danny, and if we can manage it, Molly and Ellen are immediately to set off in the coach-and-four, for Ely, where we are to take up our abode, as my father thinks it a very safe place, being so completely surrounded by marshes . . . Mrs Freeman is to stay here to take care of the house, as it will be necessary for somebody to be here.[20]

On the cliff behind the house that Mrs Freeman would be left to guard, a bonfire of gorse and pitch was ready to be fired. Beacons all round the coast of Britain were loaded with wood, with piles of wet hay nearby to provide a column of smoke by day. In early 1804, when a watcher at Home Castle in Northumberland, seeing fires on nearby moors, lit his beacon in answer, the beacons on the Scottish borders repeated the warning and volunteers dashed to their rendezvous. Walter Scott was among them, and later put the scare into *The Antiquary*, where the elderly Jonathan Oldbuck, whose only arms are a brass Roman falchion, a Renaissance blade without a handle, and a two-handed sword of the twelfth century, is woken by his sister, niece and two maids, all screaming.

'What the devil is the matter?' said he, starting up in his bed, – 'womankind in my room at this hour of night! – are ye all mad?'
    'The beacon, uncle!' said Miss McIntyre.
    'The French coming to murder us!' screamed Miss Griselda.
    'The beacon, the beacon! – The French, the French! – Murder, murder! And waur than murder!' – cried the two handmaidens, like the chorus of an opera.[21]

While the volunteers hunted for their swords, the British fleet cruising in the Channel waited for something to happen. Henry Sibthorp, who had been ashore to see his soldier brother in Canterbury barracks, told his mother in March 1804 that his ship was stationed off Dungeness, and he was hoping that Bonaparte would fall into their clutches: 'the people all talk confidently of his making the attempt at this moment, & intelligence was received the other day by two smuggling boats from Flushing that the troops were all living on board & only waiting for more moderate weather – every body here is on the look out.'[22] But by September Henry and his fellow officers on the *Euryalus* were convinced Bonaparte would never come:

We left Boulogne yesterday: all the flotilla safe moored & not in the least inclined to trouble us or move from the protection of their iron coast. I think all the editors ought to be hung at the yard arm, for raising groundless reports of invasion, it is the opinion of everyone here that the French will never attempt it.[23]

Familiarity had reduced the French camp from a threat to a show. His captain would be happy to ferry Henry's father across if he liked, Sibthorp said, 'to show him Buonaparte's mighty preparations. It is quite the rage here for parties of Ladies & gentlemen to take a trip over. Mrs B gratified her curiosity the other day . . . we ran close in shore & had a famous view.'

Whatever the sailors felt, the papers were keeping up the alarms, and during these months the MPs in Westminster began to lose faith in Addington. Grenville suggested to Pitt that he could form a new government drawn from all parties, and, although Pitt demurred, Grenville and his new ally Fox – a strange alliance of the arch-Tory and old Whig – worked behind Addington's back to bring him down. In April 1804 Pitt began speaking openly against some of the defence plans, and in May, feeling unable to win a majority, Addington resigned. 'I think Mr. Addington goes out like a gentleman,' wrote Lady Jerningham, 'accepting of no place, Title, nor Pension. The King regrets Him as an agreeable Friend, and has insisted on his keeping a small House near the Royal Domain.'[24]

Pitt proposed a coalition government that would bring in both the Grenville followers and the Foxite Whigs, but this stumbled over George III's downright refusal to have Fox in the cabinet at all, and with Fox out Grenville too stepped down. Exhausted and ill, Pitt struggled on with a lacklustre cabinet split by internal enmities.[25] When he returned to office on 10 May 1804 it was hard to see him as a match for the leader across the Channel. Eight days later, the French senate voted for Napoleon to be declared emperor. In his grand pavilion in Boulogne, he was still so confident of his invasion plans that he had a commemorative medal struck for his men. When he reviewed his eighty thousand troops in Boulogne on his birthday, 15 August, backed by the standards seized in his victories, the whole parade and his rousing speech were reported in the English papers. The press did, however, take some delight in noting that the French fleet failed to turn up and that in the evening the heavens opened and the fireworks were cancelled.

Surveying the events at Paris, Wordsworth likened the antics of the French to 'a dog/Returning to his vomit'. The establishment of the empire was confirmed by a referendum in November, and on 2 December – after marrying Josephine, so that she could be crowned beside him – Napoleon was crowned Emperor of the French by Pope Pius VII. British newspapers carried long descriptions of the ceremony, and the incredible splendour and pomp in Notre Dame. 'FINIS', William Rowbottom wrote with a flourish at the end of his diary for 1804, adding on a new line below, 'on the 2nd Bonaparte was crowned Emperor of Gaul.'

## 36. 'EVERY FARTHING I CAN GET'

Back came the income tax. To make it more palatable, for the first three years it was set at half the previous rate and divided into five separate parts, or 'schedules', listed from A to E, the basis of the modern system, running from income from land and buildings, through farming profits, public annuities and self-employment to salaries and pensions. These could be taxed in different ways at source, and the money proved far easier to collect. Despite the lower rate the income matched that of 1801.[1] Before the peace, loans had accounted for more than two thirds of military funding, but in this second war that dropped to under a third, so great was the revenue from tax. A new figure appeared in British life, the tax inspector, and behind him stood the clerks and officials of the Revenue Office, a new Civil Service department. Soon the Treasury too was reorganised, with specialised divisions and a formal, hierarchical structure. 'The taxes here are enormous,' cried one of the *Moniteur* letters, 'income, windows, houses, servants. And equipages; every thing is taxed; besides those immense duties on the various necessary articles of life, I think that a person pays full ten shillings in the pound.'[2] In London, declared Amabel Hume-Campbell, half the mansions were unoccupied because of the high taxes.[3]

With even the very rich feeling hard done by, the middling orders, manufacturers, shopkeepers and workers were struck doubly fiercely.

Trade was precarious when credit was so short. John Monkhouse's father had died in Penrith during the peace, and John moved back there from London, still dealing in wines and spirits, and helping to keep his brothers afloat. The following year, sending a draft to his brother Thomas in Preston, he apologised it was late, explaining that he needed 'every farthing of money I can get'. He had been dealing on his own behalf and had £400 to pay. 'I am a debtor in my Bankers Books – I must strain every nerve to raise this money and this with at least 1,200 Gallons on hand . . . I shall not have a farthing for any spirit merchant breathing.'[4]

John was hoping that orders would keep up and he could get rid of his debts, but business slumped everywhere: with food prices still high, only the farmers were cheerful. In Derbyshire young James Longsdon, now nearly seventeen, was leaving Mr Ashridge's school and going to Mr Blanchard's Academy in Nottingham, an entry into city life that worried his mother although she was sure he would not be 'in the bustle of it'. In April, a busy time for farmers with lambing and the great spring cattle fairs, his father missed his help but urged him to study, especially accounts and figures: 'As I said to you person-ally, *Embrace the earliest & all opportunities* of making yourself acquainted with the method of Accompts.' A good business head was needed if the farm and cotton mill and warehouse were to flourish.[5] All three Longsdon boys were soon learning French and writing exercises, pre-tending to be French dealers ordering cotton in Manchester.

The cotton business was more of a problem than the farm. In the textile districts the prices for piece-work fell and the poor rates rose. In June 1803 the second, expanded edition of Malthus's *Essay on the Principle of Population* was published, rousing more arguments. Most commentators recognised the contribution of the poor as sailors and militia and acknowledged the pain of poverty, but felt that this had little to do with their place in the economic order: nothing would be helped by imposing a minimum wage. New ideas were scarce, although in three years' time, when seven hundred thousand people were on poor relief, William Hone – who had been trying to make a living as a bookseller – set up a novel scheme called 'Tranquillity' with John Bone, one of the London Corresponding Society members who had now emerged from Coldbath Fields. It would be a savings bank, insurance office and employment registry at once. But it was too idealistic and was doomed to fail, despite support from the City, philanthropists and reformers.[6]

How to pay those who actually did receive wages? Silver and copper coins were running short, partly because people were hoarding money in case of invasion, but also because the metal itself was now more valuable than the coins' face value. Indeed coins were being melted down and sold as bulk metal. The banks looked in all directions to find ready money. The Hoare partners worried about the shortage: 'There is an amazing Scarcity both of Gold & Silver,' said a scribbled entry in the Memorandum Book for November 1803, and, a month later, 'Gold being extremely scarce the greatest Precaution is necessary in the Distribution of it. The Bankers in the City having none can pay none.' In February 1804 the situation was worse still:

The Difficulty about Gold & Silver does not diminish nor is there any to be got without a Premium: some Bankers give it for the former: it may be expedient for us to do the same, but it were better to avoid doing it publickly. The latter we have always done: but most of our Sources have dried up: a Person was sent here, Mr Hanley, No 15 Pump Roe, St Lukes, who is in the Habit of getting it from Turnpikes & other Sources.[7]

Turnpike silver was often substandard, but Hoare's made a deal with Hanley to buy £100 of silver per week for six months, paying him a guinea and a half commission.

In 1804 Matthew Boulton's Soho Mint won a government contract to produce a million of the overstamped Spanish dollars, but even Boulton began to fret about the difficulty, although he had been minting coins at Soho for the past fifteen years, including tokens for manufacturers and ironmasters, silver for Sierra Leone and penny and twopenny pieces for the government. The Royal Mint's equipment was out of date and inefficient and in 1805 the government asked Boulton to plan a new building on Tower Hill, and to supply the machines and the steam engine to work them.[8] But the new Mint would take time to build, and still the coins were short. Silversmiths and bankers began stamping their own tokens, and in the Midlands employers started paying their men by tickets or cards rather than in coin. These were quickly stopped, as they were so easily subject to forgery and fraud – men who could not read were sometimes given cards for half the amount they had earned. But then what to do? If payment was postponed it brought resentment, hunger and want.

Seeing an opportunity, forgers began work, making coins and printing notes. Convictions for forgery carried the death penalty, although this was not often applied, and simply being in possession of forged notes could bring fourteen years' transportation. Yet as the war went on, such cases multiplied. In William Rowbottom's diary trials for forgery at Lancaster assizes grew in numbers: five local men were sentenced to death in 1808, and when an appeal was turned down they were hanged at Lancaster and their bodies brought home for burial: 'There were imence numbers of people to witness there internments and expressd a deal of sorrow for their unfortunate ends. May these be the last that suffere for a similar offence.'[9]

Despite shortage of cash and fears of forgery, the private bankers kept their business. Some lucky ones, like the Hoares, expanded it. Hoare's deposits had jumped from £85,090 in 1799 to £117,278 in 1807.[10] The heavy, fat ledgers for each account ran across a range of customers, from Lord Liverpool to the Austen and Edgeworth families and from the Royal Institution, Eton College and Greenwich Hospital to Byron, who paid in the £5000 deposit for the proposed sale of Newstead – the sale never went through, but he kept the money – and Marc Isambard Brunel, who was always overdrawn after borrowing for his inventions. Hoare's were still strict on loans, though it was hard to pin down their airy, hand-waving clients: 'Duke of Hamilton asks for £10,000 to pay for Deer, Furniture &c in Scotland. Messrs H of course wished it to be temporary. The Duke would not bind himself down to say it would be so absolutely . . .' or

'The Adelphi' brothers, Henry Hugh,
Charles and Henry Merrick Hoare, in later life

'The D. of Northumberland announces his intention of drawing on us for £17,000 to pay for an estate in the North – this he says may happen in a few weeks.'[11] In 1806, when Lord Ailesbury – who had married a Hoare cousin, and was now a Groom of the Bedchamber – came to ask for a loan for Queen Charlotte of six thousand guineas to buy the Frogmore estate near Windsor, 'Mr H. hesitated & stated the Times &c. but said if he heard of any one wanting such a Mortgage he would mention it.'[12] Next day Ailesbury was back, saying that 'the Queen wants The Money & He must contrive to get it. Mr H stated the impracticability of their advancing it, upon which Lord A turned upon his heel and walked out seemingly much disappointed.' A few days later the partners relented, as long as Ailesbury stood as bondsman for the loan. It was a shrewd business decision: some years later they acquired the account for the whole royal household expenses at Windsor, salaries, tradesmen's bills and all.

The more robust country bankers, like the Gurneys and James Oakes, also continued to flourish. Oakes now had his own London agent, Ayton, Brassey & Co.; at least once a month a clerk from Bury took large sums of money up to London, £10,000 or even £20,000 in banknotes, bills and cash, taking great precautions to avoid highwaymen and footpads on the way. Oakes also had a stockbroker who placed investments for him in India Bonds, Exchequer Bills, Navy and Victualling Bills and the Omnium, a government portfolio offering stock and an annuity. A favourite investment was in India bills: a note in Oakes's bank memorandum book shows that in May 1805 they held India Bonds worth £34,000.[13] Beyond that he had a bill-broker, Thomas Richardson, a former Gurney's clerk who handled all their business in discounted bills. In 1805 he was joined by John Overend and four years later by Samuel Gurney, John of Earlham's young son. For two generations, until a disastrous crash in 1866, Overend, Gurney & Co. were the greatest discounting house in the world, 'the banker's bank'.

Every day the clerks from Fleet Street went up to the City, with bills and drafts for their brokers. Hoare's men were busy, with their work rearranged in a more orderly fashion: Mr Noble was still head clerk; under him Mr Naylor was to take charge of Exchequer Bills and the Navy Office; Mr Cottle was to take the bills for rent days four times a year, to check the ledgers, copy letters and take care of the warehouse; Mr Law to fill up the books, post the indexes of bills and 'to be at the Service of the Brothers should they require it (this will not happen very often) to clear the Decks on a Busy Day'.[14] The Stock Exchange had moved into its new building in Capel Court in 1802, and there were powerful newcomers among the bankers, brokers and stockjobbers. Abraham Ricardo's son David had begun trading on his own a decade ago and was now on the Stock Exchange Committee. The Schroder brothers, sons of a rich Hamburg merchant, set up in 1800 as agents and principals in commodity trading to Europe. New deals were made, new ventures launched, new loans raised. There may have been a shortage of cash, but with crashes and booms, collapses and revivals, the City's business thundered on.

# 37. THE BUSINESS OF DEFENCE

During the peace of 1802–3, Samuel Galton had turned back to the East India Company, asking Matthew Boulton if he could get him an introduction to the directors, and in 1803 he became a contractor to the Company. But he was happy to see war come again. As soon as it started, government officials came to ask Boulton if he could find out what the weekly output of muskets and bayonets might be if every possible man in Birmingham was pressed into making them, and Galton helped him work out an estimate. The gunmakers increased production to fourteen thousand muskets a week. The following March the Ordnance agreed new terms and prices and worked out a deal with the flint makers of Brandon in Suffolk, to supply an astounding 356,000 flints per month, offering one guinea per thousand for musket flints, £1 per thousand for carbines and pistols. But by now Galton had had enough. He was a wealthy man: his original £100 shares in the Birmingham Canal Company had doubled and trebled in value and were now worth £700 each. All the property he had built around Steelhouse Lane and in other parts of Birmingham was soaring in value and, like Boulton, he had invested heavily in the Rose Copper Company, which smelted copper in south Wales. In 1804 he retired from being an active partner in the gunmaking firm, handing it over to his eldest son, Samuel Tertius, and, like so many merchants and manufacturers, he set up as a banker.

A martial emblem for the Birmingham gunmakers, in *Bisset's Directory*, 1808

Tertius, as he was always called, had been to Cambridge and Edinburgh universities, and had worked in a Liverpool merchant house. As soon as he took over, he had to cope with making rifles, as well as the faithful India Pattern muskets. When the first rifle corps were sent to Ireland, the Ordnance had bought five thousand cheap Prussian rifled muskets, but to their dismay many were broken, the rest inferior, and they were promptly issued to foreign troops rather than British. With the support of the pioneering rifle commander Colonel Manningham, Ezekiel Baker, a master gunsmith from Whitechapel, submitted a design for a rifled carbine, which was adopted in 1802 by the Prince of Wales's 10th Light Dragoons. The prince, excited by this new toy, pressed for a special cavalry rifle and after trials in June 1803, Baker's gun was chosen. The design would be used, with modifications, for the next forty years. Gradually the Birmingham gunmakers began supplying these. In 1806, when a huge order came in, they sent 1,597 rifles, plus 15,106 rifle barrels and 11,980 locks, to be set up in London.[1]

The gunmakers increased investment and formed a contractors' cartel, the Committee of the Manufacturers of Arms and Materials for Arms, which set prices, dealt with negotiations with the Ordnance and amended the apprenticeship rules so that more men could be trained in each workshop. Finally they brought in a bounty system whereby a craftsman would bind himself to a master and agree to deliver a certain number of guns, for a bounty of up to £50 a year. Many Midlands makers were now using steam power. Ketlands in Whittal Street had long used a steam engine for barrel making and grinding; in 1803 the New Steam Mill Company was founded in Fazely, and within a few years one could visit a mill where three hundred men produced ten thousand barrels a month, using a 120-horsepower steam engine. Yet there were always difficulties, foreseen and unforeseen. If steam helped to turn out more barrels, now there was a sudden dearth of walnut for the stocks. Labourers planted trees on Ordnance stations across the country – the station at Upnor had a special Ordnance Plantation raising walnuts, ash, quickset for fences and thousands of willows. But these would never grow in time to meet demand.

The cannon masters at the Carron and Walker works also rushed back to business. The foundries and smelting works were busy, since the Navy and the Ordnance had realised that British iron was now of high quality and were ordering from home rather than from Sweden or Russia. Iron workers were needed and their wages were good. And the coal miners also did well; as the mine owners were hit by the militia draft, miners were in demand, and could move around for better pay, often brazenly breaking their contracts. In 1805, the Cumbrian and Northumbrian owners signed an agreement not to steal each other's men.

The Ordnance Board worried, however, about storage of arms and gunpowder. The invasion scare of 1798 had made them realise that nearly all their big depots were near the south coast and the Thames: the gunpowder stores at Faversham and the depot at Purfleet; Waltham Abbey on the river Lee; Woolwich Warren and the Tower of London itself. At the same time, as reserves of muskets fell, they began to think about building their own arms factory, safely inland. Weedon Bec in the steep valley of the Fawsley Water near Northampton seemed the ideal place. It was a large village, whose seven hundred or so inhabitants lived in clusters of houses along the valley bottom, or high up at Upper Weedon on the hillside to the south. The main Northampton turnpike running nearby gave a clear, if not always passable, route for the teams of horses pulling heavy field guns.[2] But the main advantage was the canal. The great project of the Grand Union, linking the canals of the Midlands with the Thames at Brentford, was still incomplete, but a spur from Weedon Bec across a high embankment to Braunston, a few miles to the north, had been finished in 1796, and at Braunston the barges could join the Oxford canal and the whole Midland network, taking them north-west to Birmingham with its Gun Quarter, or south towards the Thames and London. While a single horse could just about haul a ton on the road, on the canals it could shift twenty tons, loaded on to new seventy-foot narrowboats. Water was also a far safer way of carrying gunpowder; on the rutted roads jolts and sparks could cause explosions. Soon, they hoped, the canals would link Weedon to the new canal basin at Paddington.

In the autumn of 1802, travelling incognito, the Board's Surveyor General, Major-General Ross, had arrived in the valley, sketching the fields and meadow ground and asking casually about land and prices: it turned out that the Grand Junction partners, for example, had paid £130 an acre for meadow land, but only £80 for arable and upland pasture. Being careful not to mention any government interest in case the prices rose, Ross learned that the main landowner was Eton College and the Ordnance soon began negotiating directly with Eton's leaseholders and tenants. Some of the tenants, like the farmer Thomas Smith, were keen to sell if the price was right, but the vicar, Ross reported, said his vicarage land could not be sold, and the stubborn Mr Hewitt of Dodford was 'averse to selling any part'.[3] The rest of the area was divided among eleven tenants, who would sell their leases as long as they could still get water from the stream. Talks and cajoling continued, and in June 1803 an Act of Parliament was passed enabling the Board to take freehold possession of the Eton College lands: another Act a year later granted the Ordnance money to compensate all the proprietors.

By then the work had started, and in March 1804 Captain Robert Pilkington was appointed Commanding Royal Engineer. 'Pilky', as friends called him, had spent twelve years as an army engineer in Canada, where he was on Governor Simcoe's staff and had built Government House in York and led expeditions into the interior, as well as drinking hard with fellow officers and getting into fights. He never returned to Canada, but he kept up his connections through the Canada Club, a group of merchants, traders and others who met in the Freemasons' Tavern in London, to be entertained with 'Canadian boat songs and Indian speeches'.[4] Now his colonial days were over, and he moved to Weedon. Plans were drawn, estimates made and buildings designed: fine brick houses for the officers; storehouses, with upper floors for storing muskets; a gunpowder magazine; a branch canal with turning basins and wharves; a small arms manufactory; barracks and stables for the Royal Artillery Brigade; a hospital, workshops and offices, wells, walls and gates, and temporary cottages for the building workers.

Thomas Lepard was appointed overseer, and the first men were taken on, including an experienced carpenter, fifty-eight-year-old Robert Green, and two young labourers in their mid-twenties, Simon Rogers and William Butlin. The names of all three would still be on the Weedon books ten years later. In midsummer men dug foundations and levelled the ground, building roads and paths and drains. One by one workmen tramped over the hill or hitched a lift on carts: carpenters, bricklayers, stonemasons, plumbers and tilers. Skilled men carried their tools, while labourers came empty-handed, waiting for tasks to be allotted. Some came from local villages, others walked miles, shoving a spare work shirt into a bag and saying goodbye to their families. Several had worked on the canal and knew the area well. With Lepard, Pilkington made lists of contractors and ordered things large and small: two pairs of bellows and two anvils, six sledgehammers and six crowbars, four strong chains for raising weights, coils of tarred rope, a bell to call the workmen and bedding for the watchmen. He arranged for stone to be brought by canal from Warwickshire quarries and for good red brick from Brinklow on the Oxford canal.[5] Welsh slates were shipped from Bangor to the Mersey and then south by canal; Baltic timber came from London for the roof joists; sheets of crown glass were loaded on to Birmingham barges. A whole watery network converged on the valley, despite rows with toll-collectors who did not see why government supplies should go free, and with canal proprietors who complained that the heavy traffic and the numbers of expected troops would lead to 'a very great Expenditure of Water' and 'serious obstructions to the Trade and Navigation'.[6]

At Weedon the men began work on their own canal branch, six hundred feet long, which would let them unload goods directly into the storehouses on each side. These were huge buildings of two and three storeys, as grand as Palladian mansions, with a magazine to hold ten thousand barrels of gunpowder in a safe place nearby. By now nearly three hundred people worked here, and in January 1805 the storekeeper and Clerk of Cheque moved into the new officers' houses as soon as the smell of paint faded, the master craftsmen into smaller houses, and the workers' families into temporary cottages by the stream. There were losers here, as everywhere. Seeing his workmen ousting villagers from their lodgings, Pilkington worked out a deal with the local magistrate to house twelve families. Back came the reply from London: 'The Board cannot do anything to help relief of the poor.'[7]

Work on coastal defences also intensified. The Duke of York drew up a defence plan in August 1803, while rather bizarrely, General Dumouriez, who had wandered around Europe since his defection and had now come to England, wrote a lengthy manuscript analysing the defences in every part of the British isles and sent a copy to the War Office.[8] New funds were voted for fortifications, and between 1805 and 1808 gangs of navvies built Martello towers along the southern and eastern coasts.[9] These were modelled on the stout, round defensive towers at Mortella Point on the Corsican coast, which had so impressed Sir John Moore (who was now commanding troops in Kent) in 1794, when he saw how the thick walls and guns mounted a defence against Admiral Hood's warships. Towers had since been built in Minorca and in Ireland and now two lines were planned for England's defence, seventy-three in Kent and Sussex and another thirty for Essex and Suffolk, each with walls five feet thick or more, cannon pointing out to sea, and guns to pepper invading French troops with deadly grapeshot. An average tower contained around seven hundred thousand bricks, and the hinterland was pockmarked with brick-pits and dotted with kilns. Another plan was to flood Romney Marsh to hold back invaders, but instead, with John Rennie as consultant engineer, navvies cut the Royal Military Canal from Hythe to Rye – a mild deterrent to smugglers, if not to the French. Meanwhile great engineering works went on at Dover Castle: fieldworks and barracks, and a labyrinth of tunnels, and stairways to let troops move quickly from the castle to the shore below.

The dockyards too sprang into life. While the Ordnance Office ran the gun wharves, the Navy Board controlled the shipbuilding, repair and supplies. But they faced a mammoth task. The fleet was getting old, and only thirty-three new battleships had been launched since 1793, compared to ten each year in the 1780s. In addition, Lord St Vincent's crackdown during the Peace of Amiens had left the dockyards in disarray, and the whole great machine had to crank up again. In 1801 workers at all the royal dockyards – Deptford, Woolwich, Chatham, Portsmouth and Plymouth – had joined in a single union, or combination, to demand increases in pay. They had won some concessions but then backed down, fearing that with the peace they could lose their jobs. Now, with a new war, they could more or less settle their own terms, knowing that skilled men were short and could earn twice as much in the merchant shipyards.[10] To recruit the men they needed, over the next three years the dockyards gradually raised the top age for working in the yards to thirty-five, then forty-five, and finally abolished the limit altogether.

There were other obstacles to overcome. One was the entrenched power of the contractors of the Timber Trust, who practically mono-polised the timber supply, and had taken offence at St Vincent's intro-duction of timber masters to look after dockyard supplies, as part of his drive to stop corruption. In 1803, when contractors found their oak was being rejected on grounds of poor quality, they simply stopped supplies altogether, leaving Britain with less than a year's supply of timber and completely lacking in certain kinds of oak. When Nelson was blockading Toulon in late 1803, he wrote angrily, explaining as if to an idiot:

My crazy Fleet are getting in a very indifferent state, and others will soon follow. The finest Ships in the Service will soon be destroyed . . . if I am to watch the French, I must be at sea, and if at sea, must have bad weather; and if the Ships are not fit to stand bad weather, they are useless. I do not say much; but I do not believe that Lord St Vincent would have kept the Sea with such Ships.[11]

As soon as Pitt came back to power in early 1804, he replaced St Vincent with his old ally Dundas – made Lord Melville in 1802 – who quietly reversed all St Vincent's policies, agreed to the con-tractors' higher prices and reduced the timber masters' power in the yards.[12] The timber magnate John Larking set out to ensure supplies from Prussia and Holstein and other merchants with agents overseas imported oak plank from Russia and fir from Danzig, Riga and St Petersburg. In 1805 Samuel Bentham, brother of the philosopher Jeremy Bentham, and now the Inspector General of Naval Works, even hoped to build warships in Russia, an idea that was soon aban-doned. The Admiralty also sent a naval contractor, John Leard, who had been supplying Adriatic hemp and cordage, to buy vast quantities of oak from Croatia and from the forests along the Danube. Supplies also came from Albania and the Crimea, and across the world: cargoes of masts from Canada, hard eucalyptus, jarrah wood and Swan River mahogany from New South Wales, and dense kauri from distant New Zealand.

By 1804 there was a shipbuilding boom, with most of the work going to private yards.[13] Some of these were on the Thames, like Perry, Green and Wells, whose Blackwall yard had built ships for the East India Company since the seventeenth century.[14] But yards were busy everywhere. In the ports of Devon and Cornwall, large and small, builders hustled for contracts. In all the west country yards built nearly sixty warships. Richard Thorne from Barnstaple moved his yard to the open shore at Fremington, looking out to the mouth of the estuary, across to Lundy and the coast of south Wales. Here he built the *Delight*, a sixteen-gun sloop that sailed to the Mediterranean and the Dardanelles, and the *Ranger*, an even larger sloop. Waving crowds cheered as the ships sailed out at high tide, into the Bristol Channel.

Lord Melville focused on the navy in the same way as he had done on home defence in the invasion scare of 1803, locking himself away to go through all the information from the Admiralty and Navy Offices, and then driving through reforms. These included changing the system of repair to 'doubling' (an idea developed by Gabriel Snodgrass, Surveyor to the East India Company), which meant that instead of taking out rotten timbers, old ones were 'doubled' with three-inch oak planks and strengthened with 'iron knees, standards and iron riders'.[15] Orders went out for timber, tar, nails, canvas and rope. And in Portsmouth Marc Brunel's block-making machines took naval engineering into an age of mass production. His forty-three steam-powered machines could produce twenty-two different types of metal pulley blocks, replacing the old handmade wooden pulleys for working the rigging ropes. A large ship of the line used about a thousand blocks and the fast new machines could supply 130,000 a year, outstripping the navy's need. Yet this invention – which saved the Admiralty £24,000 in the first year alone – had taken Brunel

Rowlandson, *Perry's Dock at Blackwall*, 1806

four long years of lobbying to get approval, and then three years with
the technical wizard Henry Maudslay to build the machines to the
right standard. From the moment the block-making machines started
up, crowds came to watch them. For the dockyard men, however,
they were a threat, so easy to work that just ten semi-skilled workers
replaced 110 skilled men.[16] The man who supervised their installation
was the thirty-year-old engineer Simon Goodrich, a former draughts-
man in Samuel Bentham's office, who also built Portsmouth's Metal
Mills and a millwright's shop.[17]

The war prompted many inventions. The artillery had already
adopted Colonel Shrapnel's 'spherical case-shot' with its fuse exploding an inner shell, scattering shot as it hit, and Woolwich Arsenal was
testing rockets developed by the son of the Comptroller of the Royal
Laboratory, which proved to have considerable range but an alarming
lack of accuracy. Meanwhile the Admiralty was considering the 'catamarans' designed by the American Robert Fulton, twenty-foot-long
wooden shells, lined with lead and packed with explosive, worked by
a clockwork timer. These were tested off Boulogne in October and

November 1804 but then rejected as too risky – and 'unsporting'. The board also turned to Richard Trevithick, who was at Coalbrookdale trying to get his steam engine to drive a boat. He told Davies Giddy that men from the Admiralty had called on him 'to know if these engins wd not be good things to go into Bolong to destroy the flotels &c. in the harbour by fire ships . . . If you think you could get the Government to get it putt in to execution, I wod readily go with the engines and risque the enterprize.'[18]

Trevithick did go to the Admiralty to talk this through, but the response was slow. After waiting impatiently, he grew tired, and went back to Shropshire to get on with his other experiments. The business of defence could get on without him.

# 38. TRAFALGAR

After nearly two years of a defensive war, guarding the coast and blockading French ports, Pitt changed his policy. To break the stalemate, his government would encourage aggression in Europe, building a new coalition and subsidising the allied powers. His aim was threefold, as he explained in January 1805: to rescue countries subjugated by France and restore France to pre-revolutionary boundaries; to boost 'the security and happiness' of the recovered states, and make them buffers against French ambitions; and 'to form, at the restoration of peace, a general agreement and guarantee for the mutual protection and security of different powers, and for re-establishing a general system of public law in Europe'.[1] In April Russia was drawn in, followed by Austria in August, and negotiations continued to bring Prussia in too.

But Pitt faced trouble at home. In March 1805, St Vincent's report about the state of the navy, commissioned during the peace, was finally published.[2] Its key allegation was that during the past war Henry Dundas, Lord Melville, had been involved in financial irregularities, specifically that his Admiralty Paymaster, Alexander Trotter (the brother of the army contractor John Trotter), had used naval funds for his own transactions. This had been an accepted practice in earlier days and the money had been returned, but it was now thought reprehensible that Melville had let this slip by without comment. And perhaps, it was said, he had also used some of the money himself? On 8 April Samuel Whitbread tabled a motion of censure. After a heated debate, during which Wilberforce made a vehement speech, declaring, 'I really cannot find language sufficiently strong to express my utter detestation of such conduct,' the motion was carried and Melville had to resign.[3] His critics continued to demand his removal from the Privy Council and his impeachment or criminal prosecution, and he was impeached before the House of Lords. London society thronged to see. Thomas Fremantle's brother William got Betsey two tickets for Melville's trial, and she watched with her sister Justina from the Royal Box. 'Lord Melville appears dejected,' she wrote in her diary. 'Mr Whitbread spoke for four hours and a half – We came away from Westminster Hall at three o'clock the string of Carriages reached St James's Street.'[4] In the end Melville was acquitted of misappropriation of public funds but still labelled negligent.

When Melville left, Pitt lost one of his oldest and wiliest friends. He was further weakened in July when Henry Addington, now Lord Sidmouth, finally left the government, taking his followers with him. In Melville's place Pitt appointed the veteran Charles Middleton, now Lord Barham, 'a superannuated Methodist at the head of the Admiralty, in order to catch the votes of Wilberforce and Co., now and then,' sneered Creevey.[5] In fact Barham was sensible and efficient and after Melville's energetic work the navy was just able to meet the French threat. Then, to British alarm, in April Villeneuve's French fleet escaped from Toulon, heading, it was thought, for Martinique.

Far from thoughts of ports and fleets, on 14 August 1805 Walter Scott, Wordsworth and Humphry Davy climbed Helvellyn from Patterdale. Wordsworth, who would shortly publish a fourth edition of *Lyrical Ballads*, had recently completed a version of his long poem on 'The Growth of a Poet's Mind'. Unlike *Lyrical Ballads*, Wordsworth's poetic autobiography was impossible to publish in the current climate, with its honest memories of his early enthusiasm for the Revolution and his fury at Pitt's repression of the mid-1790s.[6] In any case, he always intended it as a forerunner to a more philosophical poem: it would eventually be published as *The Prelude* in 1850, after his death. But if Wordsworth, a married man with two children, veering towards a safe conservatism, was holding back from public gaze, the other two walkers were not. This year Davy was giving dramatic lectures at the Royal Institution on the new science of geology, his models including a volcano that spewed ash, while Scott was revelling in the astounding sales of *The Lay of the Last Minstrel*, showing, he declared casually, that the public would pay for poetry if it did not ask too much of them. Wordsworth remembered Scott grappling his way along the ridge of Striding Edge, bubbling with 'many stories and amusing anecdotes, as was his custom', while Davy, bored by literary chat, walked on to Grasmere alone.[7]

As they walked and talked of poetry, chemistry, mountains and fame, the papers were full of Nelson's pursuit of Villeneuve to the West Indies and back, an epic chase of 6600 miles. Nelson was a genuine hero to the navy. He could be a tough, demanding commander but the men thought him fair, concerned for their health, food, their share in the prize money. He was open, easy to talk to, seeking out old sailors when he visited different towns: with his one arm and bad eye he was also a battered figure, one of them. He was not afraid to speak out or take risks and his affair with Emma Hamilton merely added to his glamour, however frosty it made London high society and the Admiralty. Compared to other admirals, the seamen felt, he won fewer honours than he deserved and if he wanted to flaunt his medal from the Turkish Sultan and call himself 'Nelson and Bronte' – the Bronte dukedom granted by the king of Naples – that was fine. In the streets people mobbed and cheered him and his travels drew more crowds than those of George III.

Public idol though he was, Nelson had critics in the navy. In 1804, the *Naval Chronicle* wrote:

Should the mad project of invasion ever be attempted, the public would feel additional security from having the Hero of the Nile off our own coast. But we greatly lament that ill-judged and overweening popularity which tends to make a demigod of Lord Nelson at the expense of all other officers in the service, many of whom possess equal merit and equal abilities and equal gallantry with the noble Admiral.[8]

Nelson was back in London this summer while the *Victory* was fitted with a new rudder, and on 12 September, waiting at the Colonial Office for his instructions from Castlereagh, he bumped into Arthur Wellesley, home from India after his successes in the Maratha war: this month he would be made a Knight of the Bath. Years later Wellington remembered being appalled by Nelson's swagger until Nelson, having briefly left the room and discovered who he was, completely dropped his boasting. Amused at the transformation, by the time he left Wellington was charmed: 'luckily I saw enough to be satisfied that he really was a very superior man; but certainly a more sudden and complete metamorphosis I never saw.'[9] It was the only time they met. Nelson sailed three days later from Portsmouth.

That month, Pitt went down to see the king, who was in Weymouth, taking his family sailing on his yacht every day. Writing home, Henry Sibthorp, who was on a restful duty guarding the royal family in the brig *Liberty*, reported that they had just cheered the king, 'which we do every day in passing the yacht. The old gentleman is very hearty and quite indefatigable in his sea excursions.'[10] Next day, he told his brother Charles, Billy Pitt was there, holding a cabinet council on board the king's yacht. They had much to discuss. In late August, hearing that Villeneuve was back in Cadiz and the Brest fleet was still blockaded, ruining his plans to invade, Bonaparte gave way to a famous bout of public fury. Turning on his heel he marched his Grande Armée rapidly east to the Rhine, determined to smash Austria and Russia, part of a newly formed 'Third Coalition'. At the start of November 1805 Britain was absorbing reports that the complete Austrian army had surrendered at Ulm in Bavaria, handing over their guns and thirty thousand prisoners. No one, especially Pitt, could believe that Austria's General Mack could have surrendered. But on Sunday 3 November Pitt and Lord Mulgrave came up to Lord Malmesbury in Spring Gardens, bringing a Dutch newspaper

carrying a troubling-looking report. 'As they neither of them understood Dutch, and as all the offices were empty,' Malmesbury wrote,
'they came to me to translate it, which I did as well as I could, and I
observed but too clearly the effect it had upon Pitt, though he did his
utmost to conceal it.'[11]

But then, on 4 November, as London was reeling from the Austrian
surrender, the schooner *Pickle* docked at Falmouth. Her commander,
Captain John Richards Lapenotiere, leapt into a post-chaise and rode
to bring despatches from Admiral Collingwood to the Admiralty.
Immediately, confused rumours spread. On the morning of Thursday
7 November, Betsey Fremantle wrote, she was

Much alarmed by Nelly's ghastly appearance immediately after breakfast,
who came in to say that Dudley had brought from Winslow the account that
a most dreadful action had been fought off Cadiz, Nelson & several captains
killed, & twenty ships were taken. I really felt undescribable misery until the
arrival of the Post.

That post brought a letter from Lord Garlies, one of the Lords of the
Admiralty, congratulating her on Fremantle's safety, telling her of the
victory at Trafalgar, and of Nelson's death. In the midst of her delight
Betsy 'could not help feeling greatly distressed for the loss of poor
*Nelson*, whose loss is irreparable'.

When the London papers arrived in towns, villages and homes
across the country, people read accounts of the battle with headlines
shouting 'GLORIOUS VICTORY', and, in smaller print, 'The
Death of Lord Nelson'. Nelson's brother, a canon in Canterbury and
a well-known figure in his long black frock-coat and large shovel hat,
always went to Bristow's reading room every morning at eight for the
latest news of the fleet: but today Bristow ran to the Cathedral yard to
stop the doctor coming out and 'learning in a public newsroom of his
brother's death'.[12] In those public prints the full story was now told.
On 21 October, Nelson's fleet had finally met the French off Trafalgar. The bands of the marines, so the papers reported, had gone

into battle playing three tunes, 'Rule Britannia', 'Hearts of Oak' and Dibdin's 'Britons Strike Home'. Instead of having lines of ships sailing parallel, Nelson had employed the tactics that Howe and Jervis had used so well, breaking through the enemy line. The French and Spanish fleets lost thirty-three ships, and another seventeen were captured: their dead and wounded were said to reach fourteen thousand, compared to fifteen hundred British. But one of those British casualties was Nelson himself, who might, it was thought, have deliberately challenged death by his conspicuous clothes, making him an easy target for a sniper high in the rigging of a French ship.

James Oakes condensed the newspaper reports in a diary entry surrounded by stars, taking consolation in the fact that before Nelson died he learned that fifteen of the French ships had surrendered, and adding with much underlining, '*The Death of so brave a man & gallant an Officer occasiond a universal gloom.*' Nelson's death was felt, Southey wrote in 1814, 'as something more than a public calamity; men started at the intelligence and turned pale, as if they had heard of a loss of a dear friend.'[13]

To have been at Trafalgar, as the families of all naval men knew, was to be a hero, rich, rewarded, promoted. Although only four of the captured French ships survived the gales on the way back, parliament voted a staggering £320,000 to be distributed round the fleet. Each captain had £3300, plus prize money and gold medals, while Lloyd's Patriotic Fund handed out silver vases with designs by John Flaxman, who was soon to be commissioned to sculpt the Nelson monument in St Paul's. Officers received beautifully chased swords, and money was given to the wounded.

Those who missed the battle felt it bitterly. In early 1805 Francis Austen had been appointed flag captain to Rear-Admiral Thomas Louis in the eighty-gun *Canopus*. They had joined Nelson's fleet pursuing Villeneuve across the Atlantic but in September *Canopus* was escorting a Malta convoy and although orders came to turn back, westerly gales held them up. At home Mary Austen read Frank's long, forlorn letter, started on the eve of Trafalgar and finished after the battle. 'You perhaps may not feel this quite so forcibly as I do,' he began,

and in your satisfaction at my having avoided the danger of battle, may not much regret my losing the credit of having contributed to gain a Victory; not so, myself; I do not profess to like fighting for its own sake, but if there have been an action with the combined Fleets, I shall ever consider the day on which I sailed from the Squadron as the most inauspicious one of my life . . .

. . . Alas! My dearest Mary, all my fears are but too fully justified. The Fleets have met and after a very severe contest, a most decisive Victory has been gained by the English 27 over the Enemy's 33.[14]

Francis was stricken by Nelson's death, while rejoicing at the 'national benefit'. And he felt unlucky 'by a fatal combination of unfortunate though unavoidable events, to lose all share in the glory of a day, which surpasses all which ever went before'.

The papers were so full of naval talk that it became easy to parody, even if it seemed irreverent. On 10 December Tertius Galton wrote to his brother Hubert at Oxford, putting their entire family life and Christmas travels into navalese. 'The despatches were yesterday received at the Admiralty,' he began, 'mentioning that it was your intention in company with the Rathbone & Howard, to leave your present station on Friday the 20th inst., in order to come into Harbour to refit, previous to the heavy gales which may be expected.'[15]

'My ever Dearest and Best of Women', Thomas Fremantle wrote to Betsey from the *Neptune*, 'I am at present towing the Victory and the Admiral has just made the signal for me to go with her to Gibraltar.'[16] Nelson's body, steeped in a brandy-filled cask, was taken to Gibraltar and re-pickled in spirits of wine. As if miraculously revived, the great admiral 'made his reappearance', so Henry Sibthorp told his brother, reporting naval rumours, 'by bursting the cask in which he was confined to the utter dismay of the affrighted sentinel, who with hair erect rushed on the quarter-deck & declared the Admiral was come to life again'.[17] Eventually, on 4 November, with Nelson re-confined in fresh brandy, the *Victory* sailed for England. When it was suggested that his body be moved to a fast frigate, the sailors of the *Victory* insisted on carrying it. In Rowlandson and Woodward's print, Ben complains, 'now I think it d—d hard that as he kept us while he was alive, – that we should not be allow'd to keep him now he is dead.' Jack, keeping watch over the coffin, promises that he will never leave the *Victory* 'until he arrives in his native country' where 'his monument will be erected in the heart of every Briton'.

Woodward and Rowlandson, *Brave Tars of the Victory*, 10 January 1806

The *Victory* reached Spithead at the start of December. After the surgeon William Beatty performed an autopsy and removed the musket ball, Nelson's body was placed in a nest of three coffins: the first was made from the mainmast of the *L'Orient*, given to Nelson after the battle of the Nile; the second was of lead, and the third of wood. On 23 December, the Sheerness dockyard commissioner took the coffin upriver to Greenwich Hospital, where a hundred thousand people flocked to see Nelson lie in state in the Painted Hall. He had wished to be buried at his home village of Burnham Thorpe in Norfolk, but the government, eager to promote British heroism, planned a state funeral: the womanising and petulance that upset the Admiralty were forgotten. Two days before the ceremony Charles Lamb wrote to Hazlitt:

You know Lord Nelson is dead. He is also to be buried. And the whole town is in a fever. Seats erecting, seats to be let, sold, lent &c . . . The whole town as unsettled as a young Lady the day before being married. St Paul's virgers making their hundred pounds a day in sixpences for letting people see the scaffolding inside, & the hole where he is to be let down; which money they under the Rose share with the Dean and Praecentors at night. – Great Aquatic bustle tomorrow. Body to come up from Greenwich with Lord Mayor & City Barges. Fillets of veal predestined to be demolished at The Temple in the afternoon. All Cheswick, Pimlico & Pancras emptying out in the morning into the Temple . . . If you with your refinements were here . . . you could neither eat, sit, read nor paint, till the corpse were fairly laid.[18]

Lamb also played with the idea of the fashionable 'eldest Miss Squeeze' and how she might react, 'for she is afraid it will be too affecting. She is sure she shall turn her head away from the window as it goes by. O the immortal Man!' The vergers at St Paul's were said to be making more than a thousand pounds from the daily admissions: 'the door money is taken as at a puppet shew!' exclaimed *The Times*.[19]

On the eve of the funeral, with the wind tossing up waves on the Thames, the royal barge of Charles II, followed by a flotilla of sixty vessels, brought Nelson's body to Whitehall steps. The banks were black with people and the river was lined with vessels flying flags and firing guns. Amabel Hume-Campbell, watching from her sister's garden next to the landing place, was moved by the contrast between plain black-tarred barges and the 'gorgeous Trophies of Heraldry and war' and by the watermen holding up their oars, like soldiers presenting arms, as the coffin was landed.[20] Characteristically Amabel refused to '*romance* it' but even she shivered at the trumpets' dirge and the shower of hail that fell 'the instant the Body landed . . . & I believe all who were in the House look'd at one another with a little Superstitious Awe. Lady Lemon is sure it thundered & lighten'd, but there I believe she mistakes.'

The next day, 9 January 1806, the procession wove through London from the Admiralty to St Paul's in bright sunshine. The bier had been designed by Rudolph Ackermann to resemble Nelson's flagship, though Amabel thought it a cross between a funeral car and triumphal chariot. Behind it marched admirals, Greenwich pensioners and the sailors of the *Victory*, carrying the tattered colours they had won. The streets fell silent when the coffin appeared. At St Paul's a congregation of seven thousand watched as the coffin was lowered by a winch into the crypt below the dome. Taking the officials by surprise, when Nelson's flag was about to be lowered into the grave, the sailors taking part in the ceremony, 'with one accord rent it in pieces, that each might preserve a fragment while he lived'.[21]

A linen handkerchief, used after taking snuff, with a print showing
Nelson's funeral car on the way to St Paul's and sailors
wearing black bands round their hats

In Manchester, James Weatherley remembered:

all the Mills and workshops stopt you could scarcely see that day a lad without a ribbon round his hat with a verse or something relating to the brave Nelson some of the ribbons were Paper and some Silk the one I bought was a blue Silk one I gave sixpence for it the letters on it gold Printed verse was May Nelson's Death and Britons Glory be Repeated in future Story.[22]

The memorialising started straight away, among young and old. The thirteen-year-old George Cruikshank watched the procession from Ludgate Hill and dashed home to etch a print, helped by his father Isaac.[23] Emotional tourists viewed the tableau at Mrs Salmon's Waxworks and Madame Tussaud took her Nelson figure on tour. Even Westminster Abbey, vying with St Paul's, commissioned a wax figure.

Nelson was commemorated on plates and mugs, in books and prints and at the theatre. There was some disapproval of the theatrical shows, and not everything went according to plan. In Manchester, the theatre showed a panorama, with puppets enacting the procession, but 'owing to some imperfection in the mechanism', 'horse, foot and carriages, lords and commons, sailors, soldiers and even kings at arms, tumbled down by dozens . . . Decorous solemnity on the part of the audience was out of the question, and the funeral procession was the occasion of more laughing than generally takes place at the representation of a highly finished farce.'[24]

If theatrical entrepreneurs seized the occasion, so did artists. Gillray's *Death of Admiral Lord Nelson – in the moment of Victory* undercut solemnity by making a grief-stricken Britannia look suspiciously like Emma Hamilton in one of her 'attitudes' and Captain Hardy curiously like George III. Serious artists, however, saw Trafalgar's mix of glory and sacrifice as perfect for modern history painting. Looking back to the success of his *Death of Wolfe* over thirty years before, Benjamin West showed Nelson lying wounded on the quarterdeck, his pose like a deposition from the cross – it departed from fact, West said, because it must have 'national import' and an epic manner.[25]

Turner chose something different. He went down to Greenwich

after the *Victory* moored, talking to the men and making detailed sketches and notes. But when he came to paint the scene he set these aside and packed his smoke-filled canvas with crashing rigging and ships, with Nelson as a tiny figure slumped on deck. The dizzying perspective was important, as Turner's title made clear: *The Battle of Trafalgar, as seen from the Mizzen Starboard Shrouds of the Victory*. Although these were the *Victory*'s ropes, the viewpoint was that of the French sniper. Was this a tacit suggestion that artist and viewer – and perhaps the whole nation – were responsible for the hero's death? When Turner showed the painting in his gallery in May 1806, visitors found it noisy and disturbing. Joseph Farington said that it looked as if all the sailors had been murdered. 'I went to see Turner's picture of the Battle of Trafalgar,' wrote Betsey Fremantle, whose husband had sent her detailed letters about the action, 'it is confused and pleased me not.'[26]

## 39. ALL THE TALENTS

At the Lord Mayor's Banquet on 9 November 1805, two days after the papers carried news of Trafalgar, Pitt was toasted as the 'Saviour of Europe'. Rising to answer, he said, 'I return you thanks for the honour you have done me; but Europe is not to be saved by any single man. England has saved herself by her exertions and will, as I trust, save Europe by her example.'[1]

Fears of invasion faded, and when a *Panorama of the Invasion Port at Boulogne* was shown in Spring Gardens, it seemed like a scary bogey of the past. But the euphoria was short-lived. On 13 November the French marched into Vienna (the premiere of Beethoven's *Fidelio* a week later played to French officers in a half-empty house), and for the next month the British government, press and people waited anxiously for news. Bad weather at sea delayed the mails from Gothenburg and Hamburg, but in mid-December these brought more cheerful rumours that Bonaparte had been defeated in a major battle and was retreating towards the Danube. Some papers printed on Christmas Eve were jubilant but others continued to be wary – even John Walter, editor of *The Times*, with his web of correspondents, found it hard to get accurate accounts. 'We are on Tip-toe for public Accounts confirming the Victory in Germany,' Hester Piozzi wrote on 29 December, 'and those who do not expect a Cessation of Arms – as I do – are preparing to hear how poor Vienna is burning to the Ground by the French. That would indeed be a new and dreadful Occurrence, and the Tyrant who should propose so horrible a Measure, would be deservedly hunted from the Face of the Earth.'[2]

On New Year's Day 1806, the papers reported that Castlereagh, now Secretary of State for War and the Colonies, had received despatches informing him that Napoleon had inflicted a crushing defeat on the Austrian and Russian armies at Austerlitz, eighty miles north of Vienna, as long ago as 2 December. This was almost too much of a blow to contemplate. In Brighton, Thomas Creevey reported, the Prince of Wales stopped his ears: 'It was a funny thing to hear the Prince, when the battle had taken place, express the same opinion as was given in the London Government newspapers, that it was all over with the French – they were all sent to the devil, and the Lord knows what.'[3] His Brighton entourage were plotting the French retreat on their maps at the very moment that the Austerlitz news arrived. 'And when the truth began at last to make its appearance in the newspapers, the Prince put them all in his pockets, so that no paper was forthcoming at the Pavilion.'

'On the sad history of Austerlitz I will not dwell,' wrote Addington when he heard the news. 'There is nothing to break the gloom. Europe is France: at least the continental part of it deserves no other name.'[4] Realising that it was now vital to recall the small British force that had been sent to the Elbe, Castlereagh rushed down to see Pitt, who had been seriously ill and was recuperating in Bath. On 6 January, *The Times* quoted an article inserted by the French cabinet in the *Vienna Gazette* on 8 December:

Thus will the Emperor NAPOLEON again, a third time, give peace, not to France alone, but to the Continent, and more particularly to the Austrian States. England is at length conquered in her Allies . . . What remains but that England should consent to her share of sacrifices? The EMPEROR has conquered half of the Austrian Empire – will he surrender it without equivalents? – Shall England, sulking behind her dirty Channel, encourage the Continent in war? Shall she shed the blood, and, as far as in her lies, exhaust the Treasury of France, and suffer nothing in return? – The Emperor NAPOLEON will not suffer this.[5]

It was on his return to London, entering his house and seeing a map of Europe, that Pitt is said to have muttered (though the story has never been verified), 'Roll up that map. It will not be wanted these next ten years.' By the time of Nelson's funeral, he was emaciated and pale, hardly able to eat. Soon he was too weak to leave his house. On 23 January 1806 he died, aged forty-six.

On Pitt's death, George III asked Grenville to form a new government, and he agreed, on condition that he could enter a coalition with the followers of Fox and Addington. This time, wearily, the king gave in to Grenville's insistence that his cabinet must include Fox, who became Foreign Secretary and Leader of the Commons. Canning remarked drily that Fox was like the smallpox, 'everyone must have him once in his life', but the king was agreeably amazed to find Fox rather charming. Addington, Lord Sidmouth, became Lord Privy Seal, while Grenville's cousin William Windham took over from Castlereagh to become Secretary for War again.

The 'Ministry of All the Talents', as it became known with some irony, was immediately undermined by a flurry of unpopular moves. As always the government needed money: although enormous loans were raised through the Goldsmids for over £20 million, the new Chancellor, Henry Petty, put up income tax to 10 per cent, with allowances for children removed and a new ruling that those exempt had to pay the tax first, then claim it back, a tiring and sometimes impossible process. Then Windham pushed through his Training Act, designed to replace the scattered volunteer corps with a mass army picked annually by ballot from all able-bodied men. He planned to make an army career more attractive, with limited service for seven years, increased pay and better pension schemes for veterans and widows, but only succeeded in upsetting the gentry and the industrialists so proud of their volunteer troops. The Training Act was swiftly dropped.

Next, when the Chancellor announced a heavy excise on home-produced iron, the ironmasters organised a committee to fight him.

Their arguments were wide and wild: the duty would force people to use more timber, which was already scarce; it would stop the building of canals, bridges, and iron railways in collieries; it would harm the farmers who used iron tools; and it would weaken the arms industry and British defence. Although the Bill reached committee stage, the ironmasters won the day and it was dropped. The row caught public interest and Turner, who had patrons in South Wales, painted a Dutch scene of *A Country Blacksmith Disputing upon the Price of Iron and the Price Charged to the Butcher for Shoeing his Poney*. Though this was chiefly Turner's rivalrous riposte to David Wilkie's *Village Politicians* of 1806, to prove he could do genre scenes just as well, it made the point that iron was the stuff of war and of ordinary working lives. For blacksmiths and butchers and ploughmen, iron was the essence of England.

While Grenville's government faced troubles at home, in Europe good news and bad were bafflingly mixed. As the months passed people noticed the events that touched them and ignored others altogether. There were victories at sea, and on 25 March, William Rowbottom wrote, 'arrived the glorious news of Sir John Thomas Duckworth K B Victory February 6th 1806 upon the coast of St Domingo'.[6] Six weeks before, Duckworth's squadron had cornered a section of the Brest fleet that had escaped the blockade. His officers, the public learned, had spurred their men on by reminding them of the Nile and Trafalgar. Richard Goodwin Keats, the captain of Duckworth's flagship the *Superb*, 'brought out a portrait of Nelson, which he hung on the mizzen stay, where it remained throughout the battle untouched by the enemy's shot though dashed with the blood and brains of a seaman who was killed close beside it'.[7]

The captains, including Francis Austen, had prizes to bring home. 'My dearest Mary,' wrote Francis,

The news of an action with an enemy's squadron flies like wildfire in England, and I have no doubt but you will have heard of the one we had yesterday soon after the vessel which goes home shall arrive . . . I am in hopes this action will be the means of our speedy quitting this country, and perhaps to return to Old England. Oh, how my heart throbs at the idea![8]

From Santo Domingo the fleet sailed to Jamaica for repairs, and then home, as Francis had hoped. In July 1806, he and Mary were married and settled near the lodgings of Mrs Austen, Jane and Cassandra in Southampton. The navy returned to their patrolling, in the Mediterranean, the Channel, the West Indies and on the American coast, where the other naval Austen brother, Charles, would spend the next five years cruising on the eastern seaboard, searching American ships for deserters and intercepting trade with France. In Bermuda he married the seventeen-year-old Fanny Palmer, daughter of the island's attorney general, eventually bringing her and their two small children back to England. In the meantime, to console him in case he was homesick Jane sent a home-made rug and her copy of Scott's *Marmion*, 'very generous in me I think'.[9]

It was puzzling, even following the densely printed notices of naval and troop movements, to keep track of what was happening on all the different fronts. In the Mediterranean a small expeditionary force of about five thousand men under John Stuart, sent to help rebels in Calabria, won a startling victory on 4 July near the town of Maida. The government issued silver and gold medals, the first battle honours of this kind, and, briefly, Maida was a sensation: several girls were called Maida and a pub in the Edgware Road, named in honour of Stuart, who had been made Count of Maida, later gave its name to the whole of Maida Vale. Entering legend in a different way, Walter Scott called his favourite deerhound Maida – she was a present from his friend Glengarry, whose brother had led a Highland regiment in the battle. (The marble Maida is by his side in the Scott Monument in Edinburgh.) But Stuart's gains were soon lost. British troops retreated to Sicily, while the flamboyant Admiral Sidney Smith sailed round the Calabrian coast, attacking French batteries and landing supplies for the resistance.

On the Continent as a whole, Austerlitz opened the way, as *The Times* described it, to 'the most extraordinary crisis that has ever agitated and terrified Europe'.[10] The Russians withdrew to Poland, Austria surrendered, and on 6 August 1806 Francis II abdicated as

Emperor of the Holy Roman Empire, calling himself from now on simply Emperor of Austria. The Holy Roman Empire, which had endured since the Middle Ages, vanished. And the Third Coalition was over.

Yet six weeks later London crowds were cheering news from a different region altogether. On 21 September eight heavy wagons trundled into London: on the front of each was painted the word 'Treasure'. In St James's Square the soldiers escorting the wagons were presented with blue silk banners embroidered with 'Buenos Aires, Popham, Beresford, Victory' in gold thread. Later that day over a million dollars in Spanish gold and silver were deposited in the vaults of the Bank of England.[11] The treasure came from South America. In early 1806, the flamboyant Commodore Sir Home Riggs Popham and Lieutenant General Sir David Baird, who had sailed together in the Egypt campaign and had captured the Cape of Good Hope in a joint action, had sailed for South America, without government orders. In June, with a small band of troops, they took Buenos Aires, aiming to stir up an Argentinian rebellion against Spain. It was a maverick action, without Admiralty approval, aimed largely (Popham's finances were in a bad way) at bringing home great prizes. When Popham came back to London, leaving the Irish General Beresford to hold Buenos Aires, he made sure of his glory by sending despatches to all the London and provincial papers, and letters to the mayors of trading and manufacturing towns, describing the golden opportunities for South American trade. Speculators foresaw rich pickings.

As Foreign Secretary, Fox, the only towering presence in Grenville's cabinet, tried again to negotiate the peace he had demanded for so long. Napoleon too hoped for a general peace, based on acceptance of his continental dominance after Austerlitz. But the talks collapsed in May, with unresolved disputes over Sicily, Malta, Switzerland and Hanover. A dispirited Fox lamented that his high opinion of Bonaparte was sadly wrong. Over the summer he faded, ill and distended by dropsy, in pain from terrible gallstones and mortally weakened by cirrhosis of the liver. He died on 13 September at Chiswick House; his last words, according to his wife, were 'It don't signify, my dearest, dearest Liz'.[12]

Fox's funeral in Westminster Abbey was private, but the crowds that turned out matched those for Pitt's state mourning. Papers like Cowdroy's *Manchester Gazette* celebrated him as 'A Man as far above Praise in Death, as he was above the shafts of Malevolence in Life':

A PATRIOT, an ORATOR, a STATESMAN, and an ENGLISHMAN
. . . A Maxim of the Constitution
Cannot be named that was not written in his Heart,
And that he did not defend. Nor can any
One Class of Society be named that
Will not feel a Loss in
His Death

William Rowbottom cut out this long announcement and stuck it inside the cover of his diary for 1806.

By the time of Fox's death, the allies had revived. A new, fourth coalition formed, including Prussia, Russia, Saxony, Sweden and Britain. In August Frederick William III of Prussia had begun to mobilise, angered by Napoleon's creation of the Confederation of the Rhine, a zone of French-dominated German states, and by the execution of the nationalist pamphleteer Johann Philipp Palm. On 1 October the Prussians delivered an ultimatum to the French to withdraw all troops east of the Rhine and when this was ignored they declared war. In Britain, many people, given heart by Popham's South American treasure, rejoiced at the thought of renewed fighting. 'You will see that all Hopes of Peace are broke off,' Kitty Senhouse's nephew John Wood wrote from his Chatham barracks:

when the account was read at Lloyds on the Exchange it was received with the utmost demonstration of Joy from all ranks of People, so averse were they to the Idea of Peace with Bonaparte. It likewise shows the Resources which the Country is possess'd to carry on the War . . . The capture of Buenos Ayres in South America has opened a fine field for speculation & likewise for the Mercantile World, upwards of a Millions worth of Merchandise of various kinds is now in the Custom House in London ready to be shipped to that place.[13]

The loyalism of the shires was undented. That October James Oakes stayed late at a dinner for the new alderman at the Angel, 'all wch time we kept the Bottle going round without either tea or supper. Many very loyal, good Songs'.[14] But as the news drifted in, always a long time after events, it transpired that within a week of the Prussian declaration, Napoleon had rushed his Grande Armée of 160,000 men into a lightning campaign, crushing one branch of the Prussian army at Jena, while Marshal Davout thrashed the other at Auerstedt on the same day. At the end of the month, the French entered Berlin. Once again, Britain seemed isolated, as Wordsworth wrote in 'November, 1806':

> Another year! – another deadly blow!
> Another mighty Empire overthrown!
> And we are left, or shall be left, alone;
> The last that dare to struggle with the Foe.
> 'Tis well! from this day forward we shall know
> That in ourselves our safety must be sought.

In country rectories, London clubs and provincial reading rooms, men and women laid great maps out on the table, smoothing the folds and bending over them, studying the foreign names through their eyeglasses. Where should they draw the arrows for the French front line? Would Napoleon cross to Sweden? Or was his main aim now to crush the Russian army? And what use were maps anyway when boundaries kept changing? They heard of confrontations around the Danube and in the Balkans, where the French had made an alliance with the Turks, but all agreed that the main fighting was far to the north, just inland from the Baltic coast. As the year ended, everyone wondered: what next?

And who would lead this isolated country? After the deaths of Pitt and Fox so close together the government seemed lacklustre. In a general election in the autumn of 1806 – when Richard Heber stood unsuccessfully as an independent candidate in Oxford – the ministry gained a few seats, but no real power. In parliament the parties crystallised and their internal divisions sharpened: the old followers of Pitt were labelled 'Tory', a term intermittently used in the past, and the Whigs fractured into new groups. At Holland House, Fox's nephew Lord Holland and his clever wife Elizabeth gathered a largely aristocratic set, building links with the intellectual and literary world, particularly the circle of the *Edinburgh Review*. At the same time a reformist clique of MPs from London and the industrial districts collected around the brewer Samuel Whitbread. Known as 'The Mountain', after Robespierre and Danton's Jacobin sect, they attacked corruption and called for expansion of the franchise, public education, religious toleration and legal and penal reform. Sir Francis Burdett led an even more radical group, linking politics once more to the great public outings, processions and feast days, demonstrations on moors and in market places. Gagging Acts or not, politics would soon be on the streets again.

Clubs dedicated to Fox or to Pitt met in provincial towns at bibulous dinners. The austere but hard-drinking Pitt was turned into an evangelical martyr, embodying nationalism, godliness, authority and free trade: the jovial and dissolute Fox into a patron of liberty, freedom of thought and belief, and resistance to metropolitan cronyism and corruption. Loyalists read the *Anti-Jacobin Review*, Tories *The Times* and the evening *Courier*, while liberal Whigs read the *Morning Chronicle* and the *Edinburgh*, and began to take more notice of Cobbett's reoriented *Political Register*. Cobbett was stuffed with prejudices, including anti-Semitism, but he tore at injustice and reached the working people as no one else could. Debates raged in papers and journals, articles and book reviews, and invective and insults flew.

Soon even the jubilation over the Buenos Aires treasure began to turn sour. Popham, who had never been liked by the strait-laced naval hierarchy, was court-martialled for withdrawing his squadron from the Cape for the South American mission without permission. In the end he received only a 'severe reprimand', but Tory supporters were furious that the court martial had ever taken place, among them Jane Austen, who damned Grenville's ministry in verse:

> Of a Ministry pitiful, angry, mean,
> A gallant Commander the victim is seen.
> For Promptitude, Vigour, Success does he stand
> Condemned to receive a severe reprimand!
> To his Foes I could wish a resemblance in fate;
> That they too may suffer themselves soon or late
> The Injustice they warrant – but vain is my Spite
> *They* cannot *so* suffer, who never do right.[15]

It did seem that Grenville, and his Secretary of War William Windham, could do nothing right. In the first glow of excitement, Windham had sent four thousand more troops to South America. In February 1807 they took Montevideo but then lingered in the fever-breeding swamps while local resistance grew: when General Whitelocke and his six thousand-strong army attacked Buenos Aires again, they were forced to surrender after days of intense fighting. Among the soldiers was Thomas Perronet Thompson from Hull, who had swapped the navy for the 95th Rifles: 'We were made prisoners of war,' he told his brother John, and then released 'on condition of not serving against Spain or her allies till our return to England'.[16] The fiasco was a blow for the City men and merchants, manufacturers and workers who had hoped that South American trade would make up their losses in Europe.

On 25 March 1807 Grenville resigned, after only a year in office. The final crisis stemmed from a dispute over Lord Howick's bill to allow Roman Catholics to take commissions in the army and navy. The king vetoed even the mildest form of Catholic emancipation, and when Grenville refused to accept this, he had no other option but to go. Anti-Catholic feeling was such that people across the country sent addresses to the king congratulating him on the defeat of Howick's motion.

All the hopeful Whigs who had jostled for power were now disappointed. The previous autumn, Thomas Fremantle, pulled up by the Grenville family, had been appointed a Lord Commissioner for the Admiralty, who quickly found him a seat in the Commons, as a member for Sandwich. Betsey, who rushed to furnish their house in the Admiralty, deciding that 'ships sofas and armchairs do not make at all a mean appearance in the Drawing rooms', was extremely cross at the waste of time and expense.[17] The Whigs' chance had passed: for over twenty years, there would be Tories in power. George III now turned to William Cavendish-Bentinck, third Duke of Portland, who had been Prime Minister in 1783, almost quarter of a century earlier. Now approaching seventy, and often unwell, he was more of a figure-head than a leader and his cabinet took over decision-making, in long and sometimes acrimonious meetings: Canning as Foreign Secretary, Castlereagh as Secretary of War and Colonies again, and Hawkes-bury (Earl of Liverpool from 1808) as Home Secretary. The Chancellor of the Exchequer and Leader of the House of Commons was Spencer Perceval, 'a short, spare, pale-faced, hard, keen, sour-looking man', in Cobbett's view, 'with no knowledge of the great interest of the nation, foreign or domestic, but with a thorough knowledge of those means by which power is obtained and preserved in England, and with no scruples as to the employment of those means'.[18]

In the April elections that followed, most candidates were returned unopposed and Tory support of the king's stand against Catholic emancipation was so loud that this became known as the 'No Popery' election, a slogan scrawled on walls everywhere. Crowds threw mud at pro-Catholic candidates, corporations and clergy gave 'Protestant' addresses and, said an appalled Cobbett, 'even the cottages on the skirts of the commons and the forests heard fervent *blessings* poured out on the head of the "*good old King*, for preserving the nation from a rekindling of the *fires in Smithfield!*"'[19] As Sydney Smith noted in *Letters of Peter Plymley*, denying army commissions to Catholics was absurd: how could one rage against one's own people,

to tell them they cannot be honourable in war, because they are conscientious in religion; to stipulate (at the very moment when we should buy their hearts and swords at any price) that they must hold up the right hand in prayer and not the left; and adore one common God, by turning to the east rather than the west.[20]

On this wave of intolerance, the Tories swept grandly on. There were, however, pockets of radical resurgence: in Westminster, Fox's old constituency, Francis Burdett and the maverick naval hero Lord Cochrane won seats after a campaign brilliantly organised by Francis Place, appealing to the traders and artisans who worked around the Strand – bootmakers and tailors, drapers, cutlers, tobacconists, apothecaries and grocers. Troops were put on the alert, but there was no violence, and the triumphant electors processed through Westminster to bugles and marching bands. In Covent Garden, the buildings were so loaded with people, wrote Cobbett, 'that the chimney tops were hidden from view: hundreds were sitting or standing upon the roofs and ridges of the houses round the square'.[21]

Rowlandson and Augustus Pugin, 'St Paul's, Covent Garden at an election': Burdett is on the hustings, while sailors carry Cochrane in a boat

Reformers of the 1770s and 1780s, like Major John Cartwright, took up the cause again, calling for the free (if mythical) old Britain of the Saxons and Alfred, for annual parliaments and manhood suffrage, Magna Carta and the people's rights, the England of Robin Hood. Cartwright's hero was the seventeenth-century politician John Hampden, whose protest against taxation for ship money had helped to fire the English revolution and civil war. Cartwright would found the first of many Hampden clubs in 1812, and in June 1813, Lord Byron – who was a member of the Hampden Club – presented Cartwright's petition for suffrage to the House of Lords. The struggle for reform revived.

# 40. PRIVATE LIVES

Amid the excitement over Trafalgar, the despair at Austerlitz and the confusion of political battles in Westminster, people got on with their private lives. James Oakes, for example, had become used to being on his own. On Christmas Day 1805, when Nelson's body was lying at Greenwich, he rode over to a friend and then went to his son James and family. He arranged for his kitchen to boil twenty-six pounds of shin of beef to make '10 Gallons of good broth' for twelve poor families, and to roast fifteen pounds more, to be given to eight families of the 'better sort'. For his own household – '3 Men & 3 Maid Servants, Old Mrs Green, Mrs Smith & 2 Children, David Shadow' – he set aside more roast beef, plum pudding and pies. His diary was filled with such daily detail.

*James Oakes: 'Wednesday Janry 1 New Years Day'*

A very full market & much Business done in the Town . . . This Day I had my Son Orbell's & son James's Family from Tostock to dine with me & their 7 Child[ren], Mr & Mrs Patteson, Son John, Daughter Louisa. We had Music & the young ones dancd Minuets, Reels &ca & afterwards we made up & danced 3 or 4 Country dances. We enjoyed ourselves all very much, making very merry, being the first of the Year. Not having the Goulds with me was a very great disappointment as I hope, whilst I live, to have all my Children & grand Children pass this day with me.[1]

*Charles Lamb to William Hazlitt, 15 March 1806*

William Hazlitt, still aiming to become an artist, though becoming disillusioned, had asked Lamb to see what was around in the London auction rooms. What was Hazlitt doing idling in Shropshire, Lamb replied, 'when so many fine pictures are a going every day in London?'

Monday I visit the Marq. Lansdown's in Berkeley Square. Catalogue 2/6. Leonardos in plenty. Some other day this week, I go to see Sir Wm. Young's in Stratford place – Hulse's of Blackheath are also to be sold this month; & in May the first private collection in Europe, Welbore Ellis Agar's . . . I am afraid of your mouth watering when I tell you that Manning & I got into Anjerstein's on Wensday. *Mon dieu! – such Claudes!* Four Claudes bought for more than £10000 – those who talk of Wilson being equal to Claude are either mainly ignorant or stupid – . One of these was perfectly miraculous. What colours short of bona fide sunbeams it could be painted in, I am not earthly colourman enough to say. But I did not think it had been in the possibility of things.[2]

John Julius Angerstein, a director of Lloyd's, and chairman of the Patriotic Fund, was building up his collection. After he died in 1823, the government bought thirty-eight of his pictures – by Titian and Raphael, Claude and Poussin, Rembrandt, Rubens, Velázquez and Van Dyck – the core holding of the future National Gallery.

*Lucy Galton, 16 March 1806*

A month after Grenville formed his Ministry of All the Talents, Lucy Galton was in Bath, with her daughters Mary Anne, Sophia and Adele, waiting for her husband, Samuel, to arrive. She wrote in her large, childish hand to her youngest son, John Howard, aged eleven, who had a passion for animals and birds.

Sophia sends you a present of a book. I shall endeavour to find you another; but here are no new books of natural history . . . Do you remember Mrs Willmott's garden up the hill, above Mr Shew's? – In that garden, I hear, there is a fine aviary, there is a tame Cockatoo, & a Pelican, & several other fine Birds; but I have not seen them myself . . .

Tomorrow we change our Lodgings, for this will be too small when Papa comes. Mrs Darwin lives just over the way, & she was to have left Bath tomorrow, & then we were to have her house – but Emma is very ill, and Violetta is ill, and Hariot is ill; so I believe they will stay longer.

Farewell dear little boy – I hope you will hear from us again, very soon – Give me your hand – good night!

L Galton.[3]

The following February, Lucy told Mary Anne, John Howard had a new favourite, 'a live tortoise, which we are told by his biographer comes from Egypt. It has all the ghastly effect of an inhabitant of the Pyramids, and looks like a mummy alive.' His sisters fed cakes to the tortoise, but could not persuade him to drink: 'I believe I shall give the Gardener Goldsmith's natural history of the Tortoise that he may know how to manage him, now he is thoroughly awake in this spring weather.'[4]

## Hannah Rathbone to Hannah Greg, 11 April 1806

In early April Hannah and Samuel Greg's son Samuel died of fever: he would have been seven in May. From Liverpool, Hannah Rathbone wrote to console her:

You are my dear Friend so much the companion of my thoughts that I cannot help addressing you, tho' I cannot express the solicitude I feel for you . . . trust in the generous Being, but still there is a feeling which only Mothers know, and only those who have lost a child can conceive . . . I mourn, tho' in secret, over those who are taken away. I hope we are not the less resigned because our sense of suffering is acute.[5]

But she was not resigned. Writing these words, thinking of her own children who had died, she broke down. Her husband William told Hannah Greg that he had taken her pen away and made her stop: 'We have thrice had to drink of the same bitter cup.'

## James Longsdon, Tuesday 29 April 1806

That spring James Longsdon senior was staying at the Spread Eagle in Hanging Ditch in Manchester. He wrote to his son James, who had been buying cattle at Lancaster Fair. He was worrying about James's cold, which had looked so bad when he came back from drilling the local volunteers. 'Do take care of yourself . . .' he wrote:

I note you say the Scotch Cattle you bought at Grassington are calculated for the Hay Pasture – I wish they had been of a better stamp. I hope you will meet with a new lot of *forward* Cows for the Pasture. I flatter myself we shall be able to get our Stock in lower than they have hitherto been, but the appearance of the Weather is much in favour of the Sellers . . . do not omit giving me a line or two on the Fair day as I have before requested. When you breakfast will be the time. I want no long account.6

## Thomas Carlyle, Whitsun, 15 May 1806

Carlyle was ten, and his father took him to his new school, Annan Academy, on Whitsunday morning:

It was a bright morning, and to me full of movement, of fluttering, boundless Hopes, saddened by parting with Mother, with Home, and which afterwards were cruelly disappointed. He called once or twice in the grand schoolroom, as he chanced to have business at Annan; once sat down by me (as the master was out) and asked whether I was all well. The boys did not laugh, as I feared; perhaps durst not.7

## Francis Douce, summer 1806

In the darkest days, people tended plants. The weavers of Paisley specialised in pinks, the Sheffield cutlers in auriculas. The Royal Horticultural Society was founded in 1804. But in 1806, Francis Douce, Keeper of Manuscripts at the British Museum, moved to Charlotte Street, where the noise from his neighbour's garden drove him mad: '6 or 8 children always out & screaming', 'gates always shutting violently':

I would like a house without any opening to the street as in Eastern cities, but looking only towards a garden or back open place. When people are indoors they should literally be at home & abstracted from the streets altogether. This is in the opinion of those who love peace & tranquillity. There is time & opportunity enough of feeling the world outdoors.8

### Hester Piozzi to Revd Leonard Chappelow, 4 June 1806

Mrs Piozzi, always thirsty for news, was beginning to feel the war as a personal assault, and the new reviewers as not much better than the French:

We are not Buonaparte's subjects yet. I think few of us would outlive the day we were declared such; – it would kill *me* sooner than cold Water by half . . .

You are perfectly correct about the Malignity of Reviewers. They fall upon Friend and Foe: and Joanna Baillie being ill-treated by her own Countrymen – The Edinburghers may shew how Impossible it is for them to let any work take its fair chance with the Public that has not come from their own Junto. Lock up your verses therefore – .[9]

### Henry Angelo, 14 July 1806, the month of the Battle of Maida

On the evening of 14 July (Bastille Day) Angelo was invited to the Neapolitan Club at the Thatched House Tavern, St James's Street, a club supposedly limited to those who had visited Naples. The host was the Duke of Sussex, who 'during the time he was eating his soup, was every moment putting wine in his glass, and the rest followed his example'. The Prince of Wales was there, with Sir Sidney Smith and Admiral Halliday, and after the dinner Mr Mercer sang an Italian aria and Thomas Moore his Irish ballads:

But what seemed very much to amuse the Prince, was Sir John MacPherson's Highland war-song (probably an Ossian, one of his brother's) and to give it the true warlike effect, whilst singing, he stood up, and, what with his robust appearance, his height being above six feet, a voice like a Stentor, brandishing his arm as if he had a claymore, one would have imagined he was bidding defiance to the whole company.[10]

### Betsey Fremantle and Eugenia Campbell, 29 July 1806

A week before, Betsey's sister Eugenia had married Robert Campbell, after a suspenseful, emotional courtship. Today they were coming to stay before their wedding trip to the Western Isles. Both sisters wrote in their diaries that night:

*Betsey*

Swanbourne, Tuesday 29 July: Spent the greatest part of the day in preparations for the arrival of Les Epoux. Decorated the rooms with Flowers and smartened little Swanbourne for this gay Occasion. They did not come till ten o'clock, the Bells rang all Evening and half the night – Eugenia is not improved in her looks but appears a happy little creature – *et ils sont très tendres* –

*Eugenia*

Swanbourne, Tuesday 29 July: We had several people to breakfast with us – I made a Will, with infinite joy – then we had so many things to do, that it was past two o'Clock before we left Town – soon after nine we reached Swanbourne in the midst of the ringing of the bells and joyful shouts – I was most happy to see my Sisters altho' they *will* not treat me with *respect* –[11]

On their wedding tour Eugenia and Robert sailed through storms where the 'Sea rose Mountains high', to the Campbells' home in Islay, and then to their future home in the Kyles of Bute. Eugenia was thrilled to hear bagpipes and see barefooted people, although 'they talk chiefly Gaelic which I do not understand'.

Betsey's drawing of her house at Swanbourne

## William Rowbottom, 16–30 August 1806

Rowbottom noted events in Oldham and around: a bad month.

16th. Lancaster Assizes commenced when John Eastwood charged with murther was acquitted and five of the Warrington Soddomites where found guilty and received sentence of death

30th Oldham Rushbearing commenced . . .

John Woolstonecraft, Carter to Samuel Ogden of Swineclough, so brused by his cartwheels going over him that he died a few days after, age 55 yr. he had a brother killed by a similar accident about 18 years ago

A few days since – Shepherd, a Collier of Highgate, so burned by the fiery damp that he died a few days after

Some private lives felt the full force of law. Under the influence of evangelicalism and hysteria at 'French' ways, attitudes to homosexuality had toughened. Of the five condemned men from Warrington, two were reprieved but three were hanged at Lancaster Castle. The indictment stated that each had committed this 'detestable' crime 'not having the fear of God before his eyes, nor regarding the order of nature, but being moved and seduced by the instigation of the Devil'.[12] No one prosecuted the cart drivers, or the owner of the mine where the flammable gas killed the collier.

## Hannah Gurney, August 1806

Now a solemn nineteen, Hannah was taking stock of her desires and daydreams. 'One structure of ambition has vanished to make way for another,' she wrote. The first had been a love of riding, the second of being thought learned, 'and for this purpose how many books did I devour!'

Next succeeded mathematics, which lasted for some time, and many were the castles which I built upon the fame which I expected to acquire by discoveries in this science; but what foundation had I for these castles? This passion retired at the entrance of that for painting. As I have not long taken my leave of this object, I have clearly in my remembrance how towering were my imaginations this way; what structures, with the help of fancy, hope, and ambition, I built at this period: they are vanished, and three or four wearied pieces of canvass remain to be a sorry spectacle of the result of my folly.

Ambition, I believe, still hovers about me, marking me for its prey; but, as it wears no embodied form, I do not often feel its grasp.[13]

## Hannah Greg, 1 October 1806

October would see the French victories at Jena and Auerstadt and Napoleon's entry into Berlin. By now Hannah Greg had pulled herself back to some sort of routine after her grief for little Samuel. But she found Manchester was always a rush, with business, money and survival on its mind, and with no time to think or read. Writing to William Rathbone, she poured out her feelings about novels and the way they 'exhilirate the Spirits'. She confessed she had too much to say about this, 'because accustomed to be under restraint upon it – my husband, nor anybody I believe at Manchester approving novels, from the habit of classing all sorts together – a fit of the Gout would undo this prejudice'.[14]

## William Cobbett, November 1806

In 1805 Cobbett had bought land at Botley near Southampton, where he lived with Nancy and their four children – three more would follow. His new obsessions were farming and planting trees. When the eighteen-year-old Mary Russell Mitford visited him, she thought he was oddly like his house, 'large, high, massive, red and square'.[15] Cobbett admired Rousseau, and was determined, he said, never to make his children live a life of restraint and rebuke. At Botley they played outside or gathered round the parlour table where Nancy sewed, with the baby in a high chair:

here were ink-stands, pens, pencils, India rubber and paper, all in abundance, and everyone scrabbled about as he or she pleased. There were prints of animals of all sorts; books treating of them; others treating of gardening, of flowers, of husbandry, coursing, shooting, fishing, planting, and in short, of everything with regard to which *we had something to do*. One would be trying to imitate a bit of my writing, another *drawing* the pictures of some of our dogs or horses, a third poring over *Bewick's Quadrupeds*, and picking out what he said about them.[16]

Cobbett wrote at home, among the children: 'When they grew up to be big enough to gallop about the house I have, in wet weather, when they could not go out, written the whole day amidst noise that would made some authors half mad . . . That which you are *pleased with*, however noisy, does not disturb you.'[17]

## *Walter Scott, 16 December 1806*

By now Napoleon's army had entered Warsaw. In mid-December Scott wrote to his old student friend Adam Ferguson, in Jersey. Scott sent news of Auld Reekie and hoped that Ferguson had got rid of the typhus that 'has laid its claws upon you':

I hate to hear any of my friends talk of a disorder by its scientific name; it is a sign it has taken a little hold of his mind & that he has made further investigation about it than is consistent with the idea of its being a transient guest. I beg therefore that the Typhus may as speedily as possible assume the more humble denomination of a feverish cold . . . You know our old friend Braxie cut short one of Maconochies learned queries about the vena cava 'Hout awa' wi' your Macavas Mr. Maconochie', even so say I 'hout awa' wi' your Typhus' . . .

He envied Ferguson in Jersey, with good claret and 'Blithe French lasses with their black eyes and national vivacity scratching each other for the honour of dancing & flirting'. Charlotte, he added, sent her kindest remembrances, and he ended with news of little Walter, now five: 'the Laird of Gilnockie has got short clothes & promises to be a strapper – Believe me ever yours affectionately, Walter Scott.'[18]

\*

And so the year turned. Yet even domestic life was haunted by the war. Boney was both the bogeyman of children's nightmares and the foot-stamping child, refusing to grow up. 'Bless the Baby,' says the nurse in Rowlandson's *The Mother's Hope*, to a small boy in a tantrum, 'what an aspiring spirit – if he goes on this way – he will become a second Buonaparte!!'[19]

Woodward and Rowlandson, *The Mother's Hope*: 'I don't like dolls! –
I don't like Canary Birds – I hate Battledore and Shuttlecock.
I like Drums, and Trumpets – I won't go to School –
I will stay at home – I will have my own way in everything!!'

# 41. ABOLITION AND AFTER

On 25 March 1807, a cold, grey day with the smell of rain in the air, an event took place that made thousands cheer, among them the Rathbones and Roscoes in Liverpool, the Gurneys in Norfolk, Hannah More in Bath, and the whole of the Clapham Sect in London. After years of lobbying, the Act to Abolish the Slave Trade in all British territories finally received the Royal Assent. 'What shall we abolish next?' Wilberforce asked Henry Thornton. 'The lottery, I think,' he replied.[1]

The Act received the Royal Assent on the day Grenville resigned. It was the one great achievement of his government and it had taken many years coming. Over the past decade the planters' lobby had managed to hold back progress by exploiting the fears raised by rebellions in Santo Domingo, Grenada and St Vincent, and by arguing that if parliament abolished the British trade, it would simply fall into the hands of the French. The commitment to support Pitt's government had placed Wilberforce and his allies in some difficult situations. They knew, despite Pitt's pre-war condemnation of the trade as a 'stigma on our national character', that the army was buying slaves to fill the ranks of British regiments in the West Indies, drastically thinned by disease. Between 1795 and 1808, the regiments took around 13,400 slaves, plus two thousand women and children.[2] In parliament the abolitionists stayed silent, but privately Wilberforce wrote angrily to Pitt. This use of the trade was a 'vicious principle':

That their situation as soldiers would be beyond comparison preferable to that of plantation slaves cannot be doubted; but how can we justify buying slaves for that desirable and even humane purpose, when we reflect that the increased demand will produce a proportionately increased supply, and consequently as many more marauding expeditions, acts of individual rapine, injustice, witchcraft and condemnations, &c., as are necessary for obtaining the requisite numbers of negroes?[3]

In 1804 a new, revived committee for the abolition of the trade had begun work, and Wilberforce reintroduced his original bill of 1793, but once again it was stalled in the Lords. Determined to press on, Thomas Clarkson went on a nationwide tour, handing out pamphlets and tracts, calling meetings and gathering support. This time, campaigners had a new, pragmatic argument: allowing the slave trade to continue threatened to help the French and their allies, especially since Napoleon had restored slavery in the colonies. Abolition was patriotic. Furthermore, for those who saw French successes as a penalty for British sins, the slave trade was the chief iniquity that had brought heaven's wrath. 'The sufferings of the nations are to be regarded as the punishment of national crimes and their decline and fall as the execution of His sentence,' wrote Wilberforce in his *Letter on the Abolition of the Slave Trade*. It was time to lighten the vessel of state 'of its load of guilt and infamy'.[4] Abolition also embraced the idealised notion of British 'liberty', so central to wartime propaganda, redefining its use by Hannah More in her poem of twenty years before:

> Shall Britain, where the soul of freedom reigns,
> Forge chains for others she herself disdains?
> Forbid it, Heaven! O let the nations know
> The liberty she loves she will bestow;
> Not to herself the glorious gift confin'd,
> She spreads the blessing wide as humankind;
> And, scorning narrow views of time and place,
> Bids all be free in earth's extended space.[5]

There had been little hope of abolition under Pitt, but when Grenville's Ministry of All the Talents came into power in early 1806 James Stephen drafted a bill to bar British traders from carrying slaves to the colonies and conquered territories of European powers. Although opponents petitioned against this, Clarkson drummed up an emergency counter-petition with five times as many names. Abolition became a major issue in this year's elections. In Liverpool, William Roscoe reluctantly agreed to stand as a candidate for the reform and anti-slavery cause. To everyone's surprise, including his own, he won the seat in the face of huge opposition from local merchants, shippers and corporation. By now the evangelical 'Pious Party', under Wilberforce's leadership, controlled almost forty seats in the House of Commons, and, with the help of many sympathisers, in May 1806 they pushed through the Foreign Slave Trade Act, based on James Stephen's Bill, which banned the transport of slaves to French-controlled and foreign ports. The following month, Grenville in the Lords and Fox in the Commons won resolutions in favour of abolishing the British trade as a whole.

Wilberforce drafted the Bill for full abolition, helped by his brother-in-law James Stephen, and led the debates in the Commons, while Grenville steered it through the Lords, arguing that the trade was contrary to the principles of justice, humanity and sound policy – sound policy being the danger of shipping slaves to islands like Trinidad that might well be returned to France. This trumped opposition on strategic and economic grounds, although some of the cabinet still voted against the Bill, including Sidmouth, who feared the trade would fall into French hands. In a sop to wartime needs, the Bill specified that freed slaves could be conscripted into the British army and navy. But the moral argument was uppermost. A last-ditch petition from the Liverpool planters and merchants asked only for relief on sugar duties, and the right to barter sugar, coffee, rum and molasses with the American states, in return for timber. The Act abolishing the trade in the British empire was passed by 283 votes to sixteen on 23 March 1807 and received the Royal Assent two days later. William Roscoe arrived back in Liverpool to face traders and unemployed sailors angry at abolition, and Protestant crowds attacking his support for the Catholics. He stood down as a parliamentary candidate, continuing both fights through his pamphlets.

In July, Captain Hugh 'Mind-Your-Eye' Crow, a veteran of the Guinea trade, sailed the *Kitty's Amelia*, the last British slaving ship to leave Liverpool. Arriving at the river Bonny on the Niger delta, he found baffled British captains waiting for the next cargo of slaves, unsure if the rumours of abolition were true. They were, he told them, and the British trade would be completely banned from January 1808.[6] Four ships sailed from the Gulf of Guinea in October, protected by a British warship for the last time: from now on the warships would stop slavers, not help them. But Liverpool merchants were still importing sugar and tobacco from the Caribbean and cotton from slave-owning plantations in Brazil, and many slave-ship owners simply moved their vessels to the West Indies, South America or the Azores, or sailed under Portuguese or Spanish colours, with foreign officers and papers. Now that the trade was illegal, profits were all the greater: fast sailing schooners were still taking hundreds of slaves from the barracoons and forts, or loading them by canoes from the mangrove swamps all the way round to the Bight of Benin and the great slave port of Why-dah (modern Ouidah), where thousands were brought down from the interior of Dahomey each year. A defiant trade continued among the Liverpool captains, Thomas Clarkson reported, with ships picking up slaves in Africa alongside their official cargoes.[7] It would take a long time for this to change, and another twenty-six years for slavery itself to be abolished in all British dominions.

In Britain, people struggling to make a living in the shadow of war felt little impact from abolition. Yet it brought unforeseen consequences, the uncomfortable dilemmas of empire. In 1808 the navy launched the West Africa Squadron, sending two ships from Plymouth, a frigate and a sloop, charged with the impossible task of stopping slave ships along three thousand miles of the West African coast. Local chiefs were furious at a foreign country interfering in their long-established trade, and there were awkward international legal complications when the captains seized neutral ships. Then there was the difficulty of where the slaves freed from ships should go. While many were sent to the Bahamas or Jamaica, thousands, from many different African nations, were landed conveniently nearby in Sierra Leone.

For the evangelical leaders in Clapham this too created difficulties. They had set their sights increasingly on their work overseas, with the founding of the Church Missionary Society in 1799 and the British and Foreign Bible Society in 1804. But the experience of Zachary Macaulay, who had been Governor of Sierra Leone for five difficult years in the 1790s, persuaded them that freed slaves were not ready for self-government: 'the African nature was not yet fully civilised'. The Clapham sect believed that two things must happen. First the territory must be taken under the benign wing of the British empire: in 1808 the Sierra Leone Company was abolished and passed to the Crown. Secondly, Africans must be brought to understand the modern, 'Christian' age. To achieve this, in 1807 they founded the African Institution with the lofty aim of educating freed slaves and other Africans, spreading habits of industry and thrift, supporting commerce and putting pressure on other governments to end the trade. The Clapham leaders and their new ally, Henry Brougham, were all on the committee.

Pondering how to 'educate' men and women rescued from slavery, they accepted Macaulay's suggestion of a system of indentured apprenticeships. The 1807 Act allowed apprenticeships of up to fourteen years for slaves freed from enemy slavers, who were legally designated as 'prize'. In what sense, therefore, were they 'free'? This was the puzzle that faced the twenty-five-year-old Thomas Perronet Thompson, the new Governor of Sierra Leone.

When Thompson returned from the disastrous South American expedition, Wilberforce had recommended him for the post of governor, as a favour to his father, an old friend, now MP for Midhurst.

Thompson sailed south with high hopes in the *Mutine*, the brig that ten years ago had carried the news of the battle of the Nile to London. But when he landed at Freetown on 1 August 1808, and was hailed as governor, what he found there appalled him. Quickly, he stopped the binding as apprentices of one shipload of 'Recaptives' – whom he rechristened 'Liberated Africans' – although the previous governor, Ludlum, had approved the transaction. Within weeks, he was writing anxiously to Macaulay and James Stephen, wondering if there was an 'inaccuracy' in instructions to local agents about binding ex-slaves as apprentices. Trying to discover what the policy was, he hunted for Ludlum's commission from the Admiralty. 'In setting to rummage, among sundry musty papers', he told his fiancée Nancy, he found a commission giving him the right to hold a court for prizes, including slaves as well as 'flotsam, jettsom and ligan, and also whales, riggs and other fish of uncommon fatness'.[8]

Henry Thornton, Wilberforce, Macaulay and other members of the Sierra Leone Committee in Clapham received salt-stained letters by every ship that sailed. The following March, from 'Fort Thornton', Thompson repeated his argument that the transaction to indenture recaptives had effectively been a sale of slaves: 'the grand distinguishing point consists in the giving to the master that strong that invincible argument "he is *mine*, I *bought* him".'[9] He pointed out the danger that the Company's character would be called into question: 'All I pray for in the name of the king is, that the Company would observe their treaties, the treaties which themselves have made or which have been made for them.'[10]

He battled on, starting new settlements and farms, falling ill from fever, collecting a menagerie of animals, reading the *Edinburgh Review*, and becoming entranced by Mungo Park's *Travels in the Interior of Africa* of 1799, which painted such a detailed, yet romantic picture of the continent. He read, worked, and waited, and brooded on what had happened to Park, who had disappeared on his second journey to find the source of the Niger. Then in August 1809 the expected letter finally arrived from Castlereagh, as Secretary of the Colonies, recalling him and removing him from his post. Angry and hurt, he blamed both the local Company agents and the multiple interests of the African Institution Committee. 'At the African Institution,' he wrote that month:

They impudently declare that they have no concern either with commerce or with missions; they step into their coaches and *presto* – they are the Sierra Leone Company – *they pass* and they are the Society for Missions to Africa and the East; another transformation makes them the Society for the Suppression of Vice, a fourth carries them to the India House and a fifth lands them in the House of Commons. This marvellous property of being everywhere is not one of their least dangerous qualifications.[11]

A fortnight after this storming letter he drafted a response to Castlereagh, reporting 'the continued & increasing good conduct of all the African Inhabitants of His Majesty's Colony'. The same could not be said for the European agents, whose conduct 'has been so decidedly hostile to all order and respect for public authority, that unless the most serious notice is taken of their daring attempts at violation of public justice, a way will be left open for the introduction of such general anarchy and confusion as must ultimately be highly prejudicial to the honour and the interest of Great Britain.'[12]

In February 1810 his replacement arrived and Thompson sailed home. Back in England he became ever more bitter at the Clapham Sect, feeling that he had been sacrificed to save their reputations. Wilberforce was abashed, writing to Thomas Thompson senior, begging him to ask his son to avoid a public row. It gave him pain to send this letter, he ended, but it seemed right 'to warn you that possibly a Storm may be brewing in spite of all my Endeavours to keep things quiet'.[13] In 1811, estranged from his father, with no job and no money, with his planned marriage opposed by both families, Thompson picked up Nancy at midnight in York and they jumped into the post-chaise to London. But in only a few months, still with no money, Tom – as Nancy called him – rejoined the army while she went back to York, where Lucy, the first of their six children, was born.

In later life, after difficult and sometimes disastrous times in India and the Persian Gulf fighting Arab pirates, Thompson became part-owner of the *Westminster Review* and a noted radical MP. But he never forgot the betrayal of Sierra Leone. And he was right in suspecting a conflict of interests among the Saints. Before abolition, Zachary Macaulay had recommended that Sierra Leone should be a depot for prizes captured by the navy: in 1808 he became the local agent, taking his slice of the prize money on recaptives – £40 for a man, £30 for a woman, £10 for a child – writing them down as 'contraband goods', Crown property and available for sale as apprentices. Macaulay also bought his own ship and set up a firm trading with West Africa, acting as a contractor for army and navy provisions. By 1819, having started with nothing, he had a huge personal fortune of £100,000.

# 42. DANES AND TURKS

June 1807 was steamingly hot, with the thermometers in shady gardens reaching 99 degrees Fahrenheit (37 centigrade). City dwellers and townspeople left for the seaside, the hills and the spas. In July it was hard to get the hay in because of the heat. The children were miserable, wrote Betsey Fremantle. 'Several of the Hay Makers fainted in the Hay Fields and one poor old woman was brought home dead, we could only just sit out of doors at night, and the air even then was sultry, slept with all the doors and windows open.'[1]

As they settled in the shade over their newspapers, Betsey and scores of others followed the declining fortunes of the allies. After Jena the previous year, the Russians and Prussians had fought on, but this June the French won a towering victory over the Russian army at Friedland in north-east Prussia. This led to the strange, theatrical meeting between Napoleon and the young Tsar Alexander on a grand raft with luxurious pavilions moored in the river Niemen, flowing towards the Baltic. In the two Treaties of Tilsit, signed with Russia on 7 July 1807 and with Prussia two days later, the emperor imposed the new French-dominated 'Grand Duchy of Warsaw'. This swamped most of Poland, leaving a strip belonging to Prussia along the Baltic coast. To the west lay the new kingdom of Westphalia, including Hanover and Brunswick, of which Napoleon's brother Jerome would be king. Prussia lost almost half its lands, and was forced to pay a large levy.

Russia – wooed by promises of help against Turkey – surrendered the
Ionian islands and its Mediterranean holdings.

As reports of the Treaties of Tilsit came through, the politicos in
the clubs and at Westminster brooded over Bonaparte's next move.
It seemed likely that now that Napoleon had subdued the Austrians,
Prussians and Russians on land, he would move against Britain at sea,
probably with Russian and Danish help. Earlier in the summer, there
had been several skirmishes with the Danish navy. Waiting for news,
picking up rumours, the City of London reacted nervously. 'The Public Funds were rather higher yesterday because a report that was circulated of our forces being in possession of the Danish Capital,' wrote
Thomas Morewood when James Longsdon was thinking of selling
some government bonds in late August:

This report however not receiving official confirmations, has lost all credit
& the funds appear to be gradually drooping again – The public prospect
before us is indeed gloomy & one searches in vain to find out from what
quarter light may be expected to break in upon us. The most sanguine yet
hope for a pacific overture from France, but what kind of terms may we
reasonably look for, if a treaty is set afoot & concludes in a state of affairs
such as now exists.[2]

Next day, he added a postscript: 'We abound in rumours.' One whis-
per was that Copenhagen had surrendered after a bombardment:
'This account is said to have been rec. this forenoon at the Admiralty,
from whence it reaches the City at the close of 'Change. The Funds
rallied a little in consequence & 3% consols finished at 62 3/8 and
62½.'

The Tilsit agreement, it turned out, had specified that France
would take over the Danish navy, barring the Baltic to British shipping.
This clause was supposed to be secret, but Canning and Hawkesbury
learnt about it from their spies and immediately arranged for Admiral
Gambier to take a fleet north, with twenty-five thousand troops. The
ships waited in the sound while the British envoy, Francis Jackson,
tried to persuade the Danes to surrender their fleet until after the war,
in return for promises of protection and a subsidy towards soldiers.

The Danish government refused, and without even declaring war, on 2 September the British opened fire on Copenhagen. Wellesley's infantry stormed ashore, while the ships' great guns hurled shells and grapeshot. After three days of bombardment the Danes surrendered, and the British were in possession of their fleet: eighteen Danish ships of the line, eleven frigates, fifteen smaller ships and twenty-six gunboats. Over two thousand people died in the city, and for days the sky was red with the flames of burning buildings.[3] The British stayed in the ruined city until 21 October. Relays of soldiers stripped the beautifully organised dockyard of everything they could find: shipping, rigging, stores and ammunition. 'But with what indignation the Danes must have beheld this scene!' exclaimed Maria Edgeworth when she heard the details from their Longford neighbour Hercules Pakenham, Arthur Wellesley's brother-in law and a member of his staff. 'And how they must hate the English for ever and ever!'[4]

The attack on Copenhagen was widely condemned as an act of ruthless opportunism, 'immoral' in terms of war, as even George III admitted. It provoked horror across Europe – and won grudging, if surprised, admiration from Napoleon. A motion of censure was raised in the House of Commons, but was roundly defeated. All the British captains were awarded prize money, to be distributed among the men, but it was a problem finding crews to sail the captured gunboats home and a call went out along the east coast for volunteers, 'especially those engaged in the Greenland trade', offering a bounty. Most seamen refused, thinking it a scheme to impress them, but one man who took this up was William Scoresby, son of the famous Whitby whaling captain and later a distinguished mapper of Arctic waters. Scoresby was horrified by the smouldering houses of Copenhagen, and appalled in a different way by the carelessness of Captain John Bligh of the seventy-four gun *Alfred* (a distant relation of William Bligh of the *Bounty*), who pushed them on through such rough seas that their gunboat foundered. Bligh's fierce regime was very different from the fraternity of a whaling ship. In one case a flogging was so severe 'that the man became indifferent about his life . . . and shortly after his last punishment, which I myself witnessed, he fell from the foretop on the deck (through carelessness if not by design) and was killed on the spot. Such tyrannies loudly called for reform.'[5]

Once again, British campaigns stretched from north to south, from the Baltic to the Aegean. Turkey, once an ally, was now an enemy: the previous year Sultan Selim III and the Ottoman Porte had agreed to open the Dardanelles to French warships only. British naval captains were despatched to small Ottoman outposts in the Ionian islands to negotiate with local beys for their support. In February 1807 a British squadron managed to destroy an Ottoman fleet and anchored, briefly, opposite Constantinople, until they were driven back by the guns of the Turkish forts.

Almost immediately the Dardanelles squadron was called to take part in a new offensive, carrying an expedition from Sicily against the Ottoman regime in Egypt. Thomas Perronet Thompson's younger brother Charles, just down from Cambridge, had joined a Sicilian regiment in Malta, choosing them on the rather unwarlike basis that he wanted to learn Italian. The regiment turned out to have been recruited four years before from the hospitals, galleys and prisons of Palermo. 'In consequence all the able bodied men were felons', he told his father, 'and all the well-disposed men were halt or blind.'[6] This rough band, plus more conventional British regiments, set sail for Egypt under the command of General Mackenzie Fraser, 'an open, generous, honourable Highland chieftain . . . Everyone in the army loved Mackenzie Fraser, but no one deemed him qualified for a separate and difficult command.'[7] After landing in heavy surf, they occupied Alexandria, welcomed by the people as support against their Ottoman ruler, Muhammad Ali. But on an ill-judged march to Rosetta for supplies, following bad advice from the British resident, Misset, half the army were surrounded. No flag of truce was accepted. Harry Slessor, from the Oporto family, who had begun his army career in the Irish rebellion of 1798, was among the soldiers. 'The howling during the night in the town was most horrible,' Slessor wrote in his diary:

We daily lost men by their fire, and saw no prospect of our barbarous warfare and hardships ending. Much rather storm and come to a general action and have done with it. We suffer much from the scorching heat by day and the excessive dew by night. A few branches of the date tree shelter us a little. We lay on the ground with a blanket or great coat; often nothing but rations of salt provisions, sea biscuit and burning *acqua dente*, with soft Nile water.[8]

This lasted three weeks. Muhammad Ali's armies killed and wounded nine hundred of Fraser's men, marching their prisoners into Cairo through a palisade of stakes topped with British heads. The remaining troops, including Charles Thompson and Slessor, lingered in Alexandria until September, when they withdrew to Sicily.

It was a mortifying outcome, but it had a strange coda. Two years later, much to his surprise, Thomas Perronet Thompson met his brother Charles in London, looking very brown and stout. While garrisoning Cairo, Charles had met Muhammad Ali, who entrusted him with 'a large letter directed to that "Most Excellent & Omnipotent Lord, the Marquis of Wellesley", stating his wish to be on good terms with the British'. Charles took the package to Malta, where he was given six months' leave to take it to London. If Charles returned to Egypt, Thomas told his father:

he was to bring the Pasha a steam engine, & an engineer, & a miner (because he thinks there are emeralds in his dominion) & presents for his harem & a multitude of other matters for which the Pasha offered to give him a shipload of corn which he was to sell at Malta. The Pasha is the man who attacked & defeated the last English expedition to Egypt under Genl. Fraser.[9]

Nothing came of this message to the Marquess – and no more was heard of emeralds and steam engines, the casual desiderata of war.

The London papers, then as now, revelled in such strange stories, but even more in quotidian disasters: packs of mad dogs roving London streets and driving panicky women to mob hospitals; epidemics of blindness and typhus; gory family murders; men struck by lightning. 'The newspapers', Hester Piozzi lamented to her friend Leonard

Chappelow in October, 'I think *teem with Horrors* this Year more than I can remember. New and prodigious Crimes, portentous Meteors – We had one here, an Arrow of Fire; – sudden Deaths – Suicides: or perhaps living alone and reading old Romances leads us to Dream of Murders &c.'[10] The arrow of fire was a comet, 'the magnitude of a star', very white, with a long blazing trail.[11] It floated in the skies at dusk every evening, shaking its hoary head like a portent of pestilence and war.

That autumn more royal exiles were on their way to Britain. On 2 November, after years moving from country to country, Louis XVIII landed at Yarmouth, travelling as the Comte de Lille. The port admiral's barge brought him secretly ashore from the Swedish frigate *Freja*. Before he moved on, to settle at Hartwell in the Buckinghamshire countryside, he left a purse of fifteen guineas for the sailors who had rowed the barge, but they rejected it, writing a joint letter to Admiral Russell of the North Sea squadron:

Please Your Honour, – We holded a talk about that ther £15 that was sent us, – and hope no offence, your honour. We don't like to take it, because as how we know, fast enuff that it was the true King of France that went with your honour in the boat; and that he and our own noble King (God bless them both! And give every one his right,) is good friends now; and, besides that, your honour gived an order, long ago, not to take any money from nobody – and we never did take none.[12]

## 43. ORDERS IN COUNCIL

The war was one of commerce as well as battles on sea and land. After his victory at Jena, Napoleon controlled all the northern rivers, and the Baltic coastline. On 21 November 1806, from the capital of Prussia, so recently defeated, he had issued his Berlin Decrees, establishing the 'Continental System', forbidding British imports into any European countries allied with or controlled by France. This was prompted, he said, by the British blockade of the coast from Brest to the river Elbe that had been in place from May. All British goods would be confiscated; all ships trading with Britain or its colonies would be seized. He would starve the country out. The Berlin Decrees speeded up a disastrous collapse of the export trades. Trying to sum up the impact, William Rowbottom wrote, 'In consequence of the unparaleld victory of the French Army in totally running over the Kingdom of Prussia and seising on British Property in all places on the Continent it has consequently thrown the merchants into greatest consternation. Weaving of all denominations are falling rapidly and a universall gloom hangs over the lower class of people.'[1]

Once it was clear that Russia and Denmark would probably be drawn into supporting the Continental System, the government retaliated. If British ships were stopped so would all the others be. During 1807 the government issued a series of Orders in Council concerning trade. The first, passed by Grenville's administration on 7 January, six weeks after the Berlin Decrees, outlawed British trade with France or her allies; in February, another order banned exports of cotton and quinine to France. Later in the year, in November, Portland's government issued two new Orders declaring that all ports that denied entry to British ships would be blockaded, and that all neutral vessels who wished to trade with France had to dock first in British ports and pay customs duties and buy a licence – thus stopping them making a profit at the expense of British trade.

The international traders in Britain were, however, determined to press on. Since the peace, huge investments had been made in shipping and docks in Bristol, Liverpool, Glasgow and Hull. In London the West India Docks began taking ships at the Isle of Dogs in 1802; the London Dock Company, with the engineer John Rennie as supervisor, had completed new wharves at Wapping in 1805 for wine, brandy, tobacco and rice. Rennie also worked on the East India Docks, which opened in 1806, while the Surrey and Commercial Docks at Rotherhithe, bringing in Baltic and Scandinavian timber and grain, were being expanded every year. To build the new docks developers demolished swathes of old streets and a whole new township of seamen's lodgings grew up, housing the Indian, Lascar and Chinese seamen who were being recruited to replace British sailors impressed into the navy. These men brought new sights to London, like a four-day festival for 'Lascars of the Mahommedan persuasion' in the East End in 1805, with drums and tambourines and sword dances. And they brought trouble, with brawls and riots.[2] But the great merchant fleets, with their varied crews, grew year by year.

As soon as the Decrees and Orders came into effect, merchants began to find ways round them, persuading the government to issue thousands of licences for trade with France: the French too granted licences so that goods could be imported. But on both sides of the Channel business suffered. In French-dominated Europe, trade with the West Indies virtually ceased: only the rich could get hold of coffee

William Daniell's bird's-eye view of the Isle of Dogs, 1802: many warehouses
were still to be built. Daniell dedicated his aquatints to the chairman and
directors of the East India Company, who bought them in abundance.

and tobacco, and all but three of Hamburg's sugar-boiling factories
were closed. In Britain, goods piled up in the dockside warehouses
waiting for a chance of export.

Once ports were closed in France, the Netherlands and Italy, merchants looked for even more remote routes, sending their goods to purchasers in Europe through the Baltic countries in the north, Gibraltar
and Malta in the south and Turkey and the Ionian islands in the east.
London bankers used family contacts and trusted networks abroad to
finance mercantile smuggling, and a huge, elaborate operation developed, with secret depots in Brussels and Paris and insurance agencies
in London and Antwerp. There were great profits to be made, even if
five out of six attempts failed. At the same time, British colonial trade
increased with the West Indies, the Cape of Good Hope and India,
where the annexation of more territories led to increased imports,
especially of woollens. And new commercial treaties were signed,
such as one with Persia, whereby cloths made in Ispahan, Kashan
and Yezd were sent to Russia where they were exchanged for British
cloth, velvet and cutlery.[3] Although there was always a net loss in the
balance of payments, British trade, to the delight of City merchants,
rose steadily throughout the war.[4]

There were hidden routes to France and Germany from Lisbon and the Azores, and tons of British-made hardware was carried in neutral ships from Malta and Sicily to Trieste or Fiume. Nathan Rothschild, who had gone into partnership with another merchant, Rindskopf, in 1805, had diversified, importing and exporting colonial goods – indigo, pearls and tortoiseshell – as well as cotton.[5] But from 1807, when the Orders came into force, he too had to carry on his export business illegally. In October, he sent a consignment of coffee to Sweden via Amsterdam in an American-registered ship, using fake Dutch papers. The connection with his father-in-law, the great London merchant Nathan Barent Cohen, widened his range of goods still further. And in these tough times he was becoming increasingly interested in credit transactions, making deals with London bankers like the Goldsmids, Daniel Mocatta and the Schroder brothers.

Even Napoleon – who now employed a hundred thousand excisemen on the coasts of Europe – accepted that ships must break the rules if his own farmers and merchants were not to be ruined. In September 1808, the West Riding wool merchants reported a coup in fulfilling £40,000 worth of contracts with the French army – paid in full. French troops in Poland, it appears, were wearing boots made in Northampton as well as greatcoats of West Riding cloth. In the Baltic, the small island of Heligoland, captured after the bombardment of Copenhagen, was soon a booming centre. John Longsdon, here as an agent and writing home to his farmer father, described it as a tiny place less than a mile long, with one road, called the Lower Town, and two thousand people, five or six cows, two hundred sheep, thirty goats and some pigs.[6] But in 1810, when the British built a lighthouse there, around three hundred ships a day were calling in and the total value of products that passed through each year soon reached around £20 million. British merchants rented warehouses at high profits and local pilots made good money.[7] From Heligoland the goods were run in through Hamburg, whose port officials resented Napoleon's strict decrees. Once landed, the goods were carried further inland in double-bottomed carts and even in coffins.

The old-fashioned smuggling operations on the south coast of England also flourished, with boats setting out from small ports and coves, harassed by government cutters with their lovely names – *Griffin*, *Sea Gull*, *Lively*, *Otter*, *Tiger* and *Swallow* and *Success*. French textile companies were still largely dependent on Britain for cotton yarn and twist and plain fabric for printing, so much so that it was said that boats from Cowes dumped bales attached to chains and buoys off Calais, which were picked up by fishermen and sold as 'prize goods'.[8]

On the north coast of Kent, the desolate marshes and ancient woods on the hills behind made the shore perfect for landing contraband. Strings of farmers stood by, ready to put a light in their window if they heard the customs men coming, and willing to hide goods that couldn't be loaded on to carts straight away. One old farmer loved to tell his grandson stories of ditches between marshy meadows filled with parcels, hidden by the reeds, and how haystacks doubled in size overnight and the fields were full of the scent of tobacco before the stacks shrank again.[9] Local men of an entrepreneurial bent became rich on the trade. According to his obituary in the local paper, William Baldock 'was originally a poor boy employed to look after cows, and remarkable for dirtiness and slovenliness':

He afterwards carried the hod as a bricklayer's labourer, and at length, by dint of industry and parsimony, with some assistance, he amassed money enough to build the barracks at Canterbury, which he let to the government at the rate of 6d per week for each soldier, a practice which became so profitable that in the course of a few years the whole building became his own.[10]

As the paper put it discreetly, he then 'continued to acquire wealth in various ways'. When searches began on the coastal hiding places, Baldock's Whitstable gang moved their depot to the St Dunstan's Brewery in Canterbury, crossing through the forest by 'Cut Throat Lane'. On the turnpike, simple signals – a broomstick poked high up out of the highest chimney, a lamp in a window – sent warnings from house to house along the road. The smugglers boasted that it was impossible for the Revenue men or the Dragoons to march the quarter of a mile from the West Gate at Canterbury to St Dunstan's Church before the message reached Whitstable. When Baldock died in 1812, at the age of sixty, he was said to possess 'one million and one hundred thousand pounds'.

Baldock was not the only smuggling millionaire. Another was Zephaniah Job from the pilchard-scented fishing port of Polperro, in its deep Cornish ravine. Job started in the tin mines as a child, became a schoolmaster, and then an agent and bookkeeper for local fishermen and traders. Much of the town's money came from drift-netting for pilchards which were then cured and exported, but the fishermen, whose fast luggers could outrun the Customs boats, also smuggled goods from the Channel Islands, which were free of English customs duties, and acted as entrepôts. Once carried inland, the goods were sold on to regular traders. Job acted as an agent for Guernsey merchants, sending money over for stock, noting it down as a debit and then crediting them with the payments made to him by the smugglers. To fund all this trade he opened accounts with the less scrupulous London banking houses and drew the bills on them to pay the Guernsey spirit merchants, taking out huge loans and dealing in Navy Bills.[11] His carefully kept day books show all his expenses, the little handouts and perks and extra costs needed to win a contract, like the guinea for the clerk at the Navy Office for drawing up the contract, and payments to women to carry the corn on board. Eventually new Acts extended the British customs system to the Channel Islands but French brandy and silks still came in, and British boots and cloth and calico reached their buyers in Europe.

As 'the smuggler's banker' Job ruled the town, so accepted and respectable that he became manager of the local Trelawney estates and a friend of the family.[12] He had many sidelines. He invested in barges and boats, carrying everything from timber and bricks to linen, currants and butter, as well as sending cured fish to London and even exporting them to Italy. He also traded in lime – much needed for the poor Cornish soil – building his own extremely profitable limekilns, and he imported wheat in the food shortages, winning tenders for its supply from Plymouth dockyard.[13] Like William Baldock, Zephaniah Job died an extremely rich man.

Despite the smugglers' efforts, unsold bales of wool and cotton goods, once destined for Holland and Germany, lay in the warehouses for years. Many owners shut their mills, or worked on a four- or three-day week, and the poor rates doubled.[14] By January 1808 the Longsdons' company was facing severe losses. The second son, John, now managing the warehouse in Manchester, wrote gently to his father in Derbyshire, reassuring him that although times were hard he should take comfort in a 'loving industrious family' and should not worry about leaving them less than he had hoped. Longsdon replied in a shaky hand, thanking him for the comforting letter. But the saga ran on into the spring, when the Longsdons agreed to take five hundred acres of land in Prince Edward Island as collateral for a debt owed them by the Liverpool firm of Hepple and Hope. A year later, John set off there to see if he could make connections with American dealers, with the help of their friends the Morewoods, who had family agents there. Trade at home was still very slack: 'Cotton & goods are not much altered the former is rather stiffer and goods about the same prices. We have made no sales.' John told their Yorkshire agent:

we should not for the future give out any more warps – of course we shall not have a weaver employed in Yorkshire or Lancashire – my stock of goods is not now very considerable & I am fully of the opinion that the best manner we can now adopt will be to sell them & get our Capital as much as possible concentrated & ready to make use of on any opportunity of disposing it to advantage.[15]

It was the beginning of an unhappy slide.

Protests against the Orders in Council would dominate much of life for the next five years, linked with two other demands – the textile workers' grievances and the demands for an end of the war. The combination, which led to new demands for reform, created a resurgence in popular politics that would alter the culture. Just as significant was the shift in the site of political activity, away from London to provincial towns and cities.

In the wool industry, a select committee chaired by Wilberforce had decided firmly in 1806 against the repeated request of skilled cloth workers and small clothiers for the reinstatement of the old restrictive laws. In a virtual manifesto for *laissez-faire* capitalism, the committee insisted that manufacturers must be freed to innovate, and that the whole success of manufacturing was 'principally to be ascribed to the general spirit of enterprize and industry among a free and enlightened People, left to the unrestrained exercise of their talents in the employment of a vast capital, pushing to the utmost the principle of the division of labour; calling in all the resources of scientific research and mechanical ingenuity'.[16] The small masters and home weavers need not, the report insisted, be rooted out: the domestic industry would remain the heart of a multi-layered system. The capitalist's freedom was a part of being 'British', expressed in the language of patriotism:

The right of every man to employ the Capital he inherits, or has acquired, according to his own discretion, without molestation or obstruction, so long as he does not infringe on the rights or property of others, is one of those privileges which the free and happy Constitution of this Country has long accustomed every Briton to consider as his birthright.[17]

Yet the capitalists too were fighting the Orders, seeing them as a form of 'molestation and obstruction'. Mass meetings took place and petitions were sent to local MPs, although these were discouraged because they would show the enemy how well the blockade was working. After a huge meeting at Oldham Edge on Christmas Day 1807, constables placed an address in the Manchester papers accusing the crowds of being Jacobins and enemies of the government. Rejecting the first label, the organisers accepted the second, happy to be enemies of a cabal ruining the country. In the *Manchester Gazette*, William Cowdroy's editorial recorded it as strange 'that men who profess but one object . . . namely, our King's and Country's good – shall differ so widely about the means of obtaining that end: through war and blood, says one – through peace, commerce and manufactures, says another: – which are to be preferred, we leave history, policy, morality and above all Christianity to answer.'[18]

That month Napoleon announced his second move, the Milan Decree, an expansion of the Berlin Decrees – the very names declaring his control of Europe from south to north. Any ship, of whatever nationality, even from neutral countries, sailing from or to British ports and colonies would now be considered as British, and therefore 'lawful prize'. Britain and France were equally arrogant in assuming rights over ships from other countries, infuriating Denmark, Russia and America. In the same month, December 1807, the United States Congress, angry at the seizing of American sailors by British press gangs, passed an Embargo Act, ordering all American vessels to remain in port, except coastal ships, thus depriving Europe of American exports. Now all doors were closed.

The laying-off of hands in the textile factories, and the lack of work sent out to domestic workers, threatened to bring serious trouble. At the start of 1808 the problems of the Orders, the workers' demands and the need for peace were inextricably linked. The calls for peace were avidly discussed in the provincial papers and in national papers and journals, like the *Morning Chronicle* and the *Edinburgh Review*. William Roscoe, one of the 'Friends of Peace' based around Liverpool's Presbyterian and Unitarian chapels, published his *Considerations of the Causes, Objects, and Consequences of the Present War, and on the Expediency or the Danger of Peace with France*, pointing out the level of debt and impoverishment that the conflict had brought.[19]

Weavers' committees also raised the issue of the minimum wage, an idea supported by several manufacturers and backed by petitions. On 19 May 1808 George Rose introduced the Weavers' Minimum Wage Bill, as it became known, in the House of Commons. The Minimum Wage Bill was opposed by Spencer Perceval, then Chancellor of the Exchequer, who offered to bring in a bill of his own the following year, and by Sir Robert Peel, the son of the textile tycoon and a new MP at the age of twenty-one. When the weavers heard that the Bill had been withdrawn they began to organise, holding meetings in different towns. On 24 May, the Manchester magistrates, watching as over six thousand weavers met in St George's Fields, sent in the dragoons. Although the crowds fled, next day they gathered again, their numbers now swollen to fifteen thousand. In William Rowbottom's view they 'did not threaten any mischief but begged something to be done in order to mend their wages wich are most shameful low'.[20] This time the dragoons opened fire and one man was killed – with the soldiers later apologising and taking up a collection for his family. At the meeting, Joseph Hanson, once the proud Colonel of the Manchester and Salford Volunteers, defied the tacit rules of his class and the *laissez-faire* principles of his fellow manufacturers by addressing the weavers and supporting the minimum wage. He was arrested, tried for incitement to riot and sentenced to six months in gaol. Hanson died three years later, aged only thirty, mourned as 'a staunch friend to the cause of liberty and a true Advocate for the poor'.[21] A bronze medal of 'The Weaver's Friend' showed his profile on one side, and a loom, press and spinning wheel on the other.

On the same day as the St George's Fields meeting, crowds streamed down from the moors at Bolton and paraded the streets, carrying an effigy of Robert Peel. A strike followed: groups of weavers travelled the district, taking away spindles from the looms of weavers who had not supported their petition, so that they could not work. Protesting workers threw acid on the cloth on factory looms and staged riots in Rochdale, Blackburn, Bolton and other towns. 'This is the Bastille of Paris,' shouted Samuel Bayley, leading a crowd to rescue strikers from Rochdale gaol, 'O Glorious Revo-lu-ti-on, this is what we have long wanted'.[22] Writing to the Home Secretary, Lord Hawkesbury, from Manchester on 28 May, one magistrate said that 'the whole of the town and neighbourhood, so far as the weaving branch is concerned, are in a state of confusion. No work is carried on, and the well-disposed families, who are inclined to pursue their labour, are prevented doing so by the threats and intimidation held out to them.'[23]

At the end of the month, a handbill was pasted on walls in Royton – one of many – issued by weavers who were against the violence and who thought that it was unlikely to obtain any relief for the people in their distress:

For that distress can only be removed, by removing the cause; – which cause we have no hesitation in pronouncing is the WAR: – to prove which we need only refer to our dependance upon Commerce, and how it is obstructed by the War; – and it is our humble opinion that is impossible for either the Legislature or commercial characters to remedy the evil by any other means than that of the restoration of Peace.[24]

In that blazing summer people linked the suppression of the peace meetings and minimum wage campaign to the long years of repression of protests and workers' struggles. William Rowbottom recorded the return of one of the workers transported for 'administering illegal oaths' in 1801:

19th August – last night John Jackson of near Chaderton arived at his house after serving seven years transportation.

20th Stansfield and Buckly the unfortunate companions of the above Jackson have died some time since on the coast of Guinea the vollonteers for soldiers in preference to serving in transports.

Nothing had improved in those seven years. In July the weavers had accepted a promised increase from the masters, to be given in instalments, but a new period of misery then began, as the blockade stopped imports of raw cotton. Christmas was bleak, as Rowbottom noted, 'such are the distressedness of the times, work so low and scarce, for there are hundreds in Oldham Parish who are entirely without work'.[25] Soup kitchens were back in the streets.

# 44. LAND

William Barnard, a devout Baptist of thirty-two with a large family, was the tenant of Harlowbury Farm in Essex. In 1807 he began keeping a weather and farming diary, like his fellow farmers Randall Burroughes and James Badenach and so many others. The war's battles and treaties and bombardments did not break into this record. The only tragedy was near at hand, the death of his small son, a shadow on a plain farming day. 'I have plowed 5 acres in Great Town field & carted dung to Oldfield; my poor little boy Thomas died on the 19th at 6 AM and was buried this day in the burial ground at Forster Street.'[1]

Barnard's record was a memory aid, reminding him of the rotations in each field, the times of harvest, yields and prices, and the results of experiments, like his use of the new, lighter cast-iron plough, which allowed two horses to plough a field instead of three. Over the years he tried many different types of wheat – Kentish wheat, red wheat, small, buncle, Moravian and American and the heavy-cropping Revitt wheat from the Mediterranean. With every entry he pondered the use of his land:

My sheep are feeding off turnips 9 acres Upper Stony, they are rotten withinside for the most part tho they appear fair without; it is worthy to be remarked what a great difference there is between the usefulness of an acre of turnips used before Christmas & one that remains till March; I think I

Walker, 'Rape Threshing'. The threshers work in a circle, the leaders marked
by coloured ribbons, moving backwards, with the next two facing them.
One 'hugger' is trying to bury a woman under a load of rape

must try more coleseed for spring feed. N.B. I never had more land rolled in
one day by 2 pairs of horses.

This kind of comparison was encouraged by the monthly *Agricultural
Magazine* and by Constable's *Farmer's Magazine*, which had started publication seven years ago, in October 1800, edited by Robert Brown,
a farmer from East Lothian. The *Farmer's Magazine* was full of letters
and articles about managing crops, waste land, hedges, farm sizes and
enclosures, rents and tithes, weights and measures, liming and ploughing, prices, pests and potatoes, indeed everything that would-be progressive farmers admired. The profits to be made from grain encouraged them to use new inventions, like Andrew Meikle's threshing
machine, expensive, but saving manpower. They tried out new crops,
like the swede, which could tide the cattle over between the last of the
turnips and fresh spring grass, and used linseed cake as winter fodder. They grew more rape, which had previously been imported from
Germany and the Low Countries, sending the seed to be crushed for
oil, in mills that were now beginning to use steam engines. Rape did
especially well in the newly enclosed land, but as the seed scattered

so easily, farmers threshed it in the open fields, laying large sheets on the ground and employing crowds of threshers and reapers, carriers or 'huggers', and others to fork, sift and fill sacks. In the north, particularly, farmers started giving over more land to potatoes, hitherto unfashionable but now a staple food. Gangs of women and children dug them out, back-breaking work, and stored them in pits or under clamps of earth for the winter.

Although the harvests were better than in the terrible near-famines of the previous decade, the price of wheat stayed high, averaging around 102 shillings a quarter, the highest ever known. The price of meat was rising too. For the past three decades, long before the war, farmers had competed to breed ever fatter livestock. Lord John Russell, Duke of Bedford, Whig spokesman in the Lords and one of the most prominent agricultural improvers, held a famous annual fair for progressive farmers at Woburn lasting several days. Arthur Young wrote glowingly about the Duke's experiments in growing crops and breeding sheep and cattle, and Gillray showed him in a stockyard, declaiming, 'Ah, here's your sort! – here's your Nine-Inch Fat my boys!' Thomas Bewick, often hired to engrave prize beasts, was suspicious of the farmers' ambitions and of new agricultural societies which 'blazed forth over a great part of the Kingdom'. He admitted that their efforts to improve stock did succeed to a great extent, 'and yet I cannot help thinking that they often suffered their whimsies to overshoot the mark & in many instances, to lead them on to the *rediculous*'.[2] Eugenia Campbell, for one, snootily agreed, after being taken some time before her marriage 'to see Mr. Wenar's farm and his famous fat oxen for which he every year gets two or three prizes':

He was not at home, but his daughter as fat as the cattle, tho a civil girl did the honours of the mansion . . . she showed me the fat beasts who are fed some on oil cake and some on turnips, and look like Elephants. It is only in this country that one may see a man like Mr. Wenar, who is visited and courted by Dukes and Peers, dines at their table, and returns their dinners, and all this because he can fatten oxen better than his brethren, the other Farmers.[3]

Gillray, *Fat Cattle*. The Duke of Bedford patting his prize ox, 16 January 1802

Ten years ago James Badenach had watched as the buyers at cattle fairs round Aberdeen found prices rising beyond all expectation 'all owing to the Demand for England on account of the War &c'. He was largely right: towards the end of the war the *Farmer's Magazine* reported that Government contractors wanted 'nearly 400 fat bullocks per week for the Victualling Office, for the Royal Navy, the Prison Ships and Garrisons at Plymouth, and the War Prison on Dartmoor'.[4] This figure alone was a seventh of the annual cattle sales at Smithfield.

The same magazine declared in 1807: 'If the market value of arable has increased, that of grassland has advanced on a superlative degree. In short, a kind of mania seems to have seized the minds of grass speculators, not to be accounted for, and probably not to be cured, till the patient is weakened and exhausted by the effects of his disease.' But grass speculators, eager to cash in on the rising price of wheat or meat, found it expensive to enclose land for pastures, to grub up hedges, dig new ditches, plant fences, build new barns and sheds. They knew the yield of a crop might increase twenty times in years to come, but to offset immediate costs and to pay rising taxes, they put up their rents. These almost doubled in Wales and England, while in Scotland, where they had always been lower, they doubled and redoubled.[5] The larger tenants, especially those with long leases, could escape the rocketing cost but smaller tenants suffered. Big landowners eyed their farms like pikes eyeing minnows, or, as the *Farmer's Magazine* put it, 'as a merchant would view a pound weight of raisins'.[6] At the same time industrialists and merchants were buying land and snapping up cheap leftovers from the enclosure commissioners, then putting in agents to run the farms. The banks made substantial loans, feeding the profits back to London.

Aristocratic and gentry families with scattered estates acquired by marriage, or institutions that had received land in endowments and legacies over many years, like Oxford and Cambridge colleges, began to monitor their distant, rarely visited, estates more keenly. Since early 1806, William Knollys, who had now left the army and was married with a growing family – his wife Charlotte was pregnant almost every year for a decade – had been embroiled in a law suit to prove his title to the earldom of Banbury. The problem lay with his descent from the first Earl, whose last two sons were born when he was well into his eighties and were widely thought illegitimate. When Knollys inherited and applied to enter the House of Lords, his title was questioned. The matter was passed to the Attorney General and then to the Lords, and as William and his sisters waited, they poured their fortune into lawyers' fees until 'The Case' was eventually decided against them in 1813, and William became simple 'General Knollys' again. Politically he was a Whig and in the long legal wranglings the Tory judge Ellenborough spoke viciously against him. Bothered about money, trying to make the best of his estates in Hampshire and Yorkshire, Knollys actually visited them, unlike many absentee landlords. He had not been near his Beverley estate for years and he found many changes, old people dead, houses pulled down, 'but the Chimes are the same of the Church, and the Old Woman, the Town Crier Mrs Cotes'. He was determined to lay out money on improvements, 'and as the Improvements succeed of Course the Rent will be rais'd on short leases – this I am the more anxious to do, as it will give me the opportunity of charging the Property with Something for my dear little Girls.'[7]

These improvements and high rents made it hard for young, keen farmers to find a place. During the short-lived peace in 1802, Wordsworth's sister-in-law Joanna Hutchinson, whose dream had always been for her cousins and brothers to run their own farm, had written to her favourite cousin John Monkhouse, begging him to think of farming. 'I hear you have some notion of going to the East Indies – I was in hopes you had given up that plan long ago. I think you had better come and be a farmer somewhere hereabouts.' Their friend William Taylor took gentleman apprentices, a fashionable scheme, she told him, and three college-educated young men had trained with him and had all turned farmers. 'You might then retire upon your own estate and enjoy yourself in your own country. I wish you would think *seriously* about this John?' At the end she urged him again, 'You would be a gentleman in less than three years – two would be enough for your apprenticeship – then you would commence gentleman farmer.'[8]

Six years later, Joanna was still hoping for a farm, a permanent tie to the land. Among her brothers, the oldest, Jack, farmed on at Sockburn in County Durham, George was trying to make his way as a land agent and Henry was still at sea. Her favourite brother, Tom, had moved in 1804 to Dacre, at the foot of Ullswater, as a tenant of the farm at Park House, not far from the Eusemere home of their friends the Clarksons. This became a meeting place for all the family, including the Wordsworths, who sent their children there when they were ill. But it was hard to make a profit on the steep fellsides, and in January 1808 Tom sold his stock and began carting goods between

Penrith and Stockton. He was banking that a legacy from his rich, prickly uncle Henry might enable him to buy his own land.[9] 'God knows when we shall be settled!' Joanna wrote to John Monkhouse in August 1808, 'but I hope & trust we shall live together, for what will Fortune or situation be if we do not live with those we Love!' A few months later, she was still hoping: 'I trust now we shall be able to get a nice Farm & live together again as we used to do – for I can never be really happy till we are so.'[10]

At that point John Monkhouse was grief-stricken at the death of his wife, Joanna's childhood friend Isabella Addison, who had died the previous May only one year after their marriage. He was restless, depressed, looking for something new. In the autumn of 1808 he and Tom Hutchinson decided to try and farm together. With the high rents, good farms were scarce, and they hunted without success in Suffolk and Yorkshire. Tom then heard of one at Windermere belonging to the Bishop of Llandaff: 'Beautiful situation and good land at 30/- per acre, which I think very cheap,' but there was a difficulty with the lease.[11] John was sending him details of other places, but Tom felt they should look further afield: 'I think some of the Welsh farms will answer our purpose better than any you have yet heard of.' On the other hand, he didn't want to undertake the long journey unless there is 'some certainty'.[12]

In November Tom set out, reaching Liverpool and worrying, when he read the advertisements in the local papers, that Wales might not be cheaper after all. He wrote to warn John, 'I would not have you turn your back on every farm merely because you think it is too small for us provided you think it cheap.' By now Joanna was impatient. 'Surely something good will be produced by this journey into Wales or the duce is in it! . . . I shall be perfectly content if the place be never so ugly if it will only produce cash – I am quite tired of this wandering life.'[13] Eventually they found what they were looking for, Hindwell Farm, a few miles south of Presteigne, the county town of Radnorshire, in the hilly border country between England and Wales. Hindwell was beautiful, a plain Georgian house with an old barn, a hill behind and a lake shining in front. It had an ancient feel, with standing stones nearby and a Neolithic settlement on the slopes behind – the grassy banks in the pasture beside the farm mark a Roman frontier fort. The deep, well-drained loamy soil was fertile and rich. Altogether it promised well. The lease was signed and the two cousins moved in on Lady Day, 25 March 1809.

Joanna joined them and so did John's sister Mary Monkhouse ('M.M.'), now twenty-one. The work was hard, but the two women enjoyed it, although they were both small – two years later, when Mary Wordsworth was staying they all weighed themselves, as Mary Wordsworth reported: 'I weigh 7 stone 13 – 3 lbs more than M.M. & 2 pounds more than Joanna.'[14] On the farm, Tom began using all the latest methods. Early in a rainy August M.M. wrote: 'This is most *desperate* weather for trying the temper of us farmers but you know what we are. We have twenty acres of hay cut which if the wet weather continues a few days longer will make capital manure.'[15] They had done better than their neighbours in getting it in while the good weather lasted, and if it had continued fine two days longer 'everything wd have been good . . . however we must suppose it *"all for the best"*':

I must tell you that we have the finest crop of turnips that ever was seen in the county and people come from far and near to see them, but as they are sown with the drill which is not at all in use here the people are so bigoted in their own way of management that they cannot be persuaded there is any better.

It was not all rosy. Even here the war and the Orders in Council were biting down. On the back of M.M.'s letter to her brother Thomas Monkhouse, Tom Hutchinson scribbled his own note:

My Partner and I will thank you to get (if you can) from some well informed wool stapler his opinion concerning the probable future price of wool. My reason for this is that our wool is unsold & we see by the papers that it has had an advance . . . & find, given the turn which Spanish affairs must now take in favour of the French that it may go much higher – which is to be upon our guard against the cunning wool buyers in this country.

He had been stung, having thought that they had sold their wool 'to the agent of a Yorkshire Dealer at upwards of 2/6, but the Principal refuses to take it, it having been lower since that time. The sooner we have this information the better.'

Overcoming the variable prices, they farmed at Hindwell more or less successfully. Joanna and M.M. ran the house, taking turns to go away on long family visits. Tom joined the newly formed Radnorshire Agricultural Society, and won several prizes and premiums.[16] Their success drew more friends from the old Penrith community: Henry Addison, John Monkhouse's brother-in-law, took a farm in Wales too, and one of William Taylor's gentlemen apprentices, Francis Donaldson, a former barrister, also became a neighbour and good friend. Wordsworth, who was staying at Hindwell in August 1810, was not too sanguine about his prospects: 'He is a mild, good natured little man, of humble desires, but I much fear that humble as his desires are he will not find it easy to gratify them in the farming line; which as far as profit is concerned seems but a poor speculation.'

However gloomy he might be about their future, Wordsworth liked Hindwell, telling his wife, Mary, about the comfortable house, with its view across the pool, which 'shows beautifully the great importance of still water in landscape'. In the evening, he thought, it almost matched their own lakes. He had been fishing, and caught eleven trout, 'several of them more than half a pound a piece'.[17]

A farm seemed idyllic on a May day, with the scent of mown grass and hawthorn blossom, and cows standing with their feet in the stream, flicking their tails to get rid of the flies, but it was hard, grinding work for farmers and labourers, all year round, in all weathers. People loved the landscape they grew up in, and mourned it when they went to the cities, like Wordsworth's 'Poor Susan' seeing 'a mountain ascending, a vision of trees' when she hears a thrush sing as she walks down Cheapside. They returned to their homes in spirit, and sometimes in person, like Constable, turning his back on London and returning to paint *Dedham Vale* and the Suffolk scene. But much of the familiar landscape was changing. The wide-spreading, tangled old hedgerows were being grubbed up to make more room for crops, making larger fields bordered with thin quickset hedges, and the commons that had been open to all for centuries were fast disappearing.

The land in the wide valley around Hindwell was already an 'improved' landscape with large enclosed fields and new hedges. The war had speeded up the process of enclosure that had been happening piecemeal for the last half-century. During the war over 1,600 square miles of wastes and commons and open pasture were enclosed by Act of Parliament: the fens of Lincolnshire and Humber, the moors of the West Country and the fells and wetlands of the North. On the moors, the new owners burned gorse and heather, drained, limed and seeded to make pastures. In the Lake District new stone walls climbed higher and higher up the mountains, reflecting, as John Christian Curwen put it to the Workington Agricultural Society, a 'disposition to carry the plough much nearer heaven than what was dreamed of a few years ago'.[18]

Across the country thousands more acres were ploughed for oats, potatoes and wheat. Large farmers like the Hardys in Norfolk and Randall Burroughes in Suffolk welcomed the new Enclosure Acts in their locality, meeting with other landlords and farmers, allocating and buying land. But even they felt there was a limit. In 1807 Mary Hardy noted that her husband refused to sign a petition for a further Act, 'for inclosing the Heath Lands &c. belonging to Holt'.[19] The newly enclosed land did indeed help the war effort in providing more food, more money, more taxes. It also provided work for labourers, but often these were men and women who had been almost self-sufficient before, with a smallholding and grazing rights on the common. Now they had to come cap in hand to the farmer, hoping for wages. In theory an enclosure began with an agreement between all those who had rights to use the land, depending on the size of their holding, but the cottagers' stakes were tiny in comparison to those of the big local landowner or lord of the manor, and they were easily persuaded to sell them for a pittance. Once the land was enclosed, the cottagers lost a mass of ancient rights, established by custom and law: the right to graze their cows, to take wood for fuel, to fish in the meres, to use the reeds for thatching, to net birds and set ferrets, to catch rabbits in their burrows. There was less for the pot now. The new landlords, raising game birds on their enclosed lands, enforced the game laws with zeal, and the penalties were high.

Cobbett, farming in Botley, had come to see the value of the commons and the deprivation that enclosure could bring. He would fight for the rights of farm labourers all his life. Even dedicated improvers, like Arthur Young, could see the loss to the commoners. After the peace of 1802–3, when a parliamentary report had calculated the number of paupers in the countryside, he began exploring the effects of enclosures and high food prices and making his own suggestions about allotments for the poor that could give them a slim independence.[20] 'I had rather that all the commons of England were sunk in the sea', he wrote in *Annals of Agriculture* in 1808, 'than that the poor should in future be treated on enclosing as they have generally been hitherto.'[21]

Remembering his boyhood, John Clare wrote of paths across the heath and sheep-tracks across open pastures, of boys shouting after school, racing to play leapfrog on the 'rushy moor', or to fish in the stream, or read with a friend beside a hedge in the evening sun.[22] Clare's father often took him out of school to help with threshing in the barn, looking after the sheep or horses, scaring birds, or weeding. He traced the flight of geese across the sky and the swoop of a heron by the marsh. He watched the lolloping hare and knew the name of every copse and field. In 1809, when he was sixteen – the year that Tom Hutchinson, John Monkhouse and their sisters moved to Hindwell – an Act authorised enclosures in his neighbourhood, including the three great common fields that circled Helpston like a wheel. This too seemed like a war. Roads and right-angled hedges cut across the open land, an invasion as imperious as that of Napoleon's all-devouring troops. 'By Langley Bush I roam, but the bush hath left its hill', wrote Clare:

On Cowper Hill I stray, 'tis a desert strange and chill;
And spreading Lea Close Oak, ere decay had penned its will,
To the axe of the spoiler and self-interest fell a prey;
And Crossberry Way and old Round Oak's narrow lane
With its hollow trees like pulpits I shall never see again.
Inclosure like a Bonaparte let not a thing remain,
It levelled every bush and tree and levelled every hill
And hung the moles for traitors – though the brook is running still,
It runs a naked brook, cold and chill.

In the year of the Helpston enclosures Turner exhibited an oil in his private gallery, *Ploughing up Turnips, near Slough*. Men plough and women follow, bent double to grub up the roots, one stopping to nurse her baby in the field. A man mends a broken plough and cows munch the turnips spilling from a pannier on the ground. In the background, rising above the woods in a morning mist, is Windsor Castle. Is this a version of digging for victory, a celebration of progressive agriculture, watched over by a benign Farmer George? Or is it a scene of hardship, a slough of despond next to wide royal estates, where women and old folk toil as the young men march to war?

# VI : FIGHTING

## 1809–1815

Oh, Albuera! glorious field of grief!
As o'er thy plain the Pilgrim prick'd his steed,
Who could foresee thee, in a space so brief,
A scene where mingling foes should boast and bleed!
Peace to the perish'd! may the warrior's meed
And tears of triumph their reward prolong!
Till others fall where other chieftains lead,
Thy name shall circle round the gaping throng,
And shine in worthless lays, the theme of transient song.

Enough of battle's minions! Let them play
Their game of lives; and barter breath for fame;
Fame that will scarce reanimate their clay,
Though thousands fall to deck some single name.

BYRON, *Childe Harold*, Canto I

## 45. 'CAESAR IS EVERYWHERE'

In early 1808, keen to follow up the bombardment of Copenhagen and the seizure of the Danish fleet the year before, the British government decided to send troops to help the Swedish King Gustavus confront Russia. In May, Sir John Moore set out with ten thousand men, escorted by a naval squadron under Admiral Saumarez. But in Gothenburg, hamstrung by contradictory instructions, Moore endured weeks of convoluted negotiations with the 'mad' king, who forbade the British troops to land and eventually arrested Moore himself. He escaped, in peasant disguise, reaching the flagship to find Saumarez holding a ball for the local citizens. Furious, Moore ordered an immediate return, writing to his mother on the eve of sailing that this campaign 'has proved the most painful to me I ever served'.[1]

This spring, though, Napoleon's chief concern was not the Baltic. After trouncing the allies in the north, for the last few months he had been looking south, planning to bring Portugal and Spain into the Continental System, to throttle British trade still more. In November 1807, General Junot had taken Lisbon, after a French deal with Spain's Prime Minister, Manuel Godoy, to share Portuguese territories. The ruling Braganza family fled to Brazil with their court, their navy protected by a British squadron. Next Napoleon turned on Spain, his supposed ally, pouring in men to garrison key forts, and in March 1808 the French prompted a revolt against the Bourbon monarchy, during which Charles IV was forced to abdicate in favour of his son Ferdinand. But when the Spanish royal family were lured to Bayonne at the end of April, suspicion flared and the popular mood turned. On 2 May an uprising broke out in Madrid, suppressed with hideous violence, as Goya showed in his paintings of the charge of the Mamelukes and the shootings of 3 May. On 10 May Ferdinand and his brothers agreed to their father's decision to renounce the crown of Spain, now at Napoleon's disposal. Three weeks later, Napoleon proclaimed his elder brother Joseph to be the new king of Spain.

Soon rebellions broke out across the country, like scattered fires.[2] British men-of-war gathered off Cadiz. Aboard the *Sultan*, Tom Gill – now a first lieutenant – wrote to his sisters in the Isle of Wight in dashing rhetorical style: 'Thus is the Spanish monarchy levelled with the dust, and the genius of Bonaparte treads on the necks of another nation, and thus are seven millions more added to the unhappy wretches that bend beneath his accursed tyranny.'[3] Tom enclosed copies of Ferdinand's abdication speech and assorted addresses to the Spanish people, 'given me by the Captain to copy' – trophies for the family to circulate at home.

On George III's birthday, 4 June 1808, a day of deluging rain, people talked of little else apart from Spain. Sarah Spencer, writing to her midshipman brother Bob, vowed not to mention it, comparing herself to her irascible, bluestocking grandmother:

But I will say, like Grandma Lucan when she has talked about Buonaparte till at last she fancies he stands before her, with two heads and a long tail, 'I never will talk politicks, I protest; I never do indeed think of them; the Lord preserve us all! That's all I can say,' and then begins again directly about the Spanish Revolution . . .[4]

As Sarah said a few days later, the town 'is full of nothing but Spain, and Spanish patriots'. A delegation from the rebels in Asturias was in London, headed by the Vizconde de Materosa, 'a little, fair, fattish lad' according to Mary Berry.[5] Their visit whipped up enthusiasm, with *The Times* demanding immediate help for Spain and the Asturian deputies being hosted night and day by London grandees, although society women were struck less by their eloquence than the remarkable good looks of Materosa's aide, the olive-skinned Andrea de la Vega, 'whom everybody but me calls the green man', said Sarah.

While the delegates were in London, Sheridan gave an emotional and widely reported speech in the Commons saying that he was sure the flame of rebellion would spread, and that Britain must now act to help the Spanish: there never was 'so great an opportunity and occasion for this country to strike a bold stroke, which might end in the rescue of the world'.[6] So far, he went on, when British Governments 'should have been aiming a blow at the heart of France, there was always something else to distract the attention': instead they had been 'always employed in filching for a sugar island, or some other object of comparatively trifling moment'. Now was the time to change. The Spanish uprisings showed that a country could overthrow a tyrant, as Gillray suggested in his print of a gored Napoleon hurtling through the air in *The Spanish Bull-Fight*. Even women's magazines like *La Belle Assemblée* ran articles on the proud Spanish character and fine Spanish fashions. But, wary of their experience with the French troops, the Asturian delegation asked for money, arms and equipment, but not men. In response British plans changed – instead of going to Spain, the troops would head for Portugal, to drive out Junot's army.

Nine thousand British soldiers were already waiting in barracks at Cork, originally gathered to sail to Venezuela, to help an insurrection against the Spanish.[7] Now new instructions came. On 12 July 1808, under the command of Arthur Wellesley, trailing clouds of glory from India and Copenhagen, the men marched on to the transports and set sail for the Iberian peninsula.

Recruiting was fierce again. In Manchester, James Weatherley reckoned that forty or fifty different recruiting parties were stalking the town, who 'would trap all they could, they would Enlist them either asleep or awake'. The new troops mustered three times a week

Gillray, *The Spanish-Bull-Fight, – or – The Corsican-Matador in Danger*,
11 July 1808. Napoleon is tossed and Joseph Bonaparte trampled,
watched by George III, on the left, and other rulers, with the Pope,
the Sultan of Turkey and the Dey of Algiers

outside a pub, to be handed jackets, breeches and leggings 'all of
one size same for a Six feet man as a five foot man, some of their
breeches were as tight as a glove and some as slack as a shirt'. They
set off not to cheers but to weeping. 'I have seen them on the going
off day', Weatherley wrote, 'followed by hundreds of men women
and children lamenting and crying for they took fathers of familys
as well as single men some would go east some west some north and
south followed by friends and relatives for a few miles out of town
heartrending to see them Parting never to meet again which was too
often the case.'[8]

Thousands of men signed up for the militia, army and navy, often
through need. Two young Rowbottoms, Thomas and John, joined the
Royal Marines, with forty local men. Meeting at the 'sign of the Nelson', they set off for Woolwich followed by 'a large number of spectators and amongst them a deal of females who testified their sorrow by
a large flow of tears. The music played over the hills and far away.'[9]

The Rowbottom boys joined the marines on board the seventy-four-gun *Saint Domingo* in the Downs: and from now on Rowbottom took a keen interest in naval matters, noting every movement of the ship, taking down details from the papers and copying notes about ships from the *Traveller* magazine.

As Secretary of State for War, Castlereagh was determined to organise the military more efficiently. He sharpened up the line regiments with light infantry units, and restructured promotion, then introduced a Local Militia Act to simplify the patchwork of troops and make them more subject to central control. The Act's name was confusing, as it was not concerned with the existing militia but with forming a more organised version of the old volunteers: men would be balloted to serve for four years with as little interruption to their normal jobs as possible, with short annual training, exemption from the militia ballot, and a small payment. The novel clause was that they could transfer to the regular army for a bounty if they wished.

It was a flexible, popular move, and a brilliant conduit for army recruitment, with around ten thousand men transferring to the regulars each year. But it was the end of the glory days of the local troops: thirteen thousand small volunteer corps were replaced by some 270 units of local militia.[10] Two years later, Henry Howard of Corby Castle in Cumberland wrote in hurt tones to Lord Lonsdale about the move from the Cumberland Rangers into the local militia:

I trust government, if they no longer deem our services useful, will have the generosity to tell us so direct, & not make us feel it by inference, & that we may lay down our arms, if so wished, with the honours of war; & not give the men, with the public and in our own minds, the reproach of not fulfilling the pledge which at their call in April 1803, we made to serve as long as it was of use to the Country, during this war.[11]

And what about their uniform – which was expensive and meant to last – did it belong to the corps, or to the men? At the same time James Longsdon junior was drilling on dusty roads with the new Chatsworth Local Militia at Buxton. 'We have neither time to rest ourselves, or any thing else,' he wrote home, 'but I should never mind the duty were all the Companies more regular with their exact numbers of Men, Lists, Paying &c.'[12]

For all Castlereagh's efforts the situation was still chaotic, as Longsdon implied. When John Clare was eighteen and – in his not always reliable memory – 'the country was chin deep in the fears of invasion and every mouth was filled with the terrors which Buonaparte had spread in other countrys', he signed up for the local militia for the bounty of £2. As his troop left Helpston, he wrote later, 'our mothers parted with us as if we was going to Botany Bay and people got at their doors to bid us farewell and greet us with a sort of Jobs comfort that they doubted we shoud see Helpstone no more'. In fact they simply marched the few miles to Oundle, drilled for three weeks and drank every night:

I was one of the shortest and therefore my station is evident I was in that mixed multitude calld the battalion which they nick named 'bum tools' for what reason I cannot tell the light company was calld 'light bobs' and the granadiers 'bacon bolters' these were the names given to each other who felt as great an enmity against each other as ever they felt for the French

Absent-minded and clumsy, his head full of his poems, Clare fought with a corporal who taunted him, getting off lightly with an extra turn of guard duty. A year later he volunteered for extended service, earning an extra five shillings, which he took 'without further enquiry and never heard further about it'.

While the army, militia and volunteers were regrouping, the gunmakers hurried to make more arms. The Ordnance factories and private contractors were already overstretched, having increased their output the year before to help the allies, desperate for arms: in April 1807 Prussia alone requested forty howitzers and cannon, ten thousand muskets, three million ball cartridges and one hundred thousand flints. All this was packed off within a month.[13] Now many thousands more small arms were needed, and in the next two years the Birmingham gunsmiths would produce over a million gun barrels and locks. In the same period, to meet the demand for gunpowder for field guns and ships, the East India Company doubled its imports of saltpetre from India, to over twelve thousand tons.[14] At the huge depot at Weedon Bec the upper rooms of the storehouses were fitted with stands for muskets so that the armouries could hold a hundred thousand guns at a time. The ground-floor rooms, with special window guards, were for the 'Field Brigades' of heavy brass guns and the iron-framed gun-wagons that were dragged up the roads from Woolwich – six horses to each gun.

Twenty-three transports landed supplies and soldiers at Mondego Bay on the Portuguese coast on 5 August. The soldiers were not alone: Wellesley's campaign orders noted that there 'shall be six women to every hundred men and these shall be drawn by lot before embarkation . . . The women shall be on half rations and no wine however salt the meat.'[15] The proportion of men to women echoed the General Orders for Troops Destined for Continental Service issued the year before, which also decreed that 'They should be carefully selected, as being of good character and having the inclination and ability to render themselves useful'.[16] News of the army's progress reached London through despatches, but also – sometimes sooner – through letters from the *Times* correspondent Henry Crabb Robinson, who had already supplied the paper's editor, John Walter, with news of the fall of Danzig and the Peace of Tilsit. Now he went ahead of the troops, landing in Corunna a week before the army reached Portugal. Only four days after the army arrived, Walter was printing a first letter from 'Shores of the Bay of Biscay'.

Soon after he landed Wellesley defeated the French at Roliça, then came down to the shore to protect the reinforcements arriving from sea. On 21 August the battle on the hills of Vimeiro took place almost in full view of the fleet. 'Sent all the boats on shore to assist in taking off the wounded of our army to the hospital ships,' wrote Francis Austen in the log of the *St Albans*. 'Boats also employed in embarking French prisoners on board some of the transports.'[17] 'To be sure', wrote an excited Sarah Spencer on 3 September, 'Every detail of these Portugueze battles adds fresh glory to the name of Sir Arthur

Wellesley and his brave troops. We all talk of little else today, as the London details are arrived.'[18] But then Wellesley was superseded by new commanders, Sir Harry Burrard and Sir Hew Dalrymple. In their jostling to claim the glory, instead of accepting Junot's early offer of capitulation they left him time to negotiate. Under the Convention of Cintra that followed, twenty-six thousand French troops were sent home – in Royal Navy ships – with all their arms and booty. The deal roused fury in Britain at the generous treatment of the enemy and the betrayal of loyalties to Portugal and Spain. *The Times* hoped that 'A curse, a deep curse' might 'wring the heart and wither the hand that were base enough to devise and execute this cruel injury on their country's peace and honour', and demanded the condemnation of all involved.[19] Sarah Spencer's pen rattled with anger: 'We are full today of this deplorable news from Portugal. What a shameful piece of work that stupid Sir Hew Dalrymple has made of the capitulation!'[20] There were rumours of corruption, of deals behind closed doors, and Dalrymple, Burrard and Wellesley were summoned home to an inquiry.

Wordsworth wrote a dogged, Miltonic pamphlet attacking the government for their lack of respect for the spirit and bravery of the Spanish uprising – a rebellion that showed the true spirit of liberty – and insisting that the Convention displayed the British generals and government as 'abject, treacherous, and pernicious'.[21] His pamphlet had little impact; it was too late, too wordy, too unvaried, 'all in hot tints', thought Coleridge, 'the apple pie is made only of quinces.'[22] But the anger it expressed did not fade: 'Britannia sickens, Cintra! at thy name', wrote Byron in *Childe Harold* four years later.

And now there was a new voice of criticism, the *Examiner*, started by the publisher John Hunt, who brought in his twenty-three-year-old brother Leigh, a clerk in the War Ministry, as editor. Leigh Hunt's first book of poems, *Juvenilia*, published when he was fifteen, had caused a stir and since 1805 he had been writing weekly theatrical reviews for John's first paper, the *News*. The *Examiner* was selling over two thousand copies by the end of the year with its 'liberty-loving, liberty-advocating, liberty-eloquent articles'.[23] Its stand on Cintra was clear:

it was another example of military laziness and corruption. Why had no one been recalled? In fact the government backed the Convention, even laying down the terms, in their determination to get the French out of the peninsula so that the British could install a government in Lisbon. The official inquiry concluded that Burrard and Dalrymple had pushed it through in the face of Wellesley's opposition, a face-saving tactic that deceived no one, but let Wellesley keep his command.

While Wellesley was in London, Sir John Moore took command of the British army, now thirty thousand strong. Leaving a third of these behind in Lisbon, Moore marched north, following orders to join another contingent in Corunna and to co-operate with the Spanish armies. But by the autumn, alarmed by Junot's defeat in Portugal, Napoleon himself had arrived in Spain with a gigantic force of two hundred thousand troops. The prospect of British and Spanish success looked fainter.

Yet war-threatened Spain still drew the British. Lord Holland and his spirited wife Elizabeth, with Lord John Russell, were currently travelling across the Peninsula, deluging the British government at home with unwelcome advice and suggestions. Restless young men yearned to go there. In 1807 Tertius Galton had married Violetta, the youngest daughter of his father's old friend Erasmus Darwin, and at the end of November 1808 Tertius said goodbye to his brother Theodore, the Galtons' impulsive, warm-hearted middle son, who set off for Spain with Violetta's brother Sacheverel Darwin. Their trip, Sacheverel explained later, was 'induced by the impulse of a generous spirit to contemplate the exertions of a people struggling for their liberty'.[24] From Falmouth, the two young men would sail 'in the first packet to Corunna', said Lucy Galton:

hoping to see Madrid – the Alhambra at Granada – & Seville – & see Portugal likewise, in an Episode. They mean to pay their respects to the Knights at Malta – & to Mt Aetna in Sicily. But a little more formidable mountain is, I fear, in the way – it is Bonaparte! I think it is probable now, that they may re-embark at Corunna, & go by sea to Oporto; keeping out of harms way. Tho' perhaps it might be said now, as it was by Cicero formerly to a friend of his, who had hid himself to avoid Caesar – 'why do you think of being more secure in a Village in Asia – it is as well to come to Rome: Caesar is everywhere!'[25]

Corunna was certainly no place to head for in the winter gales of 1808. It was melancholy, wrote Sarah Spencer, to think of Napoleon 'and the horrible number of his best Generals he is stuffing Spain with'.[26] She dreamed of a stray bullet striking him, and everything going back to the way it was:

Then comes peace – long quiet peace. All ports open; no privateers to prevent coasting excursions, no expeditions, no fleets to be stationed God knows where; poor sea captains *obliged* to live at home; perhaps a journey over to Paris possible (which I own I should like vastly); no taxes to grumble at, no grievances to complain of. In short, my dream is beautiful, I assure you, quite beautiful; and I weave it over and over again, with all sorts of pretty things embroidered on it.

It was, as she said, a dream. The French took Madrid and drove Moore's expeditionary force north through the mountains. Although a retreat was the only way to save the army, the men were sullen and dispirited and spent the last stage of their trek in a frenzy of looting. When they reached Corunna in January 1809 they found the bay almost empty, with only a couple of dozen transports and two warships lying at anchor. The fleet despatched to take them home had been held back by adverse winds. In a desperate defensive battle, Moore was killed. His dying words were repeated throughout the British press: 'You know that I have always wished to die this way.' He knew that he had saved his army, at least for the moment. 'I hope the people of England will be satisfied,' he said, 'I hope my Country will do me justice.'[27] He was buried in the ramparts, and when the French took the town Marshal Soult himself ordered a monument over his grave. From then on 'Avenge Sir John Moore!' became a Peninsula rallying cry.

When the fleet finally arrived the British embarked silently, leaving behind those too badly wounded to move. Over twenty-five thousand exhausted men were crammed on to the transports. On shore, teams shot the limping cavalry horses that had survived the march, and blew up thousands of barrels of gunpowder, the huge explosion rocking the town like an earthquake. A small British rearguard held the citadel, not surrendering until the ships were safely out to sea. Francis Austen was at Spithead, as Jane told Cassandra. 'The St Albans perhaps may soon be off to help bring home what may remain by this time of our poor Army, whose state seems dreadfully critical.' She had less sympathy for Moore, whose dying words made no mention of his mother and lacked any religious note, and, she added briskly, 'Thank Heaven! we have no one to care for particularly among the Troops, no one, in fact, nearer to us than Sir John himself.'[28]

In February 1809 the last British merchants and their families in Portugal sailed home. On board ship, Harriot Slessor, whose father had been a Lisbon merchant and whose husband had served in the Portuguese army and been Governor of Oporto, recorded in her diary the chaos, emotional partings, and last views of the pine-covered hills. As she sailed over the bar, she looked back to the family's final Portuguese Christmas, when their ferocious turkey was slaughtered:

My young grandchildren had an idea that whatever came under the denomination of cruel must resemble Bonaparte; therefore they had given him that name, and for his crime had condemned him to death, for the many murders he had committed in cold blood. The sentence was confirmed by upright judges, and when the cruel tyrant was not suspecting any harm, strutting in great glory, and displaying his sleek and shining plumage in the bright sun, the wretch was seized and his head struck off with as little mercy as he had shown to others. The joy at his death was as great as if Bonaparte had fallen.[29]

In the middle of the Bay of Biscay Harriot's daughter Sophia gave birth to her third son, his arrival announced by the captain with a blast of his trumpet. The refugees were just in time. When Soult sacked Oporto on 29 March, the piled-up bodies rose above the waters of the Douro.

In April, cheering news arrived that a French fleet, on its way to supply the Peninsular troops, had been driven ashore by Cochrane's fireships in the Basque Roads off La Rochelle. The raid thrilled the public, but Cochrane was a daring maverick already at odds with the Admiralty. When he accused his commanding officer, Admiral Gambier, of not pressing home the attack, Gambier demanded a court martial to clear his name: Cochrane's naval career was finished. Meanwhile army agents and contractors had been busy gathering supplies for the new troops for Spain. The list drawn up by the Horse Guards in May showed how many things they needed: round tents with poles and pins and mallets, colour flags, powder bags, drum cases, billhooks and axes, 'Flanders kettles' and wooden water canteens, blankets, haversacks and corn sacks, bridles and nosebags for the horses, medical supplies and even a complete 'Hospital marquee and tent', at a costly £45 10s 10d.[30]

Wellesley was back in Spain that month, and the papers soon reported the defeat of Soult at Oporto and Jourdan's army at Talavera. On 4 September Wellesley was created Viscount Wellington and then Baron Douro.[31] Letters home, however, told of arguments and looting, makeshift hospitals, bloodshed and savagery. In many households brief notes arrived, notification of the death of a son or a husband, perhaps with a chit for a few shillings' pay. And often the news entered people's consciousness in strange ways. Robert Chambers, a child in 1809, remembered how in the closes and thatched cottages of Peebles, in the Scottish Borders, 'news circulated at third or fourth hand', or became oddly entwined with religious or other topics. He and his brother William listened to an elderly relative singing ballads and telling stories where 'the battle of Corunna and other prevailing news was strangely mingled with disquisition on the Jewish wars'. The Jewish history was derived from an old translation of Josephus, belonging to one Tam Fleck 'who, not particularly steady at his legitimate employment, struck out a sort of profession by going about in the evenings with his Josephus, which he read as the current news. "Weel Tam, what's the news the nicht", they would say – "Bad news, bad news," replied Tam, "Titus has begun to besiege Jerusalem, it's gaun to be a terrible business."'[32]

# 46. SCANDALS, FLANDERS AND FEVERS

The war in Spain caused violent splits: government supporters saw Wellington as a hero and urged support; manufacturers and workers, despairing of the Orders in Council, clamoured for peace. There were arguments in clubs, rows over dinner tables and fist fights in inns. In October 1808, in the *Edinburgh Review*, Francis Jeffrey argued strongly for appeasement, and Walter Scott's fury at this spurred him to join the publisher John Murray in founding the Tory *Quarterly Review* in March 1809, to press for backing of the war. Scott pulled in friends like Richard and Reginald Heber and Robert Southey, and wrote much of the first issue himself. Scott's obsession with the Peninsula was so intense, wrote his son-in-law and biographer John Lockhart,

that he never on any journey . . . omitted to take with him the largest and best map he had been able to procure of the seat of war; upon this he was perpetually poring, tracing the marches and counter-marches of the French and English by means of black and white pins; and not seldom did Mrs. Scott complain of this constant occupation of his attention and her carriage.[1]

In early 1809, when the *Quarterly Review* was launched, it was hard to support the government. The cries of mismanagement that had greeted the Convention of Cintra grew even louder after the retreat from Corunna. This barrage had been building for some time. Some months before, General John Whitelocke, who had conducted the negotiations for withdrawal from the River Plate, had been court-martialled and dismissed.[2] His trial – unlike Popham's – roused little outrage. Instead, a band of critics, led by Leigh Hunt in the *Examiner*, launched a campaign against military incompetence and bought commissions:

A young gentleman wishes to be a soldier – I beg pardon, an officer – and if he is asked what talents he possesses for command, the answer is quite ready, 'Sir I have some hundred pounds in my pocket'. It is this system which together with the dilatory privileges of seniority and the gross favouritism of the higher powers, has rendered the finest soldiers as useless as straws and shed the blood of hundreds of my gallant countrymen.[3]

The prescient Hunt also pointed to the failings of the Duke of York, the Commander in Chief, who 'maintains his mistresses upon the sale of commissions'.

Finding money to pay for commissions was a perpetual anxiety. Among the correspondence pouring into Hoare's bank were scratchy, heavily underlined letters from Lady Mansfield, worrying about Henry, her youngest son by her first marriage. 'I am particularly circumstanced from my son the Captn H. Murray's not being of age till after he went abroad,' she explained, '& am most anxious not to lose any opportunity which may offer for his Promotion':

He has now served the time allotted for advancement to a majority, & in recommending him to be on His Royal Highness the Commander in Chief's *List* for *Promotion* it is necessary to state the Money is ready, but tho' he has the money . . . I find myself under some difficulty how to act . . . unless you would have the goodness to advance the sum.

She needed £2600, and when the partners agreed she wrote with overflowing thanks, while warning them that any future promotion would mean more cost. And there were plenty more promotions to come as Henry climbed his way up, becoming a lieutenant colonel, leading the charge of the 18th Hussars at Waterloo, and ending up as a general.[4]

Stories of the cash needed to get on to promotion lists gradually flared into a scandal. In the autumn of 1808 the *Examiner* noted

Major Denis Hogan's pamphlet, an *Appeal to the Public*, in which he put his lack of promotion down to a refusal 'to kiss the petticoat'. Quoting Hogan, Hunt damned the military system as 'a dastardly carcass of corruption, full of sottishness and selfishness, preying upon the hard labour of honest men', and laid the blame squarely on the Duke of York as 'the promoter and foster-father, if not the begetter, of these corruptions'. The duke ordered a prosecution for libel, but the jury acquitted the Hunt brothers. Then in January 1809, the papers carried a report that Gwyllym Lloyd Wardle, MP for Okehampton, had laid charges before parliament that the Duke of York had colluded with his mistress, the notoriously extravagant Mary Anne Clarke – 'a damned mercenary bitch', in Cobbett's view – to sell commissions. The duke had ditched Mary Anne in 1805, keeping her sweet with a pension: when he failed to pay up in mid-1808 she spoke out, and after Wardle's accusations the Commons set up an inquiry.

In late January 1809, like a judgement from heaven, melting snow caused huge floods in the Thames valley, washing away bridges at Eton and Windsor and inundating Deptford and Lewisham. But on 1 February the headlines abandoned the swollen river for the scandalous duke. The public were agog at the reports of the committee hearings, especially the appearances of Mary Anne herself, confessing all charges and roundly implicating the duke: she received many notes asking for intimate meetings. 'There is not an Englishman but must blush to see how the best interests of the army have been sacrificed to an inglorious dalliance,' announced the *Staffordshire Advertiser*, one of a chorus of provincial papers.[5] There were plenty of good scandals in the papers that month, including the elopement of Lady Charlotte Wellesley, Wellington's sister-in-law, married with four young children, who ran off with Lady Jersey's husband, Lord Paget. But the inquiry topped this. 'Everybody was scandalized as they ought to be with the dreadful *esclandre* of Lord Paget and Lady Charlotte Wellesley,' Sarah Spencer told her brother in late March, 'but everybody has almost forgotten it as it happened a good ten days ago, and nothing is now talked of but this endless debate.'[6] The affair was the talk of the town:

'Thousands of ballads, caricatures, lives, of Mrs Clarke in every blind alley,' Charles Lamb exclaimed.[7]

It took six weeks for the Commons to try to work out how much the duke knew and although he was cleared of corruption, he resigned as Commander in Chief, only to be reinstated two years later.[8] By now Mary Anne had printed twenty thousand copies of her memoirs, and her solicitors were still holding on to the duke's letters: for returning these she won a settlement of £7000, an annuity of £400, and payment for her own son's education and, with neat irony, for his military commission. Yet this 'nonsensical business', as Lamb called it, made a crucial point: with Britain at war, corruption in the military put the whole country in danger. Cobbett filled the *Political Register* with transcripts of the Clarke evidence, enraged that British soldiers were dying under inexperienced officers who had bought their commissions, while others argued that people should challenge the 'slavery' of soldiers, just as they had fought for the abolition of the slave trade itself. As well as damning official corruption, Burdett, Cobbett and the Hunts pointed to issues like flogging to argue that the government and military establishment were betraying the very people who fought for them.

George Cruikshank's aristocrats fling Clarke's memoirs on the flames: 'Now the country will never hear of this intrigue – a Devilish expensive one tho'.

The authorities were rattled. Their subsidised papers denounced Cobbett as a spy and a traitor who ill-treated his own farm workers, and a pamphlet repeating these charges was distributed free, placed in piles in taverns and handed out to all who would take it. Gillray launched a brilliantly pointed attack in eight plates, *The Life of William Cobbett, Written by Himself*, managing to show him as 'a vain, boastful and cowardly renegade whose own words condemned him'.[9] Sarah Spencer began to despair of the ferment, where 'everybody now is either an alarmist or a reformer':

Everybody is in a constant fury. Your true alarmist, generally possessing a snug, sinecure place, or a tight little pension in a corner, keeps on screaming and howling over the danger of the nation: revolutions beginning, a set of young hot-headed boys attacking every part of the Constitution, and all sorts of 'phantoms of danger, death or dread,' are always swimming before his eyes; and he would have everything hushed up, smothered, and forgotten, always excepting the payment of his salary. Your reformer, on the contrary, is poking into all the dirty corners, routing out corruptions and abuses, till of course he gets into such a rage of disgust that he stops at nothing.[10]

*

In March, responding to his schoolboy son John Howard's request for news, Samuel Galton told him about the final days of the Clarke inquiry, and then added: 'Buonaparte has returned to Paris, & it is reported that his Troops are recalled, & that a War between France & Austria is about to break out – this his Conduct towards Spain renders highly probable.'[11] This was true. In the spring, taking advantage of French troops leaving for Spain, the Austrians went on the offensive, and formed a new, fifth, coalition. On 10 April, in freezing rain, they invaded Bavaria. Startled, Napoleon counter-attacked, driving the Austrians north across the Danube and taking the capital, Vienna, for a second time, at the start of May.

Portland's cabinet bristled with quarrels over strategy. Canning, as Foreign Secretary, wanted to concentrate all efforts in the Peninsula; Castlereagh, as Secretary for War, wanted to move into northern Europe, to help the Austrians. Castlereagh prevailed, and while Wellington was driving his troops north through Portugal that summer, a huge expedition set out for Flanders. The troops gathered in Portsmouth, where the dockyard was bursting with work, taking on more men and more clerks, like John Dickens from the Navy Pay Office in London. Even at this level a career depended on patronage, and Dickens had got his post through his father's employer, John Crewe, a friend of Canning and Sheridan, who had now taken over Canning's role as Treasurer of the Navy. Dickens was married to Frances, whose father, Thomas Barrow, had also worked in the Pay Office at Somerset House, and he walked into the busy dockyard each day from their small terraced house. Soon they had a daughter, Fanny, and a son, Charles.

Sarah Spencer, on her way to a holiday in Ryde this July, was amazed by the Portsmouth streets, a perpetual din of bells ringing, organs grinding, crockery shops, fair booths, puppet shows and drunken crowds. Grand ships of the line and dozens of small craft filled the harbour, and the town was full of soldiers waiting to board them. But at last, on 25 July, she wrote, 'the expedition sailed magnificently this morning. How thankful we are that we have no relations in it! For Heaven knows where it will go, what it will do, or when it will return; it is the largest ever sent out, they say.'[12] It was indeed the largest: 43,700 troops were heading to Walcheren island at the mouth of the Scheldt. What they would do, it was hoped, was attack the dockyards and arsenals of Antwerp and Flushing, seize the French vessels anchored there, and halt Napoleon's ambitious shipbuilding plans. Six hundred ships, large and small, including 226 ships of the line, customs cutters and even a packet ship, *The City of London*, landed the troops on the island. On 13 August Flushing surrendered to the British after a long bombardment. 'His Majestys ship Saint Domingo, Capt Gill, with Sir Richard John Strachan, led the attack against the baterrye,' wrote Rowbottom proudly. 'She had no man killed,' he added with relief, thinking of the two Rowbottom boys on board.[13]

Captain Pilkington of Weedon Bec, promoted to lieutenant colonel in the Royal Engineers, went to Flushing with the British troops, leaving Thomas Lepard in charge of the Ordnance Works. At the last minute the Board had ordered 22,000 muskets to supply the expedition and Lepard called on all the local canal carriers, including the innkeeper Thomas Barnett, who was responsible for 476 cases with 9,520 muskets.[14] Barnett heard that he could save a day's travel if he carried on down the new canal link to Brentford, rather than heading for Paddington Basin, and this would have been a good plan, had it not been for a violent thunderstorm and torrential rain in the early hours of 27 July, a day before the troops were due to leave. In the darkness and rain Barnett's barge ran aground, springing a leak and sinking: seven thousand muskets were damaged. Accepting that it was the urgency that caused Barnett's accident, the Ordnance Board paid the haulage costs and salvaged, repaired and oiled the muskets at the Tower, putting them into service at once in case they rusted. From now on the Ordnance turned to a national carrying company, Messrs Pickford of London.

The muskets were sent to Flanders, where the British campaign was stalled. The French fleet had moved to Antwerp and reinforcements had rushed to strengthen the port's defences. The troops stayed camped on Walcheren, awaiting orders. As they waited on the swampy island, attacked by swarms of mosquitoes, they fell ill: by September 8,200 men were in temporary hospitals in houses, churches and warehouses, shivering with fever, malaria and typhus, their sickness made more fatal by dysentery. In Oldham,

a letter was received from Flushing giving a dreadful account of the sickness and deaths in that country and amongst the deaths are James Woolstonecroft late of Maygate Lane and —— Bates of Oldham, both of the 52nd Regiment . . . they died of a fever wich has made great ravages in the British Army who went in the late expedition to the islands of Zealand.[15]

Benjamin Harris, who felt the effects of the Walcheren fever all his life, remembered seeing riflemen shaking so much that they could hardly walk, lying groaning in rows in a barn, 'amongst the heaps of lumpy black bread they were unable to eat'.[16]

The delay that kept the ailing army in the swamps was due to a new reversal: in July 1809, just as the British were celebrating news of Talavera and the siege of Flushing was under way, Napoleon had trounced the Austrian army at Wagram. The new coalition was over. And at home there was more scandal. In August the Prime Minister, Portland, suffered a stroke and offered to resign, but the king refused to release him. The following month the leaderless cabinet was thrown into chaos. Knowing Portland's weakness, the clever, confident Canning schemed to take his place. He had already won Portland's promise to move his rival Castlereagh from the War Office and when Castlereagh discovered this, he called Canning out. He was a crack marksman, while Canning – the only commoner in Portland's government – had never held a pistol. On Putney Heath in the clear dawn of 21 September their first shots missed, but Castlereagh insisted on a second, wounding Canning in the thigh and losing only a coat button himself. When his father heard the news he thanked Providence and damned Canning as having 'a mind replete with as much political deceit and falsehood as if bred in the school of Bonaparte'.[17] Both men resigned as Secretaries of State. The duel was kept out of the press, but the news whistled across country. From Grasmere, where he was staying with the Wordsworths and trying to edit his own paper, *The Friend*, Coleridge wrote to Daniel Stuart:

We are all greatly dejected by the present state of men & measures, & the utter hopelessness of better – Good God! What a disgrace to the nation – a *Duel* between two Cabinet Ministers on Cabinet Disputes!! And not a Breathing of its hideous Vulgarity & Immorality in any one of the Papers! – Is it possible, that such minds can be fit to govern?[18]

The loss of Canning made warmongering Tories spit. 'I suppose the Whigs will come in like a land-flood, and lay the country at the feet of Buonaparte for peace,' Walter Scott fumed, and '. . . to this you are to add all the Burdettites, men who, rather than want combustibles, will fetch brimstone from hell.'[19]

*

In September British troops began to withdraw from Flanders. Captain Pilkington, wounded during the siege of Flushing, stayed on while the main body of troops sailed home. When the order came for the last troops to leave, Pilkington took charge of wrecking Flushing's sea defences and arsenal. Soon after his return he married and became Commanding Royal Engineer at Woolwich, leaving Weedon Bec to be managed by Thomas Lepard.

The campaign had been a fiasco. Writing on military strategy, C. W. Pasley estimated the achievement so far as not much more than 'the annihilation of a part or all of our disposable military force', plus 'impotence in all the grand objects of warfare not connected with maritime power; disappointment in all our expeditions, whenever we have aimed at more than the attack of an island; want of confidence on the part of our allies; and a certain degree of contempt on the part of our enemies'.[20]

To add to the dismal outlook, Portland resigned on 4 October 1809: he died at the end of that month. In the vacuum the evangelical Spencer Perceval became Prime Minister, a gift for the print makers with his balding head and pale, skull-like face. When he tried to create a coalition cabinet, no Whigs would serve, so he appointed old Pitt loyalists, with Marquess Wellesley – Wellington's elder brother – as Foreign Secretary, and Hawkesbury as Secretary for War and Colonies. After five refusals he kept his old post as Chancellor of the Exchequer himself. No one expected Perceval's ministry to last.

## 47. GOING TO THE SHOW

As if it were a planned distraction, at this dark point of the war, with fever-weakened troops returning from Flanders and silence from Wellington in Lisbon, Britain plunged into celebrations. The occasion was George III's Jubilee on 25 October 1809. For weeks local papers had advertised special lamps and chandeliers and tin sconces to fix 'Jubilee candles' in all windows. Debtors were released, promotions were handed out, and an amnesty was announced for deserters if they agreed to rejoin their ships or regiments. Village choirs sang from church steeples at sunrise, and vicars read prayers for the king, including appeals to 'shield him from the open attacks of his enemies, and from hidden dangers'.[1] Congratulatory addresses were read by country mayors, inscribed in parchment and sent to London.

In the park at Windsor, butchers dressed in blue frocks and silk stockings cut up an ox roast and piled it on to silver plates for the royal party who 'appeared highly pleased with the novelty'. The queen gave a fete at Frogmore, where the trees were hung with coloured lanterns and, as the fireworks ended, 'as it were by magic, on the beautiful piece of water opposite the garden front of the house, two triumphal cars appeared, drawn by two sea-horses each, one occupied by Neptune, and preceded by the other with a band of music'.[2] The volunteers and militia held parades and dinners, toasting the army, since 25 October was also the anniversary of Agincourt, proposing 'A hearty supper, a good bottle, and a soft bed to the man who fights the battles of his country'.

Everywhere local dignitaries, landowners and industrialists served feasts to workers and paupers. The Jockey Club of Oldham laid on a dinner for fifty-nine elderly people, 'and when dinner was over they had each a pint of good ale there ages together amounted to 3,971 years'.[3] Houses were decorated with garlands and evergreens and triumphal arches rose across the streets. Crowds threw crackers and fireworks – one rocket in Canterbury flew through a bedroom window and set fire to a bed.[4] In London the Lord Mayor, Sir Charles Flower, gave every clerk twenty guineas, while the Royal Exchange Insurance Company gave their clerks ten guineas, their messengers five, 'and their engineers and firemen one guinea each'.[5] There was a general amnesty for prisoners of war, apart from the French, and they received money to get home. At Portsmouth nearly seven thousand prisoners were given 'threepence each by Messrs. W. Burridge and Sons, timber merchants': printed cards stated that this was to acknowledge 'the humanity shown to the British sick and wounded after the battle of Talavera'.

A month before, when crowds were buying bunting for the Royal Jubilee, there had been riots at Covent Garden. The previous year, in an appropriately martial accident, a piece of wadding from a gun fired during a performance of the crowd-pleasing *Pizarro* had set fire to the scenery, causing a terrible blaze in which over twenty people died. John Kemble, actor and manager, lost a fortune, but quickly organised the rebuilding, helped by a subscription headed by the Duke of York, the king and the Duke of Northumberland. On 18 September 1809, the new theatre opened with *Macbeth*, to be followed by a farce, *The Quaker*. But though theatregoers gasped at the chandeliers, the classical design and the statues of Greek gods, they were aghast at the hike in prices to pay for the building: the gallery had been turned into enclosed private boxes, costing £300 per year; the side boxes were up from six to seven shillings, the pit from three shillings and sixpence to four shillings. Groans and hisses, howls and jeers greeted Kemble's appearance, and protests shut the theatre completely after only six nights.

The exuberant 'O. P. Wars', demanding 'Old Prices', went on for more than two months, with slogans, banners, 'O.P.' medals, fans and caps. And the people won: after sixty-seven days Kemble put his prices down and made a public apology.[6] But although the riots were, on the whole, light-hearted, they reflected the vital importance of theatre in wartime, not simply as an entertainment, but as a place of patriotic display. There was a mania for putting on plays, in camps, on ships, in market squares and in private houses. The elite complained of the dirty, dusty, noisy theatres, where drink and flying objects tumbled on them from the gallery – orange peel, apples, nuts, glasses and even full bottles – and preferred to put on plays in their own houses. Amateur theatricals flourished, a well-known arena for moral and sexual tension, as Jane Austen showed in the production of *Lovers' Vows* in *Mansfield Park*. (Eugenia Wynne and her friends chose the popular farce *High Life below Stairs*. 'We still continue Play Mad rehearsing very ill and enraging the manager,'

George Cruikshank, *Acting Magistrates*, 18 September 1809. As the magistrates try to read the Riot Act, Kemble stands behind pleading with the placard-waving audience

her diary ran, but it was a success: 'We began it at 10 o'clock this evening and it went off with great éclat and much applause.'[7]) Austen's Fanny Price was very much a woman of her time in disapproving of theatricals on the grounds of lax morality. Evangelicals and dissenters constantly attacked the theatres as haunts of violence and vice. The Methodist minister John Styles declared that if his daughter went to the theatre, 'I should clasp my last child to my bosom, weep at the thought of innocence for ever fled, and mourn the day that made me a parent – her soul is polluted, and that is the essence of prostitution.'[8]

Announcements of plays put on by the militia or army officers often stressed that they were for the benefit of the poor, a defence against such moral outrage. Their audiences could enjoy themselves while basking in their benevolence, and feeling quietly pleased that the takings might keep down their poor rates. Forgetting public charities, benefit nights for actors also continued, happily and rowdily attended, and sometimes accompanied by offstage drama, as Rowbottom recorded:

Last night at the concert wich was for the benefit of Miss Blease & Mr Hilton at the Theatre Room Spread Eagle Oldham wich was very numerously attended by all of the beauty and fashion in the neighbourhood the gallery with one tremendous crash broke down and all fell to the bottom happily no lives were lost nor lymbs broken. Some where brused and the audience was much frightened. Several lost there shalls bonnets &c.[9]

Almost every town had its playhouse but the London theatre was still the great draw. Its lure had grown with the new war: five years before, in April 1804, James Oakes and his sister and niece Susan from Liverpool, his son James, his wife and three servants set off on a snowy morning from Bury St Edmunds. They took lodgings in Conduit Street, off Hanover Square, and since Susan had never been to London they showed her everything: 'St Pauls, Guild Hall, Bank & Tower in the City, the Opera & Play Houses, Sadler's Wells, Westminster Hall, Houses of Lords & Commons, Hyde Park, Kensington Gardens, the Green Park, Merlin's, the Cork Exhibition &ca &ca.'[10]

The Galton family also saw the exhibition of cork models of classical buildings in the 'Great Room, Spring Gardens', and thought them 'remarkably well done'. They were on a whirlwind trip that made Hubert and Adele Galton feel almost ill from so many sights and shows, including *Mother Goose* at Covent Garden, Angelica Catalani at the Opera, and a ballet of the sack of Troy, with dancers sliding down ropes, buildings collapsing and flames rising so that 'You would imagine the Theatre was on Fire'.[11]

The Galtons returned often, and so did James Oakes, who took his daughter Maria or his daughter-in-law Elizabeth to see the plays every year. They were at Drury Lane to see 'young Roscius (Master Betty, 14 years of age) play the arduous part of the Duke of Gloucester in Richard the $3^{rd}$, to the astonishment of most people who were present'. Press reports of the war were briefly rivalled by the obsession with 'the Boy Betty', a child actor who first won fame in Ireland, Scotland and the English provinces. He arrived at Covent Garden to such a rapturous reception that the Guards had to clear the way for the Prince of Wales's coach and fainting women were passed over the heads of the crowd. Pitt had wept at one performance and in 1804 closed the House of Commons early so that MPs could see Betty's Hamlet, a performance James Oakes caught with his sister in Liverpool. 'In this he was very great,' Oakes decided.[12]

The Oakeses' trips also took in Mrs Jordan in *As You Like It* and Sarah Siddons and Kemble in *Henry VIII*.[13] These were the stars everyone wanted. 'We *did* go to the play after all on Saturday,' Jane Austen told Cassandra in April 1811. She was staying with her brother Henry and Eliza in London and they had been to *The Hypocrite*, based on *Tartuffe*, at the Lyceum:

> & were well entertained . . . I have no chance of seeing Mrs Siddons. – She *did* act on Monday, but as Henry was told by the Boxkeeper that he did not think she would, the places, & all thought of it were given up. I should particularly have liked seeing her in Constance, & could swear at her with little effort for disappointing me.[14]

Thomas Perronet Thompson was also a Siddons fan, feeling he could die happy 'having seen The Stranger with Mrs Siddons & John Kemble'.[15] A week later, he was trying to get Nancy into Covent Garden 'on the night of Mrs Siddons' departure', but alas, there were no seats to be had. But Thompson admired great clowns and young starlets as much as grand tragedians:

Grimaldi has just had his benefit, & it is greatly to be regretted that he did not make his appearance as Touchstone in As You Like It . . . Now if I thought it would have an effect, I should be tempted to enter into a correspondence with Mr Grimaldi signed A.B. at the Six Clerks Coffee House & recommend it to him . . .[16]

In a short time Thompson himself would be off to the greater stage, the mountains of Spain and the Peninsular War.

The theatre was so popular that Londoners began to complain about the shortage of seats. Amabel Hume-Campbell, who was sixty in January 1811, wrote crossly with her strong, black pen, 'We have not been lucky as to the Plays we most desire & have not been able to get a Private Box yet to see Cato or King John.'[17] She had, however, been twice to see the sensational horses from Astley's Circus on stage in *Bluebeard* at Covent Garden '& think it a fine extraordinary sight'. The following year she saw Charles Kemble as Mark Antony and his brother John as Brutus in a famous production of *Julius Caesar*, admiring the Kembles' acting but deciding that the 'Great Dictator' was '*murder'd* before his fall by Egerton'.[18] And there were still more distractions:

. . . the Dresses in the first Acts, came nearer Antique Status than I had seen before – Indeed some of the Senators & Conspirators were a little puzzled, & could not walk without exhibiting their Legs. But for Charles Kemble & his Brother, I am sure they must have been the whole Day practising at a Pier Glass & adjusting their Togas according to Tommy Hope's *Costume of the Ancients*.

There were other, very different kinds of theatre in the capital, from the hell-raising sermons in churches and chapels to the halfpenny showmen setting up their booths, and the jugglers, tumblers, singers and magicians of the fairs. Spectacle was there too in strange private houses, like the little room in Pentonville where Charles Lamb saw by candlelight 'an exhibition quite uncommon in Europe . . . *A Live Rattle Snake 10 feet in Length*, and of the thickness of a big *Leg*'.[19] On the public plane, Adele Galton was entranced by the show in the parks, where it seemed that the whole world was in costume. She sent careful reports to her young brother, John Howard, of what exactly he should wear if he came to town: small hats, blue coats, primrose-coloured cashmere waistcoats, grey, brown or pepper-and-salt 'inexpressibles' – the new Regency pantaloons and trousers. If, next time she walked in Kensington Gardens, the hot weather had induced them 'to throw off their Wove inexpressibles for white Callico Drawers, I will be sure to tell you'.[20]

Away from the city and the towns the greatest crowd-pulling shows were the money-spinning pedestrian races and illegal boxing matches, which magistrates strove to close down for defying the laws on public meetings. Contests between Irish and English boxers drew noisily partisan crowds but most spectators just came for the thrill and the betting. In 1808 all the 'fancy', the sporting gentry, were waiting for the big fight between the two stars, John Gully and the huge Bob Gregson, the fifteen-stone, six-foot-tall 'Lancashire Giant'. The fans included Sarah Spencer's oldest brother John, Viscount Althorp, a swell who lived for hunting, shooting, racing and boxing. Later, to everyone's surprise, he became a solid reformist politician. Terrified that Althorp would find out, Sarah confessed to her brother Bob that in a moment of carelessness she had given away the site of the match to the disapproving Lord Buckingham at the theatre. Sure enough, next day Buckingham issued an edict, 'got out his bench of magistrates, his *posse comitatus*, his constables, and his Dunstable Volunteers, all in battle array. The peasants thought the French had landed.'[21] To Sarah's relief, the news got out and the match was quietly moved to Hertfordshire. After it Althorp was in heaven, having 'supped and slept at a small waggoner's inn near Dunstable, where likewise supped and slept Mr Gully, Mr Crib, Mr Jackson, and most of the boxing gentry . . . I hear he is in raptures at the fight, in which Mr Gregson threw his antagonist over his head. Must not that have been a sweet spectacle?' The battered Gully went back to his pub, the Plough, in Carey Street, Lincoln's Inn Fields, 'to which place he was conveyed, with all the honours accompanying victory, in the barouche belonging to a nobleman of sporting celebrity'.[22]

Another celebrity was Captain Barclay of Ury – half-brother of Samuel Galton's wife, Lucy, and second cousin to the widespread Gurney family. Over six foot and remarkably handsome, he could lift half a ton, and once 'raised a man weighing 18 stone standing on his right hand and steadied by his left, from the floor to a table'. (Strength ran in the family: his father once 'took up and threw a trespassing donkey over a hedge as he would have done a football'.[23]) Barclay had been in the limelight for a decade, since he beat Ferguson, 'a famous London walking clerk', on a race from Fenchurch Street to Windsor and back in the sweltering summer of 1798. He ran in flannel shirt, flannel trousers, lambswool stockings and thick-soled leather shoes, relaxing afterwards in slippers knitted for him in Norwich by his Quaker aunt Rachel Gurney. He won races every year and attracted stupendous bets of up to two thousand and even five thousand guineas. When the captain was billed to race a professional walker, Abraham Wood, at Newmarket in October 1807, Oakes noted, 'Orbell & wife set off in a chaise to Newmarket Races & to see the foot Race between Cap. Barclay & Wood. NB Wood Gave up abt. Noon.'[24] Henry Angelo was there too, noticing the mutters when Wood gave in after two hours: no one knew why, or 'all but the knowing ones. The blacklegs looked to others as well as their own.'[25] Like Orbell and Elizabeth, Angelo went on to Newmarket races, where he bumped into Byron and his loud student friends. Byron whisked him off to Cambridge, sending orders to St John's College 'for the good beer it was noted for', and handing tumblers to Angelo and Theodore Hook as they left for London, teetering on top of the mail coach. Angelo always remembered his old pupil's nonchalance, 'our parting, the coach driving off, his huzzas, and the twirling of his hat'.

In 1809 Captain Barclay wagered a thousand guineas with Wedderburn Webster 'to go 1,000 miles on foot in 1,000 successive hours, at the rate of a mile in each hour' at Newmarket, beginning on 30 May, with breaks overnight – six weeks of walking.[26] The betting was huge and about £100,000 changed hands. Barclay's only training was sea air and bathing in Brighton, and he set off 'with a lounging gait, making little apparent exertion, and scarcely raising his feet more than two or three inches from the ground'. When he finished, easily the winner, he had lost two stone. He spent next day at Newmarket races, then left for a night out in London. On the following evening, 17 July, he went to Ramsgate, to march off again, joining the expedition to Walcheren.

All these shows were put in the shade by the Royal Jubilee in October. But two months later it was the emperor, not the king, who swept the headlines. On 27 December 1809 Napoleon dissolved his marriage: Josephine was set aside. After escaping assassination in Vienna he had apparently decided he needed an heir, and for this a new wife. But who would he take? His first choice of Duchess Anna of Russia proved difficult – British newspaper readers learned with pleasure that the tsar's mother said she would rather drown both her daughters in the Neva than hand one to Bonaparte. A few weeks later it was announced that he would marry the eighteen-year-old Archduchess Marie-Louise, eldest daughter of the Emperor of Austria. To the alarm of aristocrats everywhere, the 'Corsican upstart' would now be linked with the Hapsburgs, one of the oldest royal families of Europe.

# 48. BURDETT AND PRESS FREEDOM

From 1809 onwards the opposition pressed the government to end the war in the Peninsula, arguing that Portugal was indefensible, Wellington's strategy was feeble and the cost was destroying the economy. In the spring of 1810 eloquent critics like Grey, Sheridan and Samuel Whitbread kept up the attack. Wellington, however, was certain that Portugal could be defended, and that it was vital to concentrate on this, rather than on pressing on into Spain: holding Lisbon would ensure that supplies could reach his army and allow it to fight on while the French forces were weakened. On his retreat to Lisbon the previous autumn he had employed thousands of labourers to build the three defensive lines of the Torres Vedras, controlling all approaches with redoubts and hilltop forts. The people evacuated from beyond the lines poured into the capital in their thousands, leaving scorched earth behind them. The whole scheme was carried out fast, and in relative secrecy, so that when the French returned, entering this barren land, they would be taken by surprise.

The main thing on the public mind, however, was not the Peninsula but anguish over the Walcheren campaign, in which only few men had been killed in conflict but four thousand had died of fever. Thousands more returned home ill and in 1809 the army hospitals admitted around thirty-six thousand men: six new hospitals were built to house them and whole barracks were given over to the sick.[1] Many suffered intermittent fever for years. Yet as soon as they were half fit the convalescents were sent back to war. Many were so weak that in February Wellington asked that no units who had been in Flanders should be sent to him at all.

In the House of Commons on 2 February, during angry debates on Walcheren, Charles Yorke (Agneta Yorke's son and the half-brother of Hardwicke, who had been Pitt's Lord Lieutenant in Ireland after the Union) moved a standing order to clear the press from the public gallery. Backing Yorke, William Windham declared that the reporting of debates was a favour, not a right. The radical London debating club the British Forum then posted up handbills advertising a debate at their next meeting and censuring Yorke's order to clear the gallery as 'an insidious and ill-timed attack upon the Liberty of the Press, as tending to aggravate the discontents of the people, and to render their Representatives objects of jealous suspicion'.[2] The Forum's secretary, John Gale Jones, an old radical orator from the London Corresponding Society and now an MP, was summoned to the Commons and charged with breach of privilege. Although he apologised, Jones was sent to Newgate: three weeks later Yorke was made a Teller of the Exchequer, a sinecure worth £2700 a year.

The hot issue was now one of freedom of speech and the people's right to be heard. In the Commons, Sir Francis Burdett questioned their right to punish Jones, and at the end of March Cobbett published a version of Burdett's speech as an open letter to his Westminster constituents, describing Jones's imprisonment as 'a most enormous Abuse of Power and most dangerous of all encroachments upon the Rights and Liberties of Englishmen'.[3] On 6 April Perceval moved to arrest Burdett for breach of privilege, but delays turned the process into a government nightmare. Burdett barricaded himself into his Piccadilly house, Thomas Cochrane arrived, unhelpfully, with a barrel of gunpowder so he could blow his assailants 'to the devil', and several thousand gathered to support Burdett. After stoning the passing coaches of his aristocratic neighbours the crowd moved on to attack the mansions of his enemies in Parliament: Charles Yorke

LANDSCAPE. Tourists flocked to sketch picturesque scenery, like the snowy mountains of Joshua Cristall's *Borrowdale*. But rural life was harsh, as George Morland showed in *Windy Day*, and many other paintings of the 1790s.

DIARISTS AND LETTER WRITERS. Amabel Hume-Campbell at the time of
her marriage, 1772, Lady Jerningham in old age, and the young
Betsey Fremantle and Sarah Spencer.

Tertius Galton; James Longsdon senior;
William Salmon, and a detail of letter to his wife Fanny.

Rowlandson's depiction of women's enthusiasm in *She will be a Soldier*, outside the King's Head Inn, and of women's despair in his drawing *The Press-Gang*.

In Gillray's *The Death of Admiral Nelson*, Captain Hardy resembles George III and the grieving Britannia Emma Hamilton, in one of her 'attitudes'. By contrast Turner's *The Battle of Trafalgar, as seen from the Mizen Starboard Shrouds of the Victory*, showed the heroic Nelson as one man among many, in the chaos of battle.

WORKING LIVES. John Sell Cotman's view of a busy Norwich market place in 1809; and Turner's scene of men and women in the turnip fields, against the background of Windsor Castle.

In *The Leader of Luddites*, a bearded worker in woman's dress waves men on while the mill burns. Yet industry could not be stopped, and George Walker's *Collier*, 1814 – the first painting of a locomotive – shows a 'steam engine lately invented by Mr Blenkinsop', at a colliery near Leeds.

George Dyer's diary entry describing Napoleon's appearance on the *Bellerophon* before his final exile. A year later, in *The Field of Waterloo*, Turner created a haunting image of the terrible loss of life in the battle, and in the whole war.

and Castlereagh in St James's Square, Lord Chatham in Hill Street, the Duke of Montrose and Lord Westminster in Grosvenor Square, Wellesley at Apsley House.

On the third morning of the riots Burdett saw a constable, balanced on a ladder, peering through his library windows, and heard soldiers break in downstairs: he was arrested reading the Magna Carta to his son, an aptly dramatic scene. He was then taken to the Tower in a coach guarded by six hundred cavalrymen wielding sabres. Watching the crowds in Green Park from the windows of Spencer House, Sarah Spencer told her brother Bob that the riot was not only in Piccadilly, but all over London. She thought she heard guns booming at the Tower:

My Bob, conceive how it made me start to hear the fine, deep distant sound of those great guns. Good heaven! If they have fired at the mob, which they say was 10,000 strong yesterday, besides all those who are now gone with Sir Francis, what horrible execution they must have made! But I hope they may only have thundered at them without ball. We are far from comfortable now, tho' the thing is done, for the people have threatened all sorts of horrors in revenge for their defeat. Well, Heaven keep the black gentry out of this quiet little nook![4]

The guns had not fired, and Burdett, she wrote later, was 'comfortable in the Tower, and neither soldiers nor blackguards are to be seen about the streets. In two more days, I dare say, it will be clean forgotten altogether.' There she was wrong. When Burdett was released from the Tower at the end of the parliamentary session in June vast crowds prepared to greet him. It was a huge, peaceful demonstration, with Burdett's blue colours and cockades, and banners with 'Magna Carta' and 'Hold to the Laws' – but to the dismay of William Hone and others on the organising committee Burdett took a back route and was rowed downriver to Wimbledon. The threatened trouble faded.[5]

One print hailed Burdett as a 'Modern St George Attacking the Monster of Despotism', and from now on the satirical print makers, who had so far aimed squarely at amusing their elite, loyalist market, began to turn on the very people who bought their work, attacking corruption, inequality and greed.[6] Government corruption, argued critics, was accompanied by brutality, even towards the soldiers who served the state. The previous year, in June 1809, mercenaries from the King's German Legion had put down a mutiny among the Cambridgeshires at Ely. Cobbett read the report of the mutineers' court martial in the *Courier*, which noted that the five ringleaders were sentenced to receive five hundred lashes each, adding that 'a stoppage for their knapsacks was the ground of complaint that excited the men to surround their officers, and demand what they deemed their arrears'.[7] The cruelty of militia discipline was well known, and many militiamen transferred to the regular army simply to escape the lash, as Robert Fairfoot and around ninety colleagues did when they moved to the Rifles from the 2nd Royal Surreys. 'I have taken the first opportunity and volunteered,' wrote one man, 'into what regiment I cared not a straw.'[8] But Ely was an exceptional outrage, and after reading the *Courier*'s report, Cobbett wrote a stinging article:

*Five hundred lashes each!* Aye that is right! Flog them: flog them! Flog them! They deserve it, and a great deal more. They deserve a flogging at every meal time . . . Base dogs! What! Mutiny for the *price of a knapsack*? . . . I do not know what sort of place Ely is; but I should really like to know how the inhabitants looked one another in the face, while this scene was exhibiting in their town.[9]

Napoleon's need to lash his troops, he continued, was often cited as showing that the people actually hated the emperor, and would willingly rise against him. So did this apply to Britain as well?

Perceval and his supporters had long been looking for an excuse to silence Cobbett. Now they could charge him with sedition. He was leaning over a gate at his farm at Botley when the writ was put in his hand. 'The beautiful field disappeared, and, in my imagination, I saw the walls of a prison. My blood boiled and cramming the paper into my pocket, I made an oath which I have kept with a little more fidelity than Tories keep their pledges.'[10] For a long time he waited, worried about how Nancy and the children would fare if he was in prison.

Rowlandson, *Libel Hunters on the Look Out*, 12 April 1810. 'The Rotten Borough
Society' trample on Magna Carta, their wall covered with bills about the
*Examiner*, the *Morning Chronicle*, Burdett and 'Enquiries into the
Expedition to Walcheren Quere if not Treason'

Then in early summer, with Burdett safely in the Tower, Perceval
arranged a date for the trial. In court Cobbett was unusually nervous,
disappointing those who had expected fiery speeches. Ellenborough
was the judge and on 15 June 1810, Cobbett was sentenced to two
years in Newgate and a massive fine of £1000. At the end of his
term he would have to give £3000 bail, and two sureties of £1000,
to keep the peace for seven years.

Taking up the same cause, in September Leigh Hunt's *Examiner*
reprinted a graphic article from the *Stamford News* entitled 'One Thousand Lashes!', asserting that even Bonaparte did not treat his troops
so badly. In November, the Hunt brothers too were charged with seditious libel. Although they were acquitted, John Drakard of the *Stamford News* was sentenced to eighteen months in gaol. In the wake of the
Hunts' trial, the nineteen-year-old Percy Bysshe Shelley, who was currently being thrown out of University College, Oxford in a row over
his pamphlet *The Necessity of Atheism*, wrote to Leigh Hunt, addressing

him as 'one of the most fearless enlighteners of the public mind at the present time'.[11] But enlightening the public was proving so dangerous that even *The Times* called for a change in the libel law, arguing that press freedom was essential to make public men accountable to the people. When Henry Holland proposed an inquiry into the Attorney General's power to frame indictments, it turned out that during the past three years there had been forty-two threats of prosecution for libel, compared to fourteen in the previous five years. Many journalists who had not already been bought were intimidated into silence.

# 49. 'BROOKES'S AND BUONAPARTE', CINTRA AND TROY

In March 1810, when *The Times* and the *Courier* were full of Napoleon's lavish marriage celebrations in Paris, and London was recovering from the Burdett riots, the Prince of Wales gave a banquet to all the Knights of the Garter at Carlton House, in rooms ablaze with candles gleaming off brand new silver plate and cut-glass chandeliers.[1] Sarah Spencer's father, who was among the guests, reported on the scene. 'Altogether it was a glorious piece of – what shall I say? – grandeur or nonsense?' wondered Sarah. 'For somehow it makes one laugh, as if it was a parcel of children playing at great people; so proud of their bits of blue ribbon, and their pretty shining playthings all about them. The Royal host worried and toasted himself till he rather clipped the King's English before it was finished.'[2] Two months later, the papers carried a different item of princely news. The Duke of Cumberland's Sardinian valet Joseph Sellis was found in his rooms with his throat cut. Cumberland, nursing a head wound, claimed Sellis had assaulted him and then killed himself: others muttered about rebuffing sexual advances. Until his rooms were shut up, smart ladies went in parties to gasp at the blood stains that covered the bed, the floor and the walls.

The concerns of this circle had not changed: title, family, money, politics, sports and scandals. There were new clubs, fashionable among gamblers, like the Cocoa Tree, and Watier's, opened by the Prince of Wales's chef and patronised by Beau Brummell and the dandies. As Byron had put it sarcastically during his year away from Cambridge in 1807, life was a round of 'Routs, Riots, Balls & Boxing matches, Dowagers & demireps, Cards & Crim-con, Parliamentary Discussion, Political Details, Masquerades, Mechanics, Argyle Street Institution & Aquatic races, Love & Lotteries, Brookes's & Buonaparte, Opera-singers and Orators, Wine, Women, Wax works, & Weathercocks'.[3] The profoundly snobbish quality bridled at the wartime fortunes of industrialists, contractors and City brokers. Even in Whig reforming circles Lady Holland sneered at the brewer Samuel Whitbread. Jane Austen painted the old-fashioned snobbery in *Pride and Prejudice*, in Lady Catherine de Bourgh, and the modern rudeness in the behaviour of Darcy and the Bingley sisters at the Assembly ball. Her readers could recognise this, just as they recognised the allure of the camps and the dangerous charm of Wickham. Maria Edgeworth, too, exposed this world in *Patronage*, published in 1813, the same year as Austen's novel, with its French refugees, soldiers and sailors, gambling and mercenary marriages: it sold out within hours on the day it was published.

But a sober mood now affected the Town. Many aristocratic families were finding the war too long and too alarming as it stretched down to embrace a second generation. Charlotte Knollys, who had waved goodbye to Sir William in the first campaigns, watched her sixteen-year-old son join the Guards in Spain. Sarah Napier, who had helped her husband at Portsmouth during the chaotic mustering of 1794 and had been widowed ten years later, now had four sons in the war: the eldest, Charles, had been captured at Corunna and then freed, and was on Wellington's staff; George and William were fighting in the Peninsula with the 52nd and 43rd regiments, while Henry was a lieutenant in the East Indies. Betsey Fremantle's nephew John, the son of her husband's brother Jack, had joined the Coldstream Guards as a fifteen-year-old ensign in 1805 and was now also in the Peninsula, writing graphic and often scathing letters.[4] Her oldest son,

Tom, was at school, but the second, Charles, joined his father's ship in 1810, aged only ten. 'To my great joy I received a few lines from Fremantle,' she wrote. He was off Cape Finisterre and said that 'Charles was delighted, had not been on board five minutes ere he was at the Mast Head, and that he climbs the Rigging as if he had been at Sea for years'.[5]

Boys not yet born at the start of the first war were joining their ships or marching away as their fathers had done, leaving mothers and sisters at home, nervous of rumours of battles, eager for promotions. Sarah Spencer's delight when her brother Bob was made lieutenant in 1810 was as keen as that of Jane and Cassandra Austen or Sophia and Charlotte Gill when their brothers had been promoted ten years before. 'I must tell you how we all thought of you and drank your precious health, and wished you all possible happiness and blessing from the bottom of our hearts yesterday,' she wrote. 'Well, Heaven bless and protect you, my dearest Lieutenant, Middy, Captain, Admiral, whatever I may live to see you – still my own darling Brother, be the title what it may!'[6] When Lord Mulgrave resigned as First Lord of the Admiralty this year many hopeful men were dismayed since, as Sarah put it, as he 'went out of office without knocking off his whole list of aspirants, which I thought was always done'.

The current ministerial reshuffle finally pushed out Lord Chatham, Pitt's dilatory elder brother, as Sarah noted:

Lord Mulgrave takes his place at the Ordnance, and Charles Yorke comes into the Admiralty; and this being considered as only a little shoving about, but no improvement in the ministry, was describ'd by somebody t'other day, by saying the King had turned his dirty shirt, and thinks he has put on a clean one: which is a very good account of it don't you think?[7]

The 'shoving about' was some balm to Yorke's mother Agneta and to her constant correspondent Amabel Hume-Campbell, who had both been horrified by the smashing of his windows in the Burdett riots.[8] Amabel was also concerned by the changes in social life, like the replacement of tea-drinking by late balls and assemblies, and the shift in the social calendar now that the opening of parliament had moved from the autumn to the New Year and the adjournment to July and August. The Season shifted with it, beginning in January and reaching a climax in early summer. This had one clear convenience, in that it left more time in the autumn for hunting, a relatively new passion, demonstrating courage and dash as well as a complete lack of sympathy for neighbours' fences, let alone foxes. Hunting was pursued with military zeal in the shires. As one devotee said: 'I need not enlarge upon the political advantages of encouraging a sport which propagates a fine breed of horse, and prevents our young men from growing quite effeminate in Bond St., nor upon the high reputation of the English horse abroad, which are perhaps the only cavalry that ever won whole battles against a very superior force.'[9]

Yet manners and appearance, even in hunting circles, had been affected by the evangelical surge. Fashionable dress was still eye-catching but flaunted an assumed modesty, rendering the very visible smart set, as one print put it in an alleged satire on French fashions, 'Les Invisibles'.[10] Men wore sober colours, plain shirts instead of lace, pantaloons instead of knee-breeches, ludicrously high collars instead of cravats; women found the flimsy materials and bare arms of the 1790s were now unthinkable, and swaddled themselves in shawls, frills and bonnets. And their pastimes were more earnest, favouring philosophy and lectures and 'charitable works', and avoiding anything bawdy, opinionated or satirical.

The riots of 1810 rattled the British aristocracy badly because of where they took place, invading their home territory of Piccadilly and St James's. Unruly crowds had stoned them and forced them to put candles in support of Burdett in their windows, and cavalry had been posted at street corners. Cobbett and others were attacking the aristocracy and landed classes as parasites living off the nation, profiting from the war, showing how they influenced elections and made vast sums out of posts, sinecures and fees, patronage, colonies and customs.[11] These, they said, were no patriots. No one felt secure.

Nash's curving Regent Street, blocking off the 'bad streets' to the east

Two years hence, when John Nash revealed his grandiose plan for Regent Street, sweeping from the new Regent's Park down Portland Place and across Piccadilly to Carlton House, it was openly conceived as a boundary dividing the mansions and squares of the elite from the slums of Bloomsbury and the artists and traders of Soho and Leicester Fields. Nash deliberately made it hard to cross the gulf, blocking off streets to the east, aiming to protect 'all the streets occupied by the higher classes and to leave out to the east all the bad streets'.[12] But they could not escape the bad streets.

The impulse of some people was to turn their backs, to get away from Britain altogether, even if it meant travelling through war-ravaged countries. In 1805 Scott's friend Reginald Heber had travelled for a year in Scandinavia and Russia, to Moscow and St Petersburg, down to the Crimea and the Black Sea. Now, in 1809 Byron and Hobhouse were also on their way, heading south rather than north. Over the past two years, ever since Byron's first collection, *Hours of Idleness*, had been savaged in the *Edinburgh Review* (he blamed Jeffrey but the critic was Henry Brougham), he had been writing *English Bards and Scotch Reviewers*, adding more stanzas in each burst of anger. Defending the practice of Pope and Dryden against modern taste he ridiculed the whole literary scene. Everyone felt his barbs: Jacobins and anti-Jacobins, Gothic writers, Scott's minstrels and the Lake poets, including the 'apostate from poetic rule', William Wordsworth,

> Who, both by precept and example shows
> That prose is verse, and verse is merely prose.

When *English Bards* came out in March 1809 to meet a flurry of attacks for its impudence, Byron turned on his heel, borrowed £5,000 from Scrope Davies's gambling winnings, and left England. With Cam Hobhouse and three servants, he sailed from Falmouth to Lisbon. The group's travels took them to Albuera and the leafy calm of Cintra, and then they rode down to Seville and Cadiz, wearing British regimental uniform for safety. In Cadiz, Byron woke on 1 August to hear the bells ringing for the victory at Talavera and to see Wellington's brother, Henry Wellesley, arrive to a rapturous reception as the new British ambassador to Spain – the fourth Wellesley brother to be involved in the war. Then Byron sailed on, past the Cape of Trafalgar and Gibraltar and into the Mediterranean, and on again, to Sardinia, Sicily and Malta, and across to the Adriatic, Albania, Greece and the Turkish coast. In the spring of 1810, while riots were shaking London, Byron's entourage boarded the *Salsette* at Smyrna, heading for Constantinople. As they waited to enter the Dardanelles, held back by storms, Byron went ashore to visit the ruins of ancient Troy. Then, on 3 May, he swam the Hellespont.

Byron would spend a further year in Greece before returning to the land of routs, riots and balls. His travels, full of affairs with both sexes, gave him copy for poems that thrilled stay-at-home Britain. First came the early cantos of *Childe Harold's Pilgrimage* and then *The Giaour*, *The Bride of Abydos* and *The Corsair*, which, Jeffrey wrote in the *Edinburgh*, 'has spread around us the blue waters and dazzling skies – the ruined temples and dusky olives – the desolated cities, and turbaned population, of modern Attica'.[13]

Meanwhile the Galton family in Birmingham were still waiting for

Theodore to return from the same region. From Corunna, he and Sacheverel Darwin had travelled through Portugal and Spain, Tangiers and Tetuán, and then east to Greece and the Ionian islands and Asia Minor, encountering pirates, robbers and plague. Theodore wanted to stay longer in Greece, wrote Sacheverel; 'he spared not labour or expense in collecting coins, vases etc. etc and determined to visit every remarkable place in Attica.'[14] But on their way home, in Malta, he contracted typhus and died in Sacheverel's arms, aged twenty-six, on 5 June 1810. The boat that he was due to arrive on brought news of his death.

The Galtons were among thousands of families mourning lost ones, dead of fever, or accidents, or from the wounds and disease of the war. And the security of the well-off families, whether they were manufacturers like the Galtons, country gentry or City men, or aristocrats caught up in Westminster politics, was shaken again in October 1810. Exactly a year after the triumphant Jubilee, anguished after the death of his youngest and favourite daughter, Amelia, George III collapsed once more into madness. In December he was still extremely ill, suffering 'violent paroxysms', as a worried Amabel Hume-Campbell reported, and hardly sleeping. All the gossip and 'twaddle' reminded her of 1789, when the opposition had seized on his illness to gain power. 'I dislike the Protestation of the Prince's highly . . . And hope we shall not hear of any *Regency Caps* invented by Ladies which I always consider'd as an Insult on Misfortune, & were retaliated by the *Bandeaux* of *God Save the King*, which I did not thoroughly approve neither.'[15] Parliament was recalled for an emergency sitting and Perceval put forward a provisional Bill to name the Prince of Wales as regent, carefully limiting his powers: he must take no major action within the year; the queen would be responsible for the king's well-being and his property would be looked after by trustees. Despite the prince's objections to these terms, Perceval steered the Bill through parliament. On 5 February, the corpulent heir, now in his fiftieth year, was named as Prince Regent.

'I wish I could give you news of our good old K.,' Amabel sighed to Agneta Yorke in May, but those around him were 'Close as Wax':

those who talk to him would sometimes think him quite well, but that the Doctors say they have never yet seen him for 24 hours together quite exempt from all symptoms of disorder, which chiefly shows itself in Irritation of Spirits, & the very Circumstance of being kept out of Power increases it.[16]

It was odd, she thought, that he seemed to have no resentment of the Prince Regent, but was vexed every time the queen held her council. 'Some say this is consistent with his old Character, for that though a good Husband & a fond Father he had but a mean Opinion of Women's Understanding.'

On 19 June 1811, to mark the official opening of the Regency, the prince mounted a fete so extravagant that even those close to him were astounded. The Carlton House Fete involved a dinner for two thousand people, including members of the Bourbon family in exile – but not his wife, whom he did not invite, nor his mother and sisters, who refused the invitation. Diamonds glittered, many borrowed back for the night from the pawnbrokers at a special high rate. To emphasise his national leadership in time of war, the prince wore a scarlet field marshal's uniform, designed by himself, embroidered from top to toe. Down the middle of the table a real stream flowed, springing from a silver fountain, with shoals of goldfish. The champagne was iced, the food lavish. For three days Carlton House was opened to the public so that they could see the decorations. On the last day the crowd was so great that several people were crushed and injured, dresses were ripped, and, said the *Morning Chronicle*, 'one lady was so completely disencumbered of all dress, a female domestic, in kind compassion, wrapped her up in an apron'.[17] So many shoes fell off that they were piled into a large tub for 'the shoeless ladies' to collect.

# 50. STORMS OF TRADE

As more bad harvests and icy winters brought fears about a repeat of the bread shortages, it proved harder to rouse middle-class charity. In Bury St Edmunds public subscriptions failed to bring in enough: '& indeed very many respectable persons had expressd their Disapprobation,' wrote James Oakes, adding that most preferred to give their money to the poor people they knew.[1] The impatient Court of Guardians raised the poor rate, planning to give four pence a week plus herrings and potatoes 'to every Poor & necessitous person in the Town, whether belonging to it or not'. Oakes bustled on with his duties as one of the Poor Law Guardians and on the committee for the Hospital, the Grammar School Committee, the Grand Jury at the Assizes and the Land Tax Commission. But his family was still his great concern. His son James and wife Elizabeth had a new son; the youngest of their three girls was twelve and this baby was clearly a surprise. On 5 March 1809 Oakes rode over to Tostock 'immediately after Breakfast to see Eliz. & the little Stranger', calling on Elizabeth's parents on the way to wish them joy.[2] After Christmas he gave a ball for all his grandchildren, large and small, something that became an annual event.

It looked as though his family and fortune were secure. He had been dealing with his stockbrokers, Lambert and Cotton of 25 Cornhill, for many years and trusted them implicitly. He was shocked, therefore, when he opened the post one Tuesday morning in April 1810 to find a letter from Cotton telling him that Lambert had shot himself the day before, and 'by an acct he had left, there were alarming Deficiencys in his Affairs, desiring my immediate presence in Town'.[3] He set off at once, and spent three days looking into everything '& found Lambert had been acting most wickedly making away the Property of myself & others to a very large Amot.' The debt was a massive £36,430 and since he could only expect three shillings in the pound he became anxious that the news might cause a run on his bank. This did not happen, but Oakes hastily moved his London account to Dawes & Co., 57 Threadneedle Street. Three months later, in July, a large West India brokers and their bankers, Brickwood, Rainer & Co., failed with debts of over half a million pounds, taking down banks in Salisbury and Exeter and five City merchant houses. In London, Oakes wrote, he 'found the City under the gretest Alarm & Bankers & Merchants coming up to Town from all Quarters to gain Information'.[4]

Every bankruptcy – of a brewer or a mill owner, an apothecary or a banker – left ripples of disaster, a swirl of unpaid debts and mortgages. As the Orders in Council hit home, some economic theorists, the 'bullionists', were anxious to get back to the gold standard, abandoned when the Bank of England stopped cash payments in 1797. Inflation, they said, came from an excess of paper money. The economist and stock trader David Ricardo made this point in letters to the *Morning Chronicle* in the autumn of 1809 and in his pamphlet *The High Price of Bullion: a Proof of the Depreciation of Bank Notes.*[5] Opponents argued to the contrary, putting forward Adam Smith's idea of 'real bills': the market itself was a sufficient regulator and there would be no danger if paper money was linked to credible mercantile dealings. But the suspicion of paper transactions undermined loan contractors, like Abraham Goldsmid, a target of Ricardo and his fellow stock-jobbers.

Goldsmid's was already a sad place: Abraham's brother Benjamin, ill and prone to depression, had hanged himself in 1808 with the cord he used to lever himself out of bed during attacks of gout. Abraham worked on alone, winning huge government loans, including one in 1810 jointly with Baring's, now run by Sir Francis's sons, Alexander and Henry, in Bishopsgate. But the Bullion Committee's recommendation and the collapse of the Amsterdam market made it hard to sell on these loans, and left Baring's and Goldsmid with huge losses. In September 1810, Goldsmid shot himself in his home. His suicide caused a City panic. Next day the *Courier* commented, 'We question whether peace or war suddenly made ever created such a bustle as the death of Mr Goldsmid.'[6] This drew an ugly rant from Cobbett in the *Register*:

Is it really true, that this man's having shot himself made the citizens of London forget almost everything else? Is it really true, that such an event put business nearly at a stand? Is it really true, that it produced an effect equal to *peace* or *war* suddenly made? And is it true: is there truth in the shameful fact, that a Jew Merchant's shooting himself produced *alarm* and *dismay* in the capital of England, which is also called, and not very improperly, perhaps, the emporium of the world?[7]

It was really true.

In the shadow of the continental blockade shares plummeted and bankruptcies rose. In 1809, hoping to save the family fortune, John Longsdon, now twenty-one, had gone to America, having been told by traders that the best things to take were 'Yorkshire Broads & low Fustian Cords and Shirtings'. He could get those on six months' credit, and bring back timber to sell. 'If we are on amicable terms with America there will be no difficulty in disposing well of the Cargo & bringing in Produce which will sell in this country – if on the contrary they pass their Act of Non-Intercourse all sorts of American Produce will be high in England.'[8] But that March, in the last days of Jefferson's presidency, under sustained pressure from local merchants Congress did indeed pass the Non-Intercourse Act, which removed the earlier embargoes on most foreign trade, but maintained those on shipping to British or French ports. John reached Halifax in Nova

Scotia that month, finding the land covered with ice and snow and the town draped in fog. After trying to settle the vexed title to their land in Prince Edward Island, he went to New York and Boston. There were many contacts but few sales: 'here as in England, business is overdone,' he wrote; 'the Manchester houses have manufactured enough to serve the world for four or five years.'[9] He could ship nothing to England that would fetch a good price, and the customs house at Boston was so strict that it was almost impossible to get a vessel off. By February 1810 he was home again, living in Islington, working for the Morewoods' merchant house in London, while his nineteen-year-old brother William looked after their affairs in Manchester.

In July John reported that in business, 'things are desperate. The whole order and system so far as relates to Manchester and some other branches are deranged.'[10] Credit and confidence seemed suspended. The Longsdons were hanging on, but only just. Both brothers wrote tenderly to their mother Elizabeth as if nothing was amiss. John told her of his daily routine and quiet Sundays, and undertook her commissions, like buying her a visiting gown of 'plain sarcanet silk or handsome printed muslin or even cotton', and a winter pelisse 'suitable for a lusty, tall person of 50, to wrap well over before, so that it is warm', and a bonnet to wear with it.[11] She knew this would be expensive, but she must have something to wear to walk to church in the winter. In return Elizabeth sent hams and shirts, news of their sister Kate and their local friends, and confided her worries over arguments between their father and James over the running of the farm.

In July 1810 Manchester was in great agitation, wrote William, after expresses from London reported the failure of more banks: two large local concerns were expected to stop trading, including their own relations, Matthew and Peter Longsdon.[12] On 14 August, William Rowbottom noted, 'At Manchester this day trade very slack on account of so many failures in London, Manchester and other places, the House of Longsden was stoped this day for a very large sum and it will materially affect the Manufacturers in Royton.'[13] The next day

John Longsdon wrote to his father that 'the storm so long gathering, seems to have burst and now we must consider how best to bear and remedy an evil we cannot avert.'[14] Matthew Longsdon & Co. owed them £13,000, considerable money for a small concern. Their father was distraught, finding many things in Matthew and Peter's conduct 'highly blameable . . . particularly their want of order and not taking their stock account, and much too extensive a spirit of adventure in their situation, with Peter spending his evenings out in parties far from respectable so regularly'.[15]

As well as personal recklessness, the Longsdon family and their fellows blamed the war, the French decrees and the British Orders in Council. Towards the end of 1810, John wrote, teeth gritted with determination:

Buonaparte is issuing decrees with more violence than ever, and enforcing his former ones with additional rigour. Determined, he seems, to exclude every thing from the Continent that has the least mark, connection, or appearance of anything that is English. In doing this he has a double satisfaction. By confiscation he recruits his finances, while he gratifies his malice. But there is a point beyond which he cannot go, and there all his revenge and hatred must have an end. To that limit he is fast hastening, and then we may regard with indifference all his threats. Our trade from that time, will, notwithstanding all his efforts to oppose it, in some degree survive.[16]

He was trying to be reassuring, but his instincts told him that the end was near. Most of the family capital had been used up, including their savings in stocks and bonds. The following year he wrote to their manager, Finch, saying that he had watched his father's property and health decline over the last five years, and felt that the right course, if he could persuade him, would be to sell up and save what they could from the wreck. They carried on for a while, with William struggling in Manchester and John going as Morewood's agent to Heligoland and then to Malta. But in March 1812 James Longsdon senior was ill, and the act of making his will seemed to make him realise they could not go on. At the end of the month, on a day of blinding snowstorms, John wrote, 'Most heavily do I take up my pen on account of the state of our Manufacture and its Finances.'[17] They had been unlucky in buying and not selling, but 'what makes the matter of more consequence is our scarcity of money'. The partnership with Finch was dissolved and the Manchester warehouse closed. James ran the farm for his father, but John and William moved to America.

Although small family firms like the Longsdons went under, canny businessmen survived. John Marshall manoeuvred his way through by clever buying. Napoleon had closed the Elbe and Weser to British ships, threatening his supply of Baltic flax, exporters in Russia and elsewhere were desperate to evade the ban and Marshall bought in bulk at low prices whenever he could, so that when there was a shortage or prices were too high his warehouses were full and he could work on while his competitors failed.[18] The woollen merchants were badly hit. In Leeds, large merchants like Lupton & Co. were still sending out orders and invoices, packing bales of cashmere and 'soldiers' cloth', but it was hard to get their money in from agents. 'Notwithstanding the promise you made when at Leeds to remit us immediately upon your return to Limerick for the goods almost four months past due,' ran one typical letter, 'we are still deprived of hearing from you; nor has any payment been made . . . We therefore are compelled to adopt such measures to enforce settlement as the law directs.'[19] A year later, they were writing to a new customer, William Marquis, who was then in Liverpool, saying they were much obliged for his order, but in 'the Critical situation of affairs' they had to curtail their correspondence, '& Indeed have established a Rule in our business, that we cannot send Goods to any Foreign port except under the Guarantee of an Established house in this Country'.[20] In the past Lupton's had been keen on trading with foreign ports. They had kept up trading links with South America since the late 1760s, and their office files were crammed with long documents in Spanish and Portuguese. They had agents in Buenos Aires and Rio de Janeiro, and as well as shipping their own wool 'to the Brazils', they carried goods for the Sheffield cutlers, sending forks, penknives, scissors, razors, screws and 'steel mount Cavalry Officers Swords'.[21] But there were problems with the climate, the nails rusted, the cloth got discoloured and disputes with local dealers led to interminable lawsuits.

Although Napoleon agreed to allow corn exports to Britain – partly to drain British funds but also to appease his own farmers – his grip had tightened on the North German ports. When the French retook Stralsund, on the Baltic coast of Germany, in 1809, they seized six hundred neutral vessels full of British goods and confiscated most of the cargoes: the following year, British warehouses were seized and burnt in the Netherlands and Italy. At the same time the rates of exchange became increasingly unfavourable, leaving Britain on the edge of a serious depression.[22] In the summer of 1810 twenty provincial banks failed, and six in London. A loss of confidence, intensified by a poor harvest and the threat of more shortages, affected stocks, trade and industry.

In this climate people turned against speculators and get-rich-quick dealers, and lost their enthusiasm for untried stock. While traditional investments like canals still held good, even they were not free from disasters: in late November 1810 the large reservoir holding water for the almost-finished Huddersfield and Ashton canal suddenly burst 'and flew in torrents down the valley', sweeping away a cottage and drowning a woman and four children.[23] Yet work on the canal went on, and at its opening the following April around five hundred investors crowded into decorated barges, sailing from Ashton-under-Lyne to Marsden in the West Riding, 'attended by a band of music playing Rule Britannia'. As they entered the tunnel they were 'loudly cheered by at least 10,000 spectators'.[24]

Canals helped the inland trade, but this could not compensate for markets lost abroad, and for the idle merchant ships. Among thousands of business casualties this year was the husband of Mary Anne Galton, Lambert Schimmelpenninck, a Dutch shipping merchant from Bristol, whom her family described as 'sensible, amiable, well read but not brilliant'.[25] Life had looked promising when the couple were married in 1806, but now Schimmelpenninck was caught up in the problems of the Bristol shipping business. He and Mary Anne looked for rescue to her Galton fortune, managing, after long and painful negotiations, to get rid of the tight conditions that her father had imposed. The ill-feeling was never healed: hard words were spoken and even Mary Anne's effervescent mother, Lucy, had had enough. She and the rest of the family cut off all contact with Mary Anne until the end of her life. But although big shipping men were hit, in smaller ports like Whitehaven, where Jack Hutchinson was hoping to make a go of it, the captains were still busy. Jack was always sanguine, and in 1810, although his farm in County Durham was suffering from drought, he sold his old hay at a good price and was off to the races. More important, he told his cousin John Monkhouse, he had two shares in a shipping company in Whitehaven. 'I have no doubt but we shall flourish,' he declared cheerfully, although 'we only have two ships at present, the Britannia in Government Pay, up the Mediterranean, & the Trident now in Whitby where she has been lengthened'.[26] The *Britannia* was a two-hundred-foot scow, and her captain William Nixon was an old family friend; the *Trident* had so far been too small to be profitable, but now she would be 'fit for any service'.

William Salmon in Chepstow was also optimistic. In 1810 he became engaged to Fanny Morgan, a local girl; he was twenty-eight and Fanny was twenty. When they were married the following March they had two miniatures painted, Fanny posed against a monument, William against a plain background, smart in his white stock, striped yellow waistcoat and gilt-buttoned blue coat. He was determined to provide Fanny with new clothes – a purple bonnet, a new pelisse – and to make enough money to stop her having to work in a shop. In time he hoped to buy a ship of his own. He would 'thrash the seas' for the next ten years then settle on land, he told her, calming her fears of storms and privateers. Heading round Land's End before beating east along the south coast, he wrote home: 'There will be several Arm'd vessels in our fleet, they all agree not going farther than Portsm'th without Convoy – my patience for a fair wind is almost exhausted – nothing but your letters will ease my mind – while I steer clear of all dangers let us be happy and thankful.'[27]

Every letter, written in howling winds or calm grey days, and sent home with the Chepstow-bound captains he met in each port, contained vehement protestations of devotion mixed with business dealings: £10 notes torn in half and the halves sent in different letters; bills due; payments made; deals done. He sent salt herrings for Fanny to trade in the town, crocks of butter, bone models and marquetry boxes made by the prisoners at Portchester, some for presents, some for a local woman to sell: 'I have purchas'd for Mrs Chapman from the French Prison toys to the Amt. of £3.4 I have bought you a Workbox, Mr Vass a frigate and Mrs V. a workbox.' He even sent a large load of old ship's rope, which was called 'paper junk', as the paper mills used rope to add to their rags and flax. 'This morning had no thoughts of writing to my Dear Belov'd Fanny,' he wrote, but 'its now 5pm fell in with a Man that has 30 tons of excellent Paper Junk at £9 per ton'. Could her uncle please ask Mr Brown – owner of the White Mill, just up the Wye from Chepstow – if he would buy '30 tons of paper Stuff and what is the most he will give for the best quality. I am confident I could clear £30 by it.'[28]

While young Captain Salmon could literally get money for old rope, for large-scale traders the only chance of balancing losses on the Continent was more trade with America. This hope was dashed in November 1810, when President Madison issued an ultimatum: Britain must repeal the Orders in three months or America would return to its strict policy of no trade with the whole of Europe. By the time this news arrived, even government supporters had become divided about the Orders. Some accepted them as a means to weaken the French economy, assert Britain's rights at sea and stop the trading rise of neutral countries, but merchants and industrialists opposed them vehemently.

The Bristol Company Copper Works near Swansea,
filling the valley with smoke

Once again, too, coinage was running short. Banknotes were exchanged for cash at less than face value and overseers of the poor issued tokens since they could get no small change. In late 1810 the Lancashire hatters were in such distress that 'some hatters gather old rags, sell matches, carry coals or any labourious business they can get imployed in'.[29] Hatters' societies across England sent money and food. At the same time, a parliamentary committee heard petitions for relief from the Bolton hand-loom weavers. Then the mule-spinners in the factories mounted a 'rolling strike' in Stalybridge, where new mills had been built along the river, and thirty miles away in Preston, where the Horrocks brothers were building their spinning empire. Until the strike was broken in the winter, money from fellow textile workers supported ten thousand people. At the start of the new year, Rowbottom wrote tartly, 'this destructive war will make thousands smart that are yet unborn.'[30]

At first a few industries, like the iron foundries, seemed invulnerable. Richard Crawshay of Cyfarthfa died in 1809, and his son

William took over, managing to weather the difficulties by building up stocks, holding on to iron when prices fell so that he could make money when they rose again. Touring south Wales, Sophia Hoare was thrilled by the amount of shipping at Swansea, including 'some very large Vessels, just getting under Weigh, and with all their Sails set, shooting the pier, which was really a very fine sight'.[31] The Vale of Glamorgan, she thought, would be beautiful 'but for the Copper and Iron Works, the smoke of which is very unpleasant and so thick one can hardly see beyond it. It is nearly the same in this respect the whole of the way to Neath.' But the smoke was thinner elsewhere. At least a quarter of the Midland iron output, particularly of nails, had gone to the American colonies and the new embargo was cruel: soon over nine thousand people were receiving poor relief in Birmingham. In the City, the ports, the textile districts and the iron foundries – everywhere – the storms of trade took their toll.

# 51. THE COMING OF THE SHEEP

In October 1810 young Howard Galton (having dropped the childish 'John Howard') was touring Scotland, pursued by letters from his mother Lucy: 'How do you like Scotch Inns & Scotch Breakfasts; above all I hope you are pleased with the People and the scenery. Be sure to write me a poetic description of the Cascades and Rocks, and woody Glens . . . Have you seen the Troshacks and Lock Catrine? Let me see them too, in your description.'[1]

Everyone, it seemed, was heading north, and it was all due to Scott. Two years before, he had published *Marmion: a Tale of Flodden Field* and then, when he was on holiday in the Trossachs with his wife and his daughter Sofia in 1809, he began *The Lady of the Lake*, his long poem set at the time of James V's battle with the clans in the early 1500s. This was published the following May. Francis Jeffrey, in the *Edinburgh Review*, said he missed the battles of *Marmion* and the picturesque sketches in the *Lay of the Last Minstrel*; 'but there is a richness and a spirit in the whole piece, which does not pervade either of these poems, – a profusion of incident, and shifting brilliancy of colouring, that reminds us of the witchery of Ariosto, – and a constant elasticity, and occasional energy, which seem to belong more peculiarly to the author now before us.'[2] By the end of the year *The Lady of the Lake* had reached four editions, with thirty thousand copies sold. The poem was full of the 'ancient Highland strain':

> Now might you see the tartans brave
> And plaids and plumage dance and wave . . .

Such lines evoked both the valour of the clans and the thrill of the Highland regiments, famed for their exploits in Egypt and the Peninsula. Readers adored it. 'It is cold and raw and damp,' wrote Sarah Spencer in May, 'so that we can't stir out, and if it were not for "The Lady of the Lake", I don't know what we should be reduced to . . . But I do so love every word that man ever wrote, that I have been enjoying the book over and over again, till I am ashamed of returning to it.'[3] Tourists dashed to the poem's setting, Loch Katrine, where the disguised King James sees Ellen rowing her skiff across the lake, gleaming in the setting sun,

> One burnished sheet of living gold,
> With promontory, creek, and bay,
> And islands that, empurpled bright,
> Floated amid the livelier light,
> And mountains that like giants stand
> To sentinel enchanted land.

For romantically minded travellers, the enchanted land began with Loch Lomond and the mountains of the Trossachs, north of Glasgow, even more than the Cairngorms to the north-west. Some people ventured west to Mull and Iona and out to the stacks of Staffa, or rode north across the Great Glen, with its Hanoverian forts, Fort William on the west, sheltering beneath Ben Nevis, Fort Augustus on Loch Ness and Fort George in the east, past Inverness. Other travellers followed in the footsteps of Johnson and Boswell, taking the road to Glenelg and across the narrow sound to Skye, and then out to the Hebrides. But few reached the lands of the far north, where strange-shaped mountains like Quinag, Suilven, Canisp and the northernmost Ben Hope surge suddenly out of wide straths, valleys, bogs and scattered lochans.

Since the Jacobite rebellions of 1745, the clan chieftains' rights had been curtailed and the Gaelic language suppressed. The main tenants, the tacksmen, rented whole glens from the clan chief and sublet their holdings to smaller tenants, who rarely had a written lease and often redivided their land among their kin. Landlords and tacksmen arranged with the drovers to drive a certain number of cattle south each year: rather than pay rent, each tenant provided a cow or more. The old clan ethos lingered, especially in the semi-feudal raising of regiments, where service was considered by those who gave their sons to the war as enshrining an understood right to the land: tenants in the MacDonald lands of Skye and North Uist were even formally listed as people 'who have been promised lands and an exchange of lands for their sons'.[4]

Some old hunting grounds had already disappeared, although they would come back under Victorian landlords with a vengeance. The revered Gaelic poet Duncan Ban MacIntyre was in his eighties in 1810. He had been a soldier and then a gamekeeper in the hills of Breadalbane in the southern Highlands around Ben More and Loch Tay, the land of Rob Roy, only a few miles from Loch Katrine, and in one of his most famous songs he bade 'Farewell to the Bens', '*Cead deireannacli nam bean*':

> As I gazed on every side of me
> I could not but be sorrowful,
> For wood and heather have run out,
> Nor live the men who flourished there.
> There's not a bird or roe there
> And the few that have not died out
> Have departed from it utterly.[5]

But the people themselves had not yet departed utterly. Far from being empty, the Highlands were full of traditional 'touns', bustling settlements of tenants and cottars and landless labourers – there were around 120 settlements on the north shore of Loch Tay alone. Farming was communal, keeping cattle grazing in the low fields in winter and moving them to the hills in summer, when the fields were used for crops, barley, beans and potatoes. The summer herdsmen lived with their families in shielings, turf or stone huts, looking after the cattle and making butter and cheese.

In the late eighteenth century the touns and shielings were almost too full, as the large potato crops had staved off hunger, allowing numbers to grow. Indeed over-population was becoming a problem, although at first the major landlords, backed by the Highland Society, were concerned *not* to lose their people. During the Peace of Amiens the government sent the engineer Thomas Telford to the coast and the central Highlands to make recommendations about roads and industry, with the aim of providing more work, so that the people would stay. This led to the digging of the Caledonian canal along the Great Glen, which employed three hundred men from Skye alone, and the building of nine hundred miles of new roads with a thousand new bridges. The Passenger Act of 1803, drawn up by Charles Hope, the Lord Advocate in Scotland, was deliberately designed to help landlords prevent emigration, laying down strict conditions for ships on the transatlantic passage.[6] But as men like the Scottish peer Lord Selkirk promoted emigration to Canada as the only solution to Highland poverty, the people began to leave, groups of families at a time, selling their cows to pay their fare.

Many tenants already had problems paying their rent with so many mouths to feed and such hard land to work. Men drifted south to the towns and took seasonal work on lowland farms or joined the army. In the war years, in the Western Isles, workers came across from the mainland to serve the growing kelp industry, combing the rocks as the tide ebbed, collecting the seaweed and burning it in open kilns on the shore; the ash was a valuable source of alkali, rising in price now that Spanish barilla was hard to get. But even here the profits were erratic and landlords and tenants borrowed money on promises of production they could not keep.[7] As the war went on the kelp industry declined and cattle prices ceased to rise. To save the situation landlords looked to another source of income – the sheep.

The cottars in the touns had always kept a few sheep, skinny and fragile, grazing with the cattle or roaming wild, but these were not

hardy enough to bring in money. Everything changed with the introduction of the sturdy black-faced Lintons and the 'Great Sheep', the
white-faced Cheviot. In his *History of Quadrupeds*, Thomas Bewick
wrote that the Cheviots were unrivalled as mountain sheep:

as well on account of their carcases and hardiness, as from the superior value
of their wool, which is in the highest estimate for cloathing . . . they thrive
on the most sterile heaths, their wool is of the most desirable texture, they
are easily fattened, and their whole conformation is so properly suited to
mountainous pasture, that we are surprised the breed has not already been
more generally diffused.[8]

The Cheviots could survive Scottish winters as well as offering good
returns in wool and mutton: they seemed a godsend to the great landlords owning thousands of acres, who saw the old communal farming
system as uneconomic. But the only way to make sheep pay was to
reduce the many small tenancies of the touns to a single holding, a
large expanse for grazing.

This had already been done to a certain extent in the borders and
southern Highlands, and successful Lowland graziers were keen to
drive north, especially as Telford's road-building made it easier to
press on with such schemes. Edinburgh intellectuals had long advo-
cated the extension of sheep farming northwards, seeing it as one way
to drag what they saw as the backward and prejudiced Highlands into
the modern era. In the *Edinburgh Magazine* in 1804 William Stevenson
(Elizabeth Gaskell's father), who had tried himself, briefly and unsuccessfully, to be a 'scientific' farmer, recommended replacing cattle by
sheep and introducing manufacturing. He also wanted to discourage
the Gaelic language, poetry and music, which worked, he said, 'to
perpetuate those prejudices which it is absolutely necessary to destroy,
before any general or permanent improvement can take place. The
prejudices and indolence of the peasantry, and the feudal interests of
the landlords, must not be suffered to interfere in the smallest degree.'[9]

Stevenson made his comments in a review of the Highland Society's *Prize Essays*. The Society itself was caught in a dilemma, determined on one hand to preserve the antiquities and culture of the clans

and on the other to improve the welfare of the people. The tension between these two aims was embodied in the attitudes of Sir John Sinclair, who was not only head of the Board of Agriculture and patron of all agricultural improvement, but also the Highland Society's president, writing an enthusiastically misguided introduction to the Society's *Poems of Ossian in the Original Gaelic* in 1807, at exactly the same time as he was forwarding schemes that would banish the Gaels from their lands. Sixteen years before, in 1791, he had launched the British Wool Society, aiming to develop a better breed of sheep for the Highlands, and he had raised Cheviots on the mountains of his own estate in Caithness, at the north-eastern tip of Scotland. In his *Statistical Account*, Sinclair assumed without question the need to abolish traditional practices. These, he thought, slowed down agricultural progress – if they went, prosperity would follow.[10] Personally, Sinclair was genuinely concerned that the changes should not displace the small tenantry; to him improvement meant sheep farming and crofting, supplemented by extra work in fishing, kelping or weaving. His theories owed much to Kirkcaldy's Adam Smith, and his words were flavoured with a particular brand of 'patriotism', a desire to build a flourishing, commercial Scottish nation.

In 1807 the newly formed Northern Association of Gentlemen Farmers and Breeders of Sheep had asked for a Royal Charter to extend their activities into Ross-shire, Sutherland and Caithness. The government agreed, offering to pay half the cost of improving the roads and bridges. Huge clearances followed the Association's decision and vast working areas of thousands of acres were created. And while the process of introducing the sheep had been gradual and relatively easy in the south, in the Highlands each clearance meant the sudden collapse of whole communities. Between 1807 and 1821 up to ten thousand people were evicted, and many were driven to emigrate.

The greatest and most notorious 'improver' was Elizabeth, Countess of Sutherland, who had brought a dowry of eight hundred thousand acres in Sutherland – vast in area but small in income – when she married George Granville Leveson-Gower, Viscount Trentham, in 1785. A chestnut-haired dynamo, five feet tall, the countess was impulsive, cultured and dominating. She had captivated people in Paris when her husband was ambassador during the Revolution, held memorable and lavish salons in London, and was greatly admired by George Canning and many other men. When her husband became Lord Stafford in 1803 and inherited the family land and fortune, including ownership of the Bridgewater canal and other lucrative networks, the couple decided to spend some of his enormous wealth on the Sutherland estates. Fired with progressive ideas, the countess undoubtedly believed, like all improvers, that she could transform her land for the better, and for the good of Scotland. If the peasants were to be dispossessed, she would build them new villages on the north coast, where they could become crofters and fishermen, and she would bring in mines and industry – what harm was there in that? This would stop emigration and the movement of the people would be done with 'tenderness', although she admitted that 'A proper degree of firmness' might be needed. In 1805, she told her husband: 'So much work is awaiting the people in the way of canals, roads and bridges, that we forsee in spite of Lord Selkirk that in a few years this Country will be benefitted by preserving its people to a reasonable degree.'[11] This proved harder than she expected. In October 1808 she wrote that they were greatly occupied with their improvement plans, but it was 'quite a wild quarter inhabited by an infinite multitude roaming at large in the old way, despising all barriers and regulations, and firmly believing in witchcraft'.[12] Four years later, faced by their stubborn resistance, she decided that 'if they will not adopt the other means of improvement universally done elsewhere they must quit it to enable others to come to it'.[13]

The task of clearing away the touns was left to the Staffords' manager, the lawyer and economist James Loch, and the agent Patrick Sellar, the most demonised figure of the clearances. Both men were from Morayshire, on Scotland's east coast, and they employed men from their home county for all the building and road-making rather than locals, another source of resentment. During 1809, several hundred families were cajoled and bullied to leave their land. If they demurred, their livelihood was threatened: in the spring, when fodder was scarce and Highland cattle depended on the young grass shooting beneath the heather, Sellar ordered huge burnings of the heather, depriving the herds of food.

The following year Lord Selkirk came to Sutherland, keen to find more emigrants, having bought a large tract of land, the Red River Colony, to help the ailing Hudson's Bay Company, in which he was a major shareholder. William Longsdon from Derbyshire hoped his efforts would raise the value of their property in Prince Edward Island, where Selkirk also had land, writing to his father, 'I observed in the newspaper an account of 500 settlers having left Scotland for Prince Edward Island under the patronage of Lord Selkirk . . . This is the second lot of emigrants that has gone out thither during the course of the present Autumn.'[14] More would follow in 1811.

In Sutherland new lots for sheep farms had already been advertised, but prospective purchasers were put off by the local fury. The factors swore in special constables, charged the cannon at Dunrobin Castle, and sent for help from Fort George near Inverness. The 21st Regiment marched across country, and the factors evicted hundreds of families to the coast, where they lived on small allotments, trying to earn money by fishing for lobster or herring. In 1813 Patrick Sellar would clear several thousand people from the inland straths of Sutherland, particularly Strathnaver, moving in with men and dogs, pulling down and burning houses. In the aftermath he was charged with arson and causing the deaths of three people, including a bedridden grandmother whose blankets caught fire as she was moved. James Loch, the Sutherlands' lawyer, argued that the people had been offered new crofts on the coast, rent-free for a year, but some came back to the glens, rebuilt their old turf huts, and had to be evicted a second time. To stop them returning 'the only course was to burn the timber'. It was not done with 'cruelty or oppression', he insisted, it was simply a regrettable casualty of improvement. The jury acquitted Sellar of any crime.

Daniell, Strathnaver, 1813: the crofts on the coast, built after the clearances

For five successive years, as the Sutherland crofter Donald MacLeod remembered with passionate indignation, this removal had continued.

The country was darkened by the smoke of the burnings, and the descendants of those who drew their swords at Bannockburn, Sheriffmuir, and Killicrankie – the children and nearest relations of those who sustained the honour of the British name in many a bloody field – the heroes of Egypt, Corunna, Toulouse, Salamanca, and Waterloo –were ruined, trampled upon, dispersed, and compelled to seek an asylum across the Atlantic; while those who remained from inability to emigrate, deprived of all the comforts of life, became paupers – beggars – a disgrace to the nation whose freedom and honour many of them had maintained by their valour and cemented with their blood.[15]

The sheep took over. Yet the Staffords did not make big money: they had drastically underestimated the cost of the clearing and were almost ruined.[16]

In these years the land acquired features that later visitors judged just as picturesque as the lost shielings, like the lines of croft houses with strips of fields down to the shore, the stone dykes climbing the mountains and the sheep pens in the valleys, built of stone from deserted touns.[17]

In May 1811 Betsey Fremantle went to visit her sisters Eugenia, Harriet and Justinia, all now married to Scottish gentry. 'I left my three little darlings fast asleep, in Bed, at five o'clock,' she wrote in her diary, 'and set out on my journey.'[18] After staying in Edinburgh, she crossed to Greenock and then to Eugenia and Robert Campbell in the Kyles of Bute, opposite Arran. Betsey was convinced that no crofters could think themselves poor. After a seven-mile walk up the glen, she wrote:

We drank some Milk at a Cottage, the inside of these Huts is dark, smoaky and gloomy, the fire blazing in the middle of the room, without a chimney, their beds fitted up the wall, all sleeping together with their cow, dog, pig and chickens, and still do not know what poverty is as the meanest cottager is possessed of a Cow, and a small piece of ground, and all the men are fishermen.[19]

There were some disappointments: 'they are dress'd like sailors, and since I have been in the Highlands I have not seen *one Kilt*.' But watching the crofters make a haystack, she decided 'these Highlanders are merry and chearful, and put me much more in mind of the peasantry in Italy, than any other'.

Scott and his readers saw the Highlands through the same rosy mist. Scott laid out his earnings from *The Lady of the Lake* on his new house, Abbotsford, near Melrose: 'I have bought a little place by Tweedside,' he told Richard Heber, 'and am busy planning, ornamenting and scheming a little cottage, where I hope we may crack a social bottle of claret, in spite of the merciless distance that separates us.'[20] In the summer of 1810 he toured the Highlands and Hebrides with friends, including his clever, loquacious cousin Jane Apreece, who would soon marry Humphry Davy. They visited Iona and Staffa, 'eternally swept by a deep and swelling sea', and Scott told Joanna Baillie that he had 'become a sort of favourite with the Hebridean boatmen, I suppose from my anxiety about their old customs'. In his honour they named a great stone at the mouth of a cave on Staffa 'the poet's stone', and consecrated it with whisky.[21]

In the same year Scott sent the Countess of Sutherland a specially bound copy of *The Lady of the Lake*. He hoped this would not disgrace her shelves, he said, which were full of 'the most beautiful & curious books in England'. So much for its appearance: 'But for the matter of the volume I must invoke your Ladyships partialities & prejudices in my favour, as a Highland Chieftainess, a Scottish Countess & if you will permit me so much honour, as a friend of the rhymer.'[22]

Yet even as he wrote this, Scott himself knew the cost of the vast clearances that this Highland chieftainess was imposing. Later, in the Preface to *Rob Roy*, he described going as a boy with his lawyer father, who had been sent to execute a writ against refractory tenants, escorted by a sergeant and six soldiers from Stirling. When they got there the house was already deserted: 'And thus it happened, oddly enough, that the author first entered the romantic scenery of Loch Katrine.'[23]

## 52. SIEGES AND PRISONERS

In the winter of 1810–11 Wellington retreated once more behind the walls of the Torres Vedras around Lisbon, but the government were confident with regard to Spain, or took pains to appear so. In letter after letter they soothed Wellington's scornful complaints about the attacks on his strategy in parliament and in the papers, and stressed their support. Passing on the gossip after an evening with Philip Yorke at Christmas, Amabel Hume-Campbell assured his mother Agneta, 'Ld Wellington keeping a French army at Bay, is more than any Power on the Continent has been able to do . . . I heard that Buonaparte grows more corpulent, & less like an Active General who would fight his own Battles, & your Son thinks none of his Commanders equal him in Military talents.'[1] But as far as the opposition could see, there was little progress.

Yet by the spring, when Amabel was ordering expensive prints of Wellington's campaigns from Colnaghi at eight guineas a set, the British seemed to be advancing.[2] Wellington had been driving the French out of Portugal, defeating General Masséna at Fuentes de Oñoro in April, and then blockading the fort of Almeida. To his fury, the French troops there managed a daring escape, blowing up the fortifications behind them. Then in early May, Sir William Beresford defeated Soult's forces at Albuera, over the Spanish border, at an appalling cost, with 4,400 out of 6,500 infantrymen killed and many more wounded. Jane Austen wrote it off briskly (and notoriously): 'How horrible it is to have so many people killed! – And what a blessing that one cares for none of them!'[3]

Wellington's impatience was well known, and after the French escape from Almeida he had told his brother William, 'I believe there is nothing on earth so stupid as a gallant officer.'[4] But John Fremantle, who was now one of his aides, told his uncle that in this mortifying situation, 'Lord Wellington exclaimed "Oh dear, oh dear!" indeed I pity him; I hear he has taken the blame chiefly on himself.'[5] Every professional soldier wanted to serve with him. John Henry Slessor, who was currently acting as Governor of Zante, the beautiful Venetian-built port on the island of Zakynthos and the main British base in the Ionian islands, handed over his post and took a boat for Italy, 'determined to get to Spain'.[6] In Bury St Edmunds James Oakes used his interest with the Duke of Grafton to obtain a lieutenancy for his wife's nephew James Harrison Baker. On 17 June Oakes noted, 'Captn Baker left me by Cambridge Coach setting off for Hull to march 120 Recruits to Portsmouth, from thence to set sail for Lisbon & join the 2nd Battalion of his Regt, the 34th, in Portugal.'[7]

Another new officer was John Longsdon's closest Derbyshire friend, John Barker, who had just left Cambridge and had thought of going into the Church: instead, to his mother's dismay, he obtained a commission through the Cavendish family as an ensign in Lord Fitzroy's 48th Foot. Old James Longsdon admired him, he said, going off to fight the 'Vile and Bloody Tyrant'.[8] But all year the 48th Foot waited for their transports. In July they were in Northampton, where Barker was fussing over his uniform, complaining that the tailor, damned scoundrel, had overcharged and sent blue pantaloons instead of white. He expected they would sail soon, the regiment's second battalion having been annihilated, and until then they must amuse themselves 'in this stupid place'. They had had one ball and expected another and he had 'made some acquaintance among the ladies' in spite of a general wariness of the army, and he and his friends hoped that 'by behaving well at church and looking dammed serious in the presence of the old ladies they may all of them be admitted into the company of the young ones'.[9] The regiment did not sail until the end of November.

For most of 1811 the situation in the Peninsula was a costly stalemate. Even with Spanish guerrilla forces harassing the French lines, the British found it hard to move on, and although Wellington defeated Masséna again at Fuentes de Oñoro in May, all attempts to storm the great border forts Ciudad Rodrigo and Badajoz, which they had taken the year before and lost again during the retreat, met French counter-offensives. Many lives were lost, many wounded men brought home. But in the autumn, when reinforcements arrived, Wellington was sent a new, powerful siege train, the artillery he needed to attack the forts. At the same time intelligence reports suggested that Napoleon was withdrawing some top regiments and posting others to Valencia, replacing them with untrained conscripts. Encouraged, Wellington renewed his assault on the fortresses. In January 1812 his troops took Ciudad Rodrigo and in March he besieged Badajoz, with its narrow streets perched on a rock above the marshy plain.

The final assault came in early April. It was made over several days in stormy weather with flooded trenches. But at last the breaches were made and the troops scrambled up the ladders under constant fire and poured into the town. The British public met the news with the usual exuberant celebrations. But they were not told what followed, when the British soldiers plunged into three days of drunken looting, violence, burning, murder and rape. For once, Wellington, usually so hard on looters, who could lose his army the goodwill of the civilian population, let the soldiers have their way, until he finally issued orders, arrested men and hanged them as an example. While some of the horror of these days reached home through letters the truth did not really emerge until a spate of soldiers' memoirs many years later. Ned Costello, a rifleman with the 95th, remembered it well. He was wounded in the assault and entered the town with blood trickling down his face, using a friend's rifle as a crutch. 'It was a dark night,' he wrote:

the shouts and oaths of drunken soldiers in quest of more liquor, the reports of fire-arms and crashing in of doors, together with the appalling shrieks of hapless women might have induced any one to have believed himself in the regions of the damned . . . the scenes of wickedness that soldiers are guilty of on capturing a besieged town are oftentimes truly diabolical, and I now, in the reflections this subject gives rise to, shudder at the past.[10]

Yet Badajoz also gave rise to one of the romantic legends of the war, the rescue of two high-born Spanish sisters by Lieutenant James Kincaid and Brigade Major Harry Smith. A few days later the twenty-four-year-old Smith married the younger sister, Juana María de Los Dolores de León, aged just fourteen. Juana rode with him through all the Peninsular campaigns, and they stayed together all their lives, in England, India and South Africa, where Smith, by now Sir Harry, became Governor of Cape Colony.

After Badajoz the army regrouped, sending the wounded to Lisbon and then home. Lists of the dead appeared in the British papers, among them the name of the exuberant Ensign John Barker, killed in the siege. Old James Longsdon immediately wrote to his son John with his condolences on the death of his friend, and three weeks later John received a letter from Lieutenant-Colonel John Wilson in Peroa in Portugal, explaining that Barker had volunteered for the Forlorn Hope – the suicidal advance guard of an attack – and had been among the first to mount the breach. He had nearly gained the top when he was shot.[11] It was John who took charge of getting his trunk and possessions sent home to the Barker family, and arranging for his back pay. That autumn, before he left to become a trading agent for the Morewoods in Malta, John impulsively proposed to a Miss Mackmurdo, then withdrew, acknowledging it had been a mistake. While John Barker was living, he told William, 'a great part of his attention and as much affection and friendship as anyone is capable of had been devoted to him – at his death he had looked for an object in whose society his finest feelings would rally.'[12] The hasty engagement had been all a mess: it was not possible to fill the gap. This was one small story of loss among thousands.

Within two months of the siege of Badajoz Wellington reached Salamanca, shadowing the French army until the decisive battle near the city on 22 July. In Britain, the response to the news of Salamanca was more than usually wild. Revellers dragged Wellington's eldest brother, the Marquess Wellesley, out of his carriage when he was on his way to see the illuminations and paraded him triumphantly through the streets, to his intense discomfort, before leaving him shaking on the doorstep of Apsley House. When the illuminations were turned off, disappointed crowds broke windows, fired guns, threw fireworks into carriages, overturned coaches and chucked fireballs, setting women's clothes on fire.

In Spain the army marched on, into Valladolid, where they were met with women carrying garlands of flowers, and then, on 12 August, into Madrid, greeted with laughter and cheering and weeping. For the past year under French occupation the city had suffered terrible famine, with Spanish partisans blocking the roads to stop supplies to the invader: over twenty thousand people had died. Yet Wellington and his officers enjoyed feasts and balls, admired Old Master paintings, went hunting in the parks and attended special bullfights (too strong for many war-hardened officers). Relations at home were regaled with accounts of Spanish glamour and kisses, and the British press was ecstatic: it was hard for opponents of the war to argue their case now.

Wellington, however, saw that his position in Madrid was weak and left the capital, heading north on the hard march to Burgos. The siege of Burgos failed, and his critics began to crow. In October he was forced to withdraw, taking his demoralised and hungry troops back to Valladolid and as far south again as Ciudad Rodrigo, leaving sick and ill soldiers and camp-followers by the roadside to fend as well as they could. 'The men's clothes were actually in rags – some one colour, some another, some in worn out helmets, some in none,' remembered William Hay, a young officer with the 12th Light Dragoons, protecting the army's rear, 'others in forage caps with handkerchiefs tied round their heads, their horses in a most woeful state, many quite unfit to carry the weight of the rider and his baggage'.[13] Finally they lurched back over the Portuguese border. James Stanhope, writing to Richard Heber in December, noted wryly,

I certainly did not expect to be cantoned in the middle of Portugal this winter . . . When one looks back on the campaign, one seeks anxiously for the reason why the tables were so rapidly turned and how it happened that we could hardly keep face before a French army which three weeks before was considered *hors de combat* for the year.[14]

In Madrid, Francisco de Goya had painted a portrait of Wellington wearing his red uniform and the new Peninsular Medal. Wellington left before the painting was finished and Goya would adapt it in 1814, adding yet more military orders. But Goya had also been etching the plates of his great and terrible series *The Disasters of War*, unpublished until 1863, over thirty years after his death. These showed the unglamorous horrors of conflict, the Spanish people facing invasion and famine: an old woman waving a knife as a soldier rapes a girl, prisoners shot by firing squad, captives tortured and mutilated – and bodies, many bodies, wrapped and waiting for burial.

Napoleon's refusal to repatriate British prisoners meant that there were virtually no exchanges, and the numbers in the hulks, prisons and parole towns grew.[15] After the Trafalgar campaign, 7,500 arrived; after Copenhagen, thousands of Danes were taken from Danish merchant vessels. Wellington was now sending a stream of prisoners from Spain, 1,100 after Ciudad Rodrigo, 3,700 from Badajoz.

The prisoners did, however, bring good to some small British towns. Wincanton in the Somerset hills was a town of farm labourers and linen weavers, flax dressers and spinners. It was a busy staging post on the London–Plymouth route but its weaving trade had collapsed and many houses lay empty. Its fortunes were transformed when it became a parole depot in 1804. The men sent there were supervised by a good-natured agent, George Messiter, a twenty-eight-year-old lawyer from a well-known local family and a partner with his brothers in the town bank.[16] Groups of officers rented empty houses and others took lodgings. The richer prisoners dined well, driving up business in the Shambles where the butchers sold meat, game and fish, while the poorer men ate at the newly set-up Restaurant pour Aspirants, a nearly meatless regime of onions and leeks, cucumbers, lettuces and dandelions, according to the season. From time to time there was a fracas when prisoners strayed over the bounds and joined battle with farmers and pitchfork-armed haymakers, but most settled into a regular, boring routine. Morning and evening the town bell rang, and the officers assembled and answered to their names. Foreign languages echoed as they 'promenaded the streets in great numbers, four abreast', remembered Henry Olding and Jonathan James, boys at the time. 'The times were then stirring,' Olding wrote later, 'and the blood in the bodies of the sleepy Somerset people flowed more quickly than ordinary. Many a gossip found his or her way into the Market Place daily, and when there was no news, went home disappointed.' The paroled men too crowded into the market to wait for the mail coach, 'and if an ensign or eagle appeared, or the word "Victory" was spoke, the prisoners who were present returned with downcast heads, and the inhabitants sent up a shout of joy'.

Here and elsewhere, paroled officers taught French, fencing and dancing, put on concerts, went to the theatre and were guests at the dinner tables of neighbouring gentry. The better off brought their army servants and sent for their wives and families. If they were Freemasons they were welcomed in the local lodges, and sometimes set up their own, like the prisoners of Ashburton in Devon, who called their Lodge 'Des Enfants de Mars et de Neptune'. In the border town of Kelso, the local Master of the Lodge 'expressed the wishes of himself and the Brethren to do anything in their power to promote the comfort and happiness of the exiles. After which he proposed the health of the Brethren who were strangers in a foreign land, which was drunk with enthusiastic applause.'[17]

The parole prisoners were welcomed for the money they brought. In Peebles, William Chambers, collecting his father's copy of the

*Edinburgh Star*, was told: 'Great news, Willie my man – terrible battles in Spain – thousands o' French prisoners – a number o' them brought to Leith, and I shouldn't wonder if some were sent here.'[18] Briefly the townspeople thrived, letting lodgings, providing food, setting up a billiard table, going to the prisoners' concerts and plays. It was tempting, Chambers's father found, to give them credit. When they were moved on – leaving with fervent promises to pay their debts when peace came – Chambers was left bankrupt. Eventually he took the family to Edinburgh and found a job managing a salt factory on the coast. In Edinburgh, William walked with his father to the ridge looking down on Valleyfield prison, near Penicuik. It was a Scottish Sabbath, shops shut, people in church. But in the 'hive of beings' below them there was no Sunday calm, 'only dimanche!'[19] The men were dressed in coarse yellow woollen clothes and red or blue cloth caps. Some danced to a fiddle, 'briskly played by a man who stood on top of a barrel':

Others were superintending cookery in big pots over open fires, which were fanned by the flapping of cocked hats. Others were fencing with sticks amid a circle of eager onlookers . . . Near one corner was a booth – a rickety concern of boards – seemingly a kind of restaurant, with the pretentious inscription 'CAFÉ DE PARIS' over the door, and a small tricolor flag was fluttering from a slender pole on the roof.

At fourteen William Chambers became a bookseller's apprentice in Edinburgh: with his brother Robert he would later start the influential *Chambers's Journal*, and found one of the great publishing firms of the next century. He never forgot the sight of the prisoners, with their dancing, their cafe and their tricolour flag.

At the same time, the hulks and land prisons were overflowing. To cope with the numbers, the new prison on Dartmoor was opened at Princetown in May 1809, the most hated gaol of all, bounded by stone walls with empty moorland stretching to the horizon, covered with snow for seven months of the year. It took five thousand men, rising to nine thousand. But although Dartmoor was impregnable, smugglers' gangs organised escapes from other prisons and hulks and from parole towns – one of the profitable trades of war. Rich parole prisoners contacted their relatives and arranged money for ransom and bribes. At Whitstable in Kent smugglers set up special escape lines, travelling the country in their carts to pick up passengers from the parole towns and take them to London wharves where they slipped on to the fishing yawls and oyster boats that sailed daily between Whitstable and Billingsgate. Landed on the shore at dusk, they walked from the coastal marshes to a farm where they were given food and clothes, and then hid in the woods until the tide was right for a boat to take them to France, one of the yawls and cutters that sailed from here weekly to Flushing, Dunkirk or Ostend. One Whitstable man, James Moore, earned enough to buy a second boat within a year. Caught in March 1810 and sentenced to join the navy, he deserted and went back to his trade. His downfall came when he was flagged down off the Goodwin Sands in December 1811, bringing silks and spirits from Dunkirk, and carrying a complete list of the prisons and parole depots, with the names of leading prisoners.[20]

The prisoners made great profits not only for the smugglers but also for dealers and traders, at the expense of village lacemakers, straw plaiters and hatmakers. These workers' greatest enemies were not the prisoners who undercut their wages, but the wholesalers in their own communities who could buy cheap and sell high. To help the straw plaiters a tax had been introduced in 1806 and plaiting was banned in the prisons, but all this did was to drive it underground. Prison guards smuggled straw in and plait out, sometimes wrapped around their bodies under their clothes, delivering the finished plait to the dealers. Some entrepreneurs bought up whole hay fields to provide the raw material: one Huntingdonshire man owned five wheat fields right by the prison at Norman Cross, and another man bought fields near Penicuik, to supply straw to the men at Valleyfield. Every now and then the militia were sent in on raids, something that haunted ten-year-old George Borrow, whose father was a lieutenant in the West Norfolk Militia at Norman Cross from 1811 to 1813. Forty years later he could still see the redcoats turning over every corner with their bayonets and marching out with their booty. Worst of all was 'the accursed bonfire on the barrack parade, of the straw plait contraband, beneath the view of those glaring eyeballs from those lofty roofs, amidst the hurrahs of the troops, frequently drowned in the curses poured down from above like a tempest shower, or the terrific war-whoop of "Vive L'Empereur".'[21]

The prisons and hulks were still a draw for tourists. In 1810, Lady Jerningham, recently widowed, was lingering sadly by the sea at Worthing until her son Edward persuaded her to 'do a little traveling'. They explored Portsmouth, and spent two hours 'in a Boat, Roving round Tremendous Men of War', entranced by the warships, the prison hulks and the ships of their Spanish allies:

Ships full of French Prisoners, Convicts in Prison Vessels with the Windows, grated with Iron, and a most noble Spanish Man of War, who was at Portsmouth to get new stores and where every individual was Spanish, and understanding no other Language. Edward had been on Board the day before, and talked Latin, with the Chaplain, a Spanish Priest. Mass is said in the ship every day, and it is really singular to English eyes and ears to See and hear them. They appeared to be numerous on Board, and in good spirits. The French Prisoners were all speaking French in their Ships, and the whole was a representation of the Confusion of Babel.[22]

Most prisoners were Catholics, but whatever their denomination, the boys in Wincanton noticed, 'they spent Sunday in playing draughts, cards, dominoes. Indeed anything to while the time away.' And more men were coming. Until 1813 the Peninsular prisoners flowed in a continuous stream. However busy they kept themselves with teaching or trades, they were homesick and sometimes desperate. In Wincanton one man went mad and another committed suicide, while others died in epidemics. Seventeen were buried in the parish churchyard, where one stone was carved with these words:

> He was a prisoner of war
> But death has made him free.

# 53. LUDDITES AND PROTESTS

By mid-1811 over ten thousand people were out of work in Lancashire. Bills for poor relief soared here and in the wool and worsted
districts of West Yorkshire, the hosiery towns of Nottinghamshire and
Leicestershire and the metal-working regions of Sheffield and the
Midlands. Corporations, manufacturers and workers sent petitions to
parliament with many thousands of signatures attacking the Orders
in Council. They were loyal subjects, the workers pointed out, and
many young men from their districts were fighting for their country,
yet they could not support their families without help. But one select
committee set up to look into the distress in relation to commercial
credit, and another that heard petitions from the weavers of Lancashire and Scotland, merely fell back on suggestions of lower wages,
changing jobs, or simply patience and endurance.[1] Why would the
government not intervene, asked the Manchester Weavers' Committee, when it had already done so with regard to corn, or with the
wages of Spitalfields weavers and London tailors? If the Commons
could not govern in their interests then reform was sorely needed.

The Nottingham framework knitters had another complaint,
asserting that their trade was being ruined, not only by Bonaparte
or the Orders, but by 'speculating, unprincipled individuals that have
made fraudulent goods, to cheat and rob the public'.[2] By 'fraudulent'
they meant work made on the new wide frames, worked by 'colts' who

had not served apprenticeships. On 11 March 1811 knitters began destroying these frames and by the end of the month there were attacks every night. Although these faded over the summer, in the autumn they began again, and manufacturers opened threatening letters from 'General Ned Ludd and the Army of Redressors'. In late November the *Nottingham Review* carried 'An Address from the Framework Knitters to the Gentlemen Hosiers of the Town of Nottingham', pointing out the dire state of the trade and the need for regulation. Special constables began patrolling, a curfew was imposed, innkeepers were ordered to close at ten o'clock, and troops were kept on constant alert. Several men stood trial at Nottingham assizes in March 1812; two were acquitted and the rest transported. By now the saboteurs were calling themselves 'Luddites'. Stories about the term differed, but the *Nottingham Review* declared that it was taken from a young Leicestershire weaver, Ned Ludd, who had smashed frames in a rage thirty years before, in 1779.[3] Soon 'General Ludd' was transformed into the mythic 'King Ludd', a Sherwood outlaw and defender of the people's rights, and 'Luddism' became a loose term for everything from machine-breaking to riots. In Luddite tracts and ballads, folklore and abuse were mixed with strict legal arguments. Their organisation was tight; like the United Englishmen they swore loyal oaths and formed secret cells as protection against spies; like the patriotic volunteers they drilled and marched, but they kept well out of sight.

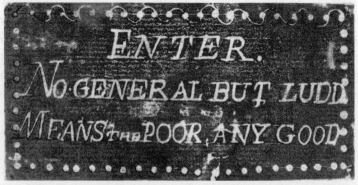

A Luddite ticket, Manchester, 1812

By the end of the year the Nottingham disturbances had inspired frame-breaking in Derbyshire, Leicestershire and Yorkshire, where the focus was on the gig-mills and cropping frames used in finishing work. Owners began guarding mills at night, waiting for the clatter of horses' hooves or the thud of marching men. In February 1812, when cloth finishers from the villages around William Cartwright's mill at Rawfolds near Cleckheaton heard that new frames were on their way, they marched out at night, stopped the wagons and hacked up the frames with axes. The authorities called in the militia but the attacks went on. The government-backed press prescribed fierce remedies – repression and imprisonment, suspension of habeas corpus, and martial law. There was a fear of the mob, the growing, impoverished masses. 'If much firmness be not displayed by the government,' wrote Wordsworth, who had spoken out so fiercely against such repression in earlier years, 'confusion & havoc & murder will break out and spread terribly.'[4] Magistrates were given new powers to hunt for arms and their spies were everywhere. In February 1812 Perceval's government brought in a Bill to make machine-breaking a capital offence.

In the Lords this Bill prompted Byron's maiden speech. He had seen the distress when he was at his Newstead estate in Nottingham-shire, and put together a sober speech with Henry Holland, who was cultivating him as a potential Whig voice in the Lords. But on the day, 27 February 1812, his words caught fire. When he was in the county recently, he admitted, not a day passed without some new act of vio-lence – but, he insisted, nothing except absolute want 'could have driven a large and once honest and industrious body of the people into the commission of excesses so hazardous to themselves, their families, and the community'. Men only destroyed looms when they became a hindrance to their livelihood: now they had to face new capital punishments, 'new snares of death'. What if this 'barbarous law' did pass?

. . . suppose one of these men, as I have seen them, – meagre with famine, sullen with despair, careless of a life which your lordships are perhaps about to value at something less than the price of a stocking-frame – suppose this man surrounded by the children for whom he is unable to procure bread at the hazard of his existence, about to be torn for ever from a family which he lately supported in peaceful industry, and which it is not his fault that he can no longer so support; suppose this man – and there are ten thousand such from whom you may select your Victims, – dragged into court to be tried for this new offence, by this new law; still there are two things wanting to convict and condemn him; and these are, in my opinion, – Twelve Butchers for a jury, and a Jefferies for a Judge![5]

Byron knew that his vehemence would raise eyebrows, as he told Hobhouse with some pride. 'I spoke very violent sentences with a sort of modest impudence, abused everything & everybody, & put the Ld. Chancellor very much out of humour, & if I may believe what I hear, have not lost any character in the experiment.'[6] But if he lost no character he also made no difference: the Destruction of Stocking Frames Act was passed in March.

A week after this speech, on 2 March, the *Morning Chronicle* published his mordant poem:

> Those villains, the weavers, are all grown refractory,
> Asking some succour for charity's sake –
> So hang them in clusters round each Manufactory,
> That will at once put an end to mistake.

Next day, the first two cantos of *Childe Harold's Pilgrimage* hit the bookshops. Byron, as he put it, 'woke up famous', and was soon acclaimed, courted and adored, the hero of high society as well as of the Nottingham frame workers.

In Lancashire, Rowbottom was gloomy. 'The old English hospitality is nearly Extinguished in every family', he wrote at the start of 1812:

at this time the lower class of people who have a family of small children are absolutely short of the common necessaries of life and a deal of familys have not left off work at all . . . to all appearances if there be an alternation of times it must be for the Better except there be commotions or civil wars which God grant may never happen in this country or Kingdom.[7]

The commotions did not take long to come, beginning in March with attacks against steam power-looms. The valleys on the borders of Lancashire and Yorkshire, where mills lay in sheltered hollows and ravines, were the most difficult to police and the strongest in their protests. But loyalties were divided, with hundreds of men also signing up as special constables. Alarmist rumours spread of a rebirth of Jacobinism and republicanism, of assassins and incendiaries. For years magistrates like the Huddersfield manufacturer Joseph Radcliffe and the Lancashire mine owner Colonel Ralph Fletcher had been employing spies to hunt out secret meetings, bombarding the Home Office with warnings of sedition. Now their letters became even more shrill.

The secret Luddite gatherings overlapped with public protests on wider subjects: the campaigns were separate, yet the authorities often confused them and lumped them together as subversive and dangerous. From the start of 1812 liberal and radical reformers in the provinces had begun to work with the 'Mountain' group of Whigs – Henry Brougham, Thomas Creevey, Major Cartwright and Samuel Whitbread – joining their demands for peace with calls for wider parliamentary representation and greater freedom of the press. In the Commons, Brougham's attack on the Orders in Council and on the East India Company monopoly mobilised the commercial classes, bringing forth eloquent spokesmen like William Roscoe from Liverpool, the cotton merchant Kirkman Finlay, Lord Provost of Glasgow, and the young banker Thomas Attwood, Birmingham's new High Bailiff. The industrial troubles, however, still seemed remote to many people in the south. In March 1812, in Bury St Edmunds, James Oakes was more concerned with young Miss Powell who ran off with a Kent recruiting officer from the 34th Regiment – they were brought back and married next day – and with arrangements for the reopening of St Mary's Church, with its new south gallery, which 'lookd remarkably well lighted up & was uncommonly full, supposed abt 3,500 Person in the Church'.[8]

This month Samuel Whitbread advised the people of Bolton to

petition parliament and the Prince Regent for peace. Their address to the prince, respectful in tone, put the blame firmly on the war for the current distress of the poor: 'Their pale and ghastly countenances – their squalid and ragged clothing . . . might possibly beget a doubt in your Royal Breast whether the most glorious results of war and victory abroad would be sufficient to compensate for such a mass of wretchedness at home.'[9] The Prince Regent may not have bothered to read this but it was printed in many local papers, whipping up support. In the next couple of months thousands signed petitions and took to the streets.

Violence erupted simultaneously on both sides of the Pennines, with Luddite attacks in Yorkshire and peace protests in Lancashire. In Yorkshire, on the night of Saturday 11 April, about fifty masked and armed men, led by George Mellor, a young cropper from Huddersfield, marched on Rawfolds Mill again, stoning the building and breaking all the windows. This time Cartwright was ready, having barricaded his mill and placed booby traps around, including barrels pierced with spikes. When the crowd drew near, his small group of defenders fired: two men were killed and many wounded. Cartwright's stand, the first by a mill owner, checked the raids and his fellow manufacturers presented him with a sword and £3000, but local people turned so firmly against him that he dared not even go to church.

Three days earlier, in Lancashire, Charles Wood, the Manchester Borough Reeve (the chief town officer), had called a meeting in the new Exchange to send a congratulatory address to the Prince Regent, not asking for peace, but praising him for keeping the Tories in power. Handbills flooded the town, calling on people to protest against this, and although the meeting to approve the address was cancelled, the demonstration went on. Samuel Bamford was there, watching the crowd, as some boys broke into the Exchange newsroom and began throwing chairs, tables and benches through the windows and smashing the chandeliers. Someone defaced the portrait of the local Whig MP Colonel Stanley, perhaps taking him for George III. At this point the Cumberland militia and a troop of Scots Greys began clearing the street: 'when, it being then warehouse time,' wrote Bamford, 'I hastened to my work'.[10]

Slowly, the militia imposed order, but in the days that followed there were more riots in Manchester and the surrounding towns, against 'the high price of provisions, the badness of trade, and the lowness of wages'.[11] These quickly became entangled with Luddite grievances against machines and mill owners. The mood was already uneasy on 20 April, when William Rowbottom noticed people setting off for the Burton brothers' house and factory at Middleton 'where they weave callicoes by steam'. The mill's workers, lying in wait, fired on a crowd of around two thousand outside the factory, 'when horrid to relate four were killed on the spot and a great number wounded'. Middleton was Bamford's home, where he lived with his wife Mimi and young daughter, and he rushed home from the warehouse, horrified to find that 'in her curiosity to watch a mob', Mimi had gone with other women 'to watch from a cottage near the factory, only yards from where one man was killed'.[12]

The next day, Rowbottom wrote, 'a large mob again assembled at Middleton armed with guns and Pistols and a very large number of colliers arrived with picks no doubt for the purpose of destroying the weaving factory'.[13] They were joined by colliers carrying mattocks. First they raided workers' houses and Emmanuel Burton's home, setting the whole place on fire, but before they could reach his father's house, the Scots Greys rode in, killing eleven men and wounding twenty-one. One of the dead had never been near a mob in his life. He was strolling through the local churchyard, stopping to read the inscription on a grave. When the sergeant saw him, 'he went down on one knee, levelled, fired, and killed the old man dead, the ball passing though his neck'.[14] These Lancashire attacks came to a climax on 24 April at Wroe and Duncroft's power-loom mill at Westhoughton near Bolton. Receiving a message that the mill was on fire, the magistrates sent in the cavalry, but when they arrived everything was calm and they left – whereupon the Luddites came back and burned it to the ground. Investigations by the Unitarian journalist John Taylor (the man who would give the massacre at St Peter's Field in 1819 the name 'Peterloo') suggested that the whole thing was instigated by government spies. Many agreed, especially as the ringleader turned king's evidence.

Across the Pennines, a few days after the burning of Westhoughton Mill, the Tory *Leeds Intelligencer* carried the headline 'Atrocious Murder'.[15] William Horsfall, who employed four hundred workers at his mill in Marsden, had been shot down as he crossed the moor on his way back from Huddersfield market. Horsfall had long used the new shearing machines, and had also been determined to track down the men who had attacked Yorkshire mills earlier, allegedly vowing that he would ride up to his saddle girths in Luddite blood. Within days a hundred suspects were rounded up and sixty-four indicted. That week the papers brought news of the storming of Badajoz, but in Yorkshire and Lancashire local battles felt just as urgent. 'The lower classes are in a most alarming state here,' a Manchester friend, James Ferriar, told Richard Heber. 'God knows where the mischief will end. The matter has quite a revolutionary appearance.'[16] Hannah Greg wrote to her son Tom:

At present it is most serious and alarming – if Ministers are not prompt at meeting the distress of the country with some measures of relief – the condescension of government may come too late. One cannot but suppose they are ignorant of the condition and of the formidable numbers of the great manufacturing districts . . . At present 10,000 Military keep and probably will keep us quiet . . . I believe your dear Father as little unpopular as any master spinner yet you will not be surprised that when he is in the dark or much past his hour, I am afraid with terror I dare not utter – but he has promised never to stay out late.[17]

In Manchester, she added, there were beggars everywhere, and although subscriptions were made for poor relief 'money will not make potatoes or flour'.

In all, twelve thousand soldiers were sent north. Local boys found this fascinating; twelve-year-old James Weatherley went out to their camp on Kersal Moor near Salford every Sunday, listening to the band, admiring the way the Buckingham and Berkshire militia made huts out of sods, and how their wives 'used to sit at the outsides with their cushions on their knees knitting Lace'.[18] Most workmen, however, saw the soldiers as men without pride, lackeys of the state. Alexander Alexander, serving in the militia, faced a barrage of abuse at an inn:

'What are you but a slave yourself to them,' shouted his accuser, 'a poor, pitiful scoundrel, who has sold himself for a shilling a day, body and mind, you cannot have a will of your own, or do one thing but what you are bid, and must go to be shot like a cock at Shrovetide, there is not a spark of spirit in thy body.'[19]

The disturbances spread to Scotland. In June Walter Scott, as Sheriff of Selkirk, told Southey, 'the country is mined below our feet'. Hearing of a weavers' meeting in Galashiels, 'for the purpose of cutting a man's web from his loom',

I apprehended the ringleaders and disconcerted the whole project; but in the course of my inquiries, imagine my surprise at discovering a bundle of letters and printed manifestoes, from which it appeared that the Manchester Weavers' Committee corresponds with every manufacturing town in the South and West of Scotland, and levies a subsidy of 2s. 6d. per man for the ostensible purpose of petitioning Parliament for redress of grievances, but doubtless to sustain them in their revolutionary movements.[20]

At the Lancaster assizes that month eight men were sentenced to hang for their part in the Manchester riots and four for the burning of the Westhoughton mill, one of them aged sixteen. The Tory *Lancaster Gazette* reported at length on the remorse 'of these deluded wretches, who felt the bitter consequence of listening to the artful insinuations of men, whose principles are at enmity with all law, human and divine'.[21] The following January, after a special assizes in York, three men found guilty of Horsfall's murder were hanged in irons. In contrast to the Lancaster paper, the radical *Leeds Mercury* recorded a dignified defiance.

The prisoners were then moved to the front of the platform, and Mellor said: 'Some of my enemies may be here, if there be, I freely forgive them, and all the world, and I hope the world will forgive me.' William Thorpe said, 'I hope none of those who are now before me, will ever come to this place.' The executioner then proceeded to perform his fatal office, and the drop fell . . .

Three men had died who 'might have lived happy and respected. They were young men on whose countenances nature had not imprinted the features of assassins'.[22]

On 12 May 1812, at about half past eleven in the morning, a tremendous explosion echoed through the villages along the Tyne. Huge flames belched from the mouths of two pits at Felling colliery. 'A slight trembling, as from an earthquake, was felt for half a mile around the workings; and the noise of the explosion, though dull, was heard to three or four miles distance, and much resembled an unsteady fire of infantry.'[23] Dust and coal and splinters of burning wood rose into the sky, causing a darkness like the coming of dusk. Crowds ran to the shafts, their footsteps printed in the ash, crying for husbands, fathers and sons. Men put their shoulders to an old rope gin, bringing up around thirty men and the bodies of two boys, 'miserably scorched and shattered'. A hundred and twenty-one men and boys were in the mine that day. It seemed at times as if the whole proud industrial world itself was murderous, its casualties as terrible as those of a burning battleship or a siege in Spain.

# 54. PRINCE, PERCEVAL, PORTLAND

The census of 1811, more detailed than the cursory survey of 1801, gave people the sense of living in a growing nation, a different feeling of scale. On 24 May, in the month of the battle of Albuera, James Oakes went to the Guildhall to meet the eight overseers and instruct them 'respecting the Population Act requiring the Numbers of Houses, Familys, Males & Females thro'out the Town to be taken by them *on one Day, Monday, the* 27.'[1] At the end of the year, William Row-bottom copied down the figures from the papers, between a note of the sailing of the *San Domingo* and a record of the usual Oldham mis-haps, like the death of John Jackson from 'a vilont pain in the head' and the arrest of two men for stealing ham: 'population of England Scotland and Wales was given in the House of Commons this month when the number of people where 11,910,000 eleven million nine hundred and ten thousand, in 1801 a like return was made to Parliament when the number where 10,171,000 ten million one hundred and seventy thousand'.[2]

The person to whom these millions were to pay allegiance, while their sad, mad king was shut away, was the Prince Regent. When the year of restrictions on the Regency was up in February 1812 everyone expected the prince to call on the Whigs, heirs of his old supporter Fox. But when they declined to drop the thorny issue of Catholic emancipation the prince turned back to Spencer Perceval and the Tories. Robert Banks Jenkinson, the former Lord Hawkesbury, who had inherited the title of Lord Liverpool on his father's death in December 1808, was Secretary for War and Colonies. Henry Addington, Lord Sidmouth, was Lord President of the Council and Castlereagh became Foreign Secretary, the disgrace of his duel forgotten. (Canning's career was still in the doldrums. He refused lesser cabinet posts, and went to Lisbon in 1814, returning two years later to be President of the Board of Trade.)

The Whigs could not forgive the prince's betrayal, and the country at large thought his extravagance and marital squabbles contemptible. Five years earlier, he had insisted on a commission of Privy Councillors, 'the Delicate Investigation', to enquire into his wife Caroline's life: she was censured, though acquitted of bearing an illegitimate child. 'The Princess's Business is Like a Cover'd volcano,' Lady Jerningham had written; 'every one wishes to talk, but it is generally understood that it is a dangerous subject of Conversation. Captain Manby is the Paramour named, and some have whispered Sir Sidney Smythe, but the Morning Post and Morning Chronicle talk of the Scandal of Defamation and seem resolved to white-wash this poor unfortunate Creature.'[3]

At the time, George III had refused to let the prince take his daughter, Princess Charlotte, away from Caroline, but now the regent whisked her away, allowing her mother to see her only once a fortnight. The following year, when Caroline's anguished letter begging to see her daughter more was published in the *Morning Chronicle*, yet another commission was appointed to question her behaviour. The depositions were printed in the papers for scandal-loving readers. Lady Melbourne wrote with some amusement to Byron: 'Have you read the *Times* of today? . . . I hear it is the fashion amongst Ladies to burn their newspapers – that the servants may not read such improprieties. They had better burn them without reading when they are first brought – that would really be acting with propriety.'[4]

Even firm Tories were appalled. Jane Austen wrote to her friend Martha Lloyd, 'Poor woman, I shall support her as long as I can, because she *is* a Woman and because I hate her husband . . . I am resolved at least always to think that she would have been respectable, if the Prince had behaved tolerably by her at first.'[5] Increasingly, the opposition – and the public – took Caroline's side.

It was now twenty years since Gillray had depicted the prince so tellingly as a voluptuary: now he was ridiculed in satires and prints as a drunken, lecherous buffoon. In March 1812, while storms were whipping across the north and grain prices were rising, and smart crowds were dancing French quadrilles and the new, shocking German waltz at Melbourne House, readers of the *Examiner* were laughing over a poem, Charles Lamb's 'Triumph of the Whale':

> Not a mightier Whale than this
> In the vast Atlantic is;
> Not a fatter fish than he
> Flounders round the polar sea.
> See his blubber – at his gills
> What a world of drink he swills.

The whale, surrounded by 'crooked Dolphins' and 'Pig-like Seals', was easy to identify – and indeed Lamb punningly named him:

> By his bulk and by his size,
> By his oily qualities,
> This (or else my eyesight fails),
> This should be the Prince of Whales.[6]

Young George Cruikshank pounced on this to produce *The Prince of Whales or the Fisherman at Anchor*, one of the large, fold-out colour frontispieces for *The Scourge: or Monthly Expositor of Imposture and Folly*, published by his friend William Jones. The print shows a shark-shaped Castlereagh leaping up while the fisherman Perceval tows the whale on a golden chain, with Sidmouth and Melville (in a tam-o'-shanter) in his boat, and the rat-faced, excluded politicians Canning and Wellesley gnawing its timbers.

In the same year, in his broadside poem 'The Devil's Walk', the

George Cruikshank, *The Prince of Whales or the Fisherman at Anchor*, 1 May 1812

twenty-year-old Shelley attacked the 'brainless King' and maudlin prince, whose 'pantaloons are like half-moons/Upon each brawny haunch'. Shelley, who had eloped with the teenage Harriet Westbrook the previous August, had been visiting Dublin, where he made provocative speeches calling for repeal of the Act of Union. In the autumn, now living in Lynmouth in Devon, he and Harriet stuffed copies of his revolutionary pamphlet *A Declaration of Rights* into bottles and into the baskets of silk-covered fire balloons, hoping they would float or fly across the Irish Sea and stir up rebellion. Shelley had no hesitation in describing the court as full of plump 'Death-birds':

> Fat as the Fiends that feed on blood
> Fresh and warm from the fields of Spain.[7]

\*

In April, a month after Lamb's poem was published, Leigh Hunt attacked the prince for his betrayal of Fox and for turning his back on the Catholics and Ireland. Ridiculing a sycophantic tribute in the *Morning Post*, Hunt pinned him down as 'a violator of his word, a libertine over head and ears in debt and disgrace, a despiser of domestic ties, the companion of gamblers and demireps, a man who has just closed half a century without a single claim on the gratitude of his country or the respect of posterity'.[8]

Inevitably this brought an indictment for libel. The Establishment now viewed the *Examiner, Political Register* and similar journals as dangerously insurrectionary. 'Nothing is more common', wrote one disdainful critic, 'than to see pasted upon the windows of the lowest pothouses, eating-houses and gin-shops, this inviting bill of political fare: "The Statesman, Cobbett and the Examiner, taken in here".'[9]

The Hunt brothers did not come to court until December, but when they did the charge stuck, despite Brougham's spirited defence and the many supporters outside. As in Cobbett's trial, the judge was Ellenborough, who told the jury that they had to choose 'whether we are to live under the dominion of libellers, or under the control of government and the law'.[10] Both brothers were sentenced to two years' imprisonment, and fined £500 plus sureties for good behaviour. John went to Coldbath Fields and Leigh to Horsemonger Lane, where he decorated his rooms with rose-patterned paper, painted clouds on the ceiling, brought in a piano and bookcases, and grew flowers in the yard outside. In this 'bower' he had companions, first his wife Marianne, until she left because their son Thornton was not well, then his sparkling sister-in-law Bess, and then Marianne again: their daughter Mary was born here, with Hunt delivering her himself 'as the hour had taken us by surprise'.[11] Hunt wrote his poetry, edited the *Examiner*, and received streams of visitors, including Benjamin Haydon, Charles and Mary Lamb, Maria Edgeworth and Hazlitt, then working as a parliamentary reporter and theatre critic for the *Morning Chronicle*, but soon one of Hunt's brilliant contributors.

Another visitor in 1813, who became a good friend, respecting Hunt's bravery and warmth while being shrewdly aware of his vanity, was Byron. Basking in celebrity after *Childe Harold*, Byron was edging towards marriage with the cool and proper Annabella Milbanke, while simultaneously falling into a much-rued relationship with Caroline Lamb and an intense affair with his half-sister Augusta. But Byron was independent, rich in his ironies. In *Childe Harold* he wrote bitterly of the wasted heroism of Albuera, 'glorious field of grief', and of Talavera, where

> Three hosts combine to offer sacrifice
> Three gaudy standards flout the pale blue skies.

The shouts are France, Spain, Albion, Victory!
The foe, the victim, and the fond ally
That fights for all, but ever fights in vain,
Are met – as if at home they could not die –
To feed the crow on Talavera's plain,
And fertilise the field that each pretends to gain.

With the bloody fields of Spain in their mind and the prospect of violence at home, Cobbett, Hunt and others attacked Perceval's policies as well as the lifestyle of the regent. The domestic focus was on the Orders in Council. After the suppression of the Manchester Exchange riots in April, the government, pushed by Brougham, established a 'Committee of the Whole House' to look at the impact of the Orders on trade and manufacture. In early May this committee began its work. But on 11 May, when Perceval was on his way to the inquiry, entering the lobby of the House of Commons 'talking and laughing', a man stepped out, drew a pistol and shot him in the heart.[12]

Perceval's assailant was no inflamed radical but an embittered merchant, John Bellingham, who had been rejected when he claimed compensation for a spell of imprisonment in Russia. After the attack, the Speaker blocked the door to the Commons and MPs quickly passed a motion calling on the Prince Regent to prosecute the murderer at once. Huge crowds gathered, the Horse Guards were summoned and at one in the morning Bellingham was taken to Newgate. The next morning, at an inquest in the Cat and Bagpipes pub at the end of Downing Street, the coroner passed a verdict of wilful murder. The newspapers were filled with eulogies of Perceval. As the news flew across the country people wrote horrified entries in their diaries. James Oakes surrounded his with stars, noting that 'the Bolt enterd his Breast. He could only say "Oh I am murdred" & died in 3 minutes.'[13] 'We have been thrown into the utmost consternation & I know not what to think or what to do with myself,' wrote Mary Wordsworth, who was staying at Hindwell with Tom and Joanna, 'having heard that Mr Perceval has been shot in the House of Commons. – this is all we know but I fear it is too true – Tom heard of it from a person who had read the dreadful news in the Hereford Paper – We have seen Monday's *Farmer's Journal* in which no such acct. appears.'[14]

Bellingham's trial took place at the end of the week, and on the following Monday, 18 May, he was executed. Cobbett, imprisoned in Newgate largely as a result of Perceval's suspicions, wrote of Bellingham's calmness on the eve of his death, as he wrote to his wife, telling her that he was sending her his watch and prayer book, and praying God to preserve her and her children. At eight in the morning people gathered in the open space below Cobbett's window. 'I saw the half-horrified countenances,' he wrote, 'I saw the mournful tears run down; and I heard the unanimous blessings. What, then, were these tears shed, and these blessings bestowed by Englishmen upon a *murderer*!' He was a murderer, certainly, Cobbett admitted, and the act could not be justified, 'but the people did not shed tears for and bless BELLINGHAM because he had committed a murder; but because his act, clearly wicked as it was in itself, had ridded them of one whom they looked upon as the leader amongst those whom they thought totally bent on the destruction of their liberties'.[15]

Byron had hired rooms opposite the gallows to watch the execution. He came back to Melbourne House for breakfast looking pale, and told Caroline Lamb, 'I have seen him suffer, and he made *no confession*.'[16]

Wordsworth, curiously, had also planned to see Bellingham die. 'The Assassin has not been executed in Palace Yard as was first proposed,' he told Mary, 'had that been the place I should this morning have been a Spectator in safety, from the top of Westminster Abbey.'[17] It was too risky, he thought, with riots anticipated, to go to see him hang at Newgate. Wordsworth was in London that summer, trying to heal a bitter rift with Coleridge, who felt he had been slighted. There was a reconciliation of sorts, but the friendship was never the same. He told Mary about Coleridge's lectures on Shakespeare, brilliant and baffling by turns. Wordsworth did not think they would bring him much profit: 'he has a world of bitter enemies, and is deplorably unpopular – besides, people of rank are very shabby for the most part, and will never pay down their five shillings when they can afford it.'

In Hindwell, Mary was far from riots. She had brought their six-year-old son Thomas – 'Totts' – to stay, writing to William in the sunshine, 'the pool dancing before me'. Earlier in the month she had told him how she let the farm workers spoil Totts, and planned to leave him with Mary Monkhouse, his godmother, of whom he was 'excessively fond', while she went on an excursion down the Wye to see Tintern Abbey.[18] But by late May, Mary felt stirrings of disquiet. Why was there no news from Grasmere? Then a letter did come, but from Dorothy to William in London, telling him that the Wordsworths' three-year-old daughter Catherine had died that morning from convulsions: they thought Mary would be able to stand the shock better if the news came from him. Wordsworth rushed to Hindwell. Later, across the top of the last letter she had written about their joy in the Hindwell summer, Mary wrote, 'Our Child had been 4 days dead.' In the coming winter they lost Totts too, from pneumonia after measles. Wordsworth told Southey, 'I dare not say in what state of mind I am; I loved the Boy with the utmost love of which my soul is capable, and he is taken from me . . . O Southey, feel for me!'[19]

Two years before, the Fremantles' six-year-old daughter Louisa had died in a similar epidemic; 'measles and scarlet fever are apprehended,' Betsey wrote miserably.[20] The lives of so many people were punctuated by the deaths of children: from a baby or a son of six to a soldier in battle, a sailor at sea. Choking stops in the flow of days. Then a jolt, a change of key and back to daily life, however haunted, to writing, weaving, banking, farming. Or political intrigue.

Perceval's death led to frantic scurrying among government and opposition groups. 'The intriguing is going on briskly,' Brougham told Creevey.[21] The forty-two-year-old Lord Liverpool reluctantly stepped into Perceval's shoes, only to resign a fortnight later after the Commons sent an address to the Prince Regent asking him to form a new, stronger ministry. There was a pause, with more discussions, debates and projected deals. There were dramas and tears on the part of the prince, who appealed in vain to Marquess Wellesley and Lord Moira, but in the end, on 8 June 1812, Liverpool took up his post: he would be Prime Minister for the next fifteen years. In the new team Castlereagh stayed on at the Foreign Office and Henry Bathurst from the Board of Trade took over Liverpool's difficult role as Secretary for War, which Wellington's brother, William Wellesley-Pole, had declined.

The situation looked grave, with unrest at home and anxiety about the Peninsula. 'From Lisbon the accounts are very unfavourable,' Creevey reported:

The American embargo has produced the greatest consternation, and our Commissariat is utterly destitute of money or credit. In addition to this, General officers write home that the ravages of the late sieges and other things have made a supply of 30,000 men from this country absolutely necessary, if Portugal is to be kept.[22]

Within a month of taking office, Liverpool's government repealed the Orders in Council, a move hailed by the *Leeds Mercury* as 'the most beneficial Victory which has been achieved during the present war'.[23] More business was done, wrote Arthur Lupton in Leeds, 'than on any day for eight years past'.[24] But the enormous relief at the revocation of the Orders was soon mixed with dismay at a new conflict.

For years, Americans had resented the trade barriers, the searching of neutral ships and the impressing of captured seamen: these were seen as insults to national pride, and although the orders were revoked with regard to American ships it was too late to stop the hostility that had built over the past. There were other grounds of resentment, particularly the way that the British gave support – and muskets – to the confederation of the Shawnee, Winnebago and other tribes, when Americans wanted to push north and west into the lands that had technically been granted to them in 1783. And ever since the War of Independence the United States had its eyes on areas of Canada that it had claimed, but not received in the final settlement. On 18 June, after Congress had argued over this for two weeks, Madison's government declared war. The news did not reach London for several weeks, and was not reported in the papers until 30 July.

*

Despite the ending of the Orders and the growing tension with America, the drive for reform went on. And so did the resistance of the authorities. In June, when thirty-eight respectable middle-class men met in Ancoats Lane in Manchester, to draw up a petition for peace, a minimum wage, an end to the Combination Acts and universal suffrage, the town's notorious deputy constable, Joseph Nadin, broke in and arrested them all. At their trial in August, they were charged with 'holding an unlawful meeting, combining for seditious purposes, tending to overthrow the government'.[25] Their leader John Knight was also charged with 'administering oaths to weavers pledging them to destroy steam looms'. All were acquitted after Henry Brougham's tough defence, and their ordeal galvanised yet more anti-government campaigns.

The opposition, though still patriotic in defying Bonaparte, now had a far broader base: the gentry were suspicious of parliament and resentful of the disbanding of the volunteers; the commercial groups were bitter about taxes and trade; the workers were fighting for their livelihoods. In the new edition of his almanac *Vox Stellarum* Henry Andrews agreed that Britain had escaped the great blows that had overwhelmed other nations, but 'We are still groaning under the Pressure of very Heavy Taxes, and other Burdens, never before known.' The country's industry and trade were crippled, Andrews wrote, 'and her Streets are filled with great Complaints, so that every Mouth is extended to execrate the War, and all its dreadful Miseries, and suffering thousands sigh for the Return of Peace'.[26] In July Henry Brougham's article 'On Peace' in the *Edinburgh* argued that war had now become a way of life, and that the invasion threat had been replaced by 'the dangers of commotion from general misery'.[27]

Then the fortunes of war changed. In mid-August, accounts of Wellington's victory at Salamanca on 22 July filled the papers. 'How happy Lady Wellington must be at this glorious victory,' wrote Maria Edgeworth. 'Had you in your paper an account of her *running* as fast as she could to Lord Bury at Lord Bathurst's when he alighted, to learn the first news of her husband! Vive l'enthousiasme.'[28] And news of Spanish victories ran alongside accounts of Napoleon's march north. In June his Grande Armée of 450,000 men crossed the river Niemen, and the following month, as his plans to advance into Russia became clear, the tsar entered into an alliance with Britain and Spain.

In early September more despatches reached the papers. 'Madrid', wrote William Rowbottom on 7 September, 'Surrendered by capitulation to Earl Wellington August 14th'. Wellington had walked into the capital without bloodshed: for once there were no casualties to grieve for. But in Britain, with anxiety about the poor harvests, men were once again joining up, not for glory but to feed their families: 'a large number of men of late inlisted into the militias and different Regements of the line', noted Rowbottom, but 'most of poor familys are in a state of actual starvation'.[29] Suicide notes, like one left by a middle-aged Lancashire man on the side of a canal with his hat and clogs, simply blamed 'the badness of the times'. Provincial towns and villages sent in yet more 'Christian petitions' for peace. On 27 August, representatives from the East Midland counties met at Loughborough in a meeting of the Friends of Peace, supported by evangelicals and Methodists, with the Belper manufacturer William Strutt in the chair.[30] Pointing out in their petition that nineteen of the past twenty years had been spent at war, they noted: 'during this melancholy period, the lives actually sacrificed by war, may, without exaggeration, be computed to have exceeded the number of all the male adults now in Great Britain, and that in the same space of time, almost every known part of the world has been visited by its dreadful agonies.'[31]

In Birmingham, Tertius Galton, gunmaker though he was, joined another manufacturer, Joseph Webster, in pulling together a committee to promote a peace petition and to correspond with the Quakers in other towns. War, these petitions pointed out, was a general as well as a specific evil, destructive of human happiness and all the best interests of mankind, 'the crime of corrupt humanity'.[32]

## 55. THREE FRONTS

The Grande Armée would first take Lithuania, Napoleon declared, then impose a peace on Moscow, then head east. He would be another Alexander. 'The end of the road is India,' he said to the Comte de Narbonne:

Just imagine, Moscow taken, Russia defeated, the Czar made over or assassinated in a palace plot . . . and then tell me that it is impossible for a large army of Frenchmen and their allies to leave Tiflis and reach the Ganges. Essentially all that is needed is a swift stroke of a French sword for the entire British mercantile apparatus in the East to collapse.[1]

But was he invincible, or was he tempting the gods? In 1812 visitors to the Royal Academy exhibition were faced with a new painting by Turner, *Snow Storm: Hannibal and his Army Crossing the Alps*. It carried an implicit reference to a work the British knew well from engravings, Jacques-Louis David's *Napoleon Crossing the Alps*, painted twelve years earlier, showing him on his horse at the St Bernard Pass, mastering the great heights in triumph. But Turner's painting, based on sketches of a thunderstorm on the Yorkshire moors, showed no great hero. Indeed Hannibal the leader had disappeared completely, unless he was one among the hundreds of tiny, struggling figures, dwarfed by the mountains, caught up in the vortex of the storm, a maelstrom of natural forces. Within a year, people would look at the painting and say: ah yes, Moscow.

British newspaper readers pored over the tsar's bold declarations that no peace would be made until every enemy soldier had left Russian soil. In September there were mentions in the press of a Russian victory at Mojaisk, but the news was unclear: it took three or four weeks for reports to reach London, with fragments coming in from messengers in Berlin, Gothenburg and Stockholm. Accounts of the inconclusive battle of Borodino were equally confused, but in late September the British public learned that Bonaparte was in Moscow, and in mid-October they heard that the city had been burned by its own citizens to prevent the invaders making it their winter head-quarters – not by the French, as *The Times* had first suggested.

No more news came for nearly two months. Finally, on 9 December, the papers carried despatches from Lord Cathcart, the ambassador in Russia, reporting that Napoleon had left Moscow in late October 'and has followed the road to Smolensko by which he came', pursued by Russian generals who were taking 'many trophies and quantities of baggage, ammunition wagons, with prisoners, and some ordnance'.[2] Napoleon had waited in Moscow for five weeks for the Russian government to agree to terms but no negotiators appeared: the Russian armies had retreated beyond the city. Eventually, too late to avoid the winter, he left Moscow, his troops following with carts loaded with plunder instead of the provisions they would need so badly. The last of his remaining troops marched out in mid-October. Just before Christmas British papers reported that Napoleon was back in Paris, having escaped in a sledge through the snow. His army, containing men from all the Napoleonic states – French, Poles, Saxons, Italians – straggled after him, harassed by bands of Cossacks and partisans, hungry, cold and frostbitten, dying by the roadside in their thousands. The following spring British readers learned that when the snow melted, the piles of bodies uncovered were quickly buried or burnt for fear of disease and the poisoning of streams and rivers. A despatch from St Petersburg in late March, published in *The Times* in early May, reported that 'Two hundred and fifty-three thousand dead bodies of the enemy have already been burnt in the Governments of Moscow,

Witepsk and Mobilow; and fifty-three thousand in the town of Wilna, and the territory adjoining'.[3]

Reports of uprisings against Napoleon in the German provinces gave the news of the disaster even more force. The northern German ports were open again – finally the blockade was easing. It was an intoxicating moment, and subscriptions were launched to help the Russian people. In the summer a Russian officer visiting London brought a Cossack soldier in his entourage. Much admired in society, he became a celebrity, and his portrait appeared in *Ackermann's Repository*, starting a craze for wide Cossack trousers among the London dandies, led by the exquisite Lord Petersham. Russia, always a mysterious destination, now had a new allure. When Sarah Spencer married the dashing reformer William Henry Lyttelton in 1813, they set off on a wedding trip of over a year, through Scandinavia to St Petersburg, where Sarah was amazed at the endless flattery of the tsar who was 'called the deliverer of the world, with as bold a *bonne foi* as if Lord Wellington and Blücher and Bernadotte had done nothing but Obey his orders!'[4] She scribbled down her conversation with Admiral Cichagov, the commander of the southern army who had been blamed for not destroying the whole French army at Berezina on their retreat. 'Very shrewd, keen, quick man, *froideur*. I suppose tells truth. Said frost did all last year: skill nothing.' In odd pages in his diary for 1813, William Rowbottom made lists:

*Miles*
From Moscow to London 1587
Paris 1561
Vienna 1081
Constantinople 1700
Naples 1490

Another list gave the numbers of the different divisions of the French army in Portugal and Spain, another the new titles of all Napoleon's generals, a bevy of dukes, and the kingdoms ruled by his family. Lists helped to make sense of the war. On 20 February, shortly after noting the executions of the Yorkshire Luddites, Rowbottom painstakingly summarised the Russian calamity:

In June 1812 Buonaparte entered Russier with an army of upwards of 400,000 men his sucsess as usual great, he took the great citty of Moscow but the citty was mostly burned which caused the invading army to retreat. A very great snow fell and a severe frost comenced wich killed great numbers of both men & horses. The Russians state the loss of the invading army to be,

killed 40 Genarals 1800 Officers of inferior rank 150,733 Rank and File Prisoners 41 Genarals, 1298 Officers of inferior rank, 167,519 Non Comissioned Officers and soldiers

1131 peices of Cannon, 2000 Baggage Wagons, 1200 Amunition Waggons, 50 Stand of Collors and 16 Eagles.

The figures from Russia were impossible to verify and Rowbottom made a different list three months later. At this stage it was not clear to him, or to anyone, that Napoleon's failure would also turn the tide of war in Spain.

Emboldened by the French retreat, in mid-March 1813 Prussia re-entered the war, with a new, formidable army, fighting what German nationalists called the Wars of Liberation. Austria joined this sixth coalition in June, Sweden in July, and Bavaria and Saxony in October. French troops were transferred from Spain, and while Napoleon frantically tried to raise more in France, Wellington planned a push forward and urgently requested reinforcements from London. In May he began his advance, waving his hat as he crossed the border and shouting, 'Farewell Portugal, I shall never see you again!'[5] The campaign trail was familiar, but this time in three weeks of marching town after town fell to the British: Salamanca, Zamora, Valladolid, Burgos. On 21 June, in the great plain of the Ebro, only eighty-five miles from France, Wellington confronted and defeated the French army at Vittoria.

Napoleon's brother Joseph Bonaparte, nominal king of Spain, and his entourage had been in Vittoria. When they fled, they left behind wagons loaded with furniture, brocaded uniforms, silver and gold coins, portraits and ledgers, horses and carriages. The victory was followed by a wave of looting as soldiers seized everything from beautifully bound books to Joseph's silver chamberpot – which would be filled with champagne on festive nights at the barracks of the Royal Hussars for generations.[6] The plundering prompted an enraged outburst and a familiar phrase from Wellington in his despatches: 'We have in the service the scum of the earth as common soldiers.'[7] There were some uncommon soldiers, too, among the looters. Colonel James Hay whisked away the painting by Van Eyck that we know as the *Arnolfini Marriage*, which he later claimed to have 'found in his lodgings' after the battle of Waterloo – he tried to persuade the Prince Regent to buy it, but then left it with a friend. Twenty years later it was bought by the National Gallery, where it still hangs.[8] And in one carriage Joseph had packed two hundred canvases of Old Master paintings, taken from the Spanish royal collection. The soldiers were using some of these as tarpaulins to cover their baggage on the mules; retrieving them, Wellington had them sent to London. When he learned their value the following year, he asked that they should be returned to the King of Spain, but no reply came from Madrid, and the Spanish ambassador in London suggested he should let things rest. Eighty-one of these paintings, including Correggio's *Agony in the Garden* and Velázquez's *The Waterseller of Seville*, adding to those already given to the 'Great Duke Wellington' on his entry into Madrid in 1812, are in Apsley House today.[9]

The despatches announcing the victory were brought back to London by the Fremantles' nephew John, now promoted to major, and details of the battle were splashed across the papers on 8 July. After the illuminations and fetes, excited patriots also celebrated new heroes, like General Cadogan, who had realised that his wounds were mortal and asked to be carried to a hill to see the fight. On 4 August, the *Morning Post* printed a poem encapsulating the kind of heroism that these army generals represented, following the model of Abercromby and Moore:

Cadogan, wounded in the fight,
Cries 'Bear, O! bear me to yon height,
That, till mine eyes can gaze no more,
Till ev'ry hope of life is o'er
I may behold the Frenchmen fly,
And hear the shouts of Victory!'

They bore the Hero to yon height:
He saw the Frenchmen put to flight!
And when 'Huzza!' the Victors cried,
He heard them with a Soldier's pride:
Bless'd his brave Countrymen, and died.[10]

Vittoria heartened Britain's allies, prompting Austria to rejoin the war. During this campaign, Wellington's confidence was also boosted by the fact that he could actually pay his troops and buy the supplies they needed. The cost of the army was huge, far higher than the subsidies to foreign powers.[11] The Spanish government and troops would only accept Spanish dollars, which William Huskisson at the Treasury obtained from Mexico and South America, through agents who often creamed money off on the way as well as making huge profits on the deal. In March 1811 Wellington had told Liverpool that lack of cash might force him to stop campaigning completely: 'Unless this army should be assisted with a very large sum of money at a very early period the distress felt by all the troops will be most severe . . . and it will be quite impossible for me to do anything.'[12] He persuaded the British government that the best thing would be to pay the subsidies directly to him: he would act as paymaster general, keeping the funds for their proper military use.

Another key step was the appointment as Commissary in Chief of John Herries, a banker's son who had studied in Leipzig and had been a clerk at the Treasury to Spencer Perceval when he was Chancellor of the Exchequer. Herries took on the staggering task of supplying Wellington's army, working with Wellington's trusted Commissary General in Spain, General Robert Kennedy. The numbers they had to cater for were huge, soaring from forty thousand men and six thousand horses in 1810 to an allied force of a hundred thousand with twenty thousand horses when Wellington marched into the foothills of the Pyrenees in late 1813.[13] Although the army could buy half of its supplies locally, convoys sailed from Britain loaded with flour and bisket – by the end of the war the army, like locusts, were devouring forty tons of bisket a day.[14]

Herries managed all this, and also began looking for people who dealt in bullion, one of whom was Nathan Rothschild. After his marriage to Hannah Barent-Cohen, Rothschild had moved to London, still trading as a merchant but also accepting and discounting bills, setting up his new bank formally in 1811 in New Court, St Swithin's Lane.[15] Working with his father Amschel and his four brothers on the Continent, he was speculating brilliantly with the volatile markets and exchange rates, and was already smuggling gold bullion to France. From late 1810 he made good use of the notorious 'guinea boats', twelve-oared galleys built by the Deal smugglers, designed for speed and stealth, which could be rowed across to France even in contrary winds, carrying as much as £30,000 of guineas at a time, bringing back lace, silk, leather gloves, brandy, wine, watches and perfume. In this late stage of the war, Napoleon actively encouraged this drain of British gold, setting up a special 'smugglers' enclosure' at Gravelines, south of Dunkirk.[16]

Soon Herries became aware of Nathan Rothschild's bullion dealings, and also heard that he had large amounts of gold available. In Rothschild's own memory, the deal was simple. 'When I was settled in London', he told Thomas Fowell Buxton:

the East India Company had 800,000 lbs of gold to sell. I went to the sale, and bought it all. I knew the Duke of Wellington must have it . . . The Government sent for me, and said they must have it. When they had got it, they did not know how to get it to Portugal. I undertook all that, and I sent it through France; and that was the best business I ever did.[17]

It was in fact not quite so easy: the shrewd, strong-nerved Rothschild was also lucky in being able to boost his capital by using his wide family connections and rapid channels of communication. In Janu-

Nathan Rothschild in 1817, after war had made him rich

ary 1814 Herries was told to give him the business of supplying Wellington's armies with money, authorising him 'in the most secret and confidential manner to collect in Germany, France and Holland the largest quantity of French gold and silver coins, not exceeding in value £600,000, which he may be able to procure within two months of the present time', to be delivered to British ships at Helvoetsluys which would then carry it to Wellington via St Jean de Luz.[18] For a commission of 2 per cent if he succeeded, Nathan was to take all risks and losses. From now on he also handled the huge payments to allies, managing his vast deals, despite the suspicion of Russian and Austrian partners, through bribery and clever control of the exchange rate.

\*

Wellington needed the money. Since the summer new troops had continued to head out to the Peninsula. In July, Thomas Perronet Thompson, now lieutenant in the 14th Light Dragoons, was writing to his wife, Nancy, as he marched to Portsmouth. When they passed the fine houses of Southampton, he said, 'grave clerical looking personages come out of them, and smug Marys; and the streets are full of middling looking girls . . . who come to stare upon us.'[19] Small boys always ran out first to watch them pass: 'I do not know why it is that children seem to think soldiers apart of the common stock and what every boy has a right to be,' wrote Thompson. Hearing of Wellington's progress he thought their job would just be to make things secure: 'I suppose we go to "make sikker". We are, as the papers tell us, 6000 infantry, 1200 horse, so that we shall go up the country in a very reverend manner. Life-guards, Hussars with whiskers, artillery, riflemen, and in short all sorts of cattle are among us.'[20] He had a wonderful warm pelisse, he reassured Nancy, and had managed to smuggle a horse on board to avoid paying for a scurvy mule in the land of Sancho Panza. His horse only came up to his elbow, but was very sweet, and should be able to carry his baggage and books, including the Arabic grammar. When Nancy reproached him with being happy to leave, he admitted that was true, in a way, as a man ought 'to follow his destinies & not withdraw from them'. Although he added, 'My heart is not much in the cause; and as far as I am personally concerned, I fight for a government I despise, and for a gulled nation.'[21]

By the time Thompson sailed British and Spanish troops were in the Pyrenees. The papers told of bloodshed in the mountain passes. In September San Sebastian was stormed, followed by a week of pillaging that nearly ruined Anglo-Spanish relations, and in the first week of October the British, Spanish and Portuguese armies crossed the river Bidassoa into France. In the fighting that followed in December, Thompson's brother Charles was killed. 'It does not seem real,' he told Nancy, 'I am yet as one stunned. Half my life is gone, and the other half is with you . . .'[22] Furious with grief, he found out where Charles was buried and dug up his body, to cut off a lock of his hair and find the gold cross he always wore.

## 56. SAILORS

All this time, during Napoleon's retreat from Russia and Wellington's advance through Spain, the campaigns in America had swung back and forth: the British stopped the invasion of Canada; the Americans held off British intrusions from the north. The war was not only a distraction from the European conflicts but an unaccustomed humiliation for the navy. At the start the United States had only eight frigates and twelve sloops, but these were extremely powerful and beautifully built and their crews were well-trained professionals, many of them deserters from the British fleet. The first blow came on 19 August 1812, with the capture of the *Guerrière* by the American *Constitution*: in Britain the moment the *Guerrière* lowered its flags and struck was cast as a major disaster. 'Never before in the history of the world', bellowed *The Times*, 'did an English frigate strike to an American . . . Good God!' Why was the British squadron not reinforced? the *Naval Chronicle* asked angrily: why was there no blockade?[1]

The autumn saw more naval surrenders, of the *Macedonian* and the *Java*. There were small victories, like Francis Austen's capture of a schooner and privateer off Boston, and occasional great ones, as when Captain Philip Broke in the *Shannon* finally captured the frigate *Chesapeake* on 1 June 1813. Broke, who was knighted on his return, was a Norfolk man, like Nelson, and a cousin of Susan, the wife of Oakes's oldest son James. In October Oakes went to a meeting at the

Guildhall in Bury St Edmunds to present Broke with a piece of Plate 'in Commemoration of his valiant Atchievements in the Shannon against American Frigates'.[2] American privateers were also operating off the Portuguese coast, seizing troop transports and supply ships, to Wellington's fury, and were even raiding the seas around Ireland and penetrating into the Channel.

The navy smarted from the strain. Their ships were old and battered, their men were tired. By contrast the French had rapidly rebuilt their fleet after Trafalgar and Santo Domingo and by 1813 Napoleon had eighty men-of-war ready for sea with thirty-five more in the shipyards. William Rowbottom, like thousands of anxious relatives, was keeping a keen eye on naval news and waiting for letters, noting in his diary that John Rowbottom had had a narrow escape from death after falling from the topgallant, hurting his foot badly – he would later be discharged with a pension – and his brother Thomas had moved to the seventy-four-gun *Duncan*, off Woolwich. Both were safe, for the moment at least. Rowbottom was now in his early fifties, suffering from the 'tyrant rheumatism', and at the start of one year he copied down a 'sovereign remedy' of rhubarb, nitre and sulphur, mixed with six ounces of treacle. But his interest in the dramas of his own community was keen as ever, whether it be pit accidents or the death from fever of fourteen-year-old Betty Clough of Top o' th' Moor. Thus the departure of the Rowbottom boys ran into the news that some villains 'stole a large quantity of Rum Brandy &c out of the bar in the Punch Bowl public house Oldham whilst Mr and Mrs Barns the landlord and landlady and a friend were amusing themselves in the parlour at a game of cribbage'. Then back to the war again.

Jane Austen, like William Rowbottom, was watching naval affairs. After her brother Charles returned from patrolling the American coast, he became flag captain to his old patron Sir Thomas Williams, now Commander in Chief at the Nore, on the *Namur*. This was a guardship off Sheerness, a receiving ship for the press gangs. To save money Charles and Fanny lived on board with their two daughters and a new baby, but it was hard on four-year-old Cassy, looking thin and ill, and suffering from seasickness as the boat rocked at anchor. The girls came to stay at Chawton in July 1813. 'Charles' little girls were with us about a month,' Jane told Francis, who was cruising in the Baltic on the *Elephant*, in a letter full of haymaking, parties and plans for the garden, '& had so endeared themselves that we were quite sorry to have them go'.[3] She also told him with pride that every copy of *Sense and Sensibility* was sold and that now she was working on *Mansfield Park*. Her new novel was full of her sailor brothers and she gave Mr Price an excited description of the *Thrush* leaving Portsmouth, sprinkled with all the names of her brothers' ships. The novel was just 'something in hand', she said, 'and by the bye shall you object to my mentioning the Elephant in it, & two or three other of your old ships? – I *have* done it, but it shall not stay, to make you angry. – They are only just mentioned.' She wrote too of the bustle of Portsmouth, the excitement of the dockyard that all visitors had to see.

Life in the dockyard, and in home postings, could be difficult at times. Charles Austen's command of the *Namur* was a grim-sounding task, yet Douglas Jerrold, the son of a Sheerness actor-manager, who joined Charles Austen's crew at the age of ten, remembered being looked after kindly, allowed to keep pigeons, to read Charles's copy of Buffon's *Historie naturelle* and to join in the ship's theatricals.[4] But the Austen family life on board did not last long. Fanny died in childbirth in September 1814 and the baby girl lived only two weeks. Grief-stricken, Charles got a posting on the *Phoenix*, chasing pirates in the eastern Mediterranean, dreaming of his children and his 'dearest Fanny'.

It was hard for sailors who never quite achieved glory and whose career, after voyages in the West and East Indies and the Mediterranean, ended in unglamorous tasks at home. Tom Gill, who had been injured in action, was happy at first with his posting to naval signals, and excited about the new developments in semaphore and telegraph. From HM Signal Vessel *Warning* off Essex in July 1811, he told his old friend John Battershall that he had 'never spent a pleasanter time', as there were scores of invitations from local people and he could dine on shore every day, 'treated with a friendliness very uncommon and that I had no right to expect'. But the building of the semaphore went slowly, and he tired of being stuck on board alone in an old ship rolling in bad weather. When his sister Charlotte was ill with typhus he was unable to see her before she died. Her loss, he said, 'is the greatest evil I have known since the death of my parents, and most bitterly do I feel it'.[5] He could not bear to write to his other sister, Sophy. He asked for a shore job to offer her a home, but Sophy told him she did not want him to do this for her sake, and he moved to another station, bitter and frustrated at missing the Mediterranean and Baltic patrols and the American war.

All this time troopships and supply ships ploughed across the Bay of Biscay. In the spring of 1811, looking from his window at North Point in Plymouth, Robert Hay watched hundreds of vessels riding at anchor in the Hamoaze, the long tidal reach of the Tamar stretching down to the docks at Devonport: 'Watermen's skiffs, Merchantmen's Yawls, Warships, launches, Pinnaces, cutters, gigs etc., were every moment landing. Porters were trudging along under their ponderous burdens. Women of pleasure flirting about in all directions watching for their prey.'[6] Sailors in their white trousers, scarlet waistcoats and blue broadcloth jackets strode past, 'with all the importance of an Indian nabob'.

At twenty-one, eight years after he had been impressed as a boy at Greenock, Hay was an experienced ship's carpenter, but he was now hiding from the press gang after swimming ashore when his ship ran aground. He was longing to leave the navy. Eventually he got a place on the merchant ship *Edward*, sailing for the Caribbean, but the fear of the gang remained. Returning on the *Edward* Hay hid among cotton bales in the hold, 'trembling like an Aspin leaf' while the gang poked the sacks with bayonets.[7] Caught by the press again in London and taken to the *Ceres* guardship at the Nore, he and a Scottish companion escaped by swimming to shore, supported by pig's bladders and guided by the brilliant comet that lit the southern counties. Stealing a boat, they crossed the estuary to Essex, where they left the boat snug in a creek, hoping it would be returned to the owner, whose name was written on the stern. From there Hay got a passage north to North Shields and then walked home to Scotland and his mother's house.

But while some men fled, young hopefuls still joined the navy, often following in their family's footsteps. In August 1813 James Oakes's fourteen-year-old grandson, Orbell Oakes junior, set off to board HMS *Boyne*. He sailed from Portsmouth to join his uncle, Captain Robert Plampin, in the *Ocean* off Toulon. A new generation were going to sea.

The navy was still operating at full stretch in the blockade of Brest, the Mediterranean and the Adriatic – in 1812 Thomas Fremantle was given command of the Adriatic squadron, combing the coasts for enemy ships and bases, capturing Fiume in 1813 and Trieste the following March. When he left the Adriatic, his command had taken a thousand guns and captured or destroyed between seven and eight hundred vessels. 'Every place on the coasts of Dalmatia, Croatia, Istria and Friuli had surrendered to some part of the squadron under my orders.'[8]

The fleet were also important protectors of the merchant ships. William Salmon was now working for the Chepstow merchant Warren Jane as master of a fast snow that shared his own name, the *William*. Throughout 1812 he had carried bark from Chepstow to Dublin, iron ore from Ulverston, coal from Swansea, timber from Plymouth, bargaining hard for every cargo, worrying about bills of lading, customs checks, insurance. On every voyage he took his apprentice Tom, whom he treated as a young brother.

The American war brought a fresh threat as privateers from New England haunted the western approaches to the Channel. In January 1813 these were becoming ever more daring, capturing one brig off the Kent coast, which was then retaken by a British frigate in full view of the shore. 'At the time of the recapture,' reported *The Times*, 'there were eleven or twelve privateers in sight, and the coast to Dungeness was in a blaze from their continual firing.'[9] Like most merchant captains Salmon wanted to sail as part of a convoy. He hoped to go on the run to Cadiz, which had never been captured by the French, despite long sieges, and from there to other ports open to the British, in Malta, Sicily, the Balearic Islands and Egypt. He might even carry guns under a government Letter of Marque, which allowed merchantmen to arm in self-defence. 'I am now on the point of Chartering for Cadiz or London,' he told Fanny in September 1812, hoping to have the *William* 'Arm'd with Guns for the Modeterenean trade . . . by joining in the Cadiz trade I shall gain Friends in Case of Imergency and soon have a larger Ship – keep all to your dear self.'[10]

Fanny dissuaded him from sailing south, but when news came of the French retreat from Moscow, Salmon joined a convoy sailing to Gothenburg in Sweden, and then to Memel in East Prussia (now Klaipeda in Lithuania), a great exporter of timber. This, he was sure, could make him good money. In late April 1813 all was settled. 'Reconcile yourself, My Dear Life, and hold with your William,' he begged,

the following Voyage, debar all misfortunes, will prove for myself and the Ship the best I every yet encountr'd with – to load a full & complete cargo of merchandize at Dublin & Dundalk for Cronstadt which is the loading port of Petersburgh for Rums 32/6 for Puncheons, for pipes Wines 32/6 Salt 40 pr ton with other goods in proportion two thirds port charges at 5 pr. Ct. primage to the Master – from Cronstadt to Dundalk – for clean Hemp & Flax £7.7.0 pr ton – Cordilla Hemp – Tallow – Brussels & other goods in proportion – Ballast Iron 30 pr ton . . .'[11]

The convoy gathered at Longhope at the mouth of Scapa Flow in the Orkneys in early June, a tumult of white sails, 150 ships with a man-of-war and two armed sloops. Other vessels joined later, and by the time they sailed round the north of Jutland the convoy had swollen to 260 ships. The seventy-four-gun *Zealous* guarded them until they reached Karlskrona in eastern Sweden, when each ship sailed on to its different destination. William landed his cargo at Kronstadt Mole in early July and filled his hold, finding Russian merchants crowding the docks, desperate to find cargo space for their hemp, wheat and tallow. He crammed his cabin and spare deck space with goods and presents:

My dear Fanny I have bought no Nonsense; I have only purchased for you & Your Sisters a pair of Russia Winter Slippers lined with Fur, likewise for your Uncle & Aunt, & a pair of Morocco slippers for Mr. Gillam. I thought I must bring something to shew I had been to Russia . . . Poor Tom has only got some bowles which are handsome altho made of wood.

The sailors and traders picked up news – of the victory at Vittoria, the ending of the continental truce and the Prussian decree, made on the assumption that Napoleon would now head for Berlin, to 'burn every town down – should Bonaparte advance'. Slowly William made his way home, waiting for the convoy in Karlskrona, where he bought some berries 'which will make the most excellent Tarts', and then beating across to the Orkneys, and south through the Scottish islands. He was working out a scheme for Fanny to join him. On 8 January 1814 he set out to join a convoy at Dublin, sending her a bill payable for £163 12s 6d – his Russian profit.

The last letter in the pile, kept carefully in the family for two hundred years, was not addressed to 'My Dear, Belov'd Fanny' but formally to 'Mrs. Salmon'. Dated 26 May 1814, it was from William Greavey, a schooner captain from Strangford in Northern Ireland. Following Fanny's request, Captain Greavey had scoured the coast, finding masts and water casks and boards, all branded 'William'. The people who collected the wreckage told him that the *William* must have foundered on the reefs around the great granite lighthouse of the South Rock, built in 1797, a few miles to the north. The violence of wind and tide had prevented any rescue and the sinking ship had drifted out to sea. Among the debris washed ashore were 'some wooden bowls, Varnish'd & Gilt denoting them to be the Manufacture of some Country to the Eastd. of the North Sea'.[12]

# 57. SWAGGER AND CIVILISATION

As soon as the news of Vittoria arrived in July 1813, the Prince Regent, so excited that he almost claimed to be directing the Spanish war himself, organised a great fete in Vauxhall Gardens, opening with a dinner for a thousand male guests – the women were told to come afterwards, at nine o'clock. Tickets sold for huge sums on the black market, the river was thick with wherries trying to land passengers and the roads were so jammed that the Duchess of York was stuck in her carriage for two hours. When the women finally got to Vauxhall there were no refreshments left. At midnight, when they tried to leave, there was equal chaos. Hearing that his wife Caroline was coming, the regent himself decided to stay away, giving a private fete in the afternoon at Carlton House, the men arriving in full dress and the women in diamonds and pearls.[1] This was sheer cowardice, thought Lord Glenbervie, who had staggered over to the Vauxhall gala at some cost. In his diary for 22 July he wrote:

I have spent the greatest part of my time in bed, having been up all night till yesterday morning at 6 o'clock at the Fete at Vauxhall in honour of the great Victory at Vittoria, planned by the Regent, but in truth given by one hundred and twenty Stewards nominated by him, who paid fifty guineas each for fifty admission tickets to be distributed gratis by them and about one thousand two hundred other persons who paid two and half guineas each for a dinner ticket.[2]

The entertainment, which Glenbervie heard cost eight thousand guineas, 'consisted only of a dinner of turtle soup, cold meat, bad fruit, indifferent wine and wretched attendance'. The tables were all 'pell-mell, nobles and tradesmen, high and low' and they were crowded on to awkward benches 'as ill-accommodated as Lord Wellington and his staff can ever have been in the bustle of a campaign'. Two more great galas for the general public were held at Vauxhall at the end of the month. Fourteen thousand people crammed into the gardens, 'which number would doubtless have been still greater,' remarked *The Times*, 'but for the thunderstorms and heavy rain which took place in the afternoon.'[3]

The star of London society this year was not Byron, but Mme de Staël, exiled by Napoleon, who arrived in June with her son and daughter, and as Glenbervie complained, 'took town by the neck'. High society ladies stood on chairs to get a glimpse of her at the Marquess of Lansdowne's party. To begin with 'Mrs. Corinne', as Byron called her, was all charm and passionate interest but by late September Glenbervie was writing that she 'was not agreeable yesterday': 'She abused English dishes – especially those at table – English customs, and, by frequent insinuations, the language and literature of England. She wants to part with her house in London, and I suspect will not stay out her twelvemonth.'[4] She did stay however. Although shattered by the death of her youngest son, killed in a duel over gambling, in June 1814 she was still overpowering the London literati and the Holland House set, dining with Sheridan, Erskine, Whitbread and the noted literary figure and poet Samuel Rogers, and deluging Byron with notes. 'I admire her abilities,' he groaned, 'but really her society is overwhelming – an avalanche that buries one in glittering nonsense – all snow and sophistry.'[5]

There was a kind of exuberance in upper-class and commercial Britain that suited de Staël, the energy of defiance, of thrusting on against all odds. The country had changed dramatically in the twenty years since Pitt had stood in the House of Commons and declared war against France on that rainy night in February 1793. For one thing, it was more brightly lit. Following William Murdoch's experiments with gas lighting in the early 1790s, Boulton and Watt in Birmingham, and the company started by Murdoch's assistant Samuel Clegg, had built gasworks to light factories and shops, while the German entrepreneur Frederick Winsor had been demonstrating its use for street lighting, rather to the alarm of many inhabitants. In 1807 Winsor had lit Pall Mall, and now, in 1812, he won a charter to open the first public gas works, the Gas, Light and Coke company. Within a few years light flickered into almost all of London's dark alleys.

George Cruikshank, *The Good Effects of Carbonic Gas*: a gassed cat slides from the roof, a bird falls from sky, people gasp for breath

Across the country civil engineers and builders were hard at work. In the capital John Rennie had designed three new bridges at Vauxhall, Southwark and the Strand, the future Waterloo Bridge. And mechanical engineers too were creating wonders. In 1805 Trevithick had made a steam engine for Wylam colliery on the Tyne, although it proved too heavy for the wooden track, and three years later he exhibited his steam locomotive 'Catch-me-who-can' on a circular track near Gower Street in London. 'There is a steam engine to run a race against a racehorse at Newmarket next meeting in October,' Sarah Spencer had told Bob in 1808, 'and they say it will certainly win. I really should like to see it. I suppose it is a sort of self-moving carriage.'[6] Then on Midsummer's Day 1812 the first practical locomotive ran at Middleton colliery near Leeds, invented by the Northumbrian John Blenkinsop, who solved the track problem with a rack and pinion system. With martial loyalty he named his first engine *Salamanca*: three others followed before the end of the war, one called *Lord Wellington*. The race was on. Soon George Stephenson built the first of his many engines, the *Blucher*, which ran at Killingworth colliery in 1814.

All this suggested prosperity, but the government were still worried about their rising budgets, and in 1812, the Chancellor, Nicholas Vansittart, increased duties on postal charges, glass and tobacco, and brought in new taxes on servants and dogs, and even on leather. This last was seen by opponents as a blow to labourers, who needed boots, and also as an absurd tax on the government's own spending, since the army and navy combined were by far the greatest purchasers. The following year came Vansittart's 'New Plan of Finance', baffling to all but a few, which involved borrowing from the City to let the Sinking Fund commissioners buy stock, and selling Exchequer Bonds when need was pressing. The juggling did supply the government with money when it was most needed, but since it often involved buying stock high and selling low, it put the Exchequer still more firmly in the bankers' hands.

Over the past five years all the banks had found that their brokerage business was increasing, bringing new tensions. At Hoare's, 'From the Increase of the Brokerage Business', the partners worried, 'vast Quantities of Letters are necessarily to be written: those of Mr Willoughby are confusedly written & many Erasures in them; this Mr H noticed.' The clerks were hopelessly overstretched – they were often detained in the City, collecting dividends and exchanging stock, so the partners reorganised their work again.[7] This looked efficient but caused jealousy among the senior clerks, and in 1813, a row broke out in the Fleet Street office. Harry Hoare, who felt he had done everything to make the clerks' lives easier, threw up his hands and declared it would be easier to employ outside brokers rather than send his men up to the City to undertake transactions themselves. Not surprisingly, the next client who came in was not greeted kindly: 'Mrs Horsley's Proceedings are disgraceful to Herself & should not be countenanced by Messrs H. Do not advance her a Sous. & let her Account be closed at the first convenient opportunity.'[8]

It was a family argument, a workplace tiff. But it was indicative of the jittery state of the banks and the City. The private banks were nervous about reserves, since the drop in the price of government stocks was prompting customers to take their money out so that they could buy them while they were low. 'Our House has stood many a rude blast,' declared Harry Hoare in 1813, 'but it cannot be concealed that our resources are alarmingly diminishing and steps must be taken to meet a crisis which seems fast approaching, but it must be done with that secret and discriminating hand which the subject and the very great importance of it demands.'[9]

The private banks had to be careful, and the unlucky ones might go under. But the big brokers in the City, like the Baring brothers and Rothschild, were minting money. David Ricardo, whose proposals for a return to the gold standard had been rejected by parliament in 1811, was now making a vast fortune as a loan contractor, joining a syndicate that won bids for a loan of £12 million in 1810, over £22 million in 1812, and an astounding £49 million in 1813.

Shrewd City men, it seemed, would always do well – in 1814 Marianne Thornton wrote to Hannah More about the death of one of her husband Henry's partners: 'Did you hear that old Mr Down is dead? He left £150,000 after educating fourteen children and marrying six daughters – so you see banking is a good trade even in these bad times.'[10]

For many, despite the Regency glitter, these were emphatically bad times. With slaughter on the battlefields and at sea, the state had a tendency to close its eyes to abuses at home. It was left to individuals and to groups of concerned people to fight for a cause. On 9 March 1812 Samuel and Hannah Greg's eldest daughter Bessy married William Rathbone, the son of their great Liverpool friends. When their daughter Elizabeth was born in March 1813, Hannah Greg and Hannah Rathbone, friends since childhood, were grandmothers together. Bessy had often stayed with the Rathbones and been swept up in the political and social campaigns of the Liverpool Unitarians, and she now flung herself into charitable work in Liverpool, setting up a Relief Society and pressing for education for the poor. She was impressed by Robert Owen's *A New View of Society* in 1813, which argued for a national education scheme. Her father Samuel had his doubts, referring disparagingly to 'Owenmania', and Hannah, after her years of teaching at Quarry Bank, was wary and realistic. Yes, she said, it had to be a national scheme, as she was well aware

that no private fortune whatever could uphold Mr O's excellent schemes (except perhaps Mr Arkwright's who thus would employ his two or three millions) and that his talents are more applicable to some public or national benefit, than to a concern of Business that requires constant attention, faculties & time, mind and anxiety, of its possessors to keep it from ruin.[11]

Several women of this new generation, like Bessy Rathbone, were determined campaigners. In 1813 Elizabeth Fry entered Newgate prison for the first time, urged to go there by Stephen Grellet, a French aristocrat who had become a Quaker minister in America. Inside, the prison was divided into men's and women's quarters. When Fry visited she saw three hundred women in two rooms, sleeping in three tiers, with few clothes, hardly any food, many with babies. The stench was terrible. Dedicated reformers had been trying for years to get better conditions in British prisons. John Howard, High Sheriff of Bedfordshire in the 1770s, was so appalled by the county prison that he raised the issue in parliament, publishing *The State of the Prisons* in 1777 and going on to visit prisons across Europe, publishing reports and detailed plans for improvement. After his death in 1790 his work began to bear fruit – at Chester the people were extremely proud of their airy prison, built on the lines he proposed, and showed it off proudly to summer visitors. But Newgate was far from alone in its unreformed state, and Elizabeth Fry and others would have to fight for another thirty years. Joe Fry was no businessman and their eleven children, dubbed affectionately 'Betsey's brats', were often farmed out to the other Gurney sisters. Like all the Gurney girls Elizabeth was determined and individual, some said eccentric: she once dragged a cow into Newgate because the women needed milk. Her campaign was based on Quaker tenets of equality, insisting that all should be treated according to the principles of humanity and justice, and above all with kindness. Her brothers Joseph and Sam – who took over the bank in Norwich when their father died in 1809 – both joined her, and so did her brother-in-law, the brewer and MP Thomas Fowell Buxton.[12] Her sister Louisa, so fervent for democracy at the age of twelve, campaigned for farm labourers, wrote on children's education and became a friend of William Blake and his young artistic admirers, the 'Ancients'.

The work in the prisons was matched by a drive to improve dispensaries and lying-in hospitals, and by a new concern for the mentally ill. Towards the end of the war William Hone and Edward Wakefield were on a committee surveying London asylums, exposing a list of abuses, embezzlement and maladministration.[13] It seemed that the war had little effect on the value put on the lives of the poor, the mad or the deviant. The criminal law had become even more dra-

conian. Outside Newgate, crowds gathered every Monday morning
to see people swing: the poor in the street, the wealthy in rented seats
at nearby windows. The governor gave a 'hanging breakfast' beforehand. On a single day in February 1814, five children between the
ages of eight and twelve were condemned to death at the Old Bailey,
one of them for burglary and stealing a pair of shoes.[14] Often these
sentences were commuted to transportation, which itself seemed like
death to many.

One word bandied about freely during these years of war, in the diaries and letters of journalists, technocrats and improvers and especially nonconformists and evangelicals, was 'civilised'. 'Uncivilised'
was used of the French sans-culottes, but also of the women in Newgate, of mobs and workers' unions, dwellers in the slums, labourers in
the countryside, the barefoot British children who stole shoes – and
indeed all children. The *Evangelical Magazine* advised parents to teach
their boys and girls that 'they are sinful polluted creatures'.[15] Whole
groups and populations could be written off in this way. Living at
Racedown in Dorset in 1795, Dorothy Wordsworth found the peasants of the West Country miserably poor: 'indeed they are not at all
beyond what might be expected in savage life.'[16] It was evident to
Edinburgh intellectuals that the 'uncivilised' Highlands of Scotland
must be dragged into the modern world. It was clear too, to a rich
tourist like Sophia Hoare, that the Welsh were impossibly backward:
they could not even speak English. Sketching in Caernarvon in 1809
she complained of being surrounded by 'dirty little Children all chattering Welch'; indeed to her amazement, all through Wales, 'it was
only now and then that the Post Boys or the Maids at the Inns could
understand us or we them'.[17] On another trip in the Brecon Beacons, she found the mountains beautiful but 'the people seem very
uncivilised indeed, and astonished beyond measure by us and our
Conveyances – they had never seen a Phaeton, and asked if it was not
what was called a London Fly'.[18] She gazed about her like a traveller
observing a remote tribe: 'Women remarkably good looking, though

short, and all wear the same dress invariable, a black beaver Hat and dark blue cloth Coat.'

Sophia's standard of civilisation stretched little further than English-speaking, cleanliness, a knowledge of smart carriages and better dress. Her mother Hester Piozzi said scathingly, when Sophia visited her in Denbighshire a year after her marriage to Henry Merrick Hoare, that they had gone 'to make the fashionable Mountain Tour of N. Wales: – The Ton Folks *do* so now o'Days; that they may say next April in London, at what *Distance* they pass'd their Summer from the Metropolis.'[19] But from now on, throughout the century, 'civilisation' was also seen as the empire-builders' mission – in Africa and India and Australia, where the aborigines employed at sheep-shearing were both praised and laughed at for covering their near nakedness in 'plenty good fellow cloth' in the white man's style.[20] In 1813, among evangelical campaigners, including Sophia's husband's cousin, the Clapham-dwelling William Hoare and his wife Louisa, this came to a head in the campaign to renegotiate the East India Company's charter.

The Company was essential to British exports, sending textiles, iron, muskets and other goods out to India and China each year in its great fleets, and bringing back grain and rice during the food shortages as well as cotton, and saltpetre for gunpowder. Now their ship trade was badly needed to offset the shortage of raw materials due to the American war. It brought in revenue too: the high duties paid on Asian imports and tea had reached over £3 million a year since 1806.[21] The Company also loaned huge sums to the government, as well as supplying guns, lending ships for transporting troops, and funding armies in India itself. But when the charter was renewed, after insistent lobbying by merchants and shipping companies, the Company lost its monopoly of trade with India and other parts of South East Asia, though it kept the Chinese trade. Other British ports gained the same status for the oriental trade as the Port of London, and the import of Indian cotton goods was banned, except for re-export. It was almost twenty years since Hannah Greg had told the Rathbones of Samuel's insistence on such a ban. 'The Muslin Manufacturers he says are apprehensive that the influx of India Piece Goods would be considerably increased by the trade being opened, to the prejudice of the Cotton Manufactory,' she had written, but it would be worth fighting the Company's monopoly if the ports demanded a prohibition on cotton imports at the same time.[22] In the end Greg won what he wanted: the import ban allowed Lancashire to capture the entire market, almost destroying a key part of the Indian economy.

The new charter had another significant element, not commercial but social, the 'pious clause', by which the Company lifted its ban on missionaries and even agreed to help them. Once the slave trade was abolished, India became a priority for the evangelicals, as Zachary Macaulay told his son Tom: 'No sooner was Africa disposed of than Asia called for our exertions: & the very day after the meeting of the African Institution, I was obliged to take active measures for calling a meeting, wh shd prevent the blessed light of Christianity from continuing to be shut out of Asia, as it had hitherto been.'[23] Wilberforce explained to the Methodist MP Joseph Butterworth that he had been appalled for years at the lack of any missionary activity in India. He trusted the renewal of the charter would open a great era, when 'it would please God to enable the friends of Christianity to be the instruments of wiping away what I have long thought, next to the Slave Trade, the foulest blot on the moral character of our country'.[24]

The Clapham Sect had enthusiastic advisers. Macaulay's elder brother Colin had spent years in India, and Clapham neighbours included John Shore, Lord Teignmouth, Governor General of India from 1793 to 1798 and President of the British and Foreign Bible Society since 1804, and Charles Grant, chairman of the directors of the East India Company. Although Grant was keen that the Company should keep its monopoly, he was a passionate advocate of the Christianising mission, and his dark, polemical account of the subcontinent, *Observations on the State of Society among the Asiatic Subjects of Great Britain*, originally published in 1792, was reprinted in the new campaign. Evangelicals on the Company's Court of Directors were supported by over nine hundred petitions with half a million signatures, particularly from Methodist congregations. Opposing these campaigners, long-serving Company officials argued that Indians must have the right and liberty to worship as they wished, without pressure to turn Christian. In practical terms, they pointed out that the best way to avoid trouble was to respect local religions and customs: the Sepoy uprising at Vellore in 1806 had been provoked by changes in Company dress code that forbade Hindus to wear religious marks on their foreheads, and required Muslims to shave off moustaches and beards and wear hats instead of turbans. Ignoring this argument, evangelicals firmly declared– as Wilberforce had done since the first attempt to impose such a clause in 1793 – that the Hindu religion was 'depraved'.

Thousands of people turned out to hear missionary sermons, while the many religious magazines carried grim descriptions of infanticide and *sati*, the burning of Hindu widows, painting Hindu culture as coloured by violence, hypocrisy, trickery and corruption, its people blinded by priests and pagan legends and superstitions. The emphasis on the plight of widows drew many women into the campaign, in Britain and in India itself. Mary Martha Sherwood had moved with her army husband from Calcutta to Cawnpore and Meerut, and had borne six more children. After her son Henry died of whooping cough in 1808, Sherwood became a fervent evangelical, setting up schools for the children of soldiers and local Indian families and founding an orphanage. She kept writing (her chronicle of Christian family life, *The Fairchild Family*, was a syrupy staple of Victorian childhoods), and in the final year of the campaign she published *Little Henry and his Bearer*, the story of the dying eight-year-old orphan Henry who achieves the conversion of his Hindu bearer Boosy:

'Sometimes I think,' said he, 'when I feel the pain which I did this morning, that I shall not live long: I think I shall die soon, Boosy. O, I wish! I wish I could persuade you to love the Lord Jesus Christ!' And then Henry, getting up, went to Boosy, and sat down upon his knee, and begged him to be a Christian.[25]

*Little Henry* was enormously popular, going through thirty-seven editions by 1850, and being translated into French, German, Spanish, Hindustani, Chinese and Sinhalese.

But India could still feel like a place of chivalry and romance. In Birmingham in May 1814, Lucy Galton was worrying about her son Howard, no longer a small boy concerned for his tortoise but now nineteen, coming in late at night, consorting with mysterious unnamed friends. As she gave him motherly advice she told him of her reading, as she always had. She was following the reviews in the *Quarterly*, waiting for Scott's *Waverley*, and letting her imagination fly:

There is another book review'd, wch I actually hunger and thirst for – it is Forbes Oriental anecdotes & drawings. He gives the most interesting account, full of facts that he witness'd himself. – He travell'd with the Mahratta army – They have all sorts of trades following the Camp – & whole streets of shops as in a town . . . It contains many Tiger stories, more terrifying than Bruce's Hyenas.[26]

Forbes was her cousin and she remembered his first going out, as a boy of sixteen. Men of a new generation were going there now, as soldiers, merchants and missionaries. One of these was Reginald Heber, who became the parson in his home village of Hodnet, married Amelia, the daughter of the Dean of St Asaph, and afterwards became Bishop of Calcutta. Frank and open and easy-going, he wrote many popular hymns, including 'Holy, holy, holy, Lord God almighty' and the fervent missionary hymn 'From Greenland's icy mountains', composed for the Society for the Propagation of the Bible. It speaks for its times.

> From Greenland's icy mountains, from India's coral strand;
> Where Afric's sunny fountains roll down their golden sand:
> From many an ancient river, from many a palmy plain,
> They call us to deliver their land from error's chain.
>
> What though the spicy breezes blow soft o'er Ceylon's isle;
> Though every prospect pleases, and only man is vile?
> In vain with lavish kindness the gifts of God are strown;
> The heathen in his blindness bows down to wood and stone.

In the debates over the East India Company in 1813 parliament was asked to consider 'whether or not the acquisition of empire carried with it a bounden duty to promote Christianity'.[27] Eight years before, when Mungo Park set off on his second, ill-fated expedition, backed by the Colonial Office, he had been hunting for a trade route, but Joseph Banks, who helped organise the trip, also saw it as a step towards empire. 'Should the undertaking be fully resolved upon', Banks wrote, 'the first step of Government must be to secure to the British throne, either by conquest or by Treaty, the whole of the Coast of Africa from Arguin to Sierra Leone.'[28] He hoped that the expedition would free people from tyrannical princes, 'inculcating in their rough minds the mild morality which is engrafted on the Tenets of our faith'.

The first territory secured to the British throne, as Banks put it, was Sierra Leone, and experience there showed how hard it was to create a godly commercial empire. Freetown was now a busy port, its British-style houses crumbling in the heat, its streets thronged with African and Arab traders, its market stalls heaped with plantains and guavas, melons and coconuts, fish, rice and maize. Ships thronged the estuary and local agents did well out of prize money and recaptives. Yet to the dismay of the Company and the African Institution, the Chief Justice, Robert Thorpe, repeated the accusations that Thomas Perronet Thompson had made when he was governor, that forced indentures were another form of slavery. His arguments were ignored. Like Thompson before him, in 1815 Thorpe was recalled, and was left without a job or a pension. From now on, guns, God and Mammon would march side by side in the making of empire.

# 58. 'WE ARE TO HAVE OUR REJOICINGS'

Suddenly the newspapers were full of hope. In the autumn of 1813 Wellington was advancing through Spain, and on 4 November 'arrived in Oldham glorious intiligence from Germany stating the total overthrow of Buonaparte in person in a genaral action near Leypsic by the Prusians, Russians Sweeds & Austrians'.[1] In Suffolk James Oakes thrilled to the same news of 'two Grand Battles . . . at which The French and her Allies were totally routed, 30,000 taken Prisoner and 35,000 Killed & Sick taken. Bonaparte made his Escape wh. a party of Cavalry to Erfurt.'[2] A fortnight later, he wrote, 'A Flagg of Truce arriv'd Yesterday at Yarmouth from Holland advising a general Insurrection & requesting the aid of this Nation.' In the same week, in Oldham, Rowbottom noted that 'the seven United States of Hollond threw off the French Yoke and declared for the Prince of Orange and their old Consititution'. Trade was taking a turn for the better, work was plentiful, and flour, meal and potatoes were down in price.

In the terrible battle of Leipzig, 'the Battle of the Nations', on 16 October 1813, the combined armies of Austria, Prussia and Russia converged upon the French. It was the largest battle Europe had ever seen, involving half a million soldiers. Up to a hundred thousand men died, and it took two weeks to clear the field of the dead. The countryside around was devastated, the people of the city died of starvation and epidemics, and the area took years to recover. It was beyond all the horrors that the British invasion propaganda had conjured. After Leipzig Napoleon retreated with the remnants of his army across the Rhine into France. While many people now pressed for peace negotiations, fiery correspondents like Edward Sterling, 'Vetus' of *The Times*, argued vehemently for the fighting to continue. Answering Vetus, Hazlitt declared bitterly that British politicians 'will not suffer the vessel of the state to enter the harbour, in the hope that they may still plunder the wreck, and prey upon the carcases. The serpent's hiss, the assassin's yell, the mowing and chattering of apes, drown the voice of peace.'[3]

Another icy winter blighted Britain. In January 1814 James Oakes was complaining that the snow was so deep, with a cold, blustering north-east wind, that all the entrances into town were blocked, no coaches could get in and the mails were stopped. The rivers were frozen, 'consequently no Navigation nor any getting up of Grain to any Market'.[4] The last of the famous Frost Fairs was held on the Thames, with a wide, brushed road across the river called 'Freezeland Street', surrounded by swings and gambling booths, bookstalls, toyshops, jugglers and gingerbread sellers and a great Wheel of Fortune.

No one could guess which way that wheel would turn. But at the end of February the weather itself seemed like an omen of change, with a sudden thaw that made it feel more like May, 'the Transition from extreme cold to really warm very extraordinary'.[5] The main concern of the men in their clubs and the groups crowding around handbills was not the weather, nor the continuing war with America, but the drive to stop the beleaguered emperor, who was fighting a brilliant rearguard action to prevent the allied Austrian, Russian and German forces crossing the borders into France. In the south those borders had already been crossed. Wellington had brought his army over the Pyrenees, and, after stopping in the heavy winter rains, on 21 February he defeated Marshal Soult at Orthez. Meanwhile representatives of the allies met at Chaumont, and were persuaded by Castlereagh, with the promise of large promised subsidies, to make Napoleon an offer, and, if he rejected it, to band together until he was defeated. Since the Treaty of Chaumont, signed on 9 March, required a return to pre-revolutionary frontiers, Napoleon swiftly turned down their terms.

The allies fought on. In April Wellington was in Toulouse. The duke's victories were the ones that children remembered: the names of Peninsular battles were etched on their minds. In Gainsborough, where Thomas Cooper was at school during 'the hottest of the war period':

our little town was kept in perpetual ferment by the news of battles, and the street would be lined with people to see old Matthew Goy, the postman, ride in with his hat covered with ribbons, and blowing his horn mightily, as he bore the news of some fresh victory, – Ciudad Rodrigo, or Badajoz, or Salamanca, or Vittoria, or St Sebastian, or Toulouse, – Miller and I were pencilling soldiers and horses, or, imaginarily, Wellington and 'Boney' – for we never heard the word 'Napoleon' at that time of day.[6]

The uncertainty affected the stock market, and helped at least one startling fraud, involving the popular naval hero and radical Thomas Cochrane, whose behaviour was still at odds with convention. In August 1812 he secretly married an orphaned sixteen-year-old, Katherine Barnes: due to doubts that this was legal, they married twice more, in 1818 and 1825 just to confirm it. Cochrane's uncle, Admiral Sir Alexander Cochrane, had employed a French exile, Captain de Berenger, as a rifle instructor for marines on his North American fleet. In February Berenger, an undisclosed bankrupt, posed as a messenger bringing despatches from Paris saying that Napoleon was dead and the war was over.[7] Immediately stocks soared. Cochrane had no idea of the fraud but had been advised to buy stocks beforehand, and since he, as well as another uncle, Andrew Cochrane-Johnstone, made a rapid killing both were arrested. Cochrane was fined, imprisoned and stripped of his naval rank and his Commons seat. He was also supposed to stand for an hour in the pillory, but this was remitted for fear his supporters might riot. The electors of Westminster, convinced of his innocence, immediately re-elected him.

In this time of suspense, ordinary life went on. 'Do not be angry with me for beginning another letter to you,' wrote Jane Austen to

Cassandra in March, 'I have read The Corsair, mended my petticoat, & have nothing else to do.'[8] There were rumours of French victories and a threatened armistice, sending people rushing to London to sell their stocks before disaster came. Once this fear was banished, there was nothing to do except wait.

On 4 April, *The Times* still carried accounts from the French papers of triumphs and prisoners. Unknown to British newspaper readers, in the last two days of March – a week before the news reached the London press – the Russians and Prussians had entered Paris. In the last stages of the battle, on 31 March, when the Russians were attacking the heights of Montmartre, General Marmont made a secret agreement with the allies and surrendered. Next day Talleyrand, now representing the exiled Bourbon monarchy, persuaded the French senate to form a provisional government: he was elected president and handed the key of the capital to the tsar. On 2 April, the new Senate declared that Napoleon was officially deposed. By now he was camped at Fontainebleau, surrounded by, as he thought, loyal troops. But he had already lost Marmont, and his marshals would not back his angry plan to march on Paris.

'The week before Easter was certainly a very agitating one,' Amabel Hume-Campbell confessed to Agneta Yorke, '& to be sure I slept but little the night after that Tuesday when three different gradations of incredible Good News came on us from Hour to Hour'.[9] The papers were peppered with contradictory reports. On Tuesday 5 April, they carried a rumour of a great battle in which the emperor had been wounded. This proved untrue. In fact, the day before, on 4 April, he had abdicated in favour of his son, the three-year-old King of Rome, but the allied powers would not accept this, and two days later he was forced to renounce the throne, unconditionally, for himself and his heirs. On the evening of 9 April, the day before Easter, a *Gazette Extraordinary* was issued by the Foreign Office, saying that despatches had arrived 'announcing the abdication of the crowns of France and Italy by Napoleon Bonaparte'. Queues formed outside booksellers and print shops, and the stock of newspapers ran out. The country

Rowlandson, 'Peace at Last', 1814

rang with bells, shone with illuminations, echoed with dinners for workers. The Gregs' house in Manchester was lit by specially bought lamps spelling the word 'Peace' over the door. 'What overpowering events!' exclaimed Richard Heber's friend John Stonard. 'Surely there will never be any more news as long as we live. The Papers will be as dull as a ledger and Politics insipid as the white of an egg.'[10]

*

The monarchs were back on their thrones. At Hartwell Louis XVIII, a portly widower of sixty, and his niece the Duchesse d'Angoulême, the only surviving child of Louis XVI and Marie Antoinette, had their bags packed into the carriages taking their exiled court to Grillon's Hotel in London. Hazlitt, admirer of Napoleon, walked through the brightly lit streets in utter gloom. Later in the year, in a long review of *The Excursion* for the *Examiner*, he acknowledged Wordsworth's poetry to be something new and important although the poetic image of rural life was far removed from the reality – 'the small-beer is sure to be sour – the milk skimmed – the meat bad'. He looked back too to the bright days when Wordsworth had welcomed the French Revolution, 'that glad dawn of the day-star of liberty': 'The dawn of that day was suddenly overcast: that season of hope is past: it is fled with the other dreams of our youth, which we cannot recall, but it has left behind its traces, which are not to be effaced by birthday odes, or the chaunting of Te Deums in all churches of Christendom.'[11]

On Easter Sunday, 18 April, the Te Deums were sung and the Lord was praised for removing the tyrant. 'Nap the Mighty is *gone to pot*,' wrote the nineteen-year-old Thomas Carlyle in amazement, with double underlining.[12] In Oldham, Rowbottom noted:

The different Manufacturers gave Diners and ale to there Respective Work people who paraded the Streets with musick and Flags with Differnt Devices. A pair of looms were Drawn in a Cart where a person was weaving Callico and a person Representing Buonaparte was winding. Every degradation was used to Insult the Memory of the fallen Monarch whose Tyrannical Career was at an end. The whole was conducted with the greatest harmony and good will, ale &c flowed in the greatest profusion.[13]

'All that has passed in France in the last few weeks!' Maria Edgeworth exclaimed, 'a revolution without bloodshed! Paris taken without being pillaged! . . . I dare say it has not escaped my aunt that the Venus de Medicis and Apollo Belvidere are both missing together: I make no remarks.'[14] But it was not all joy and glory: it took until May for James Oakes to learn that his nephew James Baker, whose commission he had obtained, had died of wounds received at the battle of Toulouse. Many families mourned sons and brothers and nephews. But others were home again. Sailors and marines were discharged – young Tom Rowbottom arrived back in Oldham, discarding his scarlet uniform of the Royal Marines after nearly six years' service. Four months before, Benjamin Harris, still not cured of his Walcheren fever, had been sent to a veterans' battalion. Now the battalion was marched to Chelsea to be disbanded. Here, Harris remembered, thousands of soldiers were lining the streets,

and lounging about before the different public-houses, with every description of wound and casualty incident to modern warfare. There hobbled the maimed light-infantry man, the heavy dragoon, the hussar, the artillery-man, the fusilier, and specimens from every regiment in the service. The Irishman, shouting and brandishing his crutch; the English soldier, reeling with drink; the Scot, with grave and melancholy visage, sitting on the steps of the public-house among the crowd, listening to the skirl of his comrades' pipes, and thinking of the blue hills of his native land. Such were Pimlico and Chelsea in 1814.[15]

A week or so later Harris was discharged, receiving his pension of sixpence a day.

The French soldiers and sailors on the hulks and in the prisons were equally jubilant at the new peace, even though their emperor was defeated, as the Peterborough newspapers reported: 'The joy produced among the prisoners of war at Norman Cross by the change of affairs in France is quite indescribably extravagant. A large white flag is set up in each of the quadrangles of the depot, under which the thousands of poor fellows, for years in confinement, dance, sing, laugh, and cry for joy, with rapturous delight.'[16] In early May another article noted that the prisoners 'are so elated at the idea of being so soon liberated, that they are all bent on selling their stock, which they do rapidly at 50% advanced prices. Many of them have realised fortunes of from £500 to £1000 each.' It was different for the French officers. Many had been on parole around Melrose, and Scott and his wife had been particularly hospitable to them. Their feeling now, Scott wrote, 'is very curious, and yet natural. Many of them, companions of Buonaparte's victories, and who hitherto have marchd with him from conquest to conquest, disbelieve the change entirely.'[17]

As soon as they could after the abdication, on 11 April, the allies signed the Treaty of Fontainebleau, exiling Napoleon to Elba, given to him as a miniature kingdom, and restoring Louis XVIII. British goods that had been piling up in warehouses on the Belgian frontiers, along the Rhine, and in Savoy were finally allowed into France. But liberals were anxious about the return of the Bourbons, fearing a return to despotism in France: 'Give thy Kings law', John Keats urged in his sonnet 'On Peace' – 'leave not uncurbed the great'. In late April Louis paid a state visit to London. 'At this present writing, Louis the Gouty is wheeling in triumph into Piccadilly, in all the pomp and rabblement of Royalty,' wrote Byron to Tom Moore. 'I had an offer of seats to see them pass; but as I have seen a Sultan going to mosque, and been at *his* reception of an ambassador, the most Christian King "hath no attractions for me".'[18] Even the loyal Amabel Hume-Campbell stayed away, partly from fear of the crowds, but also because she was not keen on the Bourbons.[19] On 24 April the lame, nervous French king left Dover for Calais on the yacht *Royal Sovereign*, entering Paris on 3 May.

As if to mark the passing of an era, on 29 May 1814 Josephine Beauharnais died in Paris, allegedly from pneumonia caught by wearing flimsy muslin to meet the tsar. Napoleon, hearing of her death in his exile on Elba, refused to come out of his room for two days.

The Peace of Paris, signed the day after Josephine's death, restored France to the borders of 1792, with slight adjustments, increasing the French population by nearly half a million, while Holland and Belgium were joined in the 'Kingdom of the Netherlands'. In June the Allied sovereigns, Frederick William III of Prussia, Tsar Alexander of Russia, Prince Metternich, the Austrian Chancellor, and the heads of various German states – plus attendant family, courtiers and hangers-on – arrived in London for the peace celebrations. With them came several generals, including the testy Russian General Platoff and the much admired Prussian General Blücher. In contrast to the apathetic reception of the returning Bourbon king, this visit caused great excitement. Orders went out that the whole route from Dover should be lit. The artist Thomas Sidney Cooper, then eleven, remembered how every house in Canterbury was lit up and flags hung across the streets. Small details stuck in his mind: how the Emperor of Russia was bald, but had a round handsome face; how Blücher 'had bits of black like sticking plaster on his face – little tufts of hair I suppose, or perhaps small wounds.'[20] Behind them came wounded soldiers, some on wooden legs or crutches, some with only one arm: 'they were treated and cheered by the populace, who smoked and drank with them; and the city was kept in a state of conviviality and uproar until midnight.'

In London, on the day of the grand procession, windows along the route were let for huge sums, bakers ran out of bread and the cows in Hyde Park were frightened by the guns and cheers and produced no milk. The Russian Grand Duchess Catherine, the tsar's sister, took over the whole of Pulteney's hotel in Piccadilly and the tsar spurned the rooms prepared for him at Carlton House to join her in the Pulteney's relative quiet. The exuberant reception overwhelmed the visitors. General Platoff, or so Creevey told his wife, was 'so cursedly provoked at the fuss' that he refused to go out: 'they are all sick to death of the way they are followed about, and above all, by the long dinners. The King of Prussia is as sulky as a bear, and scarcely returns the civilities of the populace.'[21] The Prince Regent, who laid on one of his lavish private fetes, was frantic over their reaction. Worse, this coincided with a new burst of popular sympathy for his wife, Caroline, who appeared at the opera to almost as much applause as the visiting dignitaries. 'All agree that Prinny will die or go mad,' wrote Creevey cattily. 'He is worn out with fuss, fatigue and *rage*.' Amid this chaos, White's club put on a grand ball at Burlington House, where the royal parties met politicians and bankers, among them, to Jane Austen's astonishment, her brother Henry. 'Henry at Whites!' she wrote when Cassandra told her. 'Oh, what a Henry!'[22] Betsey Fremantle was there too, gasping at the splendour: 'The rooms were brilliant, and looked like a Fairy palace . . . 2000 people set down without any inconvenience or confusion. I stayed till seven o'clock in the morng. And met almost every body I know in London.'[23] White's ball was rivalled by a great masquerade at Watier's, to which Byron went dressed as a monk, while Cam Hobhouse put on Byron's Albanian robes and Caroline Lamb appeared in mask and domino, flashing her green pantaloons.[24]

Lady Jerningham reported every stage of the visits to her daughter Charlotte. 'The Emperor of Russia is gone off', she noted finally,

with an idea of the English Ladies not being very reserved. It is said that He used to be Litterally so absorbed by them taking his Hand and staring at Him, that He said He danced meerly to be a Little more out of the way, mixing with others, than standing or Sitting in the Room. This was however in the main flattering; but the Regent was greeted only by Hisses and Groans, which must have been Less welcome.[25]

The foreign royalty fascinated people. Crowds turned out as they made forays into the provinces. In Oxford, where they trooped around the colleges, the crush at the celebratory dinner in the Radcliffe Camera was so great that hats and shoes and caps flew off, gowns and cloaks were 'torn in pieces'; the Prince Regent waved and bowed and the affable Blücher became exceedingly drunk.[26] In late June, Mary Heber, who was acting as her brother's housekeeper and general manager at Hodnet – consulting him about poor relief subscriptions, planting new trees and wondering what to do about his brute of a bull which gored horses and dismayed their neighbours – wrote to thank him for looking after her during her London visit. Particularly, she added, with sisterly irony, for his efforts 'without which I would have lived and died without seeing the Emperor of Russia'.[27] Having arrived home, she told him: 'We are to have our rejoicings here however: a Ball equal at least to Whites is to be given at Shrewsbury, & Lord Hill is to be our Emperor; it is fixed for the thirtieth & all the county will be there.'

*

Packet boats to France and Holland were filled with returning émigrés and with German soldiers who had fought with the British army.
Among them, at the end of July, were an odd trio: Percy Bysshe Shelley, leaving his wife Harriet behind, was eloping with the sixteen-year-
old Mary Godwin, taking with them Mary's elder step-sister, Claire
Clairmont. The girls were heading for the country that their mother,
Mary Wollstonecraft, had seen in the Revolution over twenty years
before. They travelled for a month, always short of money, bumping
over rutted roads through a countryside battered by war, into Switzerland and back through Germany and Holland, returning to face William Godwin's dismay and Harriet's tearful despair. The experience
marked them, as Mary acknowledged: 'The distress of the inhabitants has given a sting to my detestation of war, which none can feel
who have not travelled through a country pillaged and wasted by this
plague, which, in his pride, man inflicts upon his fellow.'[28]

In the Britain that the travellers left behind, there were balls and
peace festivals, tables in the streets, sports and games on the green.
Bury St Edmunds held a feast for four thousand poor people. The
bells rang from dawn, the sun shone:

The Town was filling at an early hour and completely throngd by ten o'clock.
They came from all parts for 20 miles round. Every carriage, Waggen, Cart
& Horse was put in requisition. The whole of the Meat was prepard a Day
or two before & of course was designed to be cold: the Plum Puddings hot.
The Tables were set all thro the Butter Market, on the Beest Market & round
the Theatre, down to the Wool Pack.[29]

Every town paper had similar stories. In Leeds, a great procession carried the proclamation of peace.[30] In Gainsborough there
was 'a grand emblematical procession', with a wagon, drawn by six
horses, holding figures 'representing Wellington, Blucher, Platoff, the
Czar Alexander, and other high personages, together with the fallen
emperor labelled "Going to Elba". There were bands of music in the
streets, a thanksgiving sermon and anthems at church, and feasting
parties at the inns, during the day, with a general illumination, bonfire, crackers, and squibs at night.'[31] Inspired by this, nine-year-old

Thomas Cooper and friends put on paper hats labelled with generals' names and went round the farms singing hymns and cheering, 'Peace and plenty! God save the King!', holding out their caps for coppers.

In the little Devon town of Ashburton on 21 July, officers from all the parole prisoners' nations joined in a guild procession: 'Shoemakers, Carpenters, Sawyers, Coopers, Blacksmiths, Butchers, Painters, Curriers, Clock-makers, Gardeners, Stocking Weavers'. The Order of Procession said it all:

> Constables, Band; Austrian Standard Bearer
> English Union Bearer; Russian Standard Bearer;
> Bearer of Standard of Peace on Horseback
> Town Arms Bearer on Horseback
> The Portreaves; Clergymen in their Gowns; Fifty Flower Girls;
> Haymakers and Agriculturalists; Four Shepperdesses;
> Woolen Manufacturers . . .
> Bearer of the French Standard;
> Union Bearer; Twenty Flower Girls; Sailors;
> Britannia in Triumphal Car drawn by Four Horses abreast . . .[32]

In Cobbett's eyes all these celebrations displayed a crazed hysteria. He raged at the balls, illuminations and processions, 'from the solemn and gawdy buffoonery of the freemasons down to the little ragged children at the Lancashire schools': 'Upwards of two thousand oxen were roasted whole and upwards of two thousand sheep. One boundless scene of extravagance and waste, and idleness and dissipation pervaded the whole Kingdome, and the people appeared to be all raving drunk, all raving mad.'[33]

To cap this 'madness' the Prince Regent announced a Grand Jubilee, to be held on 1 August, marking the centenary of Hanoverian rule and the anniversary of the battle of the Nile. In the run-up there were complaints about the neglect of the sacrifices and taxes that the war had demanded, evoked in a poem in the *Statesman* on 26 July:

For this, *I* lost an eye, an arm, a leg,
For this poor Nan, too, is compelled to beg.
Illumination! – O the shame and scandal,
*God's light they grudge, and tax my farthing candle.*

London was already *en fête*, with crowds going to see Kean at Drury Lane as Richard III, and Grimaldi in *The Wild Man* at Sadler's Wells. The prince's bonanza took over Hyde Park, Green Park and St James's Park, where a ticketing system kept the plebs out.[34] There was a revolving Temple of Concord, a mock naval engagement on the Serpentine in Hyde Park, a balloon launch with Mr Sadler from Green Park and a final firework display at ten o'clock in St James's Park. It was not quite as spectacular as hoped: Sadler's balloon descended in Mucking Marshes in Essex, the fireworks were too slow, and the Chinese pagoda caught fire and tumbled into the lake, killing two men and some swans, and drawing crowds rushing from the other parks to see it as they thought the blaze was part of the show.

All the fairground shows of Bartholomew Fair, due at the end of the month, were allowed to move to the three royal parks: swings, roundabouts, wild-beast shows, 'donkey racing, jumping in sacks, running for smocks, &c.' and even printing presses to run off special souvenirs.[35] As Charles Lamb groaned to Wordsworth, Hyde Park was turned into 'dry crumbling sand', all grass was gone, and 'booths & drinking places go all round it for a mile & half I am confident . . . the stench of liquors, *bad* tobacco, dirty people & provisions, conquers the air'.[36]

As the fairground debris was cleared from Hyde Park, the euphoria began to turn sour, like a hangover after too long a party. After all, Britain was still at war.

French prisoners went home, but British hulks and land prisons were filled with Yankee soldiers and sailors. They too fell prey to the diseases of the hulks, like the typhus that raged on the *Bahama* at Chatham, overcrowded with eight hundred men, 'weak, weary, fatigued and half-starved', wrote the surgeon Benjamin Waterhouse.

It was almost worse, he thought, because the views of the Kent hills and the banks of the Medway were so lovely, with pastures and hedges 'of a deep and beautiful green'. And they were taunted by British crews sailing past them, playing 'Yankee Doodle', and crying out that they were bound to America 'to flog the Yankees'.[37] From Chatham Waterhouse and his fellow Americans were sent to Dartmoor: 'Sorrow and sadness within; gloom, fog, or drizzly rain without.'

On 27 September 1814 the headlines read: 'Capture of the City of Washington'. That morning despatches had arrived bringing news that Major-General Robert Ross had landed at Chesapeake Bay at the end of August and occupied Washington. Expecting victory, President Madison and his wife Dolly had been holding a dinner for forty guests and fled just in time, leaving the British officers to dine in the deserted White House. The official despatches claimed that retreating American forces had set fire to a sloop in the harbour, and the fire had spread to the city; another version held that British troops had fired houses in revenge for the burning of government buildings in Canada; stories spread that Ross's men had piled chairs on the White House table and started the blaze themselves. The White House, the unfinished Capitol and the Library of Congress were all gutted before rain doused the flames. A week later, Ross realised he could not hold the charred capital, and ordered his men to withdraw. A fortnight later he was mortally wounded in a skirmish near Baltimore.

While ministers praised the Washington raid, critics were horrified. 'Willingly would we throw a veil of oblivion over our transactions at Washington,' declared the *Statesman*. 'The Cossacks spared Paris, but we spared not the capital of America.'[38] Despite some uproar in the Commons, Ross was cleared of blame. As it continued American war brought increasing losses: London financiers and bankers, the society in which Henry Austen moved, became ever gloomier, as Jane Austen reported to Martha Lloyd in September 1814. Henry's view,

& the view of those he mixes with, of Politics, is not chearful – with regard to an American war I mean; – they consider it as certain, & what is to ruin us. The [Americans] cannot be conquered, & we shall only be teaching them the skill in War which they may now want. We are to make them good Sailors & Soldiers & [gain] nothing ourselves. – If we *are* to be ruined, it cannot be helped – but I place my hope of better things on a claim to the protection of Heaven, as a Religious Nation, a Nation in spite of much Evil improving in Religion, which I cannot believe the Americans to possess.[39]

When the Treaty of Ghent with the godless Americans was finally signed on Christmas Eve there were no winners. The situation returned to its pre-war state after a terrible waste of lives on both sides. After peace was officially signed it took over two weeks for the news to reach the battlefields: in January 1815 Colonel Andrew Jackson's small army of seven hundred men defeated a large British force at New Orleans, leaving two thousand British dead or wounded. And that spring there were still thousands of American prisoners in Britain, desperate to get home. 'Our anxiety increases every day,' wrote Waterhouse on 28 February. 'We inquire of every one the news. We wait with impatience for the newspapers, and when we receive them are disappointed; not finding in them what we wish.'[40] Every now and then, he added, they saw Cobbett's *Political Register*, 'and when we do, we devour it'.

Everyone was devouring the news, and a return to peacetime normality in Britain seemed worryingly slow. One group in particular feared for their livelihoods. The farmers had made big profits from produce and rents, but now that corn prices began to fall they asked for higher tariffs on imported corn. At once manufacturers and workers protested, seeing this as a ploy to keep bread prices high. It was no more, said the farmers, than the protection afforded to industry by laws against export of machinery and duties on imported cotton and iron. James Oakes had watched the alarm of farmers in Bury market place over the past months. 'Some alteration must take place, either in Rents or prizes, or many Farmers will be ruind,' Oakes wrote in

November.[41] A Bill was introduced to ban imports when the home price of wheat fell below eighty shillings a quarter, passing the first stages in the Commons in January 1815. In the later stages of the Bill during early March crowds gathered for several days round parliament and outside ministers' houses, tearing down iron railings and scrawling 'Bread or Blood' on the walls.[42] 'I am in the greatest hurry – we are in the midst of riots – & I just saw a Charge of Cavalry from my Windows,' wrote Lady Melbourne, watching from her house opposite the Horse Guards.[43] Over a thousand infantry and cavalry were brought to London and the Life Guards charged crowds with sabres drawn. It was the start of a battle over the Corn Laws that would last for thirty years.

Taxpayers waited for a reprieve: the Property Tax – the official name for income tax – was supposed to expire in January 1815 and other wartime taxes by July. But to meet the shortfall and pay the huge national debt, the Chancellor in fact planned to raise £5 million from new and increased taxes. On 22 February dismaying news appeared: extra duties on wine and tobacco, an extra 50 per cent from bachelors on their carriages and horses, and increases on the current taxes on servants, horses for trade and pleasure, dogs and game licences, plus an increase in stamp duty, taxes on windows in warehouses and hot-houses, and on newspapers.

Earlier that month, on Thursday 2 February 1815, Leigh Hunt was at last released from gaol. Hurrying across the fields between Enfield and Edmonton, on his way to see Hunt, Charles Cowden Clarke met John Keats, now apprentice to a surgeon and apothecary in Edmonton. At the last field gate, Keats thrust a poem into Clarke's hand, 'Written on the day that Mr. Leigh Hunt left Prison':

> What though, for showing truth to flatter'd state,
> Kind Hunt was shut in prison, yet has he,
> In his immortal spirit, been as free
> As the sky-searching lark, and as elate.[44]

The flatter'd states were back in the ascendant. The previous November delegates had gathered in the Austrian capital to take part in the Congress of Vienna, deciding the terms of the peace. At the end of February 1815, after three months of complicated talks between the different nations, and countless assemblies and balls and parades, the ambassadors and dignitaries were complacent waiting for the final formal talks to begin.

Manchester celebrates Napoleon's banishment

# VII : ENDINGS

## 1815 AND BEYOND

You say that Bonyparty he's been the spoil of all,
And that we have got reason to pay for his downfall;
Well Bonyparty's dead and gone, and it is plainly shown
That we have bigger tyrants in Boneys of our own.

ANON.

# 59. TO WATERLOO AND ST HELENA

On Friday 10 March 1815, James Oakes wrote an alarmed entry in his diary. 'This morning by Mail the Acct came of Bonaparte's making good his Landing in France with 10 or 12,000 Men.'[1]

After slipping away from Elba, Napoleon had landed ten days earlier near Antibes, with six hundred men. Fanny Burney, back in Paris with her husband, later described the blindness and lack of foresight in the city: 'A torpor indiscribable, a species of stupor utterly indefinable, seemed to have enveloped the Capital with a mental mist that was impervious. Every body went about their affairs, made or received Visits, met & parted, without speaking, or, I suppose, thinking of this event as a matter of any importance.'[2]

In London, as rumours poured in, the stocks dropped 2 or 3 per cent. Every day there were new and contradictory reports: that Napoleon had reached Lyons and most of the army and navy had defected to him; that the French marshals planned to make a stand, Napoleon's army was deserting and he had been driven back south, '& great hopes were entertaind there Bonaparte would be surrounded & Brot a Prisoner, Dead or Alive, to Paris', scribbled Oakes. 'This had very much improved the Aspect of Affairs and causd general Joy. In another Post or two are in Hopes of this most desireable News being confirmd.'[3] It was not confirmed. There was no definite news for the next three days. But on Good Friday, the 24th, 'The London Papers this morning announced the Arrival of Bonaparte at Paris on Monday last, 20ᵗʰ Inst, without Opposition. Not a Gun fird.'⁴

The evening before, Louis XVIII fled again with his family. In Radnorshire, Joanna Hutchinson rode impatiently to the town, so her sister-in-law Mary told her brother Tom Monkhouse, 'in hopes of finding a newspaper to satisfy us on the report we have had of B. having entered Paris'. It was terrible not to have a paper,

at such a time as this when we are all anxiety both on this subject and the Corn laws –we have not had one since the 13ᵗʰ and therefore are in utter darkness probably made more gloomy by reports which are afloat in the neighbourhood . . . What can these wise Emperors & Kings think of themselves now, for giving such a tyranny an opportunity of once more bringing misery upon the world when they had it in them to destroy him . . .⁵

Mary was flustered but believed the farmers generally were pleased, having felt so ill-treated in the peace and fearing a drastic lowering of corn prices. More than half of them, who 'think of themselves alone and look no further than the present would be most happy to have war again'.

As Southey said towards the end of the month, 'This breaking loose of the Old Dragon has put the Corn Bill out of sight & out of mind.'⁶ The farmers were not the only ones who saw good in renewed conflict. The arms dealers checked their stocks, and Nathan Rothschild, whose government business had collapsed when Napoleon was sent to Elba, took up the business of paying Wellington's armies again, though at a reduced rate of profit, and began arranging new subsidies – the British government pledged £9 million to help the coalition fight back. But the people at large were almost paralysed with dismay. A new war meant new taxes, more hardship. The soldiers, so recently discharged, were hauled back again. Benjamin Harris, still waiting for his pension, was recalled to his battalion, 'but I was then in so miserable a plight with the remains of the fever and ague, which still attacked me every other day, that I did not answer the call, whereby I lost my pension.'⁷ The recruiting officers dashed out again, and thirty thousand troops converged on

George Walker, 'The Thirty-third Regiment'. The recruiting officer drums up men in Yorkshire outside an inn named after the Duke of Wellington

Canterbury, so many that the line of men marching to the transports stretched all the way to Deal, on the coast, where the ships were waiting in the Downs.

Waterhouse and the American prisoners also heard the news, and the few Frenchmen still in Dartmoor prison 'collected together, and shouted *Vive L'Empereur*! And the yankees joined them, with *huzza* for Bonaparte; and this we kept up incessantly, to plague the British.'[8] The treaty with America was ratified on 20 March, and American prisoners who had money were told to go to Plymouth and pay for their own passage. Those who remained in Dartmoor became increasingly angry and desperate. On 6 April, the guards discovered breaches in the wall and noticed large numbers of prisoners gathering. The agent, Captain Shortland, ordered the alarm bell to be rung and other curious prisoners poured into the square, to be faced by Shortland and fifty of the garrison. No one knew who gave the order, but firing began, with the sentries taking pot-shots from above and killing seven prisoners including fourteen-year-old Thomas Jackson, shot in the back. An embarrassed Castlereagh promised the enraged American government that transport would be speeded up and Waterhouse and his fellows finally sailed from Plymouth on St George's Day, 23 April 1815.

For the next two months, the British papers followed the fighting in Flanders and around the Rhine, and tried to keep track of the efforts of the Austrian Army of Italy to secure the Alpine passes. The May blossom came and went, and June was fine and hot. The haymaking began and smart Londoners prepared to leave for the country and the sea, and planned their tours to the Lakes or to the Highlands. Then rumours began to spread, from smugglers and cross-Channel packets, of three days of fighting south of Brussels, from 16–18 June. Captain Sutton, owner of the Belgian packets, returned from Ostend with claims of victory. Rothschild messengers also brought early bulletins, but when Nathan Rothschild told the government, no one would believe him. Knowing that his huge stocks of foreign money might no longer be needed and adding up the amounts he was owed for subsidies, Rothschild turned to the Exchange. First he signalled his agents to sell consols, his gloomy face implying a knowledge of defeat and driving prices down. When shares reached bottom he bought, knowing they would soar after the victory. Contrary to myth, he made no millions but began, at least, to recoup some of his losses.

Speculation grew, but still the government waited to hear from Wellington. Finally, at eleven at night on 21 June, Wellington's aide, Henry Percy, who had travelled without stopping, still in his blood-stained uniform, arrived in London in a chaise and four with three French eagles poking out of the windows. Hunting for Lord Bathurst, Secretary for War, Percy went to the Horse Guards, then to the Earl of Harrowby's in Grosvenor Square, where Liverpool and Bathurst were dining. After he broke the news, Liverpool whisked him on to the house of the merchant Edmund Boehm in St James's Square, where the Prince Regent was attending a grand dinner and ball. Excited crowds already filled the square, singing 'God Save the King' and the Boehms' smart guests dashed away to try and find accounts of the casualties, leaving the ballroom empty. Next morning a *London*

*Gazette Extraordinary* carried the official despatches, and the *Morning Chronicle* bore the headline 'TOTAL DEFEAT OF BONAPARTE', and continued, 'We stop the press to announce the most brilliant and complete victory ever obtained by the Duke of Wellington and which will forever exalt the Glory of the British Name.'[9]

The despatches were printed in full in the centre pages of *The Times*, describing the action and listing the known casualties. It was glorious news, James Oakes admitted, but 'the slaughter was immense on both sides'.[10] Many letters like Lady Jerningham's were written that week:

What a melancholy Victory we have gained by the Loss of so many Considerable officers! General Picton is said to have been equal to the Duke of Wellington. The poor Brave Duke of Brunswick is gone. Lord Uxbridge is reported to day to be dead, he had lost a Leg. Lord Carlisle's Son, Frederick Howard, who married two years since Miss Lambton, Granddaughter to Lady Jersey; in short as you will See in the Paper, it is innumerable to tell how many have fallen.[11]

Two days after the battle the army physician John Robert Hume estimated that fourteen thousand dead lay on the field, and many wounded men, particularly French soldiers, were still out there. 'The two nights they have been out is all in their favour,' he added bluntly. 'They will have a better chance of escaping fever this hot weather than our own people who have been carried into hospitals the first.'[12]

The papers reported that Bonaparte had dashed back to Paris determined to raise a new army. But there was no doubt that this was the end.

The public illuminations were grander than ever, with flaming tributes to Wellington and Blücher. But letters home from soldiers were sad and grim – 'how anyone escaped alive out that scene of carnage is strange,' wrote James Stanhope.[13] The celebrations were mixed with mourning, and collections were taken for the wounded and the families of those who had died.

Over the summer British tourists crossed the Channel to tour the battlefield. 'The great amusement at Bruxelles, indeed the only one except visiting the sick,' Caroline Lamb told Lady Melbourne, 'is to make large parties & go to the field of battle – & pick up a skull or an old shoe or a letter, & bring it home.'[14] Displayed in the drawing room or study, the relics were sentimentally admired. The rush of visitors included Walter Scott, aghast at the horrors of modern war; on the battlefield, where so many had been hastily buried, the smell was 'most offensive': 'the more ghastly tokens of the carnage are now removed, the bodies both of men and horses being either burned or buried. But all the ground is still torn with the shot and shells, and covered with cartridges, old hats, and shoes, and various relics of the fray which the peasants have not thought worth removing.'[15] He picked up one of the small notebooks in which all French soldiers had to enter their expenses, service and punishments, noting that the field was covered with fragments of these records. Scott published his account in *Paul's Letters to his Kinsfolk*, ostensibly a Scotsman writing home to his family: another quick bestseller.

Turner too walked round the battlefield, making sketches and taking detailed notes. But when he painted *The Field of Waterloo* three years later he showed no glorious fighting but a field of the dead. French, British and German soldiers, officers and men, lie tangled together, the armies indistinguishable from one another, while women hunt for their loved ones by the light of a flaming torch – figures of all those wives, sisters, mothers, daughters who had waited so anxiously throughout the war. Finding her dead lover, a woman flings her arms around his corpse.

On 26 June the papers announced Napoleon's second, and final, abdication. Speculations about his future buzzed for the next month. In the end it turned out that he had hoped to sail to America but found the French coast too closely patrolled by the British. At Rochefort on 15 July, where he read a British government command that he leave the country within twenty-four hours, he surrendered to Captain Maitland of the *Bellerophon*. The ship anchored in Torbay three days later, giving Napoleon his first close view of the country he had planned to invade. No strangers were allowed on board or alongside, yet people came down to the bay in their thousands, from nearby counties and from London, packing the shore and hiring boats to row out and catch a glimpse of him walking on deck. In Plymouth, where the *Bellerophon* sailed next, sailors hung out placards telling spectators that Bonaparte was at breakfast, or in his cabin, and when these read 'Coming on deck' the small boats surged forward. The water was so crammed that there were several collisions and two girls drowned when their father's boat was run down by a naval cutter.

Crowds come to see Napoleon on the *Bellerophon* in Plymouth Sound

General George Dyer of the Marines went out on the *Myrmidon*'s boat early in the evening and watched Napoleon, standing with his hat off by the gangway, looking at the crowds through his opera glass. Dyer rushed home to write down every detail: his white pantaloons and dark blue coat (some thought bottle green) with red collar and cuffs, 'buttoned close up to the throat'; his high forehead and thinning hair and 'fix'd steady look':

Colonel Bunbury arrived this day, to inform Bonaparte that he was to be sent to St. Helena, which greatly disconcerted and surprised him as he expected to have been permitted to land, and have an asylum in this Country. When I reflected on the wonderful events that had taken place I could scarcely believe (while looking at Bonaparte) that I actually saw this man who had caused so much Blood to be spilt and so much misery to all Europe and that he was at the Moment a Prisoner in a British man of War, in an English Port – But alas! How inscrutable are the ways of Providence.[16]

So overwhelmed was Dyer that his diary entry ended with a heart-felt prayer that he might look after his own family's happiness with a proper respect for the Almighty's wisdom and goodness, *'without which all human efforts must be vain!'* Eventually Napoleon was transferred to the *Northumberland*, which would take him to his banishment on St Helena in the South Atlantic. After cruising off Berry Head for a few days, the *Northumberland* sailed on Friday 11 August 1815.

Ten days later a bonfire blazed on the summit of Skiddaw, and on the mountaintop local residents, including Wordsworth and Southey, feasted on roast beef, plum pudding and punch. But if they could celebrate wholeheartedly, to countless others, including the Hollands, Byron and Hazlitt, relief at the end of war was tinged with heart-ache at the downfall of their hero, now a small strutting man on the deck of a huge ship, ploughing the Atlantic. In 'Napoleon's Farewell', Byron imagined him proud even in defeat, only conquered 'When the meteor of Conquest allured me too far':

> Farewell to thee France! When thy diadem crown'd me,
> I made thee the gem and the wonder of earth, –
> But thy weakness decrees I should leave as I found thee,
> Decay'd in thy glory, and sunk in thy worth.
> Oh! For the veteran hearts that were wasted
> In strife with the storm, when their battles were won –
> Then the Eagle, whose gaze in that moment was blasted,
> Had still soar'd with eyes fix'd on victory's sun!

In December 1815, Howard Galton came of age – he had not even been born when the wars started in February 1793. In a celebratory but sermon-like letter about the rules for adult happiness, his father Samuel wrote:

For one Moment let us consider the Fate of Buonaparte; he was a private Individual; he became the Arbiter of a greater part of the civilized World than ever existed in the time of the greatest Conquerors – of Alexander the Great, Caesar, or Gengis Khan. His success was boundless as his Wishes – But at what Expence did he effect this – 'by more than Punic Perfidy, by Cruelty the most inhuman, the Violation of all Oaths of Solemn Engagement & of all Sense of Religion, the Lives of Millions' . . . And what has been the Result to him – Banishment to a Solitary Island.[17]

What avails it, wrote the serious father, 'if a Man can gain the whole World & lose his own Soul'.

## 60. AFTERWARDS

The long negotiations of the Congress of Vienna had ground on
all through the months leading up to Waterloo. In the interminable,
meandering talks, Castlereagh, and then Wellington, who took over
from him in February 1815, argued for British interests against the
Tsar, Metternich, the Prussian Chancellor von Hardenberg, and
Talleyrand, speaking for Bourbon France. Around them circled delegates from Denmark, Spain, Sweden and Portugal, the Papal States,
Genoa, Wurtemberg and Hanover – almost every state in Europe.
Their 'Final Act', bringing together all the separate treaties, was signed
on 9 June 1815, nine days before the battle. In the summer the talks
resumed and went on until the new Treaty of Paris was finally signed
on 20 November. In the interim, Castlereagh and Wellington were
both outraged by the brutality of the Prussian army of occupation,
and although the allies – and many people in Britain – would have
liked France to pay sterner penalties, they pushed through the British
cabinet's agreed policy of 'security not revenge'. France returned to its
pre-revolutionary territory and accepted a fine of 700 million francs,
payable over five years, during which a coalition army, for which the
French had to pay, would occupy its northern departments.

The pre-war dynasties were, by and large, returned to their old
boundaries and powers. Prussia became the dominant German state,
acquiring parts of Saxony, Pomerania and Westphalia, and Austria

regained her Italian influence, taking back Lombardy and Venetia. Castlereagh declined to join the 'Holy Alliance' of Russia, Austria and Prussia, considering their agreement to govern their empires according to 'Christian principles' as mystical nonsense, and tried instead, with limited success, to win agreement to stop the international slave trade. In all this bartering the chief casualty was Poland, where some territory was divided between Prussia and Austria and the rest was controlled by Russia. Only in France was any vestige of democratic power acknowledged.

In this popular view a tyrant had been removed from Europe and Britannia ruled the waves. Britain emerged from the French wars as the leading industrial and financial nation, in control of the seas and supreme in colonial and commercial power. The empire, as it would soon be called, had gained new colonies: Trinidad and Tobago, St Lucia and Demerara in the Caribbean; the Cape of Good Hope, Mauritius and Ceylon in the Indian Ocean. The army and navy had been streamlined, the government had become more centralised, taking over power from the counties, and its creaking old departments had been overhauled, their busy clerks providing the essential back-up to the final victories.[1] And Britain now had a host of heroes: admirals like Howe, Jervis and Collingwood and dashing frigate captains like Pellew and Cochrane, with Nelson supreme above all; soldiers, the dead 'fathers of the army', the Scottish generals Abercromby and Moore, and the victorious Anglo-Irish Wellington, garlanded with honours from foreign powers. Already a duke, Wellington was granted £200,000 to buy an estate, although the final choice of Stratfield Saye was not made for another two years.

The strain of the war years, the bitter fighting in parliament and the stress of the long negotiations on the Continent played their part in the later breakdown and suicide of Castlereagh, who cut his throat with a penknife in his dressing room in Kent in 1822. But his colleagues thrust on. The Tories held on to power until 1830, with Liverpool as Prime Minister until 1827, followed briefly by Canning and Goderich and then by Wellington himself, the Iron Duke, fighting a rearguard action against the Reform Bill. This would be passed in 1832, under his successor, the Whig Prime Minister Charles Grey, now Earl Grey, who had presented the reform petition drawn up by the Friends of the People, so long ago, at the start of the wars in May 1793.

And what of the men and women glimpsed in this book? Here are some endings, a handful among the many. Thousands of sailors and soldiers drifted home, to different fortunes and futures. John Nicol, who had hidden from the press gang during the second war, was almost destitute, having failed to get his navy pension. A few years later he told his story to John Howell, who published it in Edinburgh in 1822, giving Nicol the royalties. Nicol died in 1825. At the end of his book he wrote that he could not bear the idea of the poorhouse but was quite resigned to death: 'I have been a wanderer and the child of chance all my days, and now only look for the time when I shall enter my last ship, and be anchored with a green turf upon my breast, and I care not how soon the command is given.'[2] The other Scottish sailor, Robert Hay, scooped up by the press gang in Greenock at the age of thirteen, studied navigation and then worked on the Ardrossan Canal, acting as clerk and storekeeper for eighteen years. He wrote his memoirs in 1820–1, and then articles for the weekly *Paisley Advertiser* in 1828, becoming sub-editor in 1830 and eventually editor. He died in 1847, aged fifty-eight.

Among the officers, Francis Austen came on shore in May 1814 and although still a naval officer, did not command a ship again for thirty years. He settled with Mary and their five children at Chawton House in Hampshire, owned by his brother Edward: both he and Charles were there when Jane Austen died in Winchester in 1817. In line with naval patterns of seniority Francis was regularly promoted and in 1844, aged seventy-one, returned to sea, becoming Commander in Chief of the North American and West Indian Station, sailing to the Caribbean. His flagship, the *Vindictive*, was a 'family ship': his first flag lieutenant was his son Herbert, followed by Charles's son, Charles junior, while another of Francis's sons, George, was the chaplain, and his daughters Cassandra and Fanny came to help him entertain. In 1863 he became Admiral of the Fleet. He died in August 1865, aged ninety-one. Charles Austen too remained in the navy: at seventy-one, he became Commander in Chief of the East Indies and China Station: he died of cholera in Burma, aged seventy-three.

Many army families lost members of two generations. William and Bessy Harness's son Charles, a toddler at the start of the war, qualified as a cadet and sailed to India in 1809 with his father's regiment, the 80th. In May 1815, a month before Waterloo, his transport ship was wrecked off South Africa when he was sailing back on leave. Like his father, he left to be a soldier and never came home.[3] Shipwrecks, accidents, ill-health and ordinary fatalities replaced the deaths from wounds and wartime fevers. A month after Waterloo, Betsey Fremantle and her husband set off to Paris, Geneva and Italy, where Betsey met her sister Mary, whom she had not seen since she left Naples eighteen years before. The tour was a whirl of happiness, but three years later, on 18 December 1819, her husband died of a sudden heart attack.[4] For a long time afterwards, Betsey, the incorrigible diarist, could write nothing at all. She pulled herself together as she always had, and wrote on until old age, her diary covering the coming of Victoria, the Reform Bill and even the Great Exhibition. Her son Tom became an MP, Secretary for War and Chief Secretary for Ireland, and his brother Charles raised the British flag in Western Australia (the town of Fremantle is named after him), and later became a rear admiral, controlling the transports from Balaclava during the Crimean War. Betsey died in Nice in 1857, aged seventy-nine.

By 1814 the Tower was so full of weapons that arms were diverted to Edinburgh, Chester, Dover, Chelmsford and Tynemouth, and contractors were warned to slow down manufacture. Then, in March 1815, when Napoleon returned from Elba, in a sudden panic all the orders were increased. In July, the Ordnance cancelled them all again. The gunmakers were left with stocks piled high, and no money coming in. After Waterloo the armaments store and factory at Weedon found its budget cut and its labourers dismissed. Today some buildings remain, like a ghost town. Captain Robert Pilkington became Inspector General of Fortifications, the most senior Royal Engineer post. He died in July 1834, aged sixty-nine. There was another curious coda to his wartime life. After the war, Pilkington began to develop his Canadian lands, arranging for roads to be driven into the forests and offering a hundred acres to willing settlers. Among those who took up the offer were the extended families of Thomas Lepard, Joseph Davies the miller, and the carpenter George Wilbee. After a long, difficult journey, they found a wild, untamed land, and there were failures and disasters and land disputes – many cursed Pilkington's dreams – but more Northamptonshire families came to join them and Pilkington Township is still there today.[5]

Some of the prisons closed too, although in others, including Dartmoor, the doors still clang shut. After 1815, the last prisoners from the hulks, prisons and parole towns gradually drifted home. But some remained. In Wincanton two Italians stayed on and made their homes there: Gosue Soldini, a barometer maker, and Alberto Bioletti, a hairdresser and jeweller. So did Louis Duchemin, captured on board the corvette *La Torche* in the West Indies in 1805. He married Elizabeth Clewett, a printer's daughter, in Wincanton in 1808 and after the war he worked as a French teacher. When he applied for a job in Birmingham in 1821 clergy, solicitors, surgeons and gentry from Wells, Shepton Mallet and Wincanton all sent testimonials. Louis died in Birmingham in 1855, aged seventy-eight, having spent fifty years in England.[6]

In 1815, to general amazement, it appeared that despite the long blockades industry and trade had survived and even flourished in the twenty years of conflict. Internally, the nation was more tightly linked, in a practical sense. Better roads and new bridges meant faster mail and stagecoaches, while freight could now be sent more cheaply along a network of nearly four thousand miles of canals. And the railway age was slowly approaching: in 1815 Stephenson was working on his locomotives in Newcastle and the first steamships were already running between Liverpool and Glasgow. With its industrial power, technological wizardry and financial clout Britain was squeezed out of the French wars like a pip from a lemon into a century and a half as a major world power. The wars had made hundreds of people very rich – naval admirals and captains with their prizes, gunmakers like the Galtons, mill owners like Peel, Gott, Greg and Marshall, careful bankers like the Hoares and bold City men like Rothschild, Ricardo and the Barings. At the same time thousands of people were left destitute and angry. History is as you read it. It would take twenty years and more before the first real moves towards political reform, religious toleration, education and concern for the poor, and improvement in the condition of workers.

The contractors had flourished. Claude Scott was a millionaire from his dealings in wheat. Peter Mellish, supplier of meat to the fleet, would die in 1833 leaving an estate in the Isle of Dogs and a staggering £3 million, divided between his widow and two daughters, one of whom, Margaretta, leapt up the social scale by marrying the Earl of Glengall. In 1819 John Trotter of Soho Square, storekeeper to the army, was investigated by a parliamentary committee who were horrified by his overcharging. But by then Trotter had already waved his chubby hand at the profitable war. Almost as soon as it ended, he turned his now redundant warehouse into the Soho Bazaar, where craftsmen and artisans could rent space by the day, selling everything from millinery and gloves to potted plants. His aim, he said, was patriotic, a scheme that would allow the industrious to thrive: it would help the distressed wives and daughters of army officers to make some genteel pocket money, encourage 'Female and Domestic Industry' and stop the nation pouring 'its happy and innocent virgins into the common sink of London'.[7] The bazaar stayed in Soho until 1889, when the publishers A. & C. Black took over the premises.

While some men went under, others sailed on. Hoare's Bank is still in Fleet Street, with its Brown Bess muskets in the hall. By contrast, Henry Austen's bank crashed in 1816, largely as a result of lending £6000 to the notoriously extravagant Lord Moira. But James Oakes's West Suffolk Bank survived the century until 1899, when it was bought by Capital and Counties Bank, eventually being absorbed into Lloyd's. The Gurneys also carried on, and although many of the family were ruined by the crash of Overend, Gurney & Co. which rocked the City in 1866, their bank endured until 1896, when it merged with the Quaker bank of Backhouse & Co., and then with Barclay's. The Galton bank closed earlier. In 1815, Samuel Tertius Galton was among the men who took addresses from Birmingham to the Prince Regent on the restoration of peace, but when wartime orders ceased, he gave up gunmaking altogether. The bank suffered in the financial crisis of 1825 and Tertius slowly wound it up and closed it in 1831. He retired to Leamington, and died in 1844. Violetta lived on until 1874, and their son Francis Galton became a well-known eugenicist – though not as famous as his cousin Charles Darwin.

The mill owners John Marshall, Benjamin Gott, Robert Peel and Samuel Greg added to their fortunes during the war and in the years afterwards, while the smaller firm of Longsdon disappeared entirely. John and William Longsdon set up a cotton merchant firm in Charleston, Virginia, where John died in the cholera epidemic of 1819. Their elder brother James continued to run the family farm in Derbyshire until his death in 1826, leaving his small estate to his wife Anne and their infant son Henry: at this point it appeared the family would vanish from the village, but a year later William returned from America, rich enough to pay off all the debts and buy the manor house in Little Longstone and all the land around it.[8]

In the immediate post-war years, as the Prince Regent revamped Brighton Pavilion and the new plutocrats built their mansions, the numbers in the poorhouses and workhouses soared. To William Hazlitt, writing in the *Examiner* in 1816, this was the world of the Tory, a man who read no poetry except birthday odes to the regent and celebrations of Waterloo. A Tory, he wrote bitterly, 'asserts that the present sufferings of the country' are merely trifling and temporary:

though the gaols are filled with insolvent debtors, and criminals driven to theft by urgent want, the Gazette filled with bankruptcies, agriculture declining, commerce and manufactories nearly at a stand, while thousands are emigrating to foreign countries, whole parishes deserted, the burthen of the poor rates intolerable, and yet insufficient to maintain the increasing number of the poor, and hundreds of once respectable house-holders reduced to the sad necessity of soliciting admission into the receptacles for paupers and vagabonds, and thousands wandering about in search for that employment which it is no longer in the power of the gentleman or farmer to bestow![9]

There had been inequality and oppression before the war, there was afterwards, and there is still. Yet the immediate aftermath of the Napoleonic wars was particularly grim. Later accounts, eerily precise, put the cost of the war at £1,657,854,518. This was three times the cost of all other wars since 1688 and six times the pre-war national income.[10] Over £65 million of this was paid as subsidies to allies, half during the last five years of war: to Austria, Russia, Prussia and Sweden, to Portugal and Spain, to Hanover and the German states, to Sardinia and Sicily.[11] Taxes and loans had raised millions but the remaining national debt of around £850 million would hang over governments for a generation or more.

A million men and boys from the British isles had fought in the army and navy since 1793, out of a population that grew in those twenty-two years from around ten million to fourteen million. Over 311,000 of these had died, from wounds or fever: some estimates are higher.[12] Families had lost fathers, brothers, sons: the number of orphans in the Royal Military Asylum and the Royal Naval Asylum at Greenwich was at a peak. Many of those who survived were badly injured, and the old soldier with his wooden leg or with one empty arm of his coat pinned to his side was a common sight. In 1815 around 350,000 men were demobilised, roughly one in six of the male population aged between fifteen and forty. All were looking for work in an economy that was shrinking fast. While they sang 'Rule Britannia' with gusto, their songs, like 'British Tars', were not always triumphant:

> When war at first assailed us I quickly left my trade,
> Our country was in danger, I flew to lend my aid.
> And in my country's service, long, long fatigues I bore,
> But now I'm turned adrift to starve upon my native shore.

What could the returning soldiers and sailors live on? Officers retired on half-pay, and before the end of the war there was a spate of promotions so that their pensions would be larger, but ordinary sailors paid off at the quayside when the ship came home, and privates collecting their last pay in the barracks, did not even have this. Thomas Haswell from Tyneside remembered the scores of old sailors on the quays and wharves and streets of Shields, 'the sea-dogs of Camperdown, of the Nile, of Trafalgar . . . in every state of picturesque dismemberment – one arm, one leg, one arm and one leg, or a mere trunk with neither arms nor legs . . . Hardy, patient, long-suffering fellows whose bronzed faces spoke in every line of hardship and privation.' They were cheery when spoken to but 'mostly reflective, taciturn and observant'.[13] Many were later reduced to begging, or peddling on the streets. Tom Plunket of the Rifle Brigade, invalided out after Waterloo, was given sixpence a day by Chelsea Hospital commissioners: when he protested they struck him off the list. His wife, who had been with him at Waterloo and whose face had been disfigured by a blast from an exploding ammunition wagon, was awarded a shilling a day: they tried emigrating to Canada, with no success, and Plunket was seen years later selling matches on a street corner.[14] Many others were also on the streets: William Frasier, who lost both hands in the conflict, sold bootlaces because he could not keep his large family on his allowance as a 'maimed soldier'. Plunket's old colleague Ned Costello found he could not look after his common-law French wife Augustine and their baby. 'Day after day', he wrote, 'we struggled

BOOT-LACES

J. T. Smith's drawing of William Frasier, 1817

without necessities, and I confess I saw nothing but starvation staring me in the face.'[15] Getting £5 from the Patriotic Fund, he used it to pay their fare to Calais, took them back to France and never saw them again. '"Ne m'oubliez pas", were her last words: as she squeezed my hand.'

1816 was the year without a summer, when the whole of Europe was affected by the great eruption of the Tambora volcano in Indonesia that swept clouds of ash high into the stratosphere. There was nothing but frost, mist, fog and rain and the floods and bad harvest promised hunger to come. Under the pall of grey skies discharged men hunted for work. In July sailors boarded ships in London docks, demanding that the masters remove the foreign seamen who had replaced them during the war, paraded through the streets and sent petitions to the Admiralty and the Lord Mayor. Neither took much notice, advising patience. On Tyneside, when the shipowners tried to keep wartime levels of employment and reduce pay, the Newcastle keelmen's strike paralysed the north-east coast trade all summer, demanding wartime wages and contesting the employment of cheap 'apprentices' and dangerous undermanning. Huge meetings took place: on 20 September seven thousand men gathered on Cullercoats sands, but in October the troops were called in, and the strike ended. Murmurs of radical conspiracies surfaced again: there was talk of leaders of the Nore mutiny re-emerging. It took a generation, and more strikes, until the seamen's demands were met.

The cleverest inventors could fall foul of the times. Six years before, seeing the condition of the soldiers returning from Corunna, Marc Isambard Brunel won a commission to supply boots made by a new, mechanised method of shoe production, employing disabled veterans. It was a virtual production line, the work passing along a line of twenty-five workers, from the arrival of the hide to the finished shoe. 'As each man performs but one step in the process, which implies no knowledge of what is done by those who go before, or follow him,' wrote Sir Richard Phillips, 'so the persons employed are not shoemakers, but wounded soldiers, who are able to learn their respective duties in few hours.'[16] Brunel's Battersea factory turned out a hundred pairs of shoes a day, cutting the cost by a third. But this could work only for mass sales: when the wars ended he had eighty thousand pairs on his hands. The army bought half at a discount, but still, the business went bankrupt. Yet Brunel recovered and from the 1820s to the 1840s he worked on his enormous Rotherhithe Tunnel under the Thames, with his son, Isambard Kingdom Brunel. The railways, bridges, docks and ships of the younger Brunel would become one of the abiding images of Victorian Great Britain.

Some lives took odd directions. In 1821, when Reginald Heber went off to Calcutta, his elder brother Richard became an MP for

Oxford. But four years later, when his friendship with Charles Hartshorne, nineteen years younger, brought rumours of a sexual relationship, he moved abroad for six years. Still a bibliophile, a founder of the
Roxburghe Club and the Athenaeum, known for his belief that you
needed three copies, one for show, one for use, and one to lend, Richard scoured Europe for rare books. At his death in 1833 he owned
eight houses, in London, Hodnet and Oxford, and in Paris, Brussels,
Antwerp and Ghent: in all of them every room and passage and attic
was crammed with books. Their sales spread over three years.

In that first slump farmers like the Hutchinsons and John Monkhouse
saw the price of wheat fall, and, like many, they struggled with their
rent. In 1815 George Hutchinson left his land agent's job to take a
small farm, The Porth near New Radnor, and at Hindwell Tom and
Mary Hutchinson were expecting their first child. On 15 August
Dorothy Wordsworth wrote to Catherine Clarkson:

Sara gives us a sad account of George Hutchinson's prospects – his farm is
small and Tom is sure that it will not do more than pay his rent and labourers
– or something to that effect as Sara reported. At all events it will not half
maintain his house. They at Hindwell are growing poorer every year – and
this, though they have happy contented minds, is a serious evil now that there
is a prospect of an increasing Family. I wish that Tom had not bought that
Estate in Wales – it binds them in banishment from this part of England
as long as they possess it; locks up their money at present, and pays poor
interest.[17]

The Hutchinson family farmed on. In 1819, to the horror of the
family, George married his young, illiterate, pregnant, Methodist servant Margaret, and when he got into trouble over money borrowed
from the local bank, Tom took over his farm. Eventually Tom moved
his own family to a large farm at Brinsop Court, near Hereford, where
they lived until his death in 1849. Nearby, John Monkhouse became
known as a breeder of fine Hereford cattle, rich and respected: he
died aged eighty-five, almost blind. Joanna Hutchinson, who had
wanted so much to bring them all together, lived briefly in the Isle of

Man with her sailor brother Henry. She died in 1843, aged sixty.

Even the great landlords suffered as corn prices fell and bank-rupted tenants gave up their farms. Rents tumbled, and men who had borrowed or taken out mortgages to pay for improvements found themselves in difficulties. Enclosures continued, and the game laws became ever fiercer: gamekeepers set mantraps and men were trans-ported merely for carrying a net. And while peace should have made food cheaper, the implications of the Corn Laws, introduced by Huskisson in 1815, became clear with the terrible harvest of 1816 and the hunger that followed. The Corn Laws showed how strongly the landed interest still controlled parliament despite the bevy of new MPs from industrial areas. Seven years later, following the Congress of Verona in 1822 – the final meeting of Britain, Russia, Prussia, Austria and France – Byron wrote his bitter poem *The Age of Bronze*. Condemning the cynical self-interest of Europe's rulers, he also turned on 'noble Albion' and the greed of country landowners dur-ing the wars and after:

> Alas, the Country! How shall tongue or Pen
> Bewail her now uncountry Gentlemen,
> The last to bid the Cry of warfare cease,
> The first to make a malady of peace.
> For what were all these Country patriots born?
> To hunt, and vote, and raise the price of Corn? . . .
>
> See these inglorious Cincinnati swarm,
> Farmers of war, dictators of the farm;
> *Their* ploughshare was the sword in hireling hands,
> *Their* fields manured by gore of other lands;
> Safe in their barns, these Sabine tillers sent
> Their brethren out to battle. Why? For rent!
> Year after year they voted cent for cent,
> Blood, sweat and tear-wrung millions – why? For rent!
> They roar'd, they dined, they drank, they swore they meant
> To die for England – why then live? For rent![18]

The fight against the Corn Laws would continue until the 1840s. But peace also brought loss to the butchers and bakers and market gardeners who had supplied the navy, the barracks and the prisoners of war; to the makers of shoes and uniforms; to the labourers in the dockyards and arsenals; to the clerks dismissed from their posts. Ironworks were shut down, or sold off for a fraction of their value, and eight thousand miners were laid off. For the first year or two, even work in the cotton mills declined. James Weatherley was one of many who lost his job in 1816:

... work was slack and they turned five or Six off every Saturday night for a few weeks keeping the old hands at work and there was some of their old hands that had been at the Battle of Waterloo and been discharged and they set as many of them as they could to work as they had suffered so much during the late Peninsular war.[19]

Soon the new generation of mill owners and industrialists bounced back to build more and more large steam-powered mills. And as coal was needed to power the steam engines and the new gas works, the mines revived too and men, women and children laboured in shifts of up to fourteen hours a day underground. Streets of cheap houses sprang up around industrial sites to house the influx of workers from the countryside. In the alarm at a new mass of the 'uncivilised', in 1818 the government allocated a million pounds to building new churches. But the real energy came not from the complacent leaders of the established Church, but from the dissenters, future leaders of almost every movement for reform.

The old cries of 'radical' and 'infidel' were hurled at those who challenged the authorities. Politics was out on the streets again, building on the great peace protests of the last stages of the war. From now on, any government in power would have to take notice of public opinion, and of the popular press. Every time protests were made, the people came out en masse: at Spa Fields in November and December 1816, in the Blanketeers' march from Manchester, and in the Pentridge Rising of the stocking makers, quarrymen and ironworkers of

Derbyshire in 1817. It was like the worst days of the wartime repression all over again, with the imprisonment of leaders, new 'Gagging Acts', and suspension of habeas corpus when a stone was thrown at the Prince Regent's carriage. And it was like the war too, in the use of the military – the King's Dragoon Guards cut down the Blanketeers with sabres. Two years later, at the great meeting for reform at Manchester's St Peter's Field on 16 August 1819, the Manchester and Salford Yeomanry Cavalry – local men – charged the crowd, leaving over four hundred injured and eleven to fifteen people dead, including a two-year-old boy and a mother of seven children. James Weatherley and Samuel Bamford were both there, and Bamford, a future Chartist writer, remembered with horror how the crowd tried to turn at the cries of 'Break! break! they are killing them in front and they cannot get away,' and the pause before the cavalry charged, with a sound like low thunder and a rush 'heavy and resistless as a head-long sea'.[20] At Peterloo there were veterans of the war among both the demonstrators and the cavalry, including men who had fought at Waterloo.

Parliament tightened the blasphemy laws, and yet more journalists appeared in court charged with sedition and libel. The fight for the liberty of the press went on, with many defeats and some notable victories. In 1817, when William Hone published his *Reformists' Register*, with comic parodies and attacks on state abuses, illustrated by George Cruikshank, including a mock Te Deum of thanks for the Prince Regent's escape from that errant stone, he faced three separate trials before Ellenborough. The jury acquitted him on all charges: at the end of his first trial cheers echoed round the court, '*Long live the honest jury*, and *an honest jury for ever* . . . the waving of hats, handkerchiefs, and applause continued for several minutes.'[21]

Yet it was also the case that after 1815 most people shared a feeling of being 'British' which had not existed before. The threat of invasion in 1798 and 1803, the propaganda and parades, the raising of the volunteers, and the feasts and fireworks at every victory on sea and land had fostered a spirit of nationhood as well as nationalism. Old paternalistic patterns had been fractured, between landlords and rural communities and between masters and workers, but in their place there was a new sense of solidarity in groups. This was learnt partly from the regiments and ships, and partly from the need to organise that had developed among dissenters, reformers and workers. The mass mobilisation of the war years and the huge demonstrations of the peace movement had made everyone feel involved with the affairs of the nation, and the effect on the political culture was transformative: governments and politicians had to adapt to the world of the popular press and mass opinion, in the knowledge that they could never return to the old deferential culture. This change was born of the wars, almost without people knowing it. Tolstoy's words were true of the people of Britain, as they were of the Russians:

In reality, private interests of the immediate present are always so much more important than the wider issues that they prevent the wider issues which concern the public as a whole from ever being felt – from being noticed at all, indeed. The majority of the people of that time paid no attention to the broad trend of the nation's affairs, and were influenced only by their private concerns. And it was these very people who played the most useful part in the history of their day.[22]

Even as they went on with their daily lives everyone in Britain played a part. Everyone shared in the wars.

Everyone thought of them too as 'Napoleon's wars'. His dominance over the British imagination, fostered during the invasion scares of 1798 and 1803, had soared to a zenith by 1815. That October his travelling carriage, captured at Waterloo by the Prussians, was given to the British government, complete with most of its contents – apart from a few valuable items, like diamonds found stuffed into a tea caddy. In the summer of 1816 William Bullock put it on show at his Egyptian Hall in Piccadilly, with four of Napoleon's horses to pull it. The exhibition provoked cartoons from both Gillray and Rowlandson, and drew crowds of thousands, netting Bullock £35,000. He then set off on tour with it to Bristol, Bath and other provincial towns. Later he sold the carriage to Madame Tussaud's, where it stayed in her exhibition until a fire in 1925.

Rowlandson, Napoleon's carriage at Bullock's Exhibition in the Strand

Busts of Napoleon stood on mantelpieces in London flats and country houses and appeared in the background of portraits of Whig MPs. After the war, and even more after Napoleon's death on St Helena in 1821, people collected memorabilia of all kinds – his uniform, his flags, his hat, his silver teaspoons, letters – even a tooth, and, so they say, his penis, cut off during his autopsy. The most prized were his death mask, and the last cup he used.

The wars kept their hold on the imaginations of the next generation, and beyond. Writers born in the last stages of the conflict would turn back to this period, seeking out eyewitnesses, drawing on memories, using them in history and fiction: Carlyle in *The French Revolution*, Charlotte Brontë in *Shirley*, Gaskell in *Sylvia's Lovers*, Dickens in *A Tale of Two Cities*, Thackeray in *Vanity Fair*. The battles at home left as many scars as the conflict abroad. Mary Anne Evans, George Eliot, born in 1812, was thinking of her own father Isaac, or so her husband Johnny Cross thought, when she wrote of the grey-haired father in her last fiction, *Impressions of Theophrastus Such* in 1879:

I was accustomed to hear him utter the word 'government' in a tone that charged it with awe, and made it part of my effective religion, in contrast with the word 'rebel', which seemed to carry the stamp of evil in its syllables, and, lit by the fact that Satan was the first rebel, made an argument dispensing with more detailed enquiry.[23]

As she wrote, the old sailors and soldiers who had been through it all still haunted British towns and villages. A year earlier, in 1878, when Thomas Hardy was beginning his research into these times, which would bear fruit later in *The Trumpet Major* and *The Dynasts*, he met an old man, 'a palsied pensioner'. He had enlisted as a boy in 1807 or 1808, had retreated through the snow with Moore at Corunna and had fought with Wellington at Waterloo.[24]

# PRINCIPAL EVENTS OF THE WARS

*Domestic events in Britain are shown in italics.*

**1789**
14 July      Fall of the Bastille

**1791**
20–21 June      Louis and Marie Antoinette flee, arrested at Varennes
10 July      Padua Circular issued by Austria, calling on European royalty to aid Louis XVI
17 July      National Guard kill fifty at anti-royalist demonstration in Champ de Mars
3 September      French Constitution adopted by National Assembly
1 October      Legislative Assembly established in Paris

**1792**
20 April      France declares war on Austria, Prussia and Piedmont
29 July      Duke of Brunswick issues manifesto promising to restore Louis XVI
10 August      Assault on the Tuileries; Swiss Guard massacred, Louis XVI arrested
20 September      Battle of Valmy: French defeat Prussians under Brunswick
21 September      Establishment of First French Republic and National Convention
6 November      Battle of Jemappes: French enter Brussels

**1793**
7 January      *Aliens Act passed in Britain*
21 January      Louis XVI guillotined
1 February      France declares war on Britain
7 February      France declares war on Spain
13 February      First Coalition: Britain, Austria, Prussia, Netherlands, Sardinia-Piedmont, Spain

| 14 February | British capture Tobago |
| 25 February | First British and Hanoverian troops under Duke of York sail to Flanders |
| 18–21 March | Battle of Neerwinden: British and Austrians defeat Dumouriez |
| April | Committee of Public Safety set up in Paris |
| 31 May | Expulsion of Girondins from National Convention |
| June | Civil war in the Vendée |
| July | British occupy Corsica; French royalists call on British help at Toulon |
| 28 July | Siege of Valenciennes: allied victory |
| 23 August | French order issued for conscription, *levée en masse* |
| 27 August | Lord Hood occupies Toulon |
| 8 September | Duke of York retreats from Dunkirk |
| 16 October | Marie Antoinette guillotined |
| 19 December | Napoleon captures Toulon: Hood sails to Corsica |

**1794**

| 12 May | *Hardy, Tooke, Thelwall and others charged with treason* |
| 17–18 May | Battle of Tourcoing. French victory: Austrians begin to retreat |
| 1 June | 'Glorious First of June': Howe's victory in north Atlantic |
| 26 June | Battle of Fleurus: French defeat allies, re-enter Brussels |
| 28 July | Robespierre guillotined |
| Aug.–Nov. | French advance in Netherlands, occupy Amsterdam |
| 5 October | Napoleon stops Paris rebellion: given command of Army of Interior |
| November | *London treason trials* |
| December | *Duke of York recalled, relieved of command* |

**1795**

| January | French troops conquer Netherlands: Stadtholder comes to Britain |
| 5 January | Russia and Austria agree division of Poland |
| 5 April | Prussia leaves Coalition, signs agreement with France |
| 8 April | *Prince of Wales marries Caroline of Brunswick* |
| 14 April | Last British troops leave Holland |
| 16 May | Dutch agreement with French |
| June | Expedition to help French royalists (*chouans*) in Vendée |
| August | British seize Ceylon; peace treaty between France and Sweden |
| 22 August | Directory replaces Jacobin regime in Paris; Franco-Spanish treaty |
| 16 September | British take Cape Town from Dutch |
| October | British occupy Île d'Yeu, Brittany; Vendée rebellion crushed |
|  | French annexation of Austrian Netherlands |
|  | Polish state ceases: triple division Russia, Prussia, Austria |
| November | *Bread riots* |
| December | *Treasonable Practices and Seditious Meetings Acts* |

**1796**

| February | Ceylon treaty gives rights of Dutch to East India Company |
| 23 February | Napoleon given command of Army of Italy |

| | |
|---|---|
| March | *Insurrection Act, Ireland* |
| April | Start of Napoleon's Italian campaign |
| 12–16 April | French victories in Piedmont |
| 10 May | French victory over Austrians at Lodi; new campaign in Germany |
| August | Treaty between France and Spain |
| 31 August | British navy leaves Corsica |
| 8 October | Spain declares war on Britain |
| 22 October | Malmesbury on peace mission to Paris until 21 December |
| 15–18 Nov. | Battle of Arcola, Napoleon defeats Austria |
| 17 November | Death of Catherine the Great of Russia |
| 22–29 Dec. | French fleet in Bantry Bay |

**1797**

| | |
|---|---|
| 15 January | French defeat Austrians at Rivoli |
| 2 February | Napoleon takes Mantua: end of Austrian resistance in Italy |
| February | British take Trinidad and St Lucia |
| 14 February | Admiral Jervis defeats Spanish off Cape St Vincent |
| 22 February | French land at Fishguard. *Bank of England suspends cash payments* |
| 16 April | *Spithead mutiny begins* |
| 2 May | *Mutiny at Yarmouth and the Nore* |
| 22 July | Nelson attacks Tenerife |
| Summer | Napoleon takes Venice |
| 11 October | Admiral Duncan defeats Dutch fleet at Camperdown |
| 18 October | French Treaty of Campo Formio with Austria |
| | Napoleon given command of new Armée d'Angleterre |

**1798**

| | |
|---|---|
| March | *Capture of leaders of planned Irish uprising in Dublin* |
| April | *Arrest of London Corresponding Society committee* |
| 19 May | Napoleon leaves Toulon for Egyptian campaign |
| 23 May | *Irish rebellion begins* |
| June | Napoleon occupies Malta |
| 21 June | *Irish rebels defeated at Vinegar Hill* |
| 2 July | Napoleon lands in Alexandria |
| 21 July | Battle of the Pyramids, French defeat Mamelukes |
| 1 August | Battle of the Nile at Aboukir Bay |
| 22 August | French troops land at Killala, Co. Mayo; surrender 8 September |
| 9 September | Ottomans declare war on France |
| October | French fleet intercepted at Lough Swilly, Wolfe Tone arrested |
| 24 December | Anglo-Russian treaty |

**1799**

| | |
|---|---|
| January | French in Corfu surrender to Russians and Turks |
| February | Napoleon leaves Cairo, heads for Syria |
| March–June | Coalition forces retake French gains in Italy |
| 7 March | French troops occupy Jaffa |
| 12 March | France declares war on Austria |

| | |
|---|---|
| 19 March | French besiege Acre |
| April | *Pitt introduces income tax* |
| 27–29 April | French leave Milan; Russians under Suvorov take city |
| 3 May | Tipu Sahib, Sultan of Mysore, killed at Seringapatam |
| 20 May | Sir Sidney Smith relieves Acre |
| 1 June | Second Coalition formed: Britain, Russia, Austria, Portugal, Turkey, Naples. |
| July | *First Combination Act passed (second Act passed in 1800)* |
| 23 August | Napoleon leaves Alexandria for France |
| 27 August | Anglo-Russian forces land in Den Helder: Dutch fleet surrenders |
| 19 September | Duke of York wins battle of Bergen |
| 18 October | Armistice signed, British troops leave north Holland |
| 9 November | Coup of 18 Brumaire: Directory overthrown, Consulate established |

**1800**

| | |
|---|---|
| January | *Food shortages: soup kitchens in London and provincial towns* |
| March | *Act of Union with Ireland passed in Dublin and Westminster* |
| 6 May | French army march to Italy, Napoleon crosses Alps |
| 14 June | French defeat Austrians at Marengo |
| 2 July | *Union with Ireland Act (Westminster)* |
| 1 August | *Act of Union (Dublin)* |
| 29 August | British fleet off Copenhagen |
| 3 December | Austria defeated at Hohenlinden |
| 16 December | Sweden, Denmark and Russia form League of Armed Neutrality |

**1801**

| | |
|---|---|
| 1 January | *Acts of Union of Great Britain and Ireland come into effect* |
| 9 February | Peace of Lunéville between France and Austria |
| 16 February | *Pitt resigns; Addington succeeds as prime minister* |
| 8 March | Abercromby lands in Aboukir Bay |
| 21 March | Treaty of Aranjuez between France and Spain; Spain cedes Louisiana |
| 24 March | Assassination of Tsar Paul |
| 2 April | Battle of Copenhagen, destruction of Danish navy |
| 3, 4 & 15 Aug. | Nelson unsuccessfully attacks Boulogne |
| 2 September | French surrender in Egypt |
| 1 October | Peace preliminaries signed |

**1802**

| | |
|---|---|
| 27 March | Peace treaty of Amiens. Ottoman Empire joins treaty, controls Egypt |
| July–August | *General election in Britain* |
| 2 August | Napoleon holds plebiscite, made Consul for life |
| September | France annexes Piedmont, advances into Switzerland and Germany |

**1803**

| | |
|---|---|
| 30 April | France sells Louisiana and New Orleans to USA |

| | |
|---|---|
| 11 May | France rejects British demands to evacuate Holland |
| 17 May | Embargo on French and Dutch ships in British ports |
| 18 May | Britain declares war on France |
| | French troops enter Hanover |
| 30 June | British take St Lucia and Tobago |
| June | Renewed war in India |
| September | Arthur Wellesley defeats Marathas at Assaye |
| 2 December | Armée d'Angleterre masses at Boulogne to invade England |

**1804**

| | |
|---|---|
| 15 March | Arrest of Duc d'Enghien, executed 21 March |
| 12 May | *Addington resigns; new Pitt government* |
| 18 May | Napoleon proclaimed Emperor of the French: crowned 2 December |
| 6 October | British attack Spanish treasure fleet off Cadiz |

**1805**

| | |
|---|---|
| 11 January | Britain declares war on Spain |
| 30 March | Villeneuve sails from Toulon to Cadiz and West Indies |
| April | Treaty of St Petersburg: Anglo-Russian alliance, Third Coalition, joined by Austria in August, Sweden in October |
| 11 May | Nelson begins pursuit of Villeneuve |
| 26 May | Napoleon crowned King of Italy in Milan |
| 26 August | Napoleon leaves Boulogne: Grande Armée marches to Rhine |
| Sept.–Dec. | French campaign in Austria |
| 20 October | Battle of Ulm, Austrian troops surrender |
| 21 October | Battle of Trafalgar, death of Nelson |
| 30 October | French defeat Austrians at Caldiero, Italy |
| 13 November | French occupy Vienna |
| 2 December | Napoleon defeats Russians and Austrians at Austerlitz |
| 12 December | British troops under General Cathcart land in north Germany |
| 26 December | France and Austria sign Peace of Pressburg |
| 29 December | News of Austerlitz arrives in London: Cathcart recalled |

**1806**

| | |
|---|---|
| 6 January | *Nelson's funeral* |
| 10 January | Seizure of Dutch colony at the Cape |
| 23 January | *Death of Pitt* |
| 6 February | Duckworth destroys French fleet off Santo Domingo |
| 11 February | *Grenville forms Whig Ministry of All the Talents* |
| May | British Order in Council declares blockade of coast from Brest to Elbe |
| 28 June | General Beresford captures Buenos Aires |
| 4 July | British defeat French at Maida |
| 12 July | Napoleon establishes Confederation of the Rhine |
| 26 August | Prussia orders French to withdraw from Germany: Napoleon refuses |
| 13 September | *Fox dies: Grey becomes leader of Foxite Whigs* |
| October | Fourth Coalition: Britain, Russia, Prussia |

| | |
|---|---|
| 14 October | French victories at battles of Jena and Auerstedt |
| 25 October | Napoleon enters Berlin |
| 7 November | Final Prussian surrender: Frederick William III flees to Russia |
| November | *General election in Britain – no decisive result* |
| 21 November | Napoleon's Berlin Decrees ban trade with British ports |
| 28 November | French enter Warsaw |

### 1807

| | |
|---|---|
| 7 January | British Orders in Council prohibit sea-borne trade between France and French-controlled ports: Napoleon retaliates with Milan Decree |
| 7–8 February | Battle of Preussisch-Eylau between French and Russians |
| 19 February | British ships in Dardanelles to help Russia against Turkey |
| 17 March | British invade Egypt, defeated at Rosetta |
| 25 March | *Grenville's ministry resign* |
| | *Slave trade abolished in British possessions* |
| | *Duke of Portland forms 'Tory' (ministerial) government* |
| 14 June | Battle of Friedland, French defeat large Russian force |
| 25 June | Napoleon meets Tsar Alexander at Tilsit; treaties with Russia and Prussia signed 7 and 9 July |
| 10 July | General Whitelocke's unsuccessful attack on Buenos Aires |
| 2–7 Sept. | Naval bombardment of Copenhagen |
| 27 October | Treaty of Fontainebleau: France and Spain agree to partition Portugal, Denmark signs alliance with France |
| 7 November | Russia declares war on Britain |
| 11, 17 Nov. | Further Orders in Council |
| 30 November | French troops under Junot occupy Lisbon: Braganzas flee to Brazil |
| 22 December | US Embargo Act passed |

### 1808

| | |
|---|---|
| 2 February | French occupy Rome |
| 15 March | French annex Tuscany, Parma and Piacenza |
| 18 March | French-instigated uprising in Madrid against Bourbon monarchy; abdication of Charles IV of Spain and end of Gody's ministry; Prince Ferdinand proclaimed king |
| 23 March | French occupy Madrid |
| 20 April–1 May | Charles IV of Spain and Ferdinand lured to Bayonne |
| 2 May | Anti-French riots in Madrid brutally suppressed |
| 10 May | Ferdinand VII abdicates; Spanish crown put at Napoleon's disposal |
| 17 May | British troops sent to Sweden under Sir John Moore; they return 15 July |
| 6 June | Joseph Bonaparte proclaimed King of Spain |
| July | *Mary Anne Clarke scandal breaks, re sale of army commissions* |
| 12 July | Arthur Wellesley sails to Portugal with 9,000 troops |
| 21 August | Wellesley defeats Junot at Vimeiro |
| 30 August | Convention of Cintra: French troops leave Portugal |
| 4 December | Madrid surrenders to Napoleon; Spanish Junta flees to Seville |

**1809**

| | |
|---|---|
| Jan.–March | *Parliamentary Committee investigates Clarke scandal* |
| 1 January | Napoleon leaves Spain for Paris; Soult given command in Spain |
| 5 January | Treaty of Dardanelles between Britain and Turkey |
| 16–17 Jan. | Battle of Corunna, death of Sir John Moore. British troops evacuated |
| April | Fifth Coalition: Austria and Britain. Austria declares war on France |
| 22 April | Wellesley returns to Lisbon as commander |
| 12 May | Wellesley defeats Soult at Oporto, French withdraw from Portugal |
| 13 May | Napoleon enters Vienna |
| 4 July | Wellesley enters Spain |
| 5–6 July | Napoleon defeats Austria at Wagram: armistice signed |
| 29 July | Wellesley defeats French at Talavera; is made Viscount Wellington |
| August | British expedition to Walcheren; they capture Flushing, leaving in September |
| 21 September | *Canning–Castlereagh duel; both resign from cabinet* |
| 14 October | Austrians sign Treaty of Schönbrunn with France |
| 25 October | *George III's Golden Jubilee* |
| 30 October | *Death of Portland; Spencer Perceval becomes prime minister* |

**1810**

| | |
|---|---|
| 6 January | French and Swedes sign Treaty of Paris |
| 17 February | Napoleon annexes Rome |
| 1 April | Napoleon marries Archduchess Marie-Louise |
| April | *Burdett riots in London* |
| 9 July | British capture Réunion; take Mauritius in November |
| 27 September | Battle of Busaco, British defeat Masséna's troops |
| October | Masséna begins siege of lines of Torres Vedras |
| | *George III falls ill again* |
| 17 November | Sweden declares war on Britain |
| 13 December | French annex north-west Germany, Hamburg, Lübeck and Hanover. |
| 31 December | Tsar opens Russian ports to neutral vessels |

**1811**

| | |
|---|---|
| 5 February | *Regency Act: Prince of Wales becomes regent* |
| March | *Machine-breaking in Nottingham* |
| May | Wellington defeats Masséna at Fuentes de Oñoro, besieges Badajoz and Ciudad Rodrigo. Marmont takes command of French army |
| Summer | British retreat again behind lines of Torres Vedras |

**1812**

| | |
|---|---|
| January | French troops leave Spain in preparation for Russian campaign |
| 19 January | Wellington takes Ciudad Rodrigo |
| February | *Frame-breaking Act imposes death penalty* |
| 16 March | Wellington besieges Badajoz, storms the town 6 April |
| April | Napoleon offers peace terms, British government rejects them |

| 11 May | *Perceval assassinated* |
| | Sixth Coalition, Britain, Spain, Portugal |
| 8 June | *Liverpool becomes prime minister* |
| 18 June | United States declares war on Britain |
| 24 June | Napoleon begins invasion of Russia: French troops cross the Niemen |
| 18 July | Britain signs treaties of Orebro with Russia and Sweden |
| 22 July | British victory at Salamanca |
| 12 August | Wellington enters Madrid: remains until late September |
| 16–17 August | French victory over Russians at Smolensk; Soult evacuates Andalucia |
| 7 September | Battle of Borodino between French and Russians |
| 14 September | French enter Moscow |
| 19–22 Sept. | Wellington besieges Burgos |
| 19 October | Napoleon begins retreat from Moscow |
| 5 December | Napoleon leaves retreating army and returns to Paris to raise forces |

## 1813

| February | Prussia and Russia join Sixth Coalition |
| 13 March | Russians enter Berlin |
| 17 March | Prussia declares war on France |
| 27 April | Americans capture Toronto |
| May | French leave Madrid: Napoleon wins battles of Lutzen and Bautzen |
| 1 June | HMS *Shannon* captures USS *Chesapeake* |
| 21 June | British victory at Vittoria |
| July | *East India Company charter renegotiated: Company loses monopoly of trade with Indies* |
| 26 July–1 Aug. | Battle of the Pyrenees, Soult fails to stop British advance |
| 12 August | Austria joins Sixth Coalition and declares war on France |
| 26 August | Napoleon defeats allies at Dresden |
| October | Bavaria and Saxony join coalition: allied front of 'Great Powers' |
| 16–19 Oct. | Napoleon defeated in 'Battle of the Nations' at Leipzig |
| 10 November | Battle of Nivelle, Wellington enters France |
| 24 December | Allies besiege Hamburg |
| 29 December | British troops seize and burn Buffalo |

## 1814

| January | Allies invade France |
| 10–14 Feb. | 'Six Days campaign': Napoleon defeats Blücher at Vauchamps |
| 9 March | Treaty of Chaumont between Russia, Austria, Prussia and England |
| 25 March | Combined allied armies march on Paris: |
| 30–31 March | Battle of Paris: Marmont surrenders to the allies |
| 4 April | Napoleon abdicates in favour of his son, abdicates unconditionally on 6 April |
| 10 April | British victory at Toulouse |
| 16 April | Treaty of Fontainebleau: Napoleon exiled to Elba |
| 30 May | First Peace of Paris |
| June | *Tsar, King of Prussia, Metternich and Blücher visit England* |

| 24 August | British occupy Washington, set fire to White House |
| 1 November | Congress of Vienna opens |
| 24 December | Treaty of Ghent ends Anglo-American war |

## 1815
| January | Secret defensive alliance: Austria, Great Britain, France |
| | British defeated at New Orleans |
| 26 February | Napoleon sails from Elba, lands in France 1 March |
| 20 March | Napoleon reaches Paris |
| 25 March | Seventh Coalition formed at Vienna: Russia, Britain, Austria and Prussia |
| 8 June | 'Final Act' of Congress of Vienna signed. |
| 15 June | Napoleon invades Belgium |
| 16 June | Blücher defeated at Ligny: Wellington retreats to Quatre Bras |
| 18 June | Battle of Waterloo: French defeated by Blücher and Wellington |
| 22 June | Napoleon abdicates |
| 28 June | Restoration of Louis XVIII |
| 15 July | Napoleon surrenders to British at Rochefort |
| July | Napoleon exiled to St Helena |
| 20 November | Second Treaty of Paris: separate treaties between France and allies |

## 1821
| 5 May | Napoleon dies on St Helena |

# ACKNOWLEDGEMENTS

I am indebted to many writers, past and present, as I hope my notes make clear – and I thank them all. I was particularly lucky to have had expert help in the final stages of writing from Mark Philp, whose invigorating comments stimulated my interest afresh, and from Nick Roe, whose sensitive reading, meticulous corrections and knowledge of the radical Romantics also lifted my spirits. I cannot thank them enough.

Archivists, librarians and individuals have been unfailingly generous. I am especially grateful to the Bodleian Library; the Brotherton Library, University of Leeds; Bury Record Office; the Cozens-Hardy Collection, Norfolk; the London Library; and Oldham Local Studies and Archives. Particular thanks go to Jeff Cowton of the Wordsworth Trust, Pamela Hunter of Hoare's Bank, and Michael Powell of Chetham's Library, Manchester: all three were not only immensely knowledgeable, but fun to work with, conjuring up documents I would never have found. I am also grateful to Margaret Bird for help with Mary Hardy; Elaine Chalus and Commander Charles Fremantle for information about Betsey Fremantle; Fiona Tait, Malcolm Dick and Frank James for Galton material; David Sekers and Tsilika Alexis for details about Hannah Greg and Quarry Bank; Mandy Marvin for assistance with Amabel Hume-Campbell; Andrew Thompson for the letters of Captain William Salmon; and David Williams and Joe Puleo for help on arms and gunmakers. For enjoyable conversations on many topics, from Nottingham frame-workers to pioneering map-makers, I would like to thank Iain Bain, Carmen Callil, Hugh Cunningham, Mary Evans, Clarissa Gornall, Rachel Hewitt, Roger Knight, David Kynaston, Sheila O'Connell, Lucy Peltz, Stella Tillyard and Marina Warner.

My thanks go to Gill Coleridge for her comradely help during the final stages of this book, and to Peter Straus and all at Rogers, Coleridge and White. The team at Faber have been superb, particularly my editor and friend Julian Loose; James Rose and Kate Ward for work on production and pictures; Eleanor Rees for copy-editing, Sarah Ereira for the index; Anna Pallai for launching the book into the world, and Stephen Page for his warm support. In New York I am grateful to Melanie Jackson, and to Jonathan Galassi for his encouragement.

I am, as always, grateful to Alison Samuel for her humour, sound sense and good cooking. And thank you, Hermione Lee and John Barnard, wise readers and dear friends. More than thanks, too, to my family and to Steve, without whom I cannot imagine doing anything, let alone writing.

Finally I owe inexpressible thanks to my agent, the late Deborah Rogers, for her wicked laughter, shrewd advice and friendship over many years. She is greatly missed.

# SOURCES AND ABBREVIATIONS

| | |
|---|---|
| BCA | Birmingham City Archives |
| BL | British Library, London |
| BLARS | Bedford and Luton Archives and Record Service |
| CRL | Cadbury Research Library: Special Collections, University of Birmingham |
| Bod. | Bodleian Library, Oxford |
| BUL | Brotherton Library, University of Leeds |
| CAS | Cumbria Archive Service, Carlisle |
| Chet. | Chetham Library, Manchester |
| DRO | Derbyshire Record Office |
| DUL | Durham University Library |
| Hants. ALS | Hampshire Archives, Winchester |
| HB | Hoare's Bank Archives, London |
| Herts. ALS | Hertfordshire Archives and Local Studies |
| HUL | Hull University Library, Special Collections |
| LA | Lincolnshire Archives |
| LUL | Liverpool University Library, Special Collections |
| Manch. ALS | Manchester Archives and Local Studies |
| NLS | National Library of Scotland, Edinburgh |
| NMM | National Maritime Museum, Greenwich |
| Notts. A | Nottinghamshire Archives |
| *ODNB* | *Oxford Dictionary of National Biography* |
| OL | Oldham Library |
| PRO | Public Record Office |
| PWDRO | Plymouth and West Devon Record Office |
| REL | Royal Engineers Library, Gillingham |
| SA | Shropshire Archives, Shrewsbury |
| TNA | The National Archives, Kew |
| UCL | University College London, Special Collections |
| WT | The Wordsworth Trust, Grasmere |

# SELECT BIBLIOGRAPHY

This list includes background works and some biographical sources. Other more specific titles and articles are listed in the relevant chapters.

Albion, R. G., *Forests and Sea Power: The Timber Problem of the Royal Navy, 1652–1862* (1926)

Angelo, Henry, *The Reminiscences of Henry Angelo*, 2 vols (1828–30)

Ashton, John, *English Caricature and Satire on Napoleon*, 2 vols (1884)

——, *Social England under the Regency*, 2 vols (1899)

Aspinall, Arthur, *Politics and the Press, 1780–1850* (1949, repr. 1973)

Austen, Jane, *Jane Austen's Letters*, ed. Deirdre Le Faye (1995, 4th edn 2011)

Badenach, James, *Flitting the Flakes: the Diary of J. Badenach, a Stonehaven Farmer, 1789–1797*, ed. Mowbray Pearson (1992)

Bamford, Samuel, *Autobiography*, vol. i *Early Days*, vol. ii *Passages in the Life of a Radical*, ed. W. H. Chaloner (1967)

Bannerman, G., *Merchants and the Military in Eighteenth-Century Britain: British Army Contracts and Domestic Supply* (2008)

Barker, Hannah, *Newspapers: Politics and Public Opinion in the Late Eighteenth Century* (1987)

Barrell, John, *The Dark Side of the Landscape: The Rural Poor in English Painting, 1730–1840* (1980)

——, *Imagining the King's Death: Figurative Treason, Fantasies of Regicide, 1793–96* (2000)

——, *The Spirit of Despotism: Invasions of Privacy* (2006)

Bate, Jonathan, *John Clare: A Biography* (2003)

Berkeley, Alice D. (ed.), *New Lights on the Peninsular War* (1991)

Berry, Mary, *Extracts of Journals and Correspondence of Miss Berry*, ed. Lady Theresa Lewis (1865)

Blake, William, *The Complete Poems and Prose*, ed. David V. Erdman (1980)

Blakeney, Robert, *A Boy in the Peninsular War*, ed. Julian Sturgis (1899)

Bohstedt, John, *Riots and Community Politics in England and Wales, 1790–1810* (1983)

——, *The Politics of Provisions: Food Riots, Moral Economy and Market Transition in England, c.1550–1850* (2010)

Bowen, H. V., *The Business of Empire: The East India Company and Imperial Britain, 1756–1833* (2006)

Brewer, John, *The Pleasures of the Imagination: English Culture in the Eighteenth Century* (1997)

Burke, Edmund, *The Writings and Speeches of Edmund Burke*, 12 vols, gen. ed. Paul Langford (1997–2008)

Burney, Fanny, *Journals and Letters*, vols iii–viii, 1793–1812, ed. Joyce Hemlow, Edward A. Bloom and Lillian D. Bloom, and Peter Hughes (1973–80)

Burroughes, Randall, *The Farming Journal of Randall Burroughes, 1794–1799*, ed. Susanna Wade Martins and Tom Williamson (1995)

Byron, *The Complete Poetical Works*, ed. Jerome J. McGann, 7 vols (1980–93)

——, *Byron's Letters and Journals*, ed. Leslie A. Marchand, 13 vols (1973–94)

——, *Lord Byron: Complete Miscellaneous Prose*, ed. Andrew Nicholson (1991)

Cannadine, David (ed.), *Trafalgar in History: A Battle and its Afterlife* (2006)

Chamberlain, Paul, *Hell upon Water: Prisoners of War in Britain, 1793–1815* (2008)

Chambers, William, *Memoir of William and Robert Chambers* (1884)

Chase, Malcolm, *The People's Farm: English Radical Agrarianism 1775–1840* (1988)

Clare, John, *John Clare, by Himself*, ed. Eric Robinson and David Powell (1996)

Coad, Jonathan G., *The Royal Dockyards 1690–1850* (1989)

——, *Support for the Fleet: Architecture and Engineering of the Royal Navy's Bases* (2013)

Coats, Ann and MacDougall, Philip (eds), *The Naval Mutinies of 1797: Unity and Perseverance* (2011)

Cobbett, William (ed.), *The Parliamentary History of England*, 36 vols (1806–20), vols xxv–xxxvi, 1785–1803 (succeeded by Hansard, *Parliamentary Debates*)

Cockburn, Henry, *Memorials of His Time* (1910)

Cole, Gareth, *Arming the Royal Navy, 1793–1815: The Office of Ordnance and the State* (2011)

Coleridge, Samuel Taylor, *The Complete Poems*, ed. William Keach (1997)

——, *Collected Works*, gen. ed. Kathleen Coburn, 6 vols (2001)

——, *Collected Letters*, ed. E. L. Griggs, 6 vols (1956–71)

Colley, Linda, *Britons: Forging the Nation, 1707–1837* (1997)

——, *Acts of Union, Acts of Disunion* (2014)

Collins, Bruce, *War and Empire: The Expansion of Britain, 1790–1830* (2010)

Cookson, John, *The British Armed Nation, 1793–1815* (1997)

——, *The Friends of Peace: Anti-War Liberalism in England, 1793–1815* (1982)

Cooper, Thomas, *The Life of Thomas Cooper, Written by Himself* (1872)

Cope, S. R., *Walter Boyd: A Merchant Banker in the Age of Napoleon* (1983)

Costello, Edward, *The Adventures of a Soldier; or Memoirs of Edward Costello* (1841)

Crabb Robinson, Henry, *Diary, Reminiscences and Correspondence*, ed. T. Sadler, 3 vols (1869)

Crawford, Robert, *The Bard: Robert Burns, a biography* (2009)

Creevey, Thomas, *The Creevey Papers*, ed. John Gore (1948 edn)

Cunningham, Hugh, *The Children of the Poor: Representations of Childhood since the Seventeenth Century* (1991)

——, *The Invention of Childhood* (2006)

Daunton, Martin, *Progress and Poverty: An Economic and Social History of Britain 1700–1850* (1995)

——, *Trusting Leviathan: The Politics of Taxation in Britain 1799–1814* (2001)

David, Saul, *Prince of Pleasure: The Prince of Wales and the Making of the Regency* (2000)

Devine, T. M., *Clearance and Improvement: Land, Power and People in Scotland 1700–1900* (2010)

Donald, Diana, *The Age of Caricature: Satirical Prints in the Reign of George IV* (1996)

Duffy, Michael, *Soldiers, Sugar and Seapower: The British Expeditions to the West Indies and the War against Revolutionary France* (1987)

Duffy, Michael et al., *The New Maritime History of Devon*, 2 vols (1992, 1994)

Duncan-Jones, Caroline, *Trusty and Well Beloved: The Letters Home of William Harness* (1957)

Eden, Frederick Morton, *The State of the Poor: Or, An History of the Labouring Classes in England*, 3 vols (1797)

Edgeworth, Maria, *Memoir of Maria Edgeworth*, ed. F. E. Edgeworth, 3 vols (1867 edn)

Edgeworth, R. L., *Memoirs of Richard Lovell Edgeworth, Esq.* (1820)

Ehrman, John, *The Younger Pitt*, 3 vols (1969, 1983, 1996)

Emsley, Clive, *British Society and the French Wars 1793–1815* (1979)

Emsley, Clive and Walvin, James (eds), *Artisans, Peasants and Proletarians 1760–1860* (1985)

Esdaile, Charles, *The Peninsular War: A New History* (2002)

——, *Napoleon's Wars: An International History 1803–1815* (2007)

Evans, Chris and Ryden, Goran, *Baltic Iron in the Atlantic World in the Eighteenth Century* (2007)

Farington, Joseph, *The Diary of Joseph Farington*, ed. Kenneth Garlick and Angus Macintyre, 17 vols (1978–98), vols i–xiii

Farrell, Stephen, Unwin, Melanie and Walvin, James (eds), *The British Slave Trade: Abolition, Parliament and the People* (2007)

Ferguson, Niall, *The World's Banker: The History of the House of Rothschild* (1998)

Forbes, A., *A Short History of the Army Ordnance Services*, 3 vols (1921)

Forrest, A., Hagemann, K. and Rendall J. (eds), *Soldiers, Citizens and Civilians: Experiences and Perceptions of the French Wars, 1790–1820* (2008)

Fortescue, J. W., *A History of the British Army*, 13 vols (1899–1930), vols iv–x

Fox, Celina, *The Arts of Industry in the Age of Enlightenment* (2009)

Franklin, Alexandra and Philp, Mark, *Napoleon and the Invasion of Britain*, exh. cat. (2003)

Gates, David, *The Spanish Ulcer: A History of the Peninsular War* (2002)

Gatrell, Vic, *City of Laughter: Sex and Satire in Eighteenth-century London* (2007)

——, *The First Bohemians: Life and Art in London's Golden Age* (2013)

Gawler, Jim, *Britons Strike Home: A History of Lloyd's Patriotic Fund* (1993)

Geddes, A., *Portsmouth During the Great French Wars 1770–1800* (1970)

Gee, Austin, *The British Volunteer Movement 1794–1814* (2003)

George, Dorothy M., *English Political Caricature, 1793–1832* (1959)

Gill, Stephen, *William Wordsworth: A Life* (1989)

Glenbervie, Lord, *The Diaries of Sylvester Douglas, Lord Glenbervie*, ed. F. L. Bickley, 2 vols (1928)

Glover, Richard, *Peninsular Preparation: The Reform of the British Army 1795–1809* (1963, 2008)

——, *Britain at Bay: Defence against Napoleon, 1803–1814* (1973)

Godfrey, R., *James Gillray: The Art of Caricature* (2001)

Granville, Countess (ed.), *Lord Granville Leveson Gower: Private Correspondence 1781–1821*, 2 vols (1916)

Hague, William, *William Pitt the Younger* (2004)

——, *William Wilberforce* (2008)

Hall, Catherine, *Macaulay and Son: Architects of Imperial Britain* (2012)

Hammond, J. L. and Hammond, B., *The Skilled Labourer, 1760–1832* (1919)

Hardy, Mary, *Mary Hardy's Diary*, Norfolk Record Society (1968)

——, *The Diary of Mary Hardy*, ed. Margaret Bird, 4 vols (2013)

Hare, A. J. C, *The Gurneys of Earlham* (1895)

Harling, Philip, *The Waning of 'Old Corruption': The Politics of Economical Reform in Britain, 1779–1846* (1996)

Harris, Benjamin, *Recollections of Rifleman Harris*, ed. Henry Curling (1848, 1929)

Harris, J., *The Copper King: A Biography of Thomas Williams of Llanidan* (1964)

Hay, Daisy, *The Young Romantics* (2010)

Hay, Robert, *Landsman Hay: The Memoirs of Robert Hay, 1789–1847*, ed. M. D. Hay (1953)

Hayter, Alethea, *The Backbone: Diaries of a Military Family in the Napoleonic Wars* (1993)

Hazlitt, W. M., *The Letters of William Hazlitt*, ed. H. M. Sikes (1979)

——, *The Selected Writings of William Hazlitt*, ed. Duncan Wu, 9 vols (1998)

Heber, Richard, *The Heber Letters, 1783–1832* (1950)

Hewitt, Rachel, *Map of a Nation: A Biography of the Ordnance Survey* (2011)

Hilton, Boyd, *The Age of Atonement: The Influence of Evangelicalism on Social and Economic Thought, 1795–1865* (1988)

——, *A Mad, Bad and Dangerous People? England 1783–1846* (2006)

*Hoare's Bank: A Record 1672–1955* (1955)

Hobhouse, John Cam, Lord Broughton, *Recollections of a Long Life*, ed. Lady Dorchester, 6 vols (1909–11)

Holmes, Richard, *The Age of Wonder* (2008)

Horn, Pamela, *The Rural World 1780–1850: Social Change in the English Countryside* (1980)

Hostettler, John, *Dissenters, Radicals, Heretics and Blasphemers* (2012)

Hubback, J. H. and Hubback, Edith C., *Jane Austen's Sailor Brothers* (1906)

Hunt, Tamara L., *Defining John Bull: Political Caricature and National Identity in Late Georgian England* (2003)

Hunter, Pamela, *Through the Years: Tales from Hoare's Bank Archives* (2011)

Hutchings, Victoria, *Messrs Hoare, Bankers* (2005)

Ingrams, Richard, *The Life and Adventures of William Cobbett* (2005)

Jerningham, Lady Frances, *The Jerningham Letters, 1780–1843*, ed. E. Castle, 2 vols (1896)

Johnson, L. G., *General T. Perronet Thompson* (1957)

Johnston, Kenneth, *Unusual Subjects: Pitt's Reign of Alarm and the Lost Generation of the 1790s* (2013)

Klingberg, Frank J. and Hustvedt, Sigurd B. (eds), *The Warning Drum: The British Home Front Faces Napoleon* (1944)

Knight, Roger, *The Pursuit of Victory: The Life and Achievement of Horatio Nelson* (2005)

——, *Britain against Napoleon: The Organization of Victory, 1793–1815* (2013)

Knight, Roger and Wilcox, Martin, *Sustaining the Fleet, 1793–1815: War, the British Navy and the Contractor State* (2010)

Lamb, Charles and Lamb, Mary, *The Letters of Charles and Mary Lamb*, ed. Edwin W. Marrs, 3 vols (1975–8)

——, *The Works of Charles and Mary Lamb*, ed. E. V. Lucas, 7 vols (1903–5)

Lloyd, Christopher, *The British Seaman 1200–1860: A Social Survey* (1968)

Lloyd, Clive L., *A History of Napoleonic and American Prisoners of War 1756–1816* (2007)

——, *Arts and Crafts of Napoleonic and American Prisoners of War 1756–1816* (2007)

Lockhart, J. G., *Memoirs of the Life of Sir Walter Scott* (1848)

Logue, K. J., *Popular Disturbances in Scotland, 1780–1815* (1979)

Lovett, William, *Life and Struggles of William Lovett: In his Pursuit of Bread, Knowledge & Freedom* (1967)

Lyttelton, Sarah, *Correspondence of Sarah Spencer, Lady Lyttelton, 1787–1870*, ed. Hon. Mrs Hugh Wyndham (1912)

McCalman, Iain, *Radical Underworld: Prophets, Revolutionaries and Pornographers in London, 1795–1840* (1988)

MacCarthy, Fiona, *Byron: Life and Legend* (2002)

Macdonald, Janet, *The British Navy's Victualling Board, 1793–1815: Management Competence and Incompetence* (2010)

MacDougall, Ian, *All Men are Brethren: Prisoners of War in Scotland, 1803–1814* (2008)

McLynn, Frank, *Napoleon: A Biography* (1997)

*Microcosm of London*, Rudolph Ackermann: text vols i and ii W. H. Pyne; vol. iii William Combe, illus. T. Rowlandson and A. C. Pugin, 3 vols (1809–10, 1904 edn)

Mitford, Mary Russell, *Recollections of a Literary Life*, 3 vols (1852)

More, Hannah, *Memoirs of the Life and Correspondence of Mrs Hannah More*, ed. William Roberts, 4 vols (1834)

Morriss, Roger, *The Foundations of British Maritime Ascendancy: Resources, Logistics and the State, 1755–1815* (2010)

Navickas, Katrina, *Loyalism and Radicalism in Lancashire 1798–1815* (2008)

Neeson, Janet, *Commoners: Common Right, Enclosure and Social Change in England 1700–1820* (1993)

Nicol, John, *The Life and Adventures of John Nicol, Mariner*, ed. J. Howell (1937)

Oakes, James, *The Oakes Diaries: Business, Politics and Family in Bury St. Edmunds, 1778–1827*, ed. Jane Fiske, 2 vols (1990)

O'Connell, Sheila, *The Popular Print in England, 1550–1850* (1999)

Parkinson, Cecil Northcote, *The Trade Winds: A Study of British Overseas Trade during the French Wars* (1948)

*The Parliamentary Register; or, History of the Proceedings and Debates*, ed. John Almon, John Debrett, John Stockdale (1st Series vols xxxiii–xlv, 1790–6; New Series vols i–xviii, 1796–1802)

Philips, C. H., *The East India Company, 1794–1834* (1940, repr. 1961)

Philp, Mark, *Godwin's Political Justice* (1986)

—— (ed.), *Resisting Napoleon: The British Response to the Threat of Invasion, 1797–1815* (2006)

——, *Reforming Ideas in Britain: Politics and Language in the Shadow of the French Revolution, 1789–1815* (2013)

Philp, Mark and Innes, Joanna (eds), *Re-imagining Democracy in the Age of Revolutions: America, France, Britain, Ireland, 1750–1850* (2013)

Piozzi, Hester Lynch, *The Piozzi Letters: Correspondence of Hester Lynch Piozzi, 1784–1821*, ed. Edward A. Bloom and Lillian D. Bloom, 6 vols (1989–2002)

Pitt, William, *The Speeches of the Right Honourable William Pitt*, ed. W. S. Hathaway, 4 vols (1806)

Pressnell, L. S., *Country Banking in the Industrial Revolution* (1956)

Randall, Adrian, *Before the Luddites: Custom, Community and Machinery in the English Woollen Industry 1776–1809* (2002)

——, *Riotous Assemblies: Popular Protest in Hanoverian England* (2005)

Richards, Eric, *A History of the Highland Clearances*, 2 vols (1982)

Rimmer, W. G., *Marshall's of Leeds Flax-Spinners 1788–1886* (1960)

Rodger, N. A. M., *The Wooden World: An Anatomy of the Georgian Navy* (1986, 1996 edn)

——, *The Command of the Ocean: A Naval History of Britain, 1649–1815* (2004)

Roe, Nicholas, *Wordsworth and Coleridge: The Radical Years* (1990)

——, *Fiery Heart: The First Life of Leigh Hunt* (2005)

——, *John Keats: A New Life* (2012)

Rogers, Nicholas, *The Press Gang: Naval Impressment and its Opponents in Georgian Britain* (2007)

Rowbottom, William, *The Most Dismal Times: William Rowbottom's Diary, 1787–1799*, ed. Alan Peat (1996)

Russell, Gillian, *The Theatres of War: Performance, Politics and Society, 1793–1815* (1995)

St Clair, William, *The Reading Nation and the Romantic Period* (2004)

Schimmelpenninck, Mary Anne, *The Life of Mary Anne Schimmelpenninck*, ed. Christina M. Hankin (1858)

Scott, Walter, *The Letters of Sir Walter Scott*, ed. H. J. C. Grierson, 12 vols (1932–7); online edition, Edinburgh University Library (www.walterscott.lib.ed.ac.uk)

Sekers, David, *A Lady of Cotton: Hannah Greg, Mistress of Quarry Bank Mill* (2013)

Semmel, Stuart, *Napoleon and the British* (2004)

Shelley, P. B., *The Letters of Percy Bysshe Shelley*, ed. F. L. Jones, 2 vols (1964)

——, *Complete Poetry of Percy Bysshe Shelley*, ed. Donald H. Reiman, Neil Fraistat (2007)

Sherwig, John M., *Guineas and Gunpowder: British Foreign Aid in the Wars with France, 1793–1815* (1969)

Sherwood, Mary Martha, *The Life of Mrs Sherwood*, ed. Sophia Kelly (1884)

Snell, K. D. M., *Annals of the Labouring Poor; Social Change and Agrarian England, 1660–1900* (1985)

Snow, Peter, *To War with Wellington: From the Peninsula to Waterloo* (2010)

Southam, Brian, *Jane Austen and the Navy* (2000)

Southey, Robert, *Life and Correspondence of the late Robert Southey*, ed. Charles Cuthbert Southey, 6 vols (1849)

——, *Letters from England*, ed. J. Simmons (1807, 1984)

Spence, Peter, *The Birth of Romantic Radicalism: War, Popular Politics and English Radical Reformism, 1800–1815* (1996)

Sugden, John, *Nelson: A Dream of Glory* (2004)

——, *Nelson: The Sword of Albion* (2012)

*Survey of London* (1966), available at www.british-history.ac.uk

Sutherland, John, *The Life of Walter Scott: A Critical Biography* (1995)

Svedenstierna, Eric, *Svedenstierna's Tour of Great Britain 1802–3; the Travel Diary of an Industrial Spy*, trans. E. L. Dellow (1973)

Thale, Mary (ed.), *Selections from the Papers of the London Corresponding Society, 1792–1799* (1983)

Thompson, Andrew, *Captain William Salmon, Mariner of Chepstow, Letters 1811–1814* (2002)

Thompson, E. P., *The Making of the English Working Class* (1963)

——, *Customs in Common* (1991)

Thorne, R. G. (ed.), *The History of Parliament: The House of Commons 1790–1820*, 5 vols (1986): see also Parliamentary History Online (www.histparl.ac.uk)

Urban, Mark, *The Rifles: Six Years with Wellington's Legendary Sharpshooters* (2003)

Waterhouse, Benjamin, *Journal of a Young Man of Massachusetts* (1816)

Wells, Roger, *Insurrection: The British Experience 1795–1803* (1983)

——, *Wretched Faces: Famine in Wartime England, 1793–1801* (1988)

Western, J. R., *English Militia in the Eighteenth Century* (1965)

Wharam, Alan, *The Treason Trials, 1794* (1992)

Wheeler, H. F. C., and Broadley, A. M., *Napoleon and the Invasion of England*, 2 vols (1908)

Wilberforce, Robert and Wilberforce, Samuel, *Life of William Wilberforce*, 5 vols (1838)

Williams, Beryl, *Captain Pilkington's Project: The Great Works at Weedon* (2003)

Wilson, Ben, *The Laughter of Triumph: William Hone and the Fight for the Free Press* (2006)

——, *Decency and Disorder: The Age of Cant, 1789–1837* (2007)

Wilson, R. G., *Gentlemen Merchants: The Merchant Community in Leeds 1700–1830* (1971)

Woodforde, James, *The Diary of James Woodforde*, ed. R. L. Winstanley, Peter Jameson and Heather Edwards, 17 vols (1980–2007), vols xiii–xvii

Wordsworth, Dorothy, *The Grasmere and Alfoxden Journals*, ed. Pamela Woof (2002)

Wordsworth, William, *The Cornell Wordsworth*, gen. ed. Stephen Maxfield Parrish, 21 vols (1975–2007)

Wordsworth, William and Wordsworth, Dorothy, *The Letters of William and Dorothy Wordsworth*, ed. Ernest de Selincourt, 8 vols (2nd edn, 1967–93)

Wordsworth, William and Wordsworth, Mary, *The Love Letters of William and Mary Wordsworth*, ed. Beth Darlington (1982)

Wu, Duncan, *William Hazlitt: The First Modern Man* (2008)

Wynne, Elizabeth, *The Wynne Diaries*, ed. Anne Fremantle, 3 vols (1935–40)

# NOTES

## 1. WHO TELLS THE NEWS?

1 Johannes Eckstein, *The Birmingham Book Club at the Leicester Arms*, 1792; Margaret Willes, *Reading Matters* (2008), 139
2 Quoted in St Clair, *Reading Nation*, 256
3 Mitford, *Recollections*, i, 2
4 Chambers, *Memoir*, 65
5 Dorothy Wordsworth, *Recollections of a Tour Made in Scotland*, ed. Carol Kyros Walker (1997), 75
6 BUL Marshall Papers 200/63, journal Cumberland and Scotland 1800
7 Aspinall, *Politics and the Press*, 25
8 A. Aikin, *Journal of a Tour through North Wales* (1797), 147
9 Nicol, *Life and Adventures*, 188
10 Lyttelton, *Correspondence*, 38, to Robert Spencer, October 1808
11 Bod. MSS Eng. c. 7330, 28 December 1794
12 All quotations are taken from the Oldham Library text, but an edited version for 1793–9 is in *The Most Dismal Times*, ed. Alan Peat (1996). William, b. 1757, was the oldest of six children. He married Nanny Wood, 10 November 1777. They had seven children: Michael (died as a baby) b. 1778, Ann b. 1780, William b. 1785, John b. 1788, Betty b. 1790, Thomas b. 1793, George b. 1798.
13 Wynne, *Diaries*, iii, 265, Thomas Fremantle, 30 April 1806

## 2. DOWN WITH TOM PAINE!

1 Bod. MSS Eng. lett. d. 198, 12 November, 26 December 1790
2 *Memorials and Correspondence of Charles James Fox*, ed. Lord John Russell, 4 vols (1853–7), ii, 361, to R. Fitzpatrick, 30 July 1789 (BL Add. MSS 47580, f. 139)
3 Barker, *Newspapers*, 178
4 Cobbett, *Parliamentary History*, xxviii, 351, 5 February 1790; Hague, *Pitt*, 272

5 Edmund Burke, *Speech . . . in the Debate on Army Estimates, 9 February, 1790, Comprehending a Discussion of the Present Situation of Affairs in France* (1790), 23

6 Mark Philp, correspondence, 2014

7 Edmund Burke, *Reflections on the Revolution in France*, ed. J. C. D. Clarke (1790, 2001 edn)

8 Pitt, *Speeches*, ii, 36, 17 February 1792

9 *Proclamation of the Duke of Brunswick, 25 July 1792*, Hanover Historical Texts Project (www.history.hanover.edu), 2001

10 Bod. MSS Eng. lett. d. 198/64, 24 May 1792

11 *Bath Journal*, 10 December 1792. The counties without loyalist associations were Northumberland, Cumberland, Westmorland and Rutland.

12 Bamford, *Early Days*, 44

13 *Letters and Prose Writings of William Cowper*, ed. James King and Charles Ryskamp, 5 vols (1979–86), iv, 344–5; Russell, *Theatres of War*, 23

14 Druin Burch, *Digging Up the Dead: the Life and Times of Astley Cooper* (2007), 113

15 Minutes of meeting at the Crown and Anchor, Strand, 7 December 1792, letter signed by John Frost and Joel Barlow from Paris, 28 November 1792; evidence in the trial of Thomas Hardy, 1794; *Cobbett's State Trials* (1818), xxiv, 529–30

16 Jennifer Mori, *William Pitt and the French Revolution 1785–95* (1997), 121–30

17 28 December 1792, Cobbett, *Parliamentary History*, xxx, 189; F. B. Lock, *Edmund Burke, vol. ii: 1780–1797* (2006), 439

18 Clifford Musgrave, *Life in Brighton* (1970), 108; Venetia Murray, *High Society* (1998), 6

19 Burney, *Journals and Letters*, iii, 10–11, to Mrs Waddington, 19 September 1793

20 Sherwood, *Life*, 108–9. The song was sung at all theatre performances in Paris, inspired by the response of Benjamin Franklin when asked about the American revolution, 'It'll be fine.'

21 Francis Bamford, *Dear Miss Heber: An Eighteenth Century Correspondence* (1936), 141, 5 November 1792

22 Elizabeth Sparrow, 'The Alien Office, 1792–1806', *Historical Journal* 33 (1990), 361–84, and *Secret Service: British Agents in France 1792-1815* (1999). The first superintendent was William Huskisson: in 1794, the post went to William Wickham, who set up a network of spies in Europe, and Britain.

23 OL Rowbottom, 4 January, 3 March 1793. For pantomime, see Andrew Stott, *The Pantomime Life of Joseph Grimaldi* (2009), 74

## 3. 'THE UNIVERSAL PANT FOR GLORY'

1 *Gentleman's Magazine*, Spring 1793

2 Woodforde, *Diary*, xiii, 213–14, 26 January 1793

3 Heber, *Letters*, 79, 27 January 1793

4 Ibid., 78, 5 January 1793

5 *Parliamentary Register*, xxxiv, 459

6 Badenach, *Diary*, 155, 15 February 1793

7 Thomas Jackson, *Narrative of the Eventful Life of Thomas Jackson* (1847), 40

8 Bod. MSS Eng. c. 7330, 1 November 1790

9 Philip Henry Stanhope, *Notes of Conversations with the Duke of Wellington* (1886, 1938 edn), 18, 12 November 1831

10 Jackson, *Narrative*, 5

11 Woodforde, *Diary*, xv, 36, 38, 10, 16 May 1796

12 *Times*, 9, 13, 14 July 1795

13 Huw Davies, *Wellington's Wars: The Making of a Military Genius* (2012), 4

14 The army was then made up of three regiments of Household Cavalry, twenty-seven cavalry line regiments, three regiments of Foot Guards, seventy-seven line infantry regiments.

15 Cookson, *Armed Nation*, 130–1: see chapter 'Scotland's Fame'

16 OL Rowbottom 9, 11, 23 January, 10 February 1793; Northmoor recruits 8, 18 March, 26 June

17 National militia return, 13 August 1796; PRO 30/8/244, f. 22

18 OL Rowbottom, 8 March 1793

19 See John Thelwall, 'On Barracks and Fortifications; with sketches of the character and treatment of the British Soldiery', *Tribune* 2 (1796), 92, 100

20 Clive Emsley, 'The Military and Popular Disorder in England, 1790–1815', *Journal of the Society for Army Historical Research* 61 (1983), 17

21 WT WLMS Gill 1/1, 19 November 1794

22 Western, *Militia*, 289

23 Emsley, *British Society*, 38, TNA HO 51, 147.30, Dundas to Amherst, 25 February 1793

24 F. M. Anderson (ed.), *The Constitutions and Other Select Documents Illustrative of the History of France, 1789–1907* (1908), 184–5

25 Gee, *Volunteer Movement*, 1, Westmoreland to Pitt, 8 May 1794

26 The 1794 Act authorised the king 'to accept the services of such of his loyal subjects, as chose to enroll themselves as volunteers for the defence of our inestimable constitution'.

27 James Cruikshank, *Sketch of the Incorporation of Masons . . . with much curious information regarding . . . Glasgow past and present* (1879), 304–5

28 G. Riello, *A Foot in the Past* (2006), 72–4

29 *Gentleman's Magazine* 65 (February 1795); partially quoted in Colley, *Britons*, 253–4

30 Gee, *Volunteer Movement*, 161

## 4. FLANDERS AND TOULON

1 'March of the Guards to Greenwich', 25 February 1793, *New Annual Register*, 1796

2 *Morning Post*, July 1791; Philip Ziegler, *King William IV* (1971), 78

3 *Morning Chronicle*, 26 August 1793; Russell, *Theatres of War*, 34

4 OL Rowbottom, 22, 23 January 1794

5 Bod. MSS Eng. lett. d. 198/22, 7 April 1793

6 Bod. MSS Eng. lett. d. 203, 11 March 1793

7 Bod. MSS Eng. lett. d. 203, 19 February 1793

8 CAS D SEN 26, Ann Michelson to Kitty Senhouse, 24 June 1793

9 Hants. ALS Knollys Family Papers 1/M44/110/13

10 Astley wrote two military textbooks, his account of *Places Now the Theatre of War in the Low Countries* (1794) and *Remarks on the Profession and Duties of a Soldier* (1794)

11  *The Glenbervie Journals*, ed. Walter Sichel (1910), 46, 27 October 1793

12  J. Barrow, *The Life and Correspondence of Admiral Sir William Sidney Smith*, 2 vols (1848), i, 135, Smith to Lord Hood, 20 December 1793


5. SCARLET, SHOES AND GUNS

 1  Bod. MSS Eng. lett. d. 198/23, Reginald Heber snr to Elizabeth Heber, 7 April 1793

 2  OL Rowbottom; *Wheeler's Chronicle*, 31 August 1793

 3  Herts. ALS DE/Tr/T

 4  *Survey of London* (1966), vols xxxiii and xxxiv: St Anne's, Soho, 57–9

 5  Emsley, *British Society*, 82; Forbes, *Army Ordnance Services*, i, 177–80

 6  L. D. Schwarz, *London in the Age of Industrialisation* (2004), 186

 7  TNA ADM 49/35 F. 98; Riello, *Foot in the Past*, 47

 8  Morriss, *Ascendancy*, 199; TNA ADM 160/150

 9  Hewitt, *Map of a Nation*, 137

10  Roger Knight, 'The Fleets at Trafalgar: The Margin of Superiority', in Cannadine (ed.), *Trafalgar*, 65–6

11  *Gentleman's Magazine* 68 (August 1798), 648

12  Simon Werrett, 'The Arsenal as Spectacle', *Nineteenth-Century Theatre and Film* 37, no. 1 (Summer 2010), 14–22

13  Williams, *Weedon*, 43

14  H. L. Blackmore, *British Military Firearms 1650–1850* (1961), 133

15  For Nock, see Blackmore, *Firearms*, 100–8

16  From 1804 to 1817 1,827,889 muskets, rifles, carbines, and pistols were made for the government: 3,037,644 barrels and 2,879,203 locks were sent to London, and over a million for the East India Company. *Showell's Directory of Birmingham*, 'Trades'

17  Evans and Ryden, *Baltic Iron*, 154

18  Ibid., 148–54

19  *Showell's Directory*, 'Trades'

20  See English Heritage video, 'How to fire a Brown Bess musket', available via YouTube

21  Schimmelpenninck, *Life*, 214

22  Society of Friends, Tamworth Meeting, 1790, written Epistle: BCA Galton MS 3101/B/16.2

23  Schimmelpenninck, *Life*, 256

24  Samuel Galton jnr to the Monthly Meeting in Birmingham, BCA Galton MS 3101/B/16.2: see Revolutionary Players website, Birmingham Museum and Art Gallery; also Samuel Lloyd, *The Lloyds of Birmingham* (1907), 120–32


6. BRITISH TARS

 1  Hague, *Pitt*, 341

 2  Woodforde, *Diary*, xiii, 258, 26 June 1793

 3  See J. Harris, *Copper King*, and Knight, *Britain*, 36

 4  Southam, *Jane Austen and the Navy*, 83

5  Austen, *Letters*, 29, to Cassandra Austen, 24–26 December 1798
6  Ibid., 33, to Cassandra Austen, 28 December 1798
7  See Morriss, *Ascendancy*, 235–9
8  Rogers, *Press Gang*, 54; *Newcastle Courant*, 23 February 1793
9  Rogers, *Press Gang*, 127–8; TNA HO 28/9/71
10 WT Gill Papers, Bundle 9, Thomas Gill, 'Recollections', transcript
11 LUL Rathbone Papers, II 1. 61, Samuel Greg to William Rathbone, 6 March 1793
12 Stephen Taylor, *Commander: The Life and Exploits of Britain's Greatest Frigate Commander* (2012), 79–80
13 Angelo, *Reminiscences*, ii (1830 edn), 291–3
14 Oakes, *Diaries*, i, 301, 18 June 1794
15 Russell, *Theatres of War*, 60–1
16 Others included Samuel Jerrold's theatres in Southend and Sheerness, and Sarah Baker's in Rochester: Russell, *Theatres of War*, 95–8, 104. See W. Blanchard Jerrold, *The Life and Remains of Douglas Jerrold* (1859), and Henry Francis Whitfield, *Plymouth and Devonport in Times of War and Peace* (1900)
17 Many songs are collected in Charles Dibdin the Elder, *The Naval Songster, or Jack Tar's Choice of Conviviality, for 1798* (1798) and *Songs, Naval and National, of the late Charles Dibdin* (1841). See also *Professional and Literary Memoirs of Charles Dibdin the Younger*, ed. George Speaight (1956), 26
18 Chambers, *Memoir*, 41

## 7. TRIALS AND TRIBULATIONS

1  *The Letters of Robert Burns*, ed. J. De Lancey Ferguson, 2 vols (2nd edn 1985), ii, 173–6, 8 January 1793. See Crawford, *Bard*, 363–74, and Ian McIlvanney, *Burns the Radical* (2003) for Burns's political views
2  Burns, *Letters*, ii, 182, 20 February 1793
3  Henry Cockburn, *An Examination of the Trials for Sedition which have hitherto occurred in Scotland* (1888), quoted in Hostettler, *Dissenters*, 142
4  Hostettler, *Dissenters*, 142
5  See Barrell, *Imagining the King's Death*, 150–69
6  Cockburn, *Memorials*, 116; Michael Fry on Braxfield, *ODNB*
7  Burns, *Letters*, ii, 235–6, 237, to George Thomson, *c*.30 August, 8 September 1793
8  Charles Dibdin, *Observations on a Tour Through Almost the Whole of England, and a Considerable Part of Scotland* (1801), 329
9  Scott, *Letters*, i, 30–1, to Christian Rutherford, 8 June 1794
10 Ibid., i, 34, to Christian Rutherford, 5 September 1794. See Barrell, *Imagining the King's Death*, 252–84
11 David Cressy, *Dangerous Talk: Scandalous, Seditious, and Treasonable Speech in Pre-Modern England* (2010), 245–6
12 *Politics for the People*, viii, 104, quoted in Barrell, *Imagining the King's Death*, 104
13 See Barrell, *Imagining the King's Death*, ch. 5, 'The Trial of Thomas Walker', 170–81
14 OL Rowbottom, 21 April; see also 23 July 1794, 14 March 1795

15 Thale, *Selections*, 135, 'Report from Spy Groves', 14 April 1794

16 Gill, *Wordsworth*, 85

17 Mark Philp, 'Preaching to the Unconverted: Rationality and Repression in the 1790s', *Enlightenment and Dissent* 28 (2013), 73–88

18 [William Godwin], *Cursory Strictures on the Charges Delivered by Lord Chief Justice Eyre to the Grand Jury*, 2 October 1794 (1794). For Godwin's argument and the trials see Philp, *Godwin's Political Justice*, 118–20; Barrell, *Imagining the King's Death*, chs 10–12, 285–401

19 Horace Twiss, *The Public and Private Life of Lord Chancellor Eldon, with Selections from his Correspondence* (1829, 1844 edn), i, 269–70

20 Hague, *Pitt*, 364

21 The lecture was 'Animal Vitality', delivered January 1793, later developed as 'On the Origin of Sensation': John Thelwall, *An Essay Towards a Definition of Animal Vitality* (1793): Nicholas Roe on Thelwall, *ODNB*

22 For repression of intellectual life, see Johnston, *Unusual Subjects*; for debating societies see Donna T. Andrew, *London Debating Societies, 1776–1779* (1994) and her database on debates listed in the press, via British History Online, www.british-history.ac.uk

23 Desmond King-Hele, *The Collected Letters of Erasmus Darwin* (2007), 471–2, Erasmus Darwin to Richard Lovell Edgeworth, 15 March 1795

24 Barker, *Newspapers*, 191

25 Royal Dumfries Volunteers, Minute Book: Ewart Library Dumfries: see William Will, *Robert Burns as a Volunteer* (1919), 24

26 Crawford, *Bard*, 385

27 Burns, *Letters*, ii, 382, to Maria Riddell, 1 June 1796

28 [Allan Cunningham], 'Robert Burns and Lord Byron', *Caledonian Mercury*, 16 August 1824, and originally in *London Magazine*. This may be apocryphal as the details of Cunningham's memoir were soon challenged.

## 8. WARP AND WEFT

1 Chambers, *Memoir*, 7

2 OL Rowbottom, 11 August 1793

3 Ibid., 31 December 1793

4 Ibid., 3 August, 14 September 1794

5 John Aikin, *Description of the Country for Thirty to Forty Miles round Manchester* (1795), 3

6 John Byng (1790 visit), *The Torrington Diaries*, ed. C. Bruyn Andrews, 4 vols (1934–8), ii, 172

7 Navickas, *Loyalism and Radicalism*, 24; TNA HO 42/41/1, Singleton to King, 27 May 1799

8 OL Rowbottom, 29, 31 August 1795

9 BCA B&WD/3, Folder 2, Matthew Boulton to James Watt, 21 June 1781

10 G. T. Wright, *Historical Sketches of Great Longstone* (1906), 290–3, in S. D. Chapman, 'James Longsdon (1745–1821), Farmer and Fustian Manufacturer', *Textile History* 1 (1970), 265–92

11 Chapman, 'James Longsdon', 273

12 DRO D 3580 Longsdon Family Papers, See D 3580/EF 504–9 James Longsdon Cotton Enterprize. (James Longsdon (1745–1821), James Longsdon II (1786–1827), John Longsdon (1788–1819), William Longsdon (1790–1878).) For the Morewoods, John R. Killick, 'Bolton Ogden & co', *Business History Review*, 48, 4 (Winter 1974)

13 J. Hodgson, *Textile Manufacture and Other Industries in Keighley* (1879), 226, 229

14 Elizabeth Lightbody m. Thomas Hodgson, Liverpool African merchant with cotton mills at Caton, near Lancaster; Agnes m. Thomas Pares, Leicestershire banker with textile interests in Derbyshire.

15 Chet. A.6.30, Weatherley transcript, 'Recollections'

16 Manch. ALS C/5/1/8, *Transcript of the Examination of Joseph Sefton* (1806); see also Sekers, *Hannah Greg*, 155

17 28 June 1796. Minutes of Birmingham Board of Guardians; Katrine Honeyman, *Child Workers in England, 1780–1820: Parish Apprentices and the Making of the Early Industrial Labour Force* (2007), 253

18 Coleridge, *Remarks on the Objections which have been urged against the Principle of Sir Robert Peel's Bill* (1818), in Cunningham, *Children of the Poor*, 71

19 Pat Hudson, *The Genesis of Industrial Capital: A Study of the West Riding Wool Textile Industry, c.1750–1850* (1986), 26–7

20 BUL Gott MS 194; R. G. Wilson on Gott, *ODNB*

21 BUL Marshall MS 200, 'Life'

22 Rimmer, *Marshall's*, 45

## 9. MONEY, CITY AND COUNTRY

1 David Macpherson, *Annals of Commerce, Manufactures, Fisheries and Navigation*, 4 vols (1805), iv, 266–7

2 HB 8/T/4 Outgoing Letter Book, Thanet, 7 June 1793; Farre and Rivers, 18 June 1793; Conolly, 2 July 1793

3 HB 8/T/4 Earl Spencer, 8 July 1793; George Aust, agent for Lord Hardwicke, 11 September 1793

4 HB 2/1/E/1 Memorandum Book, December 1794

5 *Hoare's Bank*, 93, Richard Colt Hoare to Henry Hoare, 1795

6 Henry Hoare of Mitcham (1750–1828), partner from 1771; Henry Hugh Hoare (1762–1841), partner from 1785; Charles Hoare (1767–1852), partner from 1787; Henry Merrick Hoare (1770–1856), partner from 1791. Joined in 1798 by William Henry Hoare (1776–1819), son of Henry of Mitcham.

7 *Hoare's Bank*, 61–2

8 Hunter, *Hoare's Bank Archives*, 39, 'Willoughby's Cordial for Old Age'

9 Charles Lamb, 'The Good Clerk' (1811), *The Works of Charles and Mary Lamb: Miscellaneous Prose, 1798–1834*, ed. E. V. Lucas (1968 repr.), 129

10 By 1820 it would top £844 million: Hilton, *Mad, Bad and Dangerous*, 113

11 See Sherwig, *Guineas and Gunpowder*, 34–53

12 *Times*, 13 December 1794. See Cope, *Boyd*, 57–9, 75–86, 102, and Martin Daunton on Boyd, *ODNB*

13 HB 2/E/1 Memorandum Book, 10 December 1794

14 *Morning Post*, 26 December 1795

15 *Morning Chronicle*, 14 April 1797
16 HB 2/E/1 Memorandum Book, 2 December 1798
17 See H. F. Barclay and A. Wilson Fox, *A History of the Barclay Family*, 3 vols (1934), and Margaret Ackrill and Leslie Hannah, *Barclays: The Business of Banking, 1690–1996* (2001)
18 Oakes, *Diaries*, i, 288, 16 January 1793
19 Ibid., i, 289, 21 January, 1, 21 February 1793
20 Ibid., i, 48
21 Ibid., i, 305, 22 October 1794
22 Gurney ledgers, Barclays Group Archives, Manchester; Oakes, *Diaries*, i, 63
23 Oakes, *Diaries*, i, 72, marginal note described by Janet Fiske
24 Ibid., i, 296, 12, 14 November 1793
25 Ibid., i, 316, 16 October 1795
26 Ibid., i, 335, 8 September 1796

## 10. 'ARE WE FORGOTTEN?'

1 Stella Tillyard, *Aristocrats: Caroline, Emily, Louisa and Sarah Lennox, 1740–1832* (1994), 365
2 Bod. MSS Eng. c. 7330, 11 January 1794
3 Bod. MSS Eng. c. 7330, 15 January 1794
4 *Times*, 19 August 1794
5 Duncan-Jones, *Harness*, 48
6 Bod. MSS Eng. c. 7330, 10 October 1794
7 Fortescue, *British Army*, iv, Part I, 899–900
8 Bod MSS Eng. lett. d. 198, 25 November 1793
9 Bod. MSS Eng. c. 7330, 10 November 1794
10 Bod. MSS Eng. c. 7330, 18 December 1794
11 Woodforde, *Diary*, xiv, 118, 25 January 1795
12 Bod. MSS Eng. c. 7330, 21 January 1795
13 Duncan-Jones, *Harness*, 69
14 Bod. MSS Eng. c. 7330, 7–16 February 1795
15 James Abercromby, Lord Dunfermline, *Sir Ralph Abercromby, K.B., 1793–1801: A Memoir by his Son* (1861), 46
16 OL Rowbottom, 5 May 1795
17 Bod. MSS Eng. c. 7330, June 1795
18 Knight, *Britain*, 72
19 Bod. MSS Eng. c. 7330, 25 October 1795
20 Fortescue, *British Army*, iv, Part I
21 Chet. Manchester petition, 1795
22 *Times*, 24 December 1795

## 11. HIGH LIFE

1 *An Historical Sketch of the French Revolution from Its Commencement to the Year 1792* (1792), and *An Historical Essay on the Ambition and Conquests of France, with Some Remarks on the French Revolution* (1797)

2  UBCRL JER/72, Lady Maria Stuart to Charlotte, 17 April 1795. For transcripts see also *Jerningham Letters*

3  David, *Prince of Pleasure*, 170

4  Bod. MSS Eng. lett. d. 199/117, 21 April 1795

5  Gatrell, *City of Laughter*, 70

6  UBCRL JER/88, to Charlotte, 21 June 1796

7  CAS D SEN 29, 1 February 1796

8  HB 2/E/1 Memorandum Book, 16 March 1796

9  *Hoare's Bank*, 98

10  HB 8/T/4, 18 July 1796

11  Wynne, *Diaries*, iii, 363, 5 March 1813

12  Quoted in Paula Byrne, '"The Unmeaning Luxuries of Bath": Urban Pleasures
in Jane Austen's World', *Persuasions: The Jane Austen Journal* 26 (2004), 13–26

13  Gatrell, *City of Laughter*, 56

14  See Barrell, *Spirit of Despotism*, 28–30

15  Angelo, *Reminiscences*, ii, 63

16  Hants. ALS 1 M44/110/128, 29 July 1794

17  Henry Dillon's regiment served in Jamaica and Haiti, disbanded 1798; Edward
Dillon's regiment, 'Dillon's Regiment of Foot', raised in northern Italy in 1795,
fought for the British in the Mediterranean, in Egypt in 1801, and in the Peninsula: René Chartrand, *Émigré & foreign troops in British service 1793–1802* (1999),
i, 12–13. For the Dillons in France and in exile, see Caroline Moorhead, *Dancing
to the Precipice: The Life of Lucie de la Tour du Pin, Eyewitness to an Era* (1999)

18  Moorhead, *Dancing to the Precipice*, 258

19  UBCRL JER/160, 163, Lady Jerningham to Charlotte, 24, 27 May 1800

20  Louvet's *Narrative of the Dangers to which I have been exposed, since the 31st May 1793*,
Madame Roland's *An Appeal to Impartial Posterity*, Helen Maria Williams's *Letters,
Containing a Sketch of the Politics of Europe . . . and of the Scenes which have passed in the
Prisons of Paris*

21  See Colley, *Britons*, 'Dominance', 149–93

## 12. FOUR FARMERS

1  Quotations from Burroughes, *Journal*, 73–91: 5, 24 January, 21 February, 9 July,
30 July 1796; 95, 19 March 1798

2  His wife Anne died in 1827. Children: Ann b. 1793, Randall Proctor b. 1795,
Diana b. 1797 and Jemima b. 1799; Ann lived until 1859, Randall and Jemima
died within a fortnight in January 1820, aged twenty-five and twenty-one.

3  Susan Ottaway, *The Decline of Life* (2007), 87

4  Burroughes, *Journal*, 67, 14 September 1795

5  Ibid., Introduction, 11; Will, TNA PROB 11/1605/48

6  Ibid., iv, 217, 4 February 1803

7  Hardy, *Diary*, iii, 41, 24 January 1794

8  Ibid., iii, 44, 7 February 1794

9  Ibid., iii, 72, 23–25 May 1794

10  Ibid., iii, 179–80, 8–11 June 1795

11  Ibid., iii, 423, Appendix D3.C

12 Quotations from Badenach, *Diary*, 236–79, 5 December, 28 July, 16 February, 14 July, 22 June 1796

13 Andrew Wight, *The Present State of Husbandry in Scotland*, 1778, repr. in David McClure (ed.), *Ayrshire in the Age of Improvement* (2002), 13

14 Quoted in McClure (ed.), *Ayrshire*, 6

15 Devine, *Clearance and Improvement*, 97–9, 115–19, 151

16 J. Farey, *General View of the Agriculture and Minerals of Derbyshire* (1811), iii, 433, 494–5

17 DRO D3580/C18, 29 November 1799

18 DRO D3580/C20, 16 March 1801

## 13. PORTSMOUTH DELIVERIES

1 Vice-Admiral Graves, Spithead, letter with comments from agent victualler, TNA ADM C/683 February 1795. The outline is given in Macdonald, *Victualling Board*, 51–2.

2 J. Duncombe, *The Life of William Cobbett* (1835), 8

3 Wilberforce, *Life*, i, 58; diary, 24 June 1794

4 Eden, *State of the Poor*, ii, 228–9

5 R. A. Morris, 'Labour Relations in the Royal Dockyards, 1801–5', *Mariners' Mirror* 62 (1976), 337–46; A. Geddes, *Portsmouth during the Great French Wars 1770–1800* (1970)

6 For the Victualling Board see Knight and Wilcox, *Sustaining the Fleet* and the National Maritime Museum database (www.nmm.ac.uk); also Janet Macdonald, *Victualling Board* and *Feeding Nelson's Navy: The True Story of Food at Sea in the Georgian Era* (2004)

7 In 1792 17,000 men were in 'sea pay': by 1801 this had reached 140,000, and by 1809 the Board were supplying 732 warships, with 146,0132 seamen and marines. Rodger, *Command of the Ocean*, 639; Macdonald, *Victualling Board*, 19

8 John Clare, *The Shepherd's Calendar*, 'July'

9 Macdonald, *Victualling Board*, 60–2

10 A visitor in 1804: Emsley, *British Society*, 109, quoting Siegfried Giedion, *Mechanization Takes Command: A Contribution to Anonymous History* (1948)

11 Macdonald, *Victualling Board*, 34: TNA ADM 112/160

12 Knight and Wilcox, *Sustaining the Fleet*, 44, 129–30

13 Notts. A 2103/6/3, 27 December 1810

14 Hermione Hobhouse, 'Northern Milwall: The Byng and Mellish estates', and 'The Mellish Estate', *Survey of London*, xliv, 418–23, 433–45

15 Government paid their bills 'by course' – meaning in the order they came in – and the bills could be sold on at a discount if the cash was needed early.

16 Woodforde, *Diary*, xvi, 154, 6 October 1799

17 For Great Yarmouth see Knight and Wilcox, *Sustaining the Fleet*, 192–209

18 Knight and Wilcox, *Sustaining the Fleet*, 196; Stephen Paget, *Memoirs and Letters of Sir James Paget* (1902), 1–2

## 14. BREAD

1 Woodforde, *Diary*, xiv, 117, 126, 23 January, 22 February 1795

2 Quotations from Burroughes, *Journal*, 50–1, 23–31 January

3 Ibid., 53, 8 March 1795

4 TNA HO 42/34/99, Welford to Portland, 6 April 1795; Emsley, *British Society*, 42

5 Bohstedt, *Politics of Provisions*, 174–7 and *Riots* ch. 2

6 Oakes, *Diaries*, i, 312, 29 April 1795

7 Emsley, *British Society*, 38, and R. Wells, 'The Militia Mutinies of 1795' in J. Rule (ed.), *Outside the Law: Studies in Crime and Order 1650–1850* (1982); see Bohstedt, *Riots*, 27–68; F. Willan, *History of the Oxfordshire Regiment of Militia* (1900), 26–3; Ian F. W. Beckett, *The Amateur Military Tradition, 1558–1945* (1991), 72 (says eighteen tried and five executed).

8 Hardy, *Diary*, iii, 290, 293, 22 July, 9 August 1796

9 Cunningham, *Children of the Poor*, 27

10 Bamford, *Early Days*, 56

11 Eden, *State of the Poor*, ii, 343

12 Heber, *Letters*, 166, Revd John Stonard to Richard Heber, 26 February 1795

13 Wells, *Wretched Faces*, 106–10

14 Sheffield handbill, 5 August 1795; Wells, *Wretched Faces*, 136

15 OL Rowbottom, 24 October 1795

16 Scott biography: Thorne, *History of Parliament*, 105; Farington, *Diary*, ii, 145; *Gentleman's Magazine*, 1830, i., 467

17 For Scott's dealings, see *Journal of the House of Commons*, 46, 379, 4 April 1791

18 Scott to Long, 13 December 1794, TNA PRO 30/8/176; also Thorne, *History of Parliament*. See Wells, *Wretched Faces*, 184–8

19 Scott's Report, 24 February 1795; Scott to Hawkesbury, 12 June, 27 July, 18 August, 8 October 1795, BL Add. MSS 38230, ff. 173, 179–80, 254–5, 265, 340–1

20 Roe, *Keats*, 9; John Thelwall, *Peaceful Discussion and and Not Tumultuary Violence the Means of Redressing National Grievances* (1795). For subsequent events and Acts see Barrell, *Imagining the King's Death*, 551–603. For divisions in the reform movement, Philp, *Reforming Ideas*, 1–39, 'The Fragmented Ideology of Reform'

21 Woodforde, *Diary*, xiv, 215–6, 29 October 1795

22 Barrell, *Imagining the King's Death*, 557: see also his *Spirit of Despotism*, 45–6

23 Gillray, *Copenhagen House*, 16 November 1795

24 See Barrell, *Spirit of Despotism*, and Johnson, *Unusual Suspects*, for the impact. For the counter-argument that a resilient elite were protecting British interests see David Andress, *The Savage Storm: Britain on the Brink in the Age of Napoleon* (2012)

25 *Correspondence of the London Corresponding Society* (1795), 66

26 Oakes, *Diaries*, i, 318, 23 November 1795

27 Joseph Cottle, *Early Recollections*, 2 vols (1837), i, 178–9

28 Quoted in David Alexander, *Richard Newton and English Caricature in the 1790s* (1998), 115

29 'Brutus', *Cursory Remarks on Mr Pitt's New Tax imposing a Guinea per Head on every Person who wears Hair-Powder* (1795); quoted in Barrell, *Spirit of Despotism*, 163, and chapter 'Hair Powder', 145–209

30  Woodforde, *Diary*, xv, 30, 20 April 1796
31  Badenach, *Diary*, 249, 24 June 1796
32  Woodforde, *Diary*, xv, 13, 15 February 1796
33  See K. D. M. Snell, 'In or Out of their Place: The Migrant Poor in English Art, 1740–1900', *Rural History* 24, No. 1 (April 2013); also Barrell, *Dark Side of the Landscape*, and ch. 5 of *Spirit of Despotism*


15. EAST AND WEST

 1  Verily Anderson, *The Northrepps Grandchildren* (1968), 85
 2  Society of Friends Archive, Louisa Gurney diary, 30 May, 19 August 1796; Hare, *Gurneys*, 53, 57
 3  OL Rowbottom, 20, 21 March 1795
 4  Patricia Y. C. E. Lin, 'Caring for the Nation's Families: British Soldiers' and Sailors' Families and the State, 1793–1815', in Forrest et al., *Soldiers, Citizens and Civilians*, 103–9
 5  LA Flinders/2, Diary and Account Book of Matthew Flinders senior, 1785–1802
 6  Bod. MSS Eng. c. 7330, 6 September 1796
 7  Duncan-Jones, *Harness*, 112
 8  Ibid., 127–9, 16 September 1797
 9  Bod. MSS Eng. c. 7330, 16 January 1800
10  CAS S SEN 29, 1 February 1796. For storms in north, see *Cumberland Paquet*, 26 January 1796. Two hundred and thirty-six ships sailed in November; only thirty-five had returned by 29 January; Knight, *Britain*, 74
11  See J. R. Ward, 'The British West Indies in the Age of Abolition, 1748–1815', *Oxford History of the British Empire* (1998), ii, 415–39
12  George Pinckard, *Notes on the West Indies, 1796* (1806 edition), 220, 451 and passim. Henry Dillon's émigré regiment, which fought in Haiti and Jamaica, was disbanded in 1798 because it had lost almost all its men to fever.
13  Chamberlain, *Hell upon Water*, 121
14  *Reading Mercury*, 13 October 1800
15  Wynne, *Diaries*, iii, 288, 21 October 1797. For bone work see Lloyd, *Arts and Crafts*: see the collection in Peterborough Museum
16  Chamberlain, *Hell upon Water*, 11, War Office papers, 6 June 1796
17  Ibid., 128, Sir William Pitt, October 1796
18  Ibid., 35, Commissioner Ambrose Searle, 19 December 1796
19  Ibid., 71, Commissioner William Otway, 19 December 1796


16. INVASIONS, SPIES AND POETS

 1  LUL Rathbone Papers II 1. 63, Hannah Greg to William Rathbone, 31 July 1796
 2  Hague, *Pitt*, 385
 3  Woodforde, *Diary*, xv, 76, 93, 10 September, 6 November 1796
 4  James Harris, Earl of Malmesbury, *Diaries and Correspondence* (1844), iii, 308
 5  Quoted in Roy Foster, 'Remembering 1798', in Ian McBride (ed.), *History and Memory in Modern Ireland* (2001), 69

6  R. L. Edgeworth, *Memoirs*, 138

7  See Marianne Elliot, *Partners in Revolution: The United Irishmen and France* (1982); also her biography *Wolfe Tone* (2012)

8  John Bew, *Castlereagh* (2011), xxiv, xxvi

9  David Worrall, *Celebrity, Performance, Reception: British Georgian Theatre as Social Assemblage* (2013), 137–42

10  Lloyd, *Prisoners of War*, 62

11  27 February 1797. Lloyd, *Prisoners of War*, 64, 66; M. B. Mirehouse, *South Pembrokeshire, History and Records* (1910), 30–3

12  Cawdor to his wife, 13 March 1797: Wheeler and Broadley, *Napoleon*, i, 65; see J. S. Kinross, *Fishguard Fiasco: An Account of the Last Invasion of Britain* (1974), and J. E. Thomas, *Britain's Last Invasion, Fishguard 1797* (2007)

13  In *Biographia Literaria* (1817), 164

14  See Johnston, *Unusual Suspects*, 255–8

15  'My first acquaintance with poets' (1823), Hazlitt, *Selected Writings*, ix, *Uncollected Essays*, 96

## 17. MUTINIES AND MILITIA

1  *Annual Register* 1797, Appendix to Chronicle, 89

2  OL Rowbottom, 22 March 1797

3  *Times*, 30 August 1796

4  *Times*, 13 March 1797

5  WT Gill Papers Bundle 9, Thomas Gill transcript, 'Recollections'

6  Oakes, *Diaries*, i, 343, 4 March 1797

7  First Quota Act, 5 March 1795: 9,769 men from counties in England and Wales; second Act, 16 March: 19,867 men from seaports, England, Scotland and Wales, 5,704 from London; third Act, 25 April: counties and burghs of Scotland, 1,814 men; fourth and fifth Acts, 11 November 1,796: coastal counties of England, 6,124 men for navy; inland counties and Wales, 6,525 men for army; Scotland, 2,108 men. Emsley, *British Society*, 53

8  Philip Harling, 'Critiques of the British War Effort, 1793–1815', in Philp (ed.), *Resisting Napoleon*, 27

9  Quoted in Harling, *Waning of 'Old Corruption'*, 102

10  Hubback, *Austen's Sailor Brothers*, 29

11  Oakes, *Diaries*, i, 349, 9 May 1797

12  Quoted in Nicholas Rogers, 'The Sea-Fencibles, Loyalism and the Reach of the State', in Philp (ed.), *Resisting Napoleon*, 51; TNA ADM 1/5125, petitions 1793–7, ADM 1/27 C370, No. 4

13  Wells, *Insurrection*, 87–102

14  Peter Padfield, *Nelson's War* (1976), 84

15  Knight and Wilcox, *Sustaining the Fleet*, 201, and for Camperdown, 183–6

16  James McGrigor, *The Autobiography and Services of Sir James McGrigor* (1861), 91; Russell, *Theatres of War*, 114

17  'Mutiny at Portsmouth', 25 April 1797, Betty T. Bennett, *British War Poetry in the Age of Romanticism, 1793–1815* (1976); digital version ed. Orianne Smith, 67

18  Wheeler and Broadley, *Napoleon*, i, 203

19 For Scottish militia, and generally, see Cookson, *Armed Nation*, 106–9, and the chapter 'Scotland's Fame', 126–52

20 See Sandy Mullay, *The Tranent Massacre* (1979, 1997 edn)

21 James Miller, *Lamp of Lothian: or, The History of Haddington* (1844), 312

22 *Courier and Evening Gazette*, London, 4 September 1797

23 *Anti-Jacobin; or, Weekly Examiner*, 27 November 1797

## 18. CASH IN HAND

1 *Times*, 27 February 1797

2 John Keyworth, 'The Old Lady of Threadneedle Street', *Bank of England Quarterly Bulletin* June 2013, 138

3 J. F. Wright, 'British Government Borrowing in Wartime, 1750–1815', *English Historical Review* 52, no. 2 (1999), 355

4 Hardy, *Diary*, iii, 343, 28 February 1797

5 HB 8/T/4, 75–7, 29 February 1797

6 HB 2/E/1 Memorandum Book, 19 January 1801

7 David Symons, 'Matthew Boulton and the Royal Mint', in Malcolm Dick (ed.), *Matthew Boulton: A Revolutionary Player* (2009), 176

8 1 March 1797. All other quotations in this paragraph are from Oakes, *Diaries*, i, 342–5, 1–23 March

9 Woodforde, *Diary*, xv, 130, 133, 16, 29 March 1797

10 Henry Bohn (ed.), *Speeches of the Right Honourable Richard Brinsley Sheridan* (1842), iii, 164, 24 March 1797

11 *Times*, 30 May 1804

12 'Lord Malmesbury's Negotiations with the French Ministers Plenipotentiary', *St James's Gazette*; Chet. Hay Scrapbook, 105

13 HB/2/E/1 Memorandum Book, 18 December 1797

14 HB/5/A/10 Private Ledger 182, 20 September 1799

15 *Piozzi Letters*, iv, 145, Sophia Thrale to Gabriel Piozzi, 21 July 1807

16 Badenach, *Diary*, 267–74, 28 February, 16 March, 10 April 1797

17 OL Rowbottom, 22 August 1797

18 Martin Daunton on Boyd, *ODNB*

19 Bod. MSS Eng. lett. d. 199, Elizabeth Heber to Reginald Heber snr, 13 February 1795

20 HB 2/E/1 Memorandum Book, 3 March 1798

21 Woodforde, *Diary*, xv, 193, 3 December 1797

## 19. AT SEA AND ON LAND

1 See Knight and Wilcox, *Sustaining the Fleet*, 201–4

2 Rogers, *Press Gang*, 111; *Morning Chronicle*, 17 October 1797

3 Burroughes, *Journal*, 106, 16 July 1798

4 *Norfolk News*, 19 July 1798

5 Paget, *Memoirs and Letters*, 2. Paget and his wife Betsey had seventeen children; the eldest, Sir James, was a distinguished surgeon, and another son, Sir George, became Regius Professor of Physic in Cambridge.

6 Robert Hay, *Memoirs*, 17

7 Lyttelton, *Correspondence*, 1–2, to the Dowager Countess Spencer, 8 June 1804

8 *John Clare by Himself*, 35

9 John Clare, in *William Hone's Every Day Book*, 1825, in John Wardroper (ed.), *The World of William Hone* (1997), 113–4

10 Thomas Sidney Cooper, *My Life*, 2 vols (1890), i, 18; David Wilkie, *The Fair at Pitlessie*, 1804 (National Gallery)

11 Henry Gunning, *Reminiscences of Cambridge*, 2 vols (1854), i, 153–8

12 Thompson, *Salmon*, 11–12; for Warren Jane, 48; Will of Warren Jane TNA/ PROB 11/158/275, 24 December 1816

13 Knight, *Britain*, 141, citing Patrick Crowhurst, *The French War on Trade: Privateering 1793–1815* (1989), 199–202

14 CAS D SEN 5/5/1/9/32, 28 August 1807

## 20. THE POWERHOUSE

1 *Aris's Birmingham Gazette*, 1 February 1796

2 Svedenstierna, *Tour*, 30

3 Folk song *c.*1800, 'John Wilkinson, Wales & the Wider World', Wrexham (2008), www.wrexham.gov.uk/English/heritage/bersham_ironworks

4 John P. Addis, *The Crawshay Dynasty: A Study in Industrial Organization and Development, 1765–1867* (1957), 16

5 J. M. W. Turner, *Ironworks, Merthyr*, 1798 (Tate)

6 See Chris Evans, *The Labyrinth of Flames: Work and Social Conflict in Early Industrial Merthyr Tydfil* (1993)

7 M. W. Thomson (ed.), *The Journeys of Sir Richard Colt Hoare through Wales and England, 1793–1810* (1983), 98

8 Output of 68,000 tons from eighty-five furnaces in 1788, rose to 250,400 tons from 221 furnaces by 1816; T. S. Ashton, *Iron and Steel in the Industrial Revolution* (1924), 98

9 Svedenstierna, *Tour*, 67

10 *Carlisle Journal*, 6 November 1802

11 Woodforde, *Diary*, xiv, 42, 11 June 1794

12 See Chris Evans, 'Gilbert Gilpin: A Witness to the South Wales Iron Industry in Its Ascendancy', *Morgannwg* 34 (1990), Welsh Journals Online. Also Gilpin to William Wilkinson, 19 July 1797, SA 1781/6/25; Chris Evans on Crawshay, *ODNB*

13 Elizabeth Fry's journal, 4 September 1798; *Memoir of the Life of Elizabeth Fry*, ed. K. Fry and R. E. Cresswell (1847), i, 58–60, 74

14 Barrie Tridner, *ODNB*

15 See Arthur Raistrick, *Dynasty of Iron Founders: the Darbys and Coalbrookdale* (1953), 159

16 Ibid., 163–4

17 Svedenstierna, *Tour*, 42; also visits to Keir 85, Sheffield 93, Walker alkali 112, whisky 126, Lasswade paper mill 134

18 Dorothy Wordsworth, *Tour in Scotland*, 49–50

## 21. 'CHECK PROUD INVASION'S BOAST'

1 Hague, *Pitt*, 407

2 *Anti-Jacobin* 1 (Monday 20 November 1797), 4, 2

3 Richard Polwhele, 'Unsex'd Females' (written 1798, pub. 1800): Polwhele's list included the 'poor maniac' Mary Wollstonecraft, Mary Hays, Anna Barbauld, Mary Robinson, Angelica Kauffman, Hester Thrale Piozzi and Charlotte Smith, recommending more conservative writers like Anna Seward and Hannah More.

4 OL Rowbottom, 19 December 1797

5 J. Holland Rose, *William Pitt and the Great War* (1911), 349

6 Wheeler and Broadley, *Napoleon*, i, 98

7 Russell, *Theatres of War*, 53; from C. B. Hogan (ed.), *London Stage*, Part 5, iii, 2043–4

8 For propaganda and idealised visions of rural life, see ch. 5, 'Cottage Politics', in Barrell, *Spirit of Despotism*

9 Advertisement for *An Address to the People . . . on the Threatened Invasion* (1798), Wheeler and Broadley, *Napoleon*, i, 73

10 See Samuel Rogers, *Table Talk*, ed. Alexander Dyve (1887), 146–51, 201–2

11 Ibid., i, 361, 24 February 1798

12 Appendix to the Chronicle, *Annual Register* 1798, 183–9, 'Circular Letter from Mr. Dundas to the Lords Lieutenants of the Counties'. Cookson, *Armed Nation*, 47–8

13 The military strength, according to an optimistic report in *The Times*, 15 January 1798, was: regular soldiers 31,824; militia (sixty-nine regiments) 45,000; fencible cavalry 13,104; fencible infantry 11,042: volunteer cavalry (252 troops) 15,120; infantry volunteers (856 companies) 51,360; supplementary militia 60,000: total 227,450.

14 *The Buckinghamshire Posse Comitatus 1798*, Buckinghamshire Record Society publication 22 (1985), www.bucksinfo.net/brs

15 Hardy, *Diary*, iv, 32, 29 April, 7 May 1798

16 Wheeler and Broadley, *Napoleon*, i, 122–3

17 Scott, *Letters*, i, 63–6, to Patrick Murray, 8 March 1797

18 Ibid., i, 75, to Christian Rutherford, October 1797

19 James Grant, *Cassell's Old and New Edinburgh*, 6 vols (1880), vi, 264

20 Oakes, *Diaries*, i, 365, 4 June 1798

21 Compared to twenty-two in the previous three years. See K. B. Pry, *'Dread the Boist'rous Gale': Theatre in Wartime Britain 1793–1802* (1894); Cookson, *Armed Nation*, 219

22 *Annual Register* 41 (1799), Chron. 22–3, 24

23 Gee, *Volunteer Movement*, 88, TNA HO 50/43, Telford to Earl of Powis, 11 June 1798

24 Wheeler and Broadley, *Napoleon*, i, 132; *Bath Chronicle*, 3 May, 17 May 1798

25 Hannah More, diary, 17 May 1798, in Hutchings, *Messrs Hoare*, 95; see also Hunter, *Hoare's Bank Archives*, 42, 'Brown Bess Muskets'

26 *Memoirs of Henry Hunt, Esq.* (1820), i, 199–200

27 Wynne, *Diaries*, iii, 2, Wednesday 5 September 1798

28 Gee, *Volunteer Movement*, 173; Farington, *Diary*, iii, 1028, 5 July 1798; also iv, 1274, 2 September 1799
29 Emsley, *British Society*, 67, quoting Holland Rose, *Pitt*, 338
30 Johnson, *Thompson*, 14

## 22. IRELAND

1 *Times*, 11 April 1798
2 Dunfermline, *Abercromby*, 94, Order of 26 February 1798; letter to his father, 107-8
3 Journal entry 10 March 1814, in MacCarthy, *Byron*, 28
4 Miles Byrne, *Memoirs of Miles Byrne: Chef de Bataillon in the Service of France*, (1863), i, 46
5 *Memoir of Maria Edgeworth*, 83
6 John Henry Slessor, 9-23 June 1798, in Hayter, *Backbone*, 40-3
7 R. L. Edgeworth, *Memoirs*, 378-9
8 *British Critic* 13 (1799), 320
9 McCalman, *Radical Underworld*, 22
10 J. Graham, *The Nation, the Law and the King: Reform Politics in England, 1789-1799*, 2 vols (2000), ii, 753: see Michael Davis, 'United Englishmen' in *ODNB*
11 Navickas, *Loyalism and Radicalism*, 144
12 LUL Rathbone Papers II 1. 65, Hannah Greg to Hannah Rathbone, April 1798
13 Peter Spencer, *Hannah Greg* (1982), Quarry Bank Mill Trust, 8; Sekers, *Hannah Greg*, 103-8
14 Ellen Melly, *Reminiscences*, in Sekers, *Hannah Greg*, 107
15 See Navickas, *Loyalism and Radicalism*, 117-32
16 *Memoir of Maria Edgeworth*, i, 98-9

## 23. THE NILE AND BEYOND

1 *Times*, 27 April 1798
2 *Times*, 27 April 1798
3 *Piozzi Letters*, ii, 525-6, to Penelope Sophia Pennington, 14 September 1798
4 Nicol, *Life and Adventures*, 174
5 *Dispatches and Letters of Vice-admiral Lord Viscount Nelson*, ed. N. H. Nicolas, 7 vols (1844-6), iii, 230, to Lord Howe, 8 January 1799
6 For this and Gillray's other apocalyptic visions, see Gatrell, *City of Laughter*, 283
7 Mike Jay, *The Atmosphere of Heaven: The Unnatural Experiments of Dr Beddoes and His Sons of Genius* (2009), 160
8 Oakes, *Diaries*, i, 369-71, 6 October, 1, 13 November 1798
9 Mark Philp, 'Politics and Memory: Nelson and Trafalgar in Popular Song' in Cannadine (ed.), *Trafalgar*, 101-2
10 Woodforde, *Diary*, xvi, 67, 29 November 1798
11 WT Gill Papers Bundle 9, Thomas Gill transcript, 'Recollections'
12 14 November 1791, R. A. Austen Leigh (ed.), *Austen Papers, 1784-1856* (1942), 144

13 Oakes, *Diaries*, i, 379, 6 September 1799
14 OL Rowbottom, 28 January 1799
15 WT WLMS Gill Papers 1/1/5–6, 21 August, 26 September 1799
16 Sugden, *Sword of Albion*, 131
17 Duncan-Jones, *Harness*, 134
18 V & A website, 'Tipu's Tiger', www.vam.ac.uk. Thanks to Nicholas Roe on Keats.
19 William Godwin, diary, 2 May 1800: http://godwindiary.bodleian.ox.ac.uk
20 Russell, *Theatres of War*, 54–6
21 *Times*, 6 June 1799

## 24. 'THE DISTRESSEDNESS OF THE TIMES'

1 Bod. MSS Eng. lett. d. 200, Elizabeth Heber to Reginald Heber snr, 4 December 1798
2 Bod. MSS Eng. lett. d. 201, note from Mary Heber, 24 September 1800
3 Hardy, *Diary*, iv, 75, 12 April 1799
4 *Norfolk Chronicle*, 10 November 1825; Hardy, *Diary*, iv, 74
5 OL Rowbottom, 1 January 1799
6 Ibid., 27 February 1799
7 Oakes, *Diaries*, i, 374, 16 April 1799
8 The gig-mill was a revolving cylinder with rows of teasels over which the cloth was wound by rollers, while the shearing frame had two pairs of shears mounted on a carriage.
9 OL Rowbottom, 15 July 1799
10 BLARS L30/24/26; Amabel Hume-Campbell (Lucas) to Agneta Yorke, 2 November 1799
11 Bamford, *Early Days*, 174–5
12 Oakes, *Diaries*, ii, 3, 8 January 1801; i, 393, 24 November 1800
13 Ibid., i, 392, 2 October 1800
14 Wynne, *Diaries*, iii, 12, 17–18 December 1799
15 John Sykes, *Local Records, or, Historical Register of Remarkable Events* (1833), ii, 1
16 OL Rowbottom, 20 April 1800
17 James Hamilton, *Turner: A Life* (1997), 146
18 WT WLMS H/1/1/8/3, Joanna Hutchinson to John Monkhouse, 9 April 1800
19 WT WLMS H/1/14/1, John Monkhouse to his grandfather, 1799
20 WT WLMS H/1/14/2, John Monkhouse to his father, 24 September 1799
21 WT WLMS H/1/14/5 John Monkhouse to Joanna Hutchinson, April 1801
22 Gee, *Volunteer Movement*, 260; TNA HO 50/50, 25 May 1801. For Brixham see R. Wells, 'The Revolt of the South-west 1800–1801: A Study in English Popular Protest', *Social History* 2, No. 6 (October 1977), 713–42
23 Sutherland, *Scott*, 94; Edgar Johnson, *Sir Walter Scott: The Great Unknown*, ii, 868–9
24 OL Rowbottom, 19 April 1801
25 *Manchester Gazette*, 14, 21 February 1801
26 Bod. MSS Eng. lett. d. 201, Reginald Heber snr to Elizabeth Heber, 12 July 1800

# Central Library
# Newport City Council

## Issue Summary

Patron: Ms Gill Edwards
Id: R145***
Date: 2/7/2019  12:57 PM

## Loaned today

Item: Z962657
Title: In these times :
Due back: 28/02/2019

Remember that your library
membership
also gives you access to free
eBooks,
eMagazines and eAudiobooks,
available
to download online any time of day or
night!

*Visit LION to renew, request
and search for books online
https://opac.newport.gov.uk*

Thank you

27 Bod. MSS Eng. lett. d. 201, Reginald Heber snr to Elizabeth Heber, 24 September 1800
28 Emsley, *British Society*, 85-6
29 Wells, *Wretched Faces*, 200: Scott to Board of Trade, 3 November 1800, and examination TNA BT 5/12, 59-75, 126-34; also L. V. Harcourt (ed.), *The Diaries and Correspondence of the Rt. Hon George Rose*, 2 vols (1860), i, 282
30 Cobbett, *Parliamentary History*, xxxiv, 1429-30
31 WT WLMS H/1/1/3, John Hutchinson to John Monkhouse, 17, 25 May 1799
32 WT WLMS H/1/8, 9, 10, John Hutchinson to John Monkhouse, 30 December 1800, October 1801, 4 December 1801
33 5 April 1801, Tandle Hill near Royton; 3 May, on the moors of Buckton Castle and Greenacres, near Oldham; 5 May, Rivington Pike near Bolton
34 Thomas Spence, 'Letter 5, 20 September 1800', in *Restorer of Society to its Natural State*, April 1801; *Political Works of Thomas Spence*, ed. H. T. Dickinson (1982)

## 25. GOD ON OUR SIDE

1 Sherwood, *Life*, 221
2 *Cheap Repository for Moral and Religious Publications*, [a prospectus], [1795]
3 Hannah More to Elizabeth Montagu, Broadley MSS, Wheeler and Broadley, *Napoleon*, i, 210
4 More, *Correspondence*, i, 473, to Zachary Macaulay, 6 January 1796
5 Thomas Paine, *The Age of Reason*, ed. Moncure Conway (2010 edition), Preface
6 Part I was published in 1794, Part II by H. D. Symonds in 1795. Both parts were republished by Daniel Eaton in 1796, and then edited by Francis Place and published in 1797 by Thomas Williams, who was indicted and sentenced to a year's hard labour: *The Autobiography of Francis Place* (1972 edn), 171, Appendix: *The Age of Reason*
7 Gregory Claeys, *Thomas Paine: Social and Political Thought* (2002), 185. In one influential riposte, *An Apology for the Bible*, Richard Watson, Bishop of Llandaff, objected less to Paine's views than to his zeal: if anything, Watson's response spread Paine's ideas still further.
8 Mark Philp, correspondence, 2014
9 Wilberforce, *A Practical View of the Prevailing Religious System of Professed Christians, in the Higher and Middle Classes in this Country, Contrasted with Real Christianity* (1797, 3rd edn 1829), 109, in Cunningham, *Invention of Childhood*, 130
10 William Cowper, *The Task*, book ii, 'The Timepiece'
11 Heber, *Letters*, 166, Revd John Stonard to Richard Heber, 26 February 1795
12 Wilberforce, *Life*, i, 149
13 Wilberforce, *Practical View* (1797), 81
14 Ibid., 180
15 Ibid., 429
16 F. K. Brown, *Fathers of the Victorians: The Age of Wilberforce* (1961) lists over 150 societies founded between 1785 and 1833; see also Hilton, *Age of Atonement*, and for the navy, Richard Blake, *Evangelicals in the Royal Navy 1775-1815: Blue Lights and Psalm-Singers* (2008)

17 Sydney Smith, *Edinburgh Review* 13 (January 1809), in *The Works of the Rev. Sydney Smith* (1859), 136

18 Oakes, *Diaries*, ii, 32, 21 November 1802

19 Quotations from *Parliamentary Register* ix, 2, 7 (11 June 1799, third reading)

20 *Parliamentary Register* viii, 4 (30 May 1799, second reading)

21 Sarah Trimmer, *The Guardian of Education* (1801), i, 2

22 Hardy, *Diary*, iv, 120–1, 18 May 1800

23 Ibid., iv, 131, 13 June 1800

24 Ibid., iv, 413, 9 December 1808

25 Lovett, *Life and Struggles*, 6

26 Bamford, *Early Days*, 4

27 Quoted in Eric Hopkins, *Childhood Transformed: Working-class Children in Nineteenth-century England* (1994), 128

28 Charlotte Bronte, *Shirley*, ch. 17, 'The School-Feast'

29 Pitt, *Speeches*, ii, 69, 74–5, 2 April 1792

30 Roger Anstey, *The Atlantic Slave Trade and British Abolition 1760–1810* (1975), 292; Barker, *Newspapers*, 174

31 BCA Galton MS 3101/B/16.2

32 Schimmelpenninck, *Life*, 151

33 Ibid., 243

34 LUL Rathbone Papers II 1.65, April 1798; Sekers, *Hannah Greg*, 73

## 26. 'GOOD MEN SHOULD NOW CLOSE RANKS'

1 Hardy, *Diary*, iv, 73, 25 March 1799

2 See Simon Schama, *Patriots and Liberators: Revolution in the Netherlands 1780–1813* (1977), 390–4

3 Pitt, *Speeches*, iv, 62, 17 February 1800

4 *Morning Post*, 12, 31 December 1799, 1 January 1800

5 *Morning Post*, 11 March 1800

6 Fox, 3 February 1800, Cobbett, *Parliamentary History*, xxxiv, 1394

7 Bod. MSS Eng. lett. d. 201, Elizabeth Heber to Reginald Heber snr, 16 May 1800

8 *Monthly Mirror* 9 (1800), 314; see Russell, *Theatres of War*, 187

9 Bod. MSS Eng. lett. c. 206, 29 October 1800, Richard Heber to his aunt Elizabeth Heber

10 WT Gill Papers Bundle 9, Thomas Gill transcript, 'Recollections'

11 Earl Camden, Memorandum on Pitt's retirement, 1803–4: Hague, *Pitt*, 468

12 Hague, *Pitt*, 461

13 *Morning Chronicle*, 9 February 1801

14 *Times*, 12 March 1801

## 27. DENMARK, EGYPT, BOULOGNE — PEACE

1 Hague, *Pitt*, 492. Canning pasquinade, *The Oracle*, *Spirit of the Public Journals*, 1803–4

2 Geoffrey Bennett, *Nelson the Commander* (1997), 187

3 See Sugden, *Sword of Albion*, 428–50

4 See ibid., 442–3. The 'blind eye' story was told by an officer to Lady Malmesbury by 18 May, and independently by Dr William Ferguson of the Rifle Corps, then in the *Elephant*.

5 Wynne, *Diaries*, iii, 37, 16 April 1801

6 Woodforde, *Diary*, xvii, 28, 16 April 1801

7 WT Gill, 2/4/1–15 Thomas Gill to John Battershall, 25 May–3 June 1801

8 Wynne, *Diaries*, iii, 49, 3 May 1801

9 Piers Mackesy, *British Victory in Egypt: The End of Napoleon's Conquest* (1995), 49; Knight, *Britain*, 201

10 Nicol, *Life and Adventures*, 179

11 Bod. MSS Eng. c. 7330, 4 September 1801

12 Sir John Sinclair, *An Account of Highland Society of London, from its establishment in May 1778, to the commencement of the year 1813* (1813). For the motion to provide medals, 17 February 1802, see p. 26

13 Richard Barnett, 'Sick City' in Mike Jay (ed.), *Medical London* (2008), 179

14 Thomas Cooper, *Life*, 10

15 *Observations on the Defence of the Thames* in *Dispatches and Letters of Vice-admiral Nelson* (1845), 426, 428

16 *Times*, 19 August 1801

17 Sugden, *Sword of Albion*, 515, to Emma Hamilton, 27 September 1801

18 DRO D3580/C26, 9 October 1801

19 OL Rowbottom, 15 October 1801; for the local ball, DRO D 3580/C27, Elizabeth Longsdon, 14 October 1801

20 *Aris's Birmingham Gazette*, October 1802

21 Heber, *Letters*, 135–6, Reginald Heber snr to Elizabeth Heber, 14 October 1801

22 Oakes, *Diaries*, ii, 14–15, 20 October 1801

23 *Norfolk Chronicle*, 5 December 1801

24 Hardy, *Diary*, iv, 183, 24 November 1801

## 28. FRANCE

1 Semmel, *Napoleon and the British*, 26; Thomas Robinson to Henry Crabb Robinson, 20 October 1801, *Diary*, i, 57

2 BLARS L30/24/42, Amabel Hume-Campbell to Agneta Yorke, 14 March 1803

3 Woodforde, *Diary*, xvii, 125, 13 April 1802: he died on 1 January 1803

4 Philip Ziegler, *Addington: A Life* (1965), 148–50

5 Chet. A.6.30, James Weatherley transcript, 'Recollections'

6 OL Rowbottom, 17 October 1801

7 Nicol, *Life and Adventures*, 185

8 Gatrell, *City of Laughter*, 241

9 Heber, *Letters*, 139, Richard Heber to Elizabeth Heber, 8 December 1802

10 BLARS L30/24/35 Amabel Hume-Campbell to Agneta Yorke, 2 January 1802

11 Farington, *Diary*, v, 1890, 1 October 1802

12 Holmes, *Wonder*, 114

13 James Sime, *William Herschel and his Work* (1890), 207. For an entertaining account of the meeting see Holmes, *Wonder*, 201

14 *Memoir of Maria Edgeworth*, i, 129, to her aunt Charlotte Sneyd, 29 October 1802

15 Burney, *Journals and Letters*, v, 313–4, Paris Diary, 5 May 1802

16 *Memoir of Maria Edgeworth*, i, 147, to her aunt Charlotte Sneyd, 8 December 1802

## 29. NEW VOICES

1 Cobbett, Letter to Lord Hawkesbury III, 16 October 1801 (pub. 1802), *Selected Writings*, ii, 26. See Semmel, *Napoleon and the British*, 270

2 'On the Character of Cobbett', Hazlitt, *Selected Writings*, vi, *Table Talk* (1821), 50–1

3 Cobbett, *Advice to Young Men* (1829), para. 39

4 WT, *Miscellanea Perthensis* (1801), 6

5 *Memoir of Maria Edgeworth*, i, 185, March 1805

6 Henry Cockburn, *Life of Lord Jeffrey* (1852), 126–7

7 *Christian Observer* i (1802), 675

8 *Christian Observer* i (1802), 813, quoted in Hall, *Macaulay and Son*, 59

9 *Anti-Jacobin Review*, vi, 113 (April–August 1800)

10 Svedenstierna, *Tour*, 10

11 John Davy (ed.), *Humphry Davy: Collected Works* (1839–40), ii, 341; see Holmes, *Wonder*, 235–304

12 Robert Southey, *Letters from England* (1807; 1838 edn, ed. J. Simmons, 1984), 453: see Gatrell, *City of Laughter*, 438

13 LA Flinders 3/5, 6, 8; 3, 5, 14 April, 10 July 1801

14 *Memoir of Maria Edgeworth*, i, 115

15 Ibid., i, 106

16 Schimmelpenninck, *Life*, 124

17 BCA Galton MS 3101/C/D/10/6/30, Summer 1807

18 BCA Galton MS 3101/C/D/10/6/123, January 1815

19 *Piozzi Letters*, iv, 158, to Revd Leonard Chappelow, 21 November 1807

20 *Edinburgh Review* i (October 1802), 'Southey's Thalaba: A Metrical Romance', 63–83

21 Epigraph from Warton, on title page of *Minstrelsy*, iii (1803)

22 Brewer, *Pleasures of the Imagination*, 658

23 Thomas Cooper, *Life*, 22

24 Chambers, *Memoir*, 53

## 30. 'ALWAYS CAPABLE OF DOING MISCHIEF'

1 BLARS L30/18/47/29, Baroness Grantham to Grantham, 5 August 1802

2 BLARS L30/18/24/52, Amabel Hume-Campbell to Agneta Yorke, 31 July 1805

3 BLARS L30/18/47/29, Mary Robinson, Baroness Grantham, to Thomas Philip Robinson, third Baron Grantham, 5 August 1802

4 Wynne, *Diaries*, iii, 67, 4 June 1802

5 John Bowles, *A Postscript to thoughts on the late general election as demonstrative of the progress of Jacobinism* (1803)

6 Oakes, *Diaries*, ii, 29, 30 September 1802

7 Marianne Elliott, *ODNB*, quoting *State Trials*, 1177. See her *Partners in Revolution: the United Irishmen and France* (1982)

8 *Speeches from the Dock, or Protests of Irish Patriotism*, 3 vols (1868), i, 61

9 For his trial, see *Political Register*, 9 June 1804

10 Bamford, *Early Days*, 189

11 Charles Buxton (ed.), *Memoirs of Sir Thomas Fowell Buxton* (1848), 343

12 Ferguson, *Rothschild*, 56, to J. A. Matti, Frankfurt, December 1802

13 Ibid., 57, to Geisenheim, 19 January 1803

14 OL Rowbottom, 18 February 1802

15 Randall, *Before the Luddites*, 158; *London Gazette*, July 1802

16. Minutes of evidence: Select Committee on Bill respecting Laws relating to Woollen Trade, 3 June 1803, *House of Commons Papers, Reports of Committees* (95), 179–80

17 Ibid., 71

18 Ibid., 227–8

19 M. B. Rose, *The Gregs of Quarry Bank Mill* (1986), 106

20 Sekers, *Hannah Greg*, 108, Bessy Greg to Mary Hodgson, November 1801

21 Journal of Elizabeth Greg, 24 July 1807, in Emily Rathbone (ed.), *Records of the Rathbone Family* (1913), 312

## 31. ALBION

1 Dorothy Wordsworth, *Journals*, 102, 28 May 1802

2 Quoted in David Kynaston, *The City of London. Vol. 1: A World of Its Own, 1815–1890* (1994), 9

3 Lamb, *Letters*, i, 248, to C. L. Manning, 3 November 1800

4 Lyttelton, *Correspondence*, 2–3, to the Dowager Countess Spencer, 17 May 1805

5 Lyttelton, *Correspondence*, 19, to Robert Spencer, 24 June 1808

6 BCA Galton MS 3101/6/3/1, 18 June 1802

7 SA Rose Boughton Papers 6683/4/344, 28 December 1813

8 Oakes, *Diaries*, ii, 13, 28, 24 August 1801, 21 August 1802

9 Ibid., ii, 82, 14 August–13 September 1806

10 Quoted in Brewer, *Pleasures of the Imagination*, 660

11 Oakes, *Diaries*, ii, 67–8, 73–76, 8 June–5 July 1805

12 Coleridge, *Letters*, i, 145–6, to Tom Poole, 24 July 1800

13 Bod. MSS Eng. lett. d. 201, Reginald Heber snr to Elizabeth Heber, 31 August 1800

14 WT WLMS Gill Papers 1/1/4, 14 August 1796

15 For these tours see Heber, *Letters*, 113–31, September/October 1800

16 Thomson (ed.), *Journeys of Sir Richard Colt Hoare*, 187–8

17 *The Ancient History of South Wiltshire* (1812)

18 BUL 200/62, Cumberland, Scotland 1803 (also notes on 1805, 1807, 1808), 10

19 BUL 200/63, Cumberland and Scotland 1800, 9

20 BUL 200/62, 35
21 HB 9/14/4 Tour through Derbyshire to the Lakes, 1802
22 Wynne, *Diaries*, iii, 332, 336, 27 May, 14–15 July 1811
23 DUL BAC 275, Diary of Hannah Gurney, 2 August–1 October 1802. All quotations from this source.
24 Matthias Dunn, *An Historical, Geological and Descriptive View of the Coal Trade of the North of England* (1844), 147
25 Sykes, *Local Records* (1833), ii, 3 September 1802
26 Southey, *Letters from England*, i, 354
27 William Combe, *The Tour of Dr Syntax in Search of the Picturesque* (1812)
28 HB AFM 9/14/4 Sophia Thrale [later Hoare], Tour through Derbyshire to the Lakes: all quotations from this source. The itinerary is given in Thomas West, *Guide to the Lakes in Cumberland, Westmoreland and Lancashire* (1789), 188–9
29 Coleridge, *Letters*, ii, 456–7, to Sara Hutchinson, 25 August 1802
30 Lamb, *Letters*, ii, 65, 69, to Coleridge, 8 September 1802, to Manning, 24 September 1802
31 Ibid., ii, 70, to Manning, 24 September 1802

## 32. INTO WAR AGAIN

1 Simon Burrows, 'The War of Words: French and British Propaganda in the Napoleonic Era', in Cannadine (ed.), *Trafalgar*, 45. By 1801 London papers sold about 20,000 copies a day, and provincial weeklies 180,000 a week.
2 Bod. MSS Eng. lett. d. 201, Elizabeth Heber to Reginald Heber snr, 31 May 1802
3 *Morning Post*, 5 October 1802
4 *Select Speeches of the Right Honourable George Canning* (1842), Appendix 561, 8 December 1802
5 Ingrams, *Cobbett*, 52
6 See Simon Burrows, *French Exile Journalism and European Politics, 1792–1814* (2000), 107–28; J.-G. Peltier, *The Trial of Jean Peltier* (1803)
7 BLARS L30/24/42, Amabel Hume-Campbell to Agneta Yorke, 14 March 1803
8 Despatch 14 March, *Annual Register*, 1803
9 *Creevey Papers* 10, Creevey to James Currie, 20 April 1803
10 Pitt, *Speeches*, iv, 234, 23 May 1803
11 Ibid., 262–3, 22 July 1803
12 HB 8/T/10 Incoming Letters, Toulouse 24 October 1803. See also J. G. Alger, *Napoleon's British Visitors and Captives, 1801–15* (1904) and John Grainger, *The Amiens Truce: Britain and Bonaparte, 1801–3* (2004)
13 HB 8/T/10 Incoming Letters, 27 May, 27 September 1804
14 Burney, *Journals and Letters*, v, 444, to Mrs Locke, 30 April 1803
15 *Memoir of Maria Edgeworth*, i, 232–3, 19 March 1810
16 Stott, *Grimaldi*, 156
17 Southey, *Life and Correspondence*, ii, 215, to Grosvenor Bedford, 12 June 1803
18 Cookson, *Armed Nation*, 175, Lord Hardwicke to C. Yorke, 3 February 1804
19 OL Rowbottom, 25 February, 16 March 1803

20 Sherwood, *Life*, 258
21 Ibid., 267–8
22 Bod. MSS Eng. c. 7330, 8 September 1802
23 Bod. MSS Eng. c. 7330, 20 December 1803

## 33. 'FINE STRAPPING FELLOWS'

1 Oakes, *Diaries*, ii, 40–2, 22 July–1 August; OL Rowbottom, 28 June, 8 July, 16 August 1803
2 Chet. broadsheet copy
3 John Clare, *Autobiographical Writings*, ed. Eric Robinson (1983), 71
4 Benjamin Harris, *Recollections*, 2–3
5 Chet. A.6.30, James Weatherley transcript, 'Recollections'
6 OL Rowbottom, 25 June 1803
7 Gee, *Volunteer Movement*, 2, 5
8 Hague, *Pitt*, 520, quoting Cleveland, *Life and Letters of the Lady Hester Stanhope* (1914), 54
9 Oakes, *Diaries*, ii, 46, 25, 29 August 1803
10 Hunter, *Hoare's Bank Archives*, 42, 'Brown Bess Muskets'
11 Cockburn, *Memorials*, 187–8
12 *Wordsworth Letters*, i, 403, Dorothy Wordsworth to Catherine Clarkson, 9 October 1803
13 WT 1/14/8, John Monkhouse to Thomas Monkhouse, 1803
14 Bamford, *Early Days*, 176, 228
15 See K. Navickas, 'The Defence of Manchester and Liverpool in 1803', in Philp (ed.), *Resisting Napoleon*, 61–6
16 Revd John Charles Cox, *Three Centuries of Derbyshire Annals* (1890), ii, 199–207
17 Diaries of John Holden, attorney's clerk, Bolton Library ZZ/530; Navickas, *Loyalism and Radicalism*, 45
18 Bod. MSS Eng. lett. d. 201, Elizabeth Heber to Reginald Heber snr, 4 August 1803
19 Bod. MSS Eng. lett. d. 201, Elizabeth Heber to Reginald Heber snr, 18 August 1803
20 Bod. MSS Eng. lett. d. 201, Reginald Heber snr to Elizabeth Heber, 31 August 1803
21 Bod. MSS Eng. lett. d. 201, Reginald Heber jnr to Richard Heber, 30 September, 7 October 1804
22 Stott, *Grimaldi*, 125. Barber was director of the County Fire Office and Provident Life Office. For drill, see *Capt. Barber's, The Duke of Cumberland's Corps of Sharp-Shooters, Instructions for the Formation and Exercise of Volunteer Sharp-Shooters* (1804)
23 Angelo, *Reminiscences*, ii, 540–1
24 Stanley Mayes, *The Great Belzoni: The Circus Strongman Who Discovered Egypt's Ancient Treasures* (2006), 45
25 Stott, *Grimaldi*, 126
26 Mark Argent (ed.), *Recollections of R. J. S. Stevens: An Organist in Georgian London* (1992), 130

27 Nicholas Roe, correspondence, 2014
28 James Wheeler, *Manchester, Its Political, Social and Commercial History* (1836), 100

## 34. PRESS GANGS AND FENCIBLES

1 Svedenstierna, *Tour*, 171
2 Wynne, *Diaries*, iii, 84–5, 24 July 1803
3 Quoted in Johnson, *Thompson*, 18
4 See Lloyd's publication *Unbroken Service*; also Gawler, *Britons Strike Home*, 119–20
5 *Times*, 21 July 1803; see Klingberg and Hustvedt, *Warning Drum*, 126–8
6 'Britons Strike Home', written for Beaumont and Fletcher's play *Bonduca* (1613)
7 *The Letters of Sir Joseph Banks: A Selection, 1768–1820*, ed. Neil Chambers (2000), 249, 8 August 1803
8 G. T. Landmann, *Adventures and Recollections* (1852), ii, 269–60
9 Nicol, *Life and Adventures*, 185, see also Eden, *State of the Poor*, ii, 164–8, 562–5 for South and North Shields
10 Lovett, *Life and Struggles*, 2
11 *Times*, 13 April 1803
12 Hay, *Memoirs*, 36
13 Joseph M. Fewster, *The Keelmen of Tyneside: Labour Organisation and Conflict in the North East Coal Industry 1600–1830* (2011), 125; *Newcastle Advertiser*, 23 April 1803
14 Sykes, *Local Records*, ii, 14, 10 May, 16 June 1803
15 Rogers, *Press Gang*, 56
16 Sherwood, *Life*, 259
17 Hardy, *Diary*, iv, 248–9; 8, 14 November 1803
18 Wynne, *Diaries*, iii, 86–7, 7 August 1803
19 Quoted in Knight, *Britain*, 254
20 Southam, *Jane Austen and the Navy*, 50; NMM MS AUS/6: 'Remarks on the coast of Kent', 12 August 1803
21 Rogers, *Press Gang*, 112–5. See A. K. Hamilton Jenkin, *Cornwall and Its People* (1970), 24–9, 93–7, and Alan G. Jamieson, 'Devon and Smuggling 1680–1850' in Duffy et al., *New Maritime History*. Also J. T. R. Johns, *The Smugglers' Banker: The Story of Jephaniah Job* (2nd edn, 2008), 27, 68–9
22 B. Brownrigg, *Life and Letters of Sir John Moore* (1923), 145–6
23 Nicol, *Life and Adventures*, 206

## 35. PANIC AND PROPAGANDA

1 McLynn, *Napoleon*, 330
2 Wheeler and Broadley, *Napoleon*, ii, 25; *St James's Chronicle*, 5 July 1803
3 UBCRL JER/305, Lady Jerningham to Charlotte, 30 October 1803
4 Wheeler and Broadley, *Napoleon*, ii, 40
5 Geoffrey Keynes (ed.), *The Letters of William Blake* (3rd edn 1980), 62
6 Blake, *Complete Poems and Prose*, 95, Preface to *Milton*
7 Sir Robert Wilson, *Narrative of the British Expedition to Egypt* (1802), title page and xxxiv

8 See Klingberg and Hustvedt, *Warning Drum*, 72, 106, 161

9 Ibid., 121

10 Semmel, *Napoleon and the British*, 48–54

11 Cobbett, *Political Register*, 26 July 1803

12 Cobbett, *Important Considerations* (1803), *Selected Writings*, ii, 90

13 Klingberg and Hustvedt, *Warning Drum*, 188–90

14 Ibid., 76–9

15 Semmel, *Napoleon and the British*, 88–9, and see 72–106, 'The Pious Proteus and the Nation's Destiny'

16 Klingberg and Hustvedt, *Warning Drum*, 179

17 Joanna Southcott, *The Long Wished for Revolution Announced to be at Hand in a book Lately published by L. Mayer* (1806), 17. (Mayer's book was *A Hint to England; or, a Prophetic Mirror, containing an explanation of prophecy that relates to the French nation, and the threatened invasion; proving Bonaparte to be the beast that arose out of the earth, with two horns like a lamb, and spake as a dragon, whose number is 666* (1803))

18 *Letters intercepted on board the Admiral Applin, captured by the French* (1804), all letters 1803: Grenville to Wellesley, 12 July, 19; Mrs Seton to her son, 17 August, 43; Wharton Kinnington to Lieut. Pitt Grissin, 19 August, 63; Miss M. Tomson to her brother, August, 46; John Maid to Gordon, 24 August, 35; John Nixon to Thomas Kegley, 18 August; M. Taylor to M. Curtis, 13 August, 41, 84. See also www.napoleon-series.org/research, Dominique Constant and Tom Homberg

19 Hare, *Gurneys*, 128, Richenda to Elizabeth Fry, 8 September 1803

20 Ibid., 130–2

21 Scott, *The Antiquary* (1815), ch. 45

22 LA 1 SIB/2/4/23, 20 February 1804

23 LA 1 SIB/2/4/27, 18 September 1804

24 UBCRL JER/324, 8 May 1804

25 For Pitt's illness see Hague, *Pitt*, 576–7

## 36. 'EVERY FARTHING I CAN GET'

1 Schedule A: land and buildings; B: produce of land; C: interest from government funds; D: profits from trade, commerce, fees and salaries; E: income from offices, annuities, pensions and stipends. Pitt's 1801 tax of 10 per cent produced £5,628,813; Addington's 5 per cent produced £5,341,907: Daunton, *Trusting Leviathan*, 184–5

2 *Letters intercepted*, 77, John Blanker to Lieutenant-Colonel Close, 22 July 1803

3 BLARS L30/24/49, Amabel Hume-Campbell to Agneta Yorke, 19 January 1804

4 WT 1/14/8 8, John Monkhouse to Thomas Monkhouse, [1803]

5 DRO D 3580/C35, 37, Elizabeth Longsdon 6 April, James Longsdon 10 April 1803

6 Wilson, *Laughter of Triumph*, 41–7

7 HB 2/E/1 Memorandum Book, November, 22 December 1803, February 1804

8 See Richard Doty, *Soho Mint and the Industrialisation of Money* (1998)

9 OL Rowbottom, 28 April 1809

10 *Hoare's Bank*, Appendix III

11 HB 2/E/2 Memorandum Book, 15 March, 13 December 1800

12 HB 2/E/2 Memorandum Book, 27, 28 February 1806. See also *Hoare's Bank*, 102: the account was in the name of the Earl of Winchelsea, Groom of the Stole.

13 Oakes, *Diaries*, i, 89, Introduction

14 HB 2/E/2, December 1802


## 37. THE BUSINESS OF DEFENCE

1 De Witt Bailey, *British Military Longarms, 1715–1825* (1971), 65–8. The Birmingham output before 1806 was 2,624: between 1804 and 1815, the total was 14,695, plus 32,582 barrels and 37,338 locks. See also D. W. Bailey and D. A. Nie, *English Gunmakers, The Birmingham and Provincial Gun Trade in the eighteenth and nineteenth century* (1978)

2 See Williams, *Weedon*, throughout, for plans and development

3 Williams, *Weedon*, 10, REL WEE 10/1 Letter Book 1

4 Quoted by Kathleen Burke, in 'Migration as a Trans-generational Affair: The Pilkington and Smith Descendants Return to Canada', in *Canadian Migration Patterns from Britain and North America*, ed. Barbara Jane Messamore (2004), 124. See also Carl Christian, *Dictionary of Canadian Biography*

5 Williams, *Weedon*, 42, REL WEE 10/1 Letter Book 2

6 Williams, *Weedon*, 45, REL WEE 10/1 Letter Book 2

7 Williams, *Weedon*, 57, REL WEE 10/1 Letter Book 2

8 See Katrina Navickas, 'Dumouriez's Memoirs on the Defences of Great Britain and Ireland', in Franklin and Philp, *Napoleon and the Invasion of Britain*, 61–3

9 Bill Clements, *Martello Towers Worldwide* (2011), 13–44

10 See Cole, *Arming the Royal Navy*, and A. Geddes, *Portsmouth During the Great French Wars 1770–1800* (1970)

11 R. G. Albion, *Forests and Sea Power* (1926), 373, and generally 316–68

12 See *Parliamentary Debates*, vii, 1806, Conduct of Earl St Vincent

13 Eighty-four per cent of warships were built in private yards between 1803 and 1815: Knight, *Britain*, 359

14 These were the *Magnificent*, *Elizabeth* and *Valiant*. For the history of the dock, see English Heritage, 'Blackwall Yard', *Survey of London*, xliii–xliv, *Poplar, Blackwall and Isle of Dogs* (1994), 535–65

15 See Roger Knight, 'The Fleets at Trafalgar', in Cannadine (ed.), *Trafalgar*, 69–70

16 Ann Coats, 'The Restoration of Portsmouth Dockyard Block Mills (built 1803), 2006–8', *Dockyards* 14, 1 (July 2009), 14–18. They were marvels of precision, with many novel features – like detachable tool bits and interchangeable sheaves and pins – that would soon became standard in machine design.

17 Jonathan Coad, *The Portsmouth Block Mills: Bentham, Brunel and the Start of the Royal Navy's Industrial Revolution* (2005). Simon Goodrich papers, Science Museum

18 Raistrick, *Iron Founders*, 165

## 38. TRAFALGAR

1 Hilton, *Mad, Bad and Dangerous*, 235
2 *10th Report of the Commission for Naval Enquiry*, February 1805
3 Hague, *Wilberforce*, 323
4 Wynne, *Diaries*, iii, 254, 29 April 1806
5 *Creevey Papers*, 23, to James Currie, 11 May 1805
6 See Johnston, *Unusual Subjects*, 250–8, for the climate of repression
7 Isabella Fenwick, note, Wordsworth, *Prose Works*, iii, 86; Gill, *Wordsworth*, 245
8 Hubback, *Austen's Sailor Brothers*, 144 (August 1804); see Maya Jasanoff, *Edge of Empire: Conquest and Collecting in the East, 1750–1850* (2006), 168
9 John Wilson Croker, *Correspondence and Diaries* (1834, repr. 1972), ii, 234
10 LA 1 SIB/2/4/41 18, 19 September 1805
11 Malmesbury, *Diaries and Correspondence*, iv, 340
12 Quoted in Audrey Bateman, *A Social History of Canterbury* (1984), 81
13 Robert Southey, *Life of Nelson* (1814, 1909 edn), 260
14 Southam, *Jane Austen and the Navy*, 95
15 BCA Galton MS 3101/C/D/6/4/1–2, 10 December 1805
16 Wynne, *Diaries*, iii, 221, 28 October 1805
17 LA 1/SIB/2/4/51, 8 December 1805
18 Lamb, *Letters*, ii, 1978, to Hazlitt, 7 January 1806
19 *Times*, 6 January 1806
20 BLARS L30/24/55, Amabel Hume-Campbell to Agneta Yorke, 12 January 1806
21 Southey, *Life of Nelson*, 260
22 Chet. A.6.30–30*, Weatherley transcript
23 This was for *Fairbairn's Edition of the Funeral*; R. L. Patten, *George Cruikshank's Life, Times and Art*, 2 vols (1992–6), i, 45
24 Russell, *Theatres of War*, 84, quoting *Thespian Review* 7 (1806), 55
25 Geoffrey Quilley, 'The Battle of the Pictures', and Marianne Czisnik, 'Commemorating Trafalgar' in Cannadine (ed.), *Trafalgar*, 121–38, 139–54. Nelson had apparently once remarked, after seeing the painting of Wolfe, that 'should he die in battle, he should like West to paint his memorial in like manner'.
26 Wynne, *Diaries*, iii, 259, 6 May 1806

## 39. ALL THE TALENTS

1 Philip Henry Stanhope, *Life of the Right Honourable William Pitt* (1867, repr. 1970), iv, 346
2 *Piozzi Letters*, iv, 87, to Lady Williams, 29 December 1805
3 *Creevey Papers*, 40
4 Addington, *Life and Correspondence*, ii, 401, 31 December 1805
5 *Times*, 6 January 1806
6 OL Rowbottom, 25 March 1806
7 Marianne Czisnik, 'Commemorating Trafalgar', in Cannadine (ed.), *Trafalgar*, 140
8 Hubback, *Austen's Sailor Brothers*, 174–5, 7 February 1806

9 Austen, *Letters*, 171, to Cassandra Austen, 10 January 1808
10 *Times*, 2 January 1806
11 *Times*, 19 and 22 September 1806: Thomas Byrne, 'British Army, Irish Soldiers: The 1806 Invasion of Buenos Aires', *Irish Migration Studies in Latin America*, March 2010, 7, iii, via www.irlandeses.org; also Ian Fletcher, *The Waters of
Oblivion: The British Invasion of the Rio de la Plata, 1806–1807* (2006)
12 L. G. Mitchell, *Charles James Fox* (1992), 237
13 CAS D SEN 5/5/1/9/50, 12 October 1796
14 Oakes, *Diaries*, ii, 83, 2 October 1806
15 Jane Austen, 'On Sir Home Popham's Sentence – April 1807', Southam, *Jane
Austen and the Navy*, 135
16 Johnson, *Thompson*, 22
17 Wynne, *Diaries*, iii, 307, 309, 19 December 1806, 18 March 1807
18 D. Gray, *Spencer Perceval: The Evangelical Prime Minister, 1762–1812* (1963), 11;
Cobbett, *History of the Regency and Reign of George IV* (1830), ch. 2, para. 77
19 Cobbett, *Regency*, ch. 2, para. 86
20 *Works of the Rev. Sydney Smith*, 3 vols (1848 edn), i, 79
21 Ingrams, *Cobbett*, 83

## 40. PRIVATE LIVES

1 Oakes, *Diaries*, ii, 73, 77
2 Lamb, *Letters*, ii, 223, to Hazlitt, 15 March 1806
3 BCA Galton MS 3101/C/D/10/6/15, March 1806
4 Schimmelpenninck, *Life*, 335; BCA Galton MS 3102/C/D/10/6/30, 15
March 1807
5 LUL Rathbone Papers VI i. 165, in Sekers, *Hannah Greg*, 129
6 DRO D3580/C46, 29 April 1806
7 Thomas Carlyle, *Reminiscences*, ed. J. A. Froude (1881), 29–30
8 Douce MSS 'Miscellanies', quoted in Todd Longstaffe-Gowan, *The London Town
Garden, 1740–1840* (2001), 146
9 *Piozzi Letters*, iv, 110, to Revd Leonard Chappelow, 4 June 1806
10 Angelo, *Reminiscences*, ii, 15
11 Wynne, *Diaries*, iii, 296, 29 July 1806
12 *Remarkable Trials at the Lancaster Assizes, held August 1806* (1806)
13 Jane Gurney Fox, *Extracts from the Journal and Letters of Hannah Chapman Backhouse*
(1858), 10–11
14 LUL Rathbone Papers II 1. 69, 1 October 1806
15 Mitford, *Recollections*, ii, 25
16 William Cobbett, *Advice to Young Men, and (incidentally) to young women . . .* (1829),
Letter 5, para. 291
17 Ibid., Letter 5, para. 258
18 Scott, *Letters*, i, 339
19 Rowlandson, *The Mother's Hope*, 1808

## 41. ABOLITION AND AFTER

1 Hague, *Wilberforce*, 354
2 War Office and Colonial Office returns: see Roger Buckley, *Slaves in Red Coats: the British West India Regiments, 1795–1815* (1979), and Anstey, *Atlantic Slave Trade*
3 R. and S. Wilberforce (eds), *The Correspondence of William Wilberforce*, 2 vols (1840), i, 310, 14 September 1804
4 *Letter on the Abolition of the Slave Trade* (1807), 4, 6; see also James Stephen, *The Dangers of the Country* (1807)
5 Hannah More, *Slavery: A Poem* (1787)
6 Sian Rees, *Sweet Water and Bitter: The Ships that Stopped the Slave Trade* (2009), 7
7 H. Roscoe, *The Life of William Roscoe* (1833), ii, 477; see Marika Sherwood, *After Abolition: Britain and the Slave Trade since 1807* (2007), 34–6
8 Johnson, *Thompson*, 44, to Nancy, 7 September 1808
9 BUL Thompson MS 277/3/45, from Z. Macaulay, 3/64, from James Stephen 10, 14 November 1808; MS 277/1/1, 4 TPT to the Company, March 1809. See also the large collection in the University of Hull Special Collections
10 BUL Thompson MS 277, TPT, draft, March 1808
11 HUL DTH 1/41, 3 August 1809, quoted in Hall, *Macaulay and Son*, 69
12 BUL Thompson MS 277/1/2, TPT to Castlereagh, draft, 14 August 1809
13 BUL Thompson MS 277/3/79, Wilberforce to Thomas Thompson snr, 28 August 1810

## 42. DANES AND TURKS

1 Wynne, *Diaries*, iii, 317, 13 July 1807
2 DRO D3580/C49, T. Morewood, 26, 27 August 1807
3 Thomas Munch-Petersen, *Defying Napoleon: How Britain Bombarded Copenhagen and Seized the Danish Fleet in 1807* (2007)
4 *Memoir of Maria Edgeworth*, i, 207, to Henry Edgeworth, 25 December 1807
5 R. E. Scoresby Jackson, *The Life of William Scoresby* (1861), 45, 58–9
6 Quoted in Johnson, *Thompson*, 72
7 Henry Bunbury, *Narratives of Some Passages in the Great War with France, 1799–1810* (1854), 287, in A. W. Massie on Fraser, *ODNB*
8 20 April 1807, in Hayter, *Backbone*, 96
9 BUL Thompson MS 1/5, TPT to his father, 10 August 1811
10 *Piozzi Letters*, iv, 158, to Revd Leonard Chappelow, 21 November 1807
11 *Times*, 2 October 1807
12 C. J. Palmer and H. Manship, *The History of Great Yarmouth* (1856), 271

## 43. ORDERS IN COUNCIL

1 OL Rowbottom, 30 November 1806
2 Jerry White, *London in the Nineteenth Century* (2007), 149
3 Judith Blow Williams, *British Commercial Policy and Trade Expansion, 1750–1850* (1972), 307

4 In 1794 imports were around £38 million p.a. and exports and re-exports £32 million; in 1806 these had reached £55.5 million and £51 million, and by 1814 £72 million and £66 million: Southam, *Jane Austen and the Navy*, 12. See *Naval Chronicle*, February–March 1812, xxvii, 254

5 Ferguson, *Rothschild*, 59

6 DRO D3580/C233, 17 September 1811

7 Alex Ritsema, *Heligoland Past and Present* (2007), 69–70

8 John B. Holroyd, Earl of Sheffield, *Orders in Council and the American Embargo* (1809), 3; see Williams, *Commercial Policy*, 348–50

9 W. Harvey, *The Seasalter Company – A Smuggling Fraternity 1740–1854* (1983), 9

10 *Kentish Observer*, 21 December 1812

11 Hilton, *Mad, Bad and Dangerous*, 152; Daunton, *Trusting Leviathan*, 349

12 J. R. Johns, *The Smugglers' Banker* (2008 edn), 37–48

13 Knight and Wilcox, *Sustaining the Fleet*, 184

14 'The diary of Joseph Rogerson' in W. B. Crump, *The Leeds Woollen Industry 1780–1820* (1931), 77–91; *The Diaries of Cornelius Ashworth, Weaver, 1782–1816*, ed. Richard Davies, Alan Petford and Janet Senior. Also F. Atkinson, *Some Aspects of the Eighteenth Century Woollen and Worsted Trade in Halifax* (1956)

15 DRO D3580/C55, 24 January 1809

16 Report and minutes of evidence on the State of the Woollen Manufacture of England, 4 July 1806: *House of Commons Papers: Reports of Committees (268)*, 7

17 Ibid., 12

18 *Cowdroy's Manchester Gazette*, 2 January 1808

19 William Roscoe, *Occasional Tracts on the War* (1810)

20 OL Rowbottom, 24 May 1808

21 Ibid., 7 September 1811

22 Emsley, *British Society*, 141

23 Arthur Aspinall, *Early English Trade Unions: Documents from the Home Office Papers* (1949), 96, R. A. Farington to Hawkesbury, 28 May 1808

24 TNA HO 42/95 f. 375, via National Archives website, www.nationalarchives. gov.uk, 'Power, Politics and Protest'

25 OL Rowbottom, 1 January 1808

## 44. LAND

1 *Seedtime & Harvest: The Diary of an Essex Farmer, William Barnard of Harlowbury, 1806–23*, ed. Joyce Jones (1992), 27, 28 March 1807

2 Thomas Bewick, *A Memoir of Thomas Bewick, Written by Himself*, ed. Iain Bain (1975), 139

3 Wynne, *Diaries*, iii, 72, 23 November 1802

4 *Farmer's Magazine* xiv (1813), 507

5 T. C. Smout, 'Scottish Landowners and Economic Growth, 1650–1850', *Scottish Journal of Political Economy* 11 (1964); Colley, *Britons*, 158

6 *Farmer's Magazine* vii (1806), 121

7 Hants. ALS 1M 44/122/7, 13 October 1806

8 WT WLMS H/1/8/14, Joanna Hutchinson to John Monkhouse, 13 January 1802

9 WT WLMS H/1/8/16, Joanna Hutchinson to John Monkhouse, 15–17 March 1808

10 WT WLMS H/1/8/17, Joanna Hutchinson to John Monkhouse, 16 August 1808

11 WT WLMS 1/5/3, Tom Hutchinson to John Monkhouse, 12 October 1808

12 WT WLMS 1/5/4, Tom Hutchinson to John Monkhouse, 15 November 1808

13 WT WLMS H/1/8/20 Joanna Hutchinson to John Monkhouse, 12 November 1808

14 Wordsworth, *Love Letters*, 117, Mary Wordsworth to William Wordsworth, 2 May 1812

15 WT WLMS H1/5/1/21, Mary Monkhouse to Thomas Monkhouse, 6 August 1809

16 R. C. B. Oliver, 'The (Wordsworth) Hutchinsons in Radnorshire and on the Border', *Radnorshire Society Transactions* 49 (1979)

17 Wordsworth, *Love Letters*, 87–8, William Wordsworth to Mary Wordsworth, 19 August 1810

18 *Farmer's Magazine* viii (1807), 243

19 Act for enclosing the 'Heaths and Commons of Holt', 30 March 1797, also 6 February 1807, Hardy, *Diary*, iii, 351, iv, 124

20 Arthur Young, *An Inquiry into the Propriety of Applying Wastes to the Maintenance and Support of the Poor* (1801), and *General Survey of the Agriculture of Norfolk* (1804)

21 *Annals of Agriculture* xxvi (1808), 214

22 'Harken that happy shout', Bate, *John Clare*, 107–9

## 45. 'CAESAR IS EVERYWHERE'

1 J. C. Moore, *Life of Lieutenant-General Sir John Moore* (1834), ii, 93, 2 July 1808

2 Esdaile, *Peninsular War*, 87

3 WT WLMS 2/4/2, 29 May 1808

4 Lyttelton, *Correspondence*, 15, to Robert Spencer, 4 June 1808

5 Lyttelton, *Correspondence*, 22, to Robert Spencer, 6 July 1808

6 Richard Brinsley Sheridan, *Speeches* (1816), v, 369–70, 15 June 1808

7 Davies, *Wellington's Wars*, 86–7

8 Chet. A.6.30*, Weatherley transcript

9 OL Rowbottom, 10 March 1809

10 Cookson, *Armed Nation*, 88: in March 1809 Castlereagh told the Commons that out of 195,161 men in the local militia, 125,000 were 'old' volunteers

11 CAS D H/C 71, 24 January 1809. See also Cumberland Rangers Muster Roll HC 1/76, and Pay Lists 1803–13, HC 1/68

12 DRO D3580/C70, 15 May 1809

13 Sherwig, *Guineas and Gunpowder*, 186

14 Collins, *War and Empire*, 250, quoting the *Commission of Military Enquiry*, Fifteenth Report; Knight, *Britain*, 369–76

15 Wellington, *Supplementary Despatches*, 11 vols (1858–64), vi, 92, 31 July 1808

16 Glover, *Britain at Bay*, 130

17 Hubback, *Austen's Sailor Brothers*, 200, 21 August 1808

18 Lyttelton, *Correspondence*, 24, 3 September 1808

19 *Times*, 19 September 1808, and *Courier*, 22 September
20 Lyttelton, *Correspondence*, 29 September 1808
21 *Wordsworth's Convention of Cintra*, ed. W. J. B. Owen (1968), 122
22 Coleridge, *Letters*, iii, 214, to Daniel Stuart, 13 June 1807
23 Charles and Mary Cowden Clarke, *Recollections of Writers* (1878); Roe, *Keats*, 32
24 F. D. S. Darwin, *Tours in Spain and the East, 1808–10* (1927)
25 BCA Galton MS 3101/C/D/10/6/54, to John Howard, 25 November 1808
26 Lyttelton, *Correspondence*, 45–6, to Robert Spencer, 16 November 1808
27 W. F. P. Napier, *History of the Peninsular War* (1856), iv, ch. 5, and Carola Oman, *Sir John Moore* (1953), 599
28 Austen, *Letters*, 180, to Cassandra Austen, 24 January 1809
29 Harriot Slessor, diary, 21 February 1809, in Hayter, *Backbone*, 211–2
30 TNA WO 26/41, Camp equipment list and prices, Horse Guards, 30 May 1809
31 He was made Earl of Wellington 28 February 1812, Marquess of Wellington after Salamanca, October 1812, and Duke of Wellington on 11 May 1814.
32 Chambers, *Memoir*, 24–5

## 46. SCANDALS, FLANDERS AND FEVERS

1 Lockhart, *Scott*, ii, 215–16
2 *Times*, 1, 3, 13, 14 September 1807. His court martial began 28 January 1808.
3 Roe, *Hunt*, 225; *Examiner*, 10 April 1808
4 HB 8/T/11, Louisa Greville, Countess of Mansfield, 8, 21 April 1806
5 *Staffordshire Advertiser*, 18 February 1809; Barker, *Newspapers*, 191
6 Lyttelton, *Correspondence*, 63, to Robert Spencer, 20 March 1809
7 Gatrell, *City of Laughter*, 496
8 The inquiry confirmed the findings of a Select Committee on Public Expenditure two years before: see Spence, *Romantic Radicalism*, 109–35, Paul Berry, *By Royal Appointment: A Biography of Mary Anne Clarke* (1970), 48–52, and Harling, *Waning of 'Old Corruption'*, ch. 4
9 Gatrell, *City of Laughter*, 221
10 Lyttelton, *Correspondence*, 69–70, to Robert Spencer, 9 May 1809
11 BCA Galton MS 3101/C/D/10/9/30, 6 March 1809
12 Lyttelton, *Correspondence*, 77, to Robert Spencer, 25 July 1809
13 OL Rowbottom, 15 August 1809
14 See Williams, *Weedon*, 87: TNA WO 47/2460 Board of Ordnance Minutes
15 OL Rowbottom, 11 October 1809
16 Benjamin Harris, *Recollections*, 174
17 Bew, *Castlereagh*, 262
18 Coleridge, *Letters*, iii, 778, to Daniel Stuart, 27 September 1809
19 Scott, *Letters*, ii, 24, to George Ellis, 26 September 1809
20 Harling, 'Critiques of the British War Effort', in Philp (ed.), *Resisting Napoleon*, 21; C. W. Pasley, *Essay on the Military Policy and Institutions of the British Empire* (1810), 160

## 47. GOING TO THE SHOW

1 Thomas Preston, *Jubilee Jottings* (1887), xiii
2 *Annual Register*, October 1809
3 OL Rowbottom, 25 October 1809
4 Thomas Sidney Cooper, *My Life*, i, 16
5 Preston, *Jubilee Jottings*, xxxiv
6 See Marc Baer, *The Theatre and Disorder in Late Georgian London* (1992)
7 Wynne, *Diaries*, iii, 247, 19, 22, 25 February 1806
8 John Styles, *Essay on the Character and Influence of the Stage on Morals and Happiness* (2nd edn 1807), in Wilson, *Decency and Disorder*, 198
9 OL Rowbottom, 28 November 1811
10 Oakes, *Diaries*, ii, 54, 23 April 1804
11 BCA Galton MS 3101/D/10/9/15, Samuel Galton to John Howard Galton, 2 June 1807
12 Oakes, *Diaries*, ii, 66–7, 30 May, 3, 5 June 1805. For Pitt and *Hamlet*, see Michael Dobson and Stanley Wells, *The Oxford Companion to Shakespeare* (2001), 44
13 Oakes, *Diaries*, ii, 79, 28 April–7 May 1806
14 Austen, *Letters*, to Cassandra Austen, 25 April 1811
15 BUL Thompson MS 177/1/6, 13 May 1812
16 BUL Thompson MS 177/1/8, 25 June 1812
17 BLARS L30/2/69, 9 May 1811
18 BLARS L30/2/71, 9 April 1812. For Hazlitt's view see John Ripley, *Julius Caesar on Stage in England and America, 1599–1973* (1980), 69
19 Lamb, *Letters*, i, 241, to Manning, 16 October 1800
20 BCA Galton MS 3101/D/1/10, summer 1812
21 Lyttelton, *Correspondence*, 10–13, to Robert Spencer, 9, 11 May 1808
22 Pierce Egan, *Boxiana* (1814, 1830 edn), i, 184
23 K. Pearson, *Life, Letters and Labours of Francis Galton*, 3 vols (1914–30), i, 30
24 Oakes, *Diaries*, ii, 100, 12 October 1807
25 Angelo, *Reminiscences*, ii, 39–40
26 UCL Galton Papers 1/1/9/1/3, cuttings from *Baily's Magazine*

## 48. BURDETT AND PRESS FREEDOM

1 The principal army hospitals were Chelsea, Gosport, Plymouth, Chatham, Deal, Isle of Wight and Selsey: new ones were built at Colchester, Harwick, Chelmsford, Dunstable, Bury St Edmunds and Southampton. Knight, *Britain*, 209
2 Handbill quoted in *Political Register*, 14 April 1810
3 *Political Register*, 24 March 1810
4 Lyttelton, *Correspondence*, 98–9, to Robert Spencer, 9, 11 April 1810; see also Cobbett's account, *Political Register*, 14 April 1810
5 Wilson, *Laughter of Triumph*, 70–1
6 See Gatrell, *City of Laughter*, 79–80, 495–520
7 *Courier*, June 1809
8 Urban, *Rifles*, 86: B. H. Liddell Hart, *The Letters of Private Wheeler* (1951), 6

9 *Political Register*, June 1809
10 Cobbett, 1835, in Ingrams, *Cobbett*, 94
11 Shelley, *Letters*, i, 54, 2 March 1811

## 49. 'BROOKES'S AND BUONAPARTE', CINTRA AND TROY

1 Report from Paris dated 17 February, in *Courier*, 12 March 1810
2 Lyttelton, *Correspondence*, 101, to Robert Spencer, Good Friday 1810
3 Byron, *Letters*, ii, 127, to Elizabeth Pigot, 13 July 1807
4 See Gareth Glover (ed.), *Wellington's Voice: The Candid Letters of Lieutenant Colonel John Fremantle, Coldstream Guards, 1808–1837* (2012). John Fremantle's stepbrother Felton Hervey and cousin Charles Bishop were also serving in Spain.
5 Wynne, *Diaries*, iii, 326, 25 September 1810
6 Lyttelton, *Correspondence*, 114, to Robert Spencer, 25 October 1810
7 Lyttelton, *Correspondence*, 102–3, to Robert Spencer, 7 May 1810
8 BLARS L30/24/67, 27 December 1810
9 David C. Itzkowitz, *Peculiar Privilege: A Social History of English Foxhunting, 1753–1885* (1977), 20
10 Gillray, *Les Invisibles*, 1810
11 Colley, *Britons*, 155
12 In Gatrell, *City of Laughter*, 81, which links the riots and Nash's plans
13 *Edinburgh Review* 23 (April–September 1814), 205, 'Lord Byron's *Corsair*, and *Bride of Abydos*'
14 *Monthly Magazine*, October 1810; *Annual Register* 1810, lii, 386–8; see F. D. S. Darwin, *Tours in Spain and the East, 1808–10* (1927), 82, 115–16
15 BLARS L30/24/67, Amabel Hume-Campbell to Agneta Yorke, 27 December 1810
16 BLARS L30/24/69, Amabel Hume-Campbell to Agneta Yorke, 9 May 1811
17 *Morning Chronicle*, 29 June 1811, in J. Ashton, *Social England*, i, 37–8

## 50. STORMS OF TRADE

1 Oakes, *Diaries*, ii, 114, 26 January 1809
2 Ibid., 115, 5 March 1809
3 Ibid., 103, 5, 13 April 1810
4 Ibid., 130–1, 20 July 1810
5 *The Works and Correspondence of David Ricardo*, ed. Piero Sraffa and M. H. Dobb (2005), iii, *Pamphlets and Papers 1809–11*
6 *Courier*, 29 September 1810
7 *Political Register*, 3 October 1810
8 DRO D3580/C55, 24 January 1809
9 DRO D3580/C82, 14 August 1809
10 DRO D3580/C111–2, 21, 26 July 1810
11 DRO D3580/C94, 128 and others
12 *London Gazette*, 7 July 1810
13 OL Rowbottom, 14 August 1810
14 DRO D3580/C115–6; 7, 15 August 1810

15  DRO D3580/C122 James Longsdon snr, 29 August
16  DRO D3580/C 135, 26 November 1810
17  DRO D3580/C
18  Marshall had two hackling machines in 1809, twenty-two in 1810, thirty-two in 1815
19  BUL Lupton & Co., Letter Book 1, to James Cumming jnr, 11 May 1810, Limerick
20  BUL Lupton & Co., Letter Book 1
21  BUL Lupton & Co., Day Book 24, 1809–14; also Box 117, South American Papers 1812–14, and Letter Book 3, 1805–10
22  See Cobbett, *Political Register*, xix, cols 123–9, xx, cols 1042–73, 1092–1163
23  OL Rowbottom, 20 November 1810
24  Navickas, *Loyalism and Radicalism*, 16; *Cowdroy's Manchester Gazette*, 13 April 1811
25  Schimmelpenninck, *Life*, i, 55
26  WT 1/1/13, John Hutchison to John Monkhouse, 16 July 1810
27  Thompson, *Salmon*, 36, Milford, 18 October 1811
28  Ibid., 37–8, 42, Portsmouth, 2 January 1812
29  OL Rowbottom, 8 December 1810
30  Ibid., 1 January 1811
31  HB AMF 19/14/1, Sophia Hoare Tour, 1809


## 51. THE COMING OF THE SHEEP

1  BCA Galton MS 3101/C/D/10/6/80, 2 October 1810
2  *Edinburgh Review* 16 (August 1810), 273–4
3  Lyttelton, *Correspondence*, 104–5, to Robert Spencer, 15 May 1810
4  Devine, *Clearance and Improvement*, 105 and 100–4: in Sutherland about 13 per cent of the inhabitants were thought to have joined the army, in Skye nearer 23 per cent.
5  A. MacLeod, trans., from *The Songs of Duncan Ban Macintyre* (1952)
6  Richards, *Highland Clearances*, ii, 212–15. See Douglas Thomas, Earl of Selkirk, *Observations on the Present State of the Highlands of Scotland* (1805)
7  Andrew McKillop, *'More Fruitful than the Soil': Army, Empire and the Scottish Highlands, 1715–1815* (2000), 135
8  Thomas Bewick, *A General History of Quadrupeds* (1790, 1807 edn), 58–9
9  *Edinburgh Review* 4 (April 1804), 74
10 Sir John Sinclair, *Statistical Account of Scotland* (1791–9), xx, 340
11 Richards, *Highland Clearances*, ii, 219, quoting R. J. Adam, *Papers on Sutherland Estate Management*, 2 vols (1972), ii, 39
12 In Eric Richards on George Granville Leveson-Gower, *ODNB*
13 Richards, *Highland Clearances*, ii, 220, quoting Adam, *Papers*, ii, 90
14 DRO D3580/C135, 26 November 1810
15 D. MacLeod, *Gloomy Memories* (1857), from *Edinburgh Weekly Chronicle*, 1840
16 See chs 10 and 11, 'The Sutherland Clearances: I, Movement en Masse' and 'II, Under New Management' in Richards, *Highland Clearances*, i, 284–363. Also Devine, *Clearance and Improvement*, and his *Clanship to Crofters' War: The Social Transformation of the Scottish Highlands* (1994)

17 Mairi Stewart and Fiona Watson, 'Land, the Landscape and People', in *Everyday Life in Scotland 1800–1900*, ed. Trevor Griffiths, Graeme Morton (2010), 24

18 Wynne, *Diaries*, iii, 333, 30 May 1811

19 Ibid., iii, 336, 14–15 July 1811

20 Heber, *Letters*, 243

21 Scott, *Letters*, ii, 360, to Joanna Baillie, 1 July 1810

22 Ibid., ii, 234, May [1810]

23 Scott, *Rob Roy* (1817), Preface

## 52. SIEGES AND PRISONERS

1 BLARS L30/24/67, Amabel Hume-Campbell to Agneta Yorke, 27 December 1810

2 BLARS L30/24/67, Amabel Hume-Campbell to Agneta Yorke, 9 May 1811

3 Austen, *Letters*, 191, to Cassandra Austen, 31 May 1811. The battle of Albuera, 18 May, was reported in the British press on 23 May.

4 Wellington, *Supplementary Despatches and Memoranda*, ed. A. R. Wellington (1860), 123, to William Wellesley Pole, 15 May 1811

5 Glover (ed.), *Wellington's Voice*, 81f

6 January 1811, in Hayter, *Backbone*, 250

7 Oakes, *Diaries*, ii, 155, 17 June 1812

8 DRO D3580, J. B. Barker, 14 February, 2, 3 May; 14, 18 July

9 DRO D3580/C228, 12 August 1811

10 Costello, *Adventures*, 177

11 DRO D3580/C286, 26 May 1812

12 DRO D3580/C314, 13 November 1812

13 Captain William Hay, *Reminiscences, 1808–15* (1901), in Snow, *Wellington*, 178

14 Heber, *Letters*, 247, James Stanhope to Richard Heber, 10 December 1812

15 Only 17,607 prisoners, from 122,440, were exchanged between 1803 and 1814; Chamberlain, *Hell upon Water*, 223

16 RBS archives (www.heritagearchives.rbs.com): U. G. and H. Messiter, Wincanton *c.*1800–1844. For the town, see G. Sweetman, *History of Wincanton* (1903), and P. Bowden, *Wincanton: Pleasant Town by the Cale* (1985)

17 Francis Abell, *Prisoners of War in Britain, 1756–1815* (1914), 355; see John Thorpe, *French Prisoners' Lodges* (1900)

18 Chambers, *Memoir*, 66

19 William Chambers, 'Early recollections', *Chambers Journal* 2 (1875), 600

20 Wallace Harvey, *Whitstable and the French Prisoners of War* (1983)

21 George Borrow, *Lavengro*, ed. Clement Shorter (1967), 39

22 UBCRL JER/546, Lady Jerningham to Charlotte, 23 September 1810

## 53. LUDDITES AND PROTESTS

1 Select Committee on Commercial Credit, Hansard, *Parliamentary Debates*, xix, 123–9, 1 March 1811; Reports from Committees, 7 March 1811, ii, *Report of the Committee on the Petition of the Weavers*, 21 June 1811

2 *Parliamentary Debates*, xxii, 2; Hammond, *Skilled Labourer*, 229

3 *Nottingham Review*, 20 December 1811

4 Gill, *Wordsworth*, 317; Wordsworth, *Love Letters*, 148, 9–13 May 1812

5 Byron, Hansard 21, cc. 971–2, 'Frame Work Bill', *House of Lords Debates*, 27 February 1812 (www.hansard.millbanksystems.com)

6 Byron, *Letters*, ii, 167, to Francis Hodgson, 5 March 1812

7 OL Rowbottom, 1 January 1812

8 Oakes, *Diaries*, ii, 153, 23 January, 8 March 1812

9 Navickas, *Loyalism and Radicalism*, 241; *Blackburn Mail*, 4 March 1812

10 Bamford, *Early Days*, 297

11 OL Rowbottom, 20 April 1812

12 Bamford, *Early Days*, 307

13 OL Rowbottom, 20, 21 April 1812

14 Bamford, *Early Days*, 307

15 *Leeds Intelligencer*, 30 April 1812

16 Heber, *Letters*, 246, James Ferriar to Richard Heber, 11 May 1812

17 Quarry Bank Mill Edward/Gore Collection, Hannah Greg to Tom Greg, 13 May 1812

18 Chet. A.6.30–30*, Weatherley transcript, 'Recollections'

19 A. Alexander, *The Life of Alexander Alexander*, ed. John Howell, 2 vols (1830), i, 215

20 Scott, *Letters*, iii, 125–6, to Robert Southey, 4 June 1812

21 *Lancaster Gazette*, 20 June 1812; article quoted in full in the ludditebicentenary. com blog archive

22 *Leeds Mercury, Extraordinary Edition*, 9 January 1813

23 Revd John Hodgson, *Funeral Sermon of the Felling Colliery Sufferers* (1813)

## 54. PRINCE, PERCEVAL, PORTLAND

1 Oakes, *Diaries*, ii, 143, 24 May 1811

2 OL Rowbottom, 17 January 1812

3 UBCRL JER/412, 27 June 1806

4 Mabel Airlie, *In Whig Society, 1775–81* (1921), 159

5 Austen, *Letters*, 504, to Martha Lloyd, 16 February 1813

6 *Examiner*, 15 March 1812

7 Shelley, 'The Devil's Walk', *Complete Poetry*, i, 403–7

8 *Examiner*, 22 March 1812

9 Semmel, *Napoleon and the British*, 12: 'Fingal', *Truth: Containing the Cast of the Seven Princes of Britain* (April 1812), 11

10 Roe, *Hunt*, 178

11 In Daisy Hay, *Young Romantics*, 26

12 C. V. Williams, *The Life and Administration of the Rt. Hon. Spencer Perceval* (1813), 224

13 Oakes, *Diaries*, ii, 155, 11 May 1812

14 Wordsworth, *Love Letters*, Mary Wordsworth to William Wordsworth, 13 May 1812

15 Cobbett, *Regency*, ch. 3, para. 132

16 Caroline Lamb's journal, in MacCarthy, *Byron*, 172

17 Wordsworth, *Love Letters*, William Wordsworth to Mary Wordsworth, 161–2, 163; 17–18 May 1812

18 Ibid., 118, Mary Wordsworth to William Wordsworth, 2–4 May 1812

19 Wordsworth, *Letters*, ii, 51, William Wordsworth to Southey, [2 December 1812]

20 Wynne, *Diaries*, iii, 326, 24 October 1810

21 *Creevey Papers*, 93, Henry Brougham to Creevey, May 1812

22 *Creevey Papers*, 97–8, to Mrs Creevey, 28 May 1812

23 *Leeds Mercury*, June 1812; Donald Read, *Press and People 1790–1850: Opinion in Three English Cities* (1993), 108

24 BUL Lupton & Co. Papers, 8 September 1812

25 William Washington, George Farquharson, *A correct report of the proceedings on the trial of thirty-eight men on a charge of administering an unlawful oath* (1812)

26 Semmel, *Napoleon and the British*, 103

27 *Edinburgh Review* (July 1812), 231

28 *Memoir of Maria Edgeworth*, i, 253, to Margaret Ruxton, 20 July 1812

29 OL Rowbottom, 25 November 1812

30 Cookson, *Friends of Peace*, 238–45

31 The petition is printed in full in 'State of Public Affairs', *Monthly Magazine* (September 1812), 261–2.

32 Cookson, *Friends of Peace*, 250, 253

## 55. THREE FRONTS

1 McLynn, *Napoleon*, 498

2 *Morning Chronicle*, 9 December 1812

3 *Times*, 6 May 1813; Thompson, *Salmon*, 67

4 Lyttelton, *Correspondence*, 176, 179, to Countess Spencer, and diary entry, 12, 27 December 1813. After Lyttelton died in 1837, Sarah became a lady-in-waiting to the young Queen Victoria, and later governess to her children. See Kate Hubbard, *Serving Victoria: Life in the Royal Household* (2012)

5 Snow, *To War with Wellington*, 188

6 See ibid., 197–200

7 John Gurwood (ed.), *The Dispatches of Field Marshal the Duke of Wellington*, 13 vols (1837–8), x, 496, 2 July 1813

8 Carola Hicks, *Girl in a Green Gown* (2011), 126–33

9 C. M. Kauffmann, *Catalogue of Paintings in Apsley House* (rev. edn 2009), 9–14

10 *Morning Post*, 4 August 1813

11 Sherwig, *Guineas and Gunpowder*, 354

12 Ferguson, *Rothschild*, 90

13 Knight and Wilcox, *Sustaining the Fleet*, 53–5

14 C. D. Hall, *British Strategy in the Napoleonic War, 1803–15* (1992), 34–5

15 Ferguson, *Rothschild*, 62–3

16 Gavin Daly, 'Napoleon and the "City of Smugglers", 1810–1814', *Historical Journal* 50, 2 (2007), 333–52

17 Buxton (ed.), *Sir Thomas Fowell Buxton*, 344

18 Ferguson, *Rothschild*, 94–5

19  BUL Thompson MS 177/1/9, 9 July 1813
20  BUL Thompson MS 177/1/9, 20 July 1813
21  BUL Thompson MS 177/1/11, 26 July 1813
22  Johnson, *Thompson*, 83, 22 December 1813


## 56. SAILORS

1  Southam, *Jane Austen and the Navy*, 260; *Naval Chronicle*, xxviii (January–July 1813), 343–4
2  Oakes, *Diaries*, ii, 173, 16 October 1813
3  Austen, *Letters*, 225–6, to Francis Austen, 3 July 1813
4  Jerrold joined the *Namur* in December 1813. Southam, *Jane Austen and the Navy*, 65–6, 272–3; see play, *The Mutiny at the Nore* (1830): Jerrold, *Life and Remains of Douglas Jerrold*
5  WT WLMS Gill Papers 2/4/10–14, October 1811–August 1812
6  Robert Hay, *Memoirs*, 190
7  Ibid., 208
8  J. K. Laughton, rev. Roger Morris, *ODNB*
9  *Times*, 2 January 1813; Thompson, *Salmon*, 68
10  Thompson, *Salmon*, 61, Dublin, 14 September 1812
11  Ibid., 93, Dublin, 25 April 1813
12  Ibid., 143–4, Strangford, 26 May 1814


## 57. SWAGGER AND CIVILISATION

1  David, *Prince of Pleasure*, 344
2  *Glenbervie Journals*, 181–3, 22 July 1813
3  *Times*, 26 July 1813
4  *Glenbervie Journals*, 208, 29 September 1813
5  Byron, *Letters*, iv, 244, journal entry, 14 February 1814
6  Lyttelton, *Correspondence*, 102–3, to Robert Spencer, June 1808
7  HB 2/E/2 20 Memorandum Book, 18 January 1811
8  HB 2/E/2 Partners' Memorandum Book, 18 January 1813
9  Hutchings, *Messrs Hoare*, 103
10  Quoted in Kynaston, *City of London Vol. 1*, 31
11  LUL Rathbone Papers VI 2.31, Hannah Greg to Bessy, 2 October 1813
12  Sir Thomas Fowell Buxton, *An inquiry whether crime and misery are produced or prevented by our present system of prison discipline* (1818), and J. J. Gurney, *Notes on a visit made to some prisons of Scotland* (1819). See also E. Fry, *Observations on the visiting, superintendence, and government of female prisoners* (1827)
13  *Report from the Committee on Madhouses in England*, 1815, Minutes of Evidence. See also Wilson, *Laughter of Triumph*, 85–8
14  Peter Boss, 'Children in the Industrial Revolution' in J. Neville Turner and Pamela Williams (eds), *The Happy Couple: Law and Literature* (1994), 45
15  Cunningham, *Children of the Poor*, 48; *Evangelical Magazine*, 1799
16  Wordsworth, *Letters*, i, 162, Dorothy Wordsworth to Jane Marshall, 30 November 1795, 162

17  HB AFM 19/14/1, July 1808, Tour to North Wales
18  HB AFM 19/14/5, 1811, Tour to Wales
19  *Thraliana*, ed. Katherine C. Balderston, 2 vols (1942), ii, 1097
20  As in the drawing 'Civilisation' in Tommy Macrae's sketchbook, 1860s, National Museum of Australia, Canberra
21  See Bowen, *The Business of Empire*, for the relationship between the Company and the state, customs duties etc., and the use of Company troops
22  LUL Rathbone Papers II 1. 60, Hannah Greg to Hannah Rathbone, n.d.
23  Hall, *Macaulay and Son* 73, Zachary Macaulay to Thomas Macaulay, 5 April 1813
24  Wilberforce, *Life*, iv, 10–11, 15 February 1812, to Joseph Butterworth; for this campaign see Hague, *Wilberforce*, 408–11
25  M. M. Sherwood, *The History of Little Henry and His Bearer* (1816 edn), 66–7
26  BCA Galton MS 3101/C/D/6/114, 23 May 1814
27  Penelope Carson, *The East India Company and Religion, 1698–1858* (2012), 3
28  Chambers (ed.), *Letters of Sir Joseph Banks*, 209, Banks to Lord Liverpool, 8 June 1799; partially quoted in Holmes, *Wonder*, 222–3

## 58. 'WE ARE TO HAVE OUR REJOICINGS'

1  OL Rowbottom, 4 November 1814
2  Oakes, *Diaries*, ii, 174, 14, 21 November 1813
3  Hazlitt, *Selected Writings*, iv, *Political Essays*, 32
4  Oakes, *Diaries*, ii, 177, 18, 20 January 1814
5  Ibid., ii, 177, 12 February 1814
6  Thomas Cooper, *Life*, 17–18
7  Andrew Lambert on Thomas Cochrane, *ODNB*
8  Austen, *Letters*, 68, to Cassandra Austen, 5 March 1814
9  BLARS L 30/24/75, Amabel Hume-Campbell to Agneta Yorke, 26 April 1814
10  Heber, *Letters*, 267, Revd John Stonard to Richard Heber, 15 April 1814
11  Quoted in Wu, *Hazlitt*, 170
12  Thomas Carlyle, *Collected Letters of Thomas and Jane Carlyle*, 37 vols (1970–2009), i, 6–7, to Robert Mitchell, 30 April 1814, i, 3
13  OL Rowbottom, April 1814
14  *Memoir of Maria Edgeworth*, i, 299–300, to Margaret Ruxton, 16 May 1814
15  Benjamin Harris, *Recollections*, 189
16  Lloyd, *Prisoners of War*, 263, 11 April 1814
17  Scott, *Letters*, iii, 442, to Morritt, 30 April 1814
18  Byron, *Letters*, iv, 100, to Tom Moore, 20 April 1814
19  BLARS L30/24/75, 26 April 1814
20  Thomas Sidney Cooper, *My Life*, i, 21
21  *Creevey Papers*, 117, to Mrs Creevey, 21 June 1814
22  Austen, *Letters*, 276, to Cassandra Austen, 23 June 1814
23  Wynne, *Diaries*, iii, 372, 20 [June] 1814
24  McCarthy, *Byron*, 217
25  UBCRL JER/766, Lady Jerningham to Charlotte, 27 June 1814

26  Christopher Danziger, 'The Big Junket', *Oxford Today* xxvi, 2 (9 Trinity 2014), 36–8

27  Bod. MSS Eng. lett. c. 105, Mary Heber to Richard Heber, 21 June 1814

28  Mary Shelley, *History of a Six Weeks Tour* (1817), in Daisy Hay, *Young Romantics*, 39

29  Oakes, *Diaries*, ii, 180, 17 June 1814

30  *Leeds Mercury*, 2 July 1814

31  Thomas Cooper, *Life*, 23–4

32  Ashburton Museum, Devon; Lloyd, *Prisoners of War*, 336

33  Cobbett, *Regency*, ch. 5, para. 277

34  Farington, *Diary*, xiii, 4569

35  Russell, *Theatres of War*, 91; Ashton, *Social England*, 206–7

36  Lamb, *Letters*, iii, 96, to William Wordsworth, 9 August 1814

37  Waterhouse, *Journal*, 101–2, 109–10

38  *Statesman*, 1814; D. Hickey, *The War of 1812: A Forgotten Conflict* (1989), 202

39  Austen, *Letters*, 285, to Martha Lloyd, 2 September 1814

40  Waterhouse, *Journal*, 237, and 195–236 for prisoners' depositions etc.

41  Oakes, *Diaries*, ii, 186–7, 16 November, 28 December 1814

42  Bohstedt, *Politics of Provisions*, 246–7

43  Viscountess Melbourne, *Byron's 'Corbeau Blanc': The Life and Letters of Lady Melbourne* (1997), Lady Melbourne to Frederick Lamb, 27 February 1815

44  Roe, *Hunt*, 225–6

## 59. TO WATERLOO AND ST HELENA

1  Oakes, *Diaries*, ii, 190, 10 March 1815

2  Burney, *Journals and Letters*, viii, 339, 'The Waterloo Journal'

3  Oakes, *Diaries*, ii, 190, 19 March 1815

4  Ibid., ii, 191, 24 March 1815

5  WT H1/5/34 Mary Hutchinson (née Monkhouse) to Tom Monkhouse, 20 March 1815

6  Robert Southey, *Collected Letters*, ed. Ian Packer and Lynda Pratt (electronic edition July 2013), iv, Letter 2578, to John May, 20 March 1815. The Corn Bill was finally passed on 23 March.

7  Benjamin Harris, *Recollections*, 189

8  Waterhouse, *Journal*, 186, mid-March 1815

9  *Morning Chronicle*, 22 June 1815; see Wu, *Hazlitt*, 179; Paul O'Keefe, *Waterloo: The Aftermath* (2014) 109–10, 131–7

10  Oakes, *Diaries*, iv, 193, 22 June 1815

11  UBCRL JER/879, Lady Jerningham to Charlotte, 23 June 1815

12  *Creevey Papers*, 143, written from journals, in 1822

13  Heber, *Letters*, 273, James Stanhope to Lady Spencer Bourget, Paris, 3 July 1815

14  Airlie, *In Whig Society*, 171

15  Scott, *Letters*, iii, 79, to the Duke of Buccleugh, August 1815

16  PWDRO 560/3, General George Dyer, diary/account book, 31 July 1815

17  BCA Galton MS 3101/C/D/10/9/53, 11 December 1815

## 60. AFTERWARDS

1 See Knight, *Britain*, 313–50, 'Government Scandal and Reform 1803–1812'
2 Nicol, *Life and Adventures*, 192
3 Duncan-Jones, *Harness*, 188–201, 'Charles and His Sisters'
4 Wynne, *Diaries*, iii, 393, Sunday 1 January 1820
5 John Robert Connon, *The Early History of Elora, Ontario* (1930), 19–26
6 Lloyd, *Arts and Crafts*, 248–9
7 Letter to the Editor, *New Monthly Magazine* 5 (February 1816), 27–8; Revd Joseph Nightingale, *The Bazaar* (1816); *Gentleman's Magazine* 103, 2 (1833), 380
8 DRO D3580/T157–166: James Longsdon's will, land purchase 1828
9 'A Modern Tory Delineated', *Examiner*, 1816: William Hazlitt, *Complete Works* (1933), xix, 175
10 Colley, *Britons*, 150
11 Sherwig, *Guineas and Gunpowder*, 367–8, Appendix, 'Subsidy Payments 1793–1815'
12 Matthew White, 'Statistics of Wars, Oppressions and Atrocities of the Nineteenth Century', *Historical Atlas of the Twentieth Century* (2011): 219,420 army, 92,386 Royal Navy
13 Rogers, *Press Gang*, 125; G. H. Haswell, *The Maister: A Century of Tyneside Life* (1896), 32; Tony Barrow, *Trafalgar Geordies and North Country Seamen of Nelson's Navy, 1793–1815* (2005), 84–5
14 Costello, *Adventures*, 26–8
15 Ibid., 311
16 Sir Richard Phillips, *A Morning's Walk from London to Kew* (1817), 48
17 Wordsworth, *Letters*, i, 247, Dorothy Wordsworth to Catherine Clarkson, 15 August 1815
18 Byron, 'The Age of Bronze' (1823)
19 Chet. A.6.30–30*, Weatherley transcript, 'Recollections'
20 Bamford, *Passages* (1844), 207
21 William Hone, *The Three Trials of William Hone* (1818), 48
22 Leo Tolstoy, *War and Peace* (1865), trans. Rosemary Edmonds (1964 edn), book 4, ch. 4, 1116
23 George Eliot, *Impressions of Theophrastus Such*, 'Looking Backward' (1879)
24 Florence Hardy, *The Early Life of Thomas Hardy, 1841–91* (1927), 161; W. F. Wright, *Shaping the Dynasts* (1967), 104

# LIST OF ILLUSTRATIONS

**COLOUR PLATES**

Plate section 1

1  James Gillray, *A Voluptuary under the horrors of digestion*, 2 July 1792
2  Gillray, *Temperance enjoying a frugal meal*, 28 July 1792
3  Gillray, *The blood of the murdered crying out for vengeance*, 16 February 1793
4  James Oakes
5  James Oakes's diary, February 1798
6  Francis Austen
7  Richard Heber
8  Hannah and Samuel Greg
9  John and Jane Marshall
10  Birmingham Loyal Association, 1798
11  Thomas Rowlandson, *Private Drilling*, 1798
12  Rowlandson, *Return of the Fleet to Great Yarmouth*, 1797
13  Louis Garneray, *Prison Hulks in Portsmouth harbour*, c.1810
14  Gillray, *High-Change in Bond Street, – ou – la politesse du grande monde*, 27 March 1796
15  Walking and evening dress, *The Gallery of Fashion*, 1794
16  Augustus Pugin and Thomas Rowlandson, *Christie's Auction Rooms*, 1809
17  Pugin and Rowlandson, *Angelo's Fencing Academy*, 1809
18  Philip James de Loutherbourg, *The Battle of the Nile*, 1800
19  Loutherbourg, *Coalbrookdale by Night*, 1801

Plate section 2

20  Joshua Cristall, *Borrowdale*, 1805
21  George Morland, *Windy Day*, 1790s
22  Amabel Hume-Campbell
23  Lady Jerningham

ABOVE  Rowlandson by J. R. Smith. James Gillray, self portrait

# LIST OF ILLUSTRATIONS

24 Betsey Fremantle

25 Sarah Spencer, by John Jackson

26 Tertius Galton

27 James Longsdon senior

28 William Salmon

29 A letter from Salmon to Fanny

30 Heinrich Schutz after Rowlandson, *She will be a soldier*, 1798

31 Rowlandson, *The Press Gang*, 1798

32 Gillray, *The Death of Admiral Nelson – in the moment of victory*, 29 December 1805

33 J. M. W. Turner, *The Battle of Trafalgar, as seen from the Mizen Starboard Shrouds of the Victory*, 1806

34 John Sell Cotman, *Norwich market-place*, 1809

35 J. M W. Turner, *Ploughing up Turnips near Slough*, 1809

36 *The Leader of Luddites*, 'by an Officer', May 1812

37 George Walker, *A Collier*, 1814

38 George Dyer's diary, 28–31 July 1815

39 Turner, *The Field of Waterloo*, 1816

## ILLUSTRATIONS IN THE TEXT

7 J. Elwood, A crowd at a print-shop window, 1790

22 James Gillray, *The dagger scene, or Plot discover'd*, December 1792

23 James Aitken, *Hell Broke Loose, or, The Murder of Louis*, 1793

31 William and Elizabeth Harness

42 *The Wags of Windsor, or Love in a Camp*, 1800

49 *Cannon Manufacture in the Royal Brass Foundry, Woolwich*, c.1778

63 George Cruikshank, *Sailors on a Cruise*, 1825

71 Mock advertisement for 'A New Tragedy', 1794

83 'Factory children', George Walker, *Costumes of Yorkshire*

90 Hoare's Bank in Fleet Street, c.1780

97 Silhouettes of the Gurney sisters, Hannah, Elizabeth and Richenda

116 Gillray, *Promised Horrors of the French Revolution*, 1796

118 Evening dresses, Nicholas Wilhelm von Heideloff, *Gallery of Fashion*, 1794

137 William Daniell, 'Yarmouth from Gorlstone', in *A Voyage round Great Britain*, 1813

146 Gillray, *Copenhagen House*, 16 November 1795

150 William Henry Pyne, a group on the road, *Microcosm*, 1808

159 Pyne, Prison hulks, *Costume of Great Britain*, 1805

167 Daniell, 'The Approach to Fishguard'

184 Gillray, *Bank-notes, paper-Money, – French Alarmists*, 1 March 1797

192 Notice of Camperdown illuminations, 18 October 1795

203 Richard Colt Hoare, 'Blaenavon Ironworks', engraved by William Coxe, for *An Historical Tour in Monmouthshire*, 1801

215 Gillray, after Dalrymple, *Consequences of a Successful French Invasion*, 1 March 1798

227 William Sadler, *The Queen's Own Royal Dublin Militia going into action at the Battle of Vinegar Hill, Wexford*, 1798

236 Rowlandson, *Nelson recreating with his Brave Tars after the Glorious Battle of the Nile*, 1798

# LIST OF ILLUSTRATIONS

245 Isaac Cruikshank, *A General Fast in consequence of the War!*, 1794

262 Mary Hardy

265 *The Cruel Treatment of the Slaves in the West Indies*, pub. John Marshall, 1793

269 W. Holland, *The Corsican Crocodile dissolving the Council of Frogs!!!*, 9 November 1799

284 Illuminations at Soho, Birmingham, 1802

293 George Cruikshank, *Seizing the Italian Relics*, 1814

302 Gillray, *Scientifick Researches! – New Discoveries in Pneumaticks! – or – an Experimental Lecture of the Powers of Air*, 23 May 1802

305 Lucy Galton

315 George Walker, 'Croppers', *The Costume of Yorkshire*, 1814

324 John 'Warwick' Smith, *Junction of the Mona and Parys Mountain Copper Mines*, 1790

330 Rowlandson, *Dr Syntax Sketching the Lake*, 1812

339 Gillray, *Maniac-Ravings – or – Little Boney in a Strong Fit*, 24 May 1803

349 Charles Williams, *Col. Cinque Port Drilling his Recruits*, 1803

358 Rowlandson, *Cattle not Insurable*, 1 December 1809

369 Anon., *Elizabeth I and Napoleon*

373 Gillray, *John Bull and the Alarmist*, 1 September 1803

382 'The Adelphi' brothers: Henry Hugh, Charles and Henry Merrick Hoare, 1830

385 *Bisset's Magnificent Guide or Grand Copper Plate Directory*, Design for Birmingham gunmakers, 1808

393 Rowlandson, *Perry's Dock at Blackwall*, 1806

402 Rowlandson, after George Woodward, *Brave Tars of the Victory and the Remains of the Lamented Nelson*, 10 January 1806

404 *The Funeral Procession of Lord Viscount Nelson, 1806*, linen snuff handkerchief

418 Rowlandson and A. C. Pugin, 'The hustings outside St Paul's, Covent Garden at an election', 1806, *The Microcosm of London*, 1808–9

425 Betsey Fremantle, 'Swanbourne'

429 Woodward and Rowlandson, *The Mother's Hope*, 1808

446 Daniell, *Docks on the Isle of Dogs near Limehouse*, 1802

456 George Walker, 'Rape Threshing', *The Costume of Yorkshire*, 1814

458 Gillray, *Fat Cattle*, 16 January 1802

472 Gillray, *The Spanish-Bull-Fight, – or – The Corsican-Matador in Danger*, 11 July 1808

484 George Cruikshank, *Burning the Memoirs*, 24 April 1809

492 George Cruikshank, *Acting Magistrates*, 18 September 1809

503 Rowlandson, *Libel Hunters on the Look out*, 12 April 1810

509 T. H. Shepherd, *Regent's Quadrant*, 16 June 1827

522 'The Bristol Company Copper Works near Swansea', from *The Principal Rivers of Wales Illustrated*, 1813

532 Daniell, 'Strathnaver', 1813

546 Luddite ticket

558 George Cruikshank, *The Prince of Whales or the Fisherman at Anchor*, in *The Scourge*, 1 May 1812

573 Nathan Rothschild, 1817

584 George Cruikshank, *The Good Effects of Carbonic Gas*, 10 December *c*.1807

599 Rowlandson, *Peace at Last*, 1814

611 'Elba room for Boney'

617 Walker, 'The 33rd Regiment', *The Costumes of Yorkshire*, 1814

621  Napoleon on the *Bellerophon* in Plymouth
633  J. T. Smith, William Frasier selling bootlaces, *Vagabondiana*, 1817
640  Rowlandson, Napoleon's carriage at Bullock's Exhibition, 1816

## PICTURE CREDITS

*Plate Sections*
These are taken from a variety of sources and I am particularly grateful to the following for permission to reproduce particular illustrations: Bury St Edmunds Record Office, 4, 5; Jane Austen's House Museum, 6; National Trust, Quarry Bank Mill, 8; Brotherton Library, University of Leeds, 9; Birmingham Museums and Art Galleries, 10; National Maritime Museum, Greenwich, 13, 31; Tate, London, 18, 33, 34, 35; Science Museum, London, 19; The Wordsworth Trust, Grasmere, 20; Fitzwilliam Museum, Cambridge, 21; The Fremantle Papers, 24; Christies and Bridgeman Art Library, 25, 27; Frank James, 26; Andrew Thompson, 28, 29; British Museum, 36; The London Library, 37; Chetham Library, Manchester, 38; Plymouth & West Devon Record Office, 38.

*Illustrations in the text*
These too are taken from several sources and I am grateful to the following: The British Museum, 7, 146, 265, 373, 472, 492, 503; London Library, 83, 137, 167, 315, 446, 456, 532, 617, 633; Semeyns de Vries van Doesburgh Foundation, Netherlands, 49; Chetham Library, Manchester, 71, 192, 546, 611; Hoare's Bank, 90, 382; Bridgeman Art Library, 227, 509; The Cozens-Hardy Collection, Norfolk, 262; National Museum of Wales, 324; The Wordsworth Trust, Grasmere, 330; Birmingham Central Library, 385; National Maritime Museum, Greenwich 404; Guildhall Library, Corporation of London 573.

*Chapter headings*
Details from Pugin and Rowlandson, *Microcosm of London*, 1809, p.vii, chs 7, 9, 39, p.713; Woodcuts by Bowles and Carver, 1790s, chs 1, 4, 10, 13, 15, 25, 36, 38, 42, p.665; William Sharp, after George Romney, ch. 2; *Loyal Volunteers of London*, 1798, ch.3; William Henry Pyne, *Microcosm: Or, A Picturesque Delineation of the Arts, Agriculture, and Manufactures of Great Britain*, 1808, chs 5, 8, 12, 19, 20, 24, 31, 37, 44, 52, 53, p.653, p.655; Pyne, *The Costume of Great Britain*, 1804, chs 14, 26, 30, 47, 50, 51, 55; glass, paintings and pottery, *The Saturday Book*, 1948, 1950, chs 6, 17, 34, 41, 56, p.643; Heideloff, *Gallery of Fashion*, ch. 11; details from works by Gillray, chs 23, 29, 48, 49, p.657, p.709; George Cruikshank, ch. 22; Henry Bunbury ch. 28; Rowlandson, ch. 46; and J. T. Smith, ch. 58; Wright, *Caricature History of the Georges*, 1876, chs 27, 43; Wheeler and Broadley, *Napoleon and the Invasion of England*, 1908, chs 21, 33; National Library of Australia, Canberra, ch. 57; Thomas Bewick, ch. 60.

# INDEX

Page numbers in *italics* show illustrations

Abercromby, Sir Ralph: character, 157; Flanders withdrawal, 106; Caribbean campaign, 156–7, 160, 172; illness, 157; Irish command, 225, 268; Dutch campaign, 268–9; Mediterranean command, 279–80; Egyptian victory, 280, 289, 292; death, 280; reputation, 280, 281, 570, 625

Aboukir, landing (1801), 280, 282

Aboukir Bay, battle (1798), *see* Nile

Ackermann, Rudolph, 404

*Ackermann's Repository*, 568

Acre, siege (1799), 240, 269

Act to Abolish the Slave Trade (1807), 430, 432–3

Adams, John, 180–1

Addington, Henry (later Lord Sidmouth): appearance and character, 276; Speaker, 215, 274; voluntary contributions proposal, 215, 216; view on Catholic emancipation, 274; ministry, 274, 276–7, 298; peace plans, 276; taxation, 290; election success (1802), 310; habeas corpus reinstatement, 311; Cobbett's criticisms, 312; Peltier case, 335; troops withdrawal issue, 336; declaration of war (1803), 339–40; resignation, 376; quits government, 396; response to Austerlitz news, 408; Lord Privy Seal, 409; slave trade policy, 432; Lord President, 556

Addison, Henry, 463

Addison, Isabella, 461

Admiralty: role, 56–7; organisation, 57; press gang policy, 59, 361; East India Company relationship, 61, 357; purchase of captured warships, 62; Boards, 133, 157; food budget, 134; Great Yarmouth port, 137; seamen's complaints, 175; Spithead mutiny, 175; signalling stations, 218; peace cuts (1802), 290; war preparations (1803), 355; Lloyd's relationship, 357; timber supplies, 391; ship repair reforms, 392, 396; experiments, 393–4; financial transactions, 395; Nelson relationship, 397, 403–4; Trafalgar news, 399; Sierra Leone policies, 435; Cochrane's career, 480; sailors' petitions (1816), 634

*Advice Suggested by the State of the Times* (Wilberforce), 371

African Institution, 434, 436, 591, 594

*The Age of Reason* (Paine), 18, 256

*Agricultural Magazine*, 456

agriculture: seasonal work, 120; beef cattle, 120, 128–9, 457, *458*; pigs, 120; sheep, 120, 123–4, 527–9; improvement, 121, 122–3, 127, 457–60, 464, 530; mowing, 121; farm workers, 121–2; harvesting, 122; rotation, 123; brewery, 124–6; hay, 126; Scottish, 127–8; ploughing, 455, 464; wheat, 455–6, 457; rape, *456*, 456–7; grass, *458–9*; enclosure, 458–9, 464–6; rents, 459, 460, 567; Scottish Highlands, 526–32; clearances, 529–32; crofts, *532*, 532–3

Aiken, John, 79

Aikin, Alexander, 7

Ailesbury, Lady, 110

Ailesbury, Lord, 382

Aitken, James, 23

Albuera, battle (1811), 535–6, 555, 559

Alderson, Amelia, 97

Alderson, James, 97

Aldini, Giovanni, 302

Alexander, Alexander, 553

Alexander, Tsar: accession, 278–9; meeting with Napoleon, 438; alliance with Britain and Spain, 565; response to French invasion, 567; reputation, 568; Paris occupation, 598, 602; London peace celebrations, 602–3, 604; Congress of Vienna, 624

Alexandria, siege, 280

Alien Act, 335

Alien Office, 21, 24

Aliens Bill (1792), 21

Allotment Office, 153

Almack's, 117

Almeida, siege (1811), 535, 536

Althorp, John Spencer, Viscount, 496–7

*L'Ambigu*, 335, 337

Amiens, Peace of (1802), 169, 289, 292, 359, 390, 527

Andrews, Henry, 371, 564

Angelo, Henry, 64, 116–17, 424, 497–8

Angerstein, John Julius, 88, 238, 421

Angoulême, Duchesse d', 600

Anna, Duchess, of Russia, 498

*Annals of Agriculture*, 123, 465

*Annual Register*, 39, 273, 338

Anstey, Christopher, 114

*Anti-Jacobin*, 181, 211–12, 300

*Anti-Jacobin Review*, 415

antiquarian interests, 90, 324

*The Antiquary* (Scott), 375

*The Appeal of the People of Ulster*, 230

*An Appeal to Impartial Posterity* (Madame Roland), 119

*Appeal to the Public* (Hogan), 483

Apreece, Jane, 533

*Archaeologica*, 324

Arden, Lord, 175

arms: supplies, 48–55; cannon manufacture, *49*, *50*, 203–4, 386; musket-making, 50–3, 385; Birmingham gunmakers, 384–6, *385*, 474; rifle manufacture, 385–6; storage, 386–7; Weedon Bec factory, 387–9; shrapnel, 393; rockets, 393; output (1807–8), 474–5; output (1814–15), 627–8

army: numbers, 33; pay, 152, 179; reports of deaths, 152–3; uniforms, 37–8, 46–8, 104; recruiting, 30–4, 37, 239; camps, 40–1, *42*, 125–6; departure for Flanders, 39–40; contractors, 46–7, 54, 384; withdrawal from Flanders (1795), 106, 108, 109; Quiberon landing, 107; Île d'Yeu expedition, 107–8; punishments, 142, 484, 502; food rations, 142; colonial war, 152; casualties, 152–3, 157, 239, 246; West Indies campaign, 156–7, 172; Clavell's mobilisation plan, 216–17; behaviour of troops in Ireland, 225–6; Egyptian campaign (1801), 280–2; wounded men, 281–2; size cut after peace (1801), 290–1; recruiting (1803), 342; rifle brigades, 343; 'Army of Reserve', 346; recruiting, 347,

471–2, 473; artillery, 393; Maida victory (1806), 411; Egyptian campaign (1807), 441–2; Portuguese expedition, 471–2, 475–6; Peninsula war, 471, 499, 535–6; Local Militia Act (1808), 473; supplies for Spanish expedition, 480; payment for promotion, 482–3, 484; Flanders expedition (1809), 486, 487, 489; Walcheren fever casualties, 487–8, 499–500; Ely militia mutiny (1809), 502; rise in enlistments, 565; Peninsula victories, 557–9, 569–70, 596; cost of, 571–3; supplies for army in Spain, 571–3; recruiting (1815), 616–17, *617*; Waterloo casualties, 619; war losses, 631; demobilisation, 631–2; life of soldiers after the war, 632–3; unemployment of suppliers, 637

Army of Reserve, 346–7

Artois, Comte d', 107

Ashridge, Revd, 128–9, 379

Association for Preserving Liberty and Property against Republicans and Levellers, 18

Astley, Philip, 44, 342

Astley's Amphitheatre, 44, 495

Atkinson, William, 60

Attwood, Thomas, 549

Auerstadt, battle (1806), 414, 427

Austen, Cassandra, 23, 58–9

Austen, Charles: character, 58; career, 58, 59, 411, 576–7; at Cowes, 273; marriage, 411, 576–7; wife's death, 577; sister's death, 626; life after war, 627

Austen, Francis: character, 58; career, 58–9, 363, 400–1, 411, 475, 479, 575; floggings, 175; marriage, 363, 411; letters, 400–1, 410; life after war, 626–7

Austen, Henry, 142, 290, 494, 603, 608–9, 630

Austen, Jane: education, 23; cousin's marriage, 21–2; brothers' careers, 58–9, 507, 576–7, 603, 608–9; dress, 238; brothers' marriages, 411; view of Moore, 479; theatre going, 494; view of Albuera battle losses, 536; view of Prince Regent's marriage, 557; everyday life, 597–8; death, 626; *Sense and Sensibility*, 577; *Pride and Prejudice*, 41, 506; *Mansfield Park*, 58, 492–3, 577; *Northanger Abbey*, 5, 114, 231, 328; *Persuasion*, 114

Austen family, 381, 411, 576–7, 626–7

Austerlitz, battle (1805), 408, 411, 412, 420

Austria: coalition against France (1792), 16–17; war with France, 17, 19; coalition against France (1793), 29; victories, 41–2; war financing, 94–5, 189, 573, 631; defeat and retreat, 102, 105, 163, 172, 186; division of Poland, 108, 625; peace treaty with France, 186; Campo Formio treaty (1797), 210;

victories against France (1799), 268; retreat, 269; Marengo battle, 272; peace treaty with France (1800), 273; British travellers, 309; alliance against France (1805), 395; Ulm army surrender (1805), 398–9; French enter Vienna, 407; Austerlitz defeat, 408, 411; surrender to France, 411; abdication of Holy Roman Emperor, 411–12; coalition against France (1809), 485; Vienna captured, 485; Wagram defeat, 488; Napoleon's marriage, 498; coalition against France (1813), 569, 571, 573; Leipzig victory, 595; Peace of Paris, 602; Congress of Vienna, 611, 624–5, 636; 'Holy Alliance', 625; Congress of Verona (1822), 636

Backhouse's bank, 96
Bacon, Anthony junior, 201, 202
Badajoz, siege and capture (1812), 537–8, 539, 540
Badenach, James: farmer, 4, 126–7, 128; diary, 30, 126–7, 455; effects of war on, 126, 188, 458; interests, 127; on prices, 150, 188, 458
Bage, John, 204
Baird, Lt-General Sir David, 412
Baker, Ezekiel, 385
Baker, James Harrison, 536, 600–1
Baldock, William, 448–9
Baltic conflict, 276–7
Bamford, Samuel: on Paine, 18; childhood employment, 80, 264, 313; family, 142–3, 264; diet, 246; reading, 308; joins volunteers, 350; on Manchester Exchange riots, 550–1; memories of Peterloo (1819), 638; Chartism, 3
Bamford family, 80, 264
Bank of England, 21, 88, 92, 182–6, 514
banking: City banking, 88–94, 381–2, 383, 446, 519; country banking, 88, 96–100, 184–5, 383, 519; bankruptcies, 46, 88, 253, 514, 516–17, 519; war loans, 94–6, 189; personal debts, 112; crisis (1797), 182–3; issue of bank notes, 183–6, *184*; bank note exchange rates, 522; brokerage business, 586; *see also* finance
bankruptcies,46, 245, 514, 515, 631
Banks, Sir Joseph, 128, 246–7, 303, 341, 357, 594
Banks-Jenkinson, Robert, Lord Hawkesbury (later Lord Liverpool), *see* Liverpool
Bantry Bay, French expedition (1796), 166, 224
Baptists, 72, 261, 262, 264, 455
Barclay, Captain, 497–8
Barclay, Tritton & Co., 96, 99, 184
Barent-Cohen, Hannah, 572
Barent Cohen, Nathan, 447
Baring, Alexander, 336, 515

Baring, Francis, 93, 336
Baring brothers, 515, 586, 629
Baring's, 93, 515
Barker, John, 536–7, 538
Barnard, William, 4, 455–6
Barnes, Katherine, 597
Barnett, Thomas, 487
barracks, 35–6
Barrow, Thomas, 486
Barrymore, Lord, 116
Bass, George, 154
Bates, Hannah, 328
Bath: social life, 114; Coleridge's sermon, 148–9
Bathurst, Henry, Lord, 563, 564, 618
Bayley, Samuel, 453
beacons, 375
Beatty, William, 402
Beaule, Marquise de, 21
Beaumont, John Barber, 352
Beddoes, Thomas, 300–1
Bedford, Lord John Russell, Duke of, *see* Russell
Bedingfield, Charlotte, 4, 110, 111, 118
Bedingfield, Sir Richard, 118
Belgrave, Lord, 260
Beliard, Abbé, 24
*Belinda* (Edgeworth), 303, 304
Bellingham, John, 560–1
Benfield, Paul, 95
Benjafield, Captain, 348–9
Bentham, Samuel, 391, 393
Benyon brothers, 87, 204
Berenger, Captain de, 597
Beresford, General, 412
Berlin Decrees (1806), 444, 445, 452
Bernard, George, 121
Berry, Mary, 470
Bertie, Admiral, 58
Betty, Master, 494
Bewick, Thomas, 303, 457, 528
Bioletti, Alberto, 628
Birch, Joseph, 310
Birmingham: Book Club, 5; riots (1791), 19; arms manufacture, 50–3, 384–6, *385*, 474; Poor Law Guardians, 84; food supplies, 143; Soho foundry, 200, 208, *284*; poor relief, 523; peace petition, 565
Birmingham Canal Company, 384
Blaenavon ironworks, 202–3, *203*
Blake, Catherine, 366–7
Blake, William, 11, 251, 366–7, 588
Blanketeers' march (1817), 637
blasphemy laws, 638
Blenkinsop, John, 585
Bligh, Captain John, 440–1
Bloomfield, Robert, 306, 308
Blücher, General, 603, 604, 619

Board of Agriculture, 123, 128
Board of Trade, 145, 556, 563
Bologna, Jack, 352, 353
Bolton, weavers' protest, 453
*Bon Ton Magazine*, 114
Bonaparte, Jerome, 438
Bonaparte, Joseph, 470, 472, 569–70
Bonaparte, Lucien, 294
Bonaparte, Napoleon, *see* Napoleon
Bone, John, 380
Boodle's club, 115
booksellers, 90, 115, 300, 307, 368
Borodino, battle (1812), 567
Borrow, George, 543
Boulton, Matthew, 54, 80, 205, 208, 380–1, 384
Boulton and Watt, 86, 87, 200, *284*, 584
Bowles, John, 259, 311
boxing, 496–7
Boyd, Benfield & Co., 95, 96
Boyd, Walter, 94–5, 187, 189
Boyle, Lord and Lady, 341
Braxfield, Lord, 68–9, 70
Brest, French fleet, 164, 166, 214, 228, 398, 579
Brighton, seaside, 319
Bristol Company Copper Works, 522
'British', feeling of being, 638–9
British and Foreign Bible Society, 434, 591
British Convention, 68, 69
*British Critic*, 228
British Forum, 500
British National Endeavour, 291
*The British Tourists* (Mavor), 321
British Wool Society, 529
*Britons Strike Home* (at Strand theatre), 356–7
broadsides, 367–9
Broke, Captain Philip, 575–6
Brontë, Charlotte, 264, 640
Brooks's club, 115
Brougham, Henry: *Edinburgh Review*, 299, 509, 564; African Institution, 434; 'Mountain' group, 549; on Orders in Council, 549, 562; defence of Hunt brothers, 559; on Perceval's death, 562; defence of peace petitioners, 564
Brown, Robert, 456
Brown Bess musket, 53, 349, 629
Brown Bread Act (1799), 246
Brummell, Beau, 37, 117, 506
Brunel, Isambard Kingdom, 634
Brunel, Marc Isambard, 381, 392–3, 634
Brunswick, Duke of, 17, 19
Buckingham, Lady, 247
Buckingham, Marquess of, 113, 496
Buenos Aires, capture and loss (1806), 412, 416
Bullock, Elizabeth, 263
Bullock, William, 639

Burdett, Francis: appearance and character, 310; marriage, 310; parliamentary seat, 310, 418; on Coldbath prisoners, 230, 310; criticisms of, 310; radical leadership, 415, 488; on flogging, 484; on freedom of speech, 500–1; supporters riot, 500–1, 505, 507, 508; arrest and imprisonment, 500–1, 503
Burdett, Sophia (Coutts), 310
Burdon, Rowland, 204
Burgos, siege (1812), 539
Burke, Edmund, 13–14, 16, 21, 22, 151
Burney, Fanny (later d'Arblay), 22–3, 295, 341–2, 615
Burns, Robert: poems, 25, 69, 76–7, 298; accusations of radicalism against, 67–8; joins volunteers, 76–7; death, 77, 220, 322; sales of poems, 306; biography, 322
Burrard, Sir Harry, 476, 477
Burrell, John, 125, 218, 244, 261, 284–5
Burroughes, Randall, 4, 120–5, 139–40, 193, 455, 464
Burton, Emmanuel, 551
Burton brothers' factory, 551
Bury New Bank, 99
Bury St Edmunds: town life, 98; naval victory celebrations, 65, 237; responses to war, 98–9; banking, 99, 184–5; food protests, 141; wheat supplies, 149; king's birthday parade, 220–1; playhouse, 242; poor rate, 247, 513; volunteers, 348–9; peace celebrations, 605
Butlin, William, 388
Butt, Mary Martha (later Mrs Sherwood), *see* Sherwood
Butterworth, Joseph, 591
Buxton, Sir Thomas Fowell, 313, 572, 588
Byng, John, 79
Byron, Lord: boxing enthusiast, 116–17, 498; on Fitzgerald, 225; bust of Napoleon, 290; Lady Jersey relationship, 310; banking, 381; suffrage petition in Lords, 419; social life, 497–8, 506; *English Bards*, 509–10; travels, 509–10; *Childe Harold*, 467, 476, 510, 548, 559–60; maiden speech in Lords, 547–8; friendship with Leigh Hunt, 559; love affairs, 559; at execution, 561; on Mme de Staël, 583; on Louis XVIII, 602; at masquerade, 604; on Napoleon's downfall, 622; *The Age of Bronze*, 636

Cadogan, General, 570–1
Caledonian canal, 527
Camden, Lord, 165
Camelford, Lord, 116
Campbell, Eugenia (Wynne), 9–10, 424–5, 457, 492, 533
Campbell, Robert, 424–5, 533
Campbell, Robert (poet), 295

Camperdown, battle (1797), 191–2, *192*, 194, 199, 200, 272
Campion, Thomas, 141
Campo Formio, Treaty (1797), 210
Canada Club, 388
canals: investments in, 86, 88, 202, 384, 519; construction, 197, 387, 389, 390, 519, 527; goods carried, 197, 202, 387, 487; towpaths, 207; aqueducts, 207; Weedon depot branch, 388–9; network, 628
Canning, George: foreign negotiations, 210; *Anti-Jacobin*, 211–12, 300; Pitt's resignation, 275; on Addington, 276; songs for Pitt's birthday, 336; on Napoleon, 337; on Fox, 409; Foreign Secretary, 417, 485; Tilsit agreement, 439; war strategy, 485; duel with Castlereagh, 488; resignation, 488; admirer of Countess of Sutherland, 530; career, 556; Prime Minister, 625
Canope, battle (1801), 280
Capot de Feuillide, Eliza, 21–2, 290
Capot de Feuillide, Jean-François, 22
Caracciolo, Francesco, 240
*Carlisle Journal*, 204
Carlos IV, King of Spain, 336
Carlyle, Thomas, 423, 640
Caroline of Brunswick, Princess of Wales (later Queen), 110–11, 556–7, 582, 603
Carron company, 200
Cartwright, Major John, 17, 419, 549
Cartwright, William, 547, 550
*Castle Rackrent* (Edgeworth), 303, 304
Castlereagh, Robert Stewart, Viscount: Irish policies, 165, 166, 273; Pitt's resignation, 275; Secretary for War and Colonies, 398, 408, 417, 435–6; Austerlitz news, 408; career, 417; recall of Thompson, 435–6; army reforms, 473, 474; war strategy, 485–6; duel with Canning, 488; resignation, 488; house attacked by rioters (1810), 501; Foreign Secretary, 556, 563; Cruikshank portrayal, 557, *558*; Chaumont treaty, 596; release of American prisoners, 617; Congress of Vienna, 624; view of 'Holy Alliance', 625; death, 625
Cathcart, Lord, 567
Catherine, Grand Duchess, 603
Catherine the Great, 108, 163
Catholic emancipation issue, 165, 274, 416–18, 555–6
cattle, 134–5
Cawdor, John Campbell, Lord, 167–8
census (1811), 555
Chalk Farm, meeting (1794), 72–3
Chambers, Robert, 4, 66, 78, 480, 542
Chambers, William, 6, 66, 78, 308, 480, 541–2

*Chambers's Journal*, 542
Chappe, Claude, 218
Charles IV, King of Spain, 470
Charlotte, Princess, 111, 556
Charlotte, Queen, 40, 64, 111, 216, 319, 382, 511–12
Charpentier, Charlotte, *see* Scott
Chatham, naval yard, 133, 134, 390
Chatham, second Earl of, 57, 501, 507
Chatterton, Thomas, 282
Chaumont, Treaty of (1814), 596–7
Chelsea Hospital, 632
*Chester Chronicle*, 75
child workers: shirtmaking, 47; shoemaking, 48; weavers, 80; in factories, 82–4, *83*, 194; Schools of Industry, 142, 143; lacemaking, 194; plaiting and bonnet making, 195; African recaptives, 437; in mines, 449, 637; agricultural work, 457; Master Betty, 494
*Childe Harold's Pilgrimage* (Byron), 510, 548, 559–60
Child's bank, 91
Chinese seamen, 445
Christian, Admiral, 156
*Christian Observer*, 299–300
Church Missionary Society, 259, 434
Cichagov, Admiral, 568
Ciudad Rodrigo, capture (1812), 537
'civilised', 589–90, 637
Clairmont, Claire, 605
Clapham Sect, 257, 299–300, 430, 434–7, 591
Clare, John, 134, 196, 308, 347, 465, 474
Clarke, Charles Cowden, 610
Clarke, Mary Anne, 483–4, *484*
Clarkson, Catherine, 635
Clarkson, Thomas, 266, 431, 432, 433
Clavell, William, 216–17
Clegg, Samuel, 584
Clegg, William, 228
Cleopatra's Needle, 281
Clewett, Elizabeth, 628
Cline, Henry, 74
cloth workers, 313–17
clubs, 115–16, 505–6
Coalbrookdale, 200, 204, 206–8, 394
coastal trade, 197–9
Cobbett, William: appearance, 297, 427; background, 297; career, 297–8; on fleet at Spithead, 131; on peace celebrations (1802), 297; *Political Register*, 298, 357, 415, 484, 515, 609; on Ireland, 312–13; libel trial and fine, 313; Napoleon's demands, 335; on merchant shipping, 357; on French atrocities, 369–70; readership, 415, 559, 609; on Perceval, 417, 560; on 'No Popery' election, 417, 418; family life,

427–8, 502; on enclosure, 465; on Clarke memoirs, 483, 484; on flogging, 484, 502; attacked by government papers, 485; on Burdett, 500; sedition trial and sentence, 502–3, 559; imprisonment, 503, 561; attacks on aristocracy, 508; on Goldsmid's suicide, 515; on Prince Regent, 560; on Bellingham's execution, 561; on peace celebrations, 606

Coburg, Prince of, 41

Cochrane, Sir Alexander, 597

Cochrane, Thomas, Lord, 175, *418*, 480, 500, 597, 625

Cochrane-Johnstone, Andrew, 597

Cockburn, Henry, 68, 70, 299, 349–50

Cockerell, Teesdale, 250

coinage, 380–1

Coke, Daniel, 310–11

Coke, Thomas, 124

Coldbath Fields prison, 230, 310, 311, 380, 559

Cole, Henrietta, 309

Coleridge, Samuel Taylor: on war reporting, 8; enlistment, 32; on child labour, 84–5; sermons, 148–9, 170; 'Kubla Khan', 161; spied on, 169; marriage, 170, 331; travels with Wordsworths, 170–1, 208–9; *Lyrical Ballads*, 170–1; on steam engine, 209; Canning's influence, 211; sense of betrayal by Revolution, 213; 'Fears in Solitude', 219; on Napoleon, 270, 337; notebooks, 302; on slave trade, 322; in Lake District, 330–1; on Wordsworth's pamphlet, 476; *The Friend*, 15, 488; Wordsworth relationship, 561

Collingwood, Admiral, 399, 625

Colonial Office, 398, 594

Colpoys, Admiral, 175–6

Colt Hoare, Sir Richard, 90, 115, 202–3, *203*, 323–4

Combe, William, 329

Combination Acts (1799, 1800), 245–6, 564

Committee of the Manufacturers of Arms and Materials for Arms, 386

communications, 196–7, 628–9

*The Complete Farmer*, 123

Confederation of the Rhine, 413

Congress of Verona (1822), 636

Congress of Vienna (1814–15), 611, 624

Constable, Archibald, 299

Constable, John, 463

'Continental System', 444, 469

Convention of Cintra (1808), 476–7, 481

Cooke, George Frederick, 352–3

Cooper, Anne, 19

Cooper, Astley, 19, 74–5, 84, 281

Cooper, Thomas, 3, 282, 307–8, 597, 606

Cooper, Thomas Sidney, 603

Copenhagen: battle (1801), 277–8; surrender (1807), 439

Copenhagen House meetings (1795), *146*, 147–8

Corn Laws, 149, 610, 616, 636–7

Cornwallis, Charles, Marquess, 273, 275, 311

Cornwallis, Admiral William, 362

*The Corsair* (Byron), 510

Cort, Henry, 201

Corunna: British expedition, 477–8; battle (1809), 478; British retreat, 478–9, 481

Costello, Ned, 537–8, 632–3

Cottle, Joseph, 149

*Courier*, 8, 178, 415, 502, 505, 515

*Courier de Londres*, 335

Coutts, Thomas, 310

Coutts' bank, 91, 112

Covent Garden theatre, 166, 214, 237, 491–2, *492*, 494–5

Cowdroy, William, 228–9, 413, 451

Cowper, William, 19, 257–8, 306

Coxe, William, 324

Crabb Robinson, Henry, 289, 475

Crawshay, Richard, 201–2, 205–6, 522

Crawshay, William, 522–3

Creevey, Thomas, 339, 396, 408, 549, 562–3, 603

Crewe, John, 486

Croke, Aunt, 105, 154, 155

Crompton's Spinning Mule, 80

Crookston, Jackie, 181

crop rotation, 123

croppers, 85, 245, 314–15, *315*

Crow, Captain Hugh 'Mind-Your-Eye', 433

Cruikshank, George: *Sailors on a Cruise*, *63*; Napoleon's artistic ambitions, *293*; print of Nelson procession, 405; Clarke's memoirs, *484*; *Acting Magistrates*, *492*; *The Prince of Wales*, 557, 558; *Carbonic Gas*, *584*; *Reformists' Register*, 638

Cruikshank, Isaac, 111, 214, 245, 405

Cumberland, Duke of, 112, 221, 291, 352, 505

Cunningham, Alexander, 68

Cunningham, Allan, 77

Currie, James, 267, 322

Curwen, John Christian, 464

Cyfarthfa, ironworks, 201, 202

Dalrymple, Sir Hew, 476, 477

Dalrymple, Lady, 43

Daniell, William, *167*, *446*, 522

d'Arblay, Comte, 22–3, 295, 341

Darby, Deborah, 206–7

Darby family, 54, 206

Dartmoor prison, 458, 542–3, 608, 617, 628

Darwin, Charles, 630

Darwin, Erasmus, 75, 165, 306, 477
Darwin, Sacheverel, 477, 511
Darwin, Violetta, 477, 630
David, Jacques-Louis, 294, 566
Davies, Joseph, 628
Davies, Scrope, 510
Davout, Marshal, 414
Davy, Humphry, 24, 237, 300–1, 302, 396–7, 533
de Staël, Mme, 583
Decaen, General, 336
*A Declaration of Rights* (Shelley), 558
Defence Bill (1803), 340
Defence of the Realm Act (1798), 217
Defenders, 165, 177
Delaval, Sir John Hussey, 89
d'Enghien, Duc, 371–2
Denmark: League of Armed Neutrality, 277; Copenhagen battle (1801), 277–8; navy, 439–40; Copenhagen surrender (1807), 439–40; Continental System, 444; Congress of Vienna, 624
Deptford, naval yard, 133, 134, 390
Despard, Colonel Edward, 311–12
Destruction of Stocking Frames Act (1812), 548
Devonshire, Georgiana, Duchess of, 292, 319
Dibdin, Charles, 66, 70, 353, 356
Dibdin, Thomas, 237
Dickens, Charles, 640
Dickens, John, 486
Dillon, Edward, 280
dissenters, 71, 256, 264, 350, 493, 637
Donaldson, Francis, 463
Douce, Francis, 423
Douglas, Sylvester (later Lord Glenbervie), 44
Dover Castle, 390
Drakard, John, 503
Drennan, William, 165
Drummond's bank, 91
Drury Lane theatre, 65–6, 222, 271, 494, 607
Duberley brothers, 47
Duchemin, Louis, 628
Duckworth, Admiral John, 410
Ducos, Roger, 269
*Dumfries Weekly Journal*, 76
Dumouriez, General Charles-François, 19, 39, 44, 389–90
Duncan, Admiral, 57, 177, 191, 193
Dundas, General Sir David, 362
Dundas, Henry (later Lord Melville): Home Secretary, 33; Secretary for War, 33, 210; building up army, 33–4; war strategy, 44, 101, 268, 276; arms supplies, 51; East India Company relationship, 51, 61; response to Fishguard invasion, 182; City relationship, 189; Grenville relationship, 210, 268, 276;

voluntary subscription, 216; defence strategy, 216, 217–18; India strategy, 240; Catholic emancipation issue, 274; Pitt's resignation, 275; view of peace terms, 289; at Admiralty, 391; ship repair issues, 391, 392, 396; accused of financial irregularities, 395–6; resignation, 396; impeachment, 396
Dundas, Robert, 67
Dunkins, corn factors, 136
Dunkirk, retreat from, 44, 56
Dyer, General George, 621–2
*The Dynasts* (Hardy), 641

East India Company: arms supplies, 51, 52; Brown Bess musket, 53; naval role, 61; shipbuilding, 61, 392; investors, 61, 145; monopoly issue, 61, 549, 590–1; banking, 91; gift to Nelson, 238; Secret Committee, 240; Napoleon concerns, 240; Indian wars, 241; territory, 241; backing for exploration, 303; Thames defences, 357; French capture mailbag, 372; contractors, 384; art collectors, 446; saltpetre imports, 475; gold sales, 572; charter renegotiated, 590–1; religious policies, 591–2, 594
Eaton, Daniel Isaac, 72, 73, 75
Eden, Sir Frederick, 132, 143
Edgeworth, Lovell, 342
Edgeworth, Maria: family background, 226; memories of Irish rebellion, 227–8; sister's birth, 232; Paris visit, 295, 296; on brother Henry's career, 299; writings, 303–4; Enlightenment values, 305; *Practical Education*, 317; Paris departure, 340; brother Lovell's detention, 342; on burning of Copenhagen, 440; *Patronage*, 506; visiting Leigh Hunt, 559; on Salamanca victory news, 564–5; on Paris surrender, 600
Edgeworth, Richard Lovell, 165, 226, 295, 303, 317
Edgeworth family, 165, 226, 227–8, 232, 340, 381
Edinburgh: old town, 70; riots, 67, 70; arrest and trial of radical leaders, 68–9; Watt trial and execution, 70; volunteers, 219–21, 349–50; United Scotsmen, 228; intellectuals, 528, 589
*Edinburgh Courant*, 76
*Edinburgh Herald*, 220
*Edinburgh Magazine*, 528
Edinburgh Philosophical Society, 127
*Edinburgh Review*, 299, 300, 415, 452, 481, 509, 510, 524, 564
Edinburgh Speculative Society, 299
*Edinburgh Star*, 6, 542
education: Quarry Bank schools, 84; Quaker girls, 97; Revd Ashridge's school, 128–9,

379; lace schools, 194; plaiting schools, 195; commercial schools, 198; Sunday schools, 255, 264; Harrow, 290; schools for children of sailors and soldiers, 291; schools for apprentices, 317

Edwards, Anne, 316

elections, general: (1796), 151; (1802), 309–10; (1806), 417–19, *418*

Elford, Mr, 140

Elgin, Lord, 341

Eliot, George (Mary Anne Evans), 640–1

Ellenborough, Lord, 311, 313, 337, 459, 503, 559, 638

Embargo Act (1807), US, 452

émigrés, 21–4; memoirs, 119; journalists, 335; returning, 605

Emmet, Robert, 312

Enclosure Acts, 464

enclosure movement, 464–6, 636

*English Bards and Scotch Reviewers* (Byron), 509–10

*Enquiry Concerning Political Justice* (Godwin), 73

*Enquiry into the Nature and Effects of the Paper Credit* (Thornton), 186

Erskine, Thomas, 74, 224, 271, 292, 583

*Essay on Irish Bulls* (Edgeworth), 303, 304

*Essay on the Principle of Population* (Malthus), 251, 379

*An Essay on the Principles of Human Action* (Hazlitt), 302

*Estimate of the Religion of the Fashionable World* (More), 255

Eton College, 387–8

*Evangelical Magazine*, 589

*Evening Mail*, 6

*Examiner*, 7, 476–7, 482–3, 503, 557, 558–9, 600, 630

*The Excursion* (Wordsworth), 600

*Fabulous Histories* (Trimmer), 261

*The Fairchild Family* (Sherwood), 592

Fairfoot, Robert, 502

fairs, 195–6

Farington, Joseph, 222–3, 293, 294, 406

Farish, Mary, 199

*Farmer's Boy* (Bloomfield), 306, 308

*Farmer's Journal*, 561

*Farmer's Magazine*, 456, 459

Farr, Oliver, 89

fashion, 105–6, 117, *118*, 119, 293, 343, 508, 568

Felling colliery explosion (1812), 554

Female Friendly Society, 259

fencibles, 77, 180, 193, 250, 362–4

Ferdinand, King of Spain, 470

Ferdinand, King of the Two Sicilies, 240

Ferguson, Adam, 428

Ferriar, James, 552

Fielden, John, 79–80

finance: national debt, 94, 188, 290, 610, 631; subsidies to allies, 29, 75, 94, 188, 273, 571, 616, 631; banking crises, 46, 88, 182–6, 188; Pitt's strategies, 88, 94–5, 188–9; war loans, 94–6, 189; gold supply, 182–6, 380, 412, 572–3; gold standard, 186, 514, 586; voluntary contributions to war chest, 215–16; investment in consols, 223; silver supply, 380; exchange rates, 519, 572, 573; cost of army, 571–3; 'New Plan of Finance', 585; cost of war, 631; *see also* banking, taxation

Finch, Ralph, 81, 517, 518

Findlatter, Alexander, 76

Finlay, Kirkman, 549

Fishguard, French invasion, 167–9, *167*, 172, 219

Fitzgerald, Lord Edward, 166, 225, 298

Fitzherbert, Maria, 21

Fitzwilliam, Lord Lieutenant, 165

Flaxman, John, 293, 294

Fleck, Tam, 480

Fletcher, Colonel Ralph, 549

Fleurus, battle (1794), 102

Flinders, Matthew, 153–4, 303

Flower, Charles, 136, 491

Flushing, siege and surrender (1809), 486, 488, 489

Foley, Thomas, 277

Fontainebleau, Treaty (1814), 602

food: prices, 140–1, 143, 144, 247–8, 252, 313, 457; shortages, 140–1, 143–4, 244–5; grain shortages, 140–1, 143–5, 149–50; riots, 141–2, 144, 247–8, 250, 252; grain imports, 145, 252, 450, 519, 609–10; Brown Bread Act, 246–7; hunger, 250–2, 636; speculators, 251–3; charitable handouts, 254; imported corn issues, 609–10

Forbes, James, 341

Foreign Office, 292

Foreign Slave Trade Act (1806), 432

forgery, 381

Fox, Charles James: on French Revolution, 13; response to rumours of Jacobin plots, 21, 22; on war loan transaction, 96; Brooks's club, 115; Angelo (fencing master), 117; opposition to 'Gagging Acts', 148; Portland departure, 151; bank notes issue, *184*; support for O'Connor, 224; on Napoleon, 270, 412; in Paris, 292, 293; dinner with Napoleon, 292; Grenville alliance, 376–7; king's view of, 376, 409; Foreign Secretary, 409, 412; peace talks, 412; opposition to slave trade, 432; death, 412–13, 414; reputation, 415

France: Revolution, 13–16, 27, *116*; émigrés, 21–4, 119; declaration of war, 28–9; *levée en masse*, 36–7, 44; Vendée rebellion, 44, 107; peace treaties (1795–6), 108, 121, 163; invasion plans, 164, 166, 167–9; British peace overtures (1797), 186–7; coup of 18 Fructidor (1797), 186–7; Campo Formio treaty (1797), 210; occupation of Switzerland, 213; Irish expedition (1798), 227; expedition to Egypt (1798), 233–4; coup of 18 and 19 Brumaire (1799), 269; naval truce proposal (1800), 272; peace treaty with Austria, 273; war declaration (1803), 339–40; Trafalgar defeat, 399–400; Austerlitz victory, 408; coalition against (1806), 413; victories (1806, 1807), 438; Treaties of Tilsit (1807), 438; army contracts, 447; navy, 576; Paris occupied by Russians and Prussians (1814), 598; Napoleon deposed by Senate, 598; return of Louis XVIII, 600, 602, 603; peace terms, 602; return of Napoleon, 615–16; Waterloo, 618–20; Napoleon's second abdication, 620

Francis II, Emperor of Austria, 270, 294, 411–12

Fraser, General Mackenzie, 441

Frasier, William, 632, *633*

Frederick, Crown Prince of Denmark, 278

Frederick, Duke of York, *see* York

Frederick William III of Prussia, 413, 602, 603

freedom: dreams of, 15; of speech, 230, 500; press, 230, 260, 500, 504, 549, 638; *see also* 'Gagging Acts', habeas corpus, liberty

*Freedom Defended* (Clegg), 228

Freemasons, 541

Fremantle, Betsey: diaries, 10, 627; correspondence, 10, 113; marriage, 9; nursing Nelson, 9–10; on French prisoners, 159; on yeomanry display, 222; on Lady Buckingham's hospitality, 247; news of Copenhagen battle, 278; news from Egypt, 279; husband's election campaign, 310; on Nottingham, 326–7; at Portsmouth, 355, 362; at Melville trial, 396; news of Trafalgar, 399; on Turner's Trafalgar picture, 406; husband's parliamentary career, 417; Swanbourne house, *425*; sister's marriage, 424–5; on summer heat, 438; family news, 506–7; in Scotland, 533; daughter's death, 562; at White's ball, 603–4; life after war, 627

Fremantle, Charles, 507, 627

Fremantle, John, 113

Fremantle, John junior, 506, 536, 570

Fremantle, Stephen, 113–14

Fremantle, Thomas: marriage, 9; wounded, 9–10; career, 113–14, 417, 579; Copenhagen battle, 278; election campaign, 310; at Portsmouth, 355; Trafalgar battle, 399, 406; escorting Nelson's body, 401; parliamentary seat, 417; son's career, 507; Adriatic Squadron command, 579; life after war, 627

Fremantle, Tom, 507, 627

Fremantle, William, 113, 396

Fremantle family, 113, 506–7, 627

*The French Revolution* (Carlyle), 640

Fricker, Edith, 331

Fricker, Sara, 170, 331

Friedland, battle (1807), 438

*The Friend*, 15, 488

Friends of Peace, 71, 564

Frost, John, 72

Fry, Elizabeth (Betsey Gurney), 97, 206–7, 374, 587–8

Fry, Joseph, 207, 374, 588

Fuentes de Oñoro, battles (1811), 535, 537

Fullarton, Colonel, 127

Fulton, Robert, 393

Fuseli, Henry, 293, 294

Gaelic language, 281, 425, 525, 526, 528–9

'Gagging Acts' (1795), 148, 228, 253, 415; petitions against, 148; new, 638

Gale, Joseph, 13

*Gallery of Fashion* (Heideloff), 117, *118*

Galton, Adele, 421, 494, 496

Galton, Francis, 630

Galton, Hubert, 306, 401, 494

Galton, (John) Howard, 421–2, 485, 496, 524, 593, 623

Galton, Lucy: family background, 53, 497; appearance, *305*; character, 54; reading, 304–5, 593; religious views, 304–5; family holidays, 306; in Bath, 421–2; tortoise care, 422; on son Theodore's travels, 477–8; daughter's financial affairs, 520; son Howard's Scottish travels, 524; advice to son Howard, 593

Galton, Mary Anne, 266–7, 304, 421–2, 519–20

Galton, Samuel junior (Samuel John): appearance, 54; career, 53–4, 384; family, 53–4; interests, 54, 304; Quaker tensions, 54–5, 207, 266–7; family holidays, 320; East India Company relationship, 384; retirement, 384; banking, 384; in Bath, 421–2; news for son, 485; daughter's financial affairs, 520; advice to son Howard, 623

Galton, Samuel senior, 51, 53, 54, 55

Galton, (Samuel) Tertius, 384–5, 401, 477, 565, 630

Galton, Sophia, 421

Galton, Theodore, 477, 511

Galton bank, 384, 630

Galton company, 51–2, 53–5, 266, 629

Galton family, 320, 421–2, 494, 510–11, 519–20, 629

Galvanism, 301, 302

Gambier, Admiral, 58, 356, 439, 480

gambling, 117, 506

game laws and gamekeepers, 636

gardening, 423

Garlies, Lord, 399

gas: lighting, *584*; works, 584, 637

Gas, Light and Coke company, 584

Gaskell, Elizabeth, 84, 528, 640

*Gazette*, 5, 63, 235

*Gazette Extraordinary*, 283

*General Magazine*, 298

*The Gentleman Farmer* (Kames), 127

*Gentleman's Magazine*, 27, 37

George III, King: education, 117; recovery from madness (1788), 5; public opinion of, 5, 147, 271; conduct of war, 39; departure of troops, 40; Spithead visit, 64; son's marriage, 110–11; birth of Princess Charlotte, 111; social life, 111–12; bankers, 112; war policy, 164; demonstrations against (1795), 147; peace petitions to, 172; response to naval mutiny, 175; contribution to war chest, 216; review of troops, 221; theatre going, 242; Napoleon's peace proposal, 270; assassination attempt, 271; attitude to Catholic emancipation, 274, 416, 417; relapse into insanity, 275; review of Black Watch, 281; artistic concerns, 294; seaside holidays, 319, 367, 398; review of troops, 354; Addington's resignation, 376; view of Fox, 376, 409; view of Copenhagen attack, 440; Jubilee (1809), 490–1, 498; madness, 511–12; son's regency, 511–12, 555

George, Prince of Wales (Prince Regent): public opinion of, 5, 557, *558*, 604, 638; social life, 21, 111–12, 424, 505, 512; dress, 37; departure of troops, 40; debts, 109–10, 112; mistresses, 110; marriage, 109–11, 556–7; Carlton House, 115; review of troops, 221; Hadfield interview, 271; review of Black Watch, 281; at Brighton, 319; cavalry rifle interest, 385; response to Austerlitz news, 408; marital squabbles, 556–7; Prince Regent, 511–12, 555; removes daughter from her mother, 556; public ridicule, 557, *558*; Liverpool ministry, 562–3; Vittoria victory celebrations, 582; peace celebrations, 603, 604; Grand Jubilee, 606–7; Waterloo news, 618; Brighton Pavilion, 630; stone thrown at, 638

Gerrald, Joseph, 69

Gibbons, William, 205

Gibraltar, victualling port, 134

Gibson, Mary (later Austen), 363, 411

Giddy, Davies, 237, 394

Gill, Jack, 36, 239, 322

Gill, Revd John, 36, 60, 173, 239, 322–3

Gill, Tom: career, 60–1, 239, 272–3, 507, 577–8; St Vincent battle, 173–4; shipwreck, 238; letters from Danish waters, 279; letters from Spanish waters, 470; naval signals posting, 577–8

Gill family, 272–3, 279, 507, 578

Gillray, James: *The dagger scene*, 22; *Promised Horrors*, 115, *116*, 214; *Copenhagen House*, *146*; *Bank-notes, paper-Money*, *184*, 185; *Political Ravishment*, 185–6; Anti-Jacobin illustrations, 211; *Consequences of a Successful French Invasion*, 214, *215*; Battle of the Nile, 235–6; prints at Calais, 292; *Scientific Researches!*, 301, *302*; *Maniac-Ravings*, 338, *339*; 'Little Boney', 367; *John Bull and the Alarmist*, 372, *373*; *Death of Nelson*, 405; *Fat Cattle*, 457, *458*; *The Spanish Bull-Fight*, 471, *472*; *The Life of William Cobbett*, 485; images of Prince Regent, 557; Napoleon's carriage, 639

Gilpin, Gilbert, 202, 206

Girtin, Thomas, 293

*Glasgow Magazine*, 76

Glenbervie, Lord, 582–3

'Glorious First of June', battle off Ushant (1794), 63–6, 73, 153, 173, 272

Goderich, Viscount, 625

Godoy, Manuel, 469

Godwin, Mary, 605

Godwin, William, 73, 75, 97, 211, 242, 299

gold standard, 186, 514, 586

gold supply, 182–6, 380, 412, 572–3

Goldsmid brothers (Benjamin and Abraham), 94, 95, 291, 447, 514–15

Goodrich, Simon, 393

*Goody Two Shoes* (at Sadler's Wells), 353

Gordon Highlanders, 281

Gosling's bank, 91

Gott, Benjamin, 85–6, 128, 314–15, *316*, 629, 630

Gould, William, 100, 176

Goya, Francisco de, 470, 540

Grafton, Duke of, 99, 536

Graham, Aaron, 178

Grand Duchy of Warsaw, 438

Grant, Charles, 591

Grant Brothers, 313

Grattan, Henry, 165, 224

Graves, Vice-Admiral, 130

Gray, Robert, 229

Great Yarmouth: anchorage (Yarmouth Roads), 131, 137–8, *137*, 177, 191, 238–9; port, 124, 134, 137, 176; Pier and Haven Commission, 193; base for blockade of Dutch fleet, 137–8, 191; landing of Dutch royal family (1795), 105; landing of prisoners, 159; naval mutiny, 176, 177; fleet at (1801), 277; landing of Louis XVIII, 443; arrival of Dutch plea for help, 595

Greavey, William, 581

Green, Robert, 388

Greg, Bessy, 317, 587

Greg, Hannah (Lightbody): view of slave trade, 267; marriage, 82; Irish visit, 230; on Italian news, 163; political views, 229–30, 231; schools for apprentices, 317, 587; son's death, 422, 427; reading, 427; on riots, 552; grandmotherhood, 587; on cotton import ban, 590

Greg, Samuel: family background, 82; marriage, 82; radical politics, 82; Quarry Bank Mill, 61, 82, 84, 86, 316–17; Irish visit, 230; on East India Company, 61; Dominica plantation, 267; 'factory colonies', 316–17; son's death, 422; views on education, 587; Indian cotton import ban, 590–1; effects of war on, 629, 630

Greg family, 82, 230, 317, 422, 587, 599

Gregson, Bob, 496–7

Grellet, Stephen, 587

Grenville, William: Foreign Secretary, 27, 210; French negotiations, 27, 28; coalition negotiations, 29; brother's patronage, 113; bank crisis, 182; foreign negotiations (1797), 210; Dundas relationship, 210, 268, 276; naval victory celebrations, 212; war strategy, 268; Pitt's resignation, 275; view of peace terms, 289; correspondence captured, 372; government negotiations (1804), 376–7; Ministry of All the Talents (1806), 409, 410, 412, 416, 421; Orders in Council, 445; opposition to slave trade, 432; resignation (1807), 416, 430

Grey, Charles, 17, 499, 626

Grimaldi, Joe, 20

Guest, John, 201

*Guide to the Lakes* (West), 330

*Guide to the Lakes* (Wordsworth), 330

Gully, John, 496–7

gunpowder stores, 387

Gurney, Bartlett, 96, 151

Gurney, Betsey, *see* Fry (Elizabeth)

Gurney, Hannah, 327–9, 426–7

Gurney, Hudson, 151–2, 340

Gurney, John, 96, 97, 151, 374–5, 588

Gurney, Joseph (brother of John), 96, 97, 327

Gurney, Joseph (son of John), 588

Gurney, Louisa, 151–2, 588

Gurney, Richard, 96–7, 151

Gurney, Richenda, 97, 152, 374

Gurney, Samuel, 383, 588

Gurney family: Quakers, 54; political views, 96–7; Earlham family, 97, 97, 329, 588; election fever (1796), 151–2; reading, 304; seaside holidays, 320, 374–5; in Lake District, 329; slave trade abolition, 430; Barclay cousin, 497; finances, 630

Gurney's bank, 96, 97, 99, 184, 383, 588, 630

Gustavus, King of Sweden, 469

Habeas Corpus Act: suspension (1794), 73, 125; partial suspension, 165; suspended again (1798), 228; reinstatement (1802), 311; press views, (1812), 547; suspension (1817), 638

Hadfield, James, 271

haircuts, 116, 149, 226

Halliday, Admiral, 424

Hamilton, Duke of, 381

Hamilton, Emma, Lady, 9, 239–40, 277, 397, 405

Hamilton, Sir William, 239–40

Hammond, George, 186

Hanover, invasion (1803), 369

Hanson, Joseph, 350, 453

Harcourt, General, 104

Hardwicke, Lord, 313, 342, 500

Hardy, Mary: appearance, 262; background, 124; diary, 124–6; marriage, 124; political views, 125; workhouse visit, 142; on bank crisis (1797), 182; on defence plans, 218; on income tax, 244; religious views, 261–3; on Austrian victories, 268; peace celebrations (1801), 284–5; trip to Hull and York, 324, 326; on volunteers, 362; on enclosures, 464

Hardy, Mary Anne, 124, 262

Hardy, Raven, 124

Hardy, Thomas (secretary of the London Corresponding Society), 17, 73, 74, 91

Hardy, Thomas (writer), 641

Hardy, William, 124–6, 464

Hardy, William junior, 124, 126

Hardy family, 284–5, 324, 326, 464

Harness, Bessy (Biggs): appearance, 31; marriage, 31; newspaper reading, 8; husband's letters, 102, 105–6, 107; husband's promotion, 103; letters from Cape and India, 154–5; husband's death, 345; son's death, 627

Harness, Charles, 31, 103, 106, 154–5, 627

Harness, William: appearance, 31; marriage, 31; on newspaper reports, 8; recruiting, 30–1; departure for Flanders, 101–2, 103; promotion, 103; on Flanders campaign, 103, 105–6; return, 106–7; Vendée expedition, 107, 154; journey to India, 154–5; on sack of Seringapatam, 241; on Egyptian campaign, 280–1; return to India, 290, 345;

death, 345; son's death, 627
Harris, Benjamin, 347, 487, 601, 616
Hartshorne, Charles, 635
Harvey, Admiral, 172
Harvey, Bagenal, 226
hatters, 522
Hawkesbury, Lord, *see* Liverpool
Hay, Colonel James, 570
Hay, Robert, 4, 193–4, 360, 578–9, 626
Hay, William, 539–40
Haydon, Benjamin, 559, 618
Hazard, Samuel, 254
Hazlitt, William: on Coleridge's sermon,
    170; painting in Paris, 293; on Cobbett,
    297; writings, 302; artistic ambitions, 421;
    journalism, 559; on possibility of peace, 596;
    on Napoleon's defeat, 600, 622; on postwar
    life, 630–1
health: army casualties, 152, 157, 281–2, 487,
    627; black prisoners, 160; typhus, 428;
    Walcheren fever, 487–8, 499–500
Health and Morals of Apprentices Act (1802),
    84, 316
Heber, Elizabeth: correspondence, 6; political
    views, 17–18; on Princess Caroline, 111; on
    taxes, 189, 243; on attempted assassination
    of king, 271; on volunteers, 351
Heber, Mary, 243, 604
Heber, Revd Reginald: correspondence, 6, 24,
    351; political views, 13, 15, 28; health, 41–
    2; on banking crisis, 46; on subscriptions for
    uniforms, 104; sister's finances, 189, 243; on
    grain speculators, 251; on Burns's biography,
    322; death, 352
Heber, Reginald junior, 352, 481, 509, 593,
    634
Heber, Richard: on Flanders campaign, 42;
    guest aboard warship, 272; in Paris, 292; in
    Liverpool, 322; in Scotland, 323, 326; on
    songs, 336; volunteer corps, 351; father's
    death, 352; election attempt, 415; Scott
    friendship, 481, 533; parliamentary career,
    634–5; life abroad, 635
Heber, Thomas, 42
Heber family, 6, 24, 42, 243, 284
Heligoland, trade centre, 447
Herries, John, 571–3
Herries Bank, 91, 189
Herschel, Caroline, 15
Herschel, William, 15, 294–5
Hervey, Lord, 283
Higginbotham, Joseph, 129
*The High Price of Bullion* (Ricardo), 514
Highland and Agricultural Society, 127
Highland Society, 281, 527, 528–9
Hill, Sir Richard, 284
Hill, Rowland, 262

Hill, Selina, 257
*Historical Register* (Sykes), 328
*Historical Tour of Monmouthshire* (Coxe), 324
*History of Cumberland* (Hutchinson), 324
Hitchens, Honour, 359
Hoare, Charles, 90, 188, *382*
Hoare, Henry 'Harry': head of bank, 89–90,
    91; attitude to loans, 89, 112; financial
    strategies, 95–6, 187; on gold supply, 183;
    volunteering, 221–2, 349; brokerage issues,
    586; death, 91
Hoare, Henry Merrick, 90, 188, *382*, 590
Hoare, Hugh, 90, 187–8, *382*
Hoare, Sophia (Thrale), 188, 326, 328, 330–1,
    523, 589, 590
Hoare, William, 96, 187, 221, 590
Hoare family, 89–90, 187–8, 221, 349, *382*,
    590, 629
Hoare's bank: building, *90*; sight of mob, 74;
    financial strategies, 88–9, 95–6; attitude to
    loans, 89, 381–2, 482; partners, 89–90,
    112; clerks, 91–2, 222, 383, 586; gold
    supply issues, 182–3, 380; attitude to bank
    notes, 183; 'sinking fund', 187; loans for
    taxes, 190; loans to detainee in France, 340–
    1; deposits, 381; brokerage business, 586;
    effects of war, 629; present day, 629
Hobhouse, John Cam, 509, 548, 604
Hobson, Hannah, 60
Hoche, General Lazare, 107, 164, 166, 224
Hogan, Major Denis, 483
Hohenlinden, battle (1800), 273
Holcroft, Thomas, 73, 97
Holden, John, 351
holidays, 195–6
Holland, Elizabeth, Lady, 415, 477, 506, 622
Holland, Lord, 415, 477, 504, 547, 622
Holland, Peter, 74–5, 84
Home Office, 21, 169, 549
Homfray, Francis, 201
Homfray, Jeremiah, 201, 206
Homfray, Samuel, 206
Hone, William, 379–80, 501, 588, 638
Hood, Admiral Lord, 44, 62, 175, 390
Hook, Theodore, 497
Hope, Charles, 527
Hope & Co., 93
Horner, Francis, 299
Horsemonger Lane prison, 559
Horsfall, William, 552, 553
Howard, Henry, 473
Howard, John, 588
Howe, Lord, 63–4, 65, 173, 175, 176, 400
Howell, John, 626
Howick, Lord, 416
Hudson, Betty, 81
Hudson's Bay Company, 531

Hughes, John, 136
Hugues, Victor, 156
Humbert, General, 227
Hume, John Robert, 619
Hume-Campbell, Amabel, Countess de Grey:
    family background, 109; royal gossip, 109;
    on disastrous harvest, 246; on taxes, 290,
    378; sister, 309; on Napoleon's temper,
    338; on arrival of Nelson's body, 403–4;
    on theatre going, 495; on changes in social
    life, 507–8; on king's madness, 511–12;
    on Napoleon's fitness, 535; on news from
    France, 598; on French state visit, 602
Hunt, Henry 'Orator', 222
Hunt, John, 7, 476, 484, 503, 559
Hunt, Leigh: writings, 476; volunteering,
    354; Examiner, 7, 476, 482; on purchase of
    commissions, 482, 483; libel prosecution
    (1808), 483; on flogging, 484, 503; seditious
    libel acquittal (1810), 503; attack on Prince
    Regent, 558; libel charge (1812), 558; trial
    and sentence, 559; imprisonment, 559;
    attack on Perceval's policies, 560; release,
    610
Hunter, John, 154
hunting, 508, 526
Huntington, Selina, Countess of, 262
Huntsman, Benjamin, 200
Huskisson, William, 571, 636
Hutchinson, George, 248, 460, 635
Hutchinson, Henry, 460, 636
Hutchinson, Joanna, 248–9, 460–3, 465, 616,
    635–6
Hutchinson, John (Jack), 248–9, 252–3, 460,
    520
Hutchinson, Mary, see Wordsworth
Hutchinson, Sara, 248, 331
Hutchinson, Tom, 248, 460–3, 465, 635
Hutchinson family, 4, 170, 248–9, 460–3, 635
Hyderabad, Nizam of, 241

Île d'Yeu expedition (1795), 107–8, 154
Illingworth, Ann, 81
Imlay, Gilbert, 20
Important Considerations for the People of this Kingdom
    (Cobbett), 369–70
Incledon, Charles, 352
India: soldiers' letters, 154–5; Mysore wars,
    241–2; Maratha war, 290, 345, 398; East
    India Company monopoly, 590; ban on
    British imports from, 590–1
India House, 93
Indian seamen, 445
invasion: fears of, 36, 163, 223, 228, 356,
    367–8, 372–4, 386–7, 392, 407, 639;
    threat, 101, 182, 223, 363, 564, 638;
    Fishguard, 167–9, 172, 219; reports of

Napoleon's plans, 213–14, 282, 366;
    defences against, 215–20, 362–4, 365–6,
    375, 376, 389–90, 392
Ireland: army recruiting, 34, 342; French
    invasion plan (1796), 164, 166, 224; United
    Irishmen, 164–6, 177, 224–5, 228, 242,
    311–12; rebellion (1798), 224–8, 232, 273;
    union with Westminster, 273–4, 310; Acts
    of Union, 274; Emmet affair, 312; Martello
    towers, 390
iron: cost of, 203; works, 200–4, 522–3, 637;
    uses of, 204–5; masters, 205–6; quality of
    British, 386
Isle of Dogs, 446

Jackson, Colonel Andrew, 609
Jackson, Francis, 439
Jackson, John 'Gentleman', 116
Jackson, Thomas (guardsman), 30
Jackson, Thomas (prisoner), 617
Jacobins, 18, 21, 43, 212, 415
James, Jonathan, 541
Jane, Warren, 198, 579
Jeffrey, Francis, 299, 306, 481, 509, 510, 524
Jemappes, battle (1792), 19
Jena, battle (1806), 414, 427, 438
Jenner, Edward, 341
Jerningham, Lady Frances: family background,
    118–19; royal gossip, 111, 556; social life,
    119; volunteering, 354; invasion fears,
    365–6; on Addington's resignation, 376;
    on French prisoners, 544; on tsar, 604; on
    Waterloo casualties, 619
Jerrold, Douglas, 577
Jervis, Admiral Sir John (later Lord St Vincent):
    Mediterranean Fleet command, 57; tactics,
    400; St Vincent victory, 172, 173–4;
    ennobled, 174; dinner with, 272; dockyard
    corruption investigation, 291, 390, 391;
    report on state of navy, 395; reputation, 625
Job, Zephaniah, 449–50
John Bull and the Alarmist (Gillray), 372, 373
Johnson, Robert, 313
Jones, James, 316
Jones, John Gale, 500
Jones, Thomas, 252
Jordaine and Shaw, 136
Jordan, Dorothy, 40, 242, 494
Josephine, Empress, 377, 498, 602
Jourdan, Marshal, 480
Jules, James, 137
Junot, General, 469, 471, 476, 477

Kames, Henry Home, Lord, 127
Kean, Edmund, 117
Keats, John, 24, 146, 241–2, 323, 602, 610
Keats, Richard Goodwin, 410

keelmen, 360–1, 634
Keir, James, 208
Keith, Admiral, 279
Kemble, Charles, 495
Kemble, John Philip, 242, 491–2, *492*, 494, 495
Kennedy, General Robert, 571
Kenton, Ben, 144
Kettle, John, 50–1
Killala, French landing (1798), 227, 228
Kilwarden, Lord, 312
Kincaid, Lieutenant James, 538
Knight, John, 564
Knights, corn factors, 136
knitters, 545–6
knitting frames, 545–7
Knollys, Charlotte, 459, 506
Knollys, William, Earl of Banbury, 43, 117, 459–60

lacemaking, 194
*The Lady of the Lake* (Scott), 524–5, 533–4
*Lady's Magazine*, 236
Lake, General, 225, 226, 228
Lake District, 325, 329, 330–1, 464
Lamb, Caroline, 559, 561, 604, 620
Lamb, Charles: India House employment, 93; sister's madness, 170; on London, 318–19; in Lake District, 331; on Nelson's funeral preparations, 403; on art auctions, 421; on Clarke scandal, 483; on rattlesnake, 496; 'Triumph of the Whale', 557, 558; prison visiting, 559; on Hyde Park, 607
Lamb, Mary, 170, 331, 559
Lambert and Cotton, stockbrokers, 513–14
Lancashire: textile industries, 78–85, 314; Irish immigrants, 231; peace meetings, 253; recruiting bands, 347; unemployment, 545; weavers, 545; Luddite violence, 551–2
*Lancaster Gazette*, 553
land: enclosures, 464–6, 636; prices, 458–9; rents, 636; financial difficulties,, 636
Landmann, George, 357–8
Lapenotiere, Captain John Richards, 399
Larking, John, 391
Lascar seamen, 445
Lawrence, Thomas, 310
*Lay of the Last Minstrel* (Scott), 307, 397, 524
League of Armed Neutrality, 277, 279
Leard, John, 391
Leclerc, General, 336
Leech, Rachel, 81
Leeds, textile industries, 85–6
*Leeds Intelligencer*, 266, 552
*Leeds Mercury*, 553–4, 563
Leigh, Augusta, 559
Leinster, battle (1798), 225

Leipzig, battle (1813), 595–6
Leopold II, Emperor, 16–17
Lepard, Thomas, 388–9, 487, 489, 628
*Letter on the Abolition of the Slave Trade* (Wilberforce), 431
*Letters from France* (Williams), 119
*Letters of Peter Plymley* (Smith), 417
Levy en Masse Act (1803), 346
Lewis, Matthew 'Monk', 307
libel, 298, 313, 483, 504, 558–9, 638, *see also* seditious libel
liberty: trees, 67, 241; cap of, 115; Clapham evangelicals' view, 300; 'British liberty', 431; to worship, 592; *see also* freedom
libraries, circulating, 303–4, 308
Lightbody, Hannah, *see* Greg
Lisbon: French capture (1808), 469; British presence, 477, 490, 499, 535, 538, 563
*Little Henry* (Sherwood), 592–3
Liverpool: town, 321; banking crisis, 46; port, 178, 321–2, 355; Irish movement, 228; slave trade, 266–7, 322, 432–3; election (1806), 432
Liverpool, Lord, 381
Liverpool, Robert Banks-Jenkinson (earlier Lord Hawkesbury), Lord: militia command, 180; Foreign Secretary, 283; Home Secretary, 417, 453; Danish strategy, 439; Secretary for War, 489, 556; Prime Minister, 562–3, 625
Lloyd, Sampson, 55
Lloyd family, 54
Lloyd's bank, 96
Lloyd's of London, 93, 238, 356, 357
Lloyd's Patriotic Fund, 192, 356–7, 400, 421, 633
Local Militia Act (1808), 473
*Local Records* (Sykes), 247
Loch, James, 530, 531
Lockhart, John, 481
Lodi, battle (1796), 163
London: clubs, 115–16; bridges, 585; planning, 509; Regent Street, *509*; peace celebrations, 602–4; Grand Jubilee, 607; Tower, *see* Tower
London, City of: naval relations, 61–2, 238; institutions, 92–3; brokers, 93–4, 383, 586–7; Pitt's dealings, 189; naval victory celebrations, 212; voluntary contributions to war chest, 215–16; evangelical influence, 259; volunteers, 353; response to Copenhagen situation, 439; bankruptcies (1810), 514
London, Treaty of (1801), 289
London Constitutional Society, 72
London Corresponding Society, 17, 67, 69, 72–3, 75, 146, 148, 229, 311, 380
London Dock Company, 445
London Highland Society, 281

London Society of Planters and Merchants, 266

Londonderry, Lady, 230

Longsdon, Elizabeth, 81, 128–9, 284, 379, 516

Longsdon, James: wool sales, 81, 128; cotton trade, 81, 128; cattle farming, 128, 129, 422–3; on peace news, 283; finances, 439, 450, 516–18; illness, 517; on soldier friend, 536, 538

Longsdon, James junior: childhood, 81, 129; education, 128–9, 283, 379; dress, 284; cattle buying, 422–3; militia drilling, 473–4; farming, 516, 518; life after war, 630

Longsdon, John: childhood, 81; education, 128, 283, 379; on Heligoland, 447; Canada expedition, 450; American business trip, 515–16; concern for family finances, 516–17; move to America, 518; friend's enlistment and death, 536, 538; life after war, 630

Longsdon, Matthew and Peter, 516–17

Longsdon, William: childhood, 81; education, 128, 283, 379; in Manchester, 516; move to America, 518; on Canadian property, 531; life after war, 630

Longsdon family, 81, 128–9, 450, 516–18, 630

Los Dolores de León, Juana María de, 538

Loughborough, Lord, 274

Louis XVI, King, 15, 16, 19, 20, 27–8, 98

Louis XVIII, King, 443, 600, 602, 616

Louis, Admiral Thomas, 400

Louisiana purchase (1803), 336

Loutherbourg, Philip de, 200, 238

L'Ouverture, Toussaint, 157

Lovett, William, 3, 363–4, 359

Lowson, Newby, 294

Luddites, 546–8, 546, 549, 551, 569

Lunar Society, 54

Lupton, Arthur, 563

Lupton & Co., 518–19

Lyrical Ballads, 306, 396

Lysons, Dr Daniel, 169

Lyttelton, William Henry, 568


Macaulay, Colin, 591

Macaulay, Tom, 257, 307

Macaulay, Zachary, 255, 257, 435–7, 591

McGrigor, James, 178

MacIntyre, Duncan Ban, 526

Mack, General, 398

Mackintosh, Sir James, 337

Macklin, Thomas, 91

MacLeod, Donald, 532

MacPherson, Sir John, 424

Madison, President, 521, 563, 608

Madrid, surrender (1812), 565

Magna Carta, 17, 419, 501, 503

Maida, battle (1806), 411, 424

mail, 197, 283, 292, 372–4

Maitland, Captain, 620

Mallet du Pan, Jacques, 223

Malmesbury, James Harris, Lord, 164, 186–7, 189, 398–9

Malta: French occupation, 234; British capture, 277; treaty provisions, 289, 336; British presence, 336, 338, 442

Malthus, Thomas, 251, 379

Manby, Captain, 556

Manchester: town, 79; radicals, 18; riots (1792), 21; mechanisation protest (1792), 87; recruiting, 34, 471–2; trial of reformers (1794), 72, 82; Lit & Phil (Literary and Philosophical Society), 79, 82; textile industry, 79–80, 81; workhouse, 142–3; food riots (1795), 144; Camperdown celebrations, 192; Irish movement, 228–9; Irish community, 231; business during peace (1802), 313; factories, 326; volunteers, 348, 350; women's war work, 354; Nelson commemoration, 405; St George's Fields meeting (1808), 453; bank failures (1810), 516–17; riots (1812), 550–1, 553, 560; poverty, 552; Ancoats Lane petitioners, 564; Peterloo (1819), 638

Manchester Chronicle, 46

Manchester Gazette, 188, 229, 413, 451

Manchester Mercury, 266

Manchester Weavers' Committee, 545

Manningham, Colonel Coote, 343, 385

Mansfield, David Murray, second Lord, 112

Mansfield, Lady, 482

Marengo, battle (1800), 272

Marie Antoinette, Queen, 16, 19, 43

Marie-Louise, Archduchess, 498

marines, 132, 472–3

Marmion (Scott), 411, 524

Marmont, General, 598

Marquis, William, 518

Marshall, John (Jack): background and career, 86–7; linen mills, 86–7, 204, 325; on Glasgow coffee room, 6; in Lake District, 324–6; holiday travels, 325–6; bulk buying, 518; finances, 629, 630

Martello towers, 390

Masséna, General, 535, 537

Materosa, Vizconde de, 470–1

Mathias, Mary and John, 168

Maudslay, Henry, 393

Mavor, William, 321

Maxwell, William, 67

medals, 281, 400, 411, 540

Meikle, Andrew, 456

Melbourne, Lady, 556, 610, 620

Mellish, Peter, 136, 629

Mellish, William, 136, 144

Mellor, George, 550

Melville, Lord, *see* Dundas

*Memoirs of Emma Courtney* (Hays), 211

Mendoza, Daniel, 116

Menou, General, 280–1, 292

Merthyr Tydfil, 202

Messiter, George, 540–1

Methodists, 249, 261–4, 350, 356, 493, 565, 591–2

Metternich, Prince, 602, 624

Michelson, Ann, 43, 156

Middleton, Charles, Lord Barham, 396

Middleton, riots (1812), 551

Milan Decree (1807), 452

Milbanke, Annabella, 559

militia: institution, 34–5; length of service, 35; exemptions, 35; ballot, 34, 35, 37, 76, 179–80, 346, 348; substitutes, 34, 35; numbers, 35, 472; recruiting, 35–6, 347; barracks, 35–6, 322, 365; allowance for wives and children, 36; uniforms, 47; shoes, 48; parades, 100, 490; MPs, 113; riot control role, 141, 180, 248, 250, 252, 314, 551; rioting, 141–2; punishments, 142, 502; West Indian prisoners, 160; billeted, 165; Irish, 166; Fishguard defence, 167–8; riots against Militia Act for Scotland, 179–81; Vinegar Hill battle (1798), 227; Orange movement, 231; regular army recruiting from, 239; sent home, 290; recalled (1803), 346; local, 473–4; plays put on by, 493; straw raids, 543–4; Luddite unrest, 547, 552–3; abused by workmen, 553

Militia Act (1757), 35

Militia Act for Scotland (1797), 179–80

Militia Acts (1803), 346

Militia Bill (1793), 28

miners, 141, 386, 637

mines: copper, 57, 205, 323, *324*; coal, 127, 204, 208, 323, 328; lead, 128, 326; salt, 135; tin, 449

'Ministry of All the Talents', 409, 421, 432

*Minstrelsy of the Scottish Border* (Scott), 307

*Miscellanea Perthensis*, 298

missionaries, 591–4

Mitford, Mary Russell, 5–6, 427

Mocatta, Daniel, 447

Moira, Francis Rawdon Hastings, Lord: Ostend expedition, 101, 102–3; Flanders campaign, 103, 104; return to London, 104; Prime Minister proposal, 210, 562; support for O'Connor, 224; bank loans, 630

*Moniteur*, 372, 378

Monkhouse, Elizabeth, 248

Monkhouse, John: apprentice in London, 248;

249–50; correspondence, 249–50, 252–3, 520; on volunteers, 350; father's death, 379; move to Penrith, 379; finances, 379; career plans, 460, 461; wife's death, 461; farming at Hindwell, 461–3, 465; sister, 462; brother-in-law, 463; life after war, 635

Monkhouse, Mary (M.M.), 462–3, 465, 562

Monkhouse, Thomas, 379, 462

Monkhouse family, 248, 249, 379, 460–3

*Monthly Magazine*, 211

Montrose, Duke of, 501

Moore, James, 543

Moore, Sir John: St Lucia command, 156; Kent command, 390; on fencibles, 363–4; Swedish expedition, 469; Spanish command, 477; expeditionary force, 477, 478; Corunna battle, 478, 641; death, 478, 479; reputation, 570, 625

Moore, Thomas (Tom), 424, 602

Moorfields, dispensary, 281

More, Hannah, 221, 254–7, 307, 370, 430, 431

Morewood, Thomas, 439

Morewood family, 81, 450

Morewoods' merchant house, 516, 517, 538

Morgan, Fanny, 520–1

Morgan, John, 95, 187

Morland, George, 150

*Morning Advertiser*, 90

*Morning Chronicle*: readership, 5, 415; war policy, 27; on mock invasion, 40–1; 'Scots wha hae', 69; on treason, 73; on war loans, 96; on Lloyd's fund, 192; on Pitt's resignation, 274–5; on peace calls, 452; on Carlton House Fete, 512; Ricardo's letters, 514; Byron's work, 548; royal gossip, 556; theatre critic, 559; Waterloo news, 618–19

*Morning Post*: on Dorothy Jordan, 40; war policy, 75; on war loans, 95; on Portsmouth mutiny, 178; on naval victory celebrations, 212; Coleridge's writings, 213, 270, 337; O'Connor's Address, 224; royal gossip, 556; tribute to Prince Regent, 558; tribute to Cadogan, 570–1

*Morning Star*, 67

Moscow, French retreat (1812), 567

'Mountain', the, 415, 549

Muhammad Ali, 441–2

Muir, Thomas, 68–9, 71

mule-spinners, 522

Mulgrave, Lord, 398, 507

Murdoch, William, 584

Murphy, Father John, 225, 226

Murray, Captain George, 173

Murray, Captain Henry, 482

Murray, John, 481

Murray, Matthew, 86

Napier, Sarah, 101, 506

Napier, William, 101, 506

Napier family, 506

Napoleon Bonaparte: recapture of Toulon,
45; balloon reconnaissance, 102, 353;
Italian campaign, 121, 163, 172–3, 186,
212; Spanish peace treaty, 121; political
career, 164, 269–70; art collection, 173,
*293*; Austrian treaties, 186, 210; Armée
d'Angleterre command, 210; reputation,
212–13, 270, 289–90, 337, 367, *429*;
invasion plans, 213, 282, 365, 377;
Egyptian expedition, 233–4, 240; coup
(1799), *269*, 270; peace proposal, 270;
Marengo victory (1800), 272; ratification of
peace preliminaries (1801), 283–4; Herschel
meeting, 294–5; appearance described, 295,
296; control of press, 335; demands British
action on journalism, 335; protectionist
policies, 335–6; colonial aims, 336; Consul
for life, 336; violent scene at Tuileries,
338, *339*; view of British defences, 365;
kidnap of Duc d'Enghien, 371–2; crowned
emperor, 377; Austerlitz victory (1805),
408; peace talks (1806), 412; Confederation
of the Rhine, 413; Jena victory, 414, 444;
view of Copenhagen attack, 440; Berlin
Decrees, 444, 452; Milan Decree, 452;
Spanish expedition, 477, 478; Vienna
entry (1809), 485; Wagram victory, 488;
marriage to Marie-Louise of Austria, 498,
505; restrictions on British trade, 518, 519;
advance on Russia, 565, 566; retreat from
Moscow, 567–8, 569; uprisings against, 568;
Leipzig defeat (1813), 595; retreat, 596;
deposed by Senate, 598; abdication, 598;
exile on Elba, 602, 616; Josephine's death,
602; escape from Elba, 615, 627; landing in
France, 615; arrival in Paris, 616; Waterloo
defeat, 619; second abdication, 620;
surrender, 620; on *Bellerophon*, 620–2, 621;
St Helena exile, 622; British responses to
his fate, 622–3; travelling carriage on show,
639, *640*; busts, 640; death (1821), 640;
memorabilia, 640

*Narrative of the British Expedition in Egypt* (Wilson),
367

*Narrative of the Dangers* (Louvet), 119

Nash, John, 86, 188, *509*

*Naval Chronicle*, 397, 575

navy: seamen, 56; pay, 153, 174–5;
warships, 57; dockyards, 57, 133, 291,
390–1; suppliers, 48, 133–7, 629, 637; food
supplies, 130–1, 140–1, 191, 193, 458;
ship's bisket, 133, 134–6, 138; rations, 134;
fresh water supplies, 138; press gangs, 59–

61, 199, 358–61; prize money, 62–3, *63*,
132, 153, 175, 400, 410, 440; punishments,
175, 440–1; West Indies expedition, 156,
172; St Vincent victory, 173; recruitment
legislation, 174; mutinies, 175–8;
Camperdown victory, 191–2; Mediterranean
expedition, 234; Nile victory (1798), 234–8;
control of Mediterranean, 238; Copenhagen
victory (1801), 277–8; Egyptian expedition,
279–80; Boulogne raid, 282–3; size cut after
peace (1801), 290–1; dockyard layoffs, 291;
preparations for war, 355–8; sea fencibles,
362–4; timber supplies, 391–2; shipbuilding
boom, 392; ship repairs, 392; 'catamarans'
tested, 393–4; Trafalgar victory (1805),
399–400; Santo Domingo victory (1806),
410; policing abolition of slave trade, 433–4;
West Africa Squadron, 433–4; Copenhagen
bombardment and capture (1807), 440;
Dardanelles squadron, 441; war losses, 631;
demobilisation, 631–2; life of sailors after
the war, 632, 633–4; unemployment of
suppliers, 637

Navy Board, 57, 133, 134, 291, 390

Navy Office, 153, 392, 449

*The Necessity of Atheism* (Shelley), 503

Nelson, Horatio: early career, 57–8; loss of
arm, 9–10; tactics, 64; St Vincent battle,
173–4; knighthood, 174; showmanship, 174,
397, 398; search for French fleet, 234; battle
of the Nile, 234–8, *236*; affair with Emma
Hamilton, 239–40, 397, 405; Sicilian
issue, 240; theatre going, 242; Copenhagen
battle, 277–80; command of defences, 282;
Boulogne raid, 282–3; support for Despard,
311; off Toulon, 357; ship repair issues,
391; pursuit of Villeneuve, 397; reputation,
397–8; meeting with Wellington, 398;
Trafalgar, 399–400; death, 399, 400; body,
401–2, *402*, 420; funeral, 403–5, *404*;
commemoration, 405–6; heroic status, 625

Netherlands: United Republic, 28, 105
Austrian, 41, 94, 210; French control, 105,
137, 519; Kingdom of, 602

*The New Bath Guide* (Anstey), 114

New Orleans, battle (1815), 609

New Ross, battle (1798), 225

New Steam Mill Company, 386

*A New View of Society* (Owen), 587

Newcastle, Duke and Dowager Duchess, 341

*Newcastle Advertiser*, 360

*Newcastle Chronicle*, 75

*Newcastle Courant*, 59

Newgate prison, 587–8

*News*, 476

newspapers and journals, 6–8, 153, 260,
298–9, 415, 442–3

Newton, Robert, 214
Nicholas, Jemima, 168
Nicholls, John, 340–1
Nicol, John: career, 60; press gang experiences, 7–8, 60, 359, 364; battle of the Nile, 235; Aboukir landings, 280; return to Edinburgh, 291; life after war, 626
Nile, battle of the (1798), 234–8, 236, 272
Nixon, William, 520
Noailles, Comtesse de, 21
Noble, John, 92
Nock, Henry, 51, 349
Non-Intercourse Act (1809), US, 515
Nore mutiny (1797), 176–8
Norfolk, Duke of, 224
Norfolk Chronicle, 284–5
Norfolk News, 193
Norman Cross prison, 158–9, 195, 543, 601
North Shields, resistance to press gang, 59
Northern Association of Gentlemen Farmers and Breeders of Sheep, 529
Northumberland, Duke of, 382
Nottingham: elections (1802), 310–11; knitters, 545–6; Luddites, 546
Nottingham Review, 546

Oakes, Charlotte, 98, 216
Oakes, Elizabeth, 320–1
Oakes, James: background and career, 97–8, 99; yarn-combing factory, 99; landtax receiver, 99; views on war, 98–9; banking, 99–100, 383, 630; social life, 99–100, 238, 414, 420; on Glorious First of June celebrations, 65; on food protests, 141; petition against Seditious Meetings Act, 148; wheat meeting, 149; on St Vincent victory, 174; on Spithead mutiny, 176; on banking crisis, 184–5; on Bury fair, 195; daughter's death, 216; voluntary subscription, 216; parade for king's birthday, 220; on theatre, 242; on cold weather, 244–5; attitude to badging the poor, 247; tour of pubs, 260; news of peace, 283; alderman election, 311; seaside holiday, 320; wife's death, 320; touring, 321; on preparations for war, 337–8; on volunteers, 349; investments, 383; on Trafalgar, 400; feeding the poor, 420; London visit, 493–4; theatre going, 494; on foot race, 497; on giving to the poor, 513; finances, 513–14; arranging lieutenancy, 536; on local happenings, 549; on census, 555; on Perceval assassination, 560; commemoration of Chesapeake capture, 575–6; on victories against French, 595; on cold weather, 596; nephew's death, 600; on wheat imports, 609–10; on Napoleon's escape, 615; on Waterloo, 619

Oakes, James, 98, 100, 420, 493, 513, 575
Oakes, Maria, 98, 100, 494
Oakes, Orbell: career, 98, 99, 321; bank notes question, 184; son's death, 216; alderman, 247; volunteer company, 348–9; social life, 420, 497
Oakes, Orbell junior, 579
Oakes family, 97–8, 100, 284, 420, 493–4, 513, 575
O'Coigley, Father James, 224, 229
O'Connor, Arthur, 166, 224, 294
Old England to Her Daughters, 370
Oldham: Paine's effigy burnt (1793), 24; recruiting, 35; poor rates, 36; weavers, 79, 454; army casualties, 152, 246, 487; volunteers, 348; local events (1806), 426; unemployment, 454; Jubilee celebrations (1809), 491; peace celebrations, 600
Oldham Edge, mass meeting (1807), 451
Olding, Henry, 541
Opie, John, 97, 242, 293
Oporto: sack (1809), 479; battle (1809), 480
Oracle and Public Advertiser, 182
Orange Order, 165, 231
Orders in Council: issued (1807), 444–5; effects, 445, 462, 481, 514, 517; protests against, 450, 451, 545, 549, 560; US demand for repeal, 521; repealed, 563
Ordnance Board: head of, 44, 48, 507; role, 48–9; members, 48–9; Woolwich Arsenal, 49–50, 49; cannon supplies, 50, 203, 474; musket supplies, 50–3, 385, 474, 487; relationship with gunmakers, 52–3, 386; contracts, 52, 133, 201, 384; bills, 93–4; iron and steel supplies, 203, 386; flint supplies, 384, 474; tree planting, 386; storage of arms, 386–7; Weedon Bec depot, 387–9, 628; gun wharves, 390; carriers, 487; orders cancelled, 627
Orthez, battle (1814), 596
Ostrach, battle (1799), 268
Otto, M. (French envoy), 283, 292, 311
Otway, Commissioner, 160
Oulart Hill, battle (1798), 225
Overend, John, 383
Overend, Gurney & Co., 383, 630
Owen, Robert, 316–17, 326, 587
Oxford, Jane Harley, Lady, 310

Paget, Sir Edward, 101–2
Paget, Lord, 483
Paget, Samuel, 138, 177, 193
Paine, Thomas: bridge design, 204; Rights of Man, 14–15, 18, 21, 256; religious views, 256; seditious libel conviction, 15; supporters, 17, 18, 165; effigy, 18, 24, 28, 69; sale of works, 72; readership, 97;

lampooned by More, 255

*Paisley Advertiser*, 626

Pakenham, Hercules, 440

Palm, Johann Philipp, 413

Palmer, Thomas Fyshe, 68–9

*Panorama of the Invasion Port at Boulogne*, 407

Paris: British visitors (1802), 292–5; British after declaration of war (1803), 340–1; Russian and Prussian entry (1814), 598; Napoleon's return (1815), 616

Paris, Peace of (1814), 602

Paris, Treaty of (1815), 624

Park, Mungo, 435, 594

Parker, Captain Edward, 283

Parker, Admiral Sir Hyde, 277

Parker, Richard, 176, 177–8

Parma, Duke of, 336

Parys copper mine, 323, *324*

Pasley, C. W., 489

Passenger Act (1803), 527

passports, 292

*Patronage* (Edgeworth), 506

Patton, William, 136

Paul II, Tsar, 163, 273, 277, 278

Peel, Robert: business career, 82, 317, 629, 630; employees, 82, 84; political views, 82, 86; factory legislation, 84; volunteer troop, 350

Peel, Robert (son of above), 82, 453

Pellew, Captain Edward, 62, 625

Peltier, Jean-Gabriel, 335, 337

Pentridge Rising (1817), 637–8

Perceval, Spencer: appearance, 417, 489; Peltier case, 337; Chancellor of Exchequer, 417, 571; minimum wage issue, 452–3; Prime Minister, 489; arrest of Burdett, 500; trial of Cobbett, 502–3; regency legislation, 511; machine-breaking legislation, 547; Prince Regent's support, 555; portrayal by Cruikshank, 557, *558*; death, 560–1, 562

Percival, Thomas, 267

Percy, Henry, 618

Perry, Green and Wells, 392, *393*

Peterloo (1819), 638

Petersham, Lord, 568

Petty, Henry, 409

Philips, John Leigh, 350

Phillip, Vice-Admiral, 363

Phillips, Sir Richard, 634

Pickford, Messrs, 487

Pictet, Marc-Auguste, 295

picturesque, the, 202, 321, 323–5, 327, 329, 532

pigs, 135

Pilkington, Robert, 4, 388–9, 486–7, 489, 628

Piozzi, Hester: daughter's marriage, 188; on French fleet, 234; reading, 306; on news

from Vienna, 407–8; on reviewers, 424; on newspaper stories, 442–3; on tourism, 590

Pitt, William: career, 13, 115; view of French Revolution, 13–14; taxation, 16, 94, 125, 189–90, 194, 205, 216, 243–4; view of slave trade, 265, 267, 430; attitude to war, 16–17, 27; Aliens Bill, 21, 22; war declaration, 28–30, 583; war strategy, 29, 56; financial strategies, 88, 94–6, 188–9; repression of radical opinion, 71; Tooke trial, 74; on Quiberon withdrawal, 107; responses to food crisis, 142, 149; poor law reform plans, 142; 'Gagging Acts', 148, 228; parliamentary majority, 151; war policies, 152, 164; on Russia, 163; invasion concerns, 163–4; response to naval mutinies, 177; response to banking crisis, 183, *184*, 185–6; peace overtures, 186–7; ill health, 210, 272, 408; heckled, 212; voluntary contribution to war chest, 216; fear of conspiracy, 228; Mediterranean expedition, 234; theatre going, 242; income tax, 243–4; Combination Acts, 245–6; offer to Cobbett, 298; rejection of Napoleon's peace plans, 270; rejection of naval truce, 272; Irish policy, 273–4; resignation, 274–5; successor, 276; view of peace terms, 289; birthday celebrations, 336; return to Commons, 339; speech on war (1803), 339–40; Colonel of the Cinque Ports, 348, *349*; view of defence plans, 376; government (1804), 376–7; theatre going, 494; naval policy, 391; war strategy (1805), 395; government (1805), 396; meeting with king, 398; response to Austrian surrender, 398–9; response to Trafalgar, 407; death, 409, 414; reputation, 415

Pitt, Sir William, 160

Pius VII, Pope, 377

Place, Francis, 418

Plampin, Captain Robert, 579

Platoff, General, 602, 603

Plunket, Tom, 632

Plymouth: naval yard, 133, 134, 390; prison hulks, 158; naval mutiny, 176; peace bonfire, 284

Pneumatic Institution, 237, 300–1

*Poems of Ossian in the Original Gaelic*, 529

Poland, partitions, 108, 438, 625

Polewhele, Revd Richard, 211

*Political Register*, 298, 357, 415, 484, 558

*Politics for the People*, 72, 75

Pollard, Jane, 324–5

Poor Law Guardians, 84, 513

poor relief: poor rates, 36, 247, 379, 450, 493, 513, 631; food in winter, 140, 206, 247, 285, 420; Speenhamland scheme, 142; workhouses and Schools of Industry, 142–3,

250, 630; Female Friendly Society, 259; numbers on poor relief (1806), 379; Weedon policy, 389; Birmingham (1809), 523; rising cost, 545; subscriptions, 552, 604; rising numbers in poorhouses and workhouses, 630

Popham, Commodore Sir Home Riggs, 412, 413, 415–16, 482

*The Porcupine*, 298

Porter, Robert Ker, 242

Porteus, Beilby, 255

Portland, Duke of: food supply issues, 140; split from Fox, 151; Home Secretary, 151; war policies, 186; estates, 253; Prime Minister (1807), 417; Orders in Council, 445; war strategy, 485; illness, 488; resignation, 489

Portsmouth: naval yard, 130–3, 134, 390; prison hulks, 158; naval mutiny, 176, 178

Portugal: French occupation, 469; British expedition, 471, 475–6; British withdrawal, 478–9; British campaign (1809), 486

potatoes, 127, 247–8, 457, 464, 527, 595

Powis, Earl of, 221

*Practical Education* (Edgeworth), 295, 317

*Practical View* (Wilberforce), 258–9

Praed & Co., 91

*The Press*, 224

press gangs, 59–61, 206, 358–62, 452, 578–9, 626

Price, Richard, 13

Priestley, Joseph, 13, 19, 54, 255

Priestley, Thomas, 84

Prince Edward Island, 450, 516, 531

print-shops, 7, 115

prisoners of war: wounded, 64; exchanges, 157, 283, 540; payment for keep, 157–8; arrival, 159; employment and crafts, 159, 194–5, 521, 541–2, 543–4, 601; black, 159–60; escapes, 168–9, 543; in Ireland, 226, 227; British civilians in France, 340–2; amnesty, 491; numbers, 540; responses to peace, 601–2, 606, 617; American, 607–8, 617–18; returning home, 617–18, 628; staying in England, 628

prisons: hulks, 158, *159*, 540, 542, 544, 607–8, 628; parole depots, 158, 194, 540–2, 628; land prisons, 158–9, 195, 540, 542–3, 544, 607–8, 628; tourists, 158, 544; Elizabeth Fry's work, 207, 587–8; Coldbath Fields, 230, 310, 311, 380, 559; closed, 628

privateers, 198–9, 355, 579–80

propaganda, British government, 367–70, *369*

Prussia: coalition against France (1792), 17, 19; coalition against France (1793), 29; war finances, 94, 631; defeats by French, 102; treaty with France, 108; Polish partition, 108, 625; trade, 145, 385, 391; League of Armed Neutrality, 277; coalition against

France (1806), 413, 414; French victories against, 414; Berlin entered by French, 414, 444; Treaty of Tilsit (1807), 438–9; arms for, 474; 'Wars of Liberation', 569; Leipzig battle (1813), 595; Paris entry, 598; peace celebrations, 602–3; Congress of Vienna, 624; 'Holy Alliance', 625; Congress of Verona (1822), 636

Pugin, Augustus, *418*

Pye, Henry James, 213

Pyne, William Henry, *150*

Pyramids, battle of the (1798), 234

Quakers: gun-making issues, 54–5, 207; members disowned, 55, 207; banks, 96, 630; restrictions on, 151; Coalbrookdale, 206–7; exempt from mobilisation, 216, 346; slavery issues, 266–7; Elizabeth Fry's work, 588

Quarry Bank Mill, 82, 84, 317, 587

*Quarterly Review*, 481, 593

Quiberon, 107, 164

Quota Acts, 174, 176

races, 497–8

Radcliffe, Ann, 307

Radcliffe, Joseph, 549

railways, 628–9

Rathbone, Hannah, 422, 430, 587

Rathbone, William, 229–30, 267, 322, 422, 427, 430

Rathbone, William junior, 587

Rawfolds Mill, 547, 550

reading, 304–8

Recamier, Madame, 292

Reeves, John, 18

*Reflections on the Revolution in France* (Burke), 13, 14

Reform Bill (1832), 626

*Reformists' Register*, 638

Regnier, Jacques, 335

religion: tracts, 254–6; Paine's position, 256; evangelical revival, 256–61; denominations, 261–3; nonconformist upbringing, 263–4; Sunday schools, 264; slave trade issues, 265–7; response to invasion threat, 370–1; missionaries, 591–4

Rennie, John, 197, 390, 445, 585

*Repository Tracts*, 254, 300

Repton, Humphry, 86, 188

Revenue Office, 378

Reynolds, William, 207–8

Reynolds family, 206

Ricardo, Abraham, 383

Ricardo, David, 383, 514, 586, 629

Richardson, Thomas, 383

Richmond, Duke of, 44, 51

Rigden, John, 136

*Rights of Man* (Paine), 14–15, 17, 18, 21, 73

Riot Act, 141, 181, 248

riots: Manchester (1792), 21, 87; Whitby
(1793), 59–60; London (1794), 33; food
protests (1795), 141–2, 143–5; militia ballot
(1797), 181; food protests (1800), 247–8,
250, 252; weavers (1808), 453–4; Covent
Garden theatre (1809), 491–2; freedom of
speech issues (1810), 500–1, 508; Luddites,
546–8, 550, 551–2; peace protests, 550;
Corn Laws, 610; Spa Fields meetings
(1816), 637; Blanketeers march (1817), 637;
Pentridge Rising (1817), 637–8; Peterloo
(1819), 638

Rippon, John, 262

Rivers, Lord, 89

roads, 196–7

*Rob Roy* (Scott), 534

Robespierre, Maximilien, 43, 102–3

Robinson, Mary, Baroness Grantham, 309–10

Robinson, Thomas, 289

Robinson, Tom, 309–10

Rochdale, food riots, 144

Rogers, Samuel, 583

Rogers, Simon, 388

Roliça, battle (1808), 475

Roscoe, William, 67, 267, 322, 432–3, 452,
549

Roscoe family, 430

Rose, George, 452

Rose, John, 207

Rose Boughton, William, 320

Rose Copper Company, 384

Rosetta Stone, 281

Ross, Major-General, 387

Ross, Major-General Robert, 608

Rothschild, Amschel, 572

Rothschild, Nathan Mayer: cloth dealing,
313–14; range of goods, 447; illegal exports,
447; bullion dealing, 572–3; government
business, 572–3, 616; broking, 586; news of
Waterloo, 618; war profits, 629; appearance
after war, *573*

Rowbottom, John, 472–3, 486, 576

Rowbottom, Thomas, 472–3, 486, 576, 601

Rowbottom, William: diaries, 8–9, 24; on Paine
controversy, 21, 24; on militia recruiting, 34,
35; on military affair, 41; on bankruptcies,
46; on weavers, 79; on women, 80; on war
deaths, 106; on food prices (1795), 144; on
victories (1797), 172; on attitudes to bank
notes, 183; on national debt, 188; on fairs,
195, 290; on London celebrations, 212; on
recruiting (1799), 239; on food shortages,
244; on cold weather (1799), 244; on food
prices (1800), 248; on peace celebrations, 283–
4; on piece-work rates, 314; on earrings,

343; on Napoleon's coronation, 377; on
hangings, 381, 425; on Santo Domingo
victory, 410; Fox's obituary, 413; on deaths,
425; on French victory, 444; on weavers'
protest, 453; on return of transportee, 454;
on unemployment, 454; on naval matters,
473; on Flushing surrender, 486; on concert
accident, 493; on bankruptcies (1810), 516;
on effects of war, 522; on food shortages
(1812), 548, 565; on mill violence, 551;
on census, 555; on Madrid surrender, 565;
lists, 568–9; on French retreat from Russia,
569; rheumatism, 576; on Holland, 595; on
victory celebrations, 600

Rowbottom family, 8–9, 472–3, 486, 576

Rowlandson, Thomas: drawing French
prisoners, 64; *Nelson recreating with his Brave
Tars, 236*; Royal Institution cartoons, 301;
*Dr Syntax* illustrations, 329, *330*; *Cattle not
Insurable, 358*; *Perry's Dock, 393*; *Brave Tars,
402*; 'St Paul's at an election', *418*; *The
Mother's Hope, 429*; *Libel Hunters, 503*; 'Peace
at Last', *599*; Napoleon's carriage, 639, *640*

Royal College of Physicians, 302

Royal Institution, 301, 381, 397

Royal Military Asylum, 291, 631

Royal Military Canal, 390

Royal Mint, 380–1

Royal Naval Asylum, 291, 631

Royal Proclamation (1792), 17–18

Royal Society, 303

Rumford, Count, 301

Russell, Admiral, 443

Russell, Lord John (later Duke of Bedford) 17,
149, 224, 457, *458*

Russia: war with France (1792), 17; coalition
against France (1793), 29; trade, 79, 81,
201–2, 386, 391, 446, 518, 580–1; Polish
partition, 108, 625; war with France (1799),
238, 268–9; League of Armed Neutrality,
277; coalition against France (1805), 395,
398; Austerlitz defeat, 408; withdrawal, 411;
coalition against France (1806), 413; Treaty
of Tilsit (1807), 438–9; Continental System,
444; alliance with Britain and Spain, 565;
French invasion, 565, 566–7, 569; French
retreat, 567–8, 569, 575; British visitors,
568; Leipzig battle (1813), 595; Paris entry,
598; peace celebrations, 602; Congress
of Vienna, 624; 'Holy Alliance', 625; war
finances, 631; Congress of Verona (1822),
636

Ryde, seaside, 319

Sadler, James, 207

St George's Fields, meeting (1808), 453

*St James's Chronicle*, 365

*St James's Gazette*, 187
St Julien, Marquise, 23
Saint-Quentin, M., 23
St Vincent, battle (1797), 173
St Vincent, Lord, *see* Jervis
Salamanca, battle (1812), 539, 564–5
Salmon, William, 4, 198, 520–1, 579–81
Salthouse, Joseph, 129
San Sebastian, storming (1813), 574
Sanderson, Sir James, 88
Santo Domingo, battle (1806), 410
Saumarez, Admiral, 469
Saunders, John Cunningham, 281–2
Sayers, James, 214
Schimmelpenninck, Lambert, 519–20
Schools of Industry, 142–3
Schroder brothers, 383, 447
Scofield, John, 366
Scoresby, William, 440–1
Scotland: Commissioners of the Annexed
    Estates, 127; textile industry, 78; agriculture,
    126–8; army recruits, 34, 37; *Statistical
    Account*, 123, 127; volunteers, 219–20;
    Scottish regiments in Egyptian campaign,
    281; Gaelic language, 281, 425, 525,
    526, 528–9; army recruiting (1803), 342;
    Highlands, 524–9; emigration, 527, 529,
    531–2; croft houses, *532*, 532–3; weavers,
    545; disturbances, 553
Scott, Charlotte (Charpentier), 220, 428, 481,
    524, 601
Scott, Claude, 144–6, 252, 629
Scott, John, 618
Scott, John (later Lord Eldon), 74
Scott, Sofia, 524
Scott, Walter: volunteer constable (1794), 70;
    volunteer in Edinburgh Light Dragoons,
    219–20; Highlander corps, 220; marriage,
    220; action against bread looters, 250;
    publisher, 299; *Minstrelsy*, 307; *Lay of the Last
    Minstrel*, 307, 397, 524; drilling, 349–50;
    invasion scare, 375; Helvellyn climb, 396–7;
    *Marmion*, 411, 524; deerhound, 411; on
    typhus, 428; war policy, 481, 488; *Quarterly
    Review*, 481; Heber friendship, 509; *Lady of
    the Lake*, 524, 533, 534; Abbotsford, 533;
    Highland and Hebrides tour, 533–4; *Rob Roy*,
    534; on weavers' disturbances, 553; *Waverley*,
    593; on French prisoners, 601–2; Waterloo
    visit, 620
Scott, Walter junior, 428
Season, the, 115, 118, 508
*The Seasons* (Thomson), 306, 308
sedition, 68–9, 106, 177, 502, 549, 638
Sedition Act, 230–1
seditious libel, 15, 72, 75, 253, 503
Seditious Meetings Bill/Act (1795), 147, 148

Selim III, Sultan, 441
Selkirk, Lord, 527, 530, 531
Sellar, Patrick, 530–1
Sellis, Joseph, 505
semaphore, 218, 577–8
Senhouse, Kitty, 111, 156, 413
Seringapatam, siege and fall, 241–2, 246
Seward, Anna, 27
sheep, 123–4, 527–33
Sheffield, food riots. 144
*Sheffield Iris*, 75
*Sheffield Register*, 13
Shelley, Percy Bysshe, 503–4, 558, 605
Sheridan, Richard Brinsley: support for
    French, 17; response to rumours of Jacobin
    plot, 21, 22; *Glorious First* staging, 65–6;
    on Quiberon disaster, 107; opposition to
    'Gagging Acts', 148; response to gold crisis,
    *184*, 185–6; support for O'Connor, 224;
    *Pizarro* production, 242; Sunday newspaper
    debate, 260–1; Hadfield interview, 271;
    volunteering, *349*; Gillray image, 372;
    Spanish policy, 471, 499; Crewe friendship,
    486; social life, 583
Sherwood, Mary Martha (Butt), 23, 254,
    343–5, *361*, 592
Sherwood, Henry, 343–4
shoemakers, 48, 132, 634, 637
Shortland, Captain (Dartmoor agent), 617
Shortland, Captain (with press gang), 60
Shrapnel, Colonel, 393
Sibthorp, Henry, 375–6
Sick and Hurt Board, 133, 135, 157
Siddons, Sarah, 242, 494–5
Sidmouth, Lord, *see* Addington
Sierra Leone, freed slaves, 434–7, 594
Sieyès, Abbé, 269
silver supply, 380
Simpson bank, 253
Sinclair, Sir John, 123, 127, 281, 529
Singleton, John, 80
Skirving, William, 68–9
slave trade, 258, 265–6, 322, 371; abolition,
    430–3, 484, 591, 625
slavery, 265–7, *265*, 431, 433
slaves, freed, 434–7
Slessor, Harriot, 479
Slessor, Harry, 441–2
Slessor, John Henry, 226, 536
Smith, Adam, 514, 529
Smith, Sir Harry, 538
Smith, J. T., *633*
Smith, John 'Warwick', *324*
Smith, Sir Sidney, 45, 240, 411, 424
Smith, Sydney, 257, 259–60, 299, 417–18
Smithfield market, 134, 136, 458
smuggling, 102, 448–50, 543, 572

Smythe, Sir Sidney, 555
snobbery, 114, 506
Snodgrass, Gabriel, 392
Soane, John, 92
societies, 17, 122
Society for Constitutional Information, 17, 20
Society for Promoting the Religious Instruction of Youth, 259
Society for the Suppression of Vice, 259
Society of Friends of the People, 17
Soldini, Gosue, 628
Somerset, Duchess of, 112
songs: revolutionary, 23, 67, 310; 'The Heart of a Tar', 66; 'The Dumfries Volunteers', 76; national anthem, 178, 213–14; ironworkers', 201–2; 'Dumplings for Bonaparte', 237; Scott's collections, 307; 'The Hull Packet', 333; for Canning, 336; 'He may come if he dare', 353; 'Britons, strike home', 356–7; broadsheets, 368; 'Farewell to the Bens', 526; 'British Tars', 632
Sons of Liberty, 229
Soult, Marshal, 478, 479, 480, 535, 596
Southcott, Joanna, 371
Southey, Robert: relationship with Coleridge, 148, 170, 331; 'English Eclogues', 150; Thalaba, 299; on Royal Institution lectures, 301; on tourism, 329; in Lake District, 331; on war, 342; on Nelson's death, 622; Quarterly Review, 481; on Napoleon's escape, 616; peace celebrations, 622
Spa Fields meetings (1816), 637
Spain: coalition against France, 29; British subsidies, 631; treaties with France, 108, 121, 163; declaration of war on Britain, 163; Louisiana deal, 336; French presence, 469–70; Bonaparte rule, 470–1; Napoleon's arrival, 477–8; French occupy Madrid, 478; Wellington's campaigns, 480, 481, 510, 535, 539–40, 569, 595; British victories, 480, 537–9, 569–71; British occupation of Madrid, 565; flight of Joseph Bonaparte, 569–70; Congress of Vienna, 624
speculators, 1, 81, 188, 251–3, 412, 458, 519
Speenhamland scheme, 142
Spence, Thomas, 253
Spencer, Earl, 57, 275, 319, 505
Spencer, Sarah (later Lady Lyttelton): family background, 319; waiting for letters, 8; on straw work, 195; social life, 319; on Spanish situation, 470–1, 478; on Portuguese situation, 475–6; on gossip, 483; on alarmists and reformers, 485; on Walcheren expedition, 486; on boxing match, 496; on Burdett riots, 501; on Garter dinner, 505; on brother's promotion, 507; reading, 525; wedding trip, 568; on steam engine race, 585

Spink and Carss, 185
Spithead mutinies (1797), 175–6
Spooner, Barbara, see Wilberforce
Stafford, George Granville Leveson-Gower, Lord, 529–32
Staffordshire Advertiser, 483
Stamford News, 503
Stanhope, Hester, 348
Stanhope, James, 540, 619
The State of the Poor (Eden), 143
The State of the Prisons (Howard), 588
Statesman, 606, 608
Statistical Account of Scotland (Sinclair), 123, 127, 529
steam power: in factories, 80, 82, 86, 87, 326, 637; in brewhouse, 134; cylinder manufacture, 200; Soho foundry, 200; coal supply, 203, 637; arms manufacture, 203, 386; shipping, 204, 394, 629; in dockyard, 207; locomotives, 303, 585, 629; in Royal Mint, 381; naval engineering, 392–3; grain mills, 456; attacks on power-looms, 549, 551, 564; after the war, 629, 637
Stephen, James, 257, 432, 435
Stephen, Sarah, 257
Stephenson, George, 585, 629
Sterling, Edward, 596
Stevens, James, 353–4
Stevenson, William, 528
Stewart, Lt-Colonel William, 343
Stock Exchange, 92, 383
Stokach, battle (1799), 268
Stonard, Revd John, 143, 258, 599
Stone, Richard, 182–3
Strachan, Sir Richard John, 486
straw, hats and plaiting, 194–5, 543–4
strikes: Combination Acts, 245–6; croppers, 314–15, 316; keelmen, 360–1, 634; weavers, 453; mule-spinners, 522
Strutt, Joseph, 351
Strutt, William, 565
Stuart, Daniel, 488
Stuart, John, Count of Maida, 411
Stuart, Lady Maria, 110
Styal, Quarry Bank Mill, 84, 317
Suffolk, Earl of, 224
Sun, 18
Susan Grey (Butt), 343
Sussex, Duke of, 291, 424
Sutherland, Elizabeth, Countess of, 529–32, 534
Suvorov, General, 268
Svedenstierna, Eric, 208, 321–2, 355
Sweden: iron trade, 201–2, 203, 386; League of Armed Neutrality, 277; coalition against France (1805), 413; British subsidies, 631; Moore's expedition (1808), 469; coalition

against France (1813), 569; Congress of Vienna, 624

Sykes, John, 247, 328, 493

*Sylvia's Lovers* (Gaskell), 640

Symington, William, 204

tailors, 47–8, 132, 351, 545

Talavera, battle (1809), 480, 488, 510, 559–60

*A Tale of Two Cities* (Dickens), 640

Talleyrand, Charles Maurice de, 234, 598, 624

*The Task* (Cowper), 257–8, 306

Tate, Admiral George, 239

Tate, Colonel William, 167

taxation: newspapers, 5, 7; receivers, 99; Pitt's policies, 16, 94, 125, 189–90, 194, 205, 216, 243–4; hair-powder, 149; assessed taxes, 189–90; land tax, 216; income tax, 243–4, 290, 378, 409, 610; Addington's first budget, 290; iron, 409–10; Vansittart's budget (1812), 585; increases (1815), 610

Taylor, Ann, 362

Taylor, William, 460, 463

Teignmouth, John Shore, Lord, 591

telegraph, shutter/semaphore, 218, 577–8

telescopes, 15, 233, 294, 367

Telford, Thomas, 197, 207, 221, 527, 528

*The Temple of Nature* (Darwin), 306

textile industries, 78–81, 313–17, 450–1

Thackeray, William Makepeace, 640

theatres: Astley's, 44, 342, 495; Drury Lane, 65–6, 222, 271, 494, 607; Plymouth, 66; Manchester, 79, 405; Bury St Edmunds, 98, 100, 242; Norwich company, 98, 196; Bath, 114; Covent Garden, 166, 214, 237, 491–2, 492, 494–5; Portsmouth, 178; *Naumachia*, 237; Lyceum, 242, 494; Sheridan's *Pizarro*, 242; Brighton, 319; Yarmouth, 319; Sadler's Wells, 353; Strand, 356; Colchester, 362; patriotic revivals, 368; London, 493–5

theatricals, amateur, 492–3

Thelwall, John: on militia barracks, 35; speech on suffrage, 72; arrest, 73; trial, 74–5; Copenhagen House speeches, *146*, 147–8; friendship with Wordsworths and Coleridge, 169

Thompson, Andrew, 291

Thompson, Charles, 441–2, 574

Thompson, Thomas Perronet: joins navy, 356; in army, 416; South American expedition, 416, 434; Governor of Sierra Leone, 434–6, 437, 594; marriage, 436; rejoins army, 436; brother's career, 442, 574; theatre going, 495; Peninsular campaign, 495, 574; later career, 437

Thompson, Thomas senior, 223, 356, 434, 436

Thomson, George, 69

Thomson, James, 306, 308

Thorne, Richard, 392

Thornton, Henry, 186, 257, 259, 318, 430, 435

Thornton, Marianne, 257, 587

Thorpe, Robert, 594

Thrale, *see* Hoare (Sophia), Piozzi (Hester)

Tilsit, treaties (1807), 438–9

timber supply, 391–2, 580

Timber Trust, 391

*The Times*: on French servants, 24; war policy, 27; on government loan, 95; on Robespierre, 102; on Poland, 108; on Crop Club, 149; on Napoleon's bulletins, 172; on French landings, 182; Bank of England jokes, 186; on Egyptian expedition, 233; on George III at theatre, 242; on Pitt's resignation, 275; on Nelson, 283; on Hyde Park parade, 354; on Lloyd's Fund, 356; on press gang, 359; on Nelson's body, 403; getting news, 407, 475; quoting French news, 408; on post-Austerlitz crisis, 411; readership, 415; Spanish policy, 471; on Cintra Convention, 476; on press freedom, 504; on Napoleon's marriage, 505; royal gossip, 556; on Moscow, 567; on American naval encounters, 575, 579; on Vauxhall gala, 583; war policy, 596; accounts from French papers, 598; Waterloo news, 619

Tipu Sultan, 240–1

Tolstoy, Leo, 639

Tone, Wolfe, 164–6, 228

Tooke, John Horne, 73, 74, 75, 97, 310

Tooley, Tim, 32

Torbay, anchorage, 272

Tories: booksellers for, 115; conservative Whigs, 309; town corporations, 311; Manchester, 350; old followers of Pitt, 415; press, 415, 481, 552, 553; in power (1807), 417–18; Catholic emancipation issue, 417, 555–6; in power (1812), 555–6; in power after war, 625; Hazlitt's view, 630–1

Torres Vedras, 499, 535

Toulon: capture and recapture, 44–5, 56; French fleet, 234; blockade (1803), 357, 391; Villeneuve's escape, 396

Toulouse, battle, 600–1

*The Tour of Dr Syntax*, 329, *330*

Tourcoing, battle (1794), 102, 271

tourism: Portsmouth prizes, 64; reasons for, 321–5, 326; Liverpool, 322–3; in search of the picturesque, 323–4, 327–8, 329–30; Lake District, 325–6, 329, 331; factories and mills, 326–7, 328–9; Tyneside, 327–8; Loch Katrine, 525; prisons and hulks, 544; Wales, 589–90; continental, 619–20

Tower of London: rumour of Jacobin plot, 21;

Ordnance Board, 48, 51–2, 387, 487, 627; prisoners, 73, 501, 503; lions, 158; Despard case, 311; impressed seamen, 360

*The Town and Country Magazine*, 114

tracts, 254–6

trade: African, 51, 52, 266–7; cotton, 79, 433, 447, 454, 590–1, 609; American, 82, 452, 515, 521, 563; grain, 143–5, 252, 450, 519, 609–10; straw, 194–5; coastal, 197–9, 634; iron, 203, 204, 590, 609; slave, see slave trade; textiles, 325, 590; convoys of merchant shipping, 357, 580; timber, 391–2, 580; South American, 412, 416, 518–19; Berlin Decrees (1806), 444, 445; Orders in Council (1807), 444–5, 450, 451, 481, 514, 517, 521, 545, 549, 560, 563; British increase during war, 446; colonial goods, 447; smuggling, 448–50; fish, 449; East India Company charter, 590–1; after the war, 628

Trafalgar, battle (1805), 399–400

Training Act (1806), 409

'Tranquillity' scheme, 380

Transport Board, 133, 157, 158

*Traveller* magazine, 473

*Travels in the Interior of Africa* (Park), 435

treason: charges, 69; trials (1794), 73–4, 146; Maidstone trial of Irish group, 224; Wolfe Tone's sentence, 228; Erskine's trial, 271; Emmet's trial, 312

Treason Act, 73

Treasonable Practices Bill/Act (1795), 147, 148

Treasury, 94, 145, 378, 571

Treasury Commissioners, 94

Trevithick, Richard, 208, 394, 585

Trimmer, Sarah, 261

Trotter, Alexander, 395

Trotter, John, 46–7, 395, 629

*True Briton*, 18, 147, 298, 300

*The Trumpet Major* (Hardy), 641

Tugwell, Thomas, 314

Turkey, 238, 240, 273, 280, 414, 441

Turner, J. M. W.: watercolours, 114–15; Cyfarthfa sketches, 202; *Battle of the Nile*, 238; uncle's business, 248; European tour (1802), 294; Girtin's funeral, 293; *Battle of Trafalgar*, 405–6; *A Country Blacksmith*, 410; *Ploughing up Turnips*, 466; *Hannibal Crossing the Alps*, 566; *The Field of Waterloo*, 620

Turner, John, 150

turnpikes, 149, 150, 387, 448

Tussaud, Madame, 405, 639

uniforms: army, 37–8, 46–8, 104; navy, 56; volunteers, 37–8, 47, 76,, 221–3, 351, 473; postwar unemployment of makers, 637

Union, Acts of (1800–1), 274

unions, 47, 245–6, 589

Unitarians, 86, 261, 267, 371, 587

United Englishmen, 228–30, 546

United Irishmen: foundation, 164–5; leaders, 68, 166, 224–5, 229, 294; Scottish contacts, 67, 68; French contacts, 166; naval mutinies, 176–7; plans for rising, 224–5; arrests, 224, 228; rebellion, 225–8; Wolfe Tone's death, 228; English fears of, 311–12

United Irishwomen, 230

United Scotsmen, 228, 230

United States: Embargo Act (1807), 452; Non-Intercourse Act (1809), 515; ultimatum (1810), 521; declaration of war (1812), 563; war, 575, 579, 608–9; navy, 575; Treaty of Ghent (1814), 609, 617

vagrants, *150*, 292

Valenciennes, siege, 42–4

Vallon, Annette, 20, 296

*Vanity Fair* (Thackeray), 640

Vansittart, Nicholas, 585

Vega, Andrea de la, 471

Venn, Henry, 257

Victor, General, 336

Victualling Board, 131, 133–8

Vienna: French capture (1805), 407; French capture (1809), 495

*Vienna Gazette*, 408

Villeneuve, Admiral, 235, 396, 397, 398, 400

Villiers, Frances, Lady Jersey, 110, 483

Vimeiro, battle (1808), 475

*A Vindication of the Rights of Men* (Wollstonecraft), 14

*A Vindication of the Rights of Woman* (Wollstonecraft), 20

Vinegar Hill, battle (1798), 226, 227

Vittoria, battle (1813), 569–71, 582

volunteers: coastal patrols, 36; raising, 37–8, 76, 170, 348–51, 638; uniforms, 37–8, 47, 76, 221–3, 351, 473; press gangs, 59, 62; Burns's experiences, 76–7; parades, 100, 220, 223, 354, 372, 490; MPs, 113, 339; Fishguard invasion, 167–8; enjoyment, 179; Scott's experiences, 219–20; drilling, 220, 222, 308, *349*, 349–52, 374, 423, 546; numbers, 221; weapons, 221, 328, 352; social life, 222–3, 490; putting down disturbances, 250; disbanded, 328; enrolling (1804), 348–51; numbers (1804), 348; oath of loyalty, 348, 349; driving livestock, 351; actors and musicians, 352–3; women, 354; sea fencibles, 362; invasion scare, 375; Training Act, 409; Local Militia Act (1808), 473–4; disbanding, 564

von Hardenberg, Chancellor, 624

*Vox Stellarum* (Andrews), 371, 564

wages: tailors, 47–8, 545; shoemakers, 48;
  weavers, 79, 244, 245, 452, 545; spinners,
  98; agricultural workers, 121–2, 132,
  140, 464; dockyard workers, 132, 390–1;
  minimum wage issue, 142, 379, 452–3,
  454, 564; army pay, 152, 179; navy pay,
  153, 174–5; farming family income,
  194; iron workers, 206, 386; petition for
  regulation, 245; Combination Acts, 245–6;
  civilian shipyards, 291; croppers, 314–15;
  payment, 380; undercut by prison labour,
  543; reduction (1811), 545; protests against
  lowness, 551; keelmen, 634
Wagram, battle (1809), 488
Wakefield, Edward, 588
Wales, 589–90
Walker, George, *83, 315, 456, 617*
Walker, Thomas, 72
Walker brothers, 200
Walsh, James, 169
Walter, John, 407, 475
war: declaration (1793), 28–9, 98;
  Parliamentary vote (1794), 125; petitions
  for peace, 108, 172; length of, 172; peace
  meetings, 253; peace (1801), 283–5; peace
  terms, 289; declaration (1803), 339–40;
  public mood (1803), 342; calls for peace
  (1808, 1809), 452, 454, 481; petitions for
  peace (1812), 550, 564, 565; peace terms,
  596–7; peace (1814), 599; territorial effects,
  624–5; cost, 631; dead and wounded, 631;
  effects of peace movement, 639
War Office, 36, 152
Ward, William, 190
Wardle, Gwyllym Lloyd, 483
Washington, British raid (1814), 608
Waterhouse, Benjamin, 607–8, 617–18
Waterloo, battle (1815), 618–20
Watt, James, 200, 294
Watt, James junior, 20, 54, 87
Watt, Robert, 70–1
*Waverley* (Scott), 593
Way, Mary, 359
weather: diaries, 455; summer (1794), 139;
  winter (1794–5), 139–40; harvest (1795),
  139, 144; spring (1799), 244–5; summer
  (1799), 246; autumn (1799), 246; winter
  (1799–1800), 247; summer (1800), 251;
  spring and summer (1802), 318; summer
  (1803), 346; summer (1807), 438; bad
  harvests and icy winters, 513; harvest (1810),
  519; spring (1812), 517; harvest (1812),
  565; winter (1813–14), 596; spring (1814),
  596; summer (1815), 618; summer (1816),
  633; harvest (1816), 633, 636

Weatherley, James: factory work, 82–3; on
  returning soldiers, 290; on volunteer
  regiments, 348; on Nelson commemoration,
  405; on recruiting parties, 471–2; visiting
  soldiers' camp, 552–3; unemployment, 637;
  at Peterloo (1819), 638
weavers: hand-loom, 33, 78–82, 313, 451,
  522; earnings, 33, 79, 245, 313–14, 452–3,
  545; farmers, 81, 193–4; steam-powered
  weaving, 82; regional specialisms, 85; food
  price protests, 141; petition for regulation
  of wages, 245; attacks on factories, 314;
  Minimum Wage Bill, 452–3; riots, 453–4;
  petitions for relief, 522, 545; Luddites, 546,
  553, 564
Weavers Minimum Wage Bill (1808), 452–3
Webster, Joseph, 565
Webster, Wedderburn, 498
Wedgwood, Josiah, 75
Wedgwood, Josiah junior, 170
Wedgwood, Tom, 20, 170
Weedon Bec arms depot, 387–9, 475, 628
Wellesley, Arthur (later Duke of Wellington), *see*
  Wellington
Wellesley, Lady Charlotte, 483
Wellesley, Henry, 510
Wellesley, Richard, Marquess, 240, 372, 442,
  489, 501, 539, 562
Wellesley-Pole, William, 536, 563
Wellington, Sir Arthur Wellesley, Duke of:
  commissions, 33; Flanders campaign, 103;
  Mysore war, 241; Assaye victory (1803),
  345; meeting with Nelson, 398; Copenhagen
  battle, 440; Peninsula expedition, 471;
  Portuguese campaign, 475–6, 477; Spanish
  victories, 480; titles, 480; reputation, 481;
  Peninsula war strategy, 499, 535–6, 539;
  Badajoz capture (1812), 537–8; Salamanca
  victory, 539, 564–5; Goya portrait, 540;
  Madrid entry, 565; Spanish victories (1813),
  569–70; on British soldiers, 31; Spanish art
  collection, 570; army finance, 571–2, 616;
  advance through Spain, 595; Orthez victory,
  596; Waterloo victory, 114, 619; Congress
  of Vienna, 624; honours, 625; Prime
  Minister, 625–6
West, Benjamin, 294, 405
West, Thomas, 330
West Indies, 156–7, 172, 445–6, 625
Westbrook, Harriet, 558, 605
Westminster, Lord, 501
*Westminster Review*, 437
Westphalia, 438
Weymouth, seaside, 319
Wheeler, James, 354
Whigs: press, 5, 415; reform clubs, 17; Foxite,
  71, 96, 151, 211, 292, 376; booksellers for,

115; 'Gagging Acts', 148; split (1794), 151; support for O'Connor, 224; conservative (Pittite), 309; Manchester, 350; new groups, 415; 'Mountain' group, 415, 549; Catholic emancipation issue, 416–17, 555–6

Whitbread, Samuel: minimum wage proposal, 142; support for O'Connor, 224; Melville case, 396; 'The Mountain' group, 415, 549; criticism of Wellesley, 499; snobbery towards, 506; Bolton peace petition, 549–50; social life, 583

Whitby, resistance to press gang, 59–60

White, Gilbert, 303

Whitelocke, General John, 416, 481–2

White's club, 115

Whitworth, Charles, Earl, 338, 339

Whitworth, Daniel, 316

widows and orphans, 291

Wight, Andrew, 127

Wight, Major, 181

Wilbee, George, 628

Wilberforce, Barbara (Spooner), 257, 259

Wilberforce, William: on Pitt, 56; on Portsmouth, 132; theatre going, 242; friendship with More, 255; religious views, 257, 258–9, 371; marriage, 259; influence, 259, 432; on Sunday newspapers, 260; speech on Melville, 396; abolition of slave trade, 430–2; Sierra Leone situation, 434–6; wool industry committee, 451; missionary policy, 591–2

Wilkes, John, 9

Wilkie, David, 196, 410

Wilkinson, James, 349

Wilkinson, John 'Iron-Mad', 200, 201, 202, 204, 205

Wilkinson, Joseph, 330

Wilkinson, William, 205–6

William, Duke of Clarence, 40

William V of Orange, 39, 269

Williams, Captain, 58

Williams, David, 178

Williams, Helen Maria, 20, 119

Williams, Thomas (industrialist), 57, 205

Williams, Thomas (sailor), 167

Williams, Sir Thomas, 576

Williams, Captain Tom, 272–3

Williamson, David, 77

Willoughby, John, 92

Willoughby, Lord, 190

Wilson, Lt-Colonel John, 538

Wilson, Sir Robert, 367

Wincanton, parole depot, 540–1, 544, 628

Windham, William: Norwich election, 151–2; war policy, 186, 298; Pitt's resignation, 275; Cobbett funding, 298; Secretary for War, 298, 409; Cobbett funding, 298; Training

Act, 409; South American strategy, 416; on press freedoms, 500

Winsor, Frederick, 584

Winterbotham, William, 72

Wolfe, Captain, 359

Wollstonecraft, Mary, 14, 20, 67, 211, 605

women: in textile industries, 80, 81–2; wartime employment, 194–5; writers pilloried, 211; aboard warships, 235; volunteers, 354; agricultural workers, 457; mineworkers, 637

Wood, Abraham, 497

Wood, Charles, 550

Wood, John, 413

Woodforde, James: on death of Louis XVI, 28; servant's enlistment, 32; on Panorama of Spithead, 56; on French occupation of Holland, 105; enjoys stolen cheese, 137; on cold weather, 139; on demonstration against George III, 147; on wheat flour shortage, 149; on beggar, 150; on invasion defences, 163, 190; on banking crisis, 185; on taxation, 190, 290; new garden roller, 205; on celebrating Nile victory, 237; on Copenhagen victory, 278; on assassination of tsar, 278

Woodward, George Moutard, 402, 429

Woolwich Arsenal, 49, 50, 393

Woolwich naval yard, 133, 134, 390

Wordsworth, Dorothy: friendship with Hutchinsons, 248; friendship with Jane Pollard, 325; on coffee house, 6; at Alfoxden, 169–70; spied on, 169; walking to Wye valley, 171; on mining village, 208–9; in Germany, 245; in Lake District, 318, 325; in Calais, 296, 318; on invasion preparations, 350; niece's death, 562; on West Country, 589; on Hindwell, 635

Wordsworth, Mary (Hutchinson): friendship with Wordsworths, 248; Alfoxden visit, 170; marriage plans, 296; marriage, 331; Hindwell visit, 462; on Perceval's assassination, 560–1; daughter's death, 562; son's death, 562; on Napoleon's return to Paris, 616

Wordsworth, Richard, 73

Wordsworth, William: friendship with Hutchinsons, 248; on French Revolution, 15, 20, 396, 600; in Paris, 20; affair with Annette Vallon, 20; daughter Caroline, 20, 296; political opinions, 73, 211; Coleridge meeting, 148; on vagrants, 150; at Alfoxden, 169–70; spied on, 169; on Pitt's repression, 169, 396, 547; *Lyrical Ballads*, 170–1, 306, 396; on mining village, 209; in Germany, 245; in Lake District, 325; 'Calais, August, 1802', 287, 296, 318; meeting Annette again, 296; plans to marry Mary, 296; *Guide*

to the Lakes, 330; marriage to Mary, 331;
on Milton, 336; drilling, 350; on fencibles,
362–3; on invasion defences, 368, 372;
on Napoleon's coronation, 377; Helvellyn
climb, 396–7; children, 397, 460, 562; on
Britain's isolation, 414; Hindwell visit, 463;
on Spanish uprising, 476; Byron on, 510;
on need for government firmness, 547; on
Bellingham's execution, 561; relationship
with Coleridge, 561; daughter's death, 562;
son's death, 562; Hazlitt on, 600; peace
celebrations, 622
workhouses, 140, 142–3, 250, 630
Wright's bank, 91
Wroe and Duncroft's mill, 551
Wynne, Eugenia, 4, see Campbell
Wynne family, 533

Yarmouth, see Great Yarmouth
Yates, William, 350

York, Duchess of, 222–3, 582
York, Frederick, Duke of: education, 117;
Flanders expedition command, 39, 40;
Flanders campaign, 41, 42–3, 44, 101,
102–3; Dunkirk retreat, 44; replaced, 104;
Abercromby's letter, 106; orders on reporting
deaths, 152; West Indies expedition, 156;
voluntary subscription, 216; review of troops,
221; Dutch campaign, 268–9; Hadfield
interview, 271; Royal Military Asylum, 291;
defence plan, 389; sale of commissions, 482,
483; mistresses, 482, 483–4; libel suit against
Hunts, 483; Covent Garden subscription, 491
Yorke, Agneta, 4, 109, 290, 338, 507, 535
Yorke, Charles, 500–1, 507
Yorke, Philip, 535
Yorkshire: textile industries, 85–7, 245, 314–
15; Luddites, 547
Young, Arthur, 123, 457, 465
Young, Thomas, 302